T0180424

Lecture Notes in Computer Science 13644

The series Lecture Notes in Computer Science (LNCS), including its subseries Lecture Notes in Artificial Intelligence (LNAI) and Lecture Notes in Bioinformatics (LNBI), has established itself as a medium for the publication of new developments in computer science and information technology research, teaching, and education.

LNCS enjoys close cooperation with the computer science R & D community, the series counts many renowned academics among its volume editors and paper authors, and collaborates with prestigious societies. Its mission is to serve this international community by providing an invaluable service, mainly focused on the publication of conference and workshop proceedings and postproceedings. LNCS commenced publication in 1973.

Jean-Jacques Rousseau · Bill Kapralos
Editors

Pattern Recognition, Computer Vision, and Image Processing

ICPR 2022 International Workshops and Challenges

Montreal, QC, Canada, August 21–25, 2022
Proceedings, Part II

 Springer

Editors
Jean-Jacques Rousseau 🆔
York University
Toronto, ON, Canada

Bill Kapralos 🆔
Ontario Tech University
Oshawa, ON, Canada

ISSN 0302-9743 ISSN 1611-3349 (electronic)
Lecture Notes in Computer Science
ISBN 978-3-031-37741-9 ISBN 978-3-031-37742-6 (eBook)
https://doi.org/10.1007/978-3-031-37742-6

This Springer imprint is published by the registered company Springer Nature Switzerland AG
The registered company address is: Gewerbestrasse 11, 6330 Cham, Switzerland

Foreword

The organizers of the 26th International Conference on Pattern Recognition (ICPR 2022) are delighted to present the Proceedings of the event. The conference took place at Palais des Congrès de Montréal in Montreal, Canada, and we are thrilled to share the outcomes of this successful event.

We would like to express our heartfelt gratitude to the International Association for Pattern Recognition (IAPR) for sponsoring the conference, which allowed us to bring together a diverse group of researchers and experts in this field. Without their support, this conference would not have been possible.

We also want to extend our special thanks to the Workshop Chairs who provided excellent leadership in organizing the workshops. We appreciate the tireless efforts they put into making the workshops a success. We would also like to acknowledge the authors and presenters of the articles and workshops for their contributions. The high quality of their work and presentations enriched the conference.

Finally, we would like to thank the attendees for their participation, which made ICPR 2022 a truly collaborative and inspiring event. We hope that the Proceedings will serve as a valuable resource for those interested in pattern recognition and inspire future research in this field.

August 2022

Henrik I. Christensen
Michael Jenkin
Cheng-Lin Liu

Preface

The 26th International Conference on Pattern Recognition Workshops (ICPRW 2022) were held at the Palais des congrès de Montréal in Montreal, Quebec, Canada on Sunday August 21, 2022, one day earlier than the main ICPR conference. 27 workshop submissions were received and were carefully reviewed by the IAPR Conferences and Meetings committee and the workshop chairs. Considering their decisions and anticipated attendance, 24 workshops were selected and 21 workshops actually took place. Many of these workshops received a sponsorship or endorsement from the International Association for Pattern Recognition (IAPR).

ICPR 2022 marked the return of the conference to its in-person format (although workshops had the option of being held in person or remotely). This meant meeting colleagues face to face again, and making new connections to support scientific collaborations and (perhaps) even new friendships. The purpose of publishing the proceedings of a scientific conference such as ICPR 2022 include to:

- Establish a permanent record of the research presented;
- Report on the current research concerns and accomplishments of the conference participants;
- Make new research visible to scientific and other publics to promote collaboration, innovation, and discovery;
- Disseminate the latest research findings to a wider audience, in support of researchers, academics, industry, and other practitioners; and,
- Support the shared goal of staying up to date with developments in the fast moving field of artificial intelligence.

These volumes constitute the refereed proceedings of the twenty-one (21) workshops that were held in conjunction with ICPR 2022. The wide range of topics that it contains is a testament to the ever-widening concerns of AI researchers as they creatively find ways to apply artificial intelligence to domains further from its historical concerns. ICPR 2022 workshops covered domains related to pattern recognition, artificial intelligence, computer vision, and image and sound analysis. Workshop contributions reflected the most recent applications related to healthcare, biometrics, ethics, multimodality, cultural heritage, imagery, affective computing, and de-escalation. The papers included in these proceedings span four volumes and stem from the following workshops:

Volume I:

T-CAP 2022: Towards a Complete Analysis of People: From Face and Body to Clothes
HBU: 12th International Workshop on Human Behavior Understanding
SSL: Theories, Applications, and Cross Modality for Self-Supervised Learning Models
MPRSS 2022: Multimodal Pattern Recognition for Social Signal Processing in Human-Computer Interaction
FAIRBIO: Fairness in Biometric Systems

AIHA: Artificial Intelligence for Healthcare Applications
MDMR: Multimodal Data for Mental Disorder Recognition

Volume II:

MANPU 2022: 5th International Workshop on coMics ANalysis, Processing and Understanding
FOREST: Image Analysis for Forest Environmental Monitoring
MMFORWILD: MultiMedia FORensics in the WILD
IMTA: 8th International Workshop on Image Mining, Theory and Applications
PRHA: Pattern Recognition in Healthcare Analytics
IML: International Workshop on Industrial Machine Learning

Volume III:

PatReCH: 3rd International Workshop on Pattern Recognition for Cultural Heritage
XAIE: 2nd Workshop on Explainable and Ethical AI
PRRS: 12th Workshop on Pattern Recognition in Remote Sensing
CVAUI: Computer Vision for Analysis of Underwater Imagery
UMDBB: Understanding and Mitigating Demographic Bias in Biometric Systems

Volume IV:

AI4MFDD: Workshop on Artificial Intelligence for Multimedia Forensics and Disinformation Detection
AI4D: AI for De-escalation: Autonomous Systems for De-escalating Conflict in Military and Civilian Contexts
AMAR: 3rd International Workshop on Applied Multimodal Affect Recognition

Writing this preface, we were acutely aware of our special responsibilities towards those who will access the Proceedings for future reference. Unlike us and the contributors to these volumes, future readers will not have the benefit of having lived through the moment in which the research was conducted and presented. As background, leading to August 2022, there were two overarching meta-stories in the news: the COVID pandemic and social justice. COVID restrictions were lifted in piecemeal fashion leading to the conference dates, and began the long tail of the end of the pandemic. For conference attendees, wearing face masks was a live issue since masks indoors remained strongly recommended. International travel was still heavily impacted by COVID restrictions, with some participants being unable to travel either due to their COVID status or to the difficulty in meeting the range of COVID testing and inoculation requirements required. The public health theme continued with a new virus called 'Monkeypox' appearing on the scene.

On social justice, the May 25, 2020 murder of George Floyd by Minneapolis police officers continued to cast its shadow. During the summer of 2022, there continued to be protests and other actions to demand an end to anti-Black racism. In parallel, in Canada, Indigenous communities led protests and actions to demand an end to anti-Indigenous racism, and to acknowledge the historical circumstances that explain the discoveries of remains of children in unmarked burial sites at former residential schools. As conference attendees and participants, we lived through this cultural moment and were marked by it. However, future readers may need to supplement these volumes with research into the circumstances in which the research was conceptualized, conducted, and received. Philosophers of science make a relevant distinction here. Since Karl Popper, they speak of the context of discovery and the context of justification. Justification in science is relatively well understood, as it relates to the collection and analysis of data in pursuit of evidence for evaluating hypotheses in conformity with norms referenced to as the 'scientific method'. However, where do the initial questions or leaps of insights come from? The context of discovery is not as well understood. Still, it is widely believed that the social and personal conditions of researchers play an active role. We included a reference to the COVID-19 pandemic and social justice movements as widely shared preoccupations at the time of ICPR 2022 to aid a future reader who may wonder about the context of discovery of what is reported.

We acknowledge that future readers will no doubt enjoy benefits that we cannot enjoy. Specifically, they may be able to better assess which lines of research presented in the Proceedings proved the more beneficial. There are also concrete things: as we write, we do not know whether we are in a COVID pandemic hiatus or at its end; future readers will know the answer to this question.

The organization of such a large conference would not be possible without the help of many people. Our special gratitude goes to the Program Chairs (Gregory Dudek, Zhouchen Lin, Simone Marinai, Ingela Nyström) for their leadership in organizing the program. Thanks go to the Track Chairs and Area Chairs who dedicated their time to the review process and the preparation of the program. We also thank the reviewers who have evaluated the papers and provided authors with valuable feedback on their research work.

Finally, we acknowledge the work of conference committee members (Local Arrangements Chair and Committee Members, Finance Chairs, Workshop Chairs, Tutorial Chairs, Challenges Chairs, Publicity Chairs, Publications Chairs, Awards Chair, Sponsorship and Exhibition Chair) who strongly contributed to make this event successful. The MCI Group, led by Anjali Mohan, made great efforts in arranging the logistics, which is highly appreciated.

August 2022   Jean-Jacques Rousseau
                                                                 Bill Kapralos

Organization

General Chairs

Henrik I. Christensen   UC San Diego, USA
Michael Jenkin   York University, Canada.
Cheng-Lin Liu   Institute of Automation of Chinese Academy of Sciences, China

Program Committee Co-chairs

Gregory Dudek   McGill University, Canada
Zhouchen Lin   Peking University, China
Simone Marinai   University of Florence, Italy
Ingela Nyström   Swedish National Infrastructure for Computing, Sweden

Invited Speakers Chairs

Alberto Del Bimbo   University of Firenze, Italy
Michael Brown   Canada
Steven Waslander   University of Toronto, Canada

Workshop Chairs

Xiang Bai   Huazhong University of Science and Technology, China
Giovanni Farinella   University of Catania, Italy
Laurence Likforman   Télécom Paris, France
Jonathan Wu   Canada

Tutorial Chairs

David Clausi   University of Waterloo, Canada
Markus Enzweiler   Esslingen University of Applied Sciences,
                                          Germany
Umapada Pal   Indian Statistical Institute, India

Local Arrangements Chair

Ioannis Rekleitis   University of South Carolina, USA

Finance Chairs

Rainer Herpers   Hochschule Bonn-Rhein-Sieg, Germany
Andrew Hogue   Ontario Tech University, Canada

Publication Chairs

Jean-Jacques Rousseau   York University, Canada
Bill Kapralos   Ontario Tech University, Canada

Awards Chair

Johana Hansen   McGill University, Canada

Sponsorship and Exhibition Chair

Hong Zhang   China

Challenges Chairs

Marco Bertini   University of Florence, Italy
Dimosthenis Karatzas   Universitat Autónoma de Barcelona, Spain

Track 1: Artificial Intelligence, Machine Learning for Pattern Analysis

Battista Biggio	Università degli Studi di Cagliari, Italy
Ambra Demontis	Università degli Studi di Cagliari, Italy
Gang Hua	Wormpex AI Research, University of Washington, USA
Dacheng Tao	University of Sydney, Australia

Track 2: Computer Vision and Robotic Perception

Olga Bellon	Universidade Federal do Parana, Brazil
Kosta Derpanis	York University, Canada
Ko Nishino	Kyoto University, Japan

Track 3: Image, Speech, Signal and Video Processing

Ana Fred	University of Lisbon, Portugal
Regina Lee	York University, Canada
Jingdong Wang	Baidu, China
Vera Yashina	Russian Academy of Sciences, Russian Federation

Track 4: Biometrics and Human-Computer Interaction

Kevin Bowyer	University of Notre Dame, USA
Kerstin Dautenhahn	University of Waterloo, Canada
Julian Fierrez	Universidad Autónoma de Madrid, Spain
Shiqi Yu	Southern University of Science and Technology, China

Track 5: Document Analysis and Recognition

Alexandra Branzan Albu	University of Victoria, Canada
Alicia Fornes	Universitat Autònoma de Barcelona, Spain
Koichi Kise	Osaka Prefecture University, Japan
Faisal Shafait	National University of Sciences and Technology, Pakistan

Track 6: Biomedical Imaging and Informatics

Hamid Abbasi   Auckland Bioengineering Institute, New Zealand
Ismail Bey Ayed   Ecole de Technologie Superieure (ETS), Canada
Lukas Käll   KTH Royal Institute of Technology, Sweden
Dinggang Shen   ShanghaiTech University, China

Towards a Complete Analysis of People: From Face and Body to Clothes (T-CAP)

Mohamed Daoudi   IMT Lille Douai, France
Roberto Vezzani   University of Modena and Reggio Emilia, Italy
Guido Borghi   University of Bologna, Italy
Marcella Cornia   University of Modena and Reggio Emilia, Italy
Claudio Ferrari   University of Parma, Italy
Federico Becattini   University of Florence, Italy
Andrea Pilzer   NVIDIA AI Technology Center, Italy

12th International Workshop on Human Behavior Understanding (HBU)

Albert Ali Salah   Utrecht University, The Netherlands
Cristina Palmero   University of Barcelona, Spain
Hugo Jair Escalante   National Institute of Astrophysics, Optics and
    Electronics, Mexico
Sergio Escalera   Universitat de Barcelona, Spain
Henning Müller   HES-SO Valais-Wallis, Switzerland

Theories, Applications, and Cross Modality for Self-Supervised Learning Models (SSL)

Yu Wang   NVIDIA, USA
Yingwei Pan   JD AI Research, China
Jingjing Zou   UC San Diego, USA
Angelica I. Aviles-Rivero   University of Cambridge, UK
Carola-Bibiane Schönlieb   University of Cambridge, UK
John Aston   University of Cambridge, UK
Ting Yao   JD AI Research, China

Multimodal Pattern Recognition of Social Signals in Human-Computer-Interaction (MPRSS 2022)

Mariofanna Milanova   University of Arkansas at Little Rock, USA
Xavier Alameda-Pineda   Inria, University of Grenoble-Alpes, France
Friedhelm Schwenker   Ulm University, Germany

Fairness in Biometric Systems (FAIRBIO)

Philipp Terhörst	Paderborn University, Germany
Kiran Raja	Norwegian University of Science and Technology, Norway
Christian Rathgeb	Hochschule Darmstadt, Germany
Abhijit Das	BITS Pilani Hyderabad, India
Ana Filipa Sequeira	INESC TEC, Portugal
Antitza Dantcheva	Inria Sophia Antipolis, France
Sambit Bakshi	National Institute of Technology Rourkela, India
Raghavendra Ramachandra	Norwegian University of Science and Technology, Norway
Naser Damer	Fraunhofer Institute for Computer Graphics Research IGD, Germany

2nd International Workshop on Artificial Intelligence for Healthcare Applications (AIHA 2022)

Nicole Dalia Cilia	Kore University of Enna, Italy
Francesco Fontanella	University of Cassino and Southern Lazio, Italy
Claudio Marrocco	University of Cassino and Southern Lazio, Italy

Workshop on Multimodal Data for Mental Disorder Recognition (MDMR)

Richang Hong	Hefei University of Technology, China
Marwa Mahmoud	University of Glasgow, UK
Bin Hu	Lanzhou University, China

ICPR 2022 Workshops: Volume II

5th International Workshop on coMics ANalysis, Processing and Understanding (MANPU 2022)

Jean-Christophe Burie	University of La Rochelle, France
Motoi Iwata	Osaka Metropolitan University, Japan
Miki Ueno	Osaka Institute of Technology, Japan

Image Analysis for Forest Environmental Monitoring (FOREST)

Alexandre Bernardino	Instituto Superior Técnico, Portugal
El Khalil Cherif	Instituto Superior Técnico, Portugal
Catarina Barata	Instituto Superior Técnico, Portugal
Alexandra Moutinho	Instituto Superior Técnico, Portugal
Maria João Sousa	Instituto Superior Técnico, Portugal
Hugo Silva	Instituto Superior de Engenharia do Porto, Portugal

MultiMedia FORensics in the WILD (MMFORWILD 2022)

Mauro Barni	University of Siena, Italy
Sebastiano Battiato	University of Catania, Italy
Giulia Boato	University of Trento, Italy
Hany Farid	University of California, Berkeley, USA
Nasir Memon	New York University, USA

Image Mining: Theory and Applications (IMTA-VIII)

Igor Gurevich	Federal Research Center Computer Science and Control of the Russian Academy of Sciences, Russian Federation
Davide Moroni	Institute of Information Science and Technologies, National Research Council of Italy, Italy

Maria Antonietta Pascali   Institute of Information Science and Technologies, National Research Council of Italy, Italy

Vera Yashina   Federal Research Center Computer Science and Control of the Russian Academy of Sciences, Russian Federation

International Workshop on Pattern Recognition in Healthcare Analytics (PRHA 2022)

Inci Baytas   Bogazici University, Turkey

Edward Choi   Korea Advanced Institute of Science and Technology, South Korea

Arzucan Ozgur   Bogazici University, Turkey

Ayse Basar   Bogazici University, Turkey

International Workshop on Industrial Machine Learning (IML)

Francesco Setti   University of Verona, Italy

Paolo Rota   University of Trento, Italy

Vittorio Murino   University of Verona, Italy

Luigi Di Stefano   University of Bologna, Italy

Massimiliano Mancini   University of Tübingen, Germany

ICPR 2022 Workshops: Volume III

3rd International Workshop on Pattern Recognition for Cultural Heritage (PatReCH 2022)

Dario Allegra   University of Catania, Italy
Mario Molinara   University of Cassino and Southern Lazio, Italy
Alessandra Scotto di Freca   University of Cassino and Southern Lazio, Italy
Filippo Stanco   University of Catania, Italy

2nd Workshop on Explainable and Ethical AI (XAIE 2022)

Romain Giot   Univ. Bordeaux, France
Jenny Benois-Pineau   Univ. Bordeaux, France
Romain Bourqui   Univ. Bordeaux, France
Dragutin Petkovic   San Francisco State University, USA

12th Workshop on Pattern Recognition in Remote Sensing (PRRS)

Ribana Roscher   University of Bonn, Germany
Charlotte Pelletier   Université Bretagne Sud, France
Sylvain Lobry   Paris Descartes University, France

Computer Vision for Analysis of Underwater Imagery (CVAUI)

Maia Hoeberechts   Ocean Networks Canada, Canada
Alexandra Branzan Albu   University of Victoria, Canada

Understanding and Mitigating Demographic Bias in Biometric Systems (UMDBB)

Ajita Rattani   Wichita State University, USA
Michael King   Florida Institute of Technology, USA

ICPR 2022 Workshops: Volume IV

AI for De-escalation: Autonomous Systems for De-escalating Conflict in Military and Civilian Contexts (AI4D)

Victor Sanchez	University of Warwick, UK
Irene Amerini	Sapienza University of Rome, Italy
Chang-Tsun Li	Deakin University, Australia
Wei Qi Yan	Auckland University of Technology, New Zealand
Yongjian Hu	South China University of Technology, China
Nicolas Sidere	La Rochelle Université, France
Jean-Jacques Rousseau	York University, Canada

3rd Workshop on Applied Multimodal Affect Recognition (AMAR)

Shaun Canavan	University of South Florida, USA
Tempestt Neal	University of South Florida, USA
Saurabh Hinduja	University of Pittsburgh, USA
Marvin Andujar	University of South Florida, USA
Lijun Yin	Binghamton University, USA

Contents – Part II

MultiMedia FORensics in the WILD (MMFORWILD 2022)

Image Mining: Theory and Applications (IMTA-VIII)

MANPU 2022: The 5th International Workshop on coMics ANalysis, Processing and Understanding

The 5th International Workshop on coMics ANalysis, Processing and Understanding (MANPU 2022)

MANPU is the main workshop related to comics. It gathers mainly researchers in the field of computer science, but also some researchers in the field of human sciences.

Comics is a medium constituted of images combined with text and graphic information in order to narrate a story. Nowadays, comic books are a widespread cultural expression all over the world.

The market of comics continues to grow, and especially the market of digital comics. For example, the market in Japan is about 5.5 billion USD, 1.2 million USD in the US and 500 million € in France. The part of the digital market has reached respectively 2 billion USD, 200 million USD and 7 million USD in these countries.

From a research point of view, comics images are attractive targets because the structure of a comics page includes various elements (such as panels, speech balloons, captions, leading characters, and so on), the drawing of which depends on the style of the author and presents a large variability. Therefore, comics image analysis is not a trivial problem and is still immature compared with other kinds of image analysis. Moreover, digital comics such as webtoons introduce new challenges in terms of analysis and indexing.

In 2016, we held the 1st MANPU in Cancun, Mexico in conjunction with ICPR 2016. In 2017, we held the 2nd MANPU in Kyoto, Japan in conjunction with ICDAR 2017. As a characteristic point, the latter part of MANPU 2017 was held in Kyoto International Manga Museum near to conference place. In 2019, we held the 3rd MANPU in Thessaloniki, Greece in conjunction with MMM 2019. In 2020, MANPU 2020 was impacted by the covid 19 crisis and has been organized as a virtual event in conjunction with ICPR 2020. We received 5 submissions for reviews, from authors belonging to 4 distinct countries. After an accurate and thorough peer-review process, we selected 4 papers for presentation at the workshop. MANPU 2020 involved researchers from eight countries.

In 2022, we received 10 submissions and accepted 8 papers after the double peer-review process. Manpu 2022 consisted of 3 sessions dealing with *"panel detection and segmentation"*, *"text analysis in Comic Album"*, *"Content Analysis in Comic Albums"*. The workshop started with an invited talk. The speaker was the deputy editor of the SHUEISHA company. He presented the strategy of the company for deploying the Manga Plus website.

Last but not least, we would like to thank the MANPU 2022 Program Committee, whose members made the workshop possible with their precise and prompt review process. We would also like to thank ICPR 2022 staffs for hosting the workshop, and the ICPR workshop/publication chairs for the valuable help and support.

August 2022

Jean-Christophe Burie
Motoi Iwata
Miki Ueno
Rita Hartel
Yusuke Matsui
Tien-Tsin Wong

Organization

General Co-chairs

Jean-Christophe Burie   University of La Rochelle, France
Motoi Iwata   Osaka Metropolitan University, Japan
Miki Ueno   Osaka Institute of Technology, Japan

Program Co-chairs

Rita Hartel   Paderborn University, Germany
Tien-Tsin Wong   The Chinese University of Hong Kong,
    Hong Kong

Ryosuke Yamanishi   Kansai University, Japan

Advisory Board

Kiyoharu Aizawa   The University of Tokyo, Japan
Koichi Kise   Osaka Prefecture University, Japan
Jean-Marc Ogier   University of La Rochelle, France
Toshihiko Yamasaki   The University of Tokyo, Japan

Program Committee

Olivier Augereau   Ecole nationale d'ingénieurs de Brest,
    France
John Bateman   University of Bremen, Germany
Ying Cao   City University of Hong Kong, Hong Kong
Mathieu Delalandre   Tours University, France
Alexander Dunst   Paderborn University, Germany
Felix Giesa   Goethe University Frankfurt, Germany
Seiji Hotta   Tokyo University of Agriculture and
    Technology, Japan
Rynson W. H. Lau   City University of Hong Kong, Hong Kong
Jochen Laubrock   University of Potsdam, Germany
Tong-Yee Lee   National Cheng-Kung University, Taiwan
Xueting Liu   The Chinese University of Hong Kong,
    Hong Kong
Muhammad Muzzamil Luqman   University of La Rochelle, France
Yusuke Matsui   The University of Tokyo, Japan
Mitsunori Matsushita   Kansai University, Japan

Naoki Mori	Osaka Metropolitan University, Japan
Mitsuharu Nagamori	University of Tsukuba, Japan
Satoshi Nakamura	Meiji University, Japan
Nhu Van Nguyen	University of La Rochelle, France
Frédéric Rayar	Tours University, France
Christophe Rigaud	University of La Rochelle, France
Yasuyuki Sumi	Future University Hakodate, Japan
John Walsh	Indiana University, USA
Yingqing Xu	Tsinghua University, China

Towards Content-Aware Pixel-Wise Comic Panel Segmentation

Hikaru Ikuta(✉), Runtian Yu, Yusuke Matsui, and Kiyoharu Aizawa

The University of Tokyo, 7–3–1 Hongo, Bunkyo-ku, Tokyo, Japan
{ikuta,r_yu,matsui,aizawa}@hal.t.u-tokyo.ac.jp
https://www.hal.t.u-tokyo.ac.jp/

Abstract. Comic panel detection is the task of identifying panel regions from a given comic image. Many comic datasets provide the borders of the panel lines as its panel region annotations, expressed in formats such as bounding boxes. However, since such panel annotations are usually not aware of the contents of the panel, they do not capture objects that extend outside of the panels, causing such objects to be partially discarded when panels are cropped along the annotations. In such applications, a content-aware annotation that contains all of the contents in each panel is suitable. In this paper, we assess the problem of content-aware comic panel detection using two types of annotations. We first create a small dataset with bounding box annotations where each region contains the entire contents of each panel, and train a detection model. We also explore training a pixel-wise instance segmentation model using synthetic data.

Keywords: Comic panel detection · Object detection · Instance segmentation

1 Introduction

Comic panel detection [7,13,14] is the task of detecting and identifying the locations of panels in a given comic image. Since panels are the main elements composing the temporal aspects of comics, identifying their regions play an important role in comic recognition tasks.

As discussed by Nhu et al. [12], most comic panel detection techniques focus on detecting the borders of the comics, ignoring the content of the comics. This becomes a problem when there are objects that extend outside of the panels, such as in Fig. 1. When the panels are cropped along the detected borders, parts of such objects become excluded from the cropped regions. Therefore, for applications where panels are cropped, it is more convenient for panel detection results to be designed so that they contain such objects that extend outside of the panels.

Nhu et al. [12] also provides a panel detection method based on semantic segmentation, allowing for content-aware panel region detection. As the authors point out in their paper, since semantic segmentation cannot distinguish between

---

H. Ikuta and R. Yu—These authors contributed equally to this work.

J.-J. Rousseau and B. Kapralos (Eds.): ICPR 2022 Workshops, LNCS 13644, pp. 7–21, 2023.
https://doi.org/10.1007/978-3-031-37742-6_1

Fig. 1. An example of an object sticking out from panels. The bounding box on the top shown in red indicates the object sticking out. Comic: Aisazu Niha Irarenai, by Yoshi Masako (Color figure online)

different panel instances, this method has a difficulty when the panel regions overlap with other panels.

In this paper, we assess the problem of objects that extend outside the panel in two ways, with bounding box detection and instance segmentation. For the bounding box detection method, we first define *extended bounding boxes* which are bounding boxes that contain all of the objects that belong to a panel including those that stick out of the panel. We then create a small comic panel dataset based on extended bounding boxes and train an object detector on the data. In the instance segmentation method, we propose a method to create pseudo-data of comic pages with pixel-wise panel instance annotations, and train an instance segmentation model using the pseudo-data. We also explore the use of a weakly supervised instance segmentation method with bounding box annotations as weak supervision.

2 Related Work

2.1 Comic Panel Detection

Previous works in comic panel detection mainly uses three types of output label annotations – rectangular bounding boxes, general quadrilaterals, and pixel-wise annotations. Rectangular bounding boxes are discussed in the work by Ogawa et al. [13], where they apply object detection methods such as SSD300 [10] to data from the Manga109 [1,11] dataset. Quadrilateral regions are discussed in the work by Xufang et al. [14]. In this method, panels are first filled in, following with finding lines that optimally split each panel, and then the shapes of each panel are finally found. Examples of pixel-wise annotations existed before the deep learning era, such as Ho et al. [7]. Methods based on deep learning that use pixel-wise annotations include Nhu et al. [12].

2.2 Object Detection

In our paper, we have used three representative methods for object detection, Faster R-CNN [18], YOLOv3 [17], and Deformable DETR [20].

Faster R-CNN is based on methods such as R-CNN [5] and Fast R-CNN [4]. This method is an end-to-end model, where modules such as region proposal and bounding box regression are combined into a single model.

YOLOv3 is based on YOLO [15] and YOLOv2 [16]. YOLOv3 uses a backbone named DarkNet-53, which has more layers than the previous DarkNet-19 from YOLOv2. Although YOLOv3's performance is lower than DarkNet-19, the inference speed is faster than a ResNet architecture with the same accuracy.

Deformable DETR is a Transformer-based method, based on DETR [2]. DETR had a large limitation of slow convergence speed and limited feature resolutions, caused by the self-attention module. Deformable DETR alleviates this problem by replacing the self-attention module with a smaller module, where only the selected key points inferred from the features are used to calculate the attention, speeding up its calculation.

2.3 Instance Segmentation

Mask R-CNN [6] is an instance segmentation method that detects the bounding boxes of the objects in a given image, and simultaneously infers a segmentation mask for each instance. It is in a way an extention of Faster R-CNN [18], where a branch for predicting an object mask is added in parallel with the bounding box recognition branch.

In our paper, we use Mask R-CNN for pixel-wise comic panel instance segmentation, using synthetically generated psuedo-data with polygonal region annotations, as described later.

2.4 Weakly Supervised Instance Segmentation

BBAM [8] (Bounding Box Attribution Map) is a method for weakly supervised instance segmentation, which is a pixel-wise instance segmentation model trained using bounding box instance labels as weak supervision. BBAM is first trained by training a bounding-box-based object detector. Using the bounding box detection results, a pseudo-ground-truth pixel-wise mask of the detected object is created, such that the mask is the smallest region of the image that produces a nearly identical bounding box as the detected bounding box. This pseudo-ground-truth label is then used for training a weakly supervised instance segmentation model.

In our paper, we use BBAM as an alternate method for object-aware pixel-wise segmentation, using panel bounding boxes as the weak supervision, as described later.

3 Extended Comic Panel Detection

In this section, we first discuss a bounding-box-based method for object-aware comic panel detection. We first define the notion of an *extended bounding box*, then

Fig. 2. Extended bounding boxes and tight bounding boxes. The inner bounding box shown in red is the tight bounding box, which follows the rectangular borders of the panel. The outer bounding box shown in green is the extended bounding box, which contains all of the objects that belong to the panel, including those that stick out of the panel. Comic: Unbalance Tokyo, by Uchida Minako (Color figure online)

create an extended panel dataset consisting of object-aware comic panel bounding boxes, and apply object detection methods to detect the extended panels.

3.1 Extended Panel Dataset

As discussed by Nhu et al. [12] and earlier in the introduction, most existing comic panel extraction methods ignore objects that stick out of the panel, such as those shown in Fig. 1. However, such a definition of bounding boxes is usually inconvenient when the user wishes to crop the panels along the bounding box, since the objects that stick out of the panel are discarded in such cases.

To account for such sticking-out cases, we first define the notion of an *extended bounding box* and a *tight bounding box*, as shown in the outer bounding box in green and the inner bounding box in red in Fig. 2, respectively. Tight bounding boxes are conventional panel bounding boxes used in datasets such as the Manga109 dataset, defined to match the lines of the panel. For non-rectangular panels, the bounding boxes are defined as the minimal rectangle that contains all of the panel lines. On the other hand, extended bounding boxes are defined as the minimal rectangle that contains all of the objects that belong to the given panel, as shown in Fig. 2.

By definition, if there are no objects that stick out of a panel, the extended and tight bounding boxes of that panel are defined to be identical. We will refer to such panels as *tight panels*. If a panel contains objects that do stick out of a panel, the extended and tight bounding boxes will differ. We will refer to such panels as *extended panels*.

Table 1. Comics from the Manga109 dataset used to create the extended bounding box dataset.

Title	Author	#Panels	#Extended Panels
Nichijou Soup	Shindou Uni	845	170
Everyday Osakana Chan	Kuniki Yuka	911	53
Saisoku!!	Matsuda Naomasa	920	330
Youchien Boueigumi	Tenya	368	18
Unbalance Tokyo	Uchida Minako	956	127
ARMS	Kato Masaki	575	274
Dual Justice	Takeyama Yusuke	783	199
Total		5358	1171

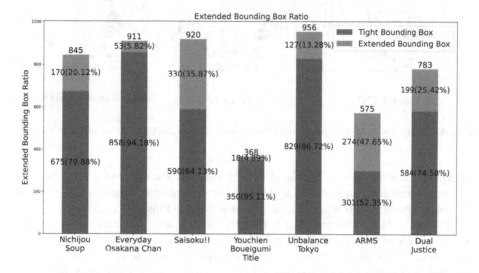

Fig. 3. Per-title frequency of extended panels.

Using this definition of extended panels, we have constructed an extended panel dataset for comic panels. We selected 7 titles from the Manga109 dataset shown in Table 1, and annotated extended panel bounding boxes according to the definition provided earlier.

3.2 The Importance of Sticking-Out Objects

Figure 3 shows the per-title frequency of extended panels, thus showing the frequency of the panels that contain sticking-out objects. The frequency of extended panels ranges from 4.89% in *Youchien Boueigumi* to 47.65% in ARMS, which is a large difference.

An interesting feature of these statistics is the relation with the theme of the comics. The titles with the smallest ratios, *Youchien Boueigumi* and *Everyday Osakana Chan* have themes based on everyday life. *Everyday Osakana Chan* is a non-fiction documentary where the author tries breeding fish at home. On the other hand, the titles with the largest ratios, *ARMS* and *Saisoku!!* have themes based on action. We hypothesize that different genres have different levels of

Table 2. AP evaluation results for the extended comic panel detection task.

Model	Backbone	#Epochs	AP (IoU=0.50 : 0.95)
Faster R-CNN [18]	ResNet50-FPN	12	0.762
YOLOv3 [17]	DarkNet-53	273	0.792
Deformable DETR [20]	ResNet50	50	**0.832**

(a) Faster R-CNN   (b) YOLOv3   (c) Deformable DETR

Fig. 4. Comparison of inference examples. Comic: Dual Justice, by Takeyama Yusuke

relevance for sticking-out panels, since objects that stick out of panels have an effect to emphasize impacts of actions of the characters, which is the cause of the large per-title differences in the frequency of sticking-out panels.

Therefore, these statistics imply that the technique of letting objects sticking out of panels is important for conveying the message of a given comic, since it is related to the genre of the comic. If the authors of the comics deliberately use this technique to express the impact of panels, it is important for comic understanding tasks to be aware of sticking-out objects. This result therefore emphasizes the importance of the object-aware panel detection task, in which sticking-out objects are properly taken into account.

3.3   Extended Panel Bounding Box Regression

Using our extended panel dataset, we train several object detection models to detect object-aware panel bounding boxes. We use Faster R-CNN [18], YOLOv3 [17], and Deformable DETR [20] as the object detection models. YOLOv3 and Deformable DETR are trained using an open source object detection toolbox MMDetection [3], based on PyTorch.

We split the entire dataset per title, with 5 titles for the training set, 1 title for the validation set, and 1 title for the test set. The backbones and the number of epochs used for training are shown in Table 2.

3.4   Results

We evaluated the average precision (AP) for each object detection model, as shown in Table 2. Examples of inference results for each method is shown in Fig. 4. As shown in Table 2, Deformable DETR achieves the best AP.

The example shown in Fig. 4 is a particularly difficult example, since it consists of both non-rectangular panels and sticking-out objects. For the speech bubble sticking out of the panel on the bottom left, Deformable DETR most accurately contains the object, while Faster R-CNN ignores the object with a largest region compared to the other models. The same follows for the corner of the panel. Note that YOLOv3 uses a different input image resolution than the other two models, causing a low-resolution result in Fig. 4 (b).

These results show that even for such difficult results, our extended-panel-based object-aware panel detection method is able to capture objects that extend outside of comic panels with a high performance. Since a separate annotation for panel borders and objects are not required for these results, this provides a relatively cost-friendly method for object-aware comic panel detection.

4   Pixel-Wise Comic Panel Segmentation

In this section, we discuss a more detailed panel detection task, the pixel-wise comic panel segmentation task. We discuss a fully supervised model based on pseudo data, and a weakly supervised pixel-wise instance segmentation model that uses bounding boxes as weak supervision.

4.1   Fully Supervised Training Using a Pseudo-Comic Dataset

In this section, we aim to train a pixel-wise object-aware panel instance segmentation model. Each pixel-wise panel mask is defined similarly as the extended panels in the previous section, where all of the objects that belong to a panel, including those that stick out of the panel, are contained in a mask for a single panel instance. However, it requires a lot of cost to manually annotate each panel instance, making it difficult to create a dataset with a size suitable for training and evaluating instance segmentation models.

To solve this problem, we propose a method to construct a psuedo-comic dataset as shown in Fig. 5, where pixel-wise annotations can be simply be obtained. The process consists of two parts, the pseudo-panel generation phase, and the pseudo-page generation phase.

Pseudo-Panels. To construct psuedo-comics, we first create a set of pseudo-panels. First, we manually extract some speech balloons from real comic pages by annotating the perimiter of each balloon as polygons. The annotation was done using Lableme [19], and the annotation format follows the style of the MS COCO dataset [9]. After obtaining the polygons, we calculate the tight bounding box for each speech balloon.

Fig. 5. Pseudo-page example by merging pseudo-panels.

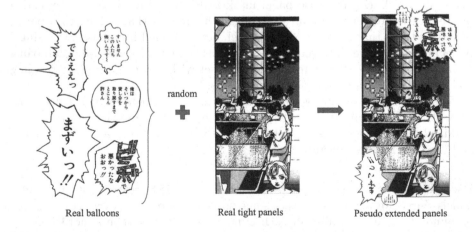

Fig. 6. The overlay process for creating pseudo-panels. Comic: Unbalance Tokyo, by Uchida Minako

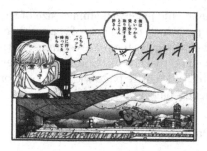 

Fig. 7. Pseudo-panel examples. The outer bounding box shown in blue is the extended bounding box, and the inner panel perimeter shown in red is the polygon annotation. Comic: ARMS, by Kato Masaki (Color figure online)

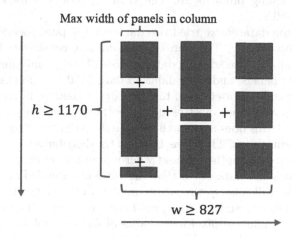

Fig. 8. The generation process of pseudo pages.

Next, for each ground-truth tight panel, i.e. for panels that do not contain any sticking-out objects, we randomly overlay the extracted speech balloons as shown in Fig. 6. The number of speech balloons, the resizing rate, the rotation, and the location of the speech balloons were randomized for each panel. We refer to these panels as pseudo-extended-panels.

Finally, we merge the polygons of all of the objects to obtain the polygon annotation of the perimeter of each pseudo-extended-panel as shown in Fig. 7. We also calculate the extended bounding box of each pseudo-extended-panel by merging all the tight bounding boxes of all the objects.

Pseudo-Pages. After obtaining a set of pseudo-panels, we construct pseudo-pages. Pseudo-pages are constructed by arranging multiple pseudo-panels so that it resembles an actual comic page.

To generate images that are close to actual comic pages, the image size of the pseudo-page is set to be close to 827 × 1170 px, which is the size of a page from the Manga109 dataset. Panels are first arranged vertically to create columns, until the height of the column exceeds or becomes equal to 1170 px. Columns are then arranged horizontally with a margin of 3px, until the entire page width exceeds or becomes equal to 827 px. An example of a pseudo-page is shown in Fig. 5.

4.2   Mask R-CNN with the Pseudo-Page Dataset

Using the pseudo-page dataset, we train a Mask R-CNN network for pixel-wise object-aware panel detection. The network is trained to detect a single object class representing the panels in the image. The batch size is set to 8, with 2 images per GPU. The backbone is ResNet50-FPN, and maximum number of epochs in the training phase is 20. The training process cost 15 min with 4 NVIDIA A100 GPUs.

For the training dataset, we tried two datasets, the pure pseudo-dataset and the mixed pseudo-dataset. The pure pseudo-dataset consists only of pseudo-pages explained above. The training data consists of 766 pseudo-pages generated from 4475 pseudo-panels, and the validation data is 50 pseudo-pages.

In the pure pseudo-dataset, all of the data in the pseudo-dataset mostly consist of extended panels since most pseudo-panels are extended panels. However, according to Fig. 3, this does not match the statistics of the extended-tight panel ratio of actual comic pages. Therefore, to make the distribution of extended-tight panels closer, we create another dataset where we mix ground-truth tight panels taken from the original dataset, so that the ratio of extended and tight panels become equal. We will refer to this as the mixed pseudo-dataset.

For the test dataset, we use two types of data, one being the pseudo-dataset. We also manually annotate pixel-wise masks of for 5 actual comic pages using polygonal annotations. We use this small dataset to evaluate our model as well.

4.3   Weakly Supervised Object-Aware Panel Detection

We also used BBAM [8] to train a weakly supervised object-aware pixel-wise panel detection model. As explained in Sect. 4.3, BBAM is a method that uses bounding box labels as weak supervision to train a pixel-wise instance segmentation model. Using the extended bounding boxes as weak supervision, we trained a BBAM network so that it behaves as an object-aware pixel-wise panel detection model.

4.4   Results

Pure Pseudo-Page Dataset. The panel detection AP (IoU=0.50:0.95) of Mask R-CNN for the pseudo-page validation dataset was 0.982 and 0.877 for the bounding box and polygon annotations, respectively. An inference example on the validation pseudo-page data is shown in Fig. 9. An inference example for Mask R-CNN and BBAM in actual manga page data is shown in Fig. 10.

(a) Inference results of a pseudo-page.

(b) A close-up view of one of the panels.

Fig. 9. An example of the inference results on the validation pseudo-page data.

From Figs. 9 and 10, we can see how the Mask R-CNN model is aware of the sticking-out objects in the image. The AP evaluation results also support the performance of the Mask R-CNN model.

The data in Fig. 10 is a difficult case where non-rectangular panels and panels without borders exist. Although Mask R-CNN detects the borderless panel, it mistakes two non-rectangular panels as one panel. However, the two non-rectangular panels on the top are detected with moderate accuracy.

On the other hand, the results by BBAM fails to detect two of the panels, and even for detected panels, and also mistakes two non-rectangular panels as one panel, which are the same pair mistaken by Mask R-CNN. BBAM captures the speech balloon that sticks out on the top side of the top right panel, but it is apparent that there is a lot of room for improvement for the BBAM model.

Mixed Pseudo-Page Dataset. The AP results for the validation data in each epoch for the pure and mixed pseudo-page dataset is shown in Fig. 11. The AP results for the small actual-page dataset is shown in Fig. 12.

Although the AP increases as the epochs proceed in the pure and mixed pseudo-page dataset as shown in Fig. 11, the opposite happens in the actual-page data, where the AP decreases as the epochs proceed as shown in Fig. 12(a) and (b).

(a) Pseudo page dataset   (b) BBAM

Fig. 10. Comparison of inference results. Comic: Aisazu Niha Irarenai, by Yoshi Masako

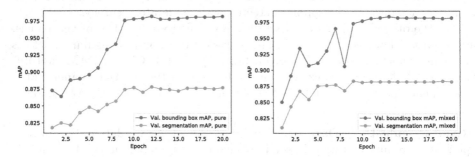

(a) Validation AP for the pure pseudo-page dataset (b) Validation AP for the mixed pseudo-page dataset

Fig. 11. The validation AP for the pure and mixed pseudo-page datasets.

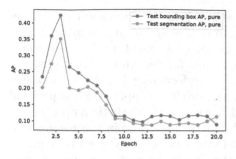 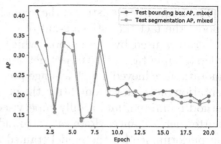

(a) Test AP for the pure pseudo-page dataset   (b) Test AP for the mixed pseudo-page dataset

Fig. 12. The AP for our small test dataset for each epoch, trained with pure and mixed pseudo-page datasets.

4.5 Discussion

As shown in the previous section, since the AP decreases for the real comic data, we hypothesize that the model trained on the synthetic data is overfitted to the pseudo-page dataset. However, it is apparent from Fig. 12 that the AP for the small actual-page dataset increases when the mixed pseudo-page dataset is used, compared to pure pseudo-page data. Therefore, the effect of adding tight panels to make the frequency of extended panels closer to actual comic data seems to be effective on making the image domains of the synthetic and actual datasets closer.

If relieving the domain differences of the synthetic data is effective, another factor that is limiting the performance may be the lack of variety of the objects used in the overlaying process. Currently, the random objects used in the pseudo-panel generation process is limited to speech balloons. Since objects such as characters extend outside of the panel as well, using a more rich variety of objects when creating the synthetic data may improve the performance for the model trained on the pseudo-comic data.

5   Conclusion

In this paper, we discussed the problem of object-aware comic panel detection, where panel regions including objects that stick out of the panel is detected. We discussed two methods, bounding-box-based object detection and instance segmentation. For the bounding box detection method, we first defined the notion of extended bounding boxes and trained an object detector based on this definition. In the instance segmentation method, we proposed a method for creating pseudo-data of comic pages with pixel-wise panel instance annotations, and trained a fully supervised instance segmentation model using the pseudo-data. We also explored the use of a weakly supervised instance segmentation method with bounding box annotations as weak supervision.

The frequency statistics of the extended panels in our extended panel dataset support the fact that sticking-out objects in comics are an important technique deliberately used by the author, which should be handled with care in comic understanding tasks. The object detection results for the extended bounding box annotations achieved a high average precision performance. For the instance segmentation method, we found that the performance for a simple weakly supervised method is limited, and a fully supervised method with synthetic data achieved a better performance. However, we found that the pixel-wise instance segmentation performance for the model trained on synthetic data has a lot of room for improvement for actual data. Improving the performance of pixel-wise instance segmentation for supervised and weakly supervised methods is a course of future work.

References

1. Aizawa, K., et al.: Building a manga dataset "manga109" with annotations for multimedia applications. IEEE MultiMedia **27**(2), 8–18 (2020). https://doi.org/10.1109/mmul.2020.2987895
2. Carion, N., Massa, F., Synnaeve, G., Usunier, N., Kirillov, A., Zagoruyko, S.: End-to-end object detection with transformers. In: Vedaldi, A., Bischof, H., Brox, T., Frahm, J.-M. (eds.) ECCV 2020. LNCS, vol. 12346, pp. 213–229. Springer, Cham (2020). https://doi.org/10.1007/978-3-030-58452-8_13
3. Chen, K., et al.: MMDetection: Open mmlab detection toolbox and benchmark. arXiv preprint arXiv:1906.07155 (2019)
4. Girshick, R.: Fast r-cnn. In: Proceedings of the IEEE International Conference on Computer Vision (ICCV) (December 2015)
5. Girshick, R., Donahue, J., Darrell, T., Malik, J.: Rich feature hierarchies for accurate object detection and semantic segmentation. In: Proceedings of the IEEE Conference on Computer Vision and Pattern Recognition (CVPR) (June 2014)
6. He, K., Gkioxari, G., Dollár, P., Girshick, R.: Mask r-cnn. In: Proceedings of the IEEE International Conference on Computer Vision, pp. 2961–2969 (2017)
7. Ho, A.K.N., Burie, J.C., Ogier, J.M.: Panel and speech balloon extraction from comic books. In: 2012 10th IAPR International Workshop on Document Analysis Systems, pp. 424–428. IEEE (2012)
8. Lee, J., Yi, J., Shin, C., Yoon, S.: Bbam: Bounding box attribution map for weakly supervised semantic and instance segmentation. In: Proceedings of the IEEE/CVF Conference on Computer Vision and Pattern Recognition, pp. 2643–2652 (2021)
9. Lin, T.-Y., et al.: Microsoft COCO: common objects in context. In: Fleet, D., Pajdla, T., Schiele, B., Tuytelaars, T. (eds.) ECCV 2014. LNCS, vol. 8693, pp. 740–755. Springer, Cham (2014). https://doi.org/10.1007/978-3-319-10602-1_48
10. Liu, W., et al.: SSD: single shot multibox detector. In: Leibe, B., Matas, J., Sebe, N., Welling, M. (eds.) ECCV 2016. LNCS, vol. 9905, pp. 21–37. Springer, Cham (2016). https://doi.org/10.1007/978-3-319-46448-0_2
11. Matsui, Y., et al.: Sketch-based manga retrieval using manga109 dataset. Multimedia Tools Appl. **76**(20), 21811–21838 (2016). https://doi.org/10.1007/s11042-016-4020-z

12. Nguyen Nhu, V., Rigaud, C., Burie, J.C.: What do we expect from comic panel extraction? In: 2019 International Conference on Document Analysis and Recognition Workshops (ICDARW). vol. 1, pp. 44–49 (2019). https://doi.org/10.1109/ICDARW.2019.00013
13. Ogawa, T., Otsubo, A., Narita, R., Matsui, Y., Yamasaki, T., Aizawa, K.: Object detection for comics using manga109 annotations (2018). https://arxiv.org/abs/1803.08670
14. Pang, X., Cao, Y., Lau, R.W., Chan, A.B.: A robust panel extraction method for manga. In: Proceedings of the 22nd ACM International Conference on Multimedia, pp. 1125–1128 (2014)
15. Redmon, J., Divvala, S., Girshick, R., Farhadi, A.: You only look once: Unified, real-time object detection. In: Proceedings of the IEEE Conference On Computer Vision And Pattern Recognition, pp. 779–788 (2016)
16. Redmon, J., Farhadi, A.: Yolo9000: better, faster, stronger. In: Proceedings of the IEEE Conference on Computer Vision and Pattern Recognition, pp. 7263–7271 (2017)
17. Redmon, J., Farhadi, A.: Yolov3: An incremental improvement (2018)
18. Ren, S., He, K., Girshick, R., Sun, J.: Faster r-cnn: towards real-time object detection with region proposal networks. Adv. Neural. Inf. Process. Syst. **28**, 91–99 (2015)
19. Wada, K.: Labelme: Image Polygonal Annotation with Python. https://doi.org/10.5281/zenodo.5711226. https://github.com/wkentaro/labelme
20. Zhu, X., Su, W., Lu, L., Li, B., Wang, X., Dai, J.: Deformable detr: Deformable transformers for end-to-end object detection. In: International Conference on Learning Representations (2021). https://openreview.net/forum?id=gZ9hCDWe6ke

A Method to Annotate Who Speaks a Text Line in Manga and Speaker-Line Dataset for Manga109

Tsubasa Sakurai(✉), Risa Ito, Kazuki Abe, and Satoshi Nakamura

School of Interdisciplinary Mathematical Sciences, Meiji University, Tokyo, Japan
rapisu283@gmail.com

Abstract. Speaker estimation in a manga is one component that needs to be recognized in conducting research using manga. To identify the speaker of a text line in a manga, a dataset of who speaks the lines is needed. In order to construct such a dataset easily, we proposed a method to annotate who speaks a text line based on characteristics of information design and the human factor. Then, we developed a prototype system, constructed a dataset that mapped between text lines and speakers in the Manga109 dataset, and distributed the dataset on the Web. Then, we analyzed the dataset and showed that the perfect match rate was about 80% when there were five annotators. In addition, we found that variation in annotation occurred even with human judgment and that this was partly due to lines requiring reference to other frames. We also found that it was difficult for annotators to map speakers in scenes involving science fiction and battles by calculating the Evaluation Consistency Indicators.

Keywords: Comic · Manga · Text Line · Speaker-Line Dataset

1 Introduction

According to the Japanese E-book Business Research Report 2020 [1], the market size of e-books is increasing yearly, and the market share of comics is more than 80% in Japan. In addition, sales of e-comics surpassed sales of print comics in 2017. As of 2021, the market size of e-comics has been expanding due to COVID-19 and other factors and enjoying manga as e-comics is becoming more common. With the spread of e-comics, there will be more and more ways to use and enjoy digital comics.

Research on processing and systems that take advantage of the fact that e-comics are available on digital terminals is also increasing. Mantra [2] performs automatic contextual translation based on image and text information of comics. Other studies have also taken into account the content of comics, such as comic searches [3], recommendations, and spoiler prevention [4]. For these studies, it is necessary to recognize the various elements of comics accurately (e.g., the area of comic frames, the area of lines, the content of lines, onomatopoeia and mimetic words, name and face of a character, facial expressions, the speaker of the lines, and relationships between characters). To promote such

© Springer Nature Switzerland AG 2023
J.-J. Rousseau and B. Kapralos (Eds.): ICPR 2022 Workshops, LNCS 13644, pp. 22–33, 2023.
https://doi.org/10.1007/978-3-031-37742-6_2

research and development, datasets annotated by many people are essential, and one of these is the Manga109 dataset [5, 6], which contains 109 comics drawn by professional cartoonists with annotations. Other examples include the *eBDtheque* dataset by Guérin et al. [7], the *COMICS* dataset by Iyyer et al. [8], and the four-frame manga dataset for the understanding story by Ueno [9]. As described above, many datasets on comics are available to the public and are used for various research purposes.

One of the issues in translating comics and performing content-based searches and recommendations with high accuracy is recognizing who speaks a line. To increase the recognition accuracy, it is very important to prepare a large dataset of who speaks the lines (hereafter, we call this "speaker-line dataset"). However, there are not enough speaker-line datasets, and it is not easy to construct such a dataset.

In this study, we propose and develop a system to construct a speaker-line dataset easily by dragging a text line and dropping it into a character's face or body area. We construct a speaker-line dataset using our system for the Manga109 dataset. We also analyze the dataset based on multiple indices to clarify fluctuations in the human evaluation and analyze situations in which judging a speaker is difficult.

The contributions of this paper are as follows:

- This paper proposes and develops a new annotation system to generate a speaker-line dataset.
- This paper constructs a speaker-line dataset with at least four annotators annotating each manga in the Manga109 dataset and distributes it.
- This paper clarifies the difficulties of generating a speaker-line dataset for people.

2 Related Work

There are various studies on techniques to recognize the elements that compose comics. Nguyen et al. [10] reexamined the definition of frames in comics and proposed a method for extracting them. Wang et al. [11] proposed to extract frames in comics and achieved high performance, accuracy, and no margins. Dubray et al. [12] automatically detected candidate speech balloons and segmentation using machine learning and achieved an F1 score of more than 0.94. Chu et al. [13] proposed a method for character face recognition, and Tolle et al. [14] proposed a method for line recognition with high accuracy. These studies used comic images and text information for recognition, and it can be said that simpler and more accurate methods are being established. A dataset that will provide the correct understanding of comics is needed to promote such research further. This study contributes to such research.

As a technique to promote the research and development of comics, Chen et al. [15] proposed an algorithm for understanding multilingual four-scene comics. Park et al. [16] analyzed the characteristics of characters to realize a comic retrieval system using the characters in comics. Such research is necessary for developing a system that considers the content of comics, and one of the techniques for understanding manga is judging the speaker. Rigaud et al. [17] proposed a method for speaker estimation based on the distance from the tail of a speech balloon. Nguyen et al. [18] proposed a Comic MTL model that learns multiple tasks and analyzes the relationship between speech balloons and characters. These studies need to recognize the relationship between lines and speakers in comics. Our study is to support such recognition by preparing the large speaker-line dataset based on the Manga109 and implementing the annotation system.

3   A Method to a Construct Speaker-Line Dataset

Constructing a speaker-line dataset is not easy because there are many speakers and a huge number of text lines in a manga. For example, in the Manga109 dataset, the total number of text lines is 147,387 in 109 mangas, the average number of text lines per manga is 1,352, the average number of speakers is 31.7, and the maximum number of speakers in a manga is 124. In order to construct the speaker-line dataset easily and quickly, we have to realize a new system to associate a speaker and a text line.

In mangas, a speech balloon and its text line are often settled near their speaker because of the aspect of information design. In addition, Fitts's law [19] and its extension to 2D [20] showed that in the action of a user pointing to a certain location, a user could point to a large target with a short distance more quickly and accurately compared with a smaller target with a long distance. Therefore, we can say that mapping between a text line and its speaker is suitable for mouse operation.

Considering these characteristics, we propose a method that enables users to map between a text line and a speaker by dragging a text line area and dropping it onto the face or body area of its speaker. We also developed our system using JavaScript, PHP, and MySQL.

Figures 1, 2, 3, and 4 show our prototype system. In Fig. 1, an annotator is dragging a text line to a face area of a character. When the annotator drops the text line onto this face area, the system registers this text line's speaker as this character.

Fig. 1. An annotator can associate a text line with a character by dragging a text line area and dropping it onto a face area of character. When the annotator starts dragging a text line on the comic, the system shows all the drop targets reference to the face area or body area of characters. In addition, when the annotator moves the mouse cursor to the drop target, the system changes the color of the drop target and shows the character's name.

Our system also considers that the speaker of the line does not appear on the same page when assigning annotations. The annotator can select the speaker from the speaker list if necessary (see Fig. 2). The annotator selects "unknown" from the speaker list if the speaker is unknown (shown in Fig. 2 by the "?" mark). In addition, select "narration" from the speaker list if the text line is narration (shown in Fig. 2 with the "microphone" mark). Fig. 3 shows the page-by-page annotation management interface. The annotator can skip a difficult text line to annotate and easily check the annotation progress in its comic. Figure 4 shows the interface for selecting and managing annotation targets.

Fig. 2. An annotator can also select a speaker from a speaker list in the comic. This function is useful when the speaker of a text line does not exist on the same page.

Fig. 3. The system shows the annotation progress in each page by changing its color.

Fig. 4. Annotation target selection user interface.

4 Speaker-Line Dataset for Manga 109

We constructed the speaker-line dataset using our system based on the Manga109 dataset. The constructed dataset is available on the Web[1].

Fifty-six annotators contributed to the construction of the dataset. The total number of speaker-line pairs assigned by these 56 annotators was 749,856, and considering that the total number of lines in all mangas in Manga109 is 147,918, there were, on average, about five annotators for each line. Furthermore, each comic was annotated by at least four annotators. Fig. 5 shows the number of annotations by each annotator. In this figure, the horizontal axis indicates the ID of the annotator who performed the annotation (sorted in descending order by the number of annotations). The vertical axis shows the number of annotations by that annotator.

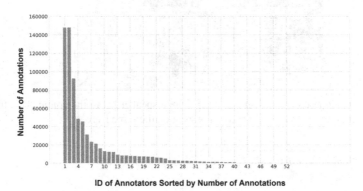

Fig. 5. Number of annotations assigned to each annotator.

The results show that the two annotators annotated nearly 150,000 lines each. The total number of lines in the target manga is 147,918, indicating that the annotators annotated almost all the lines. These results suggest that our system can adequately map lines to speakers, even with a large number of annotation targets. On the other hand, since more than half of the annotators hardly annotated anything, those annotations may not be helpful.

5 Analysis of the Dataset

5.1 Agreement Rate of the Annotations and Features of each Frame

Table 1 shows the matching or mismatching of annotations in each line by annotators in this dataset. The proportion of all annotators choosing the same character for one line was 71.1%. Table 2 shows the number and percentage of characters present with the target lines in the same frame. The presence or absence of a candidate speaker in the frame containing the line is also shown. The presence or absence of a candidate speaker

---

[1] https://nkmr.io/comic/speaker-dataset/

in a frame is determined by whether or not the corresponding line and character are depicted within ± 50px of each frame. The candidate speaker was the character with the highest number of annotations and was judged on whether it was common to the character that appeared in the frame.

Table 1. Results of annotation assignment.

Opinion	Details	Number of data	Percentage
Match	Select the same person	105,238 cases	71.1%
	Select 'Narration'	2,654 cases	1.8%
	Select 'Unknown'	30 cases	0.0%
Mismatch	Selecting different persons	25,385 cases	17.2%
	Select 'Unknown'	5,042 cases	3.4%
	Select 'Other'	874 cases	0.6%

Table 2. Number of characters and speaker candidates in each frame.

		Presence of speaker in the target frame	
		Speaker exists in the frame	Speaker does not exist in the frame
How many characters are in the target frame	No character in the frame with the target text line	0 (0.0%)	15,471 (10.8%)
	One character is present in the frame with the target text line	34,497 (24.0%)	15,798 (10.9%)
	Two or more characters exist in the frame with the target text line	66,276 (46.1%)	11,841 (8.2%)
Total		100,733 (70.0%)	43,110 (30.0%)

The results showed that the percentage of choice, "Speaker does not exist in the frame," was 30.0%. This result means that 30.0% of text lines do not appear with their speakers in the same frame. Therefore, the recognition system should find a speaker of a target text line for other frames or other pages. In addition, 34,497 cases (68.6%) of "One character is present in the frame" were classified as candidate speakers. On the other hand, 66,276 cases (84.8%) of "Two or more characters exist in the frame" were candidate speakers. This result indicates that if the number of characters per frame is low or zero, there are more opportunities to refer to other pages in the manga.

5.2 Relationship between Perfect Match Rate and Number of Annotators

In order to examine how many people should be assigned to do annotation, we compare the percentage of the perfect match rate with the number of assignees. The perfect match means that all annotators associate a target text line with the same speaker.Fig. 6 shows the perfect match rate when the first N (N = 1−6) annotators associate each target text line. The horizontal axis indicates the situation in which the first N annotators (the first two annotators, the first three annotators, and so on) annotated the lines. The vertical axis indicates the perfect match rate (percentage). The results show that the perfect match rate gradually decreases as the number of annotators increases.

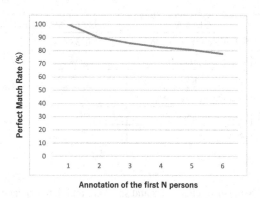

Fig. 6. The perfect match rate in each number of annotators.

5.3 Evaluation Index and Results for Speaker Mapping

To calculate the difficulty of mapping between a text line and a speaker, we define the following ECI (Evaluation Consistency Indicators) for the data in the above dataset (Eq. (1)).

$$ECI = \frac{2 \times \text{Max\_Match} \times \frac{1}{\text{Variation}}}{\text{Max\_Match} + \frac{1}{\text{Variation}}} \tag{1}$$

The ECI is the harmonic mean of "Max_Match" and inversed "Variation." The ECI is an index that indicates the blurring of evaluations in annotation assignments. Here, "Variation" means the number of speakers that annotators annotated for a given line. "Max_Match" means the maximum number of annotators who annotated the same speaker for a given line. "Max_Match" is the maximum value of the ratio calculated by dividing the number of annotators for each annotation target by the total number of annotators. For example, if eight annotators assigned character A and two assigned character B for a target text line, "Variation" is two and "Max_Match" is 0.8. We calculated these values except annotated as unknown.

In this data, if the value of Max_Match is low and the value of Variation is high, it is considered that the difference in evaluation between people is large, and the value of this indicator becomes low. Therefore, if the value of the ECI is high, it is easy to annotate the line. In contrast, it is difficult to annotate the line if the value is low.

Figure 7 shows the average of the values of the ECI for each manga, derived from the values of the ECI for all the lines in Manga109. The result shows that there is no manga with a value of 1.0. On the other hand, no manga falls below 0.8.

To confirm whether the ECI work effectively, we selected two mangas (ARMS, Joouari). We calculated the average of the values of the ECI on each page as shown in Figs. 8 and 9. In these figures, the horizontal axis indicates the number of pages, and the vertical axis indicates the average of the ECI. From these figures, it can be seen that the value of the ECI varies greatly from page to page.

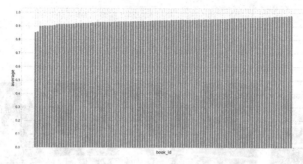

Fig. 7. Distribution of ECI in each manga.

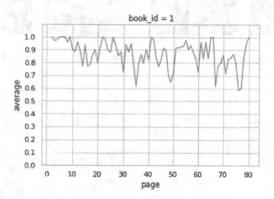

Fig. 8. Distribution of ECI in ARMS.

Figures 10 and 11 show some of the pages in Figs. 8 and 9, for which the value of the evaluation agreement index was less than 0.7. These results indicate that it is difficult for the annotator to match lines to speakers in battle scenes, dark scenes, and scenes involving spaceships with multiple passengers.

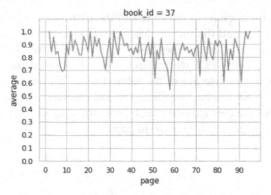

Fig. 9. Distribution of ECI in Joouari.

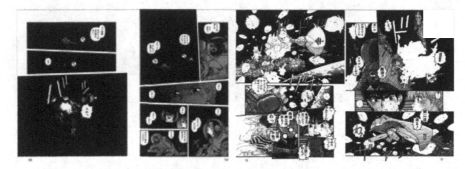

Fig. 10. Battle scenes and dark scenes are difficult to map. © Masaki Kato, ARMS

Fig. 11. Battle scenes are difficult to map. © Masakazu Ooi, Joouari

6   Discussion and Prospects

As shown in Tables 1 and 2, the perfect match for annotations was 71.1%, and the smaller the number of characters in the frame of the target lines, the lower the percentage of candidate speakers present. Therefore, it can be seen that variation in annotation occurs even in human judgment. The reason for the variation in annotation may be due to the fact that there are no speakers in the frame, and the lines need to be referred to other frames.

Figure 6 shows that the perfect match rate decreased by about 10% when comparing the case by two annotators with the case by five annotators. This result indicates that the evaluation is not appropriate just because the speaker's mapping to a line was the perfect match when there were two annotators. Therefore, a dataset constructor should design the appropriate number of annotators carefully.

Figure 7 shows scenes in which the ECI are low in all mangas. In addition, there was no manga that the ECA values was 1.0. The ECI tended to be particularly low in genres such as Science Fiction and Battle, and it was found that there were pages (scenes) with very low values, as shown in Figs. 8 and 9. In addition, it was often difficult to grasp the situation in these specific scenes, such as battle scenes and dark scenes, as shown in Figs. 10 and 11.

As a result, the following features as difficulty of association:

- Character does not exist in the frame of a target text line.
- Multiple characters exist in the same frame of a target text line.
- Many expressions indicate internal speech or physical states in the lines.
- A tail of a speech balloon does not exist.
- A tail of a speech balloon does not point toward its speaker.
- A text line is not in a speech balloon.

In summary, in constructing the speaker-line dataset, it is considered necessary to assign only one or two annotators to simple scenes that can be easily judged by anyone and assign a large number of annotators to difficult scenes such as those in Figs. 10 and 11, and to make decisions by a majority vote or other means.

The automatic estimation of annotation difficulty will be studied and realized based on the dataset constructed in our study. Suppose the automatic estimation of annotation difficulty becomes possible. If we can estimate the annotation difficulty, we will be able to change the number of annotators depending on its difficulty in each text line. In addition, we can assign a skilled person to a tough text line.

7 Conclusion

In this study, we proposed a dataset construction method to enable mapping lines and speakers in Manga109 to contribute to the study of the analysis and understanding of mangas. Then, we developed a prototype system, constructed a dataset that mapped between text lines and speakers in the Manga109 dataset, and distributed the dataset on the Web. In our dataset, 56 annotators contributed to 749,856 annotations. We analyzed the dataset to determine the rate of annotation match or mismatch, the presence or absence of candidate speakers, and how the perfect match rate changed when the number of annotators increased. Furthermore, we defined the ECI based on variation and max match rate, and analyzed scenes in which it is difficult to estimate the speaker by using these indicators manually. As a result, we found that the ECI was lower in battle scenes and scenes in which it was difficult to grasp the state of the scene like dark scenes in genres such as Science Fiction and Battle. The characteristics of the frames and lines of dialog in these scenes were also clarified.

In the future, we aim to contribute toward the automatic judgment of the speaker by clarifying the difficulty level of annotation for each line. We also plan to clarify differences in human evaluation and to consider methods for dynamically changing the number of annotations required by humans.

Acknowledgments. JSPS Grant-in-Aid partly funded this work for Scientific Research JP20K12130 and JP22K12338.

References

1. Impress Research Institute: E-book Business Research Report 2020 in Japanese. https://research.impress.co.jp/report/list/ebook/500995. Accessed 20 Oct 2021
2. Mantra. https://mangahot.jp/. Accessed 20 Oct 2021
3. Park, B., Okamoto, K., Yamashita, R., Matsushita, M.: Designing a comic exploration system using a hierarchical topic classification of reviews. Inf. Eng. Expr. **3**(2), 45–57 (2017)
4. Maki, Y., Nakamura, S.: Do manga spoilers spoil manga? In: The Sixth Asian Conference on Information Systems, pp.258–262 (2017)
5. Matsui, Y., et al.: Sketch-based manga retrieval using manga109 dataset. Multimedia Tools Appl. **76**(20), 21811–21838 (2016). https://doi.org/10.1007/s11042-016-4020-z
6. Ogawa, T., Otsubo, A., Narita, R., Matsui, Y., Yamasaki, T., Aizawa, K.: Object Detection for Comics using Manga109 Annotations, arXiv:1803.08670 (2018)
7. Guérin, C., et al.: eBDtheque: a representative database of comics. In: 12th International Conference on Document Analysis and Recognition, pp. 1145–1149 (2013)
8. Iyyer, M., et al.: The amazing mysteries of the gutter: drawing inferences between panels in comic book narratives. In: IEEE Conference on Computer Vision and Pattern Recognition, pp. 7186–7195, (2017)
9. Ueno, M.: Four-scene comic story dataset for software on creative process. In: New Trends in Intelligent Software Methodologies, Tools and Techniques, vol. 303, pp. 48–56 (2018)
10. Nguyen Nhu, V., Rigaud, C., Burie, J.: What do we expect from comic panel extraction? In: 2019 International Conference on Document Analysis and Recognition Workshops (ICDARW), vol. 1, pp. 44–49 (2019)
11. Wang, Y., Zhou, Y., Tang, Z.: Comic frame extraction via line segments combination. In: 2015 13th International Conference on Document Analysis and Recognition (ICDAR), pp. 856–860 (2015)
12. Dubray, D., Laubrock, J.: Deep CNN-based speech balloon detection and segmentation for comic books. In: 2019 International Conference on Document Analysis and Recognition (ICDAR), pp. 1237–1243 (2019)
13. Chu, W.T., Li, W.W.: Manga face detection based on deep neural networks fusing global and local information. Pattern Recogn. **86**, 62–72 (2019)
14. Tolle, H., Arai, K.: Method for real time text extraction of digital manga comic. Int. J. Image Process. **4**(6), 669–676 (2011)
15. Chen, J., Iwasaki, R., Mori, N., Okada, M., Ueno, M.: Understanding multilingual four-scene comics with deep learning methods. In: 2019 International Conference on Document Analysis and Recognition Workshops (ICDARW), pp. 32–37 (2019)
16. Park, B., Ibayashi, K., Matsushita, M.: Classifying personalities of comic characters based on egograms. In: Proceedings the 4th International Symposium on Affective Science and Engineering, and the 29th Modern Artificial Intelligence and Cognitive Science Conference, pp. 1–6 (2018)

17. Rigaud, C., et al.: Speech balloon and speaker association for comics and manga understanding. In: 13th International Conference on Document Analysis and Recognition (ICDAR), pp. 351–355, (2015)
18. Nguyen, N.V., Rigaud, C., Burie, J.C.: Comic MTL: optimized multi-task learning for comic book image analysis. Int. J. Doc. Anal. Recogn. (IJDAR), **22**, 265–284 (2019)
19. Fitts, P.M.: The information capacity of the human motor system in controlling the amplitude of movement. J. Exper. Psychol. **47**(6), 381–391 (1954)
20. MacKenzie, I.S., Buxton, W.: Extending fitts' law to two-dimensional tasks. In: Proceedings of the ACM Conference on Human Factors in Computing Systems - CHI 1992, pp. 219–226. ACM, New York (1992)

Considering Meanings and Effects of Frames Without Onomatopoeias in Japanese Comics

Riko Sugita, Minami Okajima, Takanori Komatsu[✉], and Satoshi Nakamura

Department of Frontier Media Science, Meiji University, Tokyo, Japan
tkomat@meiji.ac.jp

Abstract. Onomatopoeias - echoic, imitative, or mimetic words - are good for describing intuitive, sensitive, and ambiguous feelings that are difficult to express literally. They are often used in Japanese comics as an effective means of expression. In this study, we hypothesize that there are expressive techniques in comics such as "purposely not using onomatopoeia" and discuss the meanings and effects of frames without onomatopoeias. As a result, we confirm that frames without onomatopoeias frequently appear in significant scenes even though onomatopoeias are generally highly expressive in comics.

Keywords: Onomatopoeias · Japanese comics · Large sized frame · Enlargement of the body parts · Depiction in great detail · Background music (BGM)

1 Introduction

Onomatopoeias - echoic, imitative, or mimetic words - are an indispensable part of the Japanese language and are good for describing intuitive, sensitive, and ambiguous feelings that are difficult to express literally [1, 2]. In terms of the expressive potential of Japanese onomatopoeias, Tajima [3] argued that "Onomatopoeias, which can concisely and concretely describe a certain sound or situation, can be seen and heard everywhere on TVs, radios, newspapers, books, and magazines." Needless to say, such onomatopoeias are widely used in Japanese daily life, and moreover, they are also often used in Japanese comics as effective means of expression.

Up to now, the meanings and effects of onomatopoeias in Japanese comics have been discussed particularly from the viewpoints of linguistics or media criticism. For example, Natsume [4] focused on the higher expressiveness and creativeness of onomatopoeias in comics and discussed their expressive potential. Izawa [5] investigated the expressiveness of onomatopoeias in comics in a qualitative manner and pointed out the important roles of onomatopoeia, for example, "Compared with novels, comics lack an overwhelming amount of information, such as multiple meanings, situations, backgrounds, and so on. However, such lack of information can be compensated for just with a simple onomatopoeia word."

However, in fact, not all frames in comics use onomatopoeias for effective expression. For example, we found that the rate of frames without onomatopoeias among all

J.-J. Rousseau and B. Kapralos (Eds.): ICPR 2022 Workshops, LNCS 13644, pp. 34–47, 2023.
https://doi.org/10.1007/978-3-031-37742-6_3

frames in the first volume of the Japanese volleyball comic "Haikyu!!" was about 64.7% (specifically, 770 frames without onomatopoeias among all 1191 frames). On the basis of this finding, we then hypothesized that there are expressive techniques in comics like "purposely not using onomatopoeia." In this paper, we then investigate where onomatopoeia is NOT used in comics and discuss the meanings and effects of frames without onomatopoeias.

2 Related Works

The previous studies focusing on onomatopoeias in research field of comic computing can be roughly divided into two categories: one is "proposing novel technologies to apply the expressive potential of onomatopoeias to comics," and the other is "analyzing and considering the meanings and effects of onomatopoeias in comics."

As examples of studies of the former category, "proposing novel technologies," Hashimoto et al. [6] proposed a method for extracting onomatopoeias from frame images in comics and applying video effects to them. Matsushita et al. [7] proposed a creative tool that enables users to add motion effects to existing onomatopoeias in comics in order to build a new method for dynamically representing onomatopoeias, especially for e-comics. Sato et al. [8] also proposed a tool that can easily add animation effects to hand-written onomatopoeias when creating e-comics.

As examples of studies of the latter category, "analyzing and considering," Uchiyama [9] analyzed the characteristics of onomatopoeias appearing in speech balloons in comics by means of natural language processing methods. Hira [10] investigated the effects of onomatopoeias from the viewpoint of "movement" and reported that these onomatopoeias are not used to enhance the effects of movement like a sound effect but are used as a tool for expressing movement per se in comic works. Natsume [4] argued that the higher expressiveness and creativeness of onomatopoeias in comics are greater than imagined and reported that such onomatopoeias can produce significant effects beyond linguistic symbols that simply manipulate the readers' eye movements in comics.

It can be then said that these previous studies of both categories have focused on the existence of onomatopoeias per se. Therefore, our approach of focusing on the case where onomatopoeias are not used and considering the meanings and effects of frames without onomatopoeias is highly novel and challenging.

3 Investigation

3.1 Materials and Methods

In this study, Japanese sports comics were selected as the target of our investigation because sports comics contain more onomatopoeias than ordinary comics. Specifically, the following seven works were selected: "Aoashi," "Farewell, my dear Cramer," and "DAYS" for soccer/football, "Ahiru no sora" for basketball, "Burning kabaddi" for kabaddi, "Haikyu!!" for volleyball, and "Hanebad!" for badminton. We investigated only the first volume of each work.

We manually extracted and counted the number of frames in which onomatopoeia was not used and considered what kinds of appearance characteristics these extracted frames had and which kinds of meanings they expressed. In this paper, onomatopoeias expressed inside of speech balloons were uncounted and excluded from our investigation. Table 1 shows the total numbers of all frames and the numbers of frames without onomatopoeias in the first 100 pages of the seven target comics. This table shows that "Burning kabaddi," "Haikyu!!", and "Ahiru no sora" had relatively lower rates, from 53.7% to 63.0%, of frames without onomatopoeias (this means these three used onomatopoeias frequently). However, the other comics had higher rates between about 65.7 and 78.8%.

Table 1. Total numbers of all frames and number of frames without onomatopoeias in first 100 pages of seven comics

Title	Numbers of all frames	Numbers of frames without onomatopoeias
Aoashi	505	398 (78.8%)
Farewell, my dear…	402	309 (76.9%)
DAYS	431	193 (65.7%)
Ahiru no sora	427	269 (63.0%)
Burming kabaddi	467	251 (53.7%)
Haikyu!!	609	378 (62.1%)
Hanebad!	417	289 (69.3%)

3.2 Characteristics of Frames Without Onomatopoeias

As a result of our manual exploration into which kinds of frames do not have any onomatopoeias, we qualitatively identified that frames with the following three specific appearance characteristics had a strong tendency not to have onomatopoeias. The first characteristic is frames in which the body parts of the protagonists are depicted in an enlarged manner. Specifically, this type of frame makes readers focus on specific body actions by enlarging the significant parts of the body, like the limbs or eyes of the protagonists (Fig. 1). The second characteristic is frames that are large in size themselves. In general comics, frames with different sizes are used, but frames with extraordinarily large sizes are sometime used. In this paper, we define "large sized frame" as larger than one third the size of the page (Fig. 2). The third characteristic is frames that are depicted in great detail These frames express situations not in language but in pictures with detailed depictions (Fig. 3).

Tables 2, 3 and 4 show the numbers of frames with and without onomatopoeias in cases with and without one of three appearance characteristics, as well as the results of a Fisher's exact test on the numbers with and without onomatopoeias between the cases with and without each appearance characteristic independently.

Fig. 1. Large frame with enlarged body parts ©Haruichi Furudate 2012 "Haikyu!!".

Fig. 2. Large frame with greatly detailed depiction of protagonist's body movement ©Takeshi Hinata 2004 "Ahiru no sora"

These results indicate that frames with enlarged body parts had significantly higher rates of frames without onomatopoeias; however, those with large sized frames and greatly detailed depictions did not. Although this result seems to deviate from our qualitative observations (i.e., frames with a large size and greatly detailed depiction suppress the use of onomatopoeias), we assume the following two reasons for this deviation; one is that the numbers of frames with these two characteristics were lower that those with enlarged body parts, so there was not enough to show a statistical difference, and the other is that there is a possibility that the effects of each of these characteristics are limited and that the combination of these characteristics has an adequate effect on suppressing the use of onomatopoeias (in our statistical analysis, this adequate effect was eventually concentrated on the first characteristic, "enlarged body part"). To clarify this issue, we have to reconsider the effects of one or a combination of these appearance characteristics in our following studies.

Fig. 3. Large frame with greatly detailed depiction of protagonist's background ©Tsuyoshi Yasuda 2013 "DAYS"

Table 2. Number of frames without onomatopoeia and total number of frames with "Enlarged body parts" in first 100 pages of target comics (frames without onomatopoeia/total number of frames)

Titles	Frame with characteristic	Frame without characteristic	p-values
Aoashi	108/120 (90.0%)	297/451 (65.9%)	**p = 0.000**
Farewell, my dear...	102/126 (81.0%)	198/252 (85.3%)	p = 0.296
DAYS	105/141 (74.5%)	185/284 (65.1%)	p = 0.059
Ahiru no sora	112/147 (76.3%)	165/284 (61.7%)	**p = 0.000**
Burming kabaddi	65/95 (68.4%)	194/348 (55.7%)	**p = 0.034**
Haikyu!!	103/135 (76.3%)	345/559 (61.7%)	**p = 0.001**
Hanebad!	77/99 (77.8%)	198/296 (66.9%)	**p = 0.044**

3.3 Meanings of Frames Without Onomatopoeias

We confirmed that frames with some of the above three characteristics and without onomatopoeias frequently appeared in the following three specific situations. The first is the case when the protagonist recollects something or has a monologue or when the story is explained through narration, e.g., explaining the rules of a sport, the protagonist recalling memories or trauma, and so on (Figs. 4, 5 and 6). In such situations, it is common for the narration to objectively and unilaterally explain the above information

Table 3. Number of frames without onomatopoeia and total number of frames with "Large size frame" in first 100 pages of target comics.

Titles	Frame with characteristic	Frame without characteristic	p-values
Aoashi	72/84 (85.7%)	351/423 (83.0%)	$p = 0.182$
Farewell, my dear...	82/112 (73.2%)	235/285 (82.5%)	$p = 0.051$
DAYS	66/111 (58.4%)	230/325 (70.8%)	**$p = 0.019$**
Ahiru no sora	67/110 (60.9%)	214/327 (65.4%)	$p = 0.421$
Burming kabaddi	42/97 (43.3%)	228/388 (58.8%)	**$p = 0.008$**
Haikyu!!	62/95 (65.3%)	378/687 (64.4%)	$p = 0.908$
Hanebad!	78/104 (75.0%)	228/322 (70.8%)	$p = 0.453$

Table 4. Number of frames without onomatopoeia and total number of frames with "Greatly Detailed Depiction" in first 100 pages of target comics.

Titles	Frame with characteristic	Frame without characteristic	p-values
Aoashi	62/65 (95.4%)	395/472 (83.7%)	**$p = 0.009$**
Farewell, my dear...	85/109 (78.0%)	298/372 (80.1%)	$p = 0.685$
DAYS	53/73 (72.6%)	281/401 (70.1%)	$p = 0.780$
Ahiru no sora	57/77 (74.0%)	247/385 (64.2%)	$p = 0.114$
Burming kabaddi	21/41 (51.2%)	250/432 (57.9%)	$p = 0.414$
Haikyu!!	22/41 (53.7%)	411/642 (64.0%)	$p = 0.185$
Hanebad!	25/26 (96.2%)	278/394 (70.6%)	**$p = 0.002$**

to readers regardless of the protagonists' emotional states, so it is reasonable to not use onomatopoeias, which are good for expressing the emotional states of protagonists.

The second situation is where the protagonist's emotional state drastically changes, e.g., joy, despair, or showing resolve (Figs. 7, 8 and 9). Specific cases in sports comics are when protagonists meet new rivals or friends, become friends with others, discover new challenges during competitions, and so on. Although it seems that onomatopoeias are suitable for expressing protagonists' emotional states in detail, it is quite interesting that such onomatopoeias are not often actually used in this situation.

Fig. 4. Protagonist recollects something ©Kousuke Hamada 2013 "Hanebad!"

Fig. 5. Spoken by main protagonist to teammates ©Haruichi Furudate 2012 "Haikyu!"

The third situation involves important scenes in the story, such as the moment of a clutch performance, when the protagonists get or lose an important point, and so on (Figs. 10, 11). These frames are important to the story, so we expected that onomatopoeias that are more expressive to be frequently used; however, such onomatopoeias were rarely used. We assumed that not using such onomatopoeias succeeded in making the readers focus on the greatly detailed pictures themselves.

Fig. 6. Protagonist speaks about how to interpret game ©Kousuke Hamada 2013 "Hanebad!"

Fig. 7. Expressing friendship toward new friend ©Tsuyoshi Yasuda 2013 "DAYS"

Fig. 8. Protagonists' team loses game, and rivals point out their problems ©Haruichi Furudate 2012 "Haikyu!!"

Fig. 9. Protagonist is overwhelmed by building of his new soccer team ©Yugo Kobayashi 2015 "Aoashi"

Fig. 10. Moment decisive point is scored in match ©Kousuke Hamada 2013 "Hanebad!"

3.4 Meanings of Frames Without Onomatopoeias

On the basis of our observation, we also found that frames with frequently used ono-matopoeias appeared just before or immediately after frames without onomatopoeias (Figs. 12, 13 and 14). When frames with many onomatopoeias suddenly change to the ones without them, the reader might feel that the flow or rhythm of the story has sud-denly changed or been interrupted. This change eventually causes readers to pay stronger attention to frames without onomatopoeia. In addition, frames without onomatopoeias have specific appearance characteristics, e.g., the frame sizes are rather large, the pro-tagonist's bodies are enlarged, and the images are depicted in great detail. Therefore, these frames can effectively fascinate the readers due to the higher aesthetical potential, so frames without onomatopoeias are effectively used in important scenes in the story.

Comics usually form a story with linguistic information by using speech balloons or narration and with visual information depicted through images. Therefore, determining and switching which kinds of information should be expressed by linguistic or visual information might be a significant technique for expression in comic creations.

Fig. 11. Moment where victory is achieved by three-point shot at end of game ©Takeshi Hinata 2004 "Ahiru no sora"

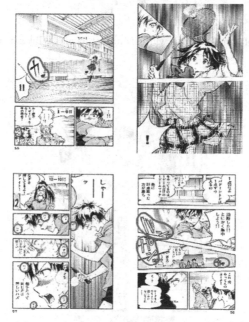

Fig. 12. Combination of frames with and without onomatopoeias (red circle indicating onomatopoeias) ©Kousuke Hamada 2013 "Hanebad!"

Fig. 13. Combination of frames with and without onomatopoeias ©Takashi Yasuda 2013 "DAYS"

Fig. 14. Combination of frames with and without onomatopoeias ©Hajime Musashino 2015 "Burning kabaddi"

4   Conclusion

We investigated where onomatopoeia is not used in Japanese sports comics and discussed the meaning and effects of frames without onomatopoeias. As a result, we qualitatively identified the appearance characteristics of frames without onomatopoeias, and we also confirmed that frames with these characteristics and without onomatopoeias frequently appeared in significant scenes in the story. Moreover, we also found that frames with many onomatopoeias appear just before or immediately after frames without them. Such contrast between frames with and without onomatopoeias eventually causes readers to pay stronger attention to frames without onomatopoeia. On the basis of the results of our investigation, we confirmed that frames without onomatopoeias feature protagonists with enlarged body parts and are depicted in great detail. Therefore, when cartoonists use visual information to express their intentions, they might depict images in certain frames in great detail. This eventually might inhibit the use of literal information including onomatopoeias.

We noticed that the effects of onomatopoeias in comics are quite similar to those of background music (BGM) in movies While BGM can enrich the nuances and intentions conveyed in a story to viewers, it can also make them focus on visual images themselves by intentionally suppressing or muting the BGM. We believe that this viewpoint, "onomatopoeias in comics = BGM in movie," could be a significant finding to understanding the flow or rhythm of a story on the basis of the meanings and effects of the frames with or without onomatopoeias.

This study was manually conducted by two of the authors. Therefore, it does not succeed in providing quantitative results but rather qualitative ones. In the near future, it will be indispensable to construct technological tools for performing quantitative analysis, e.g., extracting frames with and without onomatopoeias and annotating the meaning of the extracted frames. This will contribute to our remaining work of reconsidering the effects of one or a combination of these appearance characteristics.

In the research field of comic computing, automatically extracting important scenes from comics has been intensively studied in order to create summary generators for comics or comic content understanding. For example, Hisayuku et al. [11] defined a metadata model for objects appearing in frames in comics and realized a way of extracting scenes in accordance with the story by means of a machine learning method. Nonaka et al. [12] developed GT-Scan, which can automatically detect the frames in comic books. Whomor inc developed a comic frame cropping tool called "Mizuhanome."[1] Furthermore, Hiraoka et al. [13] estimated the importance of frames using a database on the size of frames and links between frames, and Imaizumi et al. [14] proposed a scene segmentation method based on changes in the form of protagonist groups. We assume that our significant finding of this study, that "frames without onomatopoeias indicate the important scenes of a story," can be highly valuable knowledge in creating technologies for extracting important scenes.

For example, Fig. 15 shows numbers of onomatopoeia every page in the first volume of "Haikyu!!" We show red circles where pages do not have frames with onomatopoeias, and we annotated the points of the story. It appears that these red parts could be used

---

[1] Mizuhanome URL https://whomor.com/blog/1542 (accessed 2022–05-08).

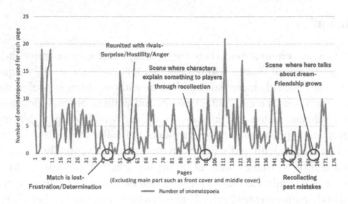

Fig. 15. Numbers of onomatopoeias per page in first volume of "Haikyu!!"

to extract the important scenes of this story, e.g., losing the match, recalling a mistake in the past, establishing friendship with teammates, and so on. Therefore, it is expected that a novel method for extracting scenes could be proposed by combining the existing techniques of the previous studies with our finding in this study.

References

1. Tamori, I.: Japanese onomatopoeias and verb-less expressions. Jimbun Ronshu **24**(2), 1–25 (1988)
2. Millington, S.: NIHONGO PERA PERA!: A User's Guide to Japanese Onomatopoeia, Charles E. Tuttle Company, Rutland, VT (1993)
3. Tajima, K.: Onomatopoeia (Giongo Gitaigo) Ni Tsuite (On Onomatopoeia (Mimetics)). Kansai Gaikokugo Daigaku Ryuugakusei-Bekka Nihongo Kyouiku Ronsyuu [Stud. Jpn. Lang. Edu. Int. Cent. Kansai Gaidai Univ.] 16, 193–205 (2006). (In Japanese)
4. Natsume, F.: Manga Ni Okeru onomatopoeia (Onomatopoeia in Manga). In: Shinohara, K., Uno, R. (eds.), Onomatopoeia Kenkyu No Shatei: Chikazuku Oto to Imi. Hitsuji Shobo, Tokyo, pp. 217–241 (2013). (In Japanese)
5. Izawa, S.: Manga Ni Okeru Onomatopoeia No Hyougenryoku (Expression of Onomatopoeia in Manga). Tokyo Joshi Daigaku Gengo Bunka Kenkyukai [Tokyo Woman's Christian University Studies in Language and Culture], pp. 217– 241 (2018). (In Japanese)
6. Hashimoto, N., Sawano H., Sato, T., Suzuki, Y., Hotta, S.: Manga No Komagazou Karano Tegaki Onomatopoeia Chushutsu to Sono Kouka Fuyo Shuhou no Teian (Extraction of handwritten onomatopoeia from comic frame images and application to visual effects). The 80th National Convention of IPSJ, no. 1, pp. 177–178 (2018). (in Japanese)
7. Matsushita, M., Imaoka, N.: Kinetic onomatopoeia generation system for creating an attractive digital comic. In: The 25th Annual Conference of the Japanese Society for Artificial Intelligence (2011)
8. Sato, K., Nakamura, S., Suzuki, M.: Denshi Comic no Hyogen wo Yutaka ni suru Tegaki Moji Animation Seisei Shuho (Handwritten Text Animation Generation Method to Enrich the Expression of Electronic Comics), JSAI2016, vol. 4, L4–4, in part 2, pp. 1–4 (2016). (in Japanese)
9. Uchiyama, S.: Manga no Serifu ya Onomatopoeia ni okeru Gengoteki Tokucyo Bunseki (Linguistic feature analysis in comic script and onomatopoeia). Memoirs of Shonan Inst. Technol. **48**(1), 63–68 (2014). (In Japanese)

10. Hira, M.: "Ugoki" wo Arawasu Manga no Onomatopoeia -"Aruku Hashiru" wo Rei to Shite- (onomatopoeia of comic express moving -e.g., working and running-). Bull. Center Jpn. Lang. Cult. **17**, 19–37 (2020). (In Japanese)
11. Hisayuku, C., Mihara, T., Nagamori, M., Sugimoto, S.: Manga metadata provider to help scene extraction by machine learning -description of frame attributes of manga and its use based on linked open data. In: The 31st Annual Conference of the Japanese Society for Artificial Intelligence (2017)
12. Nonaka, S., Sawano, T., Haneda, N.: Development of GT-Scan, the technology for automatic detection of frames in scanned comic. FUJIFILM Res. Dev. **57**, 46–49 (2012)
13. Hiraoka, T., Yamanishi, R., Nishihara, Y.: A study of frame importance detection by link relationship among frames on comics. In: The 32nd Annual Conference of the Japanese Society for Artificial Intelligence (2018)
14. Imaizumi, K., Yamanishi, R., Nishihara, Y., Ozawa, T.: Estimating groups of featured characters in comics with sequence of characters' appearance, In: Proceedings of the 2021 International Joint Workshop on Multimedia Artworks Analysis and Attractiveness Computing in Multimedia (MMArt-ACM 2021), pp. 13–18 (2021)

Can Deep Learning Approaches Detect Complex Text? Case of Onomatopoeia in Comics Albums

John Benson Louis[✉] , Jean-Christophe Burie , and Arnaud Revel

L3i Laboratory, La Rochelle University, La Rochelle, France
{john.louis,jean-christophe.burie,arnaud.revel}@univ-lr.fr

Abstract. In recent years, the use of deep learning has contributed to the development of new approaches that outperform traditional methods for many computer vision and document analysis tasks. Many text detection approaches have been proposed and target historical documents, newspapers, administrative documents but also texts in the wild.

However, some documents can present complex texts where the shape, the size and the orientation can vary within each word. Onomatopoeia are an example of these complex texts often buried in graphic elements. In this article, we present a study to determine whether the deep learning based text detection methods can tackle such complex texts. First, we selected two well-known deep learning approaches of the literature and then analysed their relevance for the detection of the onomatopoeia. In a second stage, we tried to improve their performance. The experiments show that a simple transfer learning isn't enough. The models have to consider the characteristics of the onomatopoeia. The proposed strategy show an improvement of about 40% for the detection task of the onomatopoeia.

Keywords: Text detection · Deep Learning · Onomatopoeia · Comics album

1 Introduction

Because of their many applications, text detection and recognition are two of the most popular computer vision problems. Historically, works first focused on relatively simple issues, such as typewritten text recognition. The results quickly led to the creation of high-performance text detection systems. With the appearance of neural networks, this work has been successfully extended to more complex case studies such as handwritten texts, in particular texts where the writing style of the document was variable. To date, numerous text detection systems, in particular, text buried in natural images have been proposed in order to be able to locate these texts in images. The onomatopoeias found in comics albums are an example of these complex texts, whose orientation and alignment are variable and often buried in graphic elements. Interesting work on text detection,

© Springer Nature Switzerland AG 2023
J.-J. Rousseau and B. Kapralos (Eds.): ICPR 2022 Workshops, LNCS 13644, pp. 48–60, 2023.
https://doi.org/10.1007/978-3-031-37742-6_4

in particular in bubbles [12], has been conducted around comics (cf. Fig. 1) but, does not always allow the detection of more specific texts.

In order to succeed in detecting texts buried in natural images, a considerable amount of efficient algorithms and methods have been proposed. However, successfully detecting text buried in an unnatural environment is subject to many different constraints and challenges. The purpose of this work is to determine whether the proposed methods are adapted to the case of onomatopoeia. To perform the experiments, a dataset of texts contained in natural images has been used, but a new dataset of onomatopoeia has been created. Thus, we propose in this work to explore solutions to this problem of text detection buried in comics pages.

Our main contributions are:

– Creation of an onomatopoeia image dataset. To our knowledge, this is the first onomatopoeia dataset publicly available.
– Evaluation of the relevance of two deep learning methods for detecting complex text in comics albums : onomatopoeias.
– Estimation of the ability of these methods to learn onomatopoeia characteristics in order to improve detection rate.

The following section presents related works on text detection and comic strip analysis. The Sect. 3 explains the strategy used to select the relevant methods for our study. The evaluation protocol is presented in Sect. 4 . Experiments and results are detailed in the Sect. 5. Finally, conclusions and perspectives are given in Sect. 6.

Fig. 1. Examples of onomatopoeia and text detection in BD bubbles

2   Related Works

In natural scene images, text often appears on different types of supports. It contains rich semantic information that all have their importance for the understanding of the image. The recognition of these buried texts in the images has facilitated the realization of many applications using a perception of the real world (Optical recognition and augmented reality, automatic translation in different languages...) and these reasons have aroused, for years, a great interest of the community. there are many works in the literature on text detection, in a broad sense [18, 23].

This section focuses on work dealing with embedded text detectors in natural scenes. Conventional text detection approaches rely on feature extraction with classical approaches based on stroke width transformation(SWT) [4] and the maximum stable extreme regions (MSER) [11]. These methods usually search for character candidates through edge detection or extraction of extreme edges. Zhang et al. [19] used the text local symmetry property and designed various features for text region detection. FASText [2] is a fast text detection system that adapted and modified the famous FAST key-point detector for stroke extraction. However, these historicals methods have lower performance compared to those based on deep neural networks, in terms of accuracy and adaptability, especially in difficult scenarios, for which the texts have undergone changes in orientation, alignment, perspective distortion, etc. VGG16 [14] is an architecture widely used as a backbone in many tasks that supports task-specific feature extraction, including text detection [6,16,20,21].

Huang et al. [8] proposed an algorithm that first finds candidates using MSER, and then uses a deep convolutive network as a powerful classifier to eliminate false positives. Some detectors favor the use of box regression, adapted from common object detectors. The models like TextBoxes [8] DMPNet [10] et RSDD [9] consider the rotation of the detected texts, but however, are less robust when it comes to low contrast words and for words whose characters are not proportional in size.

There are many methods and algorithms that go into creating a solution for the detection or recognition of text in the wild based on neural networks. These methods perform the learning of specific characteristics of the text. The models East and Craft also perform the extraction and learning on a certain number of criteria linked to the object (i.e. the text) to be detected. However, in European comics, as well as Japanese comics, processing more complex texts is still a topic that is not discussed or covered very much. In comics, a lot of research has been published on text detection, especially in speech bubbles [3,13] but also the detection of texts without constraints using simple text segmentation methods [3], or shape detection and recognition that includes text [5]. However, as far we know there are not really works tackling specifically the question of onomatopoeia.

3 Choice of Algorithms

Our objective is to verify if some algorithms from the literature used to detect texts buried in real scenes, have the capacity to detect onomatopoeia which are also buried texts but with particular characteristics.

We have analyzed the properties of different approaches of the literature which could consider the characteristics of the onomatopoeia, and especially their ability to detect buried text with different orientations and/or variable size. We have selected two algorithms that have demonstrated their relevance to extract text in the wild: EAST [22] and CRAFT [1]. The selected algorithms use the same backbone architecture, VGG16 [15]. Results obtained after the fine tuning on the also show that the Craft algorithm can focus mainly on the learned characteristics of the onomatopoeias, which can clearly explain in Fig. 7, third line, that it tries to detect the onomotopoeias but not the other texts on contained on the page. However, they have two different processing methods: CRAFT performs a basic detection at the character level to form the detected word, while EAST performs a detection directly at the word level.

3.1 EAST

EAST(Efficient and Accurate Scene Text Detector) [22], is a method based on a fully convolutional neural network suitable for text detection. It generates pixel-dense predictions of words or lines of text. The approach eliminates intermediate steps such as proposing candidates, forming text regions, and word partitioning. The post-processing steps only include thresholding and an NMS (Non-Max Suppression) filtering step on the predicted geometric shapes. The algorithm follows the general design of DenseBox [7], in which an image is introduced into the FCN (Fully Convolutional Network). Then several channels of text score map, at pixel level, and their geometry are generated. The network used is based on the VGG16 architecture which performs feature extraction. As detailed in Fig. 2, EAST contains multiple output channels. One of the predicted channels is a score card whose values are in the range $[0, 1]$. The other channels represent the geometric characteristics of the box that surrounds the word. The score represents confidence in the predicted geometric shape. Two geometric shapes are available for text regions: rotated box (RBOX) and quadrangle Box (QUAD). A loss function is associated for each geometric shape. A threshold is then applied to each predicted region. Region candidates with scores higher than the predefined threshold are filtered by NMS(Non-max suppression). Results after NMS processing are considered as the final output from the pipeline.

3.2 CRAFT

CRAFT (Character Region Awareness for Text Detection) [1] is designed with a convolutional neural network producing a region score for each character and an

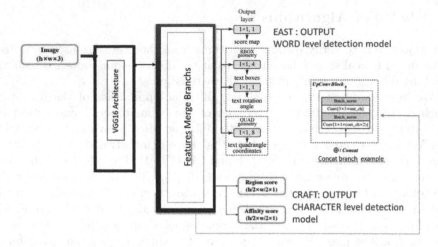

Fig. 2. Global representation of EAST and CRAFT architectures.

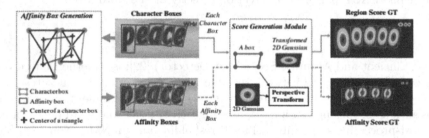

Fig. 3. Illustration of ground truth generation procedure in CRAFT from [1]

affinity score. CRAFT also adopts VGG-16 based architecture as the backbone as shown in figure Fig. 2.

The decoding segment of the CRAFT network is similar to UNet. It has jump connections that bundle low-level features. CRAFT predicts two scores for each candidate:

- Region score : score related to the location of the character.
- Affinity score : "**The Affinity**" is the degree to which one character tends to combine with another. Thus, the affinity score allows to merge or not the single characters into a single instance (a word) as detailed in Fig. 3 .

4   Experimental Procedures

The aim is to evaluate the capabilities of the methods described in the previous section to detect the onomatopoeia. Let's remember that these methods are used to detect texts in the wild with good performance.

Onomatopoeias are complex texts because they have unusual characteristics such as variable and irregular character orientations, text buried in graphics, letters that can be distorted.

several experimental protocols have been proposed to evaluate, firstly, the ability of the selected algorithms to detect onomatopoeia, and secondly, the possibility of improving the results by learning the characteristics of onomatopoeia.

4.1 Onomatopoeia Dataset Construction

As far we know there is no image dataset of onomatopoeia publicly available. To evaluate our work, we built the dataset KABOOM-ONOMATOPOEIA available at Kaboom repository.[1]. The comic book images come from the public image base COMICBOOKFX[2] that lists the sound effects of comic books. This website gathers about 1830 images of panels containing different types of onomatopoeia. These images come from American comics books of the golden and silver age (between 1936 and 1963) such as *Amazing spider-man*, *Gunsmoke Western*, *More fun comics*, etc.

Detailed Composition. To build the KABOOM-ONOMATOPOEIA image database, we have selected 700 images with different styles of onomatopoeia. To have a good representativeness, we chose onomatopoeia with different length, size, orientation and color. Our dataset consists of 500 images that contain a total of 687 onomatopoeia and 200 images that do not contain any onomatopoeia. Some samples can be seen on Fig. 5. The annotation has been carried out at character level and word level. The annotation process consisted in defining a bounding box around each character and each word by respecting the orientation or the shape of the word as seen on Fig. 6

Annotations have been realized using the online annotation tools, the VGG Image Annotator (VIA)[3]. Each polygon is composed of 8 offsets, as shown in Fig. 4.

Data Structure Used. The structure of our onomatopoeia database is described to facilitate understanding of the data and a future use for different applications. its composition is given in the following format :

- **Imnames** : Name of the image file.
- **WordBB** : word-level bounding-boxes for each image, represented by tensors of size $2 \times 4 \times NWORDS_i$, où :
  - The first dimension of size 2 correspond to x and y respectively where the x value is the position of the point with reference to the x-axis, and the y value is the position of the point with reference to the y-axis,

---

[1] https://gitlab.univ-lr.fr/jcburie/kaboom_onomatopoeia_dataset.
[2] https://www.comicbookfx.com.
[3] https://www.robots.ox.ac.uk/~vgg/software/via/via.html.

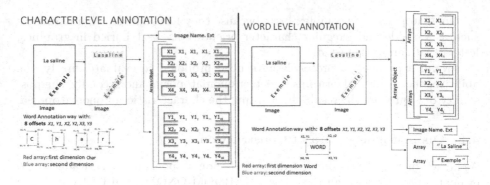

Fig. 4. Database annotation structure

- The second dimension corresponds to the 4 vertex of the bounding bow (clockwise, starting from top-left), and
- The third dimension of size NWORDS_i, corresponds to the number of words in the i_th image. In addition, each annotated word contains 8 points, being distributed in arrays each coordinate dimension separately for each word, as indicated in the Fig. 4.
- **CharBB** : character-level bounding-boxes. Each bounding box is represented by a tensor of size (red array block) $2 \times 4 \times (Bluearraysblock)NCHARS_i$ (format is same as wordBB's above)
- **Txt** : list of text strings. Each text string correspond to the transcription of the onomatopoeia.
A "character" is defined as any non-whitespace character. A "word" (an onomatopoeia) is any contiguous substring of non-whitespace characters.

5   Experiments and Results

Two types of experiments have been carried out. The first consists in a transfer learning, using pre-trained models on text in the wild dataset, to evaluate the ability of the selected algorithms to detect onomatopoeia.

In a second time, we carried out a fine-tuning to try to improve the performance of the selected algorithms by using the image of the *KABOOM-ONOMATOPOEIA* dataset.

5.1   Metric

In order to evaluate the relevance of the proposed approaches, the F1-Score is used. How is it determined as part of our evaluation ? East and Craft provide as output bounding boxes when detecting words or characters. We use the IOU (intersection over union) to estimate the relevance of the detections. The bounding boxes with an IOU greater than a threshold of 50% are considered well detected.

The bounding boxes corresponding to well detected onomatopoeia (with an IOU greater than 50%) are scored as true positive (TP). The bounding boxes of undetected onomatopoeia are scored as false negative (FN). Finally the detected bounding boxes that do not match onomatopoeia are scored as false positive (FP).

With these values, we computed precision, recall and F1-score as follow :

$$Precision = \frac{TP}{TP + FP}$$

$$Recall = \frac{TP}{TP + FN}$$

$$F1_{score} = \frac{2}{\frac{1}{Precision} + \frac{1}{Recall}}$$

5.2 Abiliy to Detect the Onomatopoeia

At this level, the objective is to evaluate whether the models trained on buried texts in the wild correctly detect onomatopoeia. For this, we made the choice to use a model pre-trained on the *Incidental Scene Text* dataset.
the *In Incidental Scene Text dataset 2015 (ICDAR Robust Reading Challenge)* [17] is used as benchmark for evaluating text detection, segmentation and recognition[4] . Let's note that the texts are mostly quasi-horizontal. This dataset contains images of variable quality: high-resolution photos with good lighting, sharpness, and variable lighting conditions. Some images contain shadows or motion effects.

Table 1. Ability to detect onomatopoeas with a model trained on the Incidental scene text [17]

Method	Precision	Recall	F-Score
EAST	42.8	48.6	**45.6**
CRAFT	60.4	45.8	**52.1**

These models trained on natural images have significant results in the detection of texts in the wild, but are they able to detect onomatopoeia? Then to determine if the knowledge stored in their respective models could be transferred to the onomatopoeia detection task, we evaluate the performance of the EAST and CRAFT method on the KABOOM-ONOMATOPOEIA dataset. More precisely, the test was carried out on 140 images of the testing set containing 149 onomatopoeias. The Table 1 shows the results of the experiment. East and Craft methods reach respectively a F-Score of 45.6% and 52.1%. We observe that

---

[4] https://rrc.cvc.uab.es/?ch=4&com=tasks.

Table 2. Performance of East and Craft on the onomatopoeia detection after training on the KABOOM-ONOMATOPOEIA data set

Method	Precision	Recall	F-Score
EAST	54.1	63	**58.2**
CRAFT	71.2	75.6	**73.4**

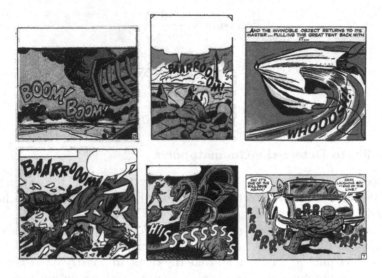

Fig. 5. Sample of KABOOM-ONOMATOPOEIA dataset

Fig. 6. Character level annotation

each method is able to detect onomatopoeia with regular shape. But many onomatopoeia of the testing set have irregular shapes, this explains the low results. We can note that CRAFT provides better results in terms of Precision and F-Score. The reason is that CRAFT works first at character level and then merge the detected characters to make up words. Thus, CRAFT can manage better

Fig. 7. Example of detection result of East(LEFT) and Craft(Right) detection

complex texts than EAST. However both methods fails when the text is too complex or too buried in the graphics elements. The Fig. 7 shows some results of this experiment.

5.3 Ability to Learn the Characteristics of Onomatopoeias

The results obtained in the previous experiment were mixed. This clearly shows that onomatopoeia have different characteristics than texts buried in natural scene images. Models must therefore incorporate these characteristics. In this new experiment, we started from the model previously trained on the **Incidental Scene Text 2015** text dataset. Then, to improve the model, we applied a training phase using the **KABOOM-ONOMATOPOEIA** data set.

To study the ability of EAST and CRAFT to learn the features of onomatopoeia. We used 560 images of the KABOOM-ONOMATOPOEIA dataset for the training and the test was done on the 140 images (149 onomatopoeia) of the testing set. For an objective comparison, the testing set used in this experiment was the same than the one used for the first experiment. A threshold of 0.5 is also used for the IOU. The Table 2 shows the results of the second experiment. The fine-tuning improves considerably the performance of both methods with a refinement of 27,6% for EAST and 40,9% for CRAFT. We can observed that CRAFT also outperforms EAST in terms of Recall and Precision. The results shows that CRAFT integrate better the characteristics of the onomatopoeia than EAST. However, CRAFT fails to detect some onomatopoeia with complex shape or textured background. These results shows that the CRAFT architecture has to be improved to consider all the specific features of the onomatopoeia.

6   Conclusion and Future Work

In this paper, we studied that ability of deep learning approaches to detect complex text and especially onomatopoeia in comics albums. We first selected two methods of the literature according to their performance on the text detection task on natural scene images. The first experiment consisted in determining if by applying transfer learning the detection of the onomatopoeia was possible. In the second experiment, we tried to improve the detection rate by considering the specific features of the onomatopoeia. The results show that the CRAFT method reach the best detection rate. However, some onomatopoeia with complex shapes are still undetected.

Results obtained after fine tuning also show that the Craft algorithm can focus mainly on the learned characteristics of onomatopoeia, which can be clearly explained in Fig. 7, third line, that it tries to detect the onomotopoeias but not the other texts on the page. In future work, we plan to adapt the CRAFT architecture by making it more expressive to consider the specific features of onomatopoeia. Moreover, we plane to study the capabilities of our approach to detect the onomatopoeia in Japanese and Korean Manga.

Acknowledgements. This work is supported by the Research National Agency (ANR) in the framework of the 2017 LabCom program (ANR 17-LCV2-0006-01) and the Region Nouvelle Aquitaine in the framework of the Scantrad project.

References

1. Baek, Y., Lee, B., Han, D., Yun, S., Lee, H.: Character Region Awareness for Text Detection. In: 2019 IEEE/CVF Conference on Computer Vision and Pattern Recognition (CVPR), pp. 9357–9366, Long Beach, CA, USA, June 2019. IEEE (2019)
2. Busta, M., Neumann, L., Matas, J.: Fastext: Efficient unconstrained scene text detector. In: Proceedings of the IEEE International Conference on Computer Vision (ICCV) December (2015)
3. Del Gobbo, J., Matuk Herrera, R.: Unconstrained text detection in manga: a new dataset and baseline. In: Bartoli, A., Fusiello, A. (eds.) ECCV 2020. LNCS, vol. 12537, pp. 629–646. Springer, Cham (2020). https://doi.org/10.1007/978-3-030-67070-2_38
4. Epshtein, B., Ofek, E., Wexler, Y.: Detecting text in natural scenes with stroke width transform. In: 2010 IEEE Computer Society Conference on Computer Vision and Pattern Recognition. IEEE, June (2010)
5. Fan, K.-C., Liu, C.-H., Wang, Y.-K.: Segmentation and classification of mixed text/graphics/image documents. Pattern Recognit. Lett. **15**(12), 1201–1209 (1994)
6. Gupta, A., Vedaldi, A., Zisserman, A.: Synthetic Data for Text Localisation in Natural Images. arXiv:1604.06646 [cs], April (2016).
7. Huang, L., Yang, Y., Deng, Y.: and Yinan Yu. Unifying landmark localization with end to end object detection, DenseBox (2015)
8. Huang, W., Qiao, Yu., Tang, X.: Robust scene text detection with convolution neural network induced MSER trees. In: Fleet, D., Pajdla, T., Schiele, B., Tuytelaars, T. (eds.) ECCV 2014. LNCS, vol. 8692, pp. 497–511. Springer, Cham (2014). https://doi.org/10.1007/978-3-319-10593-2_33
9. Liao, M., Zhu, Z., Shi, B., Xia, G.S., Bai, X.: Rotation-Sensitive Regression for Oriented Scene Text Detection (2018). Publisher: arXiv Version Number: 1
10. Liu, Y., Jin, L.: Deep Matching Prior Network: Toward Tighter Multi-oriented Text Detection (2017) Publisher: arXiv Version Number: 1
11. Neumann, L., Matas, J.: A method for text localization and recognition in real-world images. In: Kimmel, R., Klette, R., Sugimoto, A. (eds.) ACCV 2010. LNCS, vol. 6494, pp. 770–783. Springer, Heidelberg (2011). https://doi.org/10.1007/978-3-642-19318-7_60
12. Rigaud, C., Karatzas, D., Van de Weijer, J., Burie, J.C., Ogier, J.M.: Automatic Text Localisation in Scanned Comic Books. In: Proceedings of the 8th International Conference on Computer Vision Theory and Applications (VISAPP). SCITEPRESS Digital Library (2013)
13. Rigaud, C., Nguyen, N.-V., Burie, J.-C.: Text block segmentation in comic speech bubbles. In: Del Bimbo, A., Cucchiara, R., Sclaroff, S., Farinella, G.M., Mei, T., Bertini, M., Escalante, H.J., Vezzani, R. (eds.) ICPR 2021. LNCS, vol. 12666, pp. 250–261. Springer, Cham (2021). https://doi.org/10.1007/978-3-030-68780-9_22
14. Simonyan, K., Zisserman, A.: Very deep convolutional networks for large-scale image recognition. September (2014)
15. Simonyan, K., Zisserman, A.: Very Deep Convolutional Networks for Large-Scale Image Recognition. arXiv:1409.1556 [cs], April 2015. arXiv: 1409.1556

16. Tian, Z., Huang, W., He, T., He, P., Qiao, Y.: Detecting Text in Natural Image with Connectionist Text Proposal Network. arXiv:1609.03605 [cs], September (2016). arXiv: 1609.03605
17. Yao, C., et al.: Incidental scene text understanding: Recent progresses on ICDAR 2015 robust reading competition challenge 4 (2015)
18. Ye, Q., Doermann, D.: Text detection and recognition in imagery: a survey. IEEE Trans. Pattern Anal. Mach. Intell. **37**(7), 1480–1500 (2015)
19. Zhang, Z., Shen, W., Yao, C., Bai, X.: Symmetry-based text line detection in natural scenes. In: 2015 IEEE Conference on Computer Vision and Pattern Recognition (CVPR). IEEE, June (2015)
20. Zhang, Z., Zhang, C., Shen, W., Yao, C., Liu, W., Bai, X.: Multi-oriented text detection with fully convolutional networks. April (2016)
21. Zhong, Z., Jin, L., Zhang, S., Feng, Z.: DeepText: A Unified Framework for Text Proposal Generation and Text Detection in Natural Images. arXiv:1605.07314 [cs], May (2016). arXiv: 1605.07314
22. Zhou, X., et al: EAST: An Efficient and Accurate Scene Text Detector. In: 2017 IEEE Conference on Computer Vision and Pattern Recognition (CVPR), pages 2642–2651, Honolulu, HI, July 2017. IEEE (2017)
23. Zhu, Y., Yao, C., Bai, X.: Scene text detection and recognition: recent advances and future trends. Front. Comput. Sci. **10**(1), 19–36 (2016)

Automated Emotion Recognition Through Graphical Cues on Comics at Character Scale

Théodose Ruddy[(✉)], Burie Jean-Christophe, and Revel Arnaud

L3i Laboratory, SAIL Joint Laboratory, La Rochelle Université, 17042 La Rochelle
Cedex 1, France
{ruddy.theodose,jean-christophe.burie,arnaud.revel}@univ-lr.fr

Abstract. Emotions are psychological reactions to external events. Characters represented in artistic works may manifest emotions in order to replicate credible and human-like behaviors in specific situations. They also provides important hints to better understand the stakes and the tone of story. In comics, markers of emotions can be found in the dialogues or through visual cues specifically drawn by the artists. While automated emotion extraction on textual information is an active research field, few works have addressed this topic through the graphical grammar of comics (and more generally on drawings). In this paper, we propose to review the different visual tools used by artists to convey expressiveness to their characters and how they can be exploited for automated processing. Some of those cues are strongly related to the human body, its representation and mechanisms. Consequently, we propose to study developed methods for those topics on photography or captured videos. Then, we suggest contributions that aimed at facilitating the transition between real and drawn domains.

Keywords: Emotion Recognition · Document Analysis · Machine Learning · Comic Analysis

1 Introduction

Through digitization, comics books can now be processed and analysed by automatic algorithms like other types of documents. Goals are various : accessibility, archiving, facilitated translation... Multiple works have focus on extraction of comic core elements such as panels [14,19,27], speech bubbles [8,15,20], characters [6,24,30]... Most of them are restricted to the structural components analysis. Higher-level concepts such as layout understanding, story understanding and character analysis, because they rely on performances of low-level algorithms, remain less addressed. In every story, characters are the key elements. A scene evolves in a direction because of the events caused by the different protagonists. As they have to undergo specific situations along the story, the artists must illustrate their reactions to external factors as credible and life-like as possible.

© Springer Nature Switzerland AG 2023
J.-J. Rousseau and B. Kapralos (Eds.): ICPR 2022 Workshops, LNCS 13644, pp. 61–75, 2023.
https://doi.org/10.1007/978-3-031-37742-6_5

Knowing how characters feel toward specific events can provide useful cues about the stakes of the story and establish a psychological profile of each character. For accessibility purposes, knowing which emotion is represented can improve speech synthesis systems by creating voices that fit better to the scene illustrated in the frame. Moreover, felt emotion at one moment can determine the linguistic choices of a speaker, and then can be a useful indication for text translation.

Emotion recognition is an active research field that spans across all human means of communication : voice, writing, photos... However, applications of this field on comics remain scarce. Comics are multimodal medias containing both textual and visual information. Dialogues written in speech bubbles relay important pieces of information that help to understand the speaker's state of mind. Techniques developed for emotion recognition on literature can be transferred to the dialogues. However, fewer works have attempted to benefit from the graphic specificities of comic stories.

In this paper, we propose to review the different visual tools used by artists for illustrating the emotional state of their characters and how they can be exploited by automated processes. We first describe, in Sect. 2, how emotions can be represented in recognition problems and how the outputs can be expressed. Then, each category of graphic tools is introduced in Sect. 3. For the tools that are closely related to real data, we present a glimpse of methods developed for captured photos and videos. Lastly, in Sect. 4, we present methods that aims at making machine learning algorithms more robust to the transition between real and drawn images. Characters behaviours can be studied on multiple narrative levels from the story level to the character level. While the first levels induce higher levels of understanding on the story and interpersonal relations, they all rely on analysis of how each character reacts to situations. In this study we voluntarily omit social interactions and focus on indications linked to the reactions of each character independently of the others.

2   Models of Emotion

One of the first essential decision in designing an emotion recognition system is choosing which emotions are considered and how they can be represented. Multiple computational models have been proposed to interpret the perceived emotion. These models can be grouped into multiple supersets : categorical models, dimensional models and hybrids models.

Categorical Models. The categorical models define a finite set of emotions. In that case, the goal of an emotion recognition system is then to assign to the studied signal the closest emotion of the set. The main advantage of these models is that they represent emotions with simple terms. However, such models do not allow to represent more complex states that are outside of the defined set. Among the categorical models, the one proposed by Ekman [9] is the most famous model. It defines 6 basic emotions besides the neutral emotion : Anger, Happiness, Disgust, Fear, Sadness and Surprise.

Dimensional Models. In dimensional models, feelings are described in multidimensional continuous spaces, generally two for valence (positiveness or negativeness of a feeling) and arousal (the level of excitement from boredom or sleepiness to wild excitement). A feeling is then defined as a point in this multidimensional space. These models allow, in opposition with the categorical models, to represent a much broader and continuous spectrum of emotions. Such models can also allow the definition of metrics to better assess similarities between signals. However, defining emotion in a continuous space is much more complex. Each person has its own sensitivity regarding signals, hence emotion placement between participants may vary much more. The circumplex model [32] (Fig. 1a).the Self-Assessment Manikin (SAM) model [3] or the Positive Activation-Negative Activation (PANA) model [37] belong to this group of models and revolve around the concepts of valence and arousal.

Hybrid Models. Between categorical and dimensional models, hybrid models organise emotions in a hierarchical structure and state that complex emotions are combinations of more simple/basic ones, allowing to extend the emotion spectrum. For example, the Plutchik model [28] defines *dyads* as mixtures of two of the eight primary emotions. For example, in Fig. 1b, love, defined as a mixture of joy and trust is placed between them.

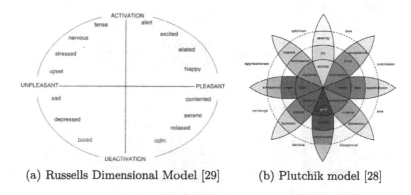

(a) Russells Dimensional Model [29]   (b) Plutchik model [28]

Fig. 1. Examples of emotion models

3   Main Visual Cues in Comics

In this section, we review the tools employed by artists to convey emotion to their characters. They can be divided into two main groups : body related signals and artificial signals.

Body related signals include facial expression and body gesture. Emotion recognition through these two signals have already been studied for years on captured photos or videos. As drawings of human and human-like characters tend to be inspired by the mechanisms and the rules of real bodies, we introduce some trends found in the literature for both topics.

Contrary to body related signals that may be associated to the way real bodies work, artificial signals are invented tools, each one having a specific function. Hence, these signals have almost no equivalent in the real world. Artificial signals include the shape of speech bubbles, symbols or even stylized effects on the background. We also included the lighting effects because they belong to stylistic effects that have no equivalent in real contexts.

3.1   Facial Expression Recognition

Facial Expression Recognition or Facial Emotion Recognition (FER) aims at the identification of the emotion felt by a subject only through facial cues. On photos, these cues are visible through specific facial movements and muscular actions. In the psychology field, Ekman [10] defined the Facial Action Coding System (FACS). In this system, muscles contractions and releases that create specific movements are coded as Action Units (AU)(Fig. 2). Each emotion then correspond a specific combination of AUs. While useful for social sciences, these features are not easily obtainable for computer vision tasks. Advances in automated FER are essentially based on machine learning techniques, often applied on raw images or videos.

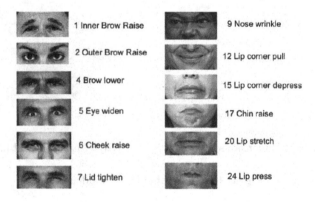

Fig. 2. Examples of Action Units (AU), extracted from [38]

Literature on FER. FER on images can be generally split into multiple phases :

– pre-processing : if the image was captured in the wild, the first step is an alignment step in order to get the focus on the face. This step can be done with a traditional face detector [34] or a deep learning-oriented one such as Faster RCNN [31] or DETR [5]. In the case of photos, a pose or lighting normalization can also be applied ;

– feature extraction
– classification

With deep learning techniques, the two last stages are often merged. The basic approach is to train a standard classification network such as ResNet [13] on the target dataset. Some approaches aim at transferring knowledge from other datasets. Ng et al. [23] experimented multiple fine-tuning strategies based on FER2013 dataset on pretrained classification networks in order to improve the emotion classification task on the smaller dataset EmotiW. Knyazev et al. [17] claimed that networks pretrained on face recognition tasks, for example on Facenet dataset, tend to produce better results after fine-tuning on FER because the network has learned to extract identity specific features from the first training that are useful for the final task.

Specifically designed blocks have also been developed in order to improve performance on FER task. For example, Zhao et al. [39] added to a feedforward network a new branch that takes the feature map of the backbone to generate a weighting map that is applied to this same feature map. Moreover, the network allows the use of a handcrafted mask in order to nullify the feature maps locations that fall into background. Supervised Scoring Ensemble (SSE) [16] defines three supervising blocks that are connected at different stages of a networks (shallow, intermediate and deep layers). The outputs of the supervision blocks are concatenated and processed by a fully connected layer to deliver the emotion output.

While facial muscles movements tend to be similar between individuals for each expression, each morphology has its own specific features that could affect the perception of some facial action. Hence, works like [21] developed multitask networks for emotion recognition and person re-identification in order to estimate features that fit better to the facial attributes instead of finding a common model for all morphologies.

Particularities of Comics. While this field is heavily investigated on photos and videos of real peoples, research on emotion recognition on drawings and comics is a lot scarcer. Most of the developed methods focus on multimodal approaches [25], with an important contribution of text. However, to the best of our knowledge, no published methods work exclusively exclusively with visual elements. First, there are few publicly available annotated datasets on comics that only target the detection of structural elements. As FER mostly relies on machine learning approaches, the availability of data is critical. Secondly, drawn characters can be illustrated in various ways, depending on the author style. Even if the most critical facial elements tend to be coherently placed on the face, visual features may vary on multiple aspects : shape, size, level of details... Nevertheless, facial actions tend to be similar between photos and drawn characters for the same expression as shown in Fig. 3.

Anger   Happiness   Sadness

Fig. 3. Expressions on real people and drawn characters. Top images come from the FER2013 dataset, bottom images were extracted from Manga109 dataset (In order ©Nakamura Chisato, ©Shirai Sanjirou, ©Shirai Sanjirou, ©Konohana Akari, ©Ide Chikae, ©Ito Shinpei).

3.2   Pose Estimation and Action Recognition

While most of the visually perceptible information comes from facial expressions, body movements can also determine how the character is feeling. Most of the body gestures have functional purposes, for interacting with the environment for example or supporting the ideas of a speech, some of them tend to reflect directly the emotional state (Fig. 4). The topic of body gesture recognition and pose estimation has been less handled for the goal of emotion recognition than its facial counterpart. Hence, there are fewer data and methods developed on this topic, even on real acquisitions. Body gesture alone is a less stable modality for emotion recognition because, unlike facial actions that tend to have universal meanings [9], their meaning can greatly vary between cultures. For example, a thumb up can represent a validation gesture in some geographical areas and an offensive sign in other ones.

Literature on Emotion Recognition from Body Gesture on Real Images/Videos. Most of the methods deal with temporal data as they do not only take the peak gesture into account but also analyze the motions (timings, intensity...) of the body parts. Hence they cannot be easily adapted to comic analysis as each frame is a snapshot of a scene.

Historically, like FER, body gesture analysis required preprocessing. The body is first detected and centered with standard detection methods. Then the different elements of the body are detected. On this step, two main paradigms exists : part based models and kinematic models. In the first one, body parts are detected independently without constraints. In the second one, the body is represented as a set of interconnected joints in order to reproduce the human body kinematics and constraints.

Fig. 4. Expressive body gestures. (Left) Head forward, clenched fists, ready for confrontation©Deguchi Ryusei ; (Middle) Hands behind, head dropped, feeling of fear/uncertainty ©Taira Masami ; (Right) Hands on face, shocking event ©Konohana Akari

Earlier works proposed multiple inputs types for their classification algorithms, most of them relying on geometric or dynamic values such as hands relative positions from a defined default pose were used for the upper body [12] or distances, accelerations, angles computed through upper body joints [33]. Neural networks fostered the use of learned features instead of handcrafted features. Barros et al. [1] exploited CNN in order to get more expressive features of the upper body and Botzheim et al. [2] used spiking networks to encode temporal events.

Regarding the output, a common trend was to simplify the emotion recognition problem. Glowinski et al. [11] chose to represent emotions according the Russells dimensional model. However, for the output of the recognition system, emotions that belong to the same quadrant were merged together.

Most of the time, body gesture signals are correlated with the ones delivered by the other communication media (speech, face). Consequently, a part of the literature aimed at data fusion problem in order to benefit from their complementarity, for example by associating audio and visual information through late fusion [26]. Caridakis et al. [4] first processed separately face and upper body images then compared the effects of middle and late fusions for the studied task.

Obstacles with Comics. The obstacles defined for FER also occur for pose estimation. Characters can have various shapes depending on the author's choices and the target audience. From realistic proportions to very stylized representations such as "Chibi" style or "Super Deformed" style, the main difficulty consists in identifying the different body parts across drawing styles and finding what is in common between characters drawn by different artists. Moreover, artists have to decide which type of shot to use for each frame. This choice can be determined by the mood they aim at or forced by limited space issues. Chosen shots must be as informative as possible. As faces convey most of the emotional information, the rest of the body tend to be less represented, leading to less data for learning algorithms.

3.3   Symbols

In order to illustrate or empathise feelings for the reader, symbols are often employed on the side of facial expression and text. Called "manpu" in japanese mangas, no consensual terminology was found to name these symbols that bring additional information about the characters. In Lexicon of Comicana [35], the author Mort Walker named symbols according to their relative position from the head. Symbols replacing the eyes are called *oculama* while icons which emerge from the head are called *emanata*.

There are numerous symbols to illustrate ideas or concepts as illustrated in Fig. 5. Some of them are integrated to the popular culture while other find their meaning in smaller communities. Consequently, symbols cannot be understood by everyone, and have to be initially explained to fully understand the reason why they were drawn for a specific situation.

Comics are generally defined by a genre and have a target audience. These two piece of information, that can be considered as metadata, may determine choices about graphic styles. Cohn and Ehly [7] show the influence of the target audience by studying the distribution of various visual morphemes on a corpus of 10 shonens and 10 shojos mangas

Fig. 5. Examples of "emotional" symbols. In order : Dropping lines for shock/depression (©Saijo Shinji), Heart for love or satisfaction (©Minamoto Tarou), Popping vein for anger (©Shirai Sanjirou), Smoke for annoyance (©Minamoto Tarou), Droplets for stressful situations (©Minamoto Tarou), Crown-like symbol for surprise (©Minamisawa Hishika)

Occasionally, symbols can be drawn in speech bubbles. This way, they do not link directly to the emotional state but act like intermediate representation of what is being told. For example, if the comic book targets younger audience, symbols can be replace offensive or insulting vocabulary without being explicit or semantically structured, as they carry the intention of the speaker.

Question and exclamation marks are special cases of symbols. In fact, they are punctuation marks, meaning that they have to be analysed as text. However, they can be found alone, in speech bubbles or next to the head when the character is surprised (an exclamation mark) or confused (a question mark) as illustrated in Fig. 6

Fig. 6. Punctuation for emotion. (Left) Confusion (©Fred) (Right) Surprise (© Shimada Hirokazu)

3.4 Speech Bubbles

Speech bubbles are one of the main links between textual and visual information. While they do not directly illustrate emotion, the shape of speech bubbles provides indications on the way the speech is heard. Consequently, it would be preferable to combine them with other visual elements for emotion recognition. Figure 7 provides examples of bubbles shapes and their function. However, there is no normalization or convention about the topic, so each artist is free to choose how to draw and use speech balloon types.

Fig. 7. Common speech bubble shapes. (Left) Spiky bubble for loud or sudden speech ©Lamisseb (Middle) "Electric" bubble for speeches heard through electronic devices ©Studio Cyborga (Right) Cloud-shaped bubble for thoughts ©Lamisseb.

3.5 Background Effects

While characters attributes remain the main tool for emotion analysis, the artists can employ background effects to highlight specific reactions. We show in Fig. 8 some examples of effects used in different mangas.

Like most of the previous graphical cues, the choice of using a background effect is up to the authors. There are no explicit rules on these effects, some techniques have been heavily used to the point that they have become tacit conventions across artists and readers. However, it is not possible to understand them without learning about them beforehand as they remain culture-specific symbols.

(a) Pitch-black background for major stakes events ©Yoshi Masako

(b) Flash on black background for surprise/realization/shock ©Shimada Hirokazu

(c) Glittering background for showing the shared happiness between the two characters ©Kuriki Shoko

(d) Twisty abstract background to illustrate the malicious intents of the characters ©Yabuno Tenya, Watanabe Tatsuya

Fig. 8. Examples of backgrounds effects used in mangas.

3.6 Lighting and Colors

In other visual arts such as photography or cinema, lighting is a powerful tool to create moods. The way the lights and the shadows are placed can change the perception of the viewer on the same face. In comics (and painting), lighting is completely defined by the artist. Shading management can be used to empathise feelings or moods the same way background effect can do (Fig. 9).

Fig. 9. Examples of specific shadings. (Left)Full shadow, no visible facial attribute for the harmful aspect ©Yagami Ken (Middle) Obscured face and smile for malicious intent ©Ishioka Shoei (Right) More detailed shading for impactful moment ©Shirai Sanjirou

In colored works, each character is illustrated with a default set of colors. However, to accentuate an effect, artists may change the default face color to another one that better matches the wanted emotion. In western comics, an angry character can be drawn with a red face, a sick or disgust one with green...

4 Robustness from Real Data to Drawings

While speech bubbles and symbols have no real world equivalents, human like characters tend to be drawn according to real mechanisms that determine the behaviour of the human body. A drawing of an existing object is firstly a simplified representation. One may suggest that a convolutional network for object classification may return the same output with a photography and a drawing of a face as they illustrate the same concept. Hence, benefiting from larger datasets built on real images would be possible as there are few data for drawings and comics. However, convolutional networks runs in a hierarchical fashion, low level features are computed and used sequentially by higher layers to produce more complex and conceptual features. Low level features include contours, local details on textures... Those features differ a lot between drawings and photos. Consequently, these divergences are propagated through the network and generate different outputs.

However, a part of literature have begun to deal with this topic. Lagunas et al. [18] studied the effects of transfer learning on a dataset of cliparts with a VGG19 pretrained on ImageNet. Wang et al. [36] suggested that, during a standard training, local features acquire a great predictive power on the early layers, the subsequent layers then resting on their predicted hypotheses. Consequently, low level features tend to take much more importance than the illustrated concept itself. Their idea was then to penalize the predictive power in the early layers by maximizing the error on predictions computed with only low level features 10. In order to evaluate their methods, the researchers also built a dataset, ImageNet-Sketch, with only web-scraped drawings and the same classes as ImageNet dataset. With the idea of dampening the effects of details on final predictions, Mishra et al. [22] evaluated the effects of an anisotropic diffusion filtering on the input image for smoothing textures without altering sharp contours.

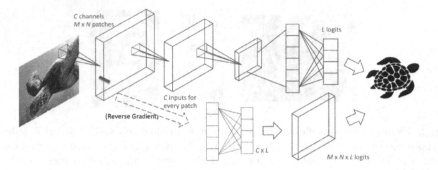

Fig. 10. Model presented in [36]. The model consists of two parts : the main global classifier (in purple), which takes into account all features locations, and a set of local classifiers (in red) for each location in early features maps. The goal is to fool the local classifiers while producing accurate predictions with the global classifier.

5   Conclusion

Emotion recognition analysis on comics is complex because multiple modalities can be intertwined in order to represent the state of mind of one character. When these ones are human-like, the face and body can by themselves provide enough information for automated processing, especially in case of realistic styles/proportions. Techniques specifically created for the comic book medium such as speech bubbles and symbols can form an important complement of information that can help to disambiguate situations. However, the tone of the work can forbid the use of "cartoony" assets. Among all the listed cues, facial information seems to be the most robust to culture changes.

We restricted the study on elements that could help to understand the state of a character during the moment of one frame. Hence, for one character, we studied the reactions to external events (other characters actions, speech...). However, the way this character affects the other was not addressed. On this topic, body gestures represent an important visual tool to analyze how characters interact between themselves. This analysis, if spread across frames, can also lead to the study of the social relationships.

Acknowledgements. This work is supported by the Research National Agency (ANR) in the framework of the 2017 LabCom program (ANR 17-LCV2-0006-01) and the Region Nouvelle Aquitaine in the framework of the EmoRecCom project.

References

1. Barros, P., Jirak, D., Weber, C., Wermter, S.: Multimodal emotional state recognition using sequence-dependent deep hierarchical features. Neural Netw. **72**, 140–151 (2015)
2. Botzheim, J., Woo, J., Tay Nuo Wi, N., Kubota, N., Yamaguchi, T.: Gestural and facial communication with smart phone based robot partner using emotional model. In: 2014 World Automation Congress (WAC), pp. 644–649 (Aug 2014)

3. Bradley, M.M., Lang, P.J.: Measuring emotion: the self-assessment manikin and the semantic differential. J. Behav. Ther. Exp. Psychiatry **25**(1), 49–59 (1994)
4. Caridakis, G., et al.: Multimodal emotion recognition from expressive faces, body gestures and speech. In: Boukis, C., Pnevmatikakis, A., Polymenakos, L. (eds.) AIAI 2007. ITIFIP, vol. 247, pp. 375–388. Springer, Boston, MA (2007). https://doi.org/10.1007/978-0-387-74161-1_41
5. Carion, N., Massa, F., Synnaeve, G., Usunier, N., Kirillov, A., Zagoruyko, S.: End-to-end object detection with transformers. In: Vedaldi, A., Bischof, H., Brox, T., Frahm, J.-M. (eds.) ECCV 2020. LNCS, vol. 12346, pp. 213–229. Springer, Cham (2020). https://doi.org/10.1007/978-3-030-58452-8_13
6. Chu, W.T., Li, W.W.: Manga FaceNet: Face Detection in Manga based on Deep Neural Network. In: Proceedings of the 2017 ACM on International Conference on Multimedia Retrieval, pp. 412–415. ACM, Bucharest Romania (Jun 2017)
7. Cohn, N., Ehly, S.: The vocabulary of manga: visual morphology in dialects of japanese visual language. J. Pragmat. **92**, 17–29 (2016)
8. Dubray, D., Laubrock, J.: Deep cnn-based speech balloon detection and segmentation for comic books. In: 2019 International Conference on Document Analysis and Recognition (ICDAR), pp. 1237–1243. IEEE (2019)
9. Ekman, P., Friesen, W.V.: Constants across cultures in the face and emotion. J. Pers. Soc. Psychol. **17**(2), 124–129 (1971)
10. Ekman, P., Rosenberg, E.L. (eds.): What the Face Reveals: Basic and Applied Studies of Spontaneous Expression Using the Facial Action Coding System (FACS). Series in Affective Science, Oxford University Press, New York, 2 edn. (2005)
11. Glowinski, D., Mortillaro, M., Scherer, K., Dael, N., Volpe, G., Camurri, A.: Towards a minimal representation of affective gestures (Extended abstract). In: 2015 International Conference on Affective Computing and Intelligent Interaction (ACII), pp. 498–504 (Sep 2015)
12. Gunes, H., Piccardi, M., Jan, T.: Face and body gesture recognition for a vision-based multimodal analyzer. In: Proceedings of the Pan-Sydney area Workshop on Visual information processing, pp. 19–28. VIP '05, Australian Computer Society Inc, AUS (Jun 2004)
13. He, K., Zhang, X., Ren, S., Sun, J.: Deep residual learning for image recognition. In: Proceedings of the IEEE Conference On Computer Vision And Pattern Recognition, pp. 770–778 (2016)
14. He, Z., et al.: An End-to-End Quadrilateral Regression Network for Comic Panel Extraction. In: Proceedings of the 26th ACM International Conference on Multimedia, pp. 887–895. MM '18, Association for Computing Machinery, New York, NY, USA (Oct 2018)
15. Ho, A.K.N., Burie, J.C., Ogier, J.M.: Panel and Speech Balloon Extraction from Comic Books. In: 2012 10th IAPR International Workshop on Document Analysis Systems, pp. 424–428. IEEE, Gold Coast, Queenslands, TBD, Australia (Mar 2012)
16. Hu, P., Cai, D., Wang, S., Yao, A., Chen, Y.: Learning supervised scoring ensemble for emotion recognition in the wild. In: Proceedings of the 19th ACM International Conference on Multimodal Interaction, pp. 553–560. ACM, Glasgow UK (Nov 2017)
17. Knyazev, B., Shvetsov, R., Efremova, N., Kuharenko, A.: Convolutional neural networks pretrained on large face recognition datasets for emotion classification from video (Nov 2017). https://arxiv.org/abs/1711.04598
18. Lagunas, M., Garces, E.: Transfer Learning for Illustration Classification. Spanish Computer Graphics Conference (CEIG), p. 9 (2017)

19. Li, L., Wang, Y., Tang, Z., Gao, L.: Automatic comic page segmentation based on polygon detection. Multimedia Tools Appl. **69**(1), 171–197 (2014)
20. Liu, X., Li, C., Zhu, H., Wong, T.T., Xu, X.: Text-aware balloon extraction from manga. Vis. Comput.: Int. J. Comput. Graph. **32**(4), 501–511 (2016)
21. Meng, Z., Liu, P., Cai, J., Han, S., Tong, Y.: Identity-Aware Convolutional Neural Network for Facial Expression Recognition. In: 2017 12th IEEE International Conference on Automatic Face & Gesture Recognition (FG 2017), pp. 558–565. IEEE, Washington, DC, DC, USA (May 2017)
22. Mishra, S., et al.: Learning Visual Representations for Transfer Learning by Suppressing Texture. arXiv:2011.01901 [cs] (Nov 2020)
23. Ng, H.W., Nguyen, V.D., Vonikakis, V., Winkler, S.: Deep Learning for Emotion Recognition on Small Datasets using Transfer Learning. In: Proceedings of the 2015 ACM on International Conference on Multimodal Interaction, pp. 443–449. ACM, Seattle Washington USA (Nov 2015)
24. Nguyen, N.V., Rigaud, C., Burie, J.C.: Comic Characters Detection Using Deep Learning. In: 2017 14th IAPR International Conference on Document Analysis and Recognition (ICDAR), pp. 41–46. IEEE, Kyoto (Nov 2017)
25. Nguyen, N.-V., Vu, X.-S., Rigaud, C., Jiang, L., Burie, J.-C.: ICDAR 2021 competition on multimodal emotion recognition on comics scenes. In: Lladós, J., Lopresti, D., Uchida, S. (eds.) ICDAR 2021. LNCS, vol. 12824, pp. 767–782. Springer, Cham (2021). https://doi.org/10.1007/978-3-030-86337-1_51
26. Noroozi, F., Marjanovic, M., Njegus, A., Escalera, S., Anbarjafari, G.: Audio-visual emotion recognition in video clips. IEEE Trans. Affect. Comput. **10**(1), 60–75 (2019)
27. Pang, X., Cao, Y., Lau, R.W., Chan, A.B.: A Robust Panel Extraction Method for Manga. In: Proceedings of the 22nd ACM international conference on Multimedia, pp. 1125–1128. ACM, Orlando Florida USA (Nov 2014)
28. Plutchik, R.: The nature of emotions: human emotions have deep evolutionary roots, a fact that may explain their complexity and provide tools for clinical practice. Am. Sci. **89**(4), 344–350 (2001)
29. Posner, J., Russell, J.A., Peterson, B.S.: The circumplex model of affect: an integrative approach to affective neuroscience, cognitive development, and psychopathology. Dev. Psychopathol. **17**(3), 715–734 (2005)
30. Qin, X., Zhou, Y., He, Z., Wang, Y., Tang, Z.: A Faster R-CNN Based Method for Comic Characters Face Detection. In: 2017 14th IAPR International Conference on Document Analysis and Recognition (ICDAR). vol. 01, pp. 1074–1080 (Nov 2017)
31. Ren, S., He, K., Girshick, R., Sun, J.: Faster r-cnn: Towards real-time object detection with region proposal networks. Advances in neural information processing systems 28 (2015)
32. Russell, J.: A circumplex model of affect. J. Pers. Soc. Psychol. **39**, 1161–1178 (1980)
33. Saha, S., Datta, S., Konar, A., Janarthanan, R.: A study on emotion recognition from body gestures using Kinect sensor. In: 2014 International Conference on Communication and Signal Processing, pp. 056–060 (Apr 2014)
34. Viola, P., Jones, M.: Rapid object detection using a boosted cascade of simple features. In: Proceedings of the 2001 IEEE Computer Society Conference on Computer Vision and Pattern Recognition. CVPR 2001. vol. 1, pp. I-511-I-518. IEEE Comput. Soc, Kauai, HI, USA (2001)
35. Walker, M.: The Lexicon of Comicana. iUniverse (2000)

36. Wang, H., Ge, S., Lipton, Z., Xing, E.P.: Learning robust global representations by penalizing local predictive power. In: Advances in Neural Information Processing Systems, vol. 32 (2019)
37. Watson, D., Tellegen, A.: Toward a consensual structure of mood. Psychol. Bull. **98**(2), 219 (1985)
38. Wu, T., Butko, N.J., Ruvulo, P., Bartlett, M.S., Movellan, J.R.: Learning to make facial expressions. In: 2009 IEEE 8th International Conference on Development and Learning, pp. 1–6. IEEE (2009)
39. Zhao, S., Cai, H., Liu, H., Zhang, J., Chen, S.: Feature selection mechanism in cnns for facial expression recognition. In: BMVC, p. 317 (2018)

Automatic Reading Order Detection of Comic Panels

Yunlong Zhang and Seiji Hotta(✉)

Department of Computer and Information Sciences, Tokyo University of Agriculture
and Technology, 2-24-16, Nakacho, Koganei, Tokyo 184-8588, Japan
s-hotta@cc.tuat.ac.jp

Abstract. Tasks such as object detection for comic content are attracting more and more attention from the public. A lot of work focuses on character detection, text recognition, or other tasks. However, only a few of them focus on the reading order detection of panels. In this paper, we review several existing sorting methods and propose a novel method based on these existing methods. Experiment results show that the proposed method outperforms the baseline methods. The proposed method can deal with pages with basic layouts easily. And sometimes has the ability to deal with some pages with complex layouts.

Keywords: Comic · Layout · Reading order

1 Introduction

In recent years, many applications related to comics have emerged. Among them, some interesting tasks have attracted a lot of public attention, for example, automatic translation and character generation. Many of these tasks need the detection and extraction of basic elements in comics, *e.g.* characters, panels, text, and speech balloons. Up to now, many works have already focused on the detection of bounding boxes [2,20], characters [4,11,18,22], speech balloons [6, 24,28], and text [3,7,25].

Although there are many effective methods for basic content extraction, the sorting of comic panels has always been ignored. In many cases, reading order is not the focus of the work, so people will ignore this problem. Even if it's necessary to deal with this issue, people just use simple methods to complete this task. These two reasons lead to there being little work about reading order.

In general, there are two kinds of reading orders. One is to read from left to right and then from top to bottom, *e.g.* American and European comics. Another is reading from right to left and then from top to bottom, *e.g.* Japanese comics. The expression of comics is not fixed, and the painting styles are also different. Sometimes we have to face complex situations. For example, as shown in Fig. 1, sometimes characters are displayed across panels, or panels overlap with each other, or panels have no clear edges. Therefore, handling the sorting by simple methods is not suitable.

© Springer Nature Switzerland AG 2023
J.-J. Rousseau and B. Kapralos (Eds.): ICPR 2022 Workshops, LNCS 13644, pp. 76–90, 2023.
https://doi.org/10.1007/978-3-031-37742-6_6

Fig. 1. The example of complex layout. [1,16] "LoveHina vol01" ©Akamatsu Ken

Each comic panel can be regarded as a scene in the story. Sorting panels according to the reading order can make scenes in order and get a complete story. Sorting numerous comic panels manually is time-consuming and not realistic. Therefore, detecting the reading order from the comic page automatically is important for other work, for example, the research of comic narrative, or the segmentation and display of comics.

Therefore, in this paper, we modify two existing methods, and propose a novel method for reading order detection of panels based on the advantage of these two methods. The novel method is designed for panels represented by bounding boxes, and this method is improved from methods of quick sort and tree structure that already existed. The proposed method combines the advantages of these two methods. In addition, we try to use the automatic classification to select the horizontal reading order in the experiment. We also try to use the panel extracted by the Feature Pyramid Network (FPN) [15] in the experiment, and observe how the proposed method performs in practical processing.

The rest of this paper is organized as follows: Sect. 2 describes some methods related to reading order detection. The proposed method is described in Sect. 3. Section 4 presents experiments and evaluations. Section 5 then offers a summary.

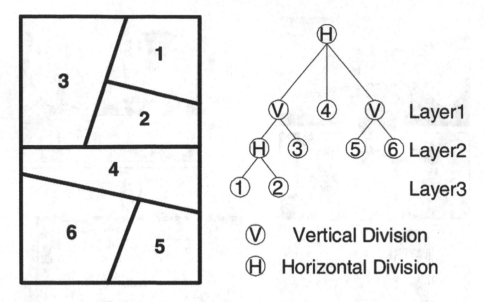

Fig. 2. Method of the tree structure. [27]

2   Related Work

The early applications of e-comic reading were designed based on personal computers or laptops. In order to display comics on cell phones with small screens, an algorithm is necessary to split panels and display them separately. At the same time, the algorithm needs to deal with the low memory capacity and high telecommunications cost of the cell phone. In 2004, Yamada *et al.* [29] proposed a compression and storing method of e-comic. Comic panels are divided and sorted according to certain rules, then compressed to files in 2 KB or 3 KB. The depth-first search is used in the process of sorting. During the search, four rules are set to judge the reading order between neighbor panels according to the dividing line between panels and the line called base line that can contain two edges of two adjacent panels. This algorithm can deal with general comic page layout. But when the layout is a little more complex, for example, when characters or speech balloons cross panels, the algorithm can not perform well.

Tanaka *et al.* [27] proposed a method of dividing panels and sorting. A large number of lines are generated on the page, and then the lines that meet certain conditions are found as the segmentation lines of panels. Segmentation lines are used to segment the page like the guillotine cut [19]. The page is alternately segmented in horizontal and vertical to generate panels, then these panels are stored in the tree structure. The reading order can be obtained simply by using the depth-first search. This process is shown in Fig. 2. However, in their work, the situation that a panel contains other panels is not included, and this algorithm is unable to deal with this particular case.

Iyyer *et al.* [13] tried to make the machine understand the narrative of comics. They collected many old comics created in the last century as datasets and applied LSTM [12] to process the image features and text features extracted from comics. Faster R-CNN [23] is used to extract panels from comics, then panels are sorted using the Morton order [17]. In the sorting, the coordinates of the panel centers are encoded, and the reading order of panels is decided by sorting these encoded coordinates. This method can only get wrong results when applied to rare and complex page layouts.

Arai *et al.* [2] designed methods of panel segmentation, sorting, and displaying for mobile devices. In order to adapt to real-time applications, the reading order is obtained by using quick sort to the coordinates of panels. Since their work is mainly about the extraction and segmentation of panels, detailed information about sorting is not provided. The coordinates of two panels are just simply compared in sorting, and the performance of this algorithm has not been tested.

Ponsard *et al.* [21] tried to apply optical character recognition (OCR) in the digital comic book viewer. They also proposed a method for reading order detection. They set five different cases to judge the order of two panels according to the relative position of the two panels. These cases include the situation where panels overlap with each other and the situation where one panel includes another.

Li *et al.* [14] proposed a method for panel extraction by line segment detection and polygon detection. They also proposed a method for reading order detection by comparing the order between two panels. The reading order is obtained by using the bubble sort algorithm. Four different geometric relationships are established based on the overlap of the projection of two panels, and three solutions of the reading order are given for these relations.

Guérin *et al.* [8] proposed a framework to handle the content of comics. They explained the relationships between panels in detail, and constructed a complete reading order detection pipeline. The reading order is obtained by using a merge sort algorithm and a topological sort. For each two panels, the reading order is detected step by step according to topological spatial relation [5] and cone shaped direction. They proposed an evaluation method for their work, and their reading order detection pipeline performed well in the experiment.

3   Proposed Method

3.1   Modified Tree Structure

We modify the method of Tanaka *et al.* [27]. Segmentation lines are generated to separate panels in their work, but this is not suitable for bounding boxes. In practical processing, bounding boxes cannot perfectly enclose panels sometimes, and these bounding boxes will overlap with each other. Therefore, it is not a good choice to use the segmentation lines to separate bounding boxes. We will not adopt the method of segmentation line generation and only use the idea of the tree structure. The modified method focuses on detecting the reading order based on the coordinates of each bounding box.

Compare the methods introduced in Sect. 2, the tree structure used by Tanaka *et al.* [27] is the only method that processes panels step by step from the whole page to the local areas. Such processing is well adapted to the global or local page layout, *i.e.*, it is easy to find which panels should be in the same row or column. We regard the panels in the same row or column as a cluster. Panels that are in the same cluster need to be found, and then these clusters will be sorted to get the reading order among rows or columns.

In the proposed method, first, the information of all bounding boxes is saved into the root node, and then the coordinates of the bounding boxes are projected to the Y-axis or X-axis. Since most comics are shown in the single-page format, we choose to project to the Y-axis first and determine which panels belong to the same row. Then to the X-axis in the subsequent recursion to determine which panels belong to the same column. The direction is changed alternately in each recursion.

Then clusters are extracted from panels. We then select the line segment with the longest length in the projection and calculate the Intersection over Minimum (IoMin) with the rest of the segments. The segment with the longest length and the segments with IoMin values larger than the preset threshold are extracted, and their corresponding panels belong to the same cluster. Then we repeat the process for the remaining line segments until all panels are assigned to corresponding clusters. The calculation of IoMin is similar to Intersection over Union (IoU). It can be defined as:

$$IoMin = \frac{Intersection(L_1, L_2)}{Min(L_1, L_2)} \qquad (1)$$

where L_1 and L_2 are segments projected by two panels, $Intersection$ (.) calculates the length of the intersection of two segments, $Min(.)$ calculates the minimum value of two segments. Because IoMin uses the minimum length instead of the union of two segments, it can get a greater score when two panels intersect each other or one is overlapped by another. Therefore, it can extract more results in the clustering than using the union of two segments, and can better show whether two panels belong to the same row or column.

Next, the order between clusters is obtained by comparing the coordinates of the cluster centers. For clusters in different rows, the reading order should be in the front if the Y-coordinate is small. For clusters in different columns, the reading order should be in the front if the X-coordinate is small. If the comic is in Japanese style, the reading order should be in the front if the X-coordinate is large. Clusters are saved in the child nodes of the current node in order.

The operations introduced above (projection, clustering, sorting, and storing) are then performed recursively on the cluster saved in each child node. This will continue until all panels are saved to the leaf nodes individually. Finally, depth-first search can be used to get the reading order of these panels.

Since the method of Tanaka *et al.* [27] can't handle the case that one panel contains others, only the default order will be output in the modified method.

3.2 Modified Quick Sort

We modify the work of Arai *et al.* [2]. The rules of comparing two panels in the quick sort are modified. Two panels to be sorted are projected to the Y-axis. For the segments after projection, the IoMin between them is calculated. If the score is greater than a preset fixed threshold, these two panels are considered to be in the same row and then we compare the X-coordinate of the center points. Otherwise, these two panels are considered to be located in different rows and then we compare the Y-coordinate of the center points. If the X-coordinate or the Y-coordinate of the center points are equal, the minimum coordinate of the bounding boxes will be used for comparison. The modified quick sort method adds the judgment of whether two panels are in the same row, and should therefore get better results than before.

3.3 Combining Two Methods

The method using quick sort does not use the actual page layout, but just simply compares the order of two panels. In the special situation that the method using tree structure can't handle, *i.e.*, panels overlapping or intersecting with others, reading order can be obtained by the quick sort method. However, for basic layouts, the tree structure method can perform better than the quick sort method. This is because the quick sort method ignores the actual page layout and it will sometimes produce incorrect results. For example, in some cases, even if two panels are in the same row, they are still judged to be located in different rows because they are not aligned horizontally.

Therefore, we combine the advantages of the two algorithms here. The novel method is based on the tree structure method and uses the modified quick sort method to deal with complex situations that the tree structure method cannot handle. This method should be suitable for basic layouts and have the ability to handle some complex layouts.

4 Experiment

4.1 Experiment of Using the Ground Truth

Different methods are tested in this experiment. We choose the quick sort method from the work of Arai *et al.* [2], the Morton order [17] used by Iyyer *et al.* [13], and the tree structure method modified from the work of Tanaka *et al.* [27] as baseline methods. Other methods require precise segmentation of the comic to get each edge of panels or need the segmentation line between panels. Therefore, these methods are not suitable for the data represented by bounding boxes and are not reimplemented in the experiment. These baseline methods, new quick sort, and tree structure + new quick sort will be tested in the experiment. The optimal threshold in the calculation of IoMin depends on the actual layouts in the dataset. In this experiment, we empirically set the threshold to 0.8.

Fig. 3. Examples of wrong results. Top left: Morton order. Top right: quick sort. Bottom left: tree structure. Bottom right: new quick sort. Images from eBDtheque [9]: (top left) *Cyborg 07: Traffic p. 4*, (top right) *Cyborg 07: Cosmozone Volume 1 p. 12*, (bottom left) *Fred: Philémon L'Arche du A p. 11*, (bottom right) *Cyborg 07: Bubblegôm Gôm La Légende des Yaouanks p. 32*.

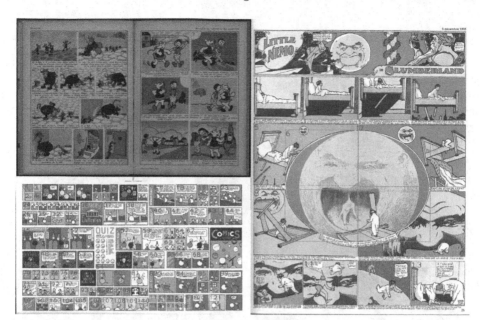

Fig. 4. Examples of wrong results obtained by tree + new quick sort. Images from eBDtheque [9]: (top left) *Alain Saint Ogan: Zig Et Puce Prosper Et Le Monstre Marin p. 16*, (bottom left) *Chris Ware: Acme novelty library p. 24*, (right) *Winsor McCay: Little Nemo Little Nemo in Slumberland p. 25*.

Because the correct reading order is not recorded in the Manga109 [1,16] dataset, the eBDtheque [9] dataset is used in the experiment. It contains 100 comic images, most of them from Europe or America, and the correct reading order of each image is recorded in the annotation. We select 88 images that read from left to right and contain more than one panel. In this experiment, we use the coordinate information recorded in the annotations for testing. The panels in each annotation are recorded in the default order (not the correct reading order), and they are input into the detector in this default order during testing. Before the test, we change the input order of these panels randomly for data augmentation. We process each image 4 times and get 352 samples used for testing finally.

The evaluation method used in this experiment is similar to the method used in the work of Guérin *et al.* [8]. In this experiment, we set the sequence of detection results for each image to be $\mathcal{P}$, where each panel is p_0, p_1... p_n, and n is the total number of panels in the sequence $\mathcal{P}$. We set the correct result, *i.e.*, the reading order sequence of the ground truth to $\mathcal{G}$, where each panel is g_0, g_1... g_m, and m is the total number of panels in the sequence $\mathcal{G}$. To evaluate the performance of each method, the calculation of accuracy has the following steps. First, check whether the first panel p_0 in the result is the same as the first panel g_0 in the ground truth. Record one correct detection if they are the

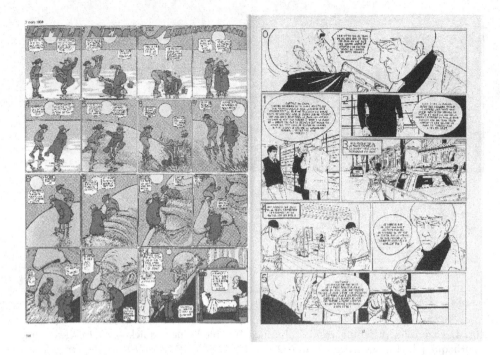

Fig. 5. Examples of correct results obtained by tree + new quick sort. Images from eBDtheque [9]: (left) *Little Nemo Little Nemo in Slumberland p. 168*, (right) *Olivier Jolivet: Boston Police L'Affaire Pradi p. 87.*

same. Then, start from the first panel until the panel before the last one, for each panel p_i, found the corresponding panel g_j in the ground truth, check whether the panel p_{i+1} is the same as panel g_{j+1}. Record one correct detection if they are the same. Finally, check if the last panel in the result is the same as the last panel in the ground truth. Record one correct detection if they are the same. For K images, the number of correct results for each image can be represented by t_k, the number of panels in each image can be represented by n_k, and the accuracy can be defined as:

$$Accuracy = \frac{\sum_{k=1}^{K} t_k}{\sum_{k=1}^{K} (n_k + 1)} \tag{2}$$

This evaluation method checks which panel is the first, which panel is the last, and which panel should be the next. It mainly focuses on the order between panels instead of the position. In addition, we calculate the 100% correct rate, *i.e.*, the proportion of pages that all panels are in the correct order.

The experiment result is shown in Table 1, the best results are written in bold. The new quick sort gets the best performance. The performance of the two proposed methods is similar, and both methods outperform the baseline methods. The new quick sort can decide if two panels should be in the same

Table 1. The experiment result of using the ground truth.

	Method	Accuracy	100% correct rate
Baseline	Morton order [17]	0.6425	40.91%
	Quick sort [2]	0.4092	25.57%
	Tree (modified) [27]	0.8717	83.52%
Proposed method	New quick sort	**0.9410**	**92.05%**
	Tree + new quick sort	0.9020	**92.05%**

row, which makes it achieves better performance than the original quick sort. This also shows that more information and more situations considered in the panel comparison can increase the accuracy. The tree structure method processes panels from the whole page to local areas. This makes it can adapt well to the global or local page layout, and can achieve better performance than the other two baseline methods. In addition, tree + new quick sort uses new quick sort to deal with complex situations, this is why it gets 0.03 accuracy larger than the modified tree method.

Wrong results for different methods are shown in Fig. 3. The method using quick sort will get wrong results when panels are not aligned. The method of Morton order needs to encode the coordinates and then use the encoded coordinates to sort. This process ignores the page layout, so the panel that should be number 4 gets number 2. The tree structure method can't handle the case of overlapping, so the second row in the example can only show the default order. Although the new quick sort has the ability to determine whether the borders are in the same row, due to disregarding the page layout, it still gets incorrect results sometimes. So the panel that should be number 9 in the example gets number 11.

The wrong results of tree + new quick sort are shown in Fig. 4 individually. Since we think comics are shown in the single-page format, wrong results will be obtained when detecting double-page comics like the top left image. The bottom left image contains more than a hundred panels, and the image on the right has a large face as an individual panel covering four surrounding panels. For images with very special layouts like these, tree + new quick sort still can't work well.

Some correct results obtained by tree + new quick sort are shown in Fig. 5. The proposed method can achieve very good results when dealing with basic layouts or slightly complex layouts.

4.2 Experiment of Combining Automatic Classification

There are two kinds of horizontal reading orders, and they are determined by the author's culture. Detecting the language used in comics to determine horizontal reading orders is a feasible approach. However, in the translated comic, the lan-

Table 2. The experiment result of combining automatic classification.

	Method	Manual		Auto	
		Accuracy	100% correct rate	Accuracy	100% correct rate
Baseline	Morton order [17]	0.6510	42.55%	0.6435	41.49%
	Quick sort [2]	0.4178	25.53%	0.4146	25.00%
	Tree (modified) [27]	0.8770	84.57%	0.8685	82.45%
Proposed method	New quick sort	**0.9434**	**92.55%**	0.9328	90.43%
	Tree + new quick sort	0.9061	**92.55%**	0.8954	90.43%

guage cannot correspond to the author's culture. Therefore, in this experiment, we try to extract image features, classify the corresponding culture, and combine it with reading order detection methods. Both manual classification and automatic classification are tested.

The ResNet101 [10] network is used as the image classifier due to its good performance in classification tasks. We select 130 images from eBDtheque [9] dataset and Manga109 [1, 16] dataset as the training set. 65 images are Japanese-style comics and 65 images are European or American comics. In addition, 58 images are selected for the testing set. We load the weights pre-trained on the ImageNet [26] dataset and then fine-tune the network using the 130 images of the training set. The classifier can achieve an accuracy of 0.96 in the test.

We add the 6 Japanese comic pages contained in eBDtheque [9] to the dataset used previously after data augmentation. In addition, the rest of the setting and evaluation methods are the same as before.

The experiment result is shown in Table 2, the best results are written in bold. The proposed methods outperform the baseline methods in both automatic classification and the manual setting. All methods of using automatic classification get lower accuracy than using the manual setting. This shows that the automatic classifier got some wrong classification results. From our observations, some comics are monochrome, and they are classified as Japanese comics in the experiment. The amount of data used to train the classifier is not large enough, and most of the Japanese comics in the dataset are monochromatic. Therefore, the size of the dataset limits the performance of the classifier.

Table 3. The experiment result of combining FPN.

	Method	F-score	100% correct rate
Baseline	Morton order [17]	0.5966	34.04%
	Quick sort [2]	0.5529	19.15%
	Tree (modified) [27]	0.6177	**40.43%**
Proposed method	New quick sort	0.6287	**40.43%**
	Tree + new quick sort	**0.6289**	**40.43%**

Fig. 6. Examples of using FPN. Top: the correct result. Bottom: the wrong result. Images from eBDtheque [9]: (top) *Cyborg 07: Bubblegôm Gôm La Légende des Yaouanks p.13*, (bottom) *Matt Fox: Chilling Tales Chilling Tales 17 Geo p.16*.

4.3   Experiment of Combining FPN

In this experiment, we want to see how these methods perform in practical use. The panels detected by FPN [15] replace the ground truth for testing. The automatic classifier used before is also used in this experiment. We use the Manga109 [1, 16] dataset for training and testing FPN [15]. 8104 images are randomly selected for training and 2026 images are used for testing. The trained detector achieves an average precision (AP) of 0.96 for panel detection. This detector extracts panels from the 94 images in eBDtheque [9] dataset and these panels are used in this experiment.

Since the number of panels in detection results may not be equal to the actual number of panels, it's necessary to modify the evaluation method. When checking whether two panels are the same, the IoU score of these two panels is calculated. If the score is greater than a certain threshold, they are considered to describe the same panel. In this experiment, this threshold was set to 0.5. Each correct detection is regarded as a true positive. We calculate the proportion of the number of true positives in the ground truth and the proportion in the detection results, *i.e.*, recall and precision, and then get the F-score for evaluation.

The experiment result is shown in Table 3, the best results are written in bold. The accuracy of all methods has dropped, but the proposed methods still achieve the best performance. Since FPN [15] is trained on the Manga109 [1, 16] dataset, miss detection or inaccurate results may be obtained when detecting images in eBDtheque [9]. Two results of using trees + new quick sort are shown in Fig. 6. When panels can be extracted accurately, the correct reading order can be obtained. Once there is a missed detection, the detection of the reading order will be influenced.

5   Conclusion

In this paper, we have proposed a novel method used for automatic reading order detection of comic panels based on existing methods. In the experiment using the eBDtheque dataset, the proposed method achieved an accuracy of 0.94 and could achieve 100% correct detection results for about 92% of the pages. In the experiments using automatic classification to determine the horizontal reading order, the accuracy of all methods dropped slightly, but the results were acceptable. We also tested using bounding boxes extracted by FPN. The accuracy of all methods had a significant drop, the proposed method achieved an accuracy of 0.62 and could achieve 100% correct detection results for about 40% of the pages. However, the proposed method still outperformed the baseline method. In the next step, we can deal with the problem of the insufficient amount of data in the eBDtheque dataset. For example, adding new comics for testing, and considering adding images with different layouts. The proposed method still can't get the correct result for some special images with complex page layouts. This problem remains for future work.

References

1. Aizawa, K., et al.: Building a manga dataset "manga109" with annotations for multimedia applications. IEEE MultiMedia **27**(2), 8–18 (2020). https://doi.org/10.1109/mmul.2020.2987895

2. Arai, K., Herman, T.: Method for automatic e-comic scene frame extraction for reading comic on mobile devices. In: 2010 Seventh International Conference on Information Technology: New Generations, pp. 370–375 (2010)
3. Aramaki, Y., Matsui, Y., Yamasaki, T., Aizawa, K.: Text detection in manga by combining connected-component-based and region-based classifications. In: 2016 IEEE International Conference on Image Processing (ICIP), pp. 2901–2905 (2016)
4. Chu, W.T., Li, W.W.: Manga FaceNet: face detection in manga based on deep neural network. In: Proceedings of the 2017 ACM on International Conference on Multimedia Retrieval (2017)
5. Cohn, A.G., Bennett, B., Gooday, J., Gotts, N.M.: Representing and reasoning with qualitative spatial relations about regions. In: Stock, O. (eds.) Spatial and Temporal Reasoning, pp. 97–134. Springer, Dordrecht (1997). https://doi.org/10.1007/978-0-585-28322-7_4
6. Dubray, D., Laubrock, J.: Deep CNN-based speech balloon detection and segmentation for comic books. In: 2019 International Conference on Document Analysis and Recognition (ICDAR), pp. 1237–1243 (2019)
7. Del Gobbo, J., Matuk Herrera, R.: Unconstrained text detection in Manga: a new dataset and baseline. In: Bartoli, A., Fusiello, A. (eds.) ECCV 2020. LNCS, vol. 12537, pp. 629–646. Springer, Cham (2020). https://doi.org/10.1007/978-3-030-67070-2_38
8. Guérin, C., Rigaud, C., Bertet, K., Revel, A.: An ontology-based framework for the automated analysis and interpretation of comic books' images. Inf. Sci. **378**, 109–130 (2017)
9. Guérin, C., et al.: eBDtheque: a representative database of comics. In: Proceedings of the 12th International Conference on Document Analysis and Recognition (ICDAR) (2013)
10. He, K., Zhang, X., Ren, S., Sun, J.: Deep residual learning for image recognition. In: 2016 IEEE Conference on Computer Vision and Pattern Recognition (CVPR), pp. 770–778 (2016)
11. Hideaki, Y., Daisuke, I., Hiroshi, W.: Face detection for comic images using the deformable part model. IIEEJ Trans. Image Electron. Visual Comput. 4(2), 95–100 (2016)
12. Hochreiter, S., Schmidhuber, J.: Long short-term memory. Neural Comput. **9**, 1735–1780 (1997)
13. Iyyer, M., et al.: The amazing mysteries of the Gutter: drawing inferences between panels in comic book narratives. In: 2017 IEEE Conference on Computer Vision and Pattern Recognition (CVPR), pp. 6478–6487 (2017)
14. Li, L., Wang, Y., Tang, Z., Liu, D.: DRR - comic image understanding based on polygon detection. In: SPIE Proceedings, vol. 8658, pp. 87–97. SPIE, February 2013
15. Lin, T.Y., Dollár, P., Girshick, R.B., He, K., Hariharan, B., Belongie, S.J.: Feature pyramid networks for object detection. In: 2017 IEEE Conference on Computer Vision and Pattern Recognition (CVPR), pp. 936–944 (2017)
16. Matsui, Y., et al.: Sketch-based manga retrieval using manga109 dataset. Multimedia Tools Appl. **76**(20), 21811–21838 (2016). https://doi.org/10.1007/s11042-016-4020-z
17. Morton, G.: A Computer Oriented Geodetic Data Base and a New Technique in File Sequencing. International Business Machines Company (1966)
18. Nguyen, N.V., Rigaud, C., Burie, J.C.: Comic characters detection using deep learning. In: 2017 14th IAPR International Conference on Document Analysis and Recognition (ICDAR), vol. 3, pp. 41–46 (2017)

19. Ono, T.: Optimizing two-dimensional guillotine cut by genetic algorithms. In: Proceedings of the Ninth AJOU-FIT-NUST Joint Seminar, pp. 40–47 (1999)
20. Pang, X., Cao, Y., Lau, R.W.H., Chan, A.B.: A robust panel extraction method for Manga. In: Proceedings of the 22nd ACM International Conference on Multimedia (2014)
21. Ponsard, C., Ramdoyal, R., Dziamski, D.: An OCR-enabled digital comic books viewer. In: Miesenberger, K., Karshmer, A., Penaz, P., Zagler, W. (eds.) ICCHP 2012. LNCS, vol. 7382, pp. 471–478. Springer, Heidelberg (2012). https://doi.org/10.1007/978-3-642-31522-0_71
22. Qin, X., Zhou, Y., He, Z., Wang, Y., Tang, Z.: A faster R-CNN based method for comic characters face detection. In: 2017 14th IAPR International Conference on Document Analysis and Recognition (ICDAR), vol. 1, pp. 1074–1080 (2017)
23. Ren, S., He, K., Girshick, R.B., Sun, J.: Faster R-CNN: towards real-time object detection with region proposal networks. IEEE Trans. Pattern Anal. Mach. Intell. **39**, 1137–1149 (2015)
24. Rigaud, C., Burie, J.-C., Ogier, J.-M.: Text-independent speech balloon segmentation for Comics and Manga. In: Lamiroy, B., Dueire Lins, R. (eds.) GREC 2015. LNCS, vol. 9657, pp. 133–147. Springer, Cham (2017). https://doi.org/10.1007/978-3-319-52159-6_10
25. Rigaud, C., Karatzas, D., van de Weijer, J., Burie, J.C., Ogier, J.M.: Automatic text localisation in scanned comic books. In: VISAPP (2013)
26. Russakovsky, O., et al.: ImageNet large scale visual recognition challenge. Int. J. Comput. Vision **115**(3), 211–252 (2015). https://doi.org/10.1007/s11263-015-0816-y
27. Tanaka, T., Shoji, K., Toyama, F., Miyamichi, J.: Layout analysis of tree-structured scene frames in comic images. In: IJCAI (2007)
28. Tanaka, T., Toyama, F., Miyamichi, J., Shoji, K.: Detection and classification of speech balloons in comic images. J. Inst. Image Inf. Television Eng. **64**, 1933–1939 (2010)
29. Yamada, M., Budiarto, R., Endo, M., Miyazaki, S.: Comic image decomposition for reading comics on cellular phones. IEICE Trans. Inf. Syst. **87-D**, 1370–1376 (2004)

Estimation of Unknown Words Using Speech and Eye Gaze When Reading Aloud Comics

Taro Takaike$^{(\boxtimes)}$ (iD), Motoi Iwata (iD), and Koichi Kise (iD)

Graduate School of Informatics, Osaka Metropolitan University, Osaka, Japan
sb22839a@st.omu.ac.jp, {imotoi,kise}@omu.ac.jp
https://imlab.jp/

Abstract. This paper proposes a method for estimating speech balloons with unknown words for English learners based on speech and eye gaze information during reading aloud Japanese comics translated into English. In this method, a headset and eye tracker are used to record speech and eye gaze information. Then we extract 47 features from them together with text information. The features are used to train a support vector machine to estimate unknown words for each speech balloon. We evaluated the proposed method by measuring data from 20 Japanese university students. As a result, we confirmed that the proposed method performs better than the estimation using only text information and that the speech and eye gaze information are effective for estimating unknown words.

Keywords: Education · Learning Support · Unknown words · Estimation · Speech · Eye gaze · Comic computing

1 Introduction

In recent years globalization has been on the rise, and the acquisition of English, the world's common language, has become indispensable. Acquiring new vocabulary is very important for learning English, and many methods have been proposed for consolidating the knowledge of acquired vocabulary. One of these methods is reading aloud. Reading aloud is a method of learning that connects vocabulary, the knowledge of grammar, and the knowledge of pronunciation by reading sentences aloud [11]. Reading aloud is expected to consolidate knowledge and help learners to use English they have learned subconsciously. However, it is time-consuming to record words of which the meanings learners do not know while reading aloud. Moreover, this can be an obstacle to reading aloud. Therefore, we propose a method to estimate words of which the meanings are unknown to learners based on the text information and the learner's behavior while reading aloud. In this paper, words of which the meanings are unknown to learners are called "unknown words". By automatically collecting unknown words, we expect that it will be easier for learners to acquire new vocabulary.

J.-J. Rousseau and B. Kapralos (Eds.): ICPR 2022 Workshops, LNCS 13644, pp. 91–106, 2023.
https://doi.org/10.1007/978-3-031-37742-6_7

The speech and eye gaze information can be recorded when reading English sentences aloud. The speech can be used to estimate unknown words by detecting unnatural pronunciation when reading unknown words aloud. The eye gaze information has been shown to be related to the level of understanding of English sentences in the study by Ohkoso et al. [5]. Therefore, we propose a method for estimating unknown words based on speech and eye gaze information.

In this study, we use Japanese comics translated into English as learning materials for reading aloud. The text in comics is placed in pieces as speech balloons. This enables us to obtain the speech and eye gaze information corresponding to small set of text enclosed in speech balloons.

Therefore, we propose a method for estimating a learner's unknown words based on the speech and eye gaze information when reading aloud Japanese comics translated into English.

In this paper, we describe related work in Sect. 2, the proposed method in Sect. 3, data measurement in Sect. 4, an evaluation in Sect. 5, and a discussion in Sect. 6, and conclude in Sect. 7.

2   Related Work

First, we introduce the studies that estimate a person's internal state or the learner's proficiency level from speech or eye gaze information. Sabu et al. estimated children's confidence from speech when reading aloud stories [9]. In this study, features such as pause, speech rate, pitch, intensity, voice quality, and enunciation were calculated from speech, and the confidence was estimated using a random forest. Zhang et al. estimated whether children were confident, confused, or hesitant from speech when performing a Lego task and talking to their tutor [12]. In this study, various speech analysis such as lexicon, prosody, spectrum, and syntax were performed, and the computed features were used to estimate the emotion by a robust classification and regression tree (CART). Martínez-Gómez et al. estimated learners' language proficiency from eye gaze information when reading [7]. Ishimaru et al. classified learners' proficiency from eye gaze information when answering questions about a physics text they had read once [6]. These studies did not use both speech and eye gaze information for estimation. In addition, these studies did not focus on the learners' state when reading Japanese comics translated into English.

Second, we introduce the studies that estimate learners' understanding level when reading Japanese comics translated into English for learning English. Daiku et al. estimated learner's understanding level for each speech balloon based on eye gaze information, micro-expressions, and word count while extensive reading of Japanese comics translated into English [3]. They measured eye gaze information with an eye tracker device and extracted micro-expression features from facial images recorded with a high-speed camera. Takahashi et al. used eye gaze information to estimate learners' understanding level for each page in Japanese comics translated into English [10]. These studies used fixation and saccade as eye gaze information and showed that eye gaze information is effective in estimating understanding level when silent reading Japanese comics translated into English. However, these studies did not use speech for understanding estimation.

The novelty of this study lies in the fact that the estimation method combining both speech and eye gaze information was realized by using comics, for which the corresponding speech and gaze information can be obtained for each speech balloon, as learning materials.

3 Proposed Method

The proposed method estimates whether an unknown word is included in each speech balloon based on the speech and eye gaze information when reading aloud Japanese comics translated into English. The reason why the unit of the estimation is speech balloon is because the extraction of features corresponding to a speech balloon is relatively easy meanwhile that corresponding to a word is difficult. Moreover, unknown words in a speech balloon can be narrowed down based on a word frequency or a learner's profile if the existence is estimated in the next step. The proposed method consists of the following four processes. First, the speech and eye gaze information are acquired using a headset and an eye tracker. Next, the obtained data is segmented and the speech and eye gaze information corresponding to each speech balloon are identified. Next, features are extracted from the segmented speech and eye gaze information. Finally, the estimator is trained and estimates whether each speech balloon contains unknown words. Each process is described in detail below.

3.1 Acquisition of Sensor Information

The speech is recorded through a microphone built into a headset worn by a learner. The headset is suitable for our method because the distance between the microphone and the mouth is always constant. It confirms the stable quality of recording. The speech is recorded and saved in wav format, which is an uncompressed audio file format. The eye tracker was placed at the bottom of the PC display to acquire eye tracking data.

3.2 Data Division and Synchronization for Each Speech Balloon

In this section, we describe how to divide the speech and eye tracking data and synchronize the divided segments with the corresponding speech balloon. The proposed method assumes that the coordinates of the speech balloon areas in the comics have been obtained in advance.

First, we describe the operations for speech. The speech is divided into speech segments using inaSpeechSegmenter [4], a CNN-based speech segmentation method. InaSpeechSegmenter can divide speech into speech segments corresponding to speech balloons more accurately than the segmentation based on silence segments. Based on inaSpeechSegmenter, speech segments with only noise

Table 1. Features used for estimation

Category	Type of features	Features
Speech	Frequency feature	Avg. of MFCC (20 dimensions) in time direction
	Features using IBM Watson	Confidence of transcription per speech balloon
		Max., min., avg. of confidence of transcription per word
		Max., min., avg. of confidence of transcription assuming the transcription is same as the text
	Reading aloud time	Reading aloud time per speech balloon
		Reading aloud time per word
Eye gaze	Fixation	Number of fixations
		Max., min., avg. of duration of fixation
	Saccade	Max., min., avg. of the lengths of saccade
		Max., min., avg. of the speed of saccade
	Gazing time	Gazing time per speech balloon
		Gazing time per word
Speech and Eye gaze	Time difference between reading aloud and gazing	Time difference in start time
		Time difference in end time
Text	Number of words	Number of words in speech balloon
	Word frequency	Max., min., avg. of word frequency

are removed. Next, the coordinates of the eye gaze at the start of the speech segment are obtained from the eye tracking data. Finally, the coordinates of the eye gaze are compared with the coordinates of the speech balloon area to synchronize the speech segment with the corresponding speech balloon. If some speech segments are synchronized with the same speech balloon, they are merged.

Next, we describe the operations for the eye tracking data. First, the raw eye tracking data is converted into fixation and saccade using the method of Buscher et al. [1]. Here, fixation is a point where an eye gaze stays for a certain period of time, and a saccade is a quick movement of an eye gaze between fixations. Next, the coordinates of the fixation are compared with the coordinates of the speech balloon area to synchronize with the corresponding speech balloon. By the above operations, the fixation and saccade for each speech balloon are obtained.

3.3   Feature Extraction

In this section, we describe a method for extracting features for estimation from speech and eye gaze information per speech balloon. Table 1 shows the 47 features used in the proposed method.

First, we describe the process for extracting features from the speech. First, Mel Frequency Cepstral Coefficients (MFCC) are calculated in the following manner. The 20 dimensions of MFCC are calculated. Then the average of each dimension on the time axis is taken as one feature. Second, we use IBM Watson[TM] Speech to Text[1] (IBM Watson) to obtain speech features considering text information. IBM Watson is an API for transcribing English speech. When

---

[1] https://www.ibm.com/jp-ja/cloud/watson-speech-to-text.

speech and text information corresponding to each speech balloon is input to IBM Watson, the output is the result of the transcription, the confidence of transcription (hereinafter called "the confidence"), and the confidence assuming that the result of the transcription is the same as the input text. The confidence are obtained for each speech balloon and each word. The confidence assuming that the transcription is the same as the input text are also obtained for each word. We employ the following values as features: the confidence per speech balloon, the maximum, minimum, and average of the confidence of the transcription per words, and the maximum, minimum, and average of the confidence assuming that the transcription is same as input text per word. Finally, the reading aloud time per speech balloon and the reading aloud time per word are employed as features. The reading aloud time per word is calculated by dividing the reading aloud time per speech balloon by the number of words in the speech balloon.

Second, we describe the process for extracting features related to eye gaze information. First, the number of fixations corresponding to each speech balloon is calculated. Second, the maximum, minimum, and average of the duration of fixation, the maximum, minimum, and average of saccade length, and the maximum, minimum, and average of saccade speed are calculated for each speech balloon and are used as the features. Finally, the gazing time per speech balloon and the gazing time per word are used as features. The gazing time per word is calculated by dividing the gazing time per speech balloon by the number of words in the speech balloon.

Third, we describe features related to both speech and eye gaze information. The difference between the start time of the reading aloud time and that of the gazing time is used as a feature. Similarly, the difference between the end time of the reading aloud time and that of the gazing time is used as a feature.

Finally, we describe the features of text information. The number of words in each speech balloon and the maximum, minimum, and average of the word frequency are used as features.

3.4   Estimation Based on Training of Estimator

In this section, we describe the training of estimator and the estimation using it. First, the estimator is trained by inputting the extracted features and binary labels indicating whether the speech balloons contain unknown words. Then, for each speech balloon, the estimator performs estimation as a binary classification problem to determine whether the speech balloon contains an unknown word.

Support vector machine (SVM) is used as the estimator. The kernel is a linear kernel. The loss function is a hinge loss. The regularization parameter C is set to 1.0. Each feature is standardized before input to the estimator. We employ sequential backward floating selection (SBFS) [8] for the feature selection so as to increase the AUPR, the AUC of the Precision-Recall curve (PR curve). SBFS introduces the operation of restoring once-deleted features into the general backward selection. By introducing this operation, SBFS can validate more feature combinations than general backward selection. Only the selected features are used for both training and estimation of the estimator.

Using the trained estimator described above, we estimate whether an unknown word is included in a speech balloon under the following three conditions: training based on speech and text information, training based on eye gaze information and text information, and training based on all features (speech, eye gaze information, and text information).

4   Data Measurement

This section describes the manner of data measurement and the detail of obtained data. The evaluation of the proposed method by using the obtained data will be described in the next section.

4.1   Outline of Data Measurement

Participants were asked to read aloud Japanese comics translated into English on a PC. The comics are displayed as a two-page spread (hereinafter called "one-page spread"). During the reading aloud, the speech and eye gaze information were recorded with a headset and an eye tracker. In the data measurement, a Jabra Evolve 30 II UC Stereo and a Tobii pro 4C were used as the headset and the eye tracker, respectively. The participants were asked to record speech balloons containing unknown words after reading aloud each episode. Then the correct labels for whether each speech balloon contained unknown words were obtained. The number of participants in the data measurement was 20, where all of them were Japanese university students. Each participant was measured twice for 60 min each time. The total time of the data measurement, including guidance and post-measurement questionnaires, was 3 h, and each participant was paid 3,000 JPY in total.

4.2   Flow of Data Measurement

Selection of a Japanese Comics Translated into English to Read Aloud. First, we asked the participants to select a Japanese comics translated into English that is read aloud during the data measurement. In order to ensure that a certain number of unknown words were included in them, the following three works were used, which contain a relatively large number of words that appear infrequently.

– Barrage (Kohei Horikoshi)
– School Judgment: Gakkyu Hotei (Nobuaki Enoki, Takeshi Obata)
– Kaguya-sama: Love Is War (Aka Akasaka)

The participants were asked to choose one of the above three works of which they had never seen the Japanese edition, the animation or the live-action movie. It is because of reducing the possibility of easily guessing the meaning of unknown words due to their knowledge of them.

Reading Aloud Practice. Next, we asked the participants to practice reading aloud in order to familiarize themselves with the sentence notations in Japanese comics translated into English. It is because most Japanese are not familiar with the writing style of the comics in which all letters are capitalized. Concretely, we asked the participants to read aloud the comics for about 15 min before measuring the data, so that the capitalization of English would not adversely affect their estimation of unknown words. During this practice, the participants were asked to read aloud the comics that was not selected for data measurement.

Concrete Manner of Data Measurement. Next, we asked the participants to read aloud the selected work. Before starting to read aloud, the participants were asked to adjust the position of a monitor and their posture so that they could read the texts in the comics without moving too close to the monitor. The distance between a participant and a monitor was around 60 cm. Then the headset and eye tracker were set up. After reading aloud each episode, the participants were asked to label speech balloons containing unknown words. Data were measured twice for 60 min.

The following four conditions were imposed on the participants. First, they were asked not to move their upper body as much as possible. Second, they were asked to read the selected work aloud with understanding the meaning. Third, they were asked to read aloud each speech balloon once. Fourth, they were asked to take a breath after reading aloud each speech balloon and not to read aloud multiple balloons consecutively. These conditions make the division of the speech described in Sect. 3.2 more accurate.

4.3 Detail of Obtained Data

Table 2 shows the number of speech balloons with the recorded speech and eye gaze information. In Table 2, "Positive" indicates the number of speech balloons with unknown words, while "Negative" indicates the number of speech balloons without unknown words. "Total" indicates the total number of recorded speech balloons, that is, the sum of "Positive" and "Negative". "Percentage of Positive" indicates the percentage of "Positive" in "Total". As shown in Table 2, we could obtain various data with individual differences. On average, the speech and eye gaze information corresponding to 334.8 speech balloons were obtained per participant, of which approximately 19.9% contains unknown words.

5 Evaluation

5.1 Evaluation Manner

We evaluated the proposed method based on user-dependent cross-validation. Three cross-validation manners were used: leave-one-episode-out cross-validation for each episode, leave-one-page-out cross-validation for each one-page spread, and leave-one-balloon-out cross-validation for each speech balloon. Since the data

Table 2. Number of data obtained in the experiment

Participant No.	Number of balloons			Percentage of Positive
	Positive	Negative	Total	
P01	43	235	278	15.5%
P02	44	277	321	13.7%
P03	40	261	301	13.3%
P04	10	80	90	11.1%
P05	88	291	379	23.2%
P06	57	298	355	16.1%
P07	47	249	296	15.9%
P08	33	197	230	14.3%
P09	62	130	192	32.3%
P10	62	181	243	25.5%
P11	22	599	621	3.5%
P12	50	259	309	16.2%
P13	56	244	300	18.7%
P14	51	270	321	15.9%
P15	95	217	312	30.4%
P16	145	179	324	44.8%
P17	84	232	316	26.6%
P18	138	172	310	44.5%
P19	36	525	561	6.4%
P20	67	569	636	10.5%
Average	61.5	273.3	334.8	19.9%

were highly biased on labels, we oversampled the training data using SMOTE [2]. The AUPR was used as the evaluation metric. Feature selection (SBFS) was applied only once for each participant based on all data of the participant before cross-validation. It is because SBFS is time-consuming, for example, SBFS costs around three weeks if we would apply it for each training in leave-one-balloon-out cross-validation. The baseline was the estimation using only the features related to the text information shown in Table 1. In this paper, we will henceforth refer to the estimation using speech and text information as "speech + text", the estimation using eye gaze information and text information as "eye gaze + text", and estimation using speech, eye gaze information, and text information as "speech + eye gaze + text".

5.2   Results

Result of Leave-One-Episode-Out Cross-Validation. Figure 1 shows the AUPRs of the three different estimations on the proposed method and baseline in leave-one-episode-out cross-validation. As shown in Fig. 1, the estimation method with the highest AUPR was "speech + eye gaze + text" for 11 participants, "eye gaze + text" for 6 participants, "speech + text" for 4 participants, and baseline for 1 participant.

The AUPRs of "speech + eye gaze + text", "speech + text" and "eye gaze + text" were larger than those of baseline for 16, 13 and 16 participants, respectively. The differences between the AUPRs of "speech + eye gaze + text" and baseline for the above 16 participants were in the range [0.02, 0.24]. On the other hand, the differences between the AUPRs of baseline and "speech + eye gaze + text" for 4 participants whose AUPRs of "speech + eye gaze + text" were lower than those of baseline were in the range [0.006, 0.04].

The AUPRs of "speech + eye gaze + text" were in the range [0.10, 0.75]. The relatively lower AUPRs of "speech + eye gaze + text" were 0.10 and 0.16 for P11 and P19, respectively. There were large gaps between the AUPRs of P11 and P19 from those of other participants.

Figure 2 shows the PR curves of "speech + eye gaze + text" for each participant in the leave-one-episode-out cross-validation. When Recall was 0.8, Precision was 0.61 for P16 who had the highest AUPR in all the participants, while Precision was 0.04 for P11 who had the lowest AUPR in all the participants.

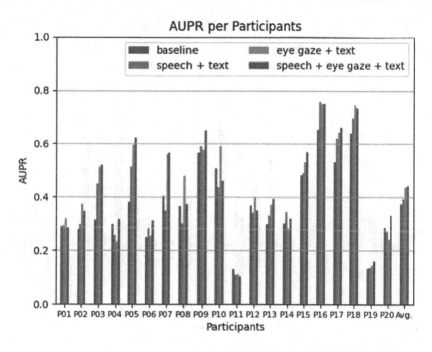

Fig. 1. Result of leave-one-episode-out cross-validation

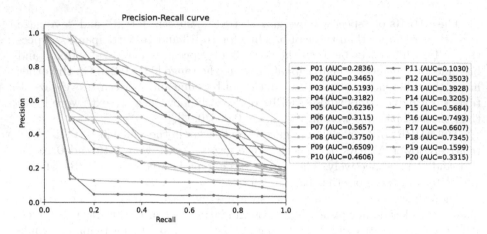

Fig. 2. Precision Recall curve for "speech + eye gaze + text" estimation in leave-one-episode-out cross-validation

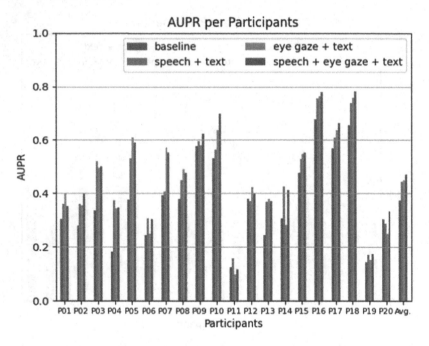

Fig. 3. Result of leave-one-page-out cross-validation

Result of Leave-One-Page-Out Cross-Validation. Figure 3 shows the AUPRs of the three different estimations on the proposed method and baseline in leave-one-page-out cross-validation. As shown in Fig. 3, the estimation method with the highest AUPR was "speech + gaze + text" for 9 participants,

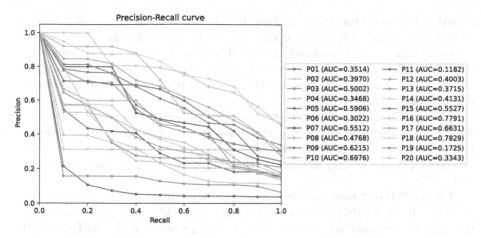

Fig. 4. Precision Recall curve for "speech + eye gaze + text" estimation in leave-one-page-out cross-validation

"gaze + text" for 6 participants, "speech + text" for 5 participants, and baseline for 0 participants.

The AUPRs of "speech + eye gaze + text", "speech + text" and "eye gaze + text" were larger than those of baseline for 19, 18 and 17 participants, respectively. The differences between the AUPRs of "speech + eye gaze + text" and baseline for the above 19 participants were in the range [0.02, 0.21]. On the other hand, the difference between the AUPRs of baseline and "speech + eye gaze + text" for P11 whose AUPR of "speech + eye gaze + text" was lower than that of baseline was 0.006.

The AUPRs of "speech + eye gaze + text" were in the range [0.12, 0.78]. The relatively lower AUPRs of "speech + eye gaze + text" were 0.12 and 0.17 for P11 and P19, respectively. There were large gaps between the AUPRs of P11 and P19 from those of other participants.

Figure 4 shows the PR curves of "speech + eye gaze + text" for each participant in the leave-one-page-out cross-validation. When Recall was 0.8, Precision was 0.68 for P18 who had the highest AUPR in all the participants, while Precision was 0.04 for P11 who had the lowest AUPR in all the participants.

Result of Leave-One-Balloon-Out Cross-Validation. Figure 5 shows the AUPRs of the three different estimations on the proposed method and baseline in leave-one-balloon-out cross-validation. As shown in Fig. 5, the estimation method with the highest AUPR was "speech + gaze + text" for 13 participants, "gaze + text" for 4 participants, "speech + text" for 3 participants, and baseline for 0 participant.

The AUPRs of "speech + eye gaze + text", "speech + text" and "eye gaze + text" were larger than those of baseline for 20, 18 and 16 participants, respectively. The differences between the AUPRs of "speech + eye gaze + text" and baseline for the above 20 participants (that is, all participants) were in the range [0.01, 0.20].

The AUPRs of "speech + eye gaze + text" were in the range [0.13, 0.80]. The relatively lower AUPRs of "speech + eye gaze + text" were 0.13 and 0.18 for P11 and P19, respectively. There were large gaps between the AUPRs of P11 and P19 from those of other participants.

Figure 6 shows the PR curves of "speech + eye gaze + text" for each participant in the leave-one-balloon-out cross-validation. When Recall was 0.8, Precision was 0.66 for P16 who had the highest AUPR in all the participants, while Precision was 0.05 for P11 who had the lowest AUPR in all the participants.

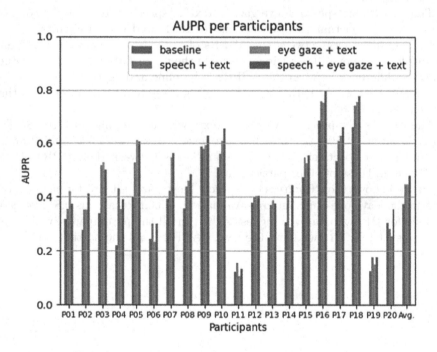

Fig. 5. Result of leave-one-balloon-out cross-validation

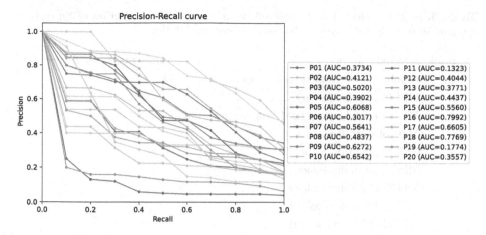

Fig. 6. Precision Recall curve for "speech + eye gaze + text" estimation in leave-one-balloon-out cross-validation

6   Discussion

6.1   Effectiveness of Speech and Eye Gaze Information

The AUPRs of "speech + eye gaze + text" in the leave-one-episode-out, leave-one-page-out, and leave-one-balloon-out cross-validation were larger than those of baseline for 16, 19 and 20 of the 20 participants, respectively. This indicates that speech and eye gaze information are effective for estimating unknown words. The AUPRs of "speech + gaze + text" for P11 and P19 were lower than those of the other participants in all cross-validations. P11 and P19 were able to obtain the data corresponding to more than 500 speech balloons. Moreover, the percentages of Positive were less than 10 percents as shown in Table 1. This suggests that the speech and eye gaze information are not effective in estimating unknown words for participants with high reading speeds and few unknown words.

6.2   Optimal Estimation Method

Among the three estimation methods, "speech + eye gaze + text" had the highest number of participants whose AUPR were larger than those of the baseline in all the cross-validations. Moreover, "speech + eye gaze + text" had the highest number of the highest AUPRs among the three estimation methods and baseline in all the cross-validations. This indicates that "speech + eye gaze + text" is generally the best estimation method among the three estimation methods in the proposed method. Only for P01, "eye gaze + text" was the estimation method with the highest AUPR in all the cross-validations. P01 had a tendency to change the pitch of the voice depending on the gender of the characters in the comics and to read aloud with emotion. This suggests that speech is not effective for estimating unknown words for the participants who change their

Table 3. Features selected by feature selection in the feature selection of "speech + eye gaze + text" in the leave-one-balloon-out cross-validation.

Rank	Selected feature	Number of selected times
1	Number of words in speech balloon	14
2	MFCC (1st dimension)	12
3	Min. of confidence of IBM Watson per word	11
	Max. of word frequency	
4	MFCC (2nd dimension)	10
	MFCC (10th dimension)	
	MFCC (13th dimension)	
	MFCC (14th dimension)	
	MFCC (18th dimension)	
	Number of fixations	
	Avg. of the speed of saccade	
	Gazeing time per speech balloon	

pitch intentionally or read aloud with emotion, and that "eye gaze + text" is the best estimation method for them. On the other hand, "speech + text" was not the estimation method with the highest AUPR in all the cross-validation for any participants. Therefore, the results of this experiment did not reveal any tendency for participants for whom eye gaze information was not effective for estimating unknown words.

6.3   Features Selected for Estimation

In this section, we consider the features selected in the "speech + eye gaze + text" estimation. Table 3 lists the top four most frequently selected features in the feature selection of "speech + eye gaze + text" in the leave-one-balloon-out cross-validation, where the maximum of the number of selected times is 20, that is, the total number of participants. All of these features in Table 3 were selected in feature selection for more than half of the participants. Among the speech features, MFCC and the minimum of the confidence per word were selected most frequently. Among the eye gaze features, the number of fixations, the average of saccade speed, and the gazing time per speech balloon were the most frequently selected. Among the text information features, the number of words in speech balloon and the maximum of word frequency were selected most frequently. On the other hand, few of the features using both speech and eye gaze information were selected. In the "speech + eye gaze + text" estimation, features were selected from all categories of speech, eye gaze, and text information.

7   Conclusion

In this paper, we proposed a method for estimating speech balloons with unknown words based on speech, eye gaze, and text information during reading aloud of Japanese comics translated into English. We conducted data measurement with 20 participants and evaluated the proposed method using the obtained data. The results demonstrated that speech and eye gaze information is effective for estimating unknown words compared with the method using only text information. Furthermore, it was found that the estimation method using all features (i.e., speech, eye gaze, and text information) won the best performance for many participants in the experiment. Future work is to develop a method that can identify which of the three estimation methods is the most suitable for a learner. Another future work is to develop a method for estimating unknown words in word unit. As described in Sect. 3, if the existence of unknown words per speech balloon is estimated, unknown words can be narrowed down based on the word frequency or the learner's profile.

Acknowledgements. This work was supported in part by grants from JST Trilateral AI Research (Grant No. JPMJCR20G3), JSPS Grant-in-Aid for Scientific Research (B) (Grant No. 20H04213), and JSPS Fund for the Promotion of Joint International Research (Fostering Joint International Research (B)) (Grant No. 20KK0235).

References

1. Buscher, G., Dengel, A., van Elst, L.: Eye movements as implicit relevance feedback. In: CHI 2008 Extended Abstracts on Human Factors in Computing Systems, pp. 2991–2996 (2008)
2. Chawla, N.V., Bowyer, K.W., Hall, L.O., Kegelmeyer, W.P.: SMOTE: synthetic minority over-sampling technique. J. Artif. Intell. Res. **16**, 321–357 (2002)
3. Daiku, Y.: Estimation of understanding and interest based on reading behavior in extensive reading with Japanese comics translated in English. In: Master Thesis of Osaka Prefecture University (2019)
4. Doukhan, D., Carrive, J., Vallet, F., Larcher, A., Meignier, S.: An open-source speaker gender detection framework for monitoring gender equality. In: 2018 IEEE International Conference on Acoustics, Speech and Signal Processing (ICASSP), pp. 5214–5218 (2018). https://doi.org/10.1109/ICASSP.2018.8461471
5. Garain, U., Pandit, O., Augereau, O., Okoso, A., Kise, K.: Identification of reader specific difficult words by analyzing eye gaze and document content. In: 2017 14th IAPR International Conference on Document Analysis and Recognition (ICDAR), vol. 1, pp. 1346–1351. IEEE (2017)
6. Ishimaru, S., Bukhari, S.S., Heisel, C., Kuhn, J., Dengel, A.: Towards an intelligent textbook: eye gaze based attention extraction on materials for learning and instruction in physics. In: Proceedings of the 2016 ACM International Joint Conference on Pervasive and Ubiquitous Computing: Adjunct, pp. 1041–1045 (2016)
7. Martínez-Gómez, P., Aizawa, A.: Recognition of understanding level and language skill using measurements of reading behavior. In: Proceedings of the 19th International Conference on Intelligent User Interfaces, pp. 95–104 (2014)

8. Pudil, P., Novovičová, J., Kittler, J.: Floating search methods in feature selection. Pattern Recogn. Lett. **15**(11), 1119–1125 (1994)
9. Sabu, K., Rao, P.: Automatic prediction of confidence level from children's oral reading recordings. In: Interspeech, pp. 3141–3145 (2020)
10. Takahashi, R.: Estimation of understanding based on eye information in extensive reading with Japanese comics translated in English. In: Graduation Thesis of Osaka Prefecture University (2021)
11. TheEnglishClub: Reading aloud in English—scientific method and tips and recommended materials for the best results (2019). https://english-club.jp/blog/english-reading-aloud/. Accessed 5 June 2022
12. Zhang, T., Hasegawa-Johnson, M., Levinson, S.E.: Children's emotion recognition in an intelligent tutoring scenario. In: Proceedings of Eighth European Conference on Speech Communication and Technology (INTERSPEECH) (2004)

Analyzing Textual Sources Attributes of Comics Based on Word Frequency and Meaning

Ryota Higuchi[✉], Ryosuke Yamanishi, and Mitsunori Matsushita

Kansai University, 2-1-1 Ryozenijicho, Takatsukishi, Osaka 569-1095, Japan
{k896930,ryama,m_mat}@kansai-u.ac.jp
https://mtstlab.org/

Abstract. The purpose of this research is to analyze the textual source attributes of explanations and reviews about comics. Comics are difficult to process in terms of the intended story because they are primarily composed of pictures and text. One of the processing methods is to analyze comics text on the Web, particularly the description of characters and reviews including the reader's impression about the comic. Sources of textual information, such as explanations or reviews, are selected according to the application of the study. However, differences among textual sources regarding comics are not taken into consideration in the analysis. This paper classifies words appearing frequently in the text semantically, with results showing that explanations include words that express the story, for example, the family structure, physical information, and sex of the characters for describing the characters. Conversely, the review frequently uses words that provide meta-information about comics, such as illustrations and style. The proposed method revealed that explanations of comics are more useful as textual sources for analyzing story information than reviews.

Keywords: Differences in Data Sources · Review Sentences of Comics · Explanation Texts of Characters · Characteristics of Comic Story

1 Introduction

1.1 Current Situation of Comics

The total number of comic books in circulation today is enormous, with more than 10,000 new comic books being published each year in Japan. A user who wants to find a new comic from a large number of comics that appeals to their interests retrieves it using web services such as e-comics and book sales websites. Typical comic retrieve methods use meta-information such as bibliographic information (e.g., title, author, journal) and genre (e.g., romantic comedy, action/adventure, human suspense) as queries. In MechaComic[1], one of

---

[1] https://sp.comics.mecha.cc, (confirmed September 2nd, 2022).

© Springer Nature Switzerland AG 2023
J.-J. Rousseau and B. Kapralos (Eds.): ICPR 2022 Workshops, LNCS 13644, pp. 107–118, 2023.
https://doi.org/10.1007/978-3-031-37742-6_8

the most popular e-comic stores in Japan, users search by tag information such as new arrivals and popular keywords ranking, genres (e.g., boys' manga, girls' manga), categories (e.g., fantasy, mystery, spin-offs). However, meta-information has no deep connection to the story. The amount of information in the meta-information is not sufficient for retrieving comics based on user preferences. As comics are cross-modal contents that contain both image information (e.g., characters and cartoons) and text information (e.g., dialogues and onomatopoeia), to recommend the comic that matches the user's interests, it is necessary to understand the story of the comic using its image and text information.

There are two approaches to understanding the story of comics. The first is a direct analysis of the images of the comic, where the story information is extracted from images of comic books by combining several procedures such as estimating comic panels [10], extracting characters [18], and constructing a dataset by adding metadata [8]. Some studies shows high extraction and estimation accuracy for individual elements; however, it is challenging to obtain story information automatically by combining these elemental technologies. For example, Manga109 [1,7] is an annotated dataset of comics that is open to the public. However, the only way to obtain story information about new comics is to use the aforementioned direct approach. The second approach is to obtain story information indirectly. This approach is realized by extracting content information from other resources and interpreting them. Studies analyzing reviews [15,17] and texts describing details of works or characters from websites [12] such as Wikipedia and Pixiv encyclopedia (pixiv 百科事典) are related to this approach. Other texts of comics on the Web exist in Q&A sentences about the comic [9], as well as in the outline of the comic in MechaComic. The advantage of the indirect approach is that considerable data exist on the We and is easy to collect.

1.2   Problem Statement

When studying content, there are multiple sources of information on the same topic. For example, in cooking informatics [4], recipes and reviews are textual sources about cooking content, while in the tourism field [2], texts about the same accommodations, such as reviews and explanations, are sources of textual information. However, few studies have considered how should choose datasets by quantitative analysis of textual source attributes.

Some types of information sources can be used to analyze comic content, such as the comics' review texts, explanations, and outline sentences. While these texts from different information sources represent the same content, the textual details vary from each source. For example, the review texts consist of descriptions intended to provide feedback and evaluation of the work, as well as the explanations and outline sentences consist of descriptions intended to provide an overview of the work. Reviews for available products provide content details to enable other people to evaluate the content before their purchases. At the same time, reviews for comics must exclude spoilers [6] to keep the entertainment values of the comics; too much detailed information about the story may be harmful to reviews of comics. Thus, it is reasonable to say that the reviews

Table 1. Explanation Sources and the number of data

Source of explanation	the number of data
Wikipedia	1,950
Niconico Pedia (ニコニコ大百科)	1,281
pixiv encyclopedia (pixiv 百科事典)	1,879
Aniotawiki (アニヲタwiki)	1,140
Sum	6,250

for comics would have less information of content itself than reviews for other products. We consider that this peculiarity is caused by the fact that comics is story-oriented content. Not only the reviews about comics, but also the explanations differ in some respects from those of general products. In the explanations of a general product, the features of the product are described in detail. Since the product is already complete, these features do not change. The explanations of comics, on the other hand, describes variable contents corresponding to the progress of the story such as the features of new characters, significant episodes and relationships between characters. As the above suggests, significant difference exist between reviews and explanations for comics rather than other products. It is, therefore, necessary to conduct a study using suitable information sources depending on the specific application that is the aim of each study. However, differences in textual sources in comics have received little attention. There are few quantitative criteria for selecting the appropriate source according to the purpose of use. To determine the criteria, this study explores what vocabulary is common (or different) between the two sources. This attempt provides two advantages. The first is that one can select appropriate information resources according to the different attributes. The second is that one has access to a large amount of data by appropriately combining different types of sources.

In this study, the attributes of each textual source about comics are analyzed by clustering frequently appearing words in the text semantically, using two analysis object sources from comics. One is explanations that convey the detail of comic content and the other is reviews that express readers' impression about the comic.

2   Analysis Method

This study analyzed attributes of different information resources from the same content. Frequently appearing words in the texts on the Web were clustered semantically using the following procedure to get the attributes:

1. Texts about comics gathered from selected websites are preprocessed.
2. Using word embedding, the vector of appearing words is acquired and a dictionary to use for classification is constructed.

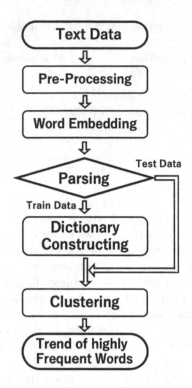

Fig. 1. Flowchart of Analysis Method

3. Words appearing frequently are clustered semantically with the dictionary obtained in Step 2.

Figure 1 shows a flowchart of the analysis method.

2.1 Dataset Construction

This study gathered explanations and reviews (6,250 each) from the Web as comic textual data. The differences in nature of description between the two types of sources are then analyzed.

First, character's explanations were collected from four types of websites, namely: Wikipedia[2], Niconico Pedia[3], pixiv encyclopedia[4], and Aniotawiki[5]. These websites consist of information written by several people, rather than a single author and the sentences on these websites includes a lot of story information about comics. Table 1 shows the number of sentences collected from each

---

[2] https://ja.wikipedia.org/wiki/ (confirmed September 2nd, 2022).
[3] https://dic.nicovideo.jp (confirmed September 2nd, 2022).
[4] https://dic.pixiv.net (confirmed September 2nd, 2022).
[5] https://w.atwiki.jp/aniwotawiki/ (confirmed September 2nd, 2022).

website. The collected explanations are about 2,067 comic characters. Most e-book and manga stores show the outline of the story for each work of comics, and it can be used as another textual resources of the story. The outline expresses the story briefly, using sentences, which is better than other sources in that they summarize all the symbolic information of the comic work but is inferior in that it is difficult to collect and may contain poor expressions. To express the comic story objectively, this study focused on explanations rather than synopsis as a more appropriate means of expression. The character explanation describes the character's actions and feelings, focusing on episodes in which the character stood out. Then, many sentences are used to explain the story in detail. This study also focused on character explanation as an appropriate means for acquiring comic story information.

Second, reviews were collected from the manga category of Sakuhin Database[6]. Among them, the top 200 most recently viewed works were included. The purpose of this site is different from shopping sites such as Amazon.com because, whilst the purpose of shopping sites is to make the customer purchase comics, the purpose of review sites like Sakuhin Database is to evaluate and collect information. Reviews from shopping sites [5] can also be used to obtain story information about comics; however, there is the risk of mixing information that has almost no connection with the story with relevant information. Therefore, this study gathered text information only from review sites. To avoid bias in the number of reviews for each work, the maximum number of reviews per work was defined as 45.

2.2   Word Segmentation and Data Cleaning

This study created a dictionary to semantically classify words in the texts. The explanations and reviews had a large variety of information such as contents of work and readers' feedback. It was thus necessary to extract this information comprehensively to research the attribute of each information source. This study focused on nouns, which can express a broad range of meanings, such as persons, things, and places. The characters' explanation contains words that describe the character's feature and content such as "Energy (元気)" and "Victory (勝利)." Reviews have words used to describe impression such "royal road (王道)" and "sentiment (感動)." Nouns in the texts were analyzed to study the attribute of each information source. Proper nouns, such as the name and technique of the appearing character, provide information that cannot be used to understand the story of comics. Therefore, these words were eliminated from the analysis texts in advance. This study used MeCab (Version0.996) as the morphological analyzer and Neologd (Version0.0.7) as the Japanese dictionary. There are also considerable proper nouns dealing with comic content. Collected texts include some words that do not describe comic content directly such as "that" and "when" in Japanese and this study defined stopwords to eliminate these words as noise. The stopword list was constructed with Slothlib [11] that holds 310 common Japanese

---

[6] https://sakuhindb.com/ (confirmed September 2nd, 2022).

Table 2. Example of characteristic words clustered together in the same class

Class A	Class B	Class C
hard battle (激戦)	black (黒)	idol (アイドル)
comrades in arms (戦友)	white (白)	shortcoming (コンプレックス)
first game (初戦)	brown (褐色)	class (クラス)
hard fight (苦戦)	complexion (顔色)	gym (ジム)
mind-game (頭脳戦)	youth (青春)	position (ポジション)
strategy (作戦)	clear (明白)	earrings (ピアス)
warring States (戦国)	white coat (白衣)	badminton (バドミントン)
battle (対戦)	love (色恋)	jungle (ジャングル)
war (戦乱)	red blood cell (赤血球)	diving (ダイビング)
war situation (戦況)	dark (暗黒)	apple (リンゴ)

words. A Japanese single word (hiragana, katakana), numbers, and symbols were also added to the list because there meanings are difficult to determine. The text data were then cleaned using the list constructed.

Low frequency words may become noise when performing semantic classification of word (described later in Sect. 2.3) used in each source. Therefore, this study removed low frequency words that appeared less than 10 times, a threshold limit that was determined empirically. The aforementioned process was then applied to both sources, explanations and reviews. The total number of unique words was 7,136 and 3,092 for explanations and reviews, respectively. Both the textual sources, each of which had 6,250 data points, were split in a ratio of 8:2 for the next classification. The number of training data and test data points was 10,000 and 2,500, respectively.

2.3   Classification of Frequently Appearing Words

This study classified the preprocessed words semantically and used Japanese Wikipedia entity vector (i.e., Wiki vector), which was proposed by Suzuki [14]. The Wiki vector was constructed using the full text of Japanese Wikipedia as

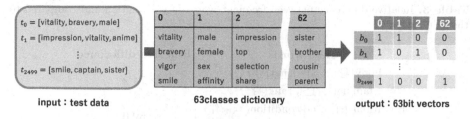

Fig. 2. Classification of Highly Frequent Words by Using the Class Dictionary

training data. The features of this vector are robust to common words and vocabulary ambiguity. The number of dimensions of the vector was set to 200, with a window size of five words. The prepared dataset was then vectorized with Wiki vector.

This study classified the word vector obtained from the aforementioned process using k-means clustering and conducted an exploratory search of the ideal number of classes from 2–100 using the elbow method. The elbow method is one of the most popular methods to determine the ideal number of classes. The results showed that 63 classes were appropriate. There were examples of characteristic word class in some of these classes (shown in Table 2). Some words that mean "battle (戦)" and "color (色)" were classified into class A and class B in the table, whilst some words in Class C were not similar in meaning or shared the common feature of being foreign words. The average number of words and the standard deviation per class was 118.8 points and 107.1 points respectively, while the maximum and minimum word counts per class was 495 and 8 points, respectively. This number shows that words belonging to each class was uneven. The resulting class sets of word was a class dictionary to use for content analysis of comics. Figure 2 shows the process of classifying frequent words using the class dictionary. The attribute of some textual sources was obtained by calculating the appearance frequency of a word in the 2,500 test data points and construing a word's meaning in the class dictionary. For example, there is "apple (リンゴ)" in class C in Table 2. When "apple" is in one test data point, it indicates that this data contains an element of class C. Then, this study can put "1" in class C in place of this data. The output data was a binary string that contains a 63 bit vectors for each of the 2,500 test data points.

3   Results and Discussion

There are two steps to consider the result. First, this study investigated the class that corresponded to the highly frequent words in each information source. Second, the appearance ratio of each class was calculated to compare some differences of attribute between the two types of sources. The relative difference for each class was defined as an absolute value of the difference ratio in each source.

Table 3. Relative difference between frequent words in explanation and compared to those in review

Class words	Relative difference
body(身), body length(身長), familiar(身近), rank(身分)	74.2
condition(条件), no condition(無条件), belief(信条), vote(票)	69.0
parent(親), brother(兄), sister(姉), cousin(従兄弟)	63.7

Table 4. Relative difference between frequent words in reviews and compared to those in explanation

Class words	Relative difference
comic(漫画), movie(映画), illustration(イラスト), style(画風)	35.5
work(作品), cartoonist(作家), drawing(作画), masterpiece(傑作)	19.8
season(節), volume(巻), generation(世代), sequel(続編)	3.1

3.1 Attribute of Explanation

There are many words that describe a character's feature and the content of works in the explanation source. Table 3 shows some classes of explanation that have a higher appearance ratio than that in review. The class of max relative difference (74%) includes many words that used "身", such as "body length (身長)" and "familiar (身近)." For example, the description in Wikipedia for "Tanjiro Kamado," who is a character from "Demon slayer (鬼滅の刃)" includes the information that "His body length is 165cm." In addition, "familiar (身近)" is often used to explain an episode that happened around the character. This word contained in the explanation source is another reason why this class showed a high percentage.

The class of the second largest relative difference includes words such as "condition (条件)" and "belief (信条)." This class has a relatively high ratio in explanations (69%) despite containing the lowest number of words (eight words) of all classes. An example of explanations containing words in this class is from the pixib encyclopedia for "Ken Kaneki" who is a character from "Tokyo Ghoul (東京喰種)." The sentence is as follows: "He proposed conditions wherein he would sacrifice himself in exchange for the freedom of his friends." Data containing this class of words tended to describe information about the story. Sometimes, the review text did not refer to the story directly to avoid spoilers, whilst words that appeared in the part describing the episode tended to appear more often in explanation sources. "Condition (条件)" also appeared frequently when describing a character's abilities. There is a description that "Raining makes the trigger conditions of his ability more severe." in the Aniotawiki describing "Roy Mustang" who is a character from "Fullmetal Alchemist (鋼の錬金術師)."

The class that corresponded to the third largest number of test data contained some words referring to family structure (e.g., parent, brother, grandchild). These words were often used to explain the relation between characters [13]. The text in the pixib encyclopedia for "Sabo" who is a character from "One Piece (ワンピース)" explains "He is Luffy's other brother. He spent his childhood with Ace and Luffy."

3.2   Attribute of Review

Review sources contained sets of words that represent meta-information about comic works such as illustration, style, and cartoonist. Table 4 shows several classes of reviews with a higher appearance ratio than that in explanation.

Review sources contained more interpretive information about how the author of the review text felt after reading the work than information relating to the story. For example, "This cartoonist style will have a great influence on future generations." The result suggest that review source could be used for research on genre analysis [3] and topic classification [16]. Genre and topic information express the category of the work, which is metadata and not data on content. Interestingly, unlike description sources, review sources do not have classes with significantly relative differences. The largest relative difference was only 35.5%. This could be because the review data included very short sentences such as "It was interesting, and I want to read it again."

Review sources have no class with a large percentage of difference relative to explanation sources. Even classes with the largest differences have values of less than approximately 40%. The results of the analysis differed significantly between the two types of information sources. The sum of the applicable classes for each source was calculated to investigate the causes. A total of 35,694 points for explanation and 20,429 points for review were calculated, indicating that explanation data corresponds to approximately 1.75 times more classes than review data. This may be owing to the fact that the adjectives were eliminated from the subject. For example, there are some descriptions using adjectives such as "the thrilling and exciting story is hot." and "the expression was scary." In this research, only common nouns were considered in the analysis. Information such as impressions of the work using adjectives was eliminated. Future work will focus on the analysis of different parts of speech.

Table 5. Class words for which the most data corresponded

hairstyle(ヘアスタイル), check(チェック), plastic model(プラモ), tire(タイヤ), character(キャラ), hip(ヒップ), waist(ウエスト), animation(アニメ), diet(ダイエット), part‑time job(バイト), cake(ケーキ), television(テレビ), motorbike(バイク), up(アップ), mascot(マスコット), rehabilitation(リハビリ), piano(ピアノ), pianist(ピアニスト), type(タイプ), captain(キャプテン), stupid(バカ), Popular(モテモテ), basket(バスケット)

3.3   Overall Discussion and Future Work

The class with the most data in all classes included a significant amount of foreign words as showed in Table 5. Approximately 73% of all data belonged to this class. This result would due to representations peculiar to the Japanese language. The Japanese language is composed of three types of characters: hiragana, katakana, and kanji. Words in this class share the superficiality of being written in katakana. Kanji are ideographic characters imported from China in the earliest times, and hiragana are phonetic characters derived from them. For this reason, things that have existed in Japan since ancient times are often expressed using a combination of kanji and hiragana. In contrast, katakana is often used to express concepts newly introduced overseas, such as "animation," or words derived from foreign languages, such as "check." There are two other classes that included a large amount of foreign words; however, the words in these classes were not semantically clustered. From this result, it is not clear whether combining sources with similar vocabulary is possible. These classifications can be improved by using a different Japanese dictionary in the future.

   Although this research embedded words in the text using Wiki vector, Hotto link Inc.[7] has built a Japanese corpus formed of SNS data such as blogs and Twitter, Japanese Wikipedia, and automatically collected web pages. Character's explanation and reviews of works include new and unknown words such as net slang and broken expressions. This corpus contains many new and unknown words and in the future, it is expected that this corpus will be applied to interpret the meaning of katakana words, such as those listed in Table 5.

4   Conclusion

This paper targeted explanation and review texts among textual information sources dealing with comic contents and analyzed sources attributes based on word frequencies. Results showed that explanation sources frequently contained words that described characters and content of works, suggesting that they are

---

[7] http://www.hottolink.co.jp/english/ (confirmed September 2nd, 2022).

a suitable source for analyzing the comic story. Conversely, review sources frequently contained words that provided meta-information about the works such as illustrations, styles, and cartoonists.

For future research, it is necessary to consider the part of speech to be focused on as the analysis target. In future research, it will be necessary to consider different parts of speech as the analysis target.

Acknowledgement. This work is supported by JSPS KAKENHI Grant Number #22K12338.

References

1. Aizawa, K., et al.: Building a manga dataset "Manga109" with annotations for multimedia applications. IEEE Multimedia **27**(2), 8–18 (2020)
2. Coenders, G., Ferrer-Rosell, B.: Compositional data analysis in tourism: review and future directions. Tour. Anal. **25**(1), 153–168 (2020)
3. Daiku, Y., Iwata, M., Augereau, O., Kise, K.: Comics story representation system based on genre. In: 2018 13th IAPR International Workshop on Document Analysis Systems (DAS), pp. 257–262 (2018)
4. Kikuchi, Y., Kumano, M., Kimura, M.: Analyzing dynamical activities of co-occurrence patterns for cooking ingredients. In: 2017 IEEE International Conference on Data Mining Workshops (ICDMW), pp. 17–24. IEEE (2017)
5. Liu, H., Wan, X.: Neural review summarization leveraging user and product information. In: Proceedings of the 28th ACM International Conference on Information and Knowledge Management, pp. 2389–2392. Association for Computing Machinery (2019)
6. Maki, Y., Shiratori, Y., Sato, K., Nakamura, S.: A method to construct coimc spoiler dataset and the analysis of comic spoilers. IEICE Technical report (2020)
7. Matsui, Y., et al.: Sketch-based manga retrieval using Manga109 dataset. Multimedia Tools Appl. **76**(20), 21811–21838 (2017)
8. Mihara, T., Hagiwara, A., Nagamori, M., Sugimoto, S.: A manga creator support tool based on a manga production process model-improving productivity by metadata. In: iConference 2014 Proceedings. iSchools (2014)
9. Moriyama, Y., Park, B., Iwaoki, S., Matsushita, M.: Designing a question-answering system for comic contents. In: Proceedings of the 1st International Workshop on CoMics ANalysis, Processing and Understanding (2016)
10. Nguyen Nhu, V., Rigaud, C., Burie, J.C.: What do we expect from comic panel extraction? In: 2019 International Conference on Document Analysis and Recognition Workshops (ICDARW), vol. 1, pp. 44–49 (2019)
11. Ohshima, H., Nakamura, S., Tanaka, K.: SlothLib: a programming library for research on web search. Database Soc. Jpn. (DBSJ Lett.) **6**(1), 113–116 (2007)
12. Park, B., Ibayashi, K., Matsushita, M.: Classifying personalities of comic characters based on egograms. In: International Symposium on Affective Science and Engineering, ISASE2018, pp. 1–6. Japan Society of Kansei Engineering (2018)
13. Ruch, W., Gander, F., Wagner, L., Giuliani, F.: The structure of character: on the relationships between character strengths and virtues. J. Posit. Psychol. **16**(1), 116–128 (2021)

14. Suzuki, M., Matsuda, K., Sekine, S., Okazaki, N., Inui, K.: Fine-grained named entity classification with Wikipedia article vectors. In: 2016 IEEE/WIC/ACM International Conference on Web Intelligence (WI), pp. 483–486. IEEE (2016)
15. Ueno, A., Kamoda, Y., Takubo, T.: A spoiler detection method for Japanese-written reviews of stories. Int. J. Innov. Comput. Inf. Control **15**(1), 189–198 (2019)
16. Xu, A., Qi, T., Dong, X.: Analysis of the Douban online review of the MCU: based on LDA topic model. J. Phys. Conf. Ser. **1437**(1), 012102 (2020)
17. Yamashita, R., Okamoto, K., Matsushita, M.: Exploratory search system based on comic content information using a hierarchical topic classification. In: Proceedings of the Asian Conference on Information Systems, pp. 310–317 (2016)
18. Yanagisawa, H., Kyogoku, K., Ravi, J., Watanabe, H.: Automatic classification of manga characters using density-based clustering. In: 2020 International Workshop on Advanced Imaging Technology (IWAIT), vol. 11515, p. 115150F. International Society for Optics and Photonics (2020)

Image Analysis for Forest Environmental Monitoring (FOREST)

Workshop on Image Analysis for Forest Environmental Monitoring (FOREST)

The workshop on Image Analysis for Forest Environmental Monitoring is the first workshop dedicated to researchers and practitioners of image analysis and pattern recognition techniques with impact in the protection of forest environments, which are key resources for sustaining life on earth. The new advances in data acquisition technologies and pattern analysis methods can provide valuable information for decision making in forest resource management policies and first response to incidents like wildfires.

Several projects worldwide are researching cost-effective ways through remote sensing and airborne or land-based sensor analysis to (semi-)automate, with modern machine learning and pattern recognition methods, many of the processes that are required to support the monitoring and decision making in forest management. In Portugal, a large research program funded by the national science foundation (FCT) is dedicated to support projects that address the multiple aspects of wildfire prevention, combat, management, and impact in people. This workshop was promoted and sponsored by FCT through projects Firefront (firefront.pt), Voamais (voamais.pt), and Eye in the Sky (eyeinthesky.tecnico.ulisboa.pt).

We received 14 submissions for review that underwent a rigorous single-blind peer-review process focused on the quality and scientific soundness of the papers. Each paper was reviewed by, at least, two independent expert reviewers. After collecting and analyzing the reviews, the workshop chairs decided to accept 12 of the submitted papers, being all presented in the full day workshop. The accepted papers cover a wide range of topics, including land cover classification, wildfire detection and monitoring, 3D reconstruction, aerial imagery georeferencing, and forest floor classification. The workshop program was completed by an invited talk on "From fire perception to fire extinguishing using aerial robots" by Prof. Luis Merino from Universidad Pablo de Olavide in Sevilla, Spain.

Extended versions of the presented papers are eligible to the special issue "Image Analysis for Forest Environmental Monitoring", also related to the workshop topics, organized in partnership with the MDPI Remote Sensing Journal.

Organization

FOREST Workshop Chairs

Alexandre Bernardino   Instituto Superior Técnico, Portugal
Alexandra Moutinho   Instituto Superior Técnico, Portugal
Bruno Damas   Naval School, Portugal
Catarina Barata   Institute for Systems and Robotics, Lisbon, Portugal
Eduardo Silva   Polytechnic Institute of Porto, Portugal
El Khalil Cherif   Institute for Systems and Robotics, Lisbon, Portugal
Maria João Sousa   Instituto Superior Técnico, Portugal

Technical Program Committee

Houda Harkat   EST Fèz, Morocco
Philippe Guiguere   Laval University, Quebec, Canada
Peter Krzystek   Munich University of Applied Sciences, Germany
Taha Ait Tchakoucht   University of Abdelmalek Essâadi, Morocco
Ricardo Ribeiro   Institute for Systems and Robotics, Lisbon, Portugal
Hakim Boulaassal   University of Abdelmalek Essâadi, Morocco
Hugo Silva   Polytechnic Institute of Porto, Portugal
Gonçalo Cruz   Air Force Academy Research Centre, Portugal
José Nascimento   Instituto de Telecomunicações, Portugal
Luís Félix   Air Force Academy Research Centre, Portugal

Sponsor

FCT – Fundação para a Ciência e Tecnologia (Portugal), through projects Firefront (PCIF/SSI/0096/2017), Voamais (PTDC/EEI-AUT/31172/2017, 02/SAICT/2017/ 31172), and Eye In the Sky (PCIF/SSI/0103/2018).

An Adversarial Method
for Semi-supervised Segmentation
of Smoke and Fire in Images

Lisa Kuhlmann[1], Milad Niknejad[2], Catarina Barata[2],
Alexandre Bernardino[2(✉)], and Gefei Zhang[1]

[1] Hochschule für Technik und Wirtschaft Berlin, Berlin, Germany
lisa_kuhlmann@aol.de, gefei.zhang@htw-berlin.de
[2] Institute for Systems and Robotics (ISR), Técnico Lisboa, Lisbon, Portugal
ana.c.fidalgo.barata@tecnico.ulisboa.pt, alex@isr.tecnico.ulisboa.pt

Abstract. Detecting and segmenting fire and smoke on images and
videos is an essential tool for autonomous systems to battle fire incidents. State-of-the-art methods based on Convolutional Neural Networks
(CNNs) require large numbers of annotated images, which are time-
consuming to obtain and need lots of human efforts. In this paper, we propose a semi-supervised method for fire and smoke segmentation using an
adversarial approach which uses a fully-supervised pretraining stage. A
dataset is also introduced containing pixel labeled and unlabeled images
of fire and smoke that can be used in semi-supervised fire and smoke
segmentation methods. Our proposed method shows improvement over
a fully-supervised segmentation method in different percentages of available labeled images for fire and smoke segmentation.

1 Introduction

Wildfire incidents have been showing an increasing trend over the past decades
worldwide. Artificial intelligence can help firefighting operations by early detection and localization of fire and smoke in images and videos. Semantic segmentation is a classical computer vision task, which assigns to every pixel a label from
a predefined category. Semantic segmentation of smoke and fire from images can
help the firefighting process by segmenting the fire or smoke regions, and indicating the location of fire or smoke spots. Localization information can be used
in different applications such as georeferencing fire location, and estimating the
progression of fire areas by predictive models.

Fire and smoke detection from video and images has been addressed clas-
sically by handcrafted features extracted from images that are classified by
data-drive models [7,15]. Recently, Convolutional Neural Networks (CNNs) have
shown state-of-the-art results for fire and smoke detection and segmentation,

This work was partially funded by the FCT projects LARSyS (UID/50009/2020),
[CEECIND/00326/2017], FIREFRONT (PCIF/SSI/0096/2017) and VOAMAIS
(PTDC/EEI-AUT/31172/2017, 02/SAICT/2017/31172).

J.-J. Rousseau and B. Kapralos (Eds.): ICPR 2022 Workshops, LNCS 13644, pp. 123–132, 2023.
https://doi.org/10.1007/978-3-031-37742-6_9

similar to many other fields in computer vision [16,21,22]. Segmentation methods such as Deeplab have been successfully used in fully-supervised fire segmentation [8]. However, fully-supervised CNN methods require a large number of labeled data in the training stage. This is more problematic in segmentation problems since each individual pixel should be labeled. The amount of pixel-level labeled data in the wildfire scenarios is currently limited, and manual labeling requires a significant amount of human effort. One solution to the problem is to use semi-supervised methods, which leverage on both large number of unlabeled images, and limited available labeled data to improve the performance of CNNs. Adversarial approaches for semi-supervised segmentation inspired by the Generative Adversarial Networks (GAN) [6] have been recently proposed. Similar to GAN, those methods consist of a generator network and a discriminator network. In adversarial semi-supervised learning, the discriminator's task is to distinguish between the ground truth segmentation mask and generated mask by the segmentation network, and the task of segmentation network is to fool the discriminator [11,12]. This process induces the generator network to produce a good segmentation of the input image.

In this paper, we propose a semi-supervised method that uses an adversarial approach to leverage unlabeled training images together with a small amount of labeled images for the task of smoke and fire segmentation. Our method is based on the work in [12], which proposes an adversarial method for semi-supervised segmentation. Our main original contribution is to use fully-supervised pretraining before the start of semi-supervised learning, which we found essential to achieve acceptable performance in our fire/smoke dataset. We also describe our dataset, which was specially curated for semi-supervised learning of fire and smoke image segmentation. The results are compared to fully-supervised models that are only trained with labeled data and show the benefits of using the semi-supervised approach with the proposed fully-supervised pretraining.

2   Related Works

Different methods have been proposed for fire detection and segmentation. Classical methods were mostly based on extracting hand-crafted features, and classifying those features using classifiers such as support vector machine (SVM) [7,15]. The features for fire and smoke detection are mainly calculated based on RGB color values of the pixels as the color is one of the main characteristics for fire and smoke [13,16,21,22].

Semantic segmentation is the task of assigning a label to each pixel in the image. Many segmentation CNNs have a encoder-decoder architecture in which a decoder network maps the image into a coarse feature map and a decoder network upsamples the features to the image dimension [2,17]. However, fully supervised segmentation based on CNNs require pixel-wise annotation, which is time-consuming and requires lots of human efforts. To mitigate this problem, many methods have been proposed to include unlabeled data or easy to obtain labels, such as image labels, in the learning process. In this paper, we

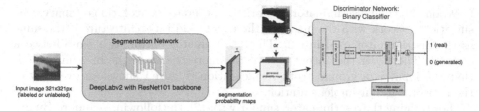

Fig. 1. Overview of the adversarial segmentation components and their inputs and outputs used in this work. The $\oplus$ denotes the concatenation of ground truth or segmentation maps with their corresponding RGB image along the channel axis. The generated segmentation map holds probability values for each pixel belonging to a certain class. The discriminator output is a probability between 0 and 1. The intermediate output* denotes a vector that is obtained before the last fully-connected layer of the discriminator.

focus on the semi-supervised approach in which the training data is a combination of unlabeled and pixel-wise labeled images. More specifically, since there are publicly available pixel-wise labeled datasets for fire [20] and smoke [1], we leverage on unlabeled data to improve the performance of the fully-supervised methods. Some semi-supervised methods for segmentation use a consistency loss between outputs of two networks with the same structure but with different parameters, and different augmented and perturbed inputs [3]. CutMix-Seg [5] uses a moving average of the parameters of the first network in the second network. [14] adds the perturbation to the output of the encoder instead of the input image. Another group of methods use adversarial approaches for semi-supervised learning [11,12,19]. In those methods the generator is usually the segmentation network, which produce the output mask. The job of the discriminator is to distinguish the generated masks from the ground-truth pixel labels. In [12], the discriminator classifies the whole masks as generated or ground truth rather than classifying each pixel. Generally, adversarial approaches encourage the segmentation network to generate pixel labels for unlabeled images which are similar to ground truth masks, thus improving the generality of the segmentation process. The discriminator can also determine the trustworthiness of segmented regions for unlabeled images, which can be used for full supervision in later stages.

3   Proposed Method

In this section, our proposed adversarial method, which is based on the work of Mittal et al. [12], is described. It consists of a segmentation network S and a discriminator network D. The role of the discriminator network is to distinguish the original masks from the ones produced by the segmentation network. The segmentation network is implemented as a DeepLabv2v [2] with a ResNet-101 backbone [9]. The discriminator network is a standard convolutional binary classification network with the masks as the input, and its architecture is the same as the discriminator used in [12]. The discriminator output is a score between 0 and 1. The closer the output is to 1, the more confident the discriminator is that the input is a ground truth segmentation. Figure 1 shows an overview of the networks in our implementation.

For training the discriminator, similarly to [12], the following standard Binary Cross Entropy (BCE) loss is used

$$L_D = \mathbb{E}_{x^\ell, y^\ell} \left[\log D(y^\ell \oplus x^\ell) \right] + \mathbb{E}_x \left[\log(1 - D(S(x) \oplus x)) \right],$$

where x^ℓ, y^ℓ denote a labeled RGB image and corresponding ground truth segmentation mask, respectively, x denotes a RGB image sampled from the labeled or unlabeled training data, $D()$ is the scalar output of the discriminator network, $S()$ is the image produced by the generator, $\oplus$ indicates the channel-wise concatenation, and $\mathbb{E}$ is the expected value operator.

The segmentation network is trained with a combination of three losses. For labeled images, the standard cross entropy loss L_{ce} is applied:

$$L_{ce} = - \mathbb{E}_{x^\ell, y^\ell} \left[y^\ell \odot \log(S(x^\ell)) \right],$$

where the $\odot$ operator denotes the sum of the pixel-wise products between the two segmentation images.

To calculate the loss for unlabeled training samples, two different losses are applied. The first one, L_{st}, adopts a self-training approach, where generated segmentation maps that are able to fool the discriminator are reused as pseudo ground truth masks to calculate the cross-entropy loss L_{ce}. The selected masks are the ones whose discriminator output $D(x)$ are above the specific threshold, which is a hyperparameter in the training process.

The second loss used for unlabeled training samples is the feature-matching loss L_{fm}, originally from [18]. This loss encourages the output masks for labeled and unlabeled data to have the same statistics as in [12], and is defined as

$$L_{fm} = | \mathbb{E}_{x^\ell, y^\ell} \left[D_k(y^\ell \oplus x^\ell) \right] - \mathbb{E}_{x^u} \left[D_k(S(x^u) \oplus x^u) \right] |,$$

where x^u denotes an unlabeled image, and $D_k(.)$ denotes the intermediate output of the discriminator at the last convolution layer (before the fully-connected layer). The intermediate output is calculated for labeled training images concatenated with their corresponding ground truth $y^\ell \oplus x^\ell$) and unlabeled samples with their corresponding generated segmentation map $S(x^u) \oplus x^u$.

The overall training loss for the generator is

$$L_S = L_{ce} + \lambda_{fm} L_{fm} + \lambda_{st} L_{st}. \tag{1}$$

Mittal et al. [12] especially emphasized the role of the self-training and feature matching losses as a important factor for balancing out the abilities of generator and discriminator.

One of the main challenges of adversarial learning approaches is balancing the generator and the discriminator. If the discriminator becomes too strong in detecting fake samples during the training process, it does not provide useful information for the generator, which prevents the generator form evolving. Unlike [12], which is a multi-class segmentation problem, our problem is a binary segmentation, and two separate networks are trained for fire and smoke. Compared to being used for the training of general benchmark datasets such as PASCAL-VOC [4], we found that training with smaller specific datasets of smoke and fire images requires strategies to balance the abilities of the discriminator and generator. In order to stabilize the performance of the CNN, we propose to add a fully-supervised pretraining step in the training stages. It has been previously practiced in [10] to stabilize the performance of semi-supervised methods. During the fully-supervised pretraining, the generator and discriminator are trained only with the labeled part of the training dataset. During this process, the generator uses only cross-entropy loss. The discriminator is trained with the collection of ground truth and segmentation masks of the labelled images.

4   Datasets and Results

In this work, we gathered two independent datasets for the segmentation of smoke and fire. For the fire dataset, we augmented the labeled Corsican dataset [20] with 416 unlabeled wildfire images from the internet. We gathered fire images from different perspectives, including aerial images. Table 1 characterizes the fire dataset by the number of images in each category.

Table 1. Overview of the fire dataset by number of images in each category

	Labeled	Unlabeled
Pixel ratio (fire/background) in %	22/78	–
Ground perspective/slightly elevated	577	295
Aerial perspective	15	121
Total number of images	592	416

For the smoke dataset, we gathered labeled images and augment them with unlabeled smoke images. For the labeled part, we gathered 105 images from the smoke dataset in [1], 18 images from the Corsican fire dataset [20], and 77 images from the internet which we annotated for smoke (total number of 200 images). To alleviate the problem of uncertainty in smoke borders, we consider an "ignore-label" in regions where the smoke concentration is very low or can not be identified as smoke. The image areas annotated with the ignore-label are not considered in the calculation of losses and evaluation metrics (See Fig. 2). In addition to the labeled images there are 148 unlabeled images collected from the internet. Table 2 characterizes the dataset used.

Table 2. Overview of the smoke dataset by number of images in each category.

	Labeled	Unlabeled
Pixel ratio (smoke/ignore-label/background) in %	27/1/72	–
Ground perspective/slightly elevated	50	39
Aerial perspective	125	109
Non-smoke	25	–
Total number of images	200	148

Original image   Ground truth   Original image   Ground truth

Fig. 2. Examples of the annotation of smoke images using white labels for smoke and grey labels for uncertain areas. (Color figure online)

In order to evaluate the performance of the proposed method, we compare three methods. The first method is the fully supervised method, in which Deeplab v3 [2] is used for the segmentation CNN. This is equivalent to using only the segmentation (generator) network in our method. The second and third methods are the proposed semi-supervised learning with and without the fully-supervised pretraining (Figs. 3 and 4, Tables 3 and 4).

The segmentation network was trained using the Stochastic Gradient Descent (SGD) with the learning rate of $2.5e - 4$, and the momentum 0.9 and the weight decay of $5e - 4$. The discriminator network was trained with the Adam optimizer with a the learning rate of $1e - 4$. In all the experiments on fire and smoke dataset, the parameters of the loss function (1), i.e. the feature matching loss weight λ_{fm} and self training loss weight λ_{st}, are set to 0.1 and 1, respectively. The generator and discriminator are trained alternately in which the alternation is done at the end of one training epoch. The experiments were conducted using a NVIDIA GeForce RTX 2080 Ti GPU with 12 GB memory, CUDA version 10.2 and Pytorch 1.5.1. Each model is trained until 8000 training iterations with a batch size of 4. In the proposed method with pretraining, the semi-supervised training starts at the 1000th iteration.

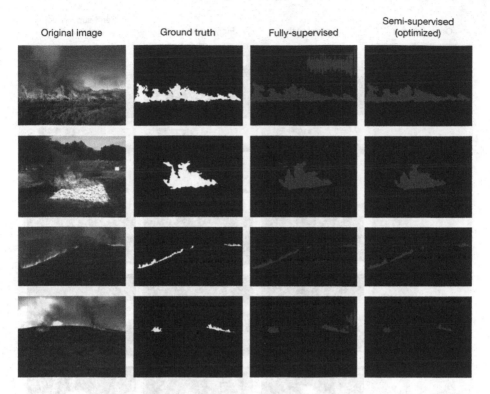

Fig. 3. Examples of segmentation of fully supervised and semi-supervised with pre-training. Semi-supervised method results in less false-positive regions.

Fire: Table 3 shows the mean Intersection over Union (mIoU) results for the fire dataset when different percentages of labeled data is available for training. The percentage is computed by the ratio between the number of labeled images and total number of images in the dataset. To have a training data for each percentage, the labeled examples are chosen randomly from the training set according to the desired percentage. For each setting the results are averaged over three random data splits. In the table, it can be seen that the semi-supervised training without pretraining yields a slightly worse result compared to fully-supervised training with only the labeled data portion of 12.5%. On the other hand, the semi-supervised method with pretraining achieves the best results. This may indicate that, without pretraining, the discriminator is much stronger than the generator and the generator might not be able to catch up with its progress. The mIoU gain of semi-supervised learning is more noticeable in the lower label ratios.

In Fig. 3, some example of segmentation results for the fully-supervised baseline and semi-supervised with pretraining are shown. It can be seen that fully-supervised learning seemingly segment more false-positive areas compared to the proposed method.

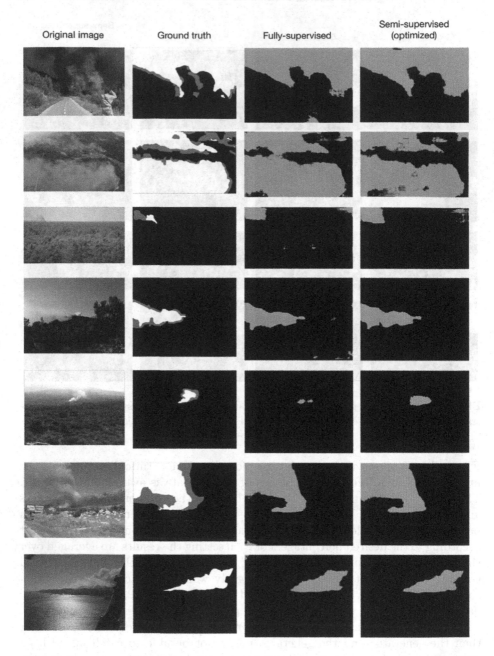

Fig. 4. Some examples of segmentation of smoke areas compared to ground-truth.

Smoke. Our gathered smoke dataset has less samples as well as less annotated samples compared to the fire dataset. The mIoU results for smoke dataset are reported in Table 4. Similar to fire, the overall performance of mIOU is better for the proposed semi-supervised method.

Table 3. Results of the proposed method compared to other methods on the fire dataset in different percentages of labeled ratio.

Method	Available labels %	mIoU
Fully Supervised	12.5%	86.2
	50%	89.3
Semi-supervised (without pretraining)	12.5%	85.9
	50%	89.1
Proposed	12.5%	**88.2**
	50%	**89.7**

Table 4. Results of the proposed method compared to other methods for the smoke dataset

Method	Available labels %	mIoU
Fully Supervised	12.5%	90.06
Semi-supervised (without pretraining)	12.5%	89.06
Proposed	12.5%	**91.8**

Figure 4 shows some segmentation examples for smoke.

5   Conclusion

This paper proposes a method for semi-supervised segmentation of fire and smoke in images using an adversarial method. We also gathered a dataset suitable for evaluation of semi-supervised segmentation methods for fire and smoke. We used a fully-supervised pretraining approach for the segmentation network, which shows noticeable improvement on the proposed method. The proposed method outperforms fully-supervised approaches for fire and smoke segmentation, in different percentages of labeled images.

References

1. Image database. https://wildfire.fesb.hr/index.php?option=com_content&view=article&id=49&Itemid=54
2. Chen, L.C., Papandreou, G., Kokkinos, I., Murphy, K., Yuille, A.L.: Deeplab: semantic image segmentation with deep convolutional nets, atrous convolution, and fully connected crfs. IEEE Trans. Pattern Anal. Mach. Intell. **40**(4), 834–848 (2017)
3. Chen, X., Yuan, Y., Zeng, G., Wang, J.: Semi-supervised semantic segmentation with cross pseudo supervision. In: Proceedings of the IEEE/CVF Conference on Computer Vision and Pattern Recognition, pp. 2613–2622 (2021)
4. Everingham, M., Gool, L.V., Williams, C.K.I., Winn, J., Zisserman, A.: The pascal visual object classes (voc) challenge. Int. J. Comput. Vision **88**(2), 303–338 (2010)

5. French, G., Aila, T., Laine, S., Mackiewicz, M., Finlayson, G.: Semi-supervised semantic segmentation needs strong, high-dimensional perturbations (2019)
6. Goodfellow, I., et al.: Generative adversarial networks. Commun. ACM **63**(11), 139–144 (2020)
7. Habiboğlu, Y.H., Günay, O., Çetin, A.E.: Covariance matrix-based fire and flame detection method in video. Mach. Vision Appl. **23**(6), 1103–1113 (2012)
8. Harkat, H., Nascimento, J.M.P., Bernardino, A.: Fire detection using residual deeplabv3+ model. In: 2021 Telecoms Conference (ConfTELE), pp. 1–6. IEEE (2021)
9. He, K., Zhang, X., Ren, S., Sun, J.: Deep residual learning for image recognition. In: 2016 IEEE Conference on Computer Vision and Pattern Recognition (CVPR), pp. 770–778 (2016). ISSN: 1063–6919
10. Hung, W.C., Tsai, Y.H., Liou, Y.T., Lin, Y.Y., Yang, M.H.: Adversarial learning for semi-supervised semantic segmentation (2018)
11. Wei-Chih Hung, Yi-Hsuan Tsai, Yan-Ting Liou, Yen-Yu Lin, and Ming-Hsuan Yang. Adversarial learning for semi-supervised semantic segmentation. arXiv preprint arXiv:1802.07934, 2018
12. Mittal, S., Tatarchenko, M., Brox, T.: Semi-supervised semantic segmentation with high-and low-level consistency. IEEE Trans. Pattern Anal. Mach. Intell. **43**(4), 1369–1379 (2019)
13. Niknejad, M., Bernardino, A.: Attention on classification for fire segmentation. In: 2021 20th IEEE International Conference on Machine Learning and Applications (ICMLA), pp. 616–621. IEEE (2021)
14. Ouali, Y., Hudelot, C., Tami, M.: Semi-supervised semantic segmentation with cross-consistency training. In: Proceedings of the IEEE/CVF Conference on Computer Vision and Pattern Recognition, pp. 12674–12684 (2020)
15. Qian, J., Fu, J., Qian, J., Yang, W., Wang, K., Cao, P.: Automatic early forest fire detection based on gaussian mixture model. In: 2018 IEEE 18th International Conference on Communication Technology (ICCT), pp. 1192–1196. IEEE (2018)
16. Ren, S., He, K., Girshick, R., Sun, J.: Faster r-cnn: towards real-time object detection with region proposal networks. In: Advances in Neural Information Processing Systems, pp. 91–99 (2015)
17. Ronneberger, O., Fischer, P., Brox, T.: U-Net: convolutional networks for biomedical image segmentation. In: Navab, N., Hornegger, J., Wells, W.M., Frangi, A.F. (eds.) MICCAI 2015. LNCS, vol. 9351, pp. 234–241. Springer, Cham (2015). https://doi.org/10.1007/978-3-319-24574-4_28
18. Salimans, T., Goodfellow, I., Zaremba, W., Cheung, V., Radford, A., Chen, X.: Improved techniques for training gans. Adv. Neural Inf. Process. Syst. **29** (2016)
19. Souly, N., Spampinato, C., Shah, M.: Semi supervised semantic segmentation using generative adversarial network. In: Proceedings of the IEEE International Conference on Computer Vision, pp. 5688–5696 (2017)
20. Toulouse, T., Rossi, L., Campana, A., Celik, T., Akhloufi, M.: Computer vision for wildfire research: an evolving image dataset for processing and analysis. Fire Saf. J. **92**, 188–194 (2017)
21. Zhang, Q., Lin, G., Zhang, Y., Gao, X., Wang, J.: Wildland forest fire smoke detection based on faster r-cnn using synthetic smoke images. Procedia Eng. **211**, 441–446 (2018)
22. Zhang, Q., Xu, J., Liang, X., Guo, H.: Deep convolutional neural networks for forest fire detection. In,: International Forum on Management, p. 2016. Atlantis Press, Education and Information Technology Application (2016)

Data-Driven Transform Based Adaptive Compressive Sensing Framework for 3D Reconstruction of Forests

Rajat C. Shinde$^{(\boxtimes)}$ (ID), Surya S. Durbha(ID), and Pratyush V. Talreja(ID)

Centre of Studies in Resources Engineering, Indian Institute of Technology, Bombay, India
{rajatshinde,sdurbha,pratyushtalreja}@iitb.ac.in

Abstract. Forests comprise a key natural resource of our natural ecosystem and play a significant role in the sustenance of living beings. LiDAR enables accurate x, y, and z measurements of the 3D surrounding. In our work, we propose a novel framework (called MEMD-CS) based on the multivariate Empirical Mode Decomposition (EMD) inspired by a Compressive Sensing (CS) framework. EMD is a data-driven transform in which the transformation basis is learned, unlike Fourier transform or wavelets having "rigid" transformation functions. We propose using the EMD-derived components as a transformation basis for the CS framework, which usually uses predefined probability distributions as priors. Our novel approach is data-agnostic and focuses on the adaptive decomposition of the input signal. We test our approach on multiple samples chosen from different forest LiDAR datasets available in the public domain. To the best of our knowledge, multivariate EMD within a compressive sensing framework is the first attempt for the LiDAR point clouds of forests. We compare our results based on the Canopy Height Model (CHM) derived from the reconstructed LiDAR point clouds.

Keywords: Data-driven transform · Canopy Height Model · Compressive Sensing · LiDAR for forests · Multivariate Empirical Mode Decomposition · Sparse Representation

1 Introduction and Related Work

LiDAR data provides accurate 3D measurements of the topographical information associated within a region; opening new research directions for solving various real-world problems. Classification of ground/non-ground points using the LiDAR-derived digital elevation models (DTMs, DSMs), 3D point cloud classification, volume estimation, and characterization are some examples.

1.1 Empirical Mode Decomposition (EMD) for LiDAR

Data transformation (such as Fourier or wavelet transform [1]) based approaches have been significant for remote sensing applications involving multispectral, hyperspectral

© Springer Nature Switzerland AG 2023
J.-J. Rousseau and B. Kapralos (Eds.): ICPR 2022 Workshops, LNCS 13644, pp. 133–141, 2023.
https://doi.org/10.1007/978-3-031-37742-6_10

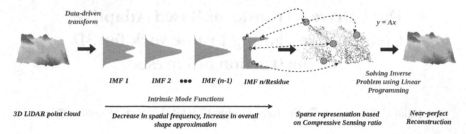

Fig. 1. Illustration of workflow for the proposed data-driven transform-based Compressive Sensing framework.

as well as LiDAR data sources. With the introduction of the data-driven paradigm, data-dependent transforms are highly applicable for unstructured datasets such as LiDAR data, unlike rigid or structured transforms. Empirical Mode Decomposition (EMD) [2, 3], originally proposed for time-series data, is a signal processing technique that is of wide use across research domains for understanding local signal characteristics and analyzing non-stationary and non-linear signals. The EMD models the input into two parts - (1) fluctuating part or the Intrinsic Mode Functions (IMFs), and (2) least (non) fluctuating part or residual function. In [4], IMFs derived from EMD of hyperspectral images are used as a feature for SVM-based classification. The authors in [5] propose a LiDAR data filtering approach for DTM generation based on the EMD applied to the DSMs derived from the LiDAR data. In [6], 3D-EMD has been proposed for hyperspectral band selection. In a more general sense, a multidimensional multivariate EMD has been proposed in the seminal work of [7, 8].

1.2   Why Compressive Sensing of LiDAR Data?

- Compressive Sensing guarantees near-perfect reconstruction from a small set of sparse measurements. Typically, LiDAR point sets show inherent sparsity due to redundancy in storage and high spatial resolution (in cms).
- Conventionally, LiDAR scans require a huge scanning time followed by pre-processing for further applications. Compressed Sensing addresses this issue of high scan time by enabling faster and more efficient acquisition followed by reconstruction.

1.3   EMD-Based Data-Driven Compressive Sensing Framework

CS theory [9, 10] allows reconstruction of signals sampled with a sampling rate greater than the Nyquist sampling criteria, given the input signal is sparse. In our earlier work [11] and [12], we explored the CS framework for reconstructing satellite images and LiDAR data to a promising extent from a few samples.

Compressive Sensing (CS) builds on two conditions required for perfect reconstruction of raw data from the small set of measurements- Sparsity and Restricted Isometry Property (RIP) [13]. All natural signals are believed to be sparse. Due to this, the CS framework is implicitly non-adaptive in its implementation. Our proposed approach addresses this issue by using an empirical transformation function and is a natural choice for modeling non-stationary and non-linear datasets such as LiDAR point clouds. The CS implementation comprises primarily two parts - (1) Sensing Matrix and (2) Measurement Matrix, where the sensing matrix should follow the Restricted Isometry Property (RIP). The generated sparse representation is then used to reconstruct the original input by solving the inverse optimization problem.

1.4 Core Contributions

- A novel Multivariate Empirical Mode Decomposition inspired adaptive Compressive Sensing framework (MEMD-CS) for sparse representation of LiDAR data of forest region.
- Generate CHM from the reconstructed point clouds and compare the evaluation results.

2 Problem Formulation

The primary focus of our work is on addressing the following three objectives associated with LiDAR point clouds of forests region with a remote sensing perspective:

- To analyze the application of a non-stationary non-adaptive and data-driven decomposition technique - Compute intrinsic mode functions (IMFs) im and the residual function r using the multivariate EMD for the point cloud $P \in \Re^{nxd}$.
- To reconstruct the point clouds from the sparse representation in the compressive sensing framework and quantitatively analyze the reconstruction results on the basis of evaluation metrics.
- To investigate the efficacy of our proposed approach based on LiDAR-derived CHM.

3 Materials and Methodology

We describe dataset details and acquired methodology for our research in the coming sections. Figure 1 illustrates the overall workflow of our proposed MEMD-CS approach.

3.1 Dataset Details

We have selected five unique samples geographically and topographically distributed over two 3D LiDAR scenes from the OpenTopography platform [14]. The LiDAR scenes are taken from the Andrews Experimental Forest, Willamette National Forest LiDAR scan acquired in August 2008 [15], and USFS Tahoe National Forest LiDAR scan acquired in 2014 [16].

3.2 Multivariate Empirical Mode Decomposition (MEMD) on the Selected Samples

The MEMD decomposes the input LiDAR sample according to the varying spatial frequency across three spatial dimensions - x, y, and z. The MEMD generates the Intrinsic Mode Functions (IMFs) and a residue function. From Eq. (1), the $im_1(x, y, z)$,

$im_2(x, y, z)...im_N(x, y, z)$ represents the N IMFs, where N also defines the EMD as an N mode decomposition. The residual function $r_N(x, y, z)$ is responsible for minimum variation and it also denotes the part with maximum amplitude.

$$f(x, y, z) = \sum_{k=1}^{N} im_k(x, y, z) + r_N(x, y, z) \tag{1}$$

The idea behind the extraction of IMFs is an iterative process, termed as Sifting. It includes computing the average envelopes of the local minima and maxima points followed by subtracting the average envelope from the original signal in that iteration. Typically, it is observed that the residual function represents the overall geometrical shape and structure of the input 3D LiDAR scene.

3.3 MEMD-CS: Compressive Sensing Framework for Sparse Representation with MEMD

The conventional Compressive Sensing approach solves the problem (P1) mentioned in Eq. (2). This problem is also termed a l_1 minimization problem and is used as a relaxed alternative to the l_0 minimization problem, which is NP-hard to solve. Prior research has shown that by solving the l_1 minimization approach, exact reconstruction can be achieved [17].

$$(\mathbf{P_1})\ min\ ||x||_1\ \mathbf{subject\ to}\ x \in \{x : Ax = y\} \tag{2}$$

where $x \in \Re^N$ is a given signal and y represents the measurements of x, which can be expressed as $y = Ax$, where A is the sensing matrix, $y \in \Re^M$ and $A \in \Re^{MxN}, M = \lfloor rN \rfloor$ with $r \in (0, 1]$ and $\lfloor \cdot \rfloor$ representing the floor function denoting greatest integer less than or equal to the product rN.

(P1) forms an underdetermined system of equations due to the fact that M < N and is solved by optimization theory using linear programming. The Problem (P1) can also be formulated as in (3) below:

$$(\mathbf{P_1})\ min\ x\ \mathbf{in}\ \frac{1}{2}||Ax - y||_2^2 + \lambda||\Psi x||_1 \tag{3}$$

where ψ represents the regularization function, λ represents the spatial regularization parameter and $||.\ ||_1$ signifies the l_1 norm. Now, replacing $\mathbf{x}$ in (3) with the tri-variate signal f from (1), we achieve Eq. (4) as described below:

$$(\mathbf{P_{gen}}) \equiv minf(x, y, z)\ \mathbf{in}\ \frac{1}{2}||A * f(x, y, z) - y||_2^2 + \lambda||\Psi f(x, y, z)||_1 \tag{4}$$

We formulate Eq. (4) as a representation of our proposed MEMD-CS framework for modeling the CS-based 3D reconstruction. Equation (4) can be solved by separating the trivariate signal into a combination of three 1D signals, considering the fact that the spatial coordinates are independent and orthogonal dimensions. This also reduces the computation time to a great extent. For solving (4), we are using the ADMM (Alternating Direction Method of Multipliers) [18] and the FISTA (Fast Iterative Shrinkage-Thresholding Algorithm) [19] algorithms due to their proven efficiency and improved accuracy.

4 Experiments and Results

We performed the CS-based recovery of the 3D LiDAR point cloud using EMD-derived residual functions. The Compressive Sensing based reconstruction of point cloud data consists of - sampling the input based on CS measurement ratios, transforming the measurements to a sparse vector space, and finally reconstructing it by solving the inverse optimization problem using linear programming.

Table 1. Evaluation results for MEMD-CS reconstruction using ADMM and FISTA solvers for the selected four samples.

Sample Dataset	MEMD-CS Using ADMM solver			MEMD-CS Using FISTA solver		
	PSNR(dB)	RMSE	H.D	PSNR(dB)	RMSE	H.D
Andrews 1	29.25	22.5	42.65	61.62	0.54	0.57
Andrews 2	28.51	20.14	36.7	61.59	0.45	0.48
Tahoe 1	31.81	51.65	52.44	61.01	1.74	1.79
Tahoe 2	21.31	173.21	173.25	61.02	1.79	1.76

We used Gaussian dictionaries for sampling the input residue function as they are proven to follow the RIP [13]. The evaluation of our proposed approach is presented based on the following metrics - PSNR (Peak Signal to Noise Ratio), RMSE (Root Mean Squared Error), and Hausdorff point cloud-to-cloud distance [20]. PSNR is considered a good measure for quantifying reconstruction results, whereas Hausdorff distance is defined as the maximum Euclidean distance from a point in one point cloud to the closest point in the other point cloud. The RMSE defines the error metric corresponding to the closeness in reconstructed output with the original output as a quadratic loss function.

In Table 1 and Fig. 2, we present quantitative and qualitative evaluation results of our proposed MEMD-CS framework, respectively. We observe that the FISTA algorithm performs much better as compared to the ADMM method. We infer that this could possibly be due to better convergence of the FISTA algorithm with the continuous signals such as the LiDAR datasets.

In order to evaluate the efficacy of our approach for a forest region, we derived the nDSM (normalized Digital Surface Model), also referred to as the CHM or Canopy Height Model. The CHM defines the surface overlapping the non-ground points of a LiDAR scan. Since we have selected the samples from a forest region, it is expected that the majority of the CHM would be tree canopy cover. For comparison, the ground truth DSM is downloaded from the OpenTopography platform, and CHM was derived from it. Similarly, CHM was generated from the reconstructed point clouds. We believe that

Ground Truth and Derivatives	Output of Proposed MEMD-CS using ADMM Solver	Output of Proposed MEMD-CS using FISTA Solver

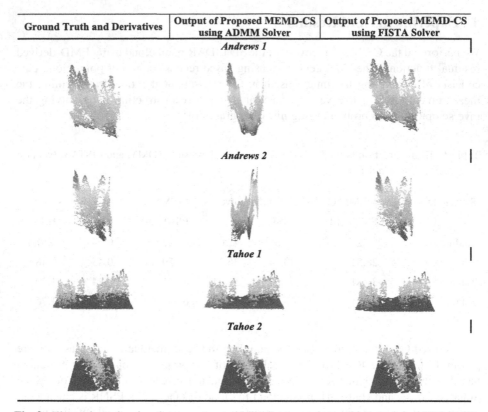

Fig. 2. Illustrations showing the reconstructed LiDAR scenes along with the original 3D LiDAR scenes.

such a comparison would help in analyzing the efficacy of our proposed approach at a local level. In Fig. 3, we present the illustrations of CHM along with the CHM derived for the reconstructed LiDAR scenes.

It is evident from the illustrations of the sites A1, A2, T1, and T2 that the reconstructed results of the FISTA approach are better as compared to the ADMM approach. We also observe that for samples of the region with topographical discontinuity, such as valley (from A1 and T1), our approach with the FISTA algorithm is able to generate the CHM properly as compared to the ADMM approach. Building upon this, we can derive individual tree metrics and map the tree canopy of the forest, which is useful for estimating forest biomass and inventory.

Andrews 1 (A1)	Andrews 2 (A2)	Tahoe 1 (T1)	Tahoe 2 (T2)

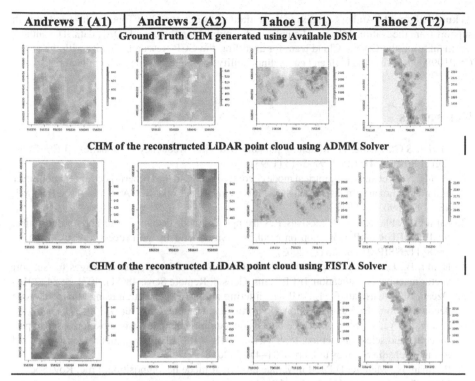

Fig. 3. Illustrations showing the CHM derived from the reconstructed LiDAR scans along with the ground truth. The ground truth CHM is generated from the DSM provided by the OpenTopography platform along with the forest LiDAR scans.

5 Conclusion

LiDAR scanning is a widely used remote sensing technology because of the advantages it provides in terms of bulk data acquisition and accurate topographical information. This has led to a recent increase in the applications of LiDAR point cloud data for forest research. The surge in active research in academia as well as industry has drastically improved the sensor design, making it more robust and reliable on the one hand and reducing the budget involved in data acquisition on the other hand. Our work explores using EMD-derived residual functions to generate sparse representations using the Compressive Sensing approach. We perform extensive experiments in reconstructing the 3D LiDAR scenes using ADMM, and FISTA approaches from the generated sparse representations. We compare the results obtained by using ADMM and FISTA approaches and observe that the FISTA-based approach (61.62 dB, $r = 0.54$) performs better than the ADMM approach (29.25 dB, $r = 22.5$). To the best of our knowledge, the application of a data-driven transform in a Compressive Sensing framework for processing forest LiDAR data is a novel contribution, and we envisage the use of our approach in applications involving near real-time processing of the acquired data.

Acknowledgment. Authors express their gratitude towards the OpenTopography Facility with support from the National Science Foundation for publishing the open LiDAR data. The authors are thankful to the Google Cloud team for awarding the GCP Research Credits with the award GCP19980904 to use the high-end computing facility for implementing the architectures.

References

1. Mallat, S.G., Zhang, Z.: Matching pursuits with time-frequency dictionaries. IEEE Trans. Signal Process. **41**(12), 3397–3415 (1993)
2. Huang, N.E., et al.: The empirical mode decomposition and the Hilbert spectrum for nonlinear and non-stationary time series analysis. Proc. Roy. Soc. Lond. Ser. A: Math. Phys. Eng. Sci. **454**(1971), 903–995 (1998)
3. Rilling, G., Flandrin, P., Goncalves, P.: On empirical mode decomposition and its algorithms. In: IEEE-EURASIP Workshop on Nonlinear Signal and Image Processing, vol. 3, no. 3, pp. 8–11. NSIP-03, Grado (I) (2003)
4. Demir, B., Ertürk, S.: Empirical mode decomposition of hyperspectral images for support vector machine classification. IEEE Trans. Geosci. Remote Sens. **48**(11), 4071–4084 (2010)
5. Özcan, A.H., Ünsalan, C.: LiDAR data filtering and DTM generation using empirical mode decomposition. IEEE J. Sel. Top. Appl. Earth Obs. Remote Sens. **10**(1), 360–371 (2016)
6. Zhang, M., Yu, W., Shen, Y.: Three-dimensional empirical mode decomposition based hyperspectral band selection method. In: IGARSS 2018–2018 IEEE International Geoscience and Remote Sensing Symposium, pp. 4701–4704 (2018)
7. Rehman, N., Mandic, D.P.: Multivariate empirical mode decomposition. Proc. Roy. Soc. A: Math. Phys. Eng. Sci. **466**(2117), 1291–1302 (2010)
8. Rehman, N., Mandic, D.P.: Empirical mode decomposition for trivariate signals. IEEE Trans. Signal Process. **58**(3), 1059–1068 (2009)
9. Donoho, D.L.: Compressed sensing. IEEE Trans. Inf. Theory **52**(4), 1289–1306 (2006)
10. Candès, E.J., Romberg, J., Tao, T.: Robust uncertainty principles: exact signal reconstruction from highly incomplete frequency information. IEEE Trans. Inf. Theory **52**(2), 489–509 (2006)
11. Shinde, R.C., Potnis, A.V., Durbha, S.S., Andugula, P.: Compressive sensing based reconstruction and pixel-level classification of very high-resolution disaster satellite imagery using deep learning. In: IGARSS 2019–2019 IEEE International Geoscience and Remote Sensing Symposium, pp. 2639–2642 (2019)
12. Shinde, R.C., Durbha, S.S., Potnis, A.V.: LiDARCSNet: a deep convolutional compressive sensing reconstruction framework for 3D airborne LiDAR point cloud. ISPRS J. Photogramm. Remote Sens. (2021). https://doi.org/10.1016/j.isprsjprs.2021.08.019
13. Lu, X., Dong, W., Wang, P., Shi, G., Xie, X.: ConvCSNet: a convolutional compressive sensing framework based on deep learning. arXiv preprint arXiv:1801.10342 (2018)
14. OpenTopography. https://opentopography.org/
15. Andrews Forest OpenTopography Link. https://portal.opentopography.org/LiDARDataset?opentopoID=OTLAS.082011.26910.1
16. Tahoe Forest OpenTopography. Link:https://portal.opentopography.org/datasetMetadata?otCollectionID=OT.032017.26910.2
17. Candes, E.J., Wakin, M.B., Boyd, S.P.: Enhancing sparsity by reweighted ℓ 1 minimization. J. Fourier Anal. Appl. **14**(5–6), 877–905 (2008)
18. Wahlberg, B., Boyd, S., Annergren, M., Wang, Y.: An ADMM algorithm for a class of total variation regularized estimation problems. IFAC Proc. Vol. **45**(16), 83–88 (2012)

19. Beck, A., Teboulle, M.: A fast iterative shrinkage-thresholding algorithm for linear inverse problems. SIAM J. Imag. Sci. **2**(1), 183–202 (2009)
20. Conci, A., Kubrusly, C.S.: Distance between sets - a survey. Adv. Math. Sci. Appl., 1–18 (2018)

Land Cover Classification for Fires Using Sentinel-2 Satellite RGB Images and Deep Transfer Learning

Ait Tchakoucht Taha[1] (iD) and El Khalil Cherif[2(✉)] (iD)

[1] School of Digital Engineering and Artificial Intelligence, Euromed University of Fes (UEMF), Fez, Morocco
t.ait-tchakoucht@ueuromed.org
[2] Institute for Systems and Robotics (ISR), Insituto Superior Technico, 1049-001 Lisboa, Portugal
c.elkhalil@uae.ac.ma

Abstract. Land cover classification is referred to as the process of identifying different types of land cover in images, generally acquired through remote sensing. It is a crucial practice to various areas such as precision agriculture, ecology, natural disaster risk assessment, urban planning and so on. The paper describes a pipeline for terrain classification for Forest Fire risk assessment using Convolutional Neural Network models and transfer learning and compares their performances on Sentinel-2 satellite Red, Blue, Green (RGB) images. The results prove the ability of transfer learning to accurately identify land cover types.

Keywords: Land cover · Remote sensing · Deep Transfer Learning

1 Introduction

Automated Earth Observation (EO) has known a growing interest to monitor land cover dynamics since the democratization of Satellite imagery and Unmanned aerial vehicles (UAVs). Researchers have exploited these tools to solve problems related to Ecology [1], Precision Agriculture [2], Disaster Management [3], Geosciences [4], Archeology [5], Water resources [6] and others. Each of the EO systems vary in their monitoring characteristics that constitute a trade-off between spectral, temporal and spatial resolutions [7].

Forest fires are one of the critical natural risks that continues to bother researchers worldwide. Currently, each year, burned areas are estimated to 420Ha distributed around the globe [8], and usually occurring in grasslands and savannah. Both climatic and anthropogenic processes contribute to forest fires as ignition factors, and can lead to loss of life, depletion in forest ecosystems, and economic loss. In consequence, more sophisticated risk assessment procedures should always be adopted and permanently updated to diminish the negative effects of this critical phenomenon. More precisely, producing maps of high-risk areas and determining fire-susceptibility for early prevention.

© Springer Nature Switzerland AG 2023
J.-J. Rousseau and B. Kapralos (Eds.): ICPR 2022 Workshops, LNCS 13644, pp. 142–150, 2023.
https://doi.org/10.1007/978-3-031-37742-6_11

Constructing such maps relies on the identification of factors that contribute to the ignition and the spread of fires, mainly, the land cover and type of vegetation (burnable/non-burnable), climate, topography, and anthropogenic characteristics of the area under study. Therefore, the objective in this contribution is to build an accurate model for land cover classification as a starter in order to locate ignition factors.

Artificial intelligence has abundantly contributed to the advances in several areas, such as Natural Language Processing and Image Classification, since the introduction of deep learning, which is currently known to yield better performances by extracting useful features from the data. Contributions in that matter are growing in number and performance to tackle regression, classification and prediction problems [9].

In this work, we present a comparative approach to classify different types of terrain, using deep learning applied on satellite data, as a first step towards designing a forest fire risk assessment model.

The rest of this paper is structured as follows: Sect. 2 discusses related studies. In Sect. 3 we describe data and methodology, and Sect. 4 reported the experimental results. Finally, Sect. 5 discusses conclusions and perspectives.

2 Related Work

Satellite imagery provides a significant amount of data that contributes to the Big Earth observation [10]. This is explained by the increased number of operational satellites and the democratization of their use [11].

Satellite imagery have been leveraged in many areas, such as agriculture, ecology, archeology, disaster management, wildlife and so on. Image classification techniques and methods fall into five categories, pixel-based, object-based, supervised, and unsupervised techniques, and Convolutional Neural Networks (CNN) [12].

Pixel-based techniques leverages properties of reflectance values for a particular pixel, then combine pixels to form land cover features. The pixel can be classified both in a supervised or unsupervised manner [13]. In supervised classification, the algorithm is based on training samples, which are already labeled, to discriminate between pixels. Most of the techniques used in this context are, maximum likelihood, minimum-distance, and parallelepiped [14]. In unsupervised techniques, pixels are grouped into clusters that share the same reflectance properties, then a domain expert attributes clusters to different land cover categories. K-means and ISODATA are among the techniques used in unsupervised classification [15]. Object-based method targets a group of pixels instead of single pixels. The images are interpreted based on image objects and their common characteristics. The method leverages spectral information, geometry, and structure aspects [16].

CNNs are special kind of deep learning techniques that have proven to produce remarkable performances in computer vision. They have been used to classify satellite imagery, as in [17] and [18], in which researchers investigate urban environment characteristics, or in [19], in an attempt to categorize different types of crops, or for archeological site detection as presented in [20].

3 Materials and Methods

Different architectures of CNN starting from a simple architecture to transfer learning architectures were used to perform land cover classification. The models are trained on RGB version of Sentinel-2 satellite imagery from EuroSat dataset and fine-tuned on validation set using Tensorflow and Keras modules in python programming language. Experiments were performed on a 64bit Windows 10 PC, with a 12 GB in RAM and an intel(R) i7 2.00, 2.6 Ghz processor.

3.1 Satellite Data

EuroSat dataset comprises multispectral images produced by Sentinel-2 satellite [21], mainly a version with 13 spectral bands and another one that is limited to RGB bands, and which is used in this study. It consists of 27,000 images of 64 × 64 pixels, categorized into 10 separate land cover as shown in Fig. 1. Figure 2 presents an overview of EuroSat RGB images. The dataset is divided into 80:10:10 ratio, respectively for training (21,600 images), validation (2700 images), and testing (2700 images).

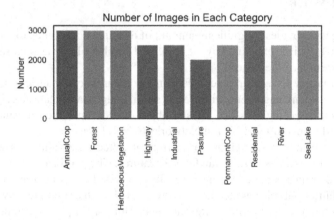

Fig. 1. Land cover categories in Eurosat Dataset.

3.2 CNN and Transfer Learning

In this research, one shallow and two deeper CNN architectures are used. The first model comprises one 2D convolutional layer with 32 convolution filters of 3 × 3 kernel and one dense layer.

MobileNet is a lightweight deep CNN architecture that uses depth-wise separable convolutions, and in which, the number of parameters is minimal in comparison with architectures that have similar depth [23].

Visual Geometry Group (VGGNet) is a very deep CNN that improves accuracy by increasing the depth to 16 weight layers with convolution filters of 3 × 3 kernel [22].

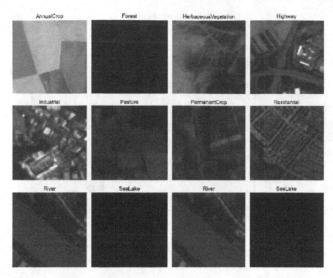

Fig. 2. Image samples of EuroSat Dataset.

It consists of five blocks of 2D convolutional layers, separated by a 2D Max Pooling blocks. The pretrained VGG-16 model was trained on the 1000 classes ImageNet dataset.

The models are trained on EuroSat RGB training set images of ($3 \times 64 \times 64$) shape, using ReLu and softmax activation functions, for 5 epochs with a batch size of 20. Regarding the model based on pretrained VGG-16, the latter layers are fine-tuned for the specific task of land cover classification on EuroSat dataset, while the first layers were made non trainable (warm start on ImageNet). Categorical cross-entropy loss function and Adam optimizer were used.

4 Experiments and Discussion

We evaluated simple and VGG-16 pretrained model on 2700 RGB images of EuroSat, based on confusion matrix in Figs. 3, 4 and 5 and Precision, Recall, and F-Score shown in Tables 1, 2 and 3.

The pretrained VGG-16 accomplishes the best performance among the three models with 96% in each metric as a weighted average over all the land cover categories, followed by MobileNet with 83% in each metric, and finally, the simple CNN model achieves a performance of 64%.

The three models (even the simpler one) performed well on SeaLake classification. This is expected as SeaLake pixels and water in general (See Fig. 2) possesses specific visible characteristics, and hence the models could accurately distinguish between water and other land cover categories.

Using the simple CNN model, performance was the poorest on River category (44% on F-Score) as one convolutional layer couldn't extract useful River features, and thus many River samples have been predicted as Highway, Pasture and PermanentCrop. This performance was considerably enhanced using pretrained MobileNet and VGG-16 (95% on F-Score), since deeper layers could capture River's high-level features.

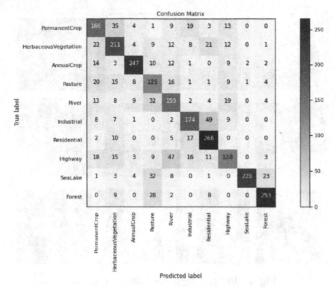

Fig. 3. Confusion matrix of the simple CNN model.

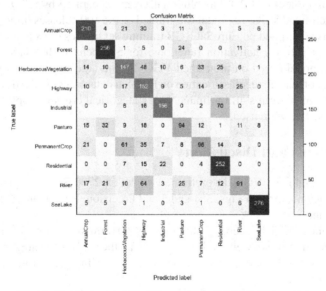

Fig. 4. Confusion matrix of the pretrained MobileNet model.

Same can be observed on Highway category, as many Highway samples were mis-classified as River, Industrial, permanentCrop, and others, since either they share the same low-level features, or there exists different land cover categories inside Highway images. The performance on Highway was improved with MobileNet (75% on F-Score), and more enhanced with VGG-16 (95% on F-Score).

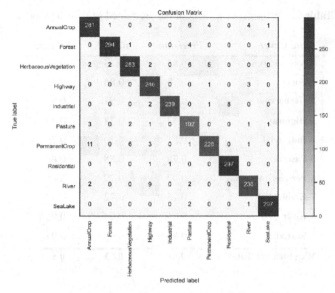

Fig. 5. Confusion matrix of pretrained VGG-16 model.

Table 1. Performance metrics of the simple CNN model.

Land Cover	Precision	Recall	F-Score
0-AnnualCrop	0.72	0.70	0.71
1-Forest	0.78	0.85	0.82
2-HerbaceousVeg	0.52	0.49	0.51
3-Highway	0.40	0.61	0.48
4-Industrial	0.74	0.62	0.68
5-Pasture	0.53	0.47	0.50
6-PermanentCrop	0.54	0.38	0.45
7-Residential	0.64	0.84	0.73
8-River	0.56	0.36	0.44
9-SeaLake	0.94	0.92	0.93
Weighted avg/Total	0.64	0.64	0.64

Pasture and Forest categories are very similar, and thus were misclassified with each other using the simple CNN model (especially Forest seen as Pasture, while Pasture is seen as Forest, PermanentCrop, HerbaceousVegetation, River and AnnualCrop, in many cases), and MobileNet, but could be accurately differentiated using VGG-16.

Table 2. Performance metrics of the pretrained MobileNet model.

Land Cover	Precision	Recall	F-Score
0-AnnualCrop	0.85	0.73	0.79
1-Forest	0.70	0.85	0.77
2-HerbaceousVeg	0.91	0.91	0.91
3-Highway	0.73	0.78	0.75
4-Industrial	0.81	0.70	0.75
5-Pasture	0.78	0.88	0.83
6-PermanentCrop	0.92	0.79	0.85
7-Residential	0.73	0.72	0.72
8-River	0.96	0.94	0.95
9-SeaLake	0.89	0.93	0.91
Weighted avg/Total	0.83	0.83	0.83

Table 3. Performance metrics of the pretrained VGG-16 model.

Land Cover	Precision	Recall	F-Score
0-AnnualCrop	0.94	0.94	0.94
1-Forest	0.99	0.98	0.98
2-HerbaceousVeg	0.97	0.94	0.96
3-Highway	0.92	0.98	0.95
4-Industrial	1.00	0.96	0.98
5-Pasture	0.90	0.96	0.93
6-PermanentCrop	0.95	0.91	0.93
7-Residential	0.97	0.99	0.98
8-River	0.96	0.94	0.95
9-SeaLake	0.99	0.99	0.99
Weighted avg/Total	0.96	0.96	0.96

Herbaceous vegetation, AnnualCrop and PermanentCrop were also confused with each other, as well as with River, Highway and Industrial at first. Nevertheless, the VGG-16 model could in most of the cases improve performance and correct misclassifications of both MobileNet and Simple CNN model.

5 Conclusion

In this paper, we investigated the ability of CNN models, and transfer learning techniques to accurately classify land cover. The experiments were performed using a simple CNN architecture, a pretrained MobileNet model and a pretrained VGG-16 model. The models were assessed on RGB images taken from EuroSat dataset. Overall, the pretrained models achieve higher performances. Pretrained VGG-16 yields the best overall results and improves classification in most of the cases as compared to the other two models, although this technique is computationally more expensive. Hence, transfer learning can be a reliable concept to be more investigated in the area of land cover classification

Moreover, The VGG-16 model run only for 5 epochs due to high computational cost, and can be more improved by adding more epochs, gradient clipping, data augmentation, early stopping, as well as learning rate fine-tuning. MobileNet can benefit as well from the former procedures, added to the advantage of being a lightweight technique. Meanwhile, more CNN architectures can be investigated and leveraged in the context of Land cover classification.

This contribution is a first step towards generating land cover maps, with segmented areas, and labeled as a specific land cover category. The former will be the first module for generating maps for forest fire risk assessment.

Acknowledgements. The authors would like to thank all the collaborators within this work, from the writing manuscript team. El Khalil Cherif would like to mention the financial support by FCT with the LARSyS—FCT project UIDB/50009/2020 and FCT project VOAMAIS (PTDC/EEIAUT/31172/2017, 02/SAICT/2017/31172).

References

1. Nhamo, L., Van Dijk, R., Magidi, J., Wiberg, D., Tshikolomo, K.: Improving the accuracy of remotely sensed irrigated areas using post-classification enhancement through UAV capability. Rem. Sens. **10**, 712 (2018)
2. Gevaert, C., Suomalainen, J.M., Tang, J., Kooistra, L.: Generation of spectral–temporal response surfaces by combining multispectral satellite and hyperspectral UAV imagery for precision agriculture applications. IEEE J. Select. Top. Appl. Earth Observ. Rem. Sens. **8**, 3140–3146 (2015)
3. Kakooei, M., Baleghi, Y.: Fusion of satellite, aircraft, and UAV data for automatic disaster damage assessment. Int. J. Rem. Sens. **38**, 2511–2534 (2017)
4. Lewis, A., et al.: The Australian geoscience data cube — foundations and lessons learned. Rem. Sens. Environ. **202**, 276–292 (2017)
5. Ding, H., et al.: A multi-resolution approach for discovery and 3-d modeling of archaeological sites using satellite imagery and a UAV-borne camera. In: American Control Conference, pp. 1359–1365 (2016)
6. Brinkhoff, J., Hornbuckle, J., Barton, J.L.: Assessment of aquatic weed in irrigation channels using UAV and satellite imagery. Water **10**, 1497 (2018)
7. Alavipanah, S.K., Matinfar, H.R., Rafiei Emam, A., Khodaei, K., Hadji Bagheri, R., Yazdan Panah, A.: Criteria of selecting satellite data for studying land resources. Desert **15**, 83–102 (2010)

8. Giglio, L., Boschetti, L., Roy, D.P., Humber, M.L., Justice, C.O.: The Collection 6 MODIS burned area mapping algorithm and product. Rem. Sens. Environ. **217**, 72–85 (2018)
9. LeCun, Y., Bengio, Y., Hinton, G.: Deep learning. Nature **521**(7553), 436–444 (2015)
10. Liu, P., Di, L., Du, Q., Wang, L.: Remote sensing big data: theory, methods and applications. Rem. Sens. **10**, 711 (2018)
11. Ghamisi, P., et al.: Multisource and multitemporal data fusion in remote sensing: a comprehensive review of the state of the art. IEEE Geosci. Rem. Sens. Mag. **7**, 6–39 (2019)
12. Ouchra, H., Belangour, A.: Satellite image classification methods and techniques: a survey. In: IEEE International Conference on Imaging Systems and Techniques (IST) (2021)
13. Dhingra, S., Kumar, D.: A review of remotely sensed satellite image classification. Int. J. Electr. Comput. Eng. **9**(3), 1720 (2019)
14. Sisodia, P.S., Tiwari, V., Kumar, A.: A comparative analysis of remote sensing image classification techniques. In: IEEE International Conference on Advances in Computing, Communications and Informatics (ICACCI), pp. 1418–1421 (2014)
15. AsthaBaxi, M.P., Potdar, M.B., Kalubarme, M.H., Agarwal, B.: Comparison of various classification techniques for satellite data. Int. J. Sci. Eng. Res. **4**(1), (2013)
16. Mohitsrivastava, N.A., Dutta, M.: Comparative analysis of pixel-based and object-based classification of high resolution remote sensing images– a review. Int. J. Eng. Trends Technol. **38**(1), 5–11 (2016)
17. Yao, Y., Liang, H., Li, X., Zhang, J., He, J.: Sensing urban land-use patterns by integrating google tensorflow and scene classification models. arXiv preprint arXiv:1708.01580 (2017)
18. Albert, A., Kaur, J., Gonzalez, M.C.: Using convolutional networks and satellite imagery to identify patterns in urban environments at a large scale. In: Proceedings of the 23rd ACM SIGKDD International Conference on Knowledge Discovery and Data Mining. ACM, pp. 1357–1366 (2017)
19. Kussul, N., Lavreniuk, M., Skakun, S., Shelestov, A.: Deep learning classification of land cover and crop types using remote sensing data. IEEE Geosci. Remote Sens. Lett. **14**(5), 778–782 (2017)
20. Caspari, G., Crespo, P.: Convolutional neural networks for archaeological site detection - finding princely tombs. J. Archaeol. Sci. **110**(1), 104998 (2019)
21. EuroSat Dataset. http://madm.dfki.de/downloads. Accessed 01 June 2022
22. Simonyan, K., Zisserman, A.: Very Deep Convolutional Networks for Large-Scale Image Recognition. https://doi.org/10.48550/arXiv.1409.1556 (2017)
23. Howard, A.G., et al.: MobileNets: Efficient Convolutional Neural Networks for Mobile Vision Applications. https://doi.org/10.48550/arXiv.1704.04861 (2017)

Landsat 8 data for forest fire monitoring: case of Mediouna forest in Tangier, Morocco

Houda Badda[1]([✉]) ⓘ, Hakim Boulaassal[1] ⓘ, El Khalil Cherif[2] ⓘ, Miriam Wahbi[1] ⓘ, Omar El Kharki[1] ⓘ, Mustapha Maatouk[1] ⓘ, and Otmane Yazidi Alaoui[1,1] ⓘ

[1] GéoTéCa, FSTT, Abdelmalek Essaadi University, Km 10, Ziaten. BP: 416, Tetouan, Morocco
baddahouda231998@gmail.com, {h.boulaassal,mwahbi,oelkharki,
mmaatouk,o.yalaoui}@uae.ac.ma
[2] Institute for Systems and Robotics (ISR), Insituto Superior Technico,
1049-001 Lisbon, Portugal
el.k.cherif@tecnico.ulisba.pt

Abstract. During the last years, many regions in North of Morocco have suffered from the spread of wildfires in summer such as Mediouna forest. Indeed, the need for Remote sensing data became more and more evident, since it provides huge regional scale data in short window time and with less cost and human resources. The challenge of this paper is to study the behavior of the Normalized Burn Ratio (NBR) index over time to determine the relationship between its variation and the Mediouna forest biomass evolution using Landsat 8 images. Moreover, we classify the burned areas, and estimate the burn severity based on spectral signatures. The monitoring of the burned areas was performed using the NBR and Burn area severity is performed using Differential Normalized Burn Ratio (dNBR). The correction of the satellite images, the calculation of the NBR index, the analysis and the mapping of the results were carried out using QGIS software. We deduced that NBR and dNBR indices are effective in monitoring Mediouna forest fires.

Keywords: Forest fire · Forest monitoring · Burn severity · Remote sensing

1 Introduction

Forest fires are one of the critical natural risks that continues to bother researchers worldwide. Currently, each year, burned areas are estimated to 420Ha distributed around the globe. Fire has a significant role in determining the structure of ecosystems, such as the evolution of the vegetation and the hydrological cycle [1]. Forest fires are a serious environmental problem in Morocco, which has recently lost thousands of hectares.

To gain insight into forest evolution, it is essential to have sufficient resources at spatial and temporal scales. The satellite remote sensing data meet greatly this requirement and thus has attracted so much researcher's interest over the past decades. Researchers have used remote sensing for many forests fire-related applications, such as [2] who assessed the reliability of satellite imagery for forest fire mapping and inventory. The

© Springer Nature Switzerland AG 2023
J.-J. Rousseau and B. Kapralos (Eds.): ICPR 2022 Workshops, LNCS 13644, pp. 151–159, 2023.
https://doi.org/10.1007/978-3-031-37742-6_12

study published by [3] MODIS (Moderate Resolution Imaging Spectroradiometer) was combined with meteorological observations in order to monitor forest fires in Chongqing. While [4] used Landsat 5 TM and Spot 4 XS images in order to compare field measurements of burn severity to numerical figures used to produce burn area reflectance classification maps.

Various studies combined remote sensing (RS) with machine learning (ML), for instance [5] used remote sensing and supervised learning to provide a neural network training for forest fires prediction in Indonesia. On the same issue, [6] used RS and ML with the ASTER digital elevation model and the Landsat 8 OLI model, to evaluate the potential of multivariate adaptive regression splines, support vector machine (SVM), and boosted regression tree to predict forest fire vulnerability in the Chaloos Rood watershed of Iran. It is also used to monitor vegetation recovery. For instance, in the study published by [7], Landsat 8 images were used with some machine learning algorithms such as the Vegetation Change Tracker algorithm to examine vegetation recovery in burned areas, alongside other machine learning algorithms such as random forest, SVM and stepwise multiple linear regression models to relate vegetation recovery to other impact triggers.

In the same context we evaluated, through this study, the performance of the normalized burn ratio (NBR) and differential normalized burn ratio (dNBR) in detecting burned areas and assessing the degree of impact of forest fire damage.

This document is organized as follows. Section 1 focuses on the study area where we describe its geographic location and forest fire history. This is followed by Sect. 2, which presents the data and methodology used throughout this paper. Finally, Sect. 3 presents our conclusions.

2   Study Area

The forest area of Mediouna, located in the Jbel Kebir west of Tangier, is known as the lung of Tangier. According to [8], the Mediouna area has been considered sensitive to forest fires because it has a very dense vegetation cover, and it is windy, which favors fire spread. Historically, this area has seen many forest fires: on 08/07/2015, 5 ha of vegetation were devastated by fire, then on 01/07/2017, fire damaged about 230 ha in less than two days [8]. Therefore, we chose this area, as it is frequently exposed to fires, which will allow us to perform relevant analyses and identify the most damaged areas that require prevention and rehabilitation. The region of interest for this paper is represented in Fig. 1.

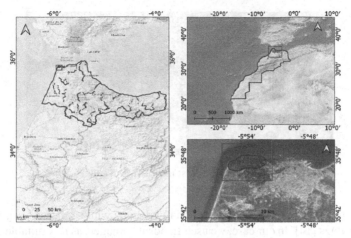

Fig. 1. Study area of Mediouna forest in Tangier – Morocco.

3   Methodology

3.1   Global Forest Change Data

The Global Forest Change (GFC) map products are an interesting approach to obtain forest maps, especially in countries where no national fire reference map exists [9]. It is produced by the University of Maryland at a resolution of 30 m × 30 m [9]. According to [9] "The maps were constructed using Landsat and HJ-1 satellite archives supplemented with ancillary data from a wide range of resources." The data are used to map forest losses between 2000 and 2021, as well as forest gains between 2000 and 2012. Forest change in the GFC database is not associated with specific causes [11]. We used the GFC database to confirm that our study area, the Mediouna forest, was heavily damaged between 2000 and 2021, as illustrated in Fig. 6. In order to have a precise idea about the year and months affected by the fire, we used the Fire Information for Resource Management System (FIRMS), so we could confirm that the forest fire is the main cause of the damage.

3.2   Fire Information for Resource Management System (FIRMS)

FIRMS is a NASA-supported application that was developed as an extension of MODIS Rapid Response [12]. The four main applications of FIRMS are: Web-based mapping services, MODIS active fire datasets, MODIS image subsets, and fire email alerts [12]. FIRMS is primarily intended for natural resource managers and provides MODIS fire data by combining remote sensing and GIS technologies [13].

We used FIRMS in our work to confirm that 2017 was a year when the Mediouna forest was damaged by fire and to have the exact months when the fire started (Fig. 2).

3.3   Determination of the Burned Areas

NBR is used to identify burned areas; to calculate it, we use the ShortWave InfraRed (SWIR) and Near InfraRed (NIR) bands. It is well known; the burned areas have high

Fig. 2. 2017 forest fire FIRMS result

reflectance in SWIR band and low reflection in NIR one while unburned vegetation has high NBR values [14]. In our case, we used Landsat 8 images, as it is suitable to provide better climate, weather, and natural hazard prediction [15]. The NBR index uses fifth (NIR) and seventh (SWIR2) Landsat 8 bands according to the following formula used for this index:

$$NBR = \frac{NIR - SWIR2}{NIR + SWIR2} \tag{1}$$

On the other hand, the dNBR index is deducted as a difference between the NBR index before and after the fire. Thus, areas not affected by the fire will have dNBR values close to zero while positive values dNBR indicate stressed or reduced vegetation in the post-fire image [16].

Table 1. Pre-fire and post-fire dates for NBR calculation.

FIRMS fire year	Fire months	Landsat satellite	Pre-fire LS Date	Post-fire LS Date
2017	June/July	8	26/06/2017	13/08/2017

After having made atmospheric corrections on the Landsat images using QGIS Semi-Automatic Classification Plugin, we calculated NBR using his formula mentioned above for the pre- and post-fire images acquired according dates indicated in Table 1. We used the results to calculate the dNBR.

4   Results and Discussion

We chose images that seemed to be suitable with low cloud cover to get the best results. After using the Band calc tool of QGIS to calculate the Pre-fire NBR (Fig. 3), which shows the Mediouna forest before the fire in 2017, and the Post- fire NBR (Fig. 4), which shows the Mediouna forest after the fire in 2017. These maps cannot present a clear idea of the forest status without running a comparison analysis in order to estimate the burn severity in Mediouna forest.

Table 2. USGS classification of dNBR severity levels (Source: https://www.usgs.gov/landsat-missions/landsat-normalized-burn-ratio)

Range	Burn severity
<-0.25	High post-fire regrowth
-0.25 to -0.1	Low post-fire regrowth
-0.1 to $+0.1$	Unburned
0.1 to 0.27	Low severity
0.27 to 0.44	Moderate-low severity
0.44 to 0.66	Moderate-high severity
>0.66	High severity

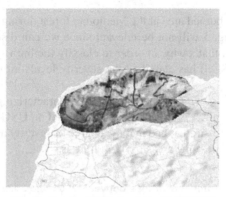

Fig. 3. Pre-fire NBR result on 26/06/2017

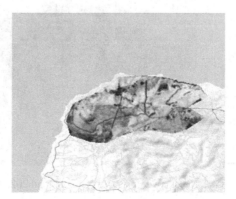

Fig. 4. Post-fire NBR result on 13/08/2017

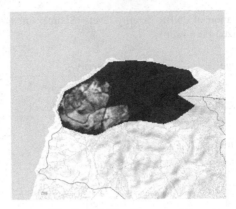

Fig. 5. dNBR primary result

Figure 5 shows the burned area at the Mediouna forest during 2017. As we can see, the interpretation of Fig. 5 will not be relevant since we can distinguish only the two colors white and black, that's why, in order to classify the burn severity, United States Geological Survey (USGS) has classified the severity levels into categories like those are illustrated in Table 2.

Figure 6 represents the GFC extent and change characterizing of forest loss, while Fig. 7 represents the result of dNBR classification based on USGS categories. We note that the results are almost similar, and that the degree of severity and the area of loss are concentrated in almost the same areas for both figures.

GFC forest cover loss between 2000 and 2021

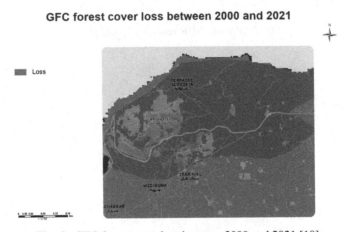

Fig. 6. GFC forest cover loss between 2000 and 2021 [10]

To have an idea of the surface of the damaged area, we calculated it and obtained that 129 ha are of moderate to high severity and 8 ha are of high severity.

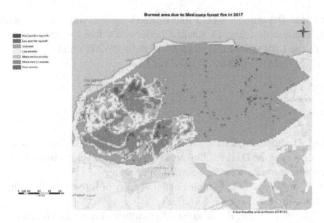

Fig. 7. Burned areas classification

5 Discussion and Conclusion

In this paper, we investigated the digitalization of the burned area in Mediouna Forest using Landsat 8 images and the NBR and dNBR indexes. The classification experiments (NBR and dNBR) showed a significant result compared to the FIRMS and GFC.

GFC showed a major loss in Mediouna forests coinciding with fire forests in the same period, we can only deduce that fire is a major reason for forest loss. This information helps decision makers to pay special attention to these vulnerable areas.

The on-going study is providing a diagnostic comparison before and after the Fire in Mediouna forest in 2017. More attention must be taken to this forest since it knows the same fire in 2020.

The fire management cycle has three phases, from prevention actions to response and the final phase of recovery and adaptation [17]. The main challenge is that it is extremely difficult to predict the spatial and temporal risk of wildfire probability based on historical data alone [18], as we did with the NBR and dNBR indices, because there are mainly four categories of wildfire factors to consider: those related to topography, climate, vegetation, and human activities [19]. Recently, the convolutional neural network (CNN) has become an emerging and prominent deep learning algorithm, giving it greater adaptation and classification capabilities as well as the ability to fully utilize neighborhood information [19]. Normally, this algorithm is used with NDVI indices with additional inputs such as temperature, slope, elevation... Considered. [19]. I think it would be interesting to use it with the NBR index to compare the accuracy of the results obtained with these two indices, in order to have visibility on the best index for forest fire prediction.

For this reason, I believe that this study should be done in the Mediouna forest in northern Morocco, which could reduce monitoring expenses and predict the vulnerable fire areas.

Acknowledgements. The authors would like to thank all the collaborators within this work, from the writing manuscript team. El Khalil Cherif would like to mention the financial support by FCT with the LARSyS—FCT project UIDB/50009/2020 and FCT project VOAMAIS (PTDC/EEIAUT/31172/2017, 02/SAICT/2017/31172).

References

1. Qiu, J., Wang, H., Shen, W., Zhang, Y., Su, H., Li, M.: Quantifying forest fire and post-fire vegetation recovery in the Daxin'anling area of Northeastern china using Landsat time-series data and machine learning. Remote Sens. **13**(4) (2021b)
2. Chuvieco, E., Congalton, R.G.: Mapping and inventory of forest fires from digital processing of tm data. Geocarto Int. **3**(4), 41–53 (2008)
3. Zhao A.H., Tang A.Z., Yang, B., Zhao, M.: Agriculture drought and forest fire monitoring in Chongqing city with modis and meteorological observations (2008)
4. Hudak, A.T., Morgan, P., Stone, C., Robichaud, P., Jain, T., Clark, J.: The relationship of field burn severity measures to satellite-derived burned area reflectance classification (BARC) maps. In: Proceedings of American Society for Photogrammetry and Remote Sensing Annual Conference (2004)
5. Suwei, Y., Massimo, L., Kuldeep, S.M.: Predicting forest fire using remote sensing data and machine learning. Assoc. Adv. Artif. Intell. (2021)
6. Kalantar, B., Ueda, N., Idrees, M.O., Janizadeh, S., Ahmadi, K., Shabani, F.: Forest fire susceptibility prediction based on machine learning models with resampling algorithms on remote sensing data. Remote Sens. **12**(22), 3682 (2020b)
7. Qiu, J., Wang, H., Shen, W., Zhang, Y., Su, H., Li, M.: Quantifying forest fire and post-fire vegetation recovery in the Daxin'anling area of northeastern china using Landsat time-series data and machine learning. Remote Sens. **13**(4), 792 (2021)
8. Jellouli, O., Bernoussi, A. S.: The impact of dynamic wind flow behavior on forest fire spread using cellular automata: application to the watershed BOUKHALEF (Morocco). Ecol. Model. **468**, 109938(2022)
9. Sannier, C., McRoberts, R.E., Fichet, L.V.: Suitability of global forest change data to report forest cover estimates at national level in Gabon. Remote Sens. Environ. **173**, 326–338 (2016)
10. Global Forest Change. https://glad.earthengine.app/view/global-forest-change. Accessed 01 July 2022
11. Castro, I., et al.: Detecting fire-caused forest loss in a Moroccan protected area. Fire, **5**(2), 51 (2022)
12. Davies, D., Ilavajhala, S., Wong, M.M., Justice, C.: Fire information for resource management system: archiving and distributing MODIS active fire data. IEEE Trans. Geosci. Remote Sens. **47**(1), 72–79 (2009)
13. Davies, D., Ilavajhala, S., Wong, M.M., Justice, C.: Fire information for resource management system: archiving and distributing MODIS active fire data. IEEE Trans. Geosci. Remote Sens. **47**(1), (2009b)
14. Meneses, B.M.: Vegetation recovery patterns in burned areas assessed with landsat 8 OLI imagery and environmental biophysical data. Fire **4**(4), 76 (2021)
15. Setyo Darmanto, N., Galang Varquez, A.C., Kanda, M.: Detection of urban environment from Landsat 8 for mesoscale modeling purposes. In: ICUC9 - 9th International Conference on Urban Climate jointly with 12th Symposium on the Urban Environment (2015)
16. Hayes, J.J., Robeson, S.M.: Spatial variability of landscape pattern change following a ponderosa pine wildfire in Northeastern New Mexico, USA. Phys. Geogr. **30**(5), 410–429 (2009)

17. Bot, K., Borges, J.G.: A systematic review of applications of machine learning techniques for wildfire management decision support. Inventions **7**(1), 15 (2022)
18. Gholami, S., Kodandapani, N., Wang, J., Lavista Ferres, J.: Where there's smoke, there's fire: wildfire risk predictive modeling via historical climate data. In: Proceedings of the AAAI Conference on Artificial Intelligence, vol. 35, no. 17, pp. 15309–15315 (2021)
19. Zhang, G., Wang, M., Liu, K.: Forest fire susceptibility modeling using a convolutional neural network for Yunnan province of China. Int. J. Disaster Risk Sci. **10**, 386–403 (2019)

Flying Wing Wildfire Tracking Using Visual Servoing and Gimbal Control

António Peres Nunes[1], Alexandra Moutinho[2](✉) [iD], and José Raul Azinheira[2] [iD]

[1] Instituto Superior Técnico, Universidade de Lisboa, Lisbon, Portugal
antoniopnunes@tecnico.ulisboa.pt
[2] IDMEC, Instituto Superior Técnico, Universidade de Lisboa, Lisbon, Portugal
{alexandra.moutinho,jose.raul.azinheira}@tecnico.ulisboa.pt

Abstract. This paper describes a vision control algorithm for flying wing wildfire tracking. The aircraft, equipped with a camera attached to a gimbal, is dropped at a given altitude by a high-altitude balloon, and then performs a gliding descent while surveying the region of interest.

The control methodology chosen was the image-based visual servoing (IBVS). An algorithm was developed to control the gliding descent trajectory, keeping the camera fixed. The results obtained for the simulations with the camera fixed validated the algorithm, although with a deviation between the position of the target in the image and its center. The stationary error was suppressed by controlling the camera rotation. The gimbal and camera were modeled, and respective Proportional-Integral controllers were designed. The algorithm was tested in a realistic simulation environment, demonstrating to effectively control the flying wing trajectory in order to guarantee wildfire monitoring.

Keywords: Visual-servoing control · Flying wing · Target tracking · Wildfire monitoring

1 Introduction

The seven hottest years on Earth have all occurred from 2014 onwards, with the temperature on the planet in 2020 being $0.98\,°C$ above the 20th-century average [5]. The temperature rise has, as a consequence, increased the number of wildfires and their severity, as pointed out by several studies [2,9]. The increased occurrence of extreme fires raises the necessity of implementing new and more efficient preventive measures [8].

To respond to this scenario, the "Eye in the Sky" project [1] emerged. This project aims to develop an unmanned aerial vehicle to provide key information to firefighters, namely georeferenced aerial imagery of active fronts and hotspots during a wildfire.

Visual servoing is often used for target tracking using a vision system, which allows controlling a robot using visual features as feedback signal [3,4]. There are different methods for visual servoing implementation, but in this work only

© Springer Nature Switzerland AG 2023
J.-J. Rousseau and B. Kapralos (Eds.): ICPR 2022 Workshops, LNCS 13644, pp. 160–170, 2023.
https://doi.org/10.1007/978-3-031-37742-6_13

the "Image-based visual servoing" method is used. Several implementations of this method are found in the literature for similar applications. For example, in [11] an "Image-based visual servoing" algorithm was developed for controlling the trajectory of the aircraft in order to track a target using a fixed camera. In [12], the degrees of freedom of a gimbal were added as a second iteration. In [10], a visual servoing flight controller for a fixed-wing UAV was developed using a command filtered back-stepping control law.

In all mentioned works, the controllers are only validated for constant altitude scenarios and constant aircraft airspeed. This work proposes an image-based visual servoing solution for wildfire tracking while performing a gliding controlled descent. This loitering trajectory around the target shall keep the target in the center of the image captured by the camera.

2 Problem Framework

The model [7] used to simulate the behavior of the flying wing is represented in Fig. 1. The models of the atmosphere, gravitation, aerodynamics, propulsion, and dynamics were deduced and integrated to form a state-space nonlinear model of the aircraft. Control and stabilization of the system were also integrated, with:

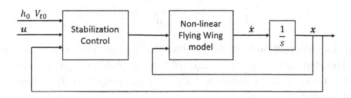

Fig. 1. Block diagram of the flying wing model and respective stabilization controller.

- System input:
$$\mathbf{u} = \begin{bmatrix} u_\phi & u_\theta \end{bmatrix}^T \tag{1}$$

The variables u_ϕ and u_θ are the requested angles, in radians, for the roll and pitch angles of the aircraft, respectively. The variables h_0 and V_{t0} represent the initial altitude and airspeed of the aircraft, respectively.
- State:
$$\mathbf{x} = \begin{bmatrix} u, v, w, p, q, r, x_n, y_n, z_n, q_0, q_1, q_2, q_3 \end{bmatrix}^T \tag{2}$$

The variables $[u, v, w]$ and $[p, q, r]$ are the linear and angular speed in the aircraft-body reference frame, respectively. The aircraft position, in North-East-Down reference frame, is represented by $[x_n, y_n, z_n]$. The aircraft altitude h can be computed as $h = -z_n$. The quaternions (q) translate the aircraft attitude, which can also be defined by Euler angles $[\phi, \theta, \psi]$.

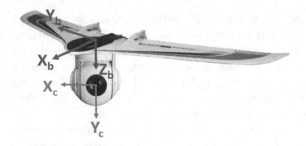

Fig. 2. Flying wing and gimbal systems (aircraft body reference frame in blue and camera reference frame in green). (Color figure online)

Figure 2 presents the flying wing and gimbal systems and their respective reference frames. The gimbal has 2 degrees of freedom and a camera attached. The pan and tilt angles of the gimbal are represented by θ_p and θ_t, respectively. The gimbal kinematic model was deduced according to the Denavit-Hartenberg convention, with the addition of one last reference frame with the Z_c axis aligned with the optical axis. The transformation matrix from the gimbal base frame, with origin in O_{gb}, to the camera frame, with origin in O_c, is represented as:

$$T_c^b = \begin{bmatrix} -s_{\theta_p} & -c_{\theta_p}s_{\theta_t} & c_{\theta_p}c_{\theta_t} & a_2c_{\theta_p}c_{\theta_t} \\ c_{\theta_p} & -s_{\theta_p}s_{\theta_t} & s_{\theta_p}c_{\theta_t} & a_2s_{\theta_p}c_{\theta_t} \\ 0 & c_{\theta_t} & s_{\theta_t} & d_1 + a_2s_{\theta_t} \\ 0 & 0 & 0 & 1 \end{bmatrix} \tag{3}$$

where c_k and s_k correspond to $\cos(k)$ and $\sin(k)$, respectively. The variables d_1 and a_2 are the distance from the origin of the aircraft body reference frame and the origin of the camera frame along Z_b and Y_b, respectively, when the gimbal pan and tilt angles are zero.

3   Visual Servoing Theory

Visual servoing control is characterized by the use of visual information, obtained by a vision system, to control the motion of a given robot. The approach adopted is based on the work of Chaumette [3], where a regulation strategy is assumed:

$$e(t) = \mathbf{s}(t) - s^* \tag{4}$$

where $\mathbf{s}(t)$ are the visual features selected and s^* are the desired values for those features, in the image frame. Then, a velocity controller is used, which relates the temporal variation of the features with the camera speed, expressed by:

$$\dot{e} = L_s V_c \tag{5}$$

where $V_c = [u_c \, v_c \, w_c \, p_c \, q_c \, r_c]^T$ and $L_s \in \mathbb{R}^{k \times 6}$ is the interaction matrix adopting the image-based visual servoing:

$$L_s = \begin{bmatrix} -\frac{f}{z_c} & 0 & \frac{x_i}{z_c} & \frac{x_i y_i}{f} & -(f + \frac{x_i^2}{f}) & y_i \\ 0 & -\frac{f}{z_c} & \frac{y_i}{z_c} & f + \frac{y_i^2}{f} & -\frac{x_i y_i}{f} & -x_i \end{bmatrix} \tag{6}$$

where x_i and y_i are the feature position in the image plane, f is the focal length and z_c is the distance from the camera to the target along the optical axis. Ensuring decoupled convergence of the error ($\dot{e} = -Ke$), the control law is finally obtained:

$$V_c = -L_s^+ K e \tag{7}$$

where $L_s^+ \in \mathbb{R}^{6 \times k}$ is the Moore-Penrose pseudoinverse of L_s and K is a diagonal matrix of positive values. In this work, z_c is considered to be always known, thus L_s^+ can be computed as:

$$L_s^+ = (L_s^T L_s)^{-1} L_s^T \tag{8}$$

4   Target Tracking Controller

4.1   Flight Section Analysis

The trajectory is divided into small straight sections, where the aircraft has a linear speed $u = V_t$ and an angular speed around Z_b of $r = \dot{\psi}$. As consequence, the flying wing performs small turns, leading to a large circular trajectory. This approach showed to be valid for wide trajectories with a slow turn rate, i.e., with a small roll angle of the aircraft. This flight mode can be used for target observation, until a certain altitude that guarantees that the aircraft can exit the trajectory and safely perform approaching and landing maneuvers. The state of the aircraft, which has been described and for which the visual servoing controller will be designed, is called the "ideal state". In this state, the aircraft has the velocity vector

$$V_b = \begin{bmatrix} V_t & 0 & 0 & 0 & 0 & \dot{\psi} \end{bmatrix}^T \tag{9}$$

and is assumed to have an attitude with zero pitch and roll angles. In Sect. 4.2, a yaw speed component $\dot{\psi}_c$ is added to account for the altitude drop during the descent, working as a feed-forward gain, to avoid large gimbal movements and keep it to fine-tuning of the target position in the image plane. A clockwise trajectory is assumed. These considerations are expressed in Fig. 3. However, the aircraft presents nonzero roll and pitch angles during flight. To account for this variation, a compensation mechanism is implemented during the controller development in Sect. 4.2.

4.2   Controller Algorithm

Attitude Compensation. An attitude compensation must be performed from the ideal state defined in Sect. 4.1, to obtain the exact error of the target in

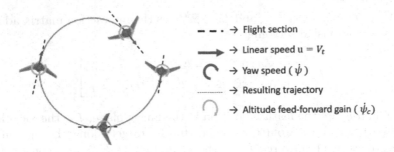

Fig. 3. Flight segment analysis with velocity vectors.

the image plane. The first step is a transformation from the pixel plane to the camera reference, assuming z_c is known, followed by a transformation to the body reference frame using (3). The compensation is applied afterwards using the actual pitch and roll angles:

$$T_{comp} = \begin{bmatrix} c_\theta & s_\theta s_\phi & s_\theta c_\phi \\ 0 & c_\phi & -s_\phi \\ -s_\theta & c_\theta s_\phi & c_\theta c_\phi \end{bmatrix} \tag{10}$$

Finally, the target coordinates are transferred back to the image plane ($e_{x,comp}$, $e_{y,comp}$), since the visual features used by the visual servoing controller are in that reference frame.

Convergence Law. According to (7), to implement decoupled error convergence in both dimensions results in:

$$\dot{e} = \begin{bmatrix} \dot{e}_x \dot{e}_y \end{bmatrix} = K \begin{bmatrix} e_{x,comp} \\ e_{y,comp} \end{bmatrix} = - \begin{bmatrix} K_1 & 0 \\ 0 & K_2 \end{bmatrix} \begin{bmatrix} e_{x,comp} \\ e_{y,comp} \end{bmatrix} \tag{11}$$

where K_1 and K_2 are positive values that affect the speed of convergence of the error in the X_i and Y_i axes, respectively.

Image-Based Visual Servoing Control Law. The control law (7) relates the velocity of the features in the image reference frame, obtained after the convergence law, to the camera velocity in the camera reference frame. However, the velocity vector of the "ideal state" defined in Sect. 4.1 presents the flight kinematics (9) in the body reference frame, thus it is necessary to perform a transformation to the camera frame, using the inverse transformation of (3). Consequently, the image Jacobian J_s is obtained by multiplying the interaction matrix with the rotation matrices from the body frame to the camera frame:

$$J_s = L_s \begin{bmatrix} R_b^c & 0_{3\times3} \\ 0_{3\times3} & R_b^c \end{bmatrix} \tag{12}$$

The last step is to substitute Eqs. (11) and (12) into the control law (7), finally yielding the desired value of $\dot{\psi}$. This procedure results into:

$$\left[V_t \ 0 \ 0 \ 0 \ 0 \ \dot{\psi}\right]^T = -J_s^+ K \dot{e} \tag{13}$$

where V_t is the reference airspeed and $\dot{\psi}$ is the controlled variable.

Altitude Feed-Forward Gain. The goal in this phase is to compute the yaw speed necessary to compensate for the altitude drop of the aircraft. The objective is to reduce the need to move the gimbal, using it for fine-tuning of the target position in the image plane.

Assuming the "ideal state", the trigonometric relationship between the radius of the trajectory and the aircraft altitude is given by:

$$\tan(\theta_t) = h(r_t)^{-1} \tag{14}$$

For a circular motion, the linear velocity is equal to the product of the angular velocity and the radius of the circumference, hence is possible to relate the yaw velocity with the linear velocity V_t:

$$V_t = \dot{\psi}_c r_t \tag{15}$$

where $\dot{\psi}_c$ is the feed-forward gain.

Substituting (14) into (15), it is possible to obtain the equation that calculates the feed-forward gain:

$$\dot{\psi}_c = V_t \tan(\theta_t) h^{-1} \tag{16}$$

In order to manipulate the convergence speed, a feedforward gain was added, which controls the radius of the trajectory:

$$\dot{\psi}_c = K_c V_t \tan(\theta_t) h^{-1} \tag{17}$$

where K_c is a positive value.

Guidance Law. The aircraft model requests a roll demand as input (1). For this reason, it is necessary to relate the yaw rate to that same angle:

$$\dot{\psi} = g \tan(u_\phi) V_t^{-1} \tag{18}$$

where g is the gravitational acceleration and considered equal to $g = 9.8 \, m/s^2$.

Rearranging (18) and adding the yaw rate terms $\dot{\psi}_i$ and $\dot{\psi}_c$, one obtains the desired input roll angle.

$$u_\phi = \arctan\left(V_t(\dot{\psi} + \dot{\psi}_c)g^{-1}\right) \tag{19}$$

Gimbal Proportional-Integral Controller. Two Proportional-Integral controllers are applied to the two gimbal actuation motors to correct the position in X_i and Y_i axes. The control actions u_x and u_y to correct the error in X_i and Y_i axes, respectively, can be computed as:

$$u_x = \left(K_{p,x} + K_{i,x}s^{-1} \right) e_x \tag{20}$$

$$u_y = \left(K_{p,y} + K_{i,y}s^{-1} \right) e_y \tag{21}$$

where K_p and K_i are the proportional and integral gains, respectively, for each controller.

Gimbal Kinematics. The following kinematic relationships can transform the control actions in image coordinates from (20) and (21), into gimbal angular control actions (u_p, u_t):

$$u_p = \arctan \left(u_x f^{-1} \right) \tag{22}$$

$$u_t = \arctan \left(u_y f^{-1} \right) \tag{23}$$

Gimbal Dynamics. It was assumed that both pan and tilt degrees of freedom of the gimbal could be represented as generic first-order systems with the following transfer function:

$$G(s) = \frac{1}{0.1s + 1} \tag{24}$$

Target Detection. The target is always detected whenever it is within the camera field of view, which depends on the camera intrinsic and extrinsic parameters. The designed controller is only activated when the target is detected, otherwise a straight trajectory shall be performed.

The final block diagram of the proposed system is represented in Fig. 4, including both visual servoing and gimbal controllers.

5   Results

This section presents simulation results obtained in a realistic environment, using *MATLAB* and *Flightgear* in order to evaluate the performance of the controller described in Sect. 4.2. Table 1 presents parameter values used, where $\theta_{p,0}$ and $\theta_{t,0}$ are the initial gimbal pan and tilt angles, respectively, and $V_{t,0}$ and h_0 are the aircraft initial airspeed and altitude, respectively.

The gains used were $K_1 = 0.6$, $K_2 = 0.6$, $K_c = 1.75$, $K_p = K_{p,x} = K_{p,y} = 10$, $K_i = K_{i,x} = K_{i,y} = 5$. The resulting trajectory of the aircraft is presented in Fig. 5, in both 3-dimensions and 2-dimensions graphics, where it is possible to see the initial straight trajectory performed until the target is detected by the camera. When detected, the aircraft performs a gliding loitering flight around the target.

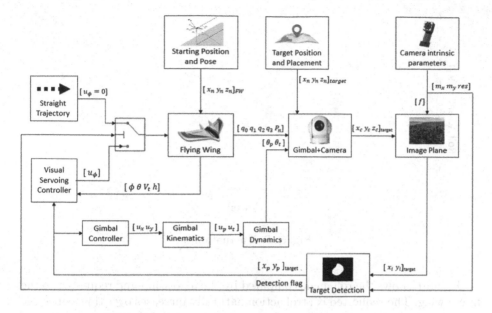

Fig. 4. Block diagram of the trajectory control solution, using a gimbal controller and a visual servoing controller.

Table 1. Simulation parameters

Parameters	Values
$P_n(target)$	$(500, 800, 0)$ [m]
$\theta_{p,0}$	90 [°]
$\theta_{t,0}$	32 [°]
$V_{t,0}$	16 [m/s]
h_0	500 [m]

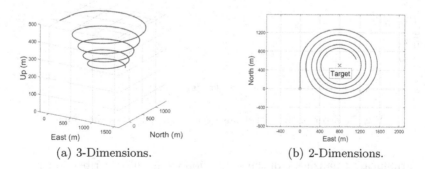

(a) 3-Dimensions.   (b) 2-Dimensions.

Fig. 5. Aircraft trajectory.

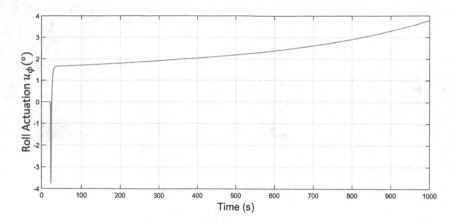

Fig. 6. Roll actuation.

Figure 6 shows the roll angle computed by the algorithm and requested to the flying wing. The requested control action naturally increases over time, since the trajectory radius decreases. Figure 7 presents the error of the target coordinates in pixels, in both X and Y dimensions, showing the convergence of the target with the image center when the error is zero. Figure 7 shows a detailed view of Fig. 8, of the error convergence.

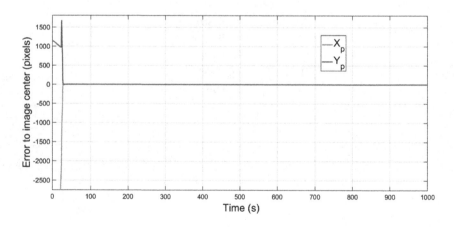

Fig. 7. Error of the target position to the center of the image.

A graphical visualization of the simulation using the described algorithm can be seen here: https://youtu.be/B0fEum37dxk.

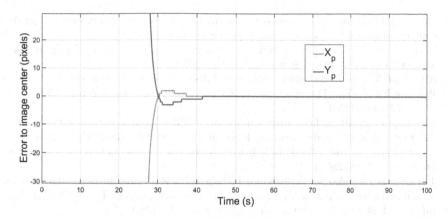

Fig. 8. Error of the target position to the center of the image (detailed view).

6   Conclusions

An algorithm for wildfire tracking with a flying-wing aircraft was successfully developed and validated in a realistic simulation environment, assuming the wildfire (target) location was known. An image-based visual servoing controller was used, recurring to a gimbal to provide supplementary degrees of freedom for the controller. More information about this work can be consulted at [6], including validation with ground moving targets. Future work includes wildfire detection and experimental validation of the proposed algorithm.

Acknowledgements. This work was supported by FCT - Fundação para a Ciência e a Tecnologia, I.P., through IDMEC, under project Eye in the Sky, PCIF/SSI/0103/2018, and under LAETA, project UIDB/50022/2020.

References

1. FCT funded project Eye in the Sky (PCIF/SSI/0103/2018). https://adai.pt/eyeinthesky/pt/entrada/. Accessed 23 Oct 2021
2. Abatzoglou, J.T., Williams, A.P.: Impact of anthropogenic climate change on wildfire across western US forests. Proc. Nat. Acad. Sci. **113**(42), 11770–11775 (2016). https://doi.org/10.1073/pnas.1607171113. https://www.pnas.org/content/113/42/11770
3. Chaumette, F.: Visual servoing. In: Encyclopedia of Robotics, pp. 1–9. Springer, Heidelberg, July 2020. https://doi.org/10.1007/978-3-642-41610-1_104-1. https://hal.inria.fr/hal-02918128
4. Hutchinson, S., Hager, G., Corke, P.: A tutorial on visual servo control. Rob. Autom. **12**, 651–670 (1996). https://doi.org/10.1109/70.538972
5. National Oceanic and Atmospheric Administration: 2020 was earth's 2nd-hottest year, just behind (2016). https://www.noaa.gov/news/2020-was-earth-s-2nd-hottest-year-just-behind-2016. Accessed 23 Oct 2021

6. Nunes, A.P.: Flying wing ground target tracking using visual servoing and gimbal control. Master's thesis, Instituto Superior Técnico (2022)
7. Parreira, J.C.L.: Modelling, simulation, analysis and stabilization of a flying wing. Master's thesis, Instituto Superior Técnico (2019)
8. Ribeiro, L.M., et al.: Extreme wildfires and disasters around the world. In: Extreme Wildfire Events and Disasters, pp. 31–51 (2020). https://doi.org/10.1016/b978-0-12-815721-3.00002-3
9. Sun, Q., et al.: Global heat stress on health, wildfires, and agricultural crops under different levels of climate warming. Environ. Int. **128**, 125–136 (2019). https://doi.org/10.1016/j.envint.2019.04.025. https://www.sciencedirect.com/science/article/pii/S0160412018328654
10. Triputra, F., Trilaksono, B., Adiono, T., Sasongko, R.: Visual servoing of fixed-wing unmanned aerial vehicle using command filtered backstepping. Int. J. Electric. Eng. Inf. **7**, 584–604 (2015). https://doi.org/10.15676/ijeei.2015.7.4.4
11. Yang, L., Liu, Z., Wang, X., Xu, Y.: An optimized image-based visual servo control for fixed-wing unmanned aerial vehicle target tracking with fixed camera. IEEE Access **7**, 68455–68468 (2019). https://doi.org/10.1109/access.2019.2918686
12. Yang, L., Liu, Z., Wang, G., Wang, X.: Image-based visual servo control for ground target tracking using a fixed-wing UAV with pan-tilt camera. In: 2020 International Conference on Unmanned Aircraft Systems (ICUAS), pp. 354–361 (2020). https://doi.org/10.1109/ICUAS48674.2020.9214071

An Overview of Tools and Algorithms Used to Classify, Detect, and Monitor Forest Area Using LiDAR Data

Wijdan Amakhchan[1]([✉]) [iD], Omar El Kharki[1] [iD], El Khalil Cherif[2] [iD],
Miriam Wahbi[1] [iD], Otmane Yazidi Alaoui[1] [iD], Mustapha Maatouk[1] [iD],
and Hakim Boulaassal[1] [iD]

[1] GéoTéCa, FSTT, Abdelmalek Essaadi University, Km 10, Ziaten. BP: 416, Tetouan, Morocco
wijdan.amakhchan@etu.uae.ac.ma, {oelkharki,mwahbi,o.yalaoui,
mmaatouk,h.boulaassal}@uae.ac.ma
[2] Institute for Systems and Robotics (ISR), Insituto Superior Technico,
1049-001 Lisbon, Portugal
el.k.cherif@tecnico.ulisba.pt

Abstract. LIght Detection and Ranging (LIDAR) is gaining popularity more and more among scientists for developing predictive models in forest areas. Lidar point cloud data has a strong potential for application to manage forest resources thanks to its high accuracy. Obviously, the forest should be given more concern, to not be destroyed, causing economic and ecological damage which affects human lives as well. Therefore, using the developed technologies to protect it is crucial. The Lidar technology is one of the most used recently to meet this requirement. To highlight the big interest of Lidar data in the forest monitoring issue, this article introduces a summary of Lidar data sources Airborne Laser scanning (ALS), Terrestrial Laser scanning (TLS) and mobile mapping system (MMS) algorithms and methods used to classify and filter the point cloud lidar data in forest areas.

Keywords: LiDAR data processing · ALS · TLS · MMS · Fire Forest

1 Introduction

LIDAR is a system that uses a distance acquisition technology using a laser beam. It is thus possible to measure the 3D coordinates X, Y and Z of a point on the surface of an object, by combining the information of distance R and orientation of the laser. By scanning many different angles with the laser, we obtain many measurement points collected in what is called a "point cloud".

Nowadays, there is a lot of improvement and variation in the techniques of monitoring, classifying the forest area, using different technologies to collect the data, mentioning LiDAR, RADAR, photogrammetry etc. This paper presents different techniques used to classify and detect individual trees from Lidar data. There are several types of LiDAR sources to collect data, the most used ones are aerial, terrestrial, and mobile mapping systems.

© Springer Nature Switzerland AG 2023
J.-J. Rousseau and B. Kapralos (Eds.): ICPR 2022 Workshops, LNCS 13644, pp. 171–182, 2023.
https://doi.org/10.1007/978-3-031-37742-6_14

An ALS is typically composed of three major components: a LiDAR instrument, GNSS receiver, and Inertial Measurement Unit (IMU). The LiDAR instrument captures ranging information which is then combined with IMU and GPS trajectory data. The result is an organized, geo-referenced point cloud [1]. Mclean et al. [2] as well used airborne lidar point cloud and GPS tracking data to study the role of canopy structure in arboreal movement in the tropical moist forest from ALS data. Also, [3] used airborne lidar point cloud to detect individual trees using lidar point cloud, the authors studied how Individual Tree Detection (ITD) results varied across diverse structural conditions in mixed-conifer forests and what this taught us about when and how to apply ITD. In the [4], the authors proceeded to the automatic detection of trees, segmentation and stem reconstruction using deep supervised machine learning from high-resolution aerial LiDAR points cloud.

TLS, based on LiDAR range measurements from a scanning system mounted on a tripod. TLS is a synthesis of technologies. They are the composite of rapid pulse lasers, precisely calibrated receivers, precision timing, high-speed micro controlled motors, and precise mirrors and advanced computing capabilities [1]. [5] proposes a new method for automatic individual tree species classification based on terrestrial lidar using Convolutional Neural Network (CNN).

Aerial systems provide large object or scene data quickly, but the data does not contain object details. Static systems provide good quality data, but it is time consuming and difficult to produce data on a large object like a street or even an entire city. Hence, Mobile Mapping Systems (MMS) appeared as a compromise between the other methods. They consist of collecting information on a terrestrial mobile platform.

A system of this type can be broken down into three parts: a perception system, a location system and a mobile platform. The perception system acquires, always, information from the scene around it. It can be composed of several sensors. The localization system always calculates the position and orientation of the system. The mobile platform is made up not only of the vehicle but also of the supports for the integrated systems, such as the power supply, the electrical connectors, and the control unit, etc. [6] used terrestrial laser mobile mapping point clouds to detect and separate the individual trees from the other scanned objects.

2   Methods and Algorithms

The techniques and the tools to collect the data have been developed in a remarkable and a fast way, this field represents a hot research spot, hence, many techniques are used that we group in four categories: resampling, filters, algorithms, and machine learning methods.

2.1   Resampling

Resampling is a revolutionary method because it deviates from the theoretical distribution. Rather, inference is based on repeated sampling within the same sample, which is why it's called resampling. The main methods used for resampling are ordinary kriging, neighborhood classification, local maximum, and triangulation with linear interpolation etc.

Ordinary kriging is the most widely used kriging method. It is used to estimate the value of a point in a region where the variogram is known. Ordinary kriging can also be used to estimate block values, or to interpolate the ground points [8].

Neighborhood Classification is a distance-based algorithm in which objects are classified based on the membership of their neighbors, it was used by Monnier et al. to classify the point cloud into vegetation and non-vegetation according to the geometrical shape of their neighborhood in order to detect and separate the individual trees from the other scanned objects of the terrestrial mobile mapping point cloud [6].

Vauhkonen et al. [9] used the location of each seed to update the neighbor cell with the highest correlation, and they repeated this operation until a local maximum of the correlation surface had been reached. For Dalponte et al. [10] each local maximum is labeled as an 'initial region' around which a tree crown can grow.

2.2 Filters

Filters are used to clean, extract, or classify data, there are several filters used with point clouds.

Liu et al. [11] used slope-based filtering and topological analysis, to filter and separate non-ground measurements from ground. Hierarchical morphological algorithm was used by Vauhkonen et al. [9] to trace the images from top to bottom by assuming the number of points to be higher where a tree crown occurs and uses as well as smoothed correlation image to detect the trees. In order to detect trees Corte et al. [12] used the tree detection function of the 'LiDAR' package using the local maximum filter as described by Popescu et al. [13]. Furthermore, local maximum filtering was applied on CHM (Canopy Height Model) rasters obtained from LiDAR data on high spatial resolution imagery to obtain tree crown tops that identify trees [14]. A low-pass filter is applied to the rasterized canopy height model CHM to smooth the surface and reduce the number of local maxima [10]. Also, Dong et al. [15] used a Gaussian filter to smooth the DHM (Digital Height Model) in order to eliminate heterogeneity in the DHM as much as possible. In addition, Yang et al. [16] used a Gaussian filtering to remove noise points from the scanned data, after acquiring the point cloud data from the experimental sites scanned by the laser scanner. The cloth simulation filtering (CSF) method was used by Zhang et al. [17] to classify the point cloud after denoising as aboveground points and ground points, then, voxelate the aboveground points to different voxel sizes to segment individual tree crowns. In addition, Progressive Morphological Filter (PMF) used to classify the point cloud data into ground and non-ground points [18].

2.3 Algorithms

Many algorithms are used for the processing and monitoring of forest area using LiDAR data, mentioning some algorithms and their definition with the references that used it:

Probabilistic Relaxation algorithm: Is an iterative algorithm in which the probability values at each point are updated for each iteration, used to homogenize probability values within the point cloud to extract the foliage and trunks [6].

RANSAC: Selects three points at random from all stem points in the bin and computes the parameters of a circle (the horizontal center position and radius) that intersects the three points used for many purposes. Monnier et al. [6] used it to detect trunk circles in horizontal projection in order to isolate individual trees. Windrim & Bryson [4] used RANSAC algorithm to selects three points at random from all stem points in the bin and computes the parameters of a circle xc, yc (the horizontal center position) and r (radius) that intersects the three points to estimate a geometric model of the tree stem. Singh et al. cluster the classified point cloud individually and filtered it using RANSAC [7].

Region growing: Region-based segmentation, surface growing algorithm is a region-based sequential image segmentation technique that assembles pixels into larger regions based on predefined seed pixels, growth criteria, and stopping conditions, used by: [10, 19, 20].

Local maximum is the height value of the function at a point is greater than (or equal to) the height anywhere else in that interval, was applied on CHM rasters obtained from LiDAR data or on high spatial resolution imagery to obtain tree crown tops. Dalponte and Coomes [10] uses a decision tree method to grow individual crowns around the local maxima for carbon mapping based on identifying individual tree crowns and species from airborne remote sensing data. Used also for tree detection by [21–23].

Spoke wheel algorithm is used to obtain the precise edges of each tree [11].

Trapezoidal method used to calculate individual volumes of tree canopy volume elements [24].

K-means algorithm is a simple unsupervised learning algorithm for solving clustering problems used by: [9, 25].

Minimum curvature algorithm is similar to the radius of curvature method in that it assumes that the wellbore is a curved path between the two survey points [25].

Kernel densities is a non-parametric method for estimating the probability density function of a random variable, used to stratify the vegetation profile and differentiate understory from the rest of the vegetation [26].

Shuffled Complex Evolution (SCE) algorithm used to optimize two site-specific coefficients to differentiate overstorey tree clusters of interest from the rest [26].

Developed Scan Labeling Algorithm (DSLA) to scan and examine the field in four directions, then detect and eliminate non-terrain points using the one-dimensional linear regression method [27].

2.4 Machine Learning Methods

Machine learning algorithms widely used for lidar data in forest area, all machine learning algorithms can be divided into three classes according to [28]: classification tree methods (Decision Trees DT, Random Forest RF), grouping and separability methods (Support Vector Machine SVM, k-nearest neighbors kNN), and rule creation and application methods (Convolutional Neural Network CNN).

RF is a collection of supervised learning algorithms for classification and regression, used in predictive modeling and machine learning techniques [37]. It collects the results and predictions of several decision trees and finally chooses the best output, either the mode of the class (the most frequent value in the decision tree results) or the mean prediction.

Kurdi et al. [29] present an overview of the applications of RF classifiers for automatic vegetation detection and modeling using LiDAR point clouds. Man et al. [30] used RF to reduce dimension and classify the combined hyperspectral and LiDAR data.

A Decision tree is one of the most popular classification and prediction tools, it's a type of supervised machine learning used to classify or make predictions based on how a previous set of questions was answered [38]. A decision tree is like a flowchart tree structure where each internal node specifies a test of an attribute, each branch represents the result of the test, and each leaf node (terminal node) contains a class label.

Džeroski et al. [39] predict forest stand height and canopy cover from Landsat and LiDAR data using decision trees to improve the accuracy and increase the spatial resolution of the supporting information to the forest monitoring system in Slovenia.

The Support Vector Machine is a non-linear classification-supervised machine learning model, which analyzes data and recognizes patterns. An SVM uses geometry to perform categorical prediction: it ranks input variables by finding an optimal separation hyperplane that maximizes the width of the margin between categories in a dataset. An SVM can be used for regression and classification analysis [40].

Nguyen et al. [31] performed a weighted SVM classifier (WSVM) for tree species recognition using ALS data as a strategy to correct the loss of distribution of tree species dependent on SVM performance and the presence of unreliable data in due to inaccurate positions of the field data and errors in the extraction of trees. Dalponte and Coomes [10] used an SVM classifier to identify tree species using features selected from the ALS and hyperspectral imagery. Individual tree crowns were delineated and classified tree species with SVM and semi-supervised SVM in boreal forests using hyperspectral and LiDAR data and proposed that higher classification accuracy could be obtained with Individual Tree Crowns (ITCs) identified in hyperspectral data [32, 33].

The K-Nearest Neighbor (kNN) algorithm is a non-parametric machine learning algorithm that belongs to the class of simple and easy-to-implement supervised learning algorithms that can be used to solve classification problems and regression [41].

Singh et al. [7] uses k-nearest neighbor (KNN) for noise filtering to identify the roof bolts in 3D point cloud data from a mobile laser scanner.

A convolutional neural network (CNN) is a type of artificial neural network based on neurons that are organized in layers and connected through weights and biases. CNN is designed to process pixel data that is used in image recognition and processing. CNN uses image recognition and classification to detect objects, recognize faces, etc.

Convolutional Neural Network (CNN) was used to automatically classify the individual tree species based on terrestrial lidar [5]. The key component is the creation step of a depth image which well describes the characteristics of each species from a point cloud. Seidel et al. [34] teste the performance of an image classification approach based on CNN with the aim to classify 3D point clouds of seven tree species based on 2D representation in a computationally efficient way.

Mayra et al. [23] compare the performance of three-dimensional convolutional neural networks (3D-CNNs) with the SVM, RF, gradient boosting machine and artificial neural network (ANN) in individual tree species classification from hyperspectral data with high spatial and spectral resolution. Medina et al. Corte et al. [12] tests four different machine learning approaches: Namely Support Vector Regression, Random Forest,

Artificial Neural Networks, and Extreme Gradient Boosting to estimate individual tree and its metrics such as diameter at breast height, total height, and timber volume from lidar point cloud. Sothe et al. [35] showed a better performance of CNN than SVM and RF when identifying tree species from the ombrophilous dense forest. Furthermore, Nezami et al. [36] also achieved high precision and recall values (higher than 0.9) when identifying three tree species using a 3D-CNN.

3 Applications of LIdar in Forest Area

LIDAR can be used in several applications in forest area due to many factories.

3.1 Applications of Machine Learning with Lidar Data

LIDAR has many applications in forest areas and using machine learning will facilitate and reduce the time of processing the data. While the point cloud consists of several classes like: vegetation, building, terrain, water etc. each one can be used in different cases and can be applied in different domains.

Vegetation Detection
Many classification algorithms are spatially developed for forest areas, Corte et al. [12] used four alternative machine learning algorithms for detecting individual trees and estimating metrics such as diameter at breast height, total height, and timber volume, researchers used an unmanned aerial vehicle lidar point cloud.

Windrim & Bryson [4] automated tree detection, segmentation and stem reconstruction using supervised machine learning from high-resolution aerial LiDAR points cloud. This method employs deep learning models that go through a series of steps, beginning with ground characterization and removal, individual tree delineation, and tree point segmentation into stem and foliage.

Tree Species Classification
Mizoguch et al. [5] propose a new method for automatic individual tree species classification based on terrestrial lidar using Convolutional Neural Network (CNN). The key component is the creation step of a depth image which well describes the characteristics of each species from a point cloud. Dalponte and Coomes [10] employ a decision tree method to develop individual crowns around local maxima for carbon mapping using airborne remote sensing data to identify specific tree crowns and species.

3.2 Application Domains of Lidar Data in Forest Area

There are many applications of lidar in forest area, we mention some of these applications:

Micro-Topography
LIDAR technology is used to calculate surface elevation values in forests. Other traditional techniques like photogrammetry are not very accurate compared to lidar. Lidar

collects this data by hitting objects precisely with laser pulses and is not obstructed by tree canopies or forest vegetation.

Alexander et al. [42] assess the influence of micro-topography and crown characteristics on treetop detection and tree heights estimation using airborne LIDAR data in a tropical forest. Zhang et al. [43] propose a novel solution for micro-topography mapping to map densely vegetated coastal environments by integrating terrestrial LiDAR with GPS surveys.

Forest Planning and Management

LIDAR can be used to measure the vertical structure of a forest canopy and can also be used to understand canopy density.

Wulder et al. [44] present the current state of LiDAR in sustainable forest management, including issues related to instrumentation, data collection, data processing, cost and attribute estimation.

Richardson et al. [45] have developed an individual tree canopy (ITC) method based on aerial LiDAR to assess forest structure by estimating the density and spatial configuration of trees. They present the strengths and limitations of the method.

Forest Fire Management

LIDAR technology is being used by fire departments all over the world to manage forest fires in several ways. For example, the technology can be used to monitor forest fire patterns, alerting the fire service to the next likely forest fire, and even putting steps in place to prevent it.

Koetz et al. [46] demonstrate the possibility for merging complimentary data samples from aerial LiDAR and image spectrometer observations to improve the classification of land cover for managing forest fires. The accuracy of the classification based on the combined imaging spectrometry and LiDAR data as compared to a pure spectral classification input is used to measure the ultimate performance of the data fusion approach.

González-Olabarria et al. [47] present a method for evaluating fire risk at the landscape level using spatially continuous information for forest management purposes in the region of Soria. This method incorporates LiDAR derived information, a forest resources inventory, understory and canopy fuel modeling, and fire behavior simulation models.

Precision Forestry

Precision forestry is the process of preparing a specific forest site in order to increase the site's productivity in terms of tree quality and overall yield. LIDAR data gives precise information about a given location and aids in the area's targeting in order to achieve this.

Šumarstvo et al. [48] present a definition of precision forestry and its surveying technologies.

Carbon Mapping

LIDAR technology can be used to provide precise data on the forest, including carbon mapping. This information is then used to calculate the quantity of carbon in a given area of the forest and to assist researchers in making changes.

Asner et Al. [49] used LiDAR data for carbon mapping in tropical forest. In order to create universal LiDAR methods for mapping carbon stocks throughout tropical forests, their research aims to assess the relative significance of various forest structural features, as well as the relationship between LiDAR data and carbon stocks in various tropical forests.

Mascaro et al. [50] analyze the degree of uncertainty in mapping forest carbon using airborne LiDAR data. Two analyses of airborne LIDAR and ground inventory data for the 50-ha forest dynamics plot on Barro Colorado Island were conducted in an attempt to better understand the reasons of the errors in LIDAR predictions of aboveground forest carbon.

Individual Tree Analysis

Individual tree properties such as tree height and crown diameter are already calculated using LIDAR data. People can use this information to assess the health of trees in each area and devise strategies for improving overall tree health.

Zhang et al. [21] propose a method to extract individual trees and estimate tree metrics using LIDAR point cloud.

Yun et al. [51] segment individual tree crown using a novel Gaussian filter and energy function minimization-based approach from airborne LiDAR data. The approach enhanced the detection rate of treetops and ITC segmentation relative to the marker-controlled watershed method, especially in complicated intersections of multiple crowns.

Controlling Deforestation

LIDAR data can be utilized to calculate the expected and actual tree output in the forest, as well as the exact difference. This information can also be utilized to explain the cause of the discrepancy, allowing researchers to put in place control measures.

Greenberg et al. [52] estimate changes in insolation under large-scale riparian deforestation using LiDAR data analysis.

Haugerud et al. [53] present some algorithms for virtual deforestation of LIDAR topographic survey data as despike algorithm, block-minimum algorithms etc. and present the advantages and the disadvantages of each.

4   Conclusion

This paper presents an overview of different Lidar technologies, airborne and terrestrial laser scanning. The lidar acquisition is almost entirely done in an automatic way. However, the challenge is staying in the processing tasks of a huge amount of point clouds depicting different object surfaces. We tried to summarize a list of algorithms and methods used commonly in forest areas, in order to monitor, detect, classify and extract information. Many applications are developed during the last years dealing with many issues resolved by Lidar technologies. Recently, many researchers suggested using machine learning algorithms to exploit artificial intelligence.

Constructing such analysis relies on the identification of factors that contribute to the spread of the fires, the land cover and type of vegetation (burnable/non-burnable), climate, topography, and anthropogenic characteristics of the forest. Considering this huge amount of data, we need to consider the big data solutions adapted according to the cloud computing algorithms. Indeed, this kind of study helps decision makers and encourages researchers for further experiments.

Due to the enormous quantity of data that LiDAR provides, it takes a long time to filter, classify, and analyze the data using the standard methods. Utilizing ML may speed up and simplify the process of creating the programs needed to analyze massive amounts of data accurately and efficiently.

The traditional fire monitoring system still has certain limitations, and the practical application of lidar data in forest fire monitoring and prevention is still very lacking specially in morocco. Hence, the next work will focus on the application of machine learning algorithms and insights gained for disaster management using LiDAR data.

Acknowledgements. The authors would like to thank all the collaborators within this work, from the writing manuscript team. El Khalil Cherif would like to mention the financial support by FCT with the LARSyS—FCT project UIDB/50009/2020 and FCT project VOAMAIS (PTDC/EEIAUT/31172/2017, 02/SAICT/2017/31172).

References

1. Fowler, A., Kadatskiy, V., Usa, R.: Accuracy and error assessment of terrestrial, mobile and airborne, p. 10 (2011)
2. McLean, K.A., et al.: Movement patterns of three arboreal primates in a Neotropical moist forest explained by LiDAR-estimated canopy structure. Landscape Ecol. **31**(8), 1849–1862 (2016). https://doi.org/10.1007/s10980-016-0367-9
3. Jeronimo, S.M.A., Kane, V.R., Churchill, D.J., McGaughey, R.J., Franklin, J.F.: Applying LiDAR individual tree detection to management of structurally diverse forest landscapes. J For. **116**(4), 336–346 (2018)
4. Windrim, L., Bryson, M.: Detection, segmentation, and model fitting of individual tree stems from airborne laser scanning of forests using deep learning. Remote Sens. **12**(9), 1469 (2020)
5. Mizoguchi, T., Ishii, A., Nakamura, H., Inoue, T., Takamatsu, H.: Lidar-based individual tree species classification using convolutional neural network, Munich, Germany, p. 103320 (2017)
6. Monnier, F., Vallet, B., Soheilian, B.: Trees detection from laser point clouds acquired in dense urban areas by a mobile mapping system. ISPRS Ann. Photogramm. Remote Sens. Spat. Inf. Sci. **3**, 245–250 (2012)
7. Singh, S.K., Raval, S., Banerjee, B.: A robust approach to identify roof bolts in 3D point cloud data captured from a mobile laser scanner. Int J Min Sci Technol. **31**(2), 303–312 (2021)
8. Li, W., Guo, Q., Jakubowski, M.K., Kelly, M.: A new method for segmenting individual trees from the lidar point cloud. Photogramm. Eng. Remote Sens. **78**(1), 75–84 (2012)
9. Vauhkonen, J., Ene, L., Gupta, S., Heinzel, J., Holmgren, J., Pitkanen, J., et al.: Comparative testing of single-tree detection algorithms under different types of forest. Forestry **85**(1), 27–40 (2012)
10. Dalponte, M., Coomes, D.A.: Tree-centric mapping of forest carbon density from airborne laser scanning and hyperspectral data. Methods Ecol. Evol. **7**(10), 1236–1245 (2016)
11. Liu, J., Shen, J., Zhao, R., Xu, S.: Extraction of individual tree crowns from airborne LiDAR data in human settlements. Math. Comput. Model. **58**(3–4), 524–535 (2013)
12. Corte, A.P.D.: Forest inventory with high-density UAV-Lidar: machine learning approaches for predicting individual tree attributes. Comput. Electron. Agric. **179**, 105815 (2020)

13. Popescu, S.C., Wynne, R.H.: Seeing the Trees in the Forest. Photogramm. Eng. Remote Sens. **70**(5), 589–604 (2004)
14. Mosin, V., Aguilar, R., Platonov, A., Vasiliev, A., Kedrov, A., Ivanov, A.: Remote sensing and machine learning for tree detection and classification in forestry applications. In: Bruzzone, L., Bovolo, F., Benediktsson, J.A. (eds.) Image and Signal Processing for Remote Sensing XXV [Internet]. Strasbourg, France: SPIE 2019, p. 14 (2019). https://doi.org/10.1117/12.253 1820
15. Dong, X., Zhang, Z., Yu, R., Tian, Q., Zhu, X.: Extraction of information about individual trees from high-spatial-resolution UAV-acquired images of an orchard. Remote Sens. **12**(1), 133 (2020)
16. Yang, X., Yang, H., Zhang, F., Fan, X., Ye, Q., Feng, Z.: A random-weighted plane-Gaussian artificial neural network. Neural Comput. Appl. **31**(12), 8681–8692 (2019). https://doi.org/10.1007/s00521-019-04457-6
17. Zhang, W., Qi, J., Wan, P., Wang, H., Xie, D., Wang, X., et al.: An easy-to-use airborne LiDAR data filtering method based on cloth simulation. Remote Sens. **8**(6), 501 (2016)
18. Zhang, K., Shu-Ching Chen, D.W., Shyu, M.L., Yan, J., Zhang, C.: A progressive morphological filter for removing nonground measurements from airborne LIDAR data. IEEE Trans. Geosci. Remote Sens. **41**(4), 872–882 (2003)
19. Hastings, J.H., Ollinger, S.V., Ouimette, A.P., Sanders-DeMott, R., Palace, M.W., Ducey, M.J., et al.: Tree species traits determine the success of LiDAR-based crown mapping in a mixed temperate forest. Remote Sens. **12**(2), 309 (2020)
20. Wang, C., Cao, A., Chen, X., et al.: Individual rubber tree segmentation based on ground-based LiDAR data and faster R-CNN of deep learning. Forests **10**(9), 793 (2019)
21. Zhang, C., Zhou, Y., Qiu, F.: Individual tree segmentation from LiDAR point clouds for urban forest inventory. Remote Sens. **7**(6), 7892–7913 (2015)
22. Zhen, Z., Quackenbush, L., Zhang, L.: Trends in automatic individual tree crown detection and delineation—evolution of LiDAR data. Remote Sens. **8**(4), 333 (2016)
23. Mäyrä, J., Keski-Saari, S., Kivinen, S., Tanhuanpää, T., Hurskainen, P., Kullberg, P., et al.: Tree species classification from airborne hyperspectral and LiDAR data using 3D convolutional neural networks. Remote Sens. Environ. **256**, 112322 (2021)
24. Berk, P., Stajnko, D., Belsak, A., Hocevar, M.: Digital evaluation of leaf area of an individual tree canopy in the apple orchard using the LIDAR measurement system. Comput. Electron. Agric. **169**, 105158 (2020)
25. Vayghan, S.S., Salmani, M., Ghasemkhani, N., Pradhan, B., Alamri, A.: Artificial intelligence techniques in extracting building and tree footprints using aerial imagery and LiDAR data. Geocarto Int. **19**, 1–29 (2020)
26. Jaskierniak, D., Lucieer, A., Kuczera, G., Turner, D., Lane, P.N.J., Benyon, R.G., et al.: Individual tree detection and crown delineation from Unmanned Aircraft System (UAS) LiDAR in structurally complex mixed species eucalypt forests. ISPRS J. Photogramm. Remote Sens. **171**, 171–187 (2021)
27. Zarea, A., Mohammadzadeh, A.: A novel building and tree detection method from LiDAR data and aerial images. IEEE J. Sel. Top Appl. Earth Obs. Remote Sens. **9**(5), 1864–1875 (2016)
28. Michałowska, M., Rapiński, J.: A review of tree species classification based on airborne LiDAR data and applied classifiers. Remote Sens. **13**(3), 353 (2021)
29. Kurdi, F.T., Amakhchan, W., Gharineiat, Z.: Random forest machine learning technique for automatic vegetation detection and modelling in LiDAR data. Int. J. Environ. Sci. Nat. Resour. **28**(2) (2021). https://juniperpublishers.com/ijesnr/IJESNR.MS.ID.556234.php
30. Man, Q., Dong, P., Yang, X., Wu, Q., Han, R.: Automatic extraction of grasses and individual trees in urban areas based on airborne hyperspectral and LiDAR data. Remote Sens. **12**(17), 2725 (2020)

31. Nguyen, H.M., Demir, B., Dalponte, M.: Weighted support vector machines for tree species classification using lidar data. In: IGARSS 2019 - 2019 IEEE International Geoscience and Remote Sensing Symposium. Yokohama, Japan, pp. 6740–6743 (2019)
32. Dalponte, M., Ørka, H.O., Ene, L.T., Gobakken, T., Næsset, E.: Tree crown delineation and tree species classification in boreal forests using hyperspectral and ALS data. Remote Sens Environ. **140**, 306–317 (2014)
33. Dalponte, M., Ene, L.T., Marconcini, M., Gobakken, T., Næsset, E.: Semi-supervised SVM for individual tree crown species classification. ISPRS J. Photogramm. Remote Sens. **110**, 77–87 (2015)
34. Seidel, D., Annighöfer, P., Thielman, A., Seifert, Q.E., Thauer, J.H., Glatthorn, J., et al.: Predicting tree species from 3D laser scanning point clouds using deep learning. Front. Plant Sci. **10**(12), 635440 (2021)
35. Sothe, C., De Almeida, C.M., Schimalski, M.B., La Rosa, L.E.C., Castro, J.D.B., Feitosa, R.Q., et al.: Comparative performance of convolutional neural network, weighted and conventional support vector machine and random forest for classifying tree species using hyperspectral and photogrammetric data. GISci. Remote Sens. **57**(3), 369–394 (2020)
36. Nezami, S., Khoramshahi, E., Nevalainen, O., Pölönen, I., Honkavaara, E.: Tree species classification of drone hyperspectral and rgb imagery with deep learning convolutional neural networks. Remote Sens. **12**, 1070 (2020)
37. Breiman, L.: Random forests. Mach Learn. **45**(1), 5–32 (2001)
38. Rokach, L., Maimon, O.: Decision trees. In: Maimon, O., Rokach, L. (eds.) Data Mining and Knowledge Discovery Handbook. Springer, New York, pp. 165–192 (2005)
39. Džeroski, S., Kobler, A., Gjorgjioski, V.: Using decision trees to predict forest stand height and canopy cover from LANDSAT and LIDAR data, p. 9 (2006)
40. Cortes, C., Vapnik, V.: Support-vector networks. Mach. Learn. **20**(3), 273–297 (1995)
41. Guo, G., Wang, H., Bell, D., Bi, Y., Greer, K.: KNN model-based approach in classification. In: Meersman, R., Tari, Z., Schmidt, D.C. (eds.) OTM 2003. LNCS, vol. 2888, pp. 986–996. Springer, Heidelberg (2003). https://doi.org/10.1007/978-3-540-39964-3_62
42. Alexander, C., Korstjens, A.H., Hill, R.A.: Influence of micro-topography and crown characteristics on tree height estimations in tropical forests based on LiDAR canopy height models. Int. J. Appl. Earth Obs. Geoinf. **65**, 105–113 (2018)
43. Zhang, X., Meng, X., Li, C., Shang, N., Wang, J., Xu, Y., et al.: Micro-topography mapping through terrestrial LiDAR in densely vegetated coastal environments. ISPRS Int. J. Geo-Inf. **10**(10), 665 (2021)
44. Wulder, M.A., Bater, C.W., Coops, N.C., Hilker, T., White, J.C.: The role of LiDAR in sustainable forest management. For. Chron. **84**(6), 807–826 (2008)
45. Richardson, J.J., Moskal, L.M.: Strengths and limitations of assessing forest density and spatial configuration with aerial LiDAR. Remote Sens. Environ. **115**(10), 2640–2651 (2011)
46. Koetz, B., Morsdorf, F., van der Linden, S., Curt, T., Allgöwer, B.: Multi-source land cover classification for forest fire management based on imaging spectrometry and LiDAR data. For. Ecol. Manag. **256**(3), 263–271 (2008)
47. González-Olabarria, J.R., Rodríguez, F., Fernández-Landa, A., Mola-Yudego, B.: Mapping fire risk in the model forest of Urbión (Spain) based on airborne LiDAR measurements. Ecol. Manag. **282**, 149–156 (2012)
48. Šumarstvo, P.: Precision forestry – definition and technologies, p. 10 (2010)
49. Asner, G.P., Mascaro, J., Muller-Landau, H.C., Vieilledent, G., Vaudry, R., Rasamoelina, M., et al.: A universal airborne LiDAR approach for tropical forest carbon mapping. Oecologia **168**(4), 1147–1160 (2012)
50. Mascaro, J., Detto, M., Asner, G.P., Muller-Landau, H.C.: Evaluating uncertainty in mapping forest carbon with airborne LiDAR. Remote Sens. Environ. **115**(12), 3770–3774 (2011)

51. Yun, T., Jiang, K., Li, G., Eichhorn, M.P., Fan, J., Liu, F., et al.: Individual tree crown segmentation from airborne LiDAR data using a novel Gaussian filter and energy function minimization-based approach. Remote Sens. Environ. **256**, 112307 (2021)
52. Greenberg, J.A., Hestir, E.L., Riano, D., Scheer, G.J., Ustin, S.L.: Using LiDAR data analysis to estimate changes in insolation under large-scale riparian deforestation1. JAWRA J. Am. Water Resour. Assoc. **48**(5), 939–948 (2012)
53. Haugerud, R.A., Harding, D.J.: Some algorithms for virtual deforestation (VDF) of LIDAR topographic survey data, p. 7 (2001)

Towards the Automation of Wildfire Monitoring with Aerial Vehicles: The FIREFRONT Project

Ricardo Ribeiro[1(✉)] , Alexandre Bernardino[1] , Gonçalo Cruz[2] ,
Diogo Silva[2] , Luís Felix[2] , João Caetano[2] , Duarte Folgado[3] ,
João Francisco[3], Nuno Simões[4], Carlos Xavier Viegas[5] ,
Domingos Xavier Viegas[5] , Houda Harkat[6] , and Jose Nascimento[7]

[1] Institute for Systems and Robotics, Instituto Superior Técnico, Lisbon, Portugal
{ribeiro,alex}@isr.tecnico.ulisboa.pt
[2] CIAFA, FAP, Sintra, Portugal
{gccruz,dasilva,lffelix,jvcaetano}@academiafa.edu.pt
[3] AeroEspaço Science Center - ACTV, Torres Vedras, Portugal
{duarte.folgado,joao.francisco}@actv.pt
[4] UAVision, Torres-Vedras, Portugal
nuno.simoes@uavision.pt
[5] ADAI, Univ Coimbra, Coimbra, Portugal
{carlos.viegas,xavier.viegas}@uc.pt
[6] UNINOVA-CTS, Monte Caparica, Portugal
houda.harkat@usmba.ac.ma
[7] IT, Lisboa, Portugal
jose.nascimento@isel.pt

Abstract. This paper describes an integrated system for wildfire monitoring with aerial vehicles. The system is composed of an airborne payload compatible with UAVs and manned aircraft and associated communication and software infrastructure. The system is able to detect fire and smoke in the payload thermal and RGB images, georeference their location in ground coordinates using telemetry (GPS, IMU), and forecast the fire front spread. We describe the progress made in the payload system, acquired datasets, fire/smoke segmentation methods, fire georeferencing, and wildfire spread modeling, providing the reader with an overview of the project and related technical publications.

Keywords: Forest Fires · Manned and Unmanned Air Vehicles · Fire and Smoke Detection · Georeferencing · Fire Prediction

1 Introduction

Forest fires are one of the biggest catastrophes of our times and the cause of huge material losses and loss of human lives. In the European Union, more than $3400\,km^2$ of land is burned by forest fires every year. On June 2017, a very large fire in the region of Pedrógão Grande, Portugal, destroyed more than $450\,km^2$ of forest and killed 66 persons [11].

© Springer Nature Switzerland AG 2023
J.-J. Rousseau and B. Kapralos (Eds.): ICPR 2022 Workshops, LNCS 13644, pp. 183–193, 2023.
https://doi.org/10.1007/978-3-031-37742-6_15

Traditional wildfire surveillance systems have limitations in fire fighting scenarios. Satellite systems are not effective during fire fighting activities due to their low temporal and/or spatial resolutions. Ground measurement devices and sensors are vulnerable to damage and have a limited view range.

Observations from manned or unmanned air vehicles can provide the right temporal and spatial scales for the monitoring of a wildfire progression. Unmanned Air Vehicles (UAVs) are able to scan the fire area from a higher and less restrictive point of view, and are much smaller and cheaper to operate. Also, manned aircraft can be an alternative when atmospheric conditions are not suitable to UAVs, such as strong winds.

The FIREFRONT project[1] (www.firefront.pt) is an initiative to help combat wildfires by using automated airborne image analysis. During fire fighting actions, manned or unmanned aerial vehicles carry the payload that observes the scenario and communicates the acquired images and localization metadata to a ground control station. See Fig. 1 for an illustration of the framework. The ground control station processes the acquired information in real-time to detect and geo-localize the fire front. This information is sent to fire simulation models that forecast the fire spread and inform the firefighting coordination team that decides the best strategies for the combat.

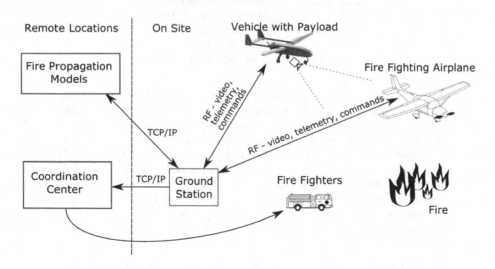

Fig. 1. Overall Architecture of the FIREFRONT project.

In this paper, we describe the progress made to date in the FIREFRONT project. In Sect. 2 we describe the payload system and data capture trials to acquire images in the visible and infrared (IR) spectrum. Those images are sent to a ground station where they are analysed to perform the detection of fire and smoke, described in Sect. 3. Detected targets are then georeferenced to ground

[1] FCT project PCIF/SSI/0096/2017.

coordinates, using methods described in Sect. 4. The georeferenced detections are used to feed dynamic fire models, described in Sect. 5, used to predict the fire front evolution. Finally, in Sect. 6 we conclude the paper, summarizing the main achievements, limitations, and plans for future developments.

In the last decades there has been large research efforts in fire and smoke detection in images [18], target georeferencing in airborne sensors [15], and fire propagation models [1]. However, there are not many fully integrated systems able to automate wildfire monitoring. One exception is the project *CICLOPE* [3] that uses fixed cameras placed on high altitude spots from where they can cover large areas of forest terrain. The surveillance system can perform remote monitoring and automatic fire and smoke detection using background subtraction, feature matching and colour analysis. This system observes the wildfires from a distance, so it is not suitable to accompany the progression of the fire fronts with detail.

2   Payload System and Data Capture

One of the main contributions of FIREFRONT project is the development of a payload specialized for wild fire detection and monitoring. As presented in Fig. 2, this payload is composed of several modules: communications, computation, image sensors and inertial sensors. The sensing module incorporates visible spectrum and long wave infrared (LWIR) cameras. The inertial module produces telemetry with the location and orientation of the payload. The images and telemetry are sent to the computation module, a NVIDIA® Jetson TX2. Despite its small size, this board offers the capability of running neural networks on the graphics processing unit (GPU). The communication module, a pDDL900 radio, allows the transmission of data to the ground and the control of payload settings.

Another relevant feature of the FIREFRONT system is the ground station that communicates with the payload. This unit provides the user interface to operate the gimbal and display the captured images and telemetry. Additionally, more complex fire detection models can be ran in the ground infrastructure. The detection results feed the fire propagation models and are shared with the firefighting entities, via a TCP/IP connection.

Two important objectives of the FIREFRONT payload is to be modular and platform agnostic. This means that, without modifications, it can be installed on a fixed wing or rotary wing aircraft, manned or unmanned (see Fig. 3). Fixed-wing UAVs, which are already monitoring wild fires in Portuguese mainland, are attractive for remote sensing applications, by offering long endurance, thus covering a large area (Fig. 3a). However, using this type of platforms in a development and testing context offers low flexibility on the choice of the take-off and landing location. To make flight operations simpler, we opted to install the payload on a hexacopter (Fig. 3b).

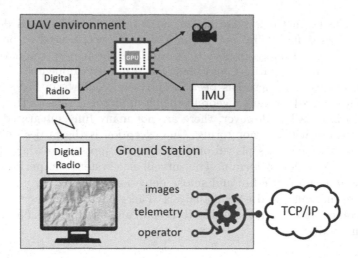

Fig. 2. Architecture of the FIREFRONT payload and ground station, with the communication among the different modules.

Fig. 3. The payload is a modular system that can be installed in several aerial vehicles. We have tested its use in a fixed wing drone (left), in a hexacopter (right) and in a manned vehicle (not shown).

Fig. 4. Two examples of the captured images. A LWIR image on the left and a RGB image on the right.

Despite the already mentioned advantages of unmanned aircraft, using manned vehicles still offers some advantages. In large wildfires over mountain terrains, the weather conditions due to orographic winds and thermal streams might exceed the unmanned vehicle's limitations. Manned aircraft can be used in these circumstances. Furthermore, they are still a viable option to allow rapid prototyping and testing of remote sensing aerial frameworks. The manned aerial vehicle used in FIREFRONT is a Reims Cessna 172 Long Range.

Since the start of the FIREFRONT project, a major concern was data gathering. Therefore, to alleviate some restrictions with airspace integration of UAVs, the first two data gathering campaigns were performed with a manned aircraft near Castanheira de Pêra, Portugal. Since the flight was manned, it allowed the crew to adjust sensors to improve the quality of the gathered images. The third campaign was performed in 2022, using a hexacopter, and allowed the test of the entire payload. The third campaign was over the same area as before, where several patches of terrain were burnt, in a controlled environment, as shown in Fig. 4.

3   Fire and Smoke Segmentation

The segmentation of fire and smoke in the acquired images is required for the accurate detection and geo-localization of the fire front. Current state-of-the-art methods for image segmentation use deep-learning approaches. However, two main challenges have to be tackled: (i) the lack of fire/smoke segmentation datasets, and the large size of the captured images. We have developed and tested several approaches to mitigate these problems. In [10] we have combined fire classification/detection models, and fire segmentation models in a quad-tree search methodology to make the search for fire/smoke regions more efficient and be able to detect small regions. Images are first divided in patches, then analysed with the classifier networks at different resolutions, and finally segmented and assembled at the original resolution to draw the exact boundaries of the fire (Fig. 5). Supervised learning approaches to train the models for classification and segmentation were applied in [5] using a combination of public datasets (Corsican [17]) and data acquired in the context of the project. To tackle the scarcity of labeled data in fire and smoke segmentation datasets, we have researched weakly supervised methods with good results in [7,8].

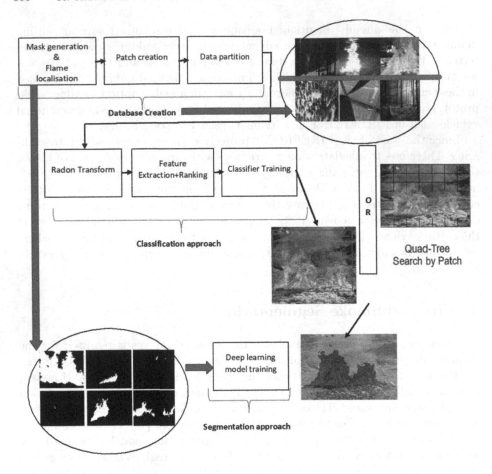

Fig. 5. Fire/smoke detection approach.

4   Georeferencing Methods

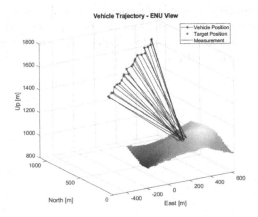

Fig. 6. Optical rays intersection with DEM during a trajectory.

Accurate localization of the positions of the fire front and the smoke origins on the ground coordinates is essential to inform the combat forces and to feed the fire spread forecast models. Telemetry data provides the location of the payload and the camera orientation and is used together with the image detection information to georeference the detections to the ground. Since the terrain is often mountainous, Digital Elevation Maps (DEM) are also used. We have developed both direct and indirect georeferecing methods. In the direct methods, the intersection of the optical ray passing through the detection image pixel is intersected with the DEM (Fig. 6) using an iterative Ray-Tracing algorithm. An Unscented Transform (UT) is used in order to characterize the geolocation uncertainty due to sensor noise. A novel Bearings-Range Extended Kalman Filter [13] is used to further reduce the target uncertainty (Fig. 7). The introduction of the range (distance from camera to target) in the filter model allowed for the improvement of the target precision when comparing to state of the art Bearings-Only methods.

Fig. 7. Target georeference uncertainty. Green cross: actual position; Red cross: estimated position; Red circle: uncertainty. (Color figure online)

Instead of only relying on telemetry data, indirect georeference methods register the image contents to known georeferenced data. For the FIREFRONT project, Structure from motion (sfm) is used to construct a 3D point cloud of the terrain (Fig. 8) from a sequence of images. The point cloud is then registered to the DEM by the Iterative Closest Point (ICP) algorithm which finds the best match between them [14].

3D scene reconstruction

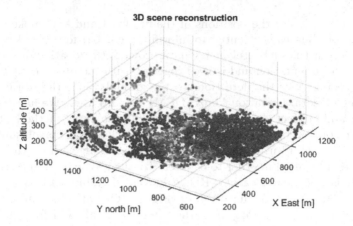

Fig. 8. Sfm reconstructed 3D point cloud.

5 Fire Propagation Models

The data acquired by the airborne sensors is relayed to a decision support tool built specifically for wildfire management. The backbone of the digital platform is the fire simulator Firestation [6], which has been improved and updated with state-of-the-art machine learning algorithms and high performance computing methods. This fire simulator employs a raster approach and uses the surface fire spread model of Rothermel [12] to determine the fire rate of spread, based on the local wind, fire, fuel and topography conditions. While fuel (type, moisture content, density, etc.) and topography (slope) can be retrieved from existing maps, fire and wind conditions, due to their dynamic nature, need to be constantly updated. Wind data (velocity and direction) is automatically fetched in real time from several sources, through developed APIs. These sources aggregate the measurements of the weather stations which are closest to the fire occurrence. These discrete measurements are then used to calculate a wind map, meaning, the wind velocity and direction for each cell in our domain.

Concerning the fire input data, in order to have reliable fire spread predictions to use in operational context, once again several data sources are used and combined, thus maximizing input data accuracy. Currently, data is acquired from official entities as well as different remote sensing platforms, manned and unmanned aircraft, high altitude balloons [16], surveillance camera systems comprising both IR and RGB sensors [2] and even smartphones [4]. All this information is relayed in standardized data formats and integrated in the digital platform, providing real-time information about the fire front location, intensity, and areas burnt. The simulator uses the input data to determine the fire rate of spread, giving information on where the fire front will be located up to 5 h in the future, as shown in Fig. 9. The simulation results are produced in less

Fig. 9. Fire spread simulation results, showing the isochronous lines and areas, which represent the fire front location and progression for a predetermined time interval. The background image represents the elevation map, while the white arrows represent the wind speed and direction.

than 3 min and can be used to aid in the coordination of the fire suppression and management efforts. In an effort to produce increasingly accurate prediction results, and compensate for possible inaccuracies in the input parameters, a methodology based on the use of evolutionary algorithms [9] compares the real fire spread with the predicted one, after a certain time, and determines a calibrated input parameter set. While at the moment only surface fire propagation is considered, we are already working on the implementation of other fire propagation mode models, including spot fires, crown fires, junction fires, fire whirls, eruptive fires, canyon fires and more.

6   Conclusions

We have presented the architecture and components of an automated solution for the monitoring of wild fires. A payload system with RGB and thermal cameras was developed as a modular component to be easily integrated in both manned and unmanned vehicles. We are acquiring extensive datasets of RGB and thermal imagery that will be prepared and released for the academic community. Fire and smoke segmentation algorithms using deep learning approaches were developed to tackle practical problems like the high resolution of the captured images, small fire or smoke spots, and the scarsity of fire and smoke segmentation datasets. Both direct and indirect geo-referecing methods were researched and evaluated in their accuracy and uncertainty in the geo-localization of the fire fronts. Fire propagation models are being developed to make use of this information in real time to provide timely and accurate prediction of the fire scenarios to the combat forces.

Until now, we have only been able to validate the system in simulated fires. Validation in real combat situation requires coordination with the combat forces and is being planned for the near future. The system still has some technical limitations, like the inability to acquire simultaneously RGB and thermal images (video channels are multiplexed). Also, the current thermal sensor is of the non-radiometric type (i.e., does not provide absolute temperature) which puts some challenges on its use.

Future work will further test the system configurations, extend the acquired datasets with more realistic wildfire scenarios, and optimize onboard implementations. We will also continue our research on semi-supervised methods of fire/smoke segmentation to circumvent the time consuming pixel-level labeling required by segmentation methods.

References

1. Bakhshaii, A., Johnson, E.: A review of a new generation of wildfire-atmosphere modeling. Can. J. For. Res. **49**(6), 565–574 (2019). https://doi.org/10.1139/cjfr-2018-0138
2. Barmpoutis, P., Papaioannou, P., Dimitropoulos, K., Grammalidis, N.: A review on early forest fire detection systems using optical remote sensing. Sensors **20**(22), 6442 (2020)
3. Batista, M., Oliveira, B., Chaves, P., Ferreira, J.C., Brandão, T.: Improved real-time wildfire detection using a surveillance system. In: Proceedings of the World Congress on Engineering 2019 WCE 2019, Lecture Notes in Engineering and Computer Science, vol. 0958, July 2019
4. Fonte, C.C., Cardoso, A., Estima, J., Almeida, J.P.D., Patriarca, J.: The FireLoc project: identification, positioning and monitoring forest fires with crowdsourced data. In: FIG e-Working Week 2021, p. 11192 (2021)
5. Harkat, H., Nascimento, J.M.P., Bernardino, A., Thariq Ahmed, H.F.: Assessing the impact of the loss function and encoder architecture for fire aerial images segmentation using Deeplabv3+. Remote Sens. **14**(9) (2022). https://doi.org/10.3390/rs14092023
6. Lopes, A., Cruz, M.G., Viegas, D.: FireStation-an integrated software system for the numerical simulation of fire spread on complex topography. Environ. Modell. Softw. **17**(3), 269–285 (2002)
7. Niknejad, M., Bernardino, A.: Attention on classification for fire segmentation. In: 2021 20th IEEE International Conference on Machine Learning and Applications (ICMLA), pp. 616–621. IEEE (2021)
8. Niknejad, M., Bernardino, A.: Weakly-supervised fire segmentation by visualizing intermediate CNN layers. arXiv preprint arXiv:2111.08401 (2021)
9. Pereira, J., Mendes, J., Júnior, J.S., Viegas, C., Paulo, J.R.: A review of genetic algorithm approaches for wildfire spread prediction calibration. Mathematics **10**(3), 300 (2022)
10. Perrolas, G., Niknejad, M., Ribeiro, R., Bernardino, A.: Scalable fire and smoke segmentation from aerial images using convolutional neural networks and quad-tree search. Sensors **22**(5), 1701 (2022)

11. Ribeiro, L.M., Rodrigues, A., Lucas, D., Viegas, D.X.: The impact on structures of the pedrógão grande fire complex in June 2017 (Portugal). Fire **3**(4) (2020)
12. Rothermel, R.C.: A mathematical model for predicting fire spread in wildland fuels, vol. 115. Intermountain Forest & Range Experiment Station, Forest Service, US Department of Agriculture (1972)
13. Santana, B., Cherif, E.K., Bernardino, A., Ribeiro, R.: Real-time georeferencing of fire front aerial images using iterative ray-tracing and the bearings-range extended Kalman filter. Sensors **22**(3) (2022)
14. Sargento, F.: Georeferencing of fire front aerial images using structure from motion and iterative closest point. Master's thesis, Instituto Superior Técnico, Lisboa, Portugal (2021)
15. Sheng, Y.: Comparative evaluation of iterative and non-iterative methods to ground coordinate determination from single aerial images. Comput. Geosci. **30**(3), 267–279 (2004). https://doi.org/10.1016/j.cageo.2003.11.003
16. Sousa, M.J., Moutinho, A., Almeida, M.: Wildfire detection using transfer learning on augmented datasets. Expert Syst. Appl. **142**, 112975 (2020)
17. Toulouse, T., Rossi, L., Campana, A., Celik, T., Akhlou, M.A.: Computer vision for wild fire research: an evolving image dataset for processing and analysis. Fire Saf. J. **92**, 188–194 (2017). https://doi.org/10.1016/j.firesaf.2017.06.012
18. Yuan, C., Zhang, Y., Liu, Z.: A survey on technologies for automatic forest fire monitoring, detection, and fighting using unmanned aerial vehicles and remote sensing techniques. Can. J. For. Res. **45**(7), 783–792 (2015). https://doi.org/10. 1139/cjfr-2014-0347

Real-Time Georeferencing of Fire Front Aerial Images Using Structure from Motion and Iterative Closest Point

Francisco Sargento, Ricardo Ribeiro⬛, El Khalil Cherif$^{(\boxtimes)}$⬛,
and Alexandre Bernardino⬛

Institute for Systems and Robotics (ISR), Instituto Superior Técnico, 1049-001
Lisbon, Portugal
francisco.sargento@tecnico.ulisboa.pt,
{ribeiro,alex}@isr.tecnico.ulisboa.pt, c.elkhalil@uae.ac.ma

Abstract. This work proposes the use of Structure-from-motion (Sfm) and Iterative Closest Point (ICP) as a forest fire georeferencing algorithm to be used with footage captured by an aerial vehicle. Sfm+ICP uses the real time video captured by an aircraft's camera, as well as its Inertial Measurement Unit (IMU) and Global Positioning System (GPS) measurements, to reconstruct a dense three dimensional (3D) point cloud of the disaster area. The Sfm reconstruction is divided in two steps to improve computational efficiency: a sparse reconstruction step using Speeded-up robust features (SURF) for camera pose estimation, and a dense reconstruction step relying on a Kanade-Lucas-Tomasi (KLT) feature tracker initialized using the minimum eigenvalue algorithm. In addition, the dense 3D reconstruction is registered to a real Digital Elevation Model (DEM) of the surrounding area, and used as the basis of the georeferencing estimates. Indeed, the algorithm was validated with a real forest fire video and compares favourably with a direct georeferencing method evaluated in the same scenario. The results demonstrate that Sfm+ICP can perform accurate 3D reconstructions while also real-time georeferencing several targets in a forest fire scenario. Furthermore, the algorithm is robust to high IMU and GPS errors, making it a far better option than optic-ray-based georeferencing for UAVs with unreliable telemetry.

Keywords: Real-time Georeferencing · Fire Front · UAV

1 Introduction

UAVs are relevant components of modern firefighting operations, which will help us fight the next waves of fire seasons. UAVs possess rapid maneuverability, extended operational range, improved personal safety and cost efficiency, when compared to other remote sensing solutions, making them particularly useful in fire monitoring and detection, given their ability to perform fire search, confirmation and observation [1]. Georeferencing algorithms are a critical aspect of

© Springer Nature Switzerland AG 2023
J.-J. Rousseau and B. Kapralos (Eds.): ICPR 2022 Workshops, LNCS 13644, pp. 194–202, 2023.
https://doi.org/10.1007/978-3-031-37742-6_16

these remote sensing systems: by locating a fire quickly and accurately, fire monitoring systems can rely on quality data to be used by fire propagation models and firefighting authorities, saving lives and property.

The current state of the art medium altitude georeferencing algorithms perform poorly in forest fire scenarios. Even the best direct georeferencing algorithms degrade quickly with altitude and even small telemetry errors, while indirect georeferencing methods are incapable of dealing with the dynamic nature of a forest fire. The unique difficulties brought by fores fires demand a georeferencing algorithm that can deal with low quality telemetry, remote environments with a severe lack of discernible landmarks, and dynamic scenes with fire and smoke continuously altering the landscape.

2 Method

This paper proposes a Sfm+ICP georeferencing method. Here, Sfm is used to reconstruct a 3D model of the fire area using techniques most similar to [2] and [3]. The reconstruction is then aligned to a known DEM of the terrain around the aircraft, similarly to [4] but with a more flexible registration algorithm that matches the down-sampled reconstructed point cloud and the up-sampled DEM. This registration is in essence similar to DEM matching [5], but instead of matching DEMs, the algorithm matches high density point clouds, which is more computationally intensive, but yields better registration results. Using Sfm allows the algorithm to densely reconstruct the operational area and consequently georeference dozens of targets at the same time with no increase in computation time. To allow real-time execution, the reconstruction process was split in two stages: a camera pose estimation stage based on sparse and reliable features, and a dense 3D reconstruction stage based on fast features. Then, ICP makes geolocalization robust to 3D reconstruction errors.

3 Experiments and Results

The dataset used to validate the algorithm is composed of a series of frames taken from a video captured by a fixed wing UAV loitering above a forest fire near Pombal, Portugal at 39.832856N -8.519885E at the 16th of August 2019, and the corresponding telemetry data. The terrain elevation surrounding the fire area can be seen in Fig. 1.

Figures 2 and 3 show two images from the dataset. This dataset was sampled at a rate 2 Hz from 15 s of continuous footage. The footage is unstable, with some sharp camera movements and video cutoffs that degrade the reconstructions quality, hence only a short part of the video was usable.

The two frames in Figs. 2 and 3 show a typical Portuguese forest fire: a small village surrounded by a dense and vast forest and a large column of smoke

Terrain elevation around the UAVision dataset location

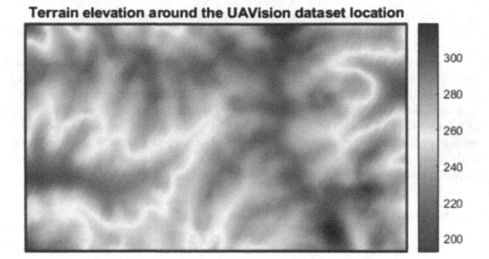

Fig. 1. Digital Elevation Model of the Experimental Site

above it. This column of smoke obscures part of the terrain under and behind it, hindering the ICP registration. At the same time, the forest surrounding the town is dense and has few distinct features, further complicating the reconstruction process. The last hindrance can be seen in Fig. 1: the terrain elevation range is only 100 m and there are no large hills to assist the ICP registration. However, the terrain is still complex and distinct enough to perform Sfm+ICP georeferencing.

Figure 4 shows the reconstructed point cloud and the true camera trajectory. The aircraft performs a coordinated turn heading northwest with a slight bank angle, naturally changing its distance to the fire in all three spatial coordinates. The camera changes its heading and pitch throughout the video in order to track the fire's progress, and inadvertently changes its rotation due to flight induced disturbances.

By comparing this reconstruction with Figs. 2 and 3, one can see that all of the village is reconstructed with a high point density. The forests surrounding it are also well represented, although with a smaller point density. The smoke seen in Figs. 2 and 3 obscures the terrain northeast of the town, and most of the smoke is not considered as a feature, with only a small amount of gray points hovering north of the town at 400 m altitude. These points should be considered outliers, as they serve no purpose for the georeferencing algorithm. The fact that a small amount of them managed to bypass the outlier removal block is not serious, as the rest of the reconstruction is close enough to the real DEM and ICP naturally discard those points.

Fig. 2. Frame 0

Fig. 3. Frame 30

Table 1 provides statistics regarding Sfm's performance with this dataset: 48 ha were reconstructed, with an average of 96 points per hectare. While this density is not as high as one might have predicted, it is more than enough to accurately georeference all the buildings in the village and several targets outside of it, as well as the fire front itself. Only 48 ha were reconstructed, however, this is mostly due to the smoke obscuring the terrain behind it.

3D scene reconstruction

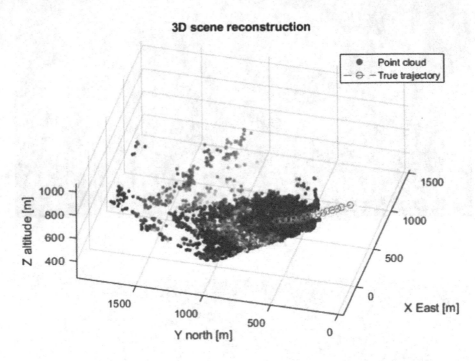

Fig. 4. 3D reconstruction and aircraft trajectory

3.1 Reconstruction Results

Table 1. Reconstruction statistics

Reconstruction area [ha]	Average points per reconstruction	Points per hectare
48	4616	96

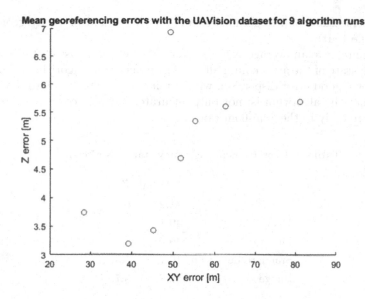

Fig. 5. Georeferencing accuracy after ICP

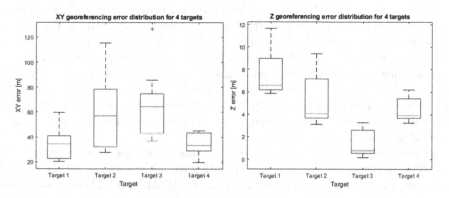

Fig. 6. XY (left) and Z (right) error for each target

3.2   Georeferencing Results

Figure 5 shows the average XY and Z errors for several sequential algorithm runs, and Table 2 presents basic statistics regarding those results. All of these runs were made sequentially and with the same inputs and tuning parameters. However, there is randomness in the output of Sfm due to the algorithm used to estimate the cameras' essential matrices, the M-estimator sample consensus (MSAC).

The georeferencing errors were obtained by comparing the position given by the Sfm+ICP algorithm with the true target position, which was manually determined using Google Earth. The targets chosen were all distinct landmarks, such as intersections and large houses, so that they could be easily georefered using Google Earth.

The results have an average XY georeferencing error of just 49.1m, which is on par with state of the art medium altitude georeferencing algorithms. The XY results show a good error dispersion, with a relatively small standard deviation, meaning that the algorithm is, not only accurate, but also consistent, as most results are roughly in the 30m-60m range.

Table 2. Georeferencing accuracy statistics after ICP

	XY [m]	Z [m]
Max	81.2	6.9
Mean	49.1	4.7
Median	49.4	4.7
Standard deviation	16.7	1.3
Range	52.7	3.7

The average Z error shown in Fig. 5 and Table 2 is just 4.7 m, and its standard deviation is only 1.3 m. These statistics demonstrate that Sfm+ICP can also consistently and accurately determine a target's elevation, even if the camera is flying at 900 m altitude. While this Z accuracy can be a useful property in some instances, a target's elevation can also be estimated by sampling a DEM at the desired coordinates. Notwithstanding, the low Z error also means that the reconstruction is consistent with the terrain, therefore the dense reconstruction is useful for more than just georeferencing, for instance, it can be used as a new dynamic map of the disaster area.

Figure 6 shows the XY and Z error distribution for the four targets georefered. The results show that the four targets have a low average XY error, and that some even have a similar accuracy as the DEM itself. There is one clear outlier reconstruction that had a very poor accuracy, however, apart from it, the algorithm performed consistently and accurately across all targets.

The Z error is also consistently low across the four targets, however, here the outlier's impact is more clear: the mean Z error of each target (represented by red lines) is much lower than the median, for every single target. While the difference between the mean and the median for each target is no more than 2 m, it shows that the vertical error is much more sensible to bad registrations than initially thought.

3.3   State of the Art Comparison

This subsection provides a comparison between the Sfm+ICP method proposed, and a state of the art direct georeferencing method. The direct method chosen was the one proposed by Santana in [6], which relies on optic-ray surface intersection. Unlike Sfm+ICP, this direct method does not perform scene reconstruction, therefore this comparison will only encompass each algorithm's georeferencing capabilities. Santana's method was chosen, since its dataset was accessible and had the same operational requirements as Sfm+ICP. The dataset used in this comparison is a Portuguese Air Force video of a forest fire near Chaves, Vila Real, at 41.631724N–7.465919E. The aircraft flies at 1920 m, roughly 3500 m away from the targets.

Table 3. Comparison between Sfm+ICP and IRT+BR-EKF

Method	RMSE [m]	μ [m]	σ [m]
Sfm+ICP	131.8	116.7	58.8
IRT+BR-EKF	157.1	148.4	24.76

Table 3 shows the position error statistics of Sfm+ICP and IRT+BR-EKF (Santana's method), taken with the same dataset. On the one hand, Sfm+ICP has a slightly lower mean error and RMSE, however, on the other hand, the direct method has a much lower standard deviation. This confirms that Sfm+ICP is more accurate on average, since it can correct the telemetry errors using the reconstruction and the knowledge of the surrounding terrain, while IRT+BR-EKF can only correct part of these errors using a Kalman filter. This contrast in the way direct and indirect methods handle telemetry errors is especially relevant in high altitude scenarios, where a small error in pitch or heading translates into hundreds of metres in georeferencing error. This can also be seen in the standard deviation of both methods: IRT+BR-EKF has a much lower result dispersion, since it uses an Extended Kalman Filter to filter the telemetry errors, thus improving the algorithm's consistency, but not its average accuracy.

4 Conclusion

This paper presented a new and robust Sfm+ICP real-time georeferencing algorithm designed for medium altitude forest fire monitoring. The algorithm showed the ability to perform a reconstruction of the area around the fire. This is the first real-time georeferencing method that can both georeference several targets, and perform a dense reconstruction of a remote environment. The method was designed to work with any medium altitude aircraft with a camera, IMU and GPS. It is also able to match state of the art algorithms accuracy-wise, even when these sensors have a high level of noise. This robustness to IMU and GPS errors is especially relevant since optic-ray-based algorithms are unable to fix these high sensor noises by themselves.

Further studies will focus on making a more precise assessment of the method by testing it in real-time with a predefined flight pattern and an accurate way to assess the algorithm's georeferencing accuracy. Indeed this endeavour would also be invaluable to other georeferencing algorithms, as all of them would be uniformly and accurately evaluated using a carefully desinged benchmark.

Acknowledgment. The authors would like to thank UAVision and the Portuguese Air Force for making available aerial footage of forest environments and firefighting scenarios. This work was partially funded by the FCT projects LARSyS (UID/50009/2020), FIREFRONT (PCIF/SSI/0096/2017) and VOAMAIS (PTDC/EEI-AUT/31172/ 2017,02/SAICT/2017/31172).

References

1. Chi, Y., Youmin, Z., Zhixiang, L.: A survey on technologies for automatic forest fire monitoring, detection, and fighting using unmanned aerial vehicles and remote sensing techniques. Can. J. For. Res. **45**(7), 783–792 (2015). https://doi.org/10.1139/cjfr-2014-0347
2. Michael, A., Hans-Erik, A., Morton, D.C., Bruce, D.C.: Quantifying boreal forest structure and composition using UAV structure from motion. For. J. **9**(3), 1–15 (2018). https://doi.org/10.3390/f9030119
3. Lhuillier, M.: Incremental fusion of structure-from-motion and gps using constrained bundle adjustment. IEEE Trans. Pattern Anal. Mach. Intell. **34**(12), 2489–2495 (2012). https://doi.org/10.1109/TPAMI.2012.157
4. Sim, D.G., Park, R.H.: Localization based on DEM matching using multiple aerial image pairs. IEEE Trans. Image Process. **11**(1), 52–55 (2002). https://doi.org/10.1109/83.977882
5. Ravanbakhsh, M., Fraser, C.S.: A comparative study of DEM registration approaches. J. Spat. Sci. **58**(1), 79–89 (2013). https://doi.org/10.1080/14498596.2012.759091
6. Santana, B., Cherif, E.K., Bernardino, A., Ribeiro, R.: Real-time georeferencing of fire front aerial images using iterative ray-tracing and the bearings-range extended kalman filter. Sensors **22**(3), 1150 (2022). https://doi.org/10.3390/s22031150

Forest Fires Identification Using Self-Supervised Learning

Sara Fernandes, Milad Niknejad[iD], Catarina Barata[✉][iD],
and Alexandre Bernardino[iD]

Institute for Systems and Robotics, Instituto Superior Técnico, Lisbon, Portugal
{sara.a.fernandes,ana.c.fidalgo.barata}@tecnico.ulisboa.pt,
alex@isr.tecnico.ulisboa.pt

Abstract. Forest fires are responsible for the destruction of thousands of hectares and infrastructures every year. To minimize their disastrous effects, it is necessary to i) accomplish and early detection and ii) ensure an efficient monitoring of the event. Automatic methods based on image analysis (acquired from surveillance towers and/or UAVs) are a useful tool to support the firefighting teams. The development of robust methods requires the acquisition of extensively labelled datasets. However, the number of publicly available images with associated annotations is low and generating labels for new data can be time-consuming. On the other hand, there are thousands of images available online, but without annotations. We propose to take advantage of these images, adopting a two phase methodology. First, a deep neural network is trained to solve a pretext task using an unlabelled dataset (self-supervised learning). Afterwards, by combining part of the learned model with a much smaller labelled dataset, the final classifier is achieved. When comparing the models only trained with the smaller dataset, the proposed methodology achieved a better performance, demonstrating the importance of a self-supervised pre-training.

Keywords: fire detection · self-supervised learning · deep learning

1 Introduction

Monitoring the evolution of forest fires is a demanding task that is still manually performed. This delays the decision making and consequent deployment and management of fire fighting teams in the field.

There is a growing interest in the development of automatic systems that leverage the information of aerial cameras (equipped in surveillance towers and/or aerial vehicles), to support the firefighting teams. Some approaches use image processing techniques [2,6,13], achieving high sensitivity. However, they strongly depend on the information provided by the user, such as camera parameters and thresholds. Furthermore, they have a high false positive rate, most likely due to environmental conditions and camera parameter changes. Recent works demonstrated the superiority of supervised deep learning (DL) methodologies [10,15].

© Springer Nature Switzerland AG 2023
J.-J. Rousseau and B. Kapralos (Eds.): ICPR 2022 Workshops, LNCS 13644, pp. 203–212, 2023.
https://doi.org/10.1007/978-3-031-37742-6_17

However, the implementation of supervised DL systems requires extensively annotated datasets. Unfortunately, such datasets are not available and, even though
there are thousands of unlabelled images available online, the process of labelling
all those images can be very expensive and highly time-consuming.

Recently, self-supervised learning (SSL) has emerged as a strategy to train DL
models using a large set of unlabelled data [9]. Such models can later be transferred to supervised tasks, where the corresponding annotated set is expected
to be much smaller. SSL handles unlabelled data through the definition of a
pretext task that a DL model must learn. Thus, synthetic labels are created
for the unlabelled dataset. According to [11], there are three families of pretext
tasks: generative, contrastive, and generative-contrastive. After learning the pretext task, the DL model can be directly applied to the supervised task (transfer
learning) or re-trained (fine-tuning).

The main goal of this work is to explore SSL as a mechanism to improve
the performance of a DL model for fire identification. We demonstrate that pretraining a DL model using a set of unlabelled images collected from online platforms significantly improves its performance. Additionally, we provide a experimental setup that: i) extensively compares three SSL techniques; and ii) evaluates the impact of the volume of unlabelled data and corresponding transformations on the performance gains achieved by SSL. Additionally, this methodology
does not require techniques such as background subtracting and can therefore
be implemented both on aerial vehicles and fixed systems such as surveillance
towers. The remainder of the paper is organizaed as follows. Section 2 describes
our approach and experimental setup. The results and presented in Sect. 3 and
Sect. 4 concludes the paper.

2   Proposed Approach

The proposed approach will be implemented in in surveillance towers and aerial
vehicles equipped with an RGB camera. It is divided into two phases. The first is
a pre-training step, where the weights of a CNN are learned using SSL. Here, the
CNN is trained to solve a pretext task using a dataset of unlabelled images. The
second stage corresponds to training the CNN to perform the target task, in this
case, fire identification. Below we further detail the main elements of each phase.

2.1   Self-supervised Phase

For the self-supervised stage, three pretext tasks were compared: a generative
and two contrastive frameworks.

Generative: Here we implemented an image reconstruction (IR) task. The idea
is to reconstruct the input image, x, using an autoencoder [8]. With this architecture, the image is first compressed using the encoder component to obtain the
representation vector in the latent space. Then, using the decoder, the image is

Table 1. Autoencoder architecture for image reconstruction pretext task.

Component	Layer	Kernel	Activation function	Output
Encoder	Conv	3×3	ReLU	$224 \times 224 \times 32$
	Avg. Pooling	2×2	–	$112 \times 112 \times 32$
	Conv	3×3	ReLU	$112 \times 112 \times 32$
	Avg. Pooling	2×2	–	$56 \times 56 \times 32$
	Conv	3×3	ReLU	$56 \times 56 \times 64$
	Avg. Pooling	2×2	–	$28 \times 28 \times 64$
	Conv	3×3	ReLU	$28 \times 28 \times 64$
	Avg. Pooling	2×2	–	$14 \times 14 \times 64$
	Conv	3×3	Tanh	$14 \times 14 \times 64$
	Avg. Pooling	2×2	–	$7 \times 7 \times 64$
Decoder	Transpose Conv	3×3	ReLU	$14 \times 14 \times 64$
	Transpose Conv	3×3	ReLU	$28 \times 28 \times 64$
	Transpose Conv	3×3	ReLU	$56 \times 56 \times 64$
	Transpose Conv	3×3	ReLU	$112 \times 112 \times 32$
	Transpose Conv	3×3	ReLU	$224 \times 224 \times 32$
	Conv	3×3	ReLU	$224 \times 224 \times 3$

reconstructed from the low dimension representation, resulting in $\hat{x}$. The architecture of the autoencoder is shown in Table 1. To train the network we used the Mean Squared Error (MSE) given by

$$\mathcal{L}_{MSE} = \frac{1}{N} \sum_{i=1}^{N} (x_i - \hat{x}_i)^2, \tag{1}$$

where N is the number of image pixels.

Contrastive: We implemented two contrastive methodologies: simCLR [4] and Barlow Twins [14]. Both methods start by applying similar random geometric and colour transformations to each image in a batch, leading to the creation of two altered copies. Then, all copies go through an encoder to extract a latent representation h. This representation will be later projected into a final embedding z using a multi-layer perceptron (MLP). The main difference between simCLR and Barlow Twins is related with the loss function used to train each of the models. simCLR aims to minimize the normalized temperature-scaled cross-entropy loss (NT-Xent)

$$\mathcal{L}_{NT} == -\log \frac{\exp(\mathrm{sim}(z_i, z_j)/\tau)}{\sum_{k=1}^{2N} \mathbb{1}_{[k \neq i]} \exp(\mathrm{sim}(z_i, z_k)/\tau)}, \tag{2}$$

Table 2. Dataset distribution per model phase.

Name	Phase	# Images	Fire [%]
A	Self-supervised	2000	–
B	Supervised	500	Positive 70
			Negative 30

where N is the batch size, i and j are a positive pair, and τ is the temperature parameter, commonly set to 0.1 [4]. The similarity between two embeddings z_i and z_j is computed using the cosine similarity

$$\text{sim}(z_i, z_j) = \frac{z_i^T z_j}{\|z_i\| \|z_j\|}. \tag{3}$$

Barlow Twins uses the cross-correlation matrix $\mathcal{C}$, computed between the embeddings

$$\mathcal{C}_{ij} \triangleq \frac{\sum_b z_{b,i}^A z_{b,j}^B}{\sqrt{\sum_b (z_{b,i}^A)^2} \sqrt{\sum_b (z_{b,j}^B)^2}}, \tag{4}$$

and tries to approximate it to the identify matrix. The loss function of Barlow Twins comprises two terms

$$\mathcal{L}_{BT} = \sum_i (1 - \mathcal{C}_{ii})^2 + \lambda \sum_i \sum_{j \neq i} \mathcal{C}_{ij}^2, \tag{5}$$

where λ is a positive constant that was set to 0.005, as proposed in the original work [14].

The encoder architecture used in both contrastive methods is the same as for the IR task (recall Table 1). We also adopt a similar architecture for the projector. In the case of simCLR, it is a MLP with two fully connected layers of 64 neurons each and a ReLU activation on the first layer. The model for Barlow Twins has one additional layer, each with 1024 neurons, and a ReLU activation on the first two. These dimensions were empirically found taking into consideration that simCLR works better with small projection heads [4], while Barlow Twins is the opposite [14].

2.2 Supervised Phase

The supervised task consists of identifying fire in an image. In this case, a small dataset with image-level annotations was used. The model comprises the encoder pre-trained using one of the SSL pretext tasks described in Sect. 2.1, and two additional layers: a global average pooling layer and a fully connected with a single neuron and sigmoid activation, since this is a binary classification task. The classification model is trained using the standard binary cross-entropy loss function

Fig. 1. Fire classification probabilities using the baseline (red) and IR (orange) models. (Color figure online)

3 Experimental Results

3.1 Dataset and Evaluation Metrics

We gathered a total of 2,500 images from various sources: 692 images came from the Portuguese Firefighters website [7], while the remaining 1,808 images are from a dataset created by our team[1]. Table 2 shows distribution of unlabelled/labelled images used in each step of our method.

The two sets were further split into training and validation sets as follows. For the SSL phase, we kept 90% of the images from set A for training and 10% to monitor the evolution of the loss functions. Set B was used in the supervised phase to train and evaluate the classifier using 10-fold cross validation. This strategy was adopted due to the reduced number of labelled images. We adopted the following evaluation metrics: average Accuracy and F-1 score.

3.2 Training Environment

All experiments were implemented using the Tensorflow [1] and Keras [5] libraries[2]. We used the Google Colab plataform [3] to run all code. The processor used was the Intel(R) Xeon(R) CPU @ 2.30 GHz, the GPU component was NVIDIA-SMI 470.74 and the maximum RAM available was 12 Gb. Regarding the SSL tasks, the autoencoder was trained for 60 epochs with a batch size of 75, while Barlow Twins was trained for 70 epochs with a batch size of 128. The authors of simCLR report that this method works best for very large batch sizes [4]. However, we did not have access to the same volume of images. To account for this limitation, we trained the model for 200 epochs and a batch size of 128.

---

[1] http://firefront.pt/.

[2] https://github.com/SaraFernandes98/Fire-Detection---Firefront The source code will be made available upon acceptance of the paper.

Table 3. Performance of the baseline and best classifiers for each pretext task.

Task	F1-Score	
	Transfer Learning	Fine - Tuning
Baseline	–	87.0 (±3.6)
IR	70.5 (±4.1)	90.9 (±3.1)
SimCLR	66.9 (±7.2)	86.9 (±5.2)
Barlow Twins	74.1 (±4.7)	88.4 (±5.0)

3.3 Comparison of Pretext Tasks

In this section we assess the impact of each SSL pretext task on the performance of the fire classifier. We start by assessing the quality of the learned features, by comparing the classifier performances using transfer learning (the weights of the encoder are frozen) and fine-tuning (see Table 3). Here, we restrict our analysis to the F1-score, since our labelled dataset is unbalanced, and this metric is more suitable to handle these situations. These results suggest that while the features learned by the three SSL approaches are suitable for the classification task, the model still benefits from a fine-tuning stage. Nevertheless, solely comparing the transfer learning scores, it is possible to see that both Barlow Twins and IR seem to learn more discriminative features than simCLR. In particular, Barlow Twins reaches the best performance. The low performance of simCLR may be justified with the lack of large batch sizes. When fine-tuning is performed, the gap between the three approaches is reduced. Nevertheless, IR and Barlow Twins still achieve better scores.

A comparison with a baseline model is also reported. The baseline model uses the same classifier as described in Sect. 2.2. However, the weights of the encoder are randomly initialized. It is clear from these results that all SSL methods allow improvements over the baseline, when fine-tuning is employed. In particular, the IR task leads to the best overall scores. It is important to stress that all results presented in this section were obtained with the best configurations for each of the approaches.

Figure 1 shows some examples of the performance of the baseline and IR classification models. The latter clearly maintains similarly or even better performances w.r.t the baseline for fire images, while at the same time is able to handle challenging negative cases like sunsets and firefighters (2nd row, 5th and 6th columns).

Table 4. Classifier performances as a function of the number of images used for training during the self-supervised phase.

# Images during self-supervised phase	Average Accuracy [%]	Average F1 Score [%]
Baseline	82.8 (±3.9)	87.0 (±3.6)
IR with 500	84.0 (±4.5)	88.1 (±3.2)
IR with 1,000	84.2 (±2.6)	88.3 (±2.4)
IR with 2,000	84.2 (±4.3)	88.5 (±3.0)

3.4 Size and Variability of the Unlabelled Dataset

This experiment aims to determine whether the number of unlabelled images available to train the SSL tasks influences the quality of the features and, consequently, the performance of the classifier. Since contrastive tasks are already known to require large amounts of data [4, 14], this experiment is only performed for the IR task. Here, we train various encoders using random samplings of $N \in \{500; 1,000; 2,000\}$ images from set A. The results for each model are shown in Table 4. In all of the experiments, the models trained using SSL surpass the baseline one. However, the number of unlabelled images does not seem to have a significant influence on the performance of the model, as the performance scores remain approximately constant. This may be due to: i) the simplicity of the SSL pretext task (IR); and ii) a lack of variability across the unlabelled images.

On a second stage, we explored alternative strategies to augment the size of the unlabelled set. While ideally we would have access to a very large set of images for the SSL phase, this may not be possible. Thus, we explore image transformations as a mechanism to artificially augment the unlabelled set and add variability to the data. In detail, we randomly sampled 1,000 images from the unlabelled set and created a copy of each of them using one or more image transformations (colour and geometric). Additionally, we perform this analysis for two augmentation ratios, 50% and 100%. The results can be seen in Fig. 2. Interestingly, the classifier's behaviour is significantly influenced by the transformations. While geometric transformations seem to have small to none impact on the performance of the classifier, models where colour transformations are employed seem to achieve better performances. Moreover, for the latter the performance also increases with the number of images. This suggests that while it may be important to have a large unlabelled set for SSL, it is also relevant for this dataset to possess diverse characteristics. In the case of fire, this diversity may seem to be related with the colour properties of the images.

Finally, we explored extensive augmentation of the 1,000 images set. The first set comprised 4,000 images: 1,000 original, 1,000 with colour transformation, 1,000 with rotations, and 1,000 with both colour and rotation. The second

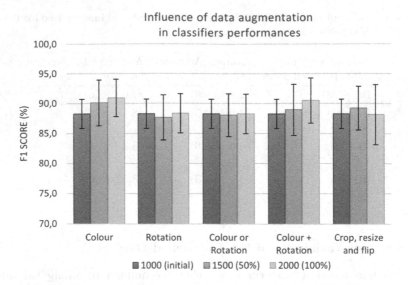

Fig. 2. Performance of pre-trained classifiers as a function of increasing the total number of images by applying transformations to 50% and 100% of the images.

comprised 5,000 images and was a combination of the previous 4,000 with 1,000 that were transformed using crop, resizing, and flip. The results can be seen in Table 5. In all cases, using data augmentation improves the results over using only the original unlabelled images. Interestingly, the best scenario is still the one where we only create a single copy using colour transformations. In fully supervised settings with small datasets, it is documented that extensive data augmentation may not meet the expected goal of increasing model performance [12]. However, it is interesting that the same can be observed in the SSL scenario. A final observation is related with the results for the 5,000 images. This set is the one that most resembles the transformations and variability that can be achieve when performing contrastive tasks (recall Sect. 2.1). Thus, it is noteworthy that it slightly outperforms Barlow Twins (see Table 3), while performing a less complex pretext task (IR).

Table 5. Classifier performances when using 1000, 2000, 4000 and 5000 images with different groups of transformations during self-supervised phase.

Transformation Groups	# Images	Average Accuracy [%]	Average F1 Score [%]
Original	1000	84.2 (±2.6)	88.1 (±3.2)
Colour	2000	87.2 (±4.5)	90.9 (±3.1)
Colour, Rotation and Original	4000	86.0 (±3.9)	89.6 (±3.8)
All	5000	86.6 (±3.9)	90.2 (±3.2)

4   Conclusion

Fire identification in aerial images is a challenging task, hampered by the lack of labelled datasets. Our work overcame this limitation using SSL. The proposed approach can be used to leverage larger sets of unlabelled images, and train a fire classification model using a small set of annotated images.

We compared three SSL methodologies: image reconstruction (generative task), simCLR, and Barlow Twins (both contrastive tasks). Our results showed that image reconstruction was the most suitable task, leading to an improvement of 3.9% for the F-1 score. Nevertheless, the other approaches also led to better performance scores than the standard supervised model, in particular Barlow Twins.

We also investigated the importance of having a large and rich set of unlabelled images. Our experiments demonstrate that, while increasing the amount of unlabelled images does not necessarily lead to an improvement in the subsequent supervised task, adding more variability through simple transformations can be useful.

In the future, we aim to explore other relevant tasks for fire monitoring, namely fire and smoke localization.

Acknowledgements. This work was partially funded by the FCT projects LARSyS (UID/50009/2020), [CEECIND/00326/2017], FIREFRONT (PCIF/SSI/0096/2017), and VOAMAIS (PTDC/EEI-AUT/31172/2017, 02/SAICT/2017/31172).

References

1. Abadi, M., et al.: TensorFlow: large-scale machine learning on heterogeneous systems (2015). https://www.tensorflow.org/, software available from tensorflow.org
2. Batista, M., Oliveira, B., Chaves, P., Ferreira, J.C., Brandao, T.: Improved real-time wildfire detection using a surveillance system. In: IAENG, pp. 520–526 (2019)
3. Bisong, E.: Google Colaboratory, pp. 59–64. Apress, Berkeley (2019)
4. Chen, T., Kornblith, S., Norouzi, M., Hinton, G.: A simple framework for contrastive learning of visual representations. In: International Conference on Machine Learning, pp. 1597–1607. PMLR (2020)
5. Chollet, F., et al.: Keras (2015). https://github.com/fchollet/keras
6. Cruz, H., Eckert, M., Meneses, J., Martínez, J.F.: Efficient forest fire detection index for application in unmanned aerial systems (UASS). Sensors **16**(6), 893 (2016)
7. Bombeiros distrito guarda, A.A.: Bombeiros portugueses. http://www.bombeiros.pt/galeria/index.php. Accessed 29 Sept 2021
8. Hinton, G.E., Salakhutdinov, R.R.: Reducing the dimensionality of data with neural networks. Science **313**(5786), 504–507 (2006)
9. Jing, L., Tian, Y.: Self-supervised visual feature learning with deep neural networks: a survey. IEEE Trans. Pattern Anal. Mach. Intell. **43**, 4037–4058 (2020)
10. Lehr, J., Gerson, C., Ajami, M., Krüger, J.: Development of a fire detection based on the analysis of video data by means of convolutional neural networks. In: Morales, A., Fierrez, J., Sánchez, J.S., Ribeiro, B. (eds.) IbPRIA 2019. LNCS, vol. 11868, pp. 497–507. Springer, Cham (2019). https://doi.org/10.1007/978-3-030-31321-0_43

11. Liu, X., et al.: Self-supervised learning: generative or contrastive. IEEE Trans. Knowl. Data Eng. **35**, 857–876 (2021)
12. Shorten, C., Khoshgoftaar, T.M.: A survey on image data augmentation for deep learning. J. Big Data **6**(1), 1–48 (2019)
13. Yuan, C., Liu, Z., Zhang, Y.: Aerial images-based forest fire detection for firefighting using optical remote sensing techniques and unmanned aerial vehicles. J. Intell. Rob. Syst. **88**(2–4), 635–654 (2017)
14. Zbontar, J., Jing, L., Misra, I., LeCun, Y., Deny, S.: Barlow twins: self-supervised learning via redundancy reduction. In: International Conference on Machine Learning (ICML), pp. 12310–12320. PMLR (2021)
15. Niknejad, M., Bernardino, A.: Attention on classification for fire segmentation. In: 2021 20th IEEE International Conference on Machine Learning and Applications (ICMLA), pp. 616–621. IEEE (2021)

Georeferencing High-Altitude Aerial Imagery

Guilherme de Melo Antunes[1], Alexandra Moutinho[2]($\boxtimes$)(iD),
and José Raul Azinheira[2](iD)

[1] Instituto Superior Técnico, Universidade de Lisboa, Lisbon, Portugal
`guilherme.antunes@tecnico.ulisboa.pt`
[2] IDMEC, Instituto Superior Técnico, Universidade de Lisboa, Lisbon, Portugal
`{alexandra.moutinho,jose.raul.azinheira}@tecnico.ulisboa.pt`

Abstract. High-altitude balloons (HAB), allied with flying-wing unmanned aerial vehicles (UAV), may play an important role in fire monitoring. Due to their aerostatic lift, a HAB may effortlessly carry an UAV to reach higher altitudes and therefore survey a wider area. Considering high-altitude UAV acquired imagery, this work presents a direct georeferencing method based on the geolocation algorithm, that consists on computing the pose of the camera with respect to the ground followed by the mapping between a 3D point and a 2D image pixel using the projection equation. Real-flight data covering diverse situations is used for evaluating the algorithm performance. The complementary filter is used on the measurements from the payload sensors to compute the necessary parameters for the direct georeferencing.

Keywords: Direct georeferencing · Aerial imagery · High altitude balloon

1 Introduction

Acquiring data regarding Earth has been an utterly important task, from the construction of the first maps to the implementation of more complex surveillance algorithms as happens today. The development of Unmanned Aerial Vehicles (UAV's), also known as drones, permitted the observation of the Earth in diverse applications, such as target location [2], agriculture [3] and fire monitoring [8]. The Eye in the Sky project [1] is an example of this latter application. This project proposes a solution composed of a HAB and an UAV equipped with remote sensing tools and telemetry sensors to survey forest fires. The high-altitude aerial view together with the correct location of the fires is key to the firefighters operating on the terrain, which makes georeferencing the aerial images acquired a crucial step.

Georeferencing can be seen as the process of assigning geographical objects to a reference frame in order to locate them on the surface of the Earth. It can be divided into two groups: direct and indirect georeferencing. Indirect georeferencing, also known as aerial triangulation, is a method used for systems that lack telemetry and remote sensing equipment. Its main characteristic is the use

© Springer Nature Switzerland AG 2023
J.-J. Rousseau and B. Kapralos (Eds.): ICPR 2022 Workshops, LNCS 13644, pp. 213–221, 2023.
https://doi.org/10.1007/978-3-031-37742-6_18

of Ground Control Points (points in the ground with well known coordinates), which requires a great manual effort, turning the process ineffective, time consuming and impossible for emergency response applications such as the Eye in the Sky project. Aerial payloads with instruments like the Global Positioning System (GPS) and Inertial Measurement Unit (IMU), allied with calibrated cameras, allow the direct estimation of the necessary parameters. In [2], a method for stationary target ground location based on the geolocation algorithm is proposed. It uses the telemetry data obtained from onboard sensors (GPS and IMU) to obtain the position and external orientation of the camera with respect to a known inertial frame (extrinsic parameters). Other researches present alternative methods for georeferencing images, by combining techniques such as feature matching algorithms and direct georeferencing. This is discussed in [4]. This paper aims to propose and implement a georeferencing algorithm capable of georeferencing high-altitude aerial images, providing information about the location of wildfires to firefighting teams operating on the terrain.

After this introduction, this paper is organized as follows: the theoretical knowledge about the algorithm is provided in Sect. 2. Section 3 defines the main equations and assumptions of the algorithm and proposes a solution for computing the UAV and camera attitude. In Sect. 4, the algorithm is evaluated using experimental data. Finally, Sect. 5 closes with some concluding remarks.

2   Background

Estimating the position and orientation of the camera is crucial for computing the location of the images captured by the UAV camera. The coordinate frames associated with this problem include (see Fig. 1) the *inertial frame* (considered to be the UTM frame), the *vehicle frame* (X_v, Y_v, Z_v) and the *body frame* (X_b, Y_b, Z_b) (with their origins in the center of mass of the drone), the *gimbal frame* (X_g, Y_g, Z_g), and the *camera frame* (located at the center of the camera with the Z axis pointing in the direction of the optical axis).

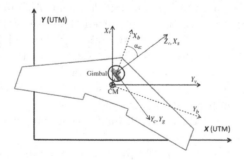

Fig. 1. A scheme showing a top view of the drone, gimbal and camera coordinate frames (adapted from [2]).

The transformation of the vehicle frame with respect to the inertial frame is given by

$$T_v^i = \begin{bmatrix} R_v^i & D_v^i \\ 0 & 1 \end{bmatrix} \tag{1}$$

with the rotation and translation being respectively

$$R_v^i = \begin{bmatrix} 0 & 1 & 0 \\ 1 & 0 & 0 \\ 0 & 0 & -1 \end{bmatrix} \quad \text{and} \quad D_v^i = \begin{bmatrix} X_{UTM} \\ Y_{UTM} \\ Alt \end{bmatrix} \tag{2}$$

where X_{UTM}, Y_{UTM} are the x and y coordinates of the UAV in UTM coordinates and Alt is its altitude. The transformation between the body frame and the vehicle frame only comprises a rotation, since both frames' origins are coincident, and is given by

$$T_b^v = \begin{bmatrix} R_b^v & 0 \\ 0 & 1 \end{bmatrix} \tag{3}$$

with

$$R_b^v = \begin{bmatrix} c_\psi c_\theta & c_\psi s_\theta s_\phi - c_\theta c_\phi & c_\psi s_\theta c_\phi + s_\psi s_\phi \\ s_\psi c_\theta & s_\phi s_\theta s_\phi + c_\psi c_\phi & s_\psi s_\theta c_\phi - c_\psi s_\phi \\ -s_\theta & c_\theta s_\phi & c_\theta c_\phi \end{bmatrix} \tag{4}$$

where ϕ, θ and ψ correspond to roll, pitch and yaw angles respectively, and s and c represent the sine and cosine functions. The transformations of the camera with respect to gimbal and of the gimbal relative to the body can be enclosed in one single matrix with

$$T_c^b = \begin{bmatrix} R_b^c & D_b^c \\ 0 & 1 \end{bmatrix} \tag{5}$$

The final transformation is:

$$T_c^b = \begin{bmatrix} c_\beta & 0 & s_\beta & a_3 s_\beta \\ s_\alpha s_\beta & s_\alpha & -s_\alpha s_\beta & -a_3 c_\beta s_\alpha - a_2 s_\alpha \\ -c_\alpha s_\beta & s_\alpha & c_\alpha c_\beta & a_3 c_\alpha c_\beta + a_2 c_\alpha + d_1 \\ 0 & 0 & 0 & 1 \end{bmatrix} \tag{6}$$

where d_1, a_2 and a_3 depend on the gimbal setup, and α and β are the pan and tilt angles respectively. The detailed demonstration can be seen in [6].

3   Georeferencing Algorithm

3.1   Image Georeferencing

The objective of the proposed algorithm ([2]) is to obtain the ground location (latitude/longitude) of each pixel in the image, p_{obj}^i. For that, it is necessary to obtain the transformation of the camera with respect to the inertial frame, T_c^i. The position of the UAV is given by the payload GPS in the WGS84 model and then converted to UTM. The orientation angles (roll, pitch and yaw) may be obtained from the IMU and the gimbal parameters can be accessed from the flight controller. The mapping of a point in the 3D world to the image pixel frame can be computed from

$$\Lambda q = K_{int} p_{obj}^C \tag{7}$$

where K_{int} is the camera intrinsic parameters matrix, $q = [x_{im} \quad y_{im} \quad 1 \quad 1]^T$ is the 4×1 homogeneous vector of each pixel coordinate in pixel units, Λ is a 4×4 diagonal homogeneous matrix containing the image depth of a specific location and p_{obj}^C is the vector of the 3D coordinates of a feature visible in a specific pixel with respect to the camera frame. Substituting the transformations defined in Sect. 2 one obtains

$$\Lambda q = K_{int} p_{obj}^C = K_{int} T_b^c T_v^b T_i^v p_{obj}^i \tag{8}$$

Solving for p_{obj}^i

$$p_{obj}^i = [T_v^i T_b^v T_c^b] K_{int}^{-1} \Lambda q \tag{9}$$

which allows to georeference every pixel in the image. To apply (9), first the image depth λ needs to be calculated. Considering p_{cc}^C as the vector containing the coordinates of the camera center with respect to the camera frame, it is possible to transpose these coordinates to the inertial frame, using the transformations described before:

$$p_{cc}^i = \begin{bmatrix} X_{cc}^i \\ Y_{cc}^i \\ Z_{cc}^i \\ 1 \end{bmatrix} = [T_v^i T_b^v T_c^b] p_{cc}^C \tag{10}$$

with $p_{cc}^C = (0 \ 0 \ 0 \ 1)^T$. The coordinates of each pixel in the image (in UTM coordinates) with respect to the inertial frame, can be obtained by

$$q_{obj}^i = \begin{bmatrix} X_{obj}^i \\ Y_{obj}^i \\ Z_{obj}^i \\ 1 \end{bmatrix} = [T_v^i T_b^v T_c^b] K_{int}^{-1} q \tag{11}$$

Looking at Fig. 2 and assuming a flat Earth model, it is possible to obtain a relation between the image depth (λ) and the Z components of q_{obj}^i and p_{cc}^i, given by:

$$\lambda = \frac{Z_{cc}^i}{(Z_{cc}^i - Z_{obj}^i)} \tag{12}$$

Having the image depth of each pixel, one can finally compute their coordinates with respect to the inertial frame. To obtain the latitude/longitude it is necessary to convert the UTM coordinates to the WGS84 system.

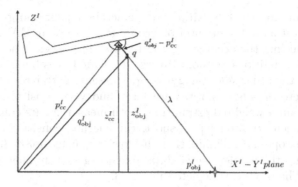

Fig. 2. Image depth estimation using flat Earth model (adapted from [2]).

3.2 Attitude Estimation

For implementing the georeferencing algorithm it is crucial that the orientation of the camera in each frame is correctly computed. This can be done ideally by using a 9DOF IMU, composed of 3DOF accelerometers, gyroscopes and magnetometers. However, many experimental setups, like the one described in Sect. 4, may not include magnetometers, which causes the yaw angle to be not correctly observable.

The accelerometer is a device that can measure both static and dynamic acceleration (usually in m/s^2) and can be used to compute roll and pitch angles using the following equations

$$\theta^a = \arctan(-\frac{\hat{a}_x}{\sqrt{\hat{a}_y^2 + \hat{a}_z^2}}) \tag{13}$$

$$\phi^a = \arctan(\frac{\hat{a}_y}{\hat{a}_z}) \tag{14}$$

where $\hat{a}_x, \hat{a}_y$ and $\hat{a}_z$ are the x, y and z calibrated components of the measured acceleration. Another sensor that composes the IMU is called gyroscope and measures the angular velocity about a particular axis, commonly in deg/s or rad/s. It can be used to compute the roll, pitch and yaw angles by simply integrating the angular velocities about each sensing axis

$$\phi^g_{n+1} = \phi^g_n + \hat{g}_x \Delta t \tag{15}$$

$$\theta^g_{n+1} = \theta^g_n + \hat{g}_y \Delta t \tag{16}$$

$$\psi^g_{n+1} = \psi^g_n + \hat{g}_y \Delta t \tag{17}$$

with $\hat{g}_x$, $\hat{g}_y$, and $\hat{g}_z$ being the calibrated gyroscope data, the subscript n the current value of the angle and Δt the time interval between the present value (n) and next angle estimation ($n + 1$). Although the accelerometer and gyroscope alone can be used to estimate the orientation (roll and pitch) of an UAV, they present limitations regarding the accuracy of the results. The accelerometer works better under static conditions, without diverse dynamic forces being applied at the same time. On the other side, the gyroscope presents better results in dynamic conditions, where the angular rates are large and vary consistently over time. In order to obtain a weighted estimation, both measurements can be combined using a complementary filter [7]. In short, this method consists of high-pass filtering the gyroscope data, eliminating the low frequency noises (e.g. bias) and low-pass filtering the accelerometer data, excluding high frequency noises (e.g. sensor noise). The process is depicted in Fig. 3.

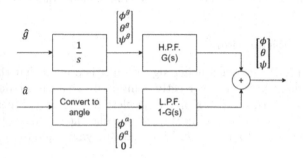

Fig. 3. Complemetary Filter Scheme.

3.3   Georeferencing Application

In order to allow the implementation of the proposed solution in a simple and interactive form, an application was elaborated in [6]. Figure 4 illustrates the main window, where the images can be georeferenced. The input data consists on the image to be georeferenced, the camera intrinsic parameters (introduced after selecting the appropriate camera model), UAV flying data consisting of position and orientation and finally gimbal orientation parameters, as described in Sect. 2.

4   Experimental Results

To test the presented solution for georeferencing high altitude acquired images, a field test was done. The setup consisted of a camera (GoPro Hero 7 Black) attached to a high altitude flying balloon, using a small rope. This camera has integrated 3DOF accelerometers and gyroscopes, and a GPS, that provide data regarding acceleration, angular velocity and position, which are saved together as metadata in the video file. The settings used for the video were a resolution of

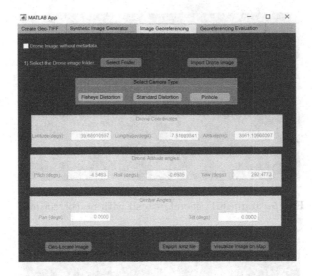

Fig. 4. Georeferencing Application - Tab to georeference the UAV acquired image.

Table 1. Georeferencing evaluation results.

Image Name	RMSE X(m)	RMSE Y(m)	MAE X (m)	MAE Y (m)	Max X (m)	Max Y (m)	Min X(m)	Min Y(m)
frame901	1111.40	246.42	988.54	239.88	1452.90	326.84	63.26	154.60
frame936	1955.70	526.65	1916.20	509.19	2276.40	617.69	1394.60	245.92

Table 2. Georeferencing evaluation results after yaw and position correction.

Image Name	RMSE X(m)	RMSE Y(m)	MAE X (m)	MAE Y (m)	Max X (m)	Max Y (m)	Min X(m)	Min Y(m)
frame901	49.11	66.20	48.10	57.40	62.51	122.86	39.38	35.03
frame936	155.38	84.73	151.54	84.66	181.88	90.86	92.83	81.73

1080p (height of 1080 and width of 1920 pixels), at 50 fps (frames per second), with a linear FOV (field of view). Since it was not possible to have a stabilization system (gimbal) for the camera, it will be assumed that there is no gimbal and the camera frame has the same origin as the body and vehicle frames. Therefore, T_c^b is given by the identity matrix.

The georeferencing process was evaluated by applying SIFT [5] to UAV images georeferenced by this algorithm and Google Earth georeferenced images (ground-truth) to identify and match similar features. Distinct metrics were then computed based on the latitude/longitude coordinates of the matching features.

Table 1 shows the baseline results obtained for two of the acquired images at an altitude around 2000 m (Fig. 5). There is a clear error in the georeferencing process as can be seen from the computed metrics. For the X direction, the maximum and minimum distanced between points were 1452.90 and 63.26 m for "frame910" and 2276.40 and 1394.60 for "frame936". For the Y direction, the maximum and minimum values are closer, but still present a large distance.

Fig. 5. "frame901" georeferenced with no corrections.

Fig. 6. "frame901" georeferenced after yaw and position correction overlay on Google Earth.

Comparing the mean absolute error (MAE) in X with MAE in Y for both images, the results suggest a higher displacement in the horizontal direction, which can be related to the fact that the correct yaw angle estimation was not possible, due to the absence of a device to complement the measurements from the gyroscope. The miscalculation of this angle has a negative impact on the overall georeferencing process, since the previous is highly dependent on the accurate estimation of the camera orientation with respect to the ground.

Table 2 illustrates the same metrics after correcting the yaw and possible latitude/longitude errors (Fig. 6). The results show a great enhancement in the computed metrics after the applied adjustments. For an altitude around 2000 m, the algorithm was able to obtain a MAE of 48.10 m for the horizontal X direction and 57.40 for the vertical Y one. The clear enhancements after the compensation of the yaw and position suggest that the algorithm is capable of obtaining satisfying georeferencing results at high altitudes with simple matrix calculations and low computation time.

5   Conclusions

This paper presented a georeferencing algorithm capable of locating high-altitude acquired images on the surface of the Earth. First, the base of the algorithm was explained, by resuming the different transformations between UAV, camera and gimbal frames. Then, the main assumptions and equations of the algorithm were depicted. A method for computing the attitude of the drone with respect to the ground was also proposed, by implementing the complementary filter. The baseline results obtained using experimental data were not very accurate, due to the experimental setups conditions, which did not allow to correctly estimate the yaw angle, leading to large errors in the georeferencing process. Nevertheless, after correcting these and possible position errors for a set of 6 distinct images, the obtained metrics displayed large enhancements, with the average values for the RMSE being 142.61 and 98.03 m and for MAE 124.3 and 89.58 m, for the X and Y directions, respectively.

Acknowledgements. This work was supported by FCT - Fundação para a Ciência e a Tecnologia, I.P., through IDMEC, under project Eye in the Sky, PCIF/SSI/0103/2018, and under LAETA, project UIDB/50022/2020.

References

1. Eye in the sky project. https://adai.pt/eyeinthesky/
2. Barber, D.B., Redding, J.D., McLain, T.W., Beard, R.W., Taylor, C.N.: Vision-based target geo-location using a fixed-wing miniature air vehicle. J. Intell. Robot. Syst.: Theory Appli. **47**, 361–382 (12 2006). https://doi.org/10.1007/s10846-006-9088-7
3. Gómez-Candón, D., Castro, A.I.D., López-Granados, F.: Assessing the accuracy of mosaics from unmanned aerial vehicle (UAV) imagery for precision agriculture purposes in wheat. Precision Agricult. **15**, 44–56 (2 2014). https://doi.org/10.1007/s11119-013-9335-4
4. Hamidi, M., Samadzadegan, F.: Precise 3d geo-location of UAV images using geo-referenced data. Int. Archives Photogramm., Remote Sens. Spatial Inform. Sci. - ISPRS Archives **40**, 269–275 (2015). https://doi.org/10.5194/isprsarchives-XL-1-W5-269-2015
5. Lowe, D.G.: Distinctive image features from scale-invariant keypoints. Int. J. Comput. Vision **60**(2), 91–110 (2004)
6. de Melo Antunes, G.: Georeferencing Aerial Imagery. Master's thesis, Instituto Superior Técnico, Universidade de Lisboa (2022)
7. Narkhede, P., Poddar, S., Walambe, R., Ghinea, G., Kotecha, K.: Cascaded complementary filter architecture for sensor fusion in attitude estimation. Sensors **21**, 1–18 (3 2021). https://doi.org/10.3390/s21061937
8. de Sousa, J.V.R., Gamboa, P.V.: Aerial forest fire detection and monitoring using a small uav. KnE Engineering, pp. 242–256 (2020)

Wildfires Detection and Segmentation Using Deep CNNs and Vision Transformers

Rafik Ghali[ID] and Moulay A. Akhloufi[✉][ID]

Perception, Robotics, and Intelligent Machines Research Group (PRIME),
Department of Computer Science, Université de Moncton, Moncton, NB, Canada
{rafik.ghali,moulay.akhloufi}@umoncton.ca

Abstract. Wildfires are an important natural risk which causes enormous damage to the environment. Many researchers are working to improve firefighting using AI. Various vision-based fire detection methods have been proposed to detect fire. However, these techniques are still limited when it comes to identifying the precise fire's shape as well as small fire areas. For such, we propose deep wildland fire detection and segmentation models based on deep Convolutional Neural Networks (CNNs) and vision Transformers. A novel deep ensemble learning method, which combines EfficientNet-B5 and DenseNet-201 models, is proposed to identify and classify wildfires on aerial images. Vision Transformers (TransUNet, MedT, and TransFire) are adopted in segmenting fire pixels and in detecting the precise shape of the fire areas using aerial and ground images. The achieved results are promising and show the potential of using deep CNNs and vision Transformers for forest fire detection and segmentation.

Keywords: Forest fires detection · Wildfire segmentation · CNN · Vision Transformer · Deep Learning · UAV images

1 Introduction

Forest fires cause important human and financial losses, the death of animals, and the destruction of wood and houses. Fires affect 350 million to 450 million hectares every year [7]. In Canada, 2021 has been one of busiest fire seasons with 6,224 causing the destruction of 4.18 million hectares [28].

In order to reduce these alarming numbers, various fire detection systems have been developed to identify forest fires. The first existing fire detection systems employed numerous fire sensing technologies such as gas, flame, heat, and smoke detectors. While these systems managed to detect fire, they faced some limitations related to coverage areas and slow time response [9]. Fortunately, the aforementioned problems were partially solved by using vision sensors that detect visual features of fires such as shape, color, and dynamic texture of flame. In this context, a plethora of models were proposed to segment forest fires. Color space methods like YCbCr [27] and RGB [6], are the first methods used

© Springer Nature Switzerland AG 2023
J.-J. Rousseau and B. Kapralos (Eds.): ICPR 2022 Workshops, LNCS 13644, pp. 222–232, 2023.
https://doi.org/10.1007/978-3-031-37742-6_19

to detect visual fire features. However, they suffer from some limitations such as false alarms.

Recently, fire detection and segmentation showed impressive progress thanks to the use of deep learning (DL) techniques, especially Convolutional Neural Networks (CNNs) [10,13]. DL-based fire detection methods are successfully employed to detect the color of wildfire and its geometrical features such as angle, shape, height, and width using ground an aerial images [11,12,17]. Their excellent results help to develop metrology tools, which can be used in modeling fire and providing the necessary inputs to the mathematical propagation models. Nonetheless, there are still challenging cases such as small object size and background complexity.

To overcome these problems, we present in this paper a novel deep ensemble learning method to detect and classify wildfire using aerial images. This method employs DenseNet-201 [23] and EfficientNet-B5 [14] models as a backbone for extracting forest fire features. In addition, vision Transformers determine the global dependencies between input patches using an attention mechanism. They showed excellent potential in various image processing tasks such as image super-resolution [31], medical imaging [24], and object detection [4]. For such, two vision-based Transformers that are TransUNet [5] and MedT [26] are adopt to detect and segment wildfire pixels using ground images in order to exploit their strengths. TransUNet [5] and TransFire are also employed in segmenting forest fire pixels and detecting the precise shape of fire on aerial images.

2   Related Works

Numerous contributions to fire detection and segmentation using DL on ground and aerial images are available in the literature. Lee et al. [15] employed five deep CNNs that are AlexNet, GoogLeNet, VGG13, a modified GoogLeNet, and a modified VGG13 to detect forest fires in aerial images. GoogLeNet and the modified GoogLeNet obtained a high performance. Shamsoshoara et al. [20] proposed a novel method based on the Xception model for wildfire classification. Using FLAME dataset [19] and data augmentation techniques (horizontal flip and rotation), this method achieved an accuracy of 76.23%. Srinivas et al. [21] proposed a novel method, which integrates CNN and Fog computing to detect forest fire using aerial images at an early stage. The proposed CNN consists of six convolutional layers followed by the ReLU activation function and max-pooling layers, three fully connected layers, and a sigmoid classifier that determines the output as Fire or Non-Fire. This method showed a high accuracy of 95.07% and faster response time. Wu et al. [29] used a pretrained MobileNetv2, which is an extended version of MobileNetv1 model to detect both smoke and fire on aerial monitoring systems. An accuracy of 99.3% was obtained outperforming an AlexNet model.

DL methods were also used to efficiently detect fire pixels in the whole image and determine the precise shape of the fire areas using ground and aerial images. Akhloufi et al. [1] proposed a deep convolutional neural network for wildland fire segmentation based on U-Net model. An accuracy of 97% and an F1-score of 91% are obtained using CorsicanFire dataset [25]. Shamsoshoara et al. [20] presented a method based on U-Net for wildfire segmentation on aerial images.

Using FLAME dataset and a dropout strategy, U-Net achieved an F1-score of 87.75%. Bochkov et al. [3] proposed a novel model, wUUNet (wide-UUNet concatenative), to detect fire regions and flame areas on ground images. Two UNet networks are employed. The first U-Net identifies fire areas as binary segmentation. The second method detects fire colors such as orange, red, yellow as multiclass segmentation using input images and the output of the first U-Net. this model outperformed UNet network by +2% and +3% in the case of binary segmentation and multiclass segmentation, respectively. In [16], DeepLabV3 model is employed in localizing and segmenting fire areas. This model achieved a high fire segmentation rate using 1775 fire images and a large number of non-fire images from SUN397 database [30]. Barmpoutis et al. [2] proposed a 360-degree remote sensing system base on two DeepLab V3+ models to segment both fire and smoke. Using 150 360-degree images of urban and forest areas, experimental results achieved an F1-score of 94.6% surpassing recent works such as DeepLabV3+. These results proved the efficiency of the proposed system in segmenting fire/smoke using aerial images and reducing the false-positive rate [2]. Frizzi et al. [8] also developed a method based on VGG16 to segment both smoke and fire. An accuracy of 93.4% and segmentation time per image of 21.1 s are reached outperforming previous published models and proving the efficiency of this method in detecting and classifying fire/smoke pixels on aerial images.

3   Materials and Methods

In this section, we present the proposed model for forest fire classification on aerial images and the proposed methods for wildfire segmentation using aerial and ground images. We also describe the training dataset and evaluation metrics used in this work.

3.1   Proposed Method for Fire Classification

To detect and classify fire, we propose a novel method based on deep ensemble learning (EL) using EfficientNet-B5 and DenseNet-201 models [12]. EfficientNet-B5 [23] proved its ability in reducing the parameters and Floating-Point Operations Per Second using an effective scaling method that employs a compound coefficient to uniformly scale model resolution, depth, and width. It showed excellent accuracy outperforming Xception, PNASNet, ResNeXt-101, and InceptionV3, V4. DenseNet [14] connects each layer to all preceding layers to create diversified feature maps. Using extracted features of all complexity levels, DenseNet shows interesting results in numerous competitive object recognition tasks such as SVHN (Street View House Numbers), ImageNet, CIFAR-10, and CIFAR-100 [14].

First, the proposed method is fed with RGB aerial images. EfficientNet-B5 and DenseNet-201 [14] models were employed as a backbone to extract two feature maps. Next, the feature maps of the two models are concatenated. The concatenated map was then fed to an average pooling layer. Then, a dropout of

0.2 was employed to avoid overfitting. Finally, a Sigmoid function was applied to classify the input image into Fire or Non-Fire classes.

3.2 Proposed Method for Fire Segmentation Using Ground Images

To segment fire pixels, we adopted two vision Transformers that are TransUNet and MedT (Medical Transformer) [11].

TransUNet [5] is a hybrid CNN-Transformer model. It adopted a high resolution of local features extracted by a CNN and the global information encoded by Transformers. This model employs a Hybrid CNN-Transformer as an encoder. First, CNN model, ResNet-50, extracts the features. Then, patch embedding is employed to encode the positional information. The Transformer encoder contains twelve Transformer layers, which include a Multihead Self-Attention (MSA), a normalization layer, and a Multi-Layer Perceptron (MLP). The skip-connections from the encoder and the output of the Transformer are feeding the decoder, which consists of multiple 3*3 convolutional layers, ReLU activations, and upsamling operator.

MedT [26] was proposed in order to segment medical images with no requirement of a large learning data. It is based on two concepts that are gated position-sensitive axial attention and LoGo (Local-Global) training methodology. Gated position-sensitive axial attention was employed to determine long-range interactions between the input features. LoGo training methodology used two branches (global branch and local branch) to extract feature maps. The first branch contains two encoders and two decoders. The second includes five encoders and five decoders. The input of these branches is extracted with a convolutional block, which contains convolutional layers, ReLU activation functions, and batch normalization.

3.3 Proposed Method for Fire Segmentation Using Aerial Images

We employed two vision Transformers that are TransUNet and TransFire to segment wildfire on aerial images [12].

TransFire is a modified MedT architecture. It was developed to overcome the memory problem of MedT and to prevent overfitting. It includes one encoder and one decoder in the global branch. It also employs a dropout strategy in the local global branch (after the fourth first encoders and the last decoder), in the global branch (after the decoder), and in each input of both of these branches.

3.4 Dataset

Two datasets that are CorsicanFire [25] and FLAME dataset are used in this work. CorsicanFire dataset [25] is used to train and evaluate our proposed segmentation methods on ground images. It consists of 1135 RGB images collected in various areas with their corresponding binary mask.

FLAME (Fire Luminosity Airborne-based Machine learning Evaluation) dataset [19] is also used to train and test the proposed methods for wildfire detection and segmentation on aerial images. It contains aerial images and raw heat-map footage captured by visible spectrum and thermal cameras onboard multiple drones with different zoom and viewpoints. It consists of 48,010 RGB images, which are split into 30,155 Fire images and 17,855 Non-Fire images. In addition, it includes 2003 RGB images and their corresponding binary mask.

3.5 Evaluation Metrics

We evaluate our proposed method using the two following metrics:

- *Accuracy* is the proportion of the correct predictions over the total predictions' number, as shown in Eq. (1).

$$Accuracy = \frac{TP + TN}{TP + FP + TN + FN} \tag{1}$$

  where TN is the true negative rate, TP is the true positive rate, FP is the false positive rate, and FN is the false negative rate.
- *F1-score* combines precision and recall metrics to determine the model's performance, as given by Eq. (2).

$$F1 - score = \frac{2 * Precision * Recall}{Precision + Recall} \tag{2}$$

$$Precision = \frac{TP}{TP + FP} \tag{3}$$

$$Recall = \frac{TP}{TP + FN} \tag{4}$$

4   Results and Discussion

We developed the models using Pytorch [18] on a machine with NVIDIA Geforce RTX 2080Ti GPU. For all experiments, we used the Dice loss function [22], which maximizes the overlap between the predicted mask and the input mask. For wildfire classification, learning data were divided into three sets: train (31,515 images), validation (7,878 images), and test (8,617 images). For wildfire segmentation, data was split as presented in Table 1.

4.1   Wildfire Detection Results

Table 2 presents a comparative analysis of our proposed method and deep CNN methods using aerial images. We can see that our proposed EL method achieved the best accuracy with 85.12% and the best F1-score with 84.77%, thanks to diversified features extracted by EfficientNet-B5 and DenseNet-201 models. It outperformed recent models (MobileNetV3-Large, DensNet-169, EfficientNet-B5, Xception, and InceptionV3). It proved its accurate efficiency in detecting wildfires on aerial images overcoming challenging problems such as uneven object intensity and background complexity.

Table 1. Data subsets.

Image subsets	CorsicanFire dataset	FLAME dataset
Training	815	1401
Validation	111	201
Testing	209	401

Table 2. Performance evaluation of wildfire detection models on aerial images.

Models	Accuracy (%)	F1-score (%)
Xception	78.41	78.12
Xception [20]	76.23	—
EfficientNet-B5	75.82	73.90
InceptionV3	80.88	79.53
DenseNet169	80.62	79.40
MobileNetV3-Large	65.10	60.91
Proposed ensemble model (EL)	**85.12**	**84.77**

4.2 Wildfire Segmentation Results

In this section, we discuss the proposed fire segmentation methods using aerial and ground images.

Table 3 reports a comparative analysis of TransUNet, MedT, U-Net, and EfficientSeg using CorsicanFire dataset. We can see that vision Transformers (TransUNet and MedT) achieved the best results compared to deep CNN models (EfficientSeg and U-Net). In addition, TransUNet segments very well fire pixels even better than manual annotation, as shown in Fig. 1. It correctly distinguishes between fire and background under different conditions such as the presence of smoke, different weather conditions proving their potential in detecting small fire areas and identifying the precise shape of wildfire.

Table 4 presents the results of wildfire segmentation models using FLAME dataset. We can see that TransUNet and TransFire achieved higher results, outperforming EfficientSeg and U-Net, thanks to their ability to extract finer details of the input images and to determine long-range interactions within features. In addition, TransUNet and TransFire proved their excellent capacity in segmenting wildfire pixels on aerial images, detecting and localizing the small fire areas, as shown in Fig. 2.

Fig. 1. Results of TransUNet using ground images. From top to bottom: RGB images, their corresponding mask, and the predicted images by TransUNet.

Table 3. Performance evaluation of wildfire segmentation models using ground images.

Models	Accuracy (%)	F1-score (%)
TransUNet	**98.5**	**97.5**
MedT	98.2	96.0
EfficientSeg	96.0	95.0
U-Net	97.0	94.0

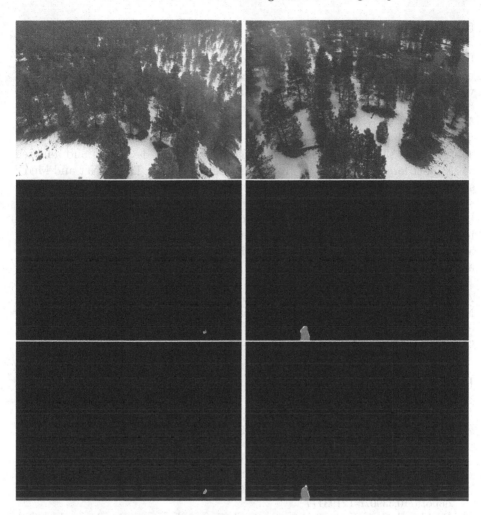

Fig. 2. Results of TransUNet and TransFire using aerial images. From top to bottom: RGB images, the predicted images by TransUNet, and the predicted images by Trans-Fire. Orange depicts true positives, yellow shows false positives, and red represents false negatives. (Color figure online)

Table 4. Performance evaluation of wildfire segmentation models using aerial images.

Models	Accuracy (%)	F1-score (%)
TransUNet	**99.90**	**99.90**
TransFire	**99.83**	**99.82**
EfficientSeg	99.66	99.63
U-Net	99.00	99.00

5   Conclusion

In this paper, we present deep wildfire models for forest fire detection and segmentation on aerial and ground images. A novel ensemble learning method, which combines DenseNet-201 and EfficientNet-B5 models, was proposed to detect wildfires. The proposed ensemble learning method showed a higher performance (F1-score of 84.77%) outperforming recent published models and confirming its ability to detect wildfires using aerial images. Furthermore, vision Transformers (TransUNet, MedT, and TransFire) were developed and adapted to segment forest fire pixels on ground and aerial images. TransUNet and MedT showed an excellent performance achieving an F1-score of 97.5% and 96.0% in segmenting wildfire pixels and detecting fire areas using ground images respectively. TransFire and TransUNet also proved their excellent potential by obtaining respectively an F1-score of 99.82% and 99.9% in segmenting forest fires using aerial images and in overcoming challenging cases such as background complexity and small wildfire areas.

Acknowledgment. This research was enabled in part by support provided by the Natural Sciences and Engineering Research Council of Canada (NSERC) funding reference number RGPIN-2018-06233 and by the support of WestGrid (www.westgrid. ca/) and Compute Canada (www.computecanada.ca).

References

1. Akhloufi, M.A., Tokime, R.B., Elassady, H.: Wildland fires detection and segmentation using deep learning. In: Pattern Recognition And Tracking xxix. vol. 10649, p. 106490B. Proc. SPIE (2018)
2. Barmpoutis, P., Stathaki, T., Dimitropoulos, K., Grammalidis, N.: Early fire detection based on aerial 360-degree sensors, deep convolution neural networks and exploitation of fire dynamic textures. Remote Sens. **12**(19), 3177 (2020). https:// doi.org/10.3390/rs12193177
3. Bochkov, V.S., Kataeva, L.Y.: wuunet: advanced fully convolutional neural network for multiclass fire segmentation. Symmetry **13**(1), 98 (2021). https://doi.org/10. 3390/sym13010098
4. Carion, N., Massa, F., Synnaeve, G., Usunier, N., Kirillov, A., Zagoruyko, S.: End-to-end object detection with transformers. In: Computer Vision - ECCV, pp. 213–229 (2020)
5. Chen, J., et al.: Transunet: Transformers make strong encoders for medical image segmentation. CoRR abs/2102.04306 (2021). https://arxiv.org/abs/2102.04306
6. Chen, T.H., Wu, P.H., Chiou, Y.C.: An early fire-detection method based on image processing. In: International Conference on Image Processing, 2004. ICIP '04, pp. 1707–1710 (2004)
7. Dimitropoulos, S.: Fighting fire with science. Nature **576**(7786), 328–329 (2019). https://doi.org/10.1038/d41586-019-03747-2
8. Frizzi, S., Bouchouicha, M., Ginoux, J.M., Moreau, E., Sayadi, M.: Convolutional neural network for smoke and fire semantic segmentation. IET Image Proc. **15**(3), 634–647 (2021). https://doi.org/10.1049/ipr2.12046

9. Gaur, A., et al.: Fire sensing technologies: a review. IEEE Sens. J. **19**(9), 3191–3202 (2019). https://doi.org/10.1109/JSEN.2019.2894665
10. Ghali, R., Akhloufi, M.A., Jmal, M., Mseddi, W.S., Attia, R.: Forest fires segmentation using deep convolutional neural networks. In: IEEE International Conference on Systems, Man, and Cybernetics (SMC), pp. 2109–2114 (2021)
11. Ghali, R., Akhloufi, M.A., Jmal, M., Souidene Mseddi, W., Attia, R.: Wildfire segmentation using deep vision transformers. Remote Sens. **13**(17), 3527 (2021). https://doi.org/10.3390/rs13173527
12. Ghali, R., Akhloufi, M.A., Mseddi, W.S.: Deep learning and transformer approaches for uav-based wildfire detection and segmentation. Sensors **22**(5), 1977 (2022). https://doi.org/10.3390/s22051977
13. Ghali, R., Jmal, M., Souidene Mseddi, W., Attia, R.: Recent advances in fire detection and monitoring systems: A review. In: Proceedings of the 18th International Conference on Sciences of Electronics, Technologies of Information and Telecommunications (SETIT'18), Vol. 1, pp. 332–340 (2018)
14. Huang, G., Liu, Z., van der Maaten, L., Weinberger, K.Q.: Densely connected convolutional networks. In: Proceedings of the IEEE Conference on Computer Vision and Pattern Recognition (CVPR), pp. 4700–4708 (2017)
15. Lee, W., Kim, S., Lee, Y.T., Lee, H.W., Choi, M.: Deep neural networks for wild fire detection with unmanned aerial vehicle. In: IEEE International Conference on Consumer Electronics (ICCE), pp. 252–253 (2017)
16. Mlích, J., Koplík, K., Hradiš, M., Zemčík, P.: Fire segmentation in still images. In: International Conference on Advanced Concepts for Intelligent Vision Systems, pp. 27–37 (2020)
17. Mseddi, W.S., Ghali, R., Jmal, M., Attia, R.: Fire detection and segmentation using yolov5 and u-net. In: 29th European Signal Processing Conference (EUSIPCO), pp. 741–745 (2021)
18. Paszke, A., et al.: Pytorch: An imperative style, high-performance deep learning library. In: Advances in Neural Information Processing Systems 32: Annual Conference on Neural Information Processing Systems 2019, NeurIPS 2019, December 8–14, 2019, Vancouver, BC, Canada, pp. 8024–8035 (2019)
19. Shamsoshoara, A., Afghah, F., Razi, A., Zheng, L., Fulé, P., Blasch, E.: The flame dataset: Aerial imagery pile burn detection using drones (uavs). IEEE Dataport (2020). https://doi.org/10.21227/qad6-r683
20. Shamsoshoara, A., Afghah, F., Razi, A., Zheng, L., Fulé, P.Z., Blasch, E.: Aerial imagery pile burn detection using deep learning: the flame dataset. Comput. Netw. **193**, 108001 (2021). https://doi.org/10.1016/j.comnet.2021.108001
21. Srinivas, K., Dua, M.: Fog computing and deep cnn based efficient approach to early forest fire detection with unmanned aerial vehicles. In: Inventive Computation Technologies, pp. 646–652 (2020)
22. Sudre, C.H., Li, W., Vercauteren, T., Ourselin, S., Jorge Cardoso, M.: Generalised dice overlap as a deep learning loss function for highly unbalanced segmentations. In: Deep Learning in Medical Image Analysis and Multimodal Learning for Clinical Decision Support, pp. 240–248 (2017)
23. Tan, M., Le, Q.: EfficientNet: Rethinking model scaling for convolutional neural networks. In: Proceedings of the 36th International Conference on Machine Learning, pp. 6105–6114 (2019)
24. Tang, Y., et al.: Self-supervised pre-training of swin transformers for 3d medical image analysis. In: Proceedings of the IEEE/CVF Conference on Computer Vision and Pattern Recognition (CVPR), pp. 20730–20740 (2022)

25. Toulouse, T., Rossi, L., Campana, A., Celik, T., Akhloufi, M.A.: Computer vision for wildfire research: an evolving image dataset for processing and analysis. Fire Saf. J. **92**, 188–194 (2017). https://doi.org/10.1016/j.firesaf.2017.06.012

26. Valanarasu, J.M.J., Oza, P., Hacihaliloglu, I., Patel, V.M.: Medical transformer: Gated axial-attention for medical image segmentation. CoRR abs/2102.10662 (2021). https://arxiv.org/abs/2102.10662

27. Wang, D., Cui, X., Park, E., Jin, C., Kim, H.: Adaptive flame detection using randomness testing and robust features. Fire Saf. J. **55**, 116–125 (2013). https://doi.org/10.1016/j.firesaf.2012.10.011

28. Woodward, A.: Natural resources canada. https://cwfis.cfs.nrcan.gc.ca/report/ lAccessed 15 May 2022

29. Wu, H., Li, H., Shamsoshoara, A., Razi, A., Afghah, F.: Transfer learning for wildfire identification in uav imagery. In: 54th Annual Conference on Information Sciences and Systems (CISS), pp. 1–6 (2020)

30. Xiao, J., Hays, J., Ehinger, K.A., Oliva, A., Torralba, A.: Sun database: Large-scale scene recognition from abbey to zoo. In: 2010 IEEE Computer Society Conference on Computer Vision and Pattern Recognition, pp. 3485–3492 (2010)

31. Yang, F., Yang, H., Fu, J., Lu, H., Guo, B.: Learning texture transformer network for image super-resolution. In: Proceedings of the IEEE/CVF Conference on Computer Vision and Pattern Recognition (CVPR), pp. 5791–5800 (2020)

Towards Multi-class Forest Floor Analysis

Maximilian Johenneken[1(✉)], Ahmad Drak[1], Mihir Mulye[1], Taha Gharaibeh[2], and Alexander Asteroth[1]

[1] Institute of Technology, Resource and Energy-efficient Engineering (TREE) Bonn-Rhein-Sieg University of Applied Sciences (H-BRS), Sankt Augustin, Germany
maximilian.johenneken@h-brs.de
[2] Yarmouk University, Irbid, Jordan

Abstract. Climate change induced events such as drought lead to stress in forest trees, causing major catastrophic outbreaks of bark beetle insects. Current efforts to mitigate the infestation is to mass log an affected area. As a result the forest floor of a post-harvest area is cluttered with various objects such as tree logs and twigs. This study is aimed towards exploring basic computer vision methods that make use of shape, elevation and color to detect and segment objects on the forest floor. Such methods have advantages over learning methods due to their simplicity and speed in producing initial usable results, in addition to the low requirement of computational resources and training data. The highest intersection over union result of the multi-class detection and segmentation method is 0.64 for the road class. Such methods prove the feasibility of deploying basic computer vision techniques to acquire fast and reliable results.

Keywords: UAV · forest floor analysis · remote sensing

1 Introduction

In recent years Central Europe faced devastating climate change induced extreme events such as drought and heat. As a result forest trees become stressed which causes a deadly outbreak of insects such as bark beetles [15]. In Germany in particular, a mere 21% of the surveyed trees in forests did not show signs of health degradation and worsening conditions [15]. Consequently the respective forest management authorities focused on handling the affected areas by mass logging, leading to large-scale gaps in forests as seen in Fig. 1. The health status of trees and bark beetle infestations is of particular interest since forests directly affect the local ecosystems, in addition to the global climate with respect to global carbon stocks [11].

Equally as important for local foresters is the state of the forest floor resulting from the mass logging to contain an outbreak. The state of the forest floor dictates the spatial suitability of the reforesting efforts, such as determining the locations of planting new seeds or seedlings. As seen in Fig. 1, the forest floor is

© Springer Nature Switzerland AG 2023
J.-J. Rousseau and B. Kapralos (Eds.): ICPR 2022 Workshops, LNCS 13644, pp. 233–242, 2023.
https://doi.org/10.1007/978-3-031-37742-6_20

Fig. 1. Example of a forest affected by bark beetle infestation and the resulting mass logging to control the deadly outbreak. Several objects can be seen on the forest floor, such as logs, tree stumps and various vegetation.

cluttered with various objects such as branches, tree stumps, twigs and various plants. Automatic detection and classification of the objects aids in quantifying their underlying spatial distribution, in addition to an estimate of the extent of the efforts needed to reforest an affected area, such as initial cost estimates. In addition, it is possible to estimate the biomass volume (and inherently the carbon content) by deploying modelling methods using the characteristics of the detected objects, such as width of a tree stump [2]. Moreover, vegetation detection (e.g. invasive plants and weeds) is of major interest to foresters as it allows to control and set the conditions for tree growth [2]. The aggregated data due to forest floor analysis gives insight and aids in developing guidelines and intuitions for the involved stakeholders.

Remote sensing offers the opportunity to investigate the condition of forests and the effect of damage in a scalable manner. Typically satellite-based data are utilized but are generally not suited for local objectives such detection of small sized objects (e.g. branches and twigs) [5]. This is due to the relatively low spatial and temporal resolution. On the other hand data sensed by Unmanned Aerial Vehicles (UAVs) has a higher spatial resolution and a faster data acquisition time, which can be used to analyze the forest floor and quantify the spatial extent of the cluttered objects [5].

Previous work on utilizing UAV-based remote sensing data for forest floor analysis includes [12] where the authors developed a method to automatically detect, segment, classify and measure the diameter of tree stumps using computer vision techniques with a maximum of 80% accuracy. In [9] a method for detecting fallen logs was presented based on Hough transform and line template matching. An accuracy of 95% was achieved, however the authors emphasize the negative effect of the isolated pixels on the performance of the Hough transform. While the above methods focused on computer vision approaches to solving the problem, the authors of [16] utilize machine learning techniques to detect and segment woody debris. Several variants of convolutional neural networks were tested with the best performing architecture selected for deployment.

This study is aimed towards exploring basic computer vision methods that make use of shape, elevation and color to detect and segment objects on the forest floor. Such methods are to be utilized as opposed to machine learning methods due to their simplicity and speed in producing initial usable results, in addition to the low requirement of computational resources and training data compared to machine learning techniques. Learning techniques can be explored at a later stage that complement this work. An important factor to consider are the stakeholders such as public or private foresters that are not just interested in the quantified results from the deployed methods, but most importantly into the understanding and explainability of the results. The challenges associated with the suggested approach are mainly related to the clutter and the occlusion amongst the different classes. A total of 7 different classes of objects are targeted in this study as they are the most prevalent, namely vegetation, roads, logs, wood piles, tree stumps, fallen trees and ground. As far as the authors are aware, no such work can be identified that attempts to detect and segment the aforementioned multiple classes using only computer vision techniques.

The study is organized as follows, Sect. 2 explains the different methods used for detection and segmentation. Section 3 enumerates the achieved results, while discussions and conclusions are followed in Sect. 4.

2 Methods

An overview of the workflow and approach presented in this study is depicted in Fig. 2.

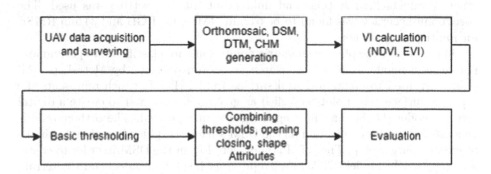

Fig. 2. The proposed workflow. Digital surface model (DSM), digital terrain model (DTM), canopy height model (CHM), vegetation index (VI), Normalized Difference Vegetation Index (NDVI), Enhanced Vegetation Index (EVI).

2.1   Study Area and Remotely Sensed Data

The post-harvest site used for testing and evaluation of the methods is located in Northrhine Westphalia, Germany. Prior to harvest, the site contained a coniferous forest monoculture (Picea abies), with a total area of 7.7 hectares. The data was acquired in the early Autumn of 2021 as part of a week long survey in different forest sites. The area contains a small stream and is moderately sloped.

Two UAV platforms DJI Mavic 2 [14] and DJI M300 [3] were deployed to acquire data. The Mavic 2 has a 20MP RGB sensor. The M300 was equipped with a Parrot Sequoia multi-spectral camera [10] (1.6 MP global shutter, Green (550±20 nm), Red (660±20 nm), Red-edge (735±5 nm), Near infrared (NIR, 790 nm±20 nm), 16-bit encoding). Flights were conducted in a row by row pattern at 40.0 m above ground level with a forward and side overlap of 90% for the RGB camera. The multi-spectral camera was setup to trigger by distance every 8.0 m. All cameras faced nadir direction. To improve and check the geometric accuracy of the processed data, 21 reference markers were placed throughout the site. The position was determined using a real time kinematics global navigation satellite system (Emlid Reach RS2+ and M2/M+ [4]).

2.2   Post-Processing and Data Annotation

The data is post-processed in order to create spectral orthomosaics and digital elevation models using 3D reconstruction methods (Metashape, Agisoft LLC [1]). The data from the RGB and multi-spectral cameras was processed separately. Structure from motion is applied to determine external and internal parameters of the images. Bundle adjustment is then applied using accuracy constraints on the surveyed reference markers and image coordinates to improve the overall geometric accuracy. A multi-view-stereo algorithm generates depths maps, which are then used to create a dense 3D point cloud. The alignment between multi-spectral and RGB imagery was established with reference markers. For both image products high settings and mild point filtering setting was used. The checkpoint accuracy was found to be 51 mm RMSE for RGB and 34 mm RMSE for multispectral bands.

The points of the photogrammetric point cloud are classified into ground and non-ground points using a local search algorithm provided by Metashape. All points are used to create a digital surface model (DSM) which represents the topmost surface. The points classified as ground are selected to create a digital terrain model (DTM) and missing areas are interpolated. The orthomosaic is generated by orthorectification on the DSM surface and blending of orthophotos to create a larger map. The DTM is subtracted from the DSM in order to create a canopy height model (CHM) that represents heights of objects on the terrain surface. To include small height changes that are omitted in the ground point classification, spatial low-pass filter at 1.0 m was applied to the DTM (following the approach of local surface models presented in [8]) before subtracting it from the DSM. All image products were exported as GeoTiff with a ground sampling distance (GSD) of 50.0 mm in UTM32N coordinate system.

The RGB orthomosaic was used for manual annotation of the data to serve as ground truth for performance evaluation, assuming that humans are capable to discern the investigated classes. Based on the class characteristics different data annotation strategies were selected. Polygonal annotations were used for the wood piles, roads, logs and tree stumps classes. Point annotations were used for classes that were abundantly present in the study field and when the instance outline could not be clearly distinguished. Ten 10×10 m plots were randomly sampled from orthomosaic of the study site. Within these plots all wood stumps and logs were annotated, in addition to selecting 10 random points with a minimum spacing of 1.0 m for annotation. To enlarge the ground truth for the point-annotated classes additional plots were sampled to reach a total point sample of 570. Roads, wood piles and fallen trees were annotated for the whole site.

2.3 Vegetation Index and Canopy Height Model Thresholds

The QGIS Raster Calculator [13] was utilized for simple thresholding operations in order to segment the different classes. The normalized difference vegetation index (NDVI) $[-1, 1]$ was used for the vegetation segmentation by applying a threshold. Pixels with an NDVI response above the threshold were considered as vegetation. In order to determine a reasonable threshold multiple values x were selected and tested $x \in [0.05, 0.1, ..., 0.4]$, as depicted in Fig. 3.

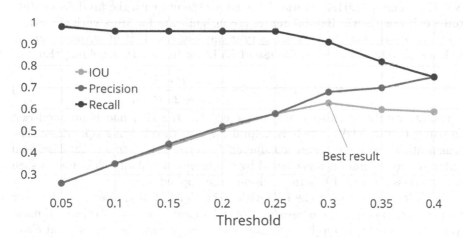

Fig. 3. The Figure shows the influence of NDVI threshold on the actual performance and trading off false positives (precision) and false negatives (recall). Intersection over union (IOU) measures the overlap between predicted segmentation and ground truth on pixel-level.

CHM thresholding was explored in order to separate the different classes such as twig clusters, logs, fallen trees, wood piles and roads by their common height. It can be thought of as slicing the 3D space into layers and assign each slice a class. This basic segmentation was observed to result in high class recall with low precision. In order to improve the separability of the classes additional features were used.

In addition, the slope of the CHM was calculated and thresholded at 5.0°. This mask was combined with CHM thresholded at 0.08m to get an improved segmentation of the ground class.

2.4 Additional Computer Vision Operations

More advanced processing was applied with python scripts using Rasterio, NumPy and OpenCV Python libraries. In order to segment roads and wood-based classes a combination of multiple layers and processing steps such as dilation, erosion, and thresholding of shape based attributes was tested.

In addition to the NDVI, the enhanced vegetation index (EVI) was used for segmentation with thresholding. EVI was proposed as improved version of NDVI to account for canopy background signals [6]. It was observed that the EVI calculation was ill-conditioned. EVI calculation requires a blue channel from the RGB orthomosaic which is not perfectly aligned with the multi-spectral images. Additionally, the blue channel was not calibrated along with the multi-spectral channel and would need manual brightness changes.

The lack of blue channel in some cases has led to search for approaches to correct the NDVI without the need of a blue band. A two-band EVI called EVI2 [7] (values $[-1.04, 2.5]$) was designed for the use with the MODIS satellite product. It was shown that differences are insignificant for areas with low atmospheric influence. For our UAV imagery it was assumed that atmospheric errors are insignificant, which led to the use of EVI2 for further thresholding (Eq. 1).

$$EVI \cong EVI2 = 2.5 * \frac{NIR - R}{NIR + 2.4R + 1} \tag{1}$$

Quantitatively speaking it was observed that the EVI had higher contrast compared to the NDVI which is helpful for any thresholding operation. The segmentation procedures were conducted for each class separately. The final multi-class segmentation was created by combining the binary class masks such that the class results with high precision were applied last.

For twigs segmentation the EVI with a threshold of -0.12 was used. As most other class segmentation are based on this EVI mask it was set to the final mask layer first and overwritten by consecutive segmentations. As for the road class, it was assumed that a road segment has at least an area of 900 pixels ($2.25\,m^2$), with no more than 5.0° slope, a very low EVI response ($EVI < -0.12$) and are located on top of the terrain surface ($CHM < 0.01\,m$).

Wood piles are considered as large regions with low EVI response and an object height between 0.2 m and 5.0 m. This definition can also include piles of logs that were arranged in the field by the harvester. Opening and closing operations were applied to remove small conglomerates of logs and create a compact representation of the remaining masks. Wood piles need a combined size of at least 4500 pixels($11.25\,m^2$).

Log segmentation was performed by selecting areas with low EVI response and thresholding CHM (0.045 m < CHM < 0.7 m). Contours with an area less then 10 pixels (i.e. size of a footprint) were discarded. Contours with an area less than 50 pixels (0.125 m^2) were considered as logs only if the ratio between long and short sides exceeds 3:1. Next a closing operation was applied to all other contours. Contours with a side length shorter than 160 pixels (8 m) were considered logs. Fallen trees were considered as those contours which exceeded 160 pixel (8 m) and had a length to width ratio of more than 10:1.

As for tree stump segmentation pixels with low EVI response and a CHM value between 0.2 m and 3.0 m were selected. The contours were closed and those smaller than 9 pixels (i.e. size of a napkin) and larger than 400 pixels (1 m^2) were discarded. Tree stumps were considered as having a side length ratio of less than 1.7:1.

2.5   Methods Evaluation

The class segmentations are evaluated by comparing them to the manually anno- tated data which serves as ground truth. For the point-based annotation data the closest pixel value is extracted from the segmentation. The Jaccard-Index (Inter- section over Union, IOU), Precision and Recall metrics were used for pixel-based performance assessment.

3   Results

After evaluating thresholding of the NDVI at multiple levels as seen in Fig. 3, the best performing threshold was found to be 0.3 with an IOU of 0.63 (n = 55 points). Applying only a threshold on the CHM was found to be inadequately performing for most classes. Only the log (0.08 m < CHM < 0.7 m) and ground segmentation (CHM < 0.08 m) reached a notable segmentation performance of 0.23 IOU and 0.38 IOU respectively. The segmented classes tend to have have a high recall but low precision.

Using a combination of VIs and CHM together with post processing for each of the classes yields improved segmentation performance for most classes as shown in Table 1.

Examples of forest floor segmentation are shown in Fig. 4. The low perfor- mance of twigs segmentation is explained by confusion with road pixels and other woody debris classes. The photogrammetric surface reconstruction is known to be limited in accuracy. Therefore logs and trees stumps with an inadequate rep- resentation in the CHM get misclassified as twigs. The twigs also have a very low EVI response similar to roads and bare soil. These areas tend to get misclassified as twigs on parts of road that are rough and uneven.

Detection performance of fallen trees is very low. The long thin shape of the tree trunks makes the segmentation mask prone to being split by erosion or opening operations such that fallen trees are mis-classified as logs. The ground truth annotation considers the dead tree crown as part of the annotation which

Table 1. Performance metrics for each of the classes and overall performance measured with intersection over union (IOU), precision and recall metrics on pixel-level (50mm ground sampling distance).

	IOU	Precision	Recall
Vegetation	0.63	0.91	0.68
Fallen Tree	0.02	0.02	0.26
Logs	0.32	0.37	0.69
Ground	0.42	0.91	0.44
Road	0.64	0.64	1.00
Twigs	0.12	0.12	0.77
Wood Pile	0.46	0.76	0.54
Tree stump	0.32	0.37	0.71
Mean	0.37	0.51	0.64

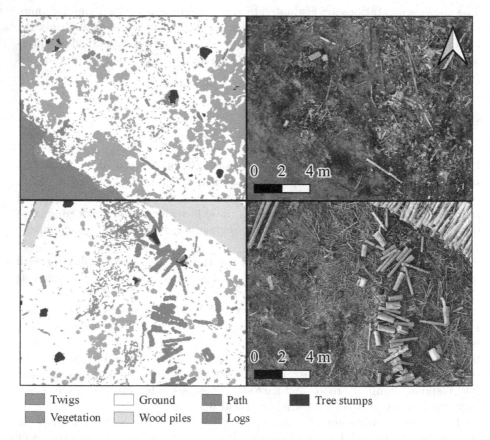

Twigs   Ground   Path   Tree stumps
Vegetation   Wood piles   Logs

Fig. 4. Forest floor semantic segmentation into different classes and corresponding RGB image.

doesn't have a characteristic response in EVI, NDVI or CHM. Therefore large parts of the tree crown cannot be selected with thresholding.

4 Discussion and Conclusions

In this study we explored typical computer vision methods that make use of shape, elevation and color to detect and segment objects on the forest floor in post-harvest sites using UAV-based sensed data. The results suggest that a dense segmentation of the forest floor is achievable with basic computer vision operations. The resulting segmentation output can be used for producing initial usable results with low requirement of computational resources and training data. However, the results also showed that more heterogeneous objects such as fallen trees which consist of the plucked stump, trunk and crown are poorly recognized. Differentiating vegetation into more specific classes such as grass patches was initially targeted. By visual comparison of RGB and multi-spectral responses it was discovered that grass patches in the observed field were mostly yellow with a low NDVI response. These characteristics are similar to ground regions in the site, and thus segmentation of grass patches with thresholding was not possible with methods explored in this study. The segmentation of herbaceous plants, moss and ferns likely requires methods that rely heavily on texture features. The method performs poorly for objects that are clustered due to the limited ability to split these clusters into separated objects with opening and selection based on shape attributes. The thresholds and order of operations were based on trial and error on a single site as well as considering class characteristics. Thresholds on object heights, size and shape are expected to be independent of the site. The thresholds on VI index values (NDVI, EVI2) are expected to change based on the lighting conditions because radiometric calibration was not applied. We argue that it is feasible to apply the method as an interactive tool to post-harvest areas to quickly generate a dense segmentation. In addition adapting thresholds (see Fig. 3) allows for trading off class precision and recall which aids in countering changing site conditions. However, we expect that the segmentation performance is to be affected by the time passed between harvest and survey.

The results of this study serve as a baseline for comparison and evaluation of future methods such as machine learning techniques. Forest floor analysis supports the verification of forest management practices and could serve as a basis for analysing silvicultural practices for reafforestation. Building upon these initial results, and applying learning-based methods will be the focal point of future work. In addition to refining the vegetation segmentation into more specific vegetation categories.

Acknowledgments. We thank the Ministry for Environment, Agriculture, Conservation and Consumer Protection of the State of North Rhine-Westphalia for funding our work and the state company Wood and Forest NRW for providing access to the forest sites and support.

References

1. Agisoft LLC: Agisoft Metashape User Manual - Professional Edition, Version 1.7 (2021)
2. Dainelli, R., Toscano, P., Di Gennaro, S.F., Matese, A.: Recent advances in unmanned aerial vehicles forest remote sensing-a systematic review. Part II: Res. Appl. Forests **12**(4), 397 (2021)
3. DJI: MATRICE 300 RTK - Specifications - DJI (2022), https://www.dji.com/matrice-300/specs
4. Emlid: Reach M2 and M+ | RTK GNSS/GPS modules for high-precision mapping (2022). https://emlid.com/reach/
5. Guimarães, N., Pádua, L., Marques, P., Silva, N., Peres, E., Sousa, J.J.: Forestry remote sensing from unmanned aerial vehicles: a review focusing on the data. Process. Potentialities. Remote Sens. **12**(6), 1046 (2020)
6. Huete, A., Didan, K., Miura, T., Rodriguez, E.P., Gao, X., Ferreira, L.G.: Overview of the radiometric and biophysical performance of the MODIS vegetation indices. Remote Sens. Environ. **83**(1), 195–213 (2002)
7. Jiang, Z., Huete, A.R., Didan, K., Miura, T.: Development of a two-band enhanced vegetation index without a blue band. Remote Sens. Environ. **112**(10), 3833–3845 (2008)
8. Johenneken, M., Drak, A., Herpers, R., Asteroth, A.: Multimodal Segmentation Neural Network to Determine the Cause of Damage to Grasslands. In: 2021 International Conference on Software, Telecommunications and Computer Networks (SoftCOM), pp. 1–6 (Sep 2021), iSSN: 1847–358X
9. Panagiotidis, D., Abdollahnejad, A., Surový, P., Kuželka, K.: Detection of fallen logs from high-resolution UAV Images. New Zealand J. Forestry Sci. **49** (2019)
10. Parrot: Parrot Sequoia (2022). https://www.parrot.com/en/shop/accessories-spare-parts/other-drones/sequoia
11. Philipp, M., Wegmann, M., Kübert-Flock, C.: Quantifying the Response of German Forests to Drought Events via Satellite Imagery. Remote Sens. **13**(9), 1845 (may 2021)
12. Puliti, S., Talbot, B., Astrup, R.: Tree-stump detection, segmentation, classification, and measurement using unmanned aerial vehicle (uav) imagery. Forests **9**(3), 102 (2018)
13. QGIS Development Team: QGIS Geographic Information System. QGIS Association (2022). https://www.qgis.org
14. SZ Dji Technology Co., Ltd: Mavic 2 - Specifications - DJI (2022). https://www.dji.com/de/mavic-2/info#specs
15. Thonfeld, F., et al.: A first assessment of canopy cover loss in germany's forests after the 2018–2020 drought years. Remote Sens. **14**(3), 562 (2022)
16. Windrim, L., Bryson, M., McLean, M., Randle, J., Stone, C.: Automated Mapping of Woody Debris over Harvested Forest Plantations Using UAVs, High-Resolution Imagery, and Machine Learning. Remote, Sens (2019)

MultiMedia FORensics in the WILD
(MMFORWILD 2022)

The 2nd Workshop on MultiMedia FORensics in the Wild

The protection of images, video, and audio data from illegal use (e.g. misinformation), as well as its exploitation in forensics and intelligence, have become serious challenges as the sheer data volume renders a full manual inspection impossible. The 2nd edition of the MMForWILD workshop aimed at bringing together researchers from both academia and industry, to share recent advances in this field. The workshop accepted seven full papers.

- Combining Automatic Speaker Verification and Prosody Analysis for Synthetic Speech Detection.
  Luigi Attorresi; Davide Salvi; Clara Borrelli; Paolo Bestagini; Stefano Tubaro

- Towards Unconstrained Audio Splicing Detection and Localization with Neural Networks
  Denise Moussa; Germans Hirsch; Christian Riess

- Comprint: Image Forgery Detection and Localization using Compression Fingerprints
  Hannes Mareen; Dante Vanden Bussche; Fabrizio Guillaro; Davide Cozzolino; Glenn Van Wallendael; Peter Lambert; Luisa Verdoliva

- Misalignment Estimation in Non-Aligned Double JPEG Scenario Based on AC Histogram Analysis
  Giovanni Puglisi; Sebastiano Battiato

- H4VDM: H.264 Video Device Matching
  Ziyue Xiang; Paolo Bestagini; Stefano Tubaro; Edward Delp

- GBDF: Gender Balanced DeepFake Dataset Towards Fair DeepFake Detection
  Aakash Varma Nadimpalli; Ajita Rattani

- Attacking and Defending Printer Source Attribution Classifiers in the Physical Domain
  Anselmo Ferreira; Mauro Barni

Organization

Workshop Chairs

Mauro Barni
University of Siena, Italy
barni@dii.unisi.it

Sebastiano Battiato
University of Catania, Italy
battiato@dmi.unict.it

Giulia Boato
University of Trento, Italy
giulia.boato@unitn.it

Hany Farid
University of California, Berkeley, USA
hfarid@berkeley.edu

Nasir Memon
New York University, USA
nm1214@nyu.edu

Publication Chair

Alessandro Orti
University of Catania, Italy
ortis@dmi.unict.it

Combining Automatic Speaker Verification and Prosody Analysis for Synthetic Speech Detection

Luigi Attorresi⬡, Davide Salvi(✉)⬡, Clara Borrelli⬡, Paolo Bestagini⬡,
and Stefano Tubaro⬡

Dipartimento di Elettronica, Informazione e Bioingegneria, Politecnico di Milano,
Milan, Italy
luigi.attorresi@mail.polimi.it,
{davide.salvi,clara.borrelli,paolo.bestagini,stefano.tubaro}@polimi.it

Abstract. The rapid spread of media content synthesis technology and the potentially damaging impact of audio and video deepfakes on people's lives have raised the need to implement systems able to detect these forgeries automatically. In this work we present a novel approach for synthetic speech detection, exploiting the combination of two high-level semantic properties of the human voice. On one side, we focus on speaker identity cues and represent them as speaker embeddings extracted using a state-of-the-art method for the automatic speaker verification task. On the other side, voice prosody, intended as variations in rhythm, pitch or accent in speech, is extracted through a specialized encoder. We show that the combination of these two embeddings fed to a supervised binary classifier allows the detection of deepfake speech generated with both Text-to-Speech and Voice Conversion techniques. Our results show improvements over the considered baselines, good generalization properties over multiple datasets and robustness to audio compression.

Keywords: Synthetic Speech Detection · Deepfake · Audio Forensics · Prosody · Speaker Verification

1 Introduction

The term deepfake (DF) refers to a category of synthetic multimedia content generated through Deep Learning (DL) techniques that depict individuals in actions and behaviors that do not belong to them. In recent years, the fast development in this technology has made it increasingly realistic and accessible. This enables producing manipulated media that are almost impossible to distinguish from the original ones [30]. These improvements result in exciting and futuristic scenarios but also represent a potential tool for malicious purposes [35,47]. There are several cases where DF videos have been employed in the creation of non-consensual adult material [13], fake political news [16] or damage people's reputation [41]. Likewise, with the increasing quality and accessibility of speech synthesis techniques, namely Text-to-Speech (TTS) and Voice Conversion (VC), DF voices

© Springer Nature Switzerland AG 2023
J.-J. Rousseau and B. Kapralos (Eds.): ICPR 2022 Workshops, LNCS 13644, pp. 247–263, 2023.
https://doi.org/10.1007/978-3-031-37742-6_21

have emerged and proved equally dangerous. The difference between these techniques is the starting point of the synthesis process, which is text for TTS and voice for VC. Both of them proved to be capable of fooling recognition systems into accessing the victim's personal information and committing frauds [14] or by providing support for voice phishing attacks [28].

Given the threat posed by these technologies, there is an urgent need to develop systems able to detect their misbehaving use. Several state-of-the-art methods have been proposed to face this problem for both videos and audio recordings [4,7,21,27,43]. These can be divided into two main groups. The first one includes methods that focus on low-level characteristics of the signal [15,24,51], looking for artifacts introduced by the generators at the pixel or sample level. These artifacts are interpreted as hidden fingerprints left by the synthesis process that we can leverage to determine the authenticity of a given media content. For example, the method proposed in [26] detects synthesized speech by looking for artifacts through high-order spectral analysis. It performs quadrature-phase coupling in the estimated bicoherence and a series of test statistics for Gaussianity and linearity, assuming that an authentic recording has higher non-linearity than a counterfeited one. Similarly, [5] addresses the same problem by combining a set of features that model speech as an autoregressive process and evaluating the effect of including bicoherence as well, which proved useful in [1]. The authors perform both closed-set and open-set tests and show how their combination provides an accuracy gain in the considered scenarios. The work of [46] aims to secure Automatic Speaker Verification (ASV) systems against playback attacks, which claim the victims' identity by playing back their voice recorded without consent. The method leverages the noise pattern of the audio channel considering noises from intermediate recording and playback devices in the authentic recordings.

The second group of DF detectors relies on more semantically meaningful features and exploits high-level inconsistencies to discriminate DFs, assuming their weakness in emulating the finest aspects of human nature. As an example, [23] focuses on the detection of the lack of natural eye blinking in synthesized videos, whereas [8] looks for semantic mismatches between the audio and video modalities, such as the absence of lip-syncing. The authors of [49] perform face-swap DF detection by comparing two different estimates of the subject's head pose and detect a DF whenever there is an apparent difference between them, indicated by a mismatch of landmark locations. Similarly, [11] detects fake videos by modeling how people move as they speak, while [2] addresses the same problem combining static and temporal bio-metrics based on face recognition and expressions/head movements. The authors of [10] show how synthetic voices lack natural emotional behavior and can be discriminated by feeding a classifier with high-level features obtained from a Speech Emotion Recognition (SER) system. Finally, the work presented in [18] encompasses the two previous approaches by exploiting audio and visual emotion analysis to detect joint audio-visual DFs.

In this paper, we adopt a semantic approach to perform DF speech detection. We partially take inspiration from the work presented in [2], where face-swap DFs are identified by looking at the mismatch between facial recognition static cues and behavioral bio-metrics based on expression and head movement. Our scenario considers speaker identification aspects together with speech prosody, defined as all the information present in a speech signal but not specified in the text (e.g., temporal variations in rhythm, intonation, stress, style, etc.). This constitutes a basis we can leverage to identify DF speech generated via different technologies that may be flawed in one semantic aspect or the other. In particular, we represent the identity of the speaker extracting a set of embedding through a recent ASV network [12]. At the same time, we obtain the bio-metric behavior that corresponds to the speech prosody through the use of an encoder network originally proposed for speech synthesis [36]. Differently from [2], we do not define a reference set for the identity-behavioral mapping, but we feed the concatenation of speaker and prosody embeddings to a simple supervised classifier, adopting an approach similar to that proposed in [10]. We believe that combining two semantic representations as speaker-identity and prosody can model both the voice's physiological and behavioral characteristics. Our detector proves capable of detecting synthetic speech samples generated with both TTS and VC techniques. Furthermore, our detector shows good generalization properties when we test it on unseen datasets or MP3-compressed recordings.

2   Proposed System

In this work, we propose a method for synthetic speech detection named *Proso-Speaker*. This predicts if a speech recording is authentic or has been synthetically generated by analyzing the audio signal only.

Formally, given a discrete-time input speech signal $\mathbf{x}$ sampled with sampling frequency F_s, the goal is to predict the associated label y such that

$$y \in \{\mathrm{REAL}, \mathrm{DF}\}, \tag{1}$$

where REAL identifies authentic speech samples, while DF corresponds to speech that has been synthetically generated, either using TTS or VC technique. Figure 1 shows the pipeline of the proposed system. As mentioned, our approach leverages the difficulty of DFs in generating complex semantic aspects of voice naturally. Hence, the proposed *ProsoSpeaker* method relies on a rich set of high-level features extracted from the input x and obtained as the concatenation of two embedding vectors extracted from two different networks architectures. We will refer to each one of them as *speaker* ($\mathbf{f}_s$) and *prosody* ($\mathbf{f}_p$) embeddings. This representation is then used as input to a simple supervised classifier, which outputs for each input $\mathbf{x}$ a prediction of the label y. In the following we provide additional details about each step of the pipeline depicted in Fig. 1.

2.1   Speaker Embedding Extraction

The principle of VC algorithms is to operate on pristine speech signals and modify their frequency content to match a target identity. We believe that this kind of forgeries could leave traces in the speaker timbre quality that we can

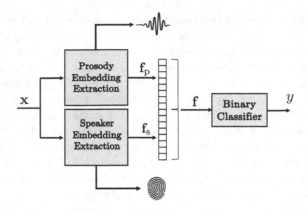

Fig. 1. Pipeline of the proposed *ProsoSpeaker* system.

leverage to perform synthetic speech detection. We propose to do so through a feature set that describes each voice's unique fingerprint in a compact fashion, extracting the spectro-temporal characteristics of the analyzed spokesperson, i.e., timbre specific properties or pitch contour of the voice. This feature set, that we indicate with $\mathbf{f_s}$, is extracted exploiting a state-of-the-art network [12] originally proposed for a speaker recognition task. The proposed speaker embeddings can spot voice anomalies and allow us to discriminate between real and synthetic tracks generated through VC engines, as we will prove in the results section.

As mentioned, speaker embeddings are defined and computed using the ECAPA-Time Delay Neural Network (TDNN) model, firstly proposed in [12] for ASV. This model, that takes as input the Mel-frequency Cepstral Coefficients (MFCCs) of the input signal, enhances the typical X-vectors architectures [37, 38, 50] and outperforms state-of-the-art TDNN based systems. The architecture is inspired by the latest trends in face verification and computer vision as it includes residual blocks [17] to skip connections and exploit multi-layer information, and squeeze-excitation blocks [19] that explicitly model channel inter-dependencies. In addition, the model extends the temporal attention mechanism presented in [31] to be channel-dependent and better adapt to global attributes, e.g., noise or recording conditions. This design allows the network to achieve higher generalization ability, capture high-level properties, and improve performance while significantly reducing the number of model parameters. We use this model as an embedding extractor by first training it for the original task (i.e., ASV) and then feeding the considered input $\mathbf{x}$ to the trained network. We then assume as embedding representation the output of the network discarding the final classification layer, hence adopting a transfer-learning strategy. In particular, the variable length signal $\mathbf{x}$ is first pre-processed, i.e., transformed in time-frequency domain applying a Short Time Fourier Transform (STFT) with window length W_s and hop size H_s. From the resulting spectrogram $\mathbf{X}$ we compute a set of MFCCs, i.e.,

$$\mathbf{X}_{\mathrm{MFCC}} = \mathrm{MFCC}(\mathbf{x}) \in \mathbb{R}^{M \times B}, \tag{2}$$

where M corresponds to the number of time windows and B is the total number of mel-frequency cepstrum coefficients. This feature map is then used as input to the trained ECAPA-TDNN network, which projects it into the fixed-length speaker embedding $\mathbf{f}_s$ of dimension N_s.

2.2   Prosody Embedding Extraction

Complementary to the aspects described by the speaker embeddings, we believe that high-level prosodic aspects, like speech signal variations in rhythm, intonation and style, constitute another aspect we can leverage to discriminate deepfake speech tracks. In particular, prosody measures an intrinsic human voice characteristic that we assume TTS synthesis algorithms struggle at recreating. In fact, despite the recent advances, synthetic prosody has different quality and intensity w.r.t. to human speech, and this difference can be captured using a set of prosody embeddings. This assumption is later proved by the obtained results. The prosody embedding vector $\mathbf{f}_p$ we propose corresponds to the result of the reference encoder of the model presented in [36], which we will refer to as prosody encoder.

The prosody encoder [36] was initially introduced to improve the naturalness of the voices synthesized by Tacotron [44,45] enhancing their prosody controls. The whole Tacotron model receives a text as input and generates speech depending on the speaker's identity considered in the training phase. In contrast, the encoder takes as input the mel-spectrogram transform of a reference signal conveying the desired prosody and extracts a fixed-length learned representation. This is used to condition the synthesis, making it possibly more expressive. The authors show that the results match the prosody with fine temporal detail even when the target and reference speakers are different. The prosody encoder comprises a 6-layer stack of 2D convolutions with batch normalization, followed by a Gated Recurrent Unit (GRU) layer to summarize the variable-length sequence. Finally, a fully-connected layer extracts the embeddings in the desired dimension. This design sufficiently bottlenecks the input information such that the encoder is forced to learn a compact representation of prosody. For this work, we train Tacotron and prosody encoder jointly by synthesizing target audio signals, provided as input to both, and using the reconstruction error as loss function. Once the prosody encoder is trained, we use it as an embedding extractor, feeding as input the mel-spectrogram of the input signal $\mathbf{x}$

$$\mathbf{X}_{\mathrm{mel}} = \mathrm{MelSpec}(\mathbf{x}) \in \mathbb{R}^{M \times K}, \tag{3}$$

where M is the number of time windows and K corresponds to the total number of frequency bins, extracted with window size W_p and hop size H_p. The output of the prosody encoder is the vector $\mathbf{f}_p$ of length N_p.

2.3 Binary Classifier

As shown in Fig. 1, the final part of the *ProsoSpeaker* pipeline is a supervised binary classifier. We concatenate the two embeddings $\mathbf{f}_s$ and $\mathbf{f}_p$ obtaining a final feature vector

$$\mathbf{f} = [\mathbf{f}_s, \mathbf{f}_p] \in \mathbb{R}^{N_s + N_p}, \tag{4}$$

which is fed to the classification stage. The supervised classifier is trained to predict the class y of the input speech $\mathbf{x}$. We decide to adopt a simple classification front-end because we mostly rely on the discriminative capacity of the rich proposed feature set. Moreover, it is worth noting that any supervised classifier algorithm can be used at this stage, as our pipeline is classifier-independent.

3 Experimental Setup

In this section we provide the reader some insights on the evaluation setup used to assess the performances of the *ProsoSpeaker* detector. We first describe the dataset used for training and testing the system. Then, we specify all the training parameters for both the back-end (i.e., the embedding extractors) and front-end (i.e., the binary supervised classifier). Finally, we describe the training process and the selected baselines.

3.1 Dataset Description

In this section we introduce the datasets involved in the training and testing phases of the presented work, which in total counts almost 800000 tracks. We considered multiple datasets containing tracks of both REAL (i.e., authentic) and DF (i.e., synthetic) classes, aiming to test the proposed method's generalization properties. We set the sampling frequency F_s to 16 kHz during all the experiments, hence if necessary, down-sampling the audio tracks. In the following we provide further details for each dataset that will be later useful in interpreting the experimental results.

ASVspoof 2019 [42] is a speech audio dataset containing both real and synthetic tracks. It has been released for the ASVspoof challenge, in which participants compete to implement the best anti-spoofing system for ASV. Here we consider the Logical Access (LA) partition of the dataset, further divided in *train*, *dev* and *eval*, which includes spoofing atalzantot2019deeptacks generated through TTS, VC and TTS/VC hybrid techniques. Each partition comprises authentic signals along with speech samples generated with 19 different synthesis algorithms. The *train* and *dev* partitions have been created using the same set of synthesis algorithms (named $A01$, $A02$, ..., $A06$), while the *eval* partition includes samples generated with different techniques ($A07$, ..., $A19$). We use *train* and *dev* partitions for training and fine-tuning the proposed method, while *eval* partition is used in test.

An updated version of the dataset was released in 2021 ([48]). Nevertheless, we decided not to consider it since, at the time of writing, it is distributed only with REAL/DF labels, while no information is available about the generation strategy adopted for each audio track.

LibriSpeech [32] is a dataset containing about 1000 h of authentic speech from different speakers. From this corpus we considered the subset *train-clean-100*. We include audio tracks from this dataset in the training set.

LJSpeech (LJS) [20] is a dataset containing short audio tracks of REAL speech recorded from a single speaker reciting pieces from non-fiction books. This dataset is part of the test set.

Cloud2019 is a collection of TTS generated audio signals proposed in [25]. It includes tracks from different speech generators available as cloud services: Amazon AWS Polly (PO), Google Cloud Standard (GS), Google CloudWaveNet (GW), Microsoft Azure (AZ) and IBM Watson (WA). We include this dataset in the test set as DF signals.

Interactive Emotional Dyadic Motion Capture (IEMOCAP) (IEM) [6] is a dataset originally designed for the SER task. The data were recorded during scripted and improvised conversations by 10 actors. It contains video and audio signals annotated with information about the speakers' facial expressions and head movements. We include this dataset in the test set as authentic signals.

Table 1 reports the train and test split used for the front-end binary classifier and the type of speech signal, REAL or DF, included in each dataset.

Table 1. Composition of the training, development and test sets for the proposed experiments.

Dataset	N. Tracks	REAL	DF	Train	Dev	Test
ASVspoof 2019	121 458	✗	✗	✗	✗	✗
LibriSpeech	28 539	✗		✗		
LJSpeech	13 100	✗				✗
Cloud2019	11 888		✗			✗
IEMOCAP	10 039	✗				✗
Total	185 024	64 159	120 865	53 919	24 844	106 264

3.2 Training

Our system involves the training of three independent blocks: the ECAPA-TDNN network, the prosody encoder, the final binary classifier. Regarding the speaker embedding extractor, we use a version of ECAPA-TDNN available at [34], which uses Additive Margin Softmax Loss and is trained on VoxCeleb 1 [29] and VoxCeleb 2 [9] datasets. As mentioned in Sect. 2.1, the input waveform x, to be used as input to ECAPA-TDNN network, must be first transformed in its MFCC representation $\mathbf{X}_{\mathrm{MFCC}}$. For this operation we consider $B = 80$ MFCCs extracted with $W_s = 25$ ms windows with hop size $H_s = 10$ ms, leading to a

$M \times 80$ representation, where the number of windows M depends on the length of the audio. The final embedding vector $\mathbf{f}_s$ has dimension $N_s = 192$. For the prosody embedding extractor, we train the prosody encoder on Blizzard 2013 dataset [22], following the training procedure detailed in [36]. For computational issues, we modify only one parameter value, the mini-batch size, that in our training process is equal to 8. Before feeding it to the encoder, the input signal $\mathbf{x}$ is transformed into a mel-spectrogram $\mathbf{X}_{\mathrm{mel}}$ using window length $W_p = 50$ ms and hop size $H_p = 12.5$ ms. The number of frequency bins used is $K = 80$. This lead to a final input of dimension $M \times 80$. The resulting embedding vector $\mathbf{f}_p$ has length and $N_p = 128$. The final concatenated feature set is $\mathbf{f}$ of length $N = N_s + N_p = 320$. This vector is standardized using z-score, i.e., removing the mean and scaling to unit variance, and acts as input to the binary classifier. The supervised classification algorithm we adopt is Support Vector Machine (SVM) classifier, following the training-development partition detailed in Table 1. To find the best set of hyper-parameters we performed a grid search on development partition using balanced accuracy as a metric. We considered the following parameters: $C \in [0.01, 0.1, 1, 10, 100]$, kernel coefficient $\gamma \in [1/N, 1/(N * \sigma_{\mathbf{f}}^2)]$, where N is dimensionality of the feature vector $\mathbf{f}$ and $\sigma_{\mathbf{f}}^2$ is the variance of $\mathbf{f}$ over the training dataset. In addition, we vary the kernel type between radial basis function kernel, polynomial kernel and sigmoid kernel. The best configuration proved to be $C = 100$, $\gamma = 1/(N * \sigma_{\mathbf{f}}^2)$ and using radial basis function kernel.

3.3   Baselines

To test the validity of our method, we compare its performances with those of three different baselines. The first one is RawNet2 [40], a state-of-the-art end-to-end neural network that operates on raw waveforms. It has been first proposed for the ASVspoof 2019 challenge and included as a baseline in the ASVspoof 2021 challenge both for LA and DF tasks. The second and third baselines are variants of ResNet [17], a residual Convolutional Neural Network that creates shortcuts between layers by skipping connections that help stabilize training. We consider two versions of the ResNet, fed with different representations of the input audio track, as presented in [3]. The first one, referenced as Spec-ResNet, takes as input the log-magnitude representation of the STFT of the considered audio. The second one, called MFCC-ResNet, is fed with the MFCCs of the input data, together with their first and second derivatives. Input transformation and training strategy for these two networks are implemented following [3]. The three baselines considered are based on different representations of the input data, allowing us to have an orthogonal approach to the problem. All the models share the same training set we adopted for the proposed method.

4   Results

In this section we assess the performances of *ProsoSpeaker* detector, measuring the performances of the method in terms of Receiver Operating Characteristic (ROC) curves, Area Under the Curve (AUC), Equal Error Rate (EER) and

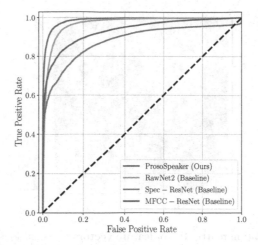

Fig. 2. ROC curves for the proposed method and the considered baselines, evaluated on ASVspoof 2019 LA *eval* set.

balanced accuracy. Optimal performances are reached when AUC and balanced accuracy are equal to one, while EER is equal to 0. All the models presented in the following have been trained on the same dataset, obtained by the union of ASVspoof 2019 LA and LibriSpeech, as shown in Table 1.

4.1 Baseline Comparison

As a first experiment, we compare the results obtained using the proposed method with those of the considered baselines on the LA *eval* partition of the ASVspoof 2019 dataset. Figure 2 shows the ROC curves of the three detectors and Table 2 shows the corresponding AUC, EER and balanced accuracy values. *ProsoSpeaker* detector outperforms all the three baselines in the considered metrics. In particular, the most remarkable improvement is seen over Spec-ResNet with a difference of about 15% for EER and balanced accuracy, 10 for AUC. A significant gain is also shown concerning RawNet2. Here, our method improves by almost 3% over EER and balanced accuracy, while 2 over AUC.

Table 2. EER, AUC and balanced accuracy values for the proposed *ProsoSpeaker* method and the considered baselines, evaluated on ASVspoof 2019 LA *eval* set.

Model	EER %	AUC	Bal. Acc. %
RawNet2 (Baseline)	8.15	97.09	91.66
MFCC-ResNet (Baseline)	13.98	93.52	84.96
Spec-ResNet (Baseline)	18.75	88.31	79.50
ProsoSpeaker (Ours)	**5.39**	**98.85**	**94.43**

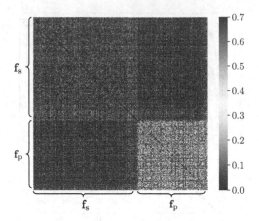

Fig. 3. Cross-correlation matrix $\mathbf{R}_{\mathbf{ff}}$ of feature vectors $\mathbf{f}$ realizations of ASVspoof 2019 *eval* set.

4.2   Embedding Analysis and Ablation Study

In this second experiment we further analyze the characteristics and the importance of each embedding subset, namely the prosody embeddings $\mathbf{f}_\mathrm{p}$ and the speaker embeddings $\mathbf{f}_\mathrm{s}$, used in *ProsoSpeaker* method.

The first question may be how much speaker and prosody embeddings differ from each other to avoid the computation of redundant information. To do so, we measure the sample Pearson correlation coefficient $r_{f_i f_j}$ for each pair of elements (f_i, f_j) of the vector $\mathbf{f} = [f_0, f_1, ..., f_{N-1}]$ over the test dataset. The resulting matrix $\mathbf{R}_{\mathbf{ff}}$ describes both cross-correlation between prosody and speaker embeddings $\mathbf{R}_{\mathbf{f}_\mathrm{s} \mathbf{f}_\mathrm{p}} = \mathbf{R}_{\mathbf{f}_\mathrm{p} \mathbf{f}_\mathrm{s}}^T$ both auto-correlations of each embedding vector $\mathbf{R}_{\mathbf{f}_\mathrm{p} \mathbf{f}_\mathrm{p}}$ and $\mathbf{R}_{\mathbf{f}_\mathrm{s} \mathbf{f}_\mathrm{s}}$. Figure 3 shows the results of this analysis computed in the ASVspoof 2019 *eval* partition. The diagonal has been set to 0 for visualization purposes. There, we can identify two rectangular regions, one at the top left, corresponding to $\mathbf{R}_{\mathbf{f}_\mathrm{s} \mathbf{f}_\mathrm{s}}$, and one at the bottom right, corresponding to $\mathbf{R}_{\mathbf{f}_\mathrm{p} \mathbf{f}_\mathrm{p}}$. Although the elements of $\mathbf{f}_\mathrm{p}$ have a higher degree of internal correlation than those of $\mathbf{f}_\mathrm{s}$, with mean value $\mu(\mathbf{R}_{\mathbf{f}_\mathrm{p} \mathbf{f}_\mathrm{p}}) = 0.21$ and standard deviation $\sigma(\mathbf{R}_{\mathbf{f}_\mathrm{p} \mathbf{f}_\mathrm{p}}) = 0.08$, respectively, the cross coefficients present low values, with an average value of $\mu(\mathbf{R}_{\mathbf{f}_\mathrm{s} \mathbf{f}_\mathrm{p}}) = 0.07$. This means that the two embedding vectors do not strongly correlate with each other and do not share much information. The spectro-temporal and prosodic characteristics we are considering have turned out to be orthogonal to each other, benefiting our detector.

Given these results, we test how the embedding types perform individually in different scenarios. In this analysis, we consider three distinct models, all based on the proposed architecture, differing only for the embeddings subset that the final SVM classifier receives as input. The first model, that we indicate with *Prosody Emb*, is fully-prosodic and based on $\mathbf{f}_\mathrm{p}$ only. The second only considers the speaker information of $\mathbf{f}_\mathrm{s}$ and we indicate it as *Speaker Emb*. The third model is the complete one, i.e., *ProsoSpeaker*, and it performs classification using the

Table 3. EER, AUC and Balanced Accuracy values for the three models (*ProsoSpeaker, Speaker Emb, Prosody Emb*) tested on the three scenarios (TTS, VC, ALL).

	(a) TTS			(b) VC			(c) ALL		
	EER	AUC	BA	EER	AUC	BA	EER	AUC	BA
ProsoSpeaker	**4.93**	**99.02**	**94.77**	**6.70**	**98.29**	**93.28**	**5.39**	**98.85**	**94.43**
Prosody Emb	8.58	96.68	90.64	30.04	76.35	66.44	15.13	91.99	85.05
Speaker Emb	26.21	81.64	74.62	9.82	96.53	88.20	22.88	85.08	77.75

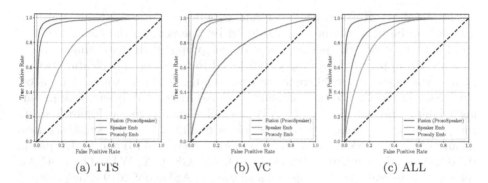

(a) TTS   (b) VC   (c) ALL

Fig. 4. ROC curves obtained for the three models using different embeddings (*ProsoSpeaker, Speaker Emb, Prosody Emb*) and tested on the three scenarios (TTS, VC, ALL).

concatenation of $\mathbf{f_p}$ and $\mathbf{f_s}$. All three models are trained on the same dataset, i.e., ASVspoof 2019 + LibriSpeech, with the same parameters. We then considered three test scenarios, depending on the synthesis techniques used to generate the synthetic speech signals of the test set. In the first scenario (a) we consider only speech tracks created with TTS techniques; in the second scenario (b) only speech tracks created with VC techniques; in the third scenario (c) both synthesis techniques are considered. All the tracks for the three scenarios are selected from ASVspoof 2019 dataset. Table 3 and Fig. 4 show the binary classification performances of this analysis, the first in terms of EER, AUC and balance accuracy obtained for the three models in the three test scenarios, the second showing the corresponding ROC curves.

The predictions of the two partial models are orthogonal to each other and each performs better on a distinct scenario. In particular, prosodic embeddings $\mathbf{f_p}$ can discriminate speech signals generated with TTS algorithms well but are less effective with VC methods, while speaker embeddings $\mathbf{f_s}$ achieves better results in the VC case than TTS. From these results we can confirm our initial hypothesis, i.e., that each one of the two speech generation techniques fails in reproducing one of the semantic features encoded by $\mathbf{f_s}$ or $\mathbf{f_p}$. On one side, TTS systems struggle at recreating natural sounding prosody, starting from a pure textual input, and hence prosody embeddings are effectively discriminating them from real speech. On the other hand, VC techniques manipulate an authentic speech sample to impersonate a target speaker, introducing artifacts in the timbre qualities that can be detected leveraging speaker embeddings. Nonetheless, the fusion of the two embeddings improves the predictions in all the considered scenarios, reaching an AUC = 0.99 in the case of the complete dataset. We can conclude that the concatenation of the two embeddings provides a more comprehensive and significant representation of the input speech signal, leading to higher binary classification performances.

4.3 Generalization

In this third set of experiments, we aim to analyze the consistency and generalization ability of the proposed method by augmenting the considered test set. First, we verify the performances of the proposed detector singularly on each algorithm present in ASVspoof 2019 *eval* to check the classification performances consistency over different synthesis strategies. Then, we want to assess *ProsoSpeaker*'s generalization capabilities across multiple datasets, unseen during training and external to the ASVspoof challenge corpora. Figure 5 shows the percentage of correct attribution values obtained for each synthesis algorithm included in ASVspoof 2019 *eval* set (A07, A08, ..., A13) and for LJSpeech, IEMOCAP and Cloud2019 (divided in PO, AZ, GS, GW, WA). The label AU corresponds to real speech samples distributed in ASVspoof 2019. The proposed method is successful in almost all the considered cases, with a percentage of correct attribution value always higher than 0.80. This means that *ProsoSpeaker* has good generalization capabilities, and we can consider it a reliable method. The only exception is represented by the TTS generator IBM Watson, included in Cloud2019, where the accuracy is equal to 0.50. We believe this issue is due to the fact that the IBM TTS method is specifically trained considering a "prosodic-phonology" approach for generating expressive speech [33], hence deceiving our detection method.

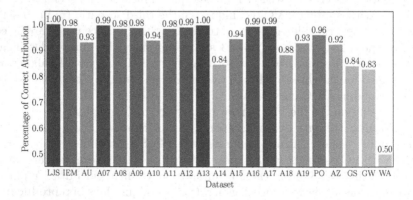

Fig. 5. Bar plot of the percentage of correct attribution values of the proposed model on each partition of each considered dataset.

4.4 Robustness Analysis

Some additional tests are finally necessary to verify the robustness of the proposed method to common signal manipulation, i.e., compression. In fact, in a real-world scenario, many operations can be performed to hide the artifacts introduced by deepfake generation algorithms, like, for instance, lossy compression. Some signal information is lost by compressing an audio track, including traces that may help deepfake detectors determine the signal's authenticity. Since our method does not rely on low-level signal characteristics but analyzes semantic features, we hypothesize that compression should not affect its performance significantly. In practice, speaker and prosody embeddings should be only partially impacted by this type of data augmentation and keep their discriminative potential. To test such aspect, we create three versions of the ASVspoof 2019 LA *eval* dataset using MP3 compression at different bitrates, namely 128 kBits/s, 64 kBits/s and 32 kBits/s, using SoX tool [39]. Table 4 shows the correspondent AUC, EER and balanced accuracy values for different compression bitrates. The detector's performance deteriorates as we increase the compression factor, observing AUC and EER values dropping by 2 and 4%, respectively, between the two extreme cases. Balanced accuracy decreases significantly when compression is firstly introduced, with a drop of 4% between the no-compression and 128 kBits/s cases. At the same time, it maintains stable values when the bitrate decreases, falling only by 1% between 128 and 32 kBit/s cases. We can conclude that, overall, the proposed system, thanks to its high-level semantic approach, is able to maintain its effectiveness even in presence of heavy signal compression.

Table 4. ROC AUC, EER and Bal. Acc. values computed on compressed versions of ASVspoof 2019 LA *eval* at different bitrates.

Compression Rate	ROC AUC	EER %	Bal. Acc. %
No Compression	98.86	5.21	94.40
128 kBits/s	98.35	6.96	89.83
64 kBits/s	98.13	7.12	89.68
32 kBits/s	96.77	9.81	88.50

5 Conclusions

In this paper we presented a novel method to perform DF speech detection. Adopting a semantic approach, we based our system on the concatenation of high-level features, denoted as speaker and prosody embeddings. This representation is used as input to a fast supervised binary classifier that predicts whether the speech signal is authentic or synthetically generated. We have shown that the performance of the proposed method outperforms those of the state-of-the-art considered baselines. In addition to that, it presents good generalization properties and is robust to real-world audio manipulation, as lossy compression. Moreover, through an ablation study, we observed how speaker and prosody embeddings perform individually in different scenarios and why their combination is the more effective strategy, achieving higher classification performances. The obtained results validate the idea of exploiting semantic features to discriminate deepfakes and highlight some of the aspects on which speech generators still fail.

Acknowledgements. This work was supported by the PREMIER project, funded by the Italian Ministry of Education, University, and Research within the PRIN 2017 program. This material is based on research sponsored by DARPA and Air Force Research Laboratory (AFRL) under agreement number FA8750-20-2-1004. The U.S. Government is authorized to reproduce and distribute reprints for Governmental purposes notwithstanding any copyright notation thereon. The views and conclusions contained herein are those of the authors and should not be interpreted as necessarily representing the official policies or endorsements, either expressed or implied, of DARPA and Air Force Research Laboratory (AFRL) or the U.S. Government.

References

1. Agarwal, S., Farid, H.: Detecting deep-fake videos from aural and oral dynamics. In: IEEE/CVF Conference on Computer Vision and Pattern Recognition (CVPR) (2021)
2. Agarwal, S., Farid, H., El-Gaaly, T., Lim, S.N.: Detecting deep-fake videos from appearance and behavior. In: IEEE International Workshop on Information Forensics and Security (WIFS) (2020)
3. Alzantot, M., Wang, Z., Srivastava, M.B.: Deep residual neural networks for audio spoofing detection. In: Conference of the International Speech Communication Association (INTERSPEECH) (2019)
4. Bonettini, N., Cannas, E.D., Mandelli, S., Bondi, L., Bestagini, P., Tubaro, S.: Video face manipulation detection through ensemble of CNNs. In: International Conference on Pattern Recognition (ICPR) (2021)
5. Borrelli, C., Bestagini, P., Antonacci, F., Sarti, A., Tubaro, S.: Synthetic speech detection through short-term and long-term prediction traces. EURASIP J. Inf. Secur. **2021**(1), 1–14 (2021). https://doi.org/10.1186/s13635-021-00116-3
6. Busso, C., et al.: IEMOCAP: interactive emotional dyadic motion capture database. Lang. Resour. Eval. **42**(4), 335–359 (2008)
7. Chen, T., Kumar, A., Nagarsheth, P., Sivaraman, G., Khoury, E.: Generalization of audio deepfake detection. In: Odyssey Speaker and Language Recognition Workshop (2020)
8. Chugh, K., Gupta, P., Dhall, A., Subramanian, R.: Not made for each other-audio-visual dissonance-based deepfake detection and localization. In: International Conference on Multimedia (ACM) (2020)
9. Chung, J.S., Nagrani, A., Zisserman, A.: VoxCeleb2: deep speaker recognition. In: Conference of the International Speech Communication Association (INTERSPEECH) (2018)
10. Conti, E., et al.: Deepfake speech detection through emotion recognition: a semantic approach. In: IEEE International Conference on Acoustics, Speech and Signal Processing (ICASSP) (2022)

11. Cozzolino, D., Rössler, A., Thies, J., Nießner, M., Verdoliva, L.: ID-Reveal: identity-aware deepfake video detection. In: IEEE/CVF Conference on Computer Vision and Pattern Recognition (CVPR) (2021)
12. Desplanques, B., Thienpondt, J., Demuynck, K.: ECAPA-TDNN: emphasized channel attention, propagation and aggregation in TDNN based speaker verification. In: Conference of the International Speech Communication Association (INTERSPEECH) (2020)
13. Forbes: Deepfakes, revenge porn, and the impact on women. https://www.forbes.com/sites/chenxiwang/2019/11/01/deepfakes-revenge-porn-and-the-impact-on-women/?sh=45b66a961f53
14. Forbes: Fraudsters Cloned Company Director's Voice In 35$ Million Bank Heist, Police Find. https://www.forbes.com/sites/thomasbrewster/2021/10/14/huge-bank-fraud-uses-deep-fake-voice-tech-to-steal-millions
15. Gao, Y., Vuong, T., Elyasi, M., Bharaj, G., Singh, R.: Generalized spoofing detection inspired from audio generation artifacts. In: Conference of the International Speech Communication Association (INTERSPEECH) (2021)
16. The Guardian: The rise of the deepfake and the threat to democracy. https://www.theguardian.com/technology/ng-interactive/2019/jun/22/the-rise-of-the-deepfake-and-the-threat-to-democracy
17. He, K., Zhang, X., Ren, S., Sun, J.: Deep residual learning for image recognition. In: IEEE Conference on Computer Vision and Pattern Recognition (CVPR) (2016)
18. Hosler, B., et al.: Do deepfakes feel emotions? A semantic approach to detecting deepfakes via emotional inconsistencies. In: IEEE Conference on Computer Vision and Pattern Recognition (CVPR) (2021)
19. Hu, J., Shen, L., Sun, G.: Squeeze-and-excitation networks. In: IEEE Conference on Computer Vision and Pattern Recognition (CVPR) (2018)
20. Ito, K., Johnson, L.: The LJ Speech Dataset (2017). https://keithito.com/LJ-Speech-Dataset/
21. Kamble, M.R., Sailor, H.B., Patil, H.A., Li, H.: Advances in anti-spoofing: from the perspective of ASVspoof challenges. APSIPA Trans. Signal Inf. Process. (2020)
22. King, S., Karaiskos, V.: The Blizzard challenge 2013. In: Blizzard Challenge Workshop (2013)
23. Li, Y., Chang, M.C., Lyu, S.: In Ictu Oculi: exposing AI created fake videos by detecting eye blinking. In: IEEE International Workshop on Information Forensics and Security (WIFS) (2018)
24. Li, Y., Lyu, S.: Exposing deepfake videos by detecting face warping artifacts. In: IEEE Conference on Computer Vision and Pattern Recognition (CVPR) (2018)
25. Lieto, A., et al.: "Hello? Who Am I Talking to?" A shallow CNN approach for Human vs. Bot speech classification. In: IEEE International Conference on Acoustics, Speech and Signal Processing (ICASSP) (2019)
26. Malik, H.: Securing voice-driven interfaces against fake (cloned) audio attacks. In: IEEE Conference on Multimedia Information Processing and Retrieval (MIPR) (2019)
27. Masood, M., Nawaz, M., Malik, K.M., Javed, A., Irtaza, A.: Deepfakes generation and detection: state-of-the-art, open challenges, countermeasures, and way forward. arXiv preprint arXiv:2103.00484 (2021)
28. Mimecast: Why Deepfakes are Revolutionizing the World of Phishing. https://www.mimecast.com/blog/deepfakes-revolutionizing-phishing
29. Nagrani, A., Chung, J.S., Zisserman, A.: VoxCeleb: a large-scale speaker identification dataset. In: Conference of the International Speech Communication Association (INTERSPEECH) (2017)

30. NewScientist: Fake faces created by AI look more trustworthy than real people. https://www.newscientist.com/article/2308312-fake-faces-created-by-ai-look-more-trustworthy-than-real-people/
31. Okabe, K., Koshinaka, T., Shinoda, K.: Attentive statistics pooling for deep speaker embedding. In: Conference of the International Speech Communication Association (INTERSPEECH) (2018)
32. Panayotov, V., Chen, G., Povey, D., Khudanpur, S.: LibriSpeech: an ASR corpus based on public domain audio books. In: IEEE International Conference on Acoustics, Speech and Signal Processing (ICASSP) (2015)
33. Pitrelli, J.F., Bakis, R., Eide, E.M., Fernandez, R., Hamza, W., Picheny, M.A.: The IBM expressive text-to-speech synthesis system for American English. IEEE Trans. Audio Speech Lang. Process. **14**(4), 1099–1108 (2006)
34. Ravanelli, M., et al.: SpeechBrain: a general-purpose speech toolkit. arXiv:2106.04624 (2021)
35. de Ruiter, A.: The distinct wrong of deepfakes. Philos. Technol. **34**(4), 1311–1332 (2021)
36. Skerry-Ryan, R., et al.: Towards end-to-end prosody transfer for expressive speech synthesis with tacotron. In: International Conference on Machine Learning (ICML) (2018)
37. Snyder, D., Garcia-Romero, D., Sell, G., McCree, A., Povey, D., Khudanpur, S.: Speaker recognition for multi-speaker conversations using X-vectors. In: IEEE International Conference on Acoustics, Speech and Signal Processing (ICASSP) (2019)
38. Snyder, D., Garcia-Romero, D., Sell, G., Povey, D., Khudanpur, S.: X-vectors: robust DNN embeddings for speaker recognition. In: IEEE International Conference on Acoustics, Speech and Signal Processing (ICASSP) (2018)
39. SoX Sound eXchange. http://sox.sourceforge.net
40. Tak, H., Patino, J., Todisco, M., Nautsch, A., Evans, N., Larcher, A.: End-to-end anti-spoofing with RawNet2. In: IEEE International Conference on Acoustics, Speech and Signal Processing (ICASSP) (2021)
41. The New York Times: Pennsylvania Woman Accused of Using Deepfake Technology to Harass Cheerleaders. https://www.nytimes.com/2021/03/14/us/raffaela-spone-victory-vipers-deepfake.html
42. Todisco, M., et al.: ASVspoof 2019: future horizons in spoofed and fake audio detection. In: Conference of the International Speech Communication Association (INTERSPEECH) (2019)
43. Verdoliva, L.: Media forensics and deepfakes: an overview. IEEE J. Sel. Topics Signal Process. **14**(5), 910–932 (2020)
44. Wang, Y., et al.: Tacotron: towards end-to-end speech synthesis. In: Conference of the International Speech Communication Association (INTERSPEECH) (2017)
45. Wang, Y., et al.: Style tokens: unsupervised style modeling, control and transfer in end-to-end speech synthesis. In: International Conference on Machine Learning (ICML) (2018)
46. Wang, Z.F., Wei, G., He, Q.H.: Channel pattern noise based playback attack detection algorithm for speaker recognition. In: IEEE International Conference on Machine Learning and Cybernetics (ICMLC) (2011)
47. Westerlund, M.: The emergence of deepfake technology: a review. Technol. Innov. Manage. Rev. **9**(11) (2019)
48. Yamagishi, J., et al.: ASVspoof 2021: accelerating progress in spoofed and deepfake speech detection. In: Automatic Speaker Verification and Spoofing Countermeasures Challenge (2021)

49. Yang, X., Li, Y., Lyu, S.: Exposing deep fakes using inconsistent head poses. In: IEEE International Conference on Acoustics, Speech and Signal Processing (ICASSP) (2019)
50. Zeinali, H., Wang, S., Silnova, A., Matějka, P., Plchot, O.: BUT system description to VoxCeleb speaker recognition challenge 2019. In: The VoxCeleb Challenge Workshop (2019)
51. Zhang, X., Karaman, S., Chang, S.F.: Detecting and simulating artifacts in GAN fake images. In: IEEE International Workshop on Information Forensics and Security (WIFS) (2019)

Towards Unconstrained Audio Splicing Detection and Localization with Neural Networks

Denise Moussa[1,2]([envelope]) [iD], Germans Hirsch[2], and Christian Riess[2] [iD]

[1] Federal Criminal Police Office (BKA), Wiesbaden, Germany
[2] Friedrich-Alexander Universität Erlangen-Nürnberg, Erlangen, Germany
{denise.moussa,christian.riess}@fau.de

Abstract. Freely available and easy-to-use audio editing tools make it straightforward to perform audio splicing. Convincing forgeries can be created by combining various speech samples from the same person. Detection of such splices is important both in the public sector when considering misinformation, and in a legal context to verify the integrity of evidence. Unfortunately, most existing detection algorithms for audio splicing use handcrafted features and make specific assumptions. However, criminal investigators are often faced with audio samples from unconstrained sources with unknown characteristics, which raises the need for more generally applicable methods.

With this work, we aim to take a first step towards unconstrained audio splicing detection to address this need. We simulate various attack scenarios in the form of post-processing operations that may disguise splicing. We propose a Transformer sequence-to-sequence (seq2seq) network for splicing detection and localization. Our extensive evaluation shows that the proposed method outperforms existing dedicated approaches for splicing detection [3,10] as well as the general-purpose networks EfficientNet [28] and RegNet [25]. Our source code is available at: https://www.cs1.tf.fau.de/research/multimedia-security/code

Keywords: Audio Splicing Detection · Forensics · Deep Learning

1 Introduction

With steadily improving technical methods, it became increasingly easier to convincingly manipulate multimedia content. In the era of social media platforms, where huge amounts of images, audio snippets and videos are distributed, well-crafted pieces of maliciously manipulated content may quickly spread over the internet. Forged multimedia content also becomes increasingly relevant in a legal context, such as criminal investigations. Hereby, multimedia material may serve as clue or evidence. Hence, it is of increasing importance to research and to deploy methods for ensuring the integrity and authenticity of such data.

D. Moussa and C. Riess—Both authors contributed equally to this work.

© Springer Nature Switzerland AG 2023
J.-J. Rousseau and B. Kapralos (Eds.): ICPR 2022 Workshops, LNCS 13644, pp. 264–280, 2023.
https://doi.org/10.1007/978-3-031-37742-6_22

Plausible multimedia forgeries can be created with several deep learning (DL) methods. Examples are approaches for changing the attributes of a given image of a human face [32], for swapping the face of persons in photographs [21], or for face reenactment [21,29]. Another impressive demonstration was shown recently on video synthesis: given a speech recording and image of an individual's face, lip synthesis can even create a video of the individual that gives the speech [4]. To create fake audio, voice conversion and speech synthesis have been proposed. Voice conversion transforms the speech of one person to sound like the voice of another person [9]. Speech synthesis generates fully synthetic audio in the voice of a specific individual [11].

In this work, we analyze audio splicing, which describes the processes of inserting, deleting or concatenating audio signals. This tampering technique is arguably one of the easiest to perform, as it can also be done by laypeople using freely available audio editing tools like Audacity [1] or Oceanaudio [22]. Despite the simplicity of creation, audio splicing can pose a serious threat. In some situations, even small changes can already alter the semantics of statements in a speech. For example, removing the negation particle 'not' may flip a negated statement into a positive statement.

Many existing works use hand-crafted features to extract specific character-istics for audio splicing detection or localization (Sect. 2.1). One weakness of hand-crafted features is that they are typically only applicable within relatively narrow bounds around their designed purpose. For example, methods intended for finding differences in recording devices do not indicate splicing if the same device is employed. As a second example, classification of recording environments is unable to detect splicing from static surroundings. However, DL techniques make it feasible to learn features that fit more complex data distributions, and thereby to overcome the constraints of manual feature selection. Surprisingly, DL methods have so far barely been explored for audio splicing detection.

With this work, we aim at closing this gap and propose a Transformer [31] seq2seq architecture to make a first step towards unconstrained audio splicing detection and localization. We analyze different attack scenarios in the form of post-processing operations that may be applied to disguise splicing. This includes MP3 and AMR-NB single and multi compression, additive synthetic and real noise. Our forgery settings also cover audio compositions with samples from different environments, same environments and – particularly difficult to differentiate – anechoic environments. We compare to a recent method that uses handcrafted features [3], and to the neural network by Jadhav et al. [10], which to our knowledge is the only other end-to-end approach to forensic audio splic-ing detection. Our method also outperforms the state-of-the-art general-purpose models EfficientNet [28] and RegNet [25]. Our main contributions are:

- We present a robust end-to-end trainable seq2seq model for audio splicing detection and localization.
- For evaluation, we propose a challenging data set that covers a large variety of forgery scenarios for the task of unconstrained audio splicing detection and localization.

2 Related Work

We distinguish two types of methods for audio splicing detection and localization. First, we review methods that manually extract features in Sect. 2.1. Second, we review DL methods in Sect. 2.2.

2.1 Methods with Manual Feature Selection

Most related works on audio splicing detection rely on specific handcrafted features. As such, the feature response is inherently explainable, but the methods can typically only be used in very specific application scenarios. For example, Yang et al. focus specifically on MP3 encoded audio [34]. They localize splicing in the signals by identifying inconsistencies in the offsets of the encoded audio frames. Cooper et al. target uncompressed audio, where they search discontinuities in the high frequencies of the audio waveform [5].

Some other approaches detect splicing by analyzing noise levels in the audio signal. For instance, Pan et al. compute global and local noise levels of audio data and identify abnormal changes in the noise level [24]. Meng et al. adopt a similar approach and compute local noise levels w.r.t. each syllable in the speech signal [19]. Different from those works, Yan et al. [33] recently targeted composite audio with signals from different sources but with similar or equal signal-to-noise ratio (SNR). This work locates splicing points from the variances of Mel frequency cepstral coefficients (MFCCs).

Cuccovillo et al. [6] perform splicing detection based on microphone classification. They exploit the fact that source files from different devices exhibit characteristic traces in the signal.

Several works analyze the electric network frequency (ENF). Esquef et al. use ENF analysis to exclusively target splices in silent (non-voice-active) positions in the signal [8]. However, ENF traces are weak and may be occluded by high noise. Hence, Lin et al. apply a spectral phase analysis instead which exhibits better robustness towards noise corruptions [13]. Lin et al. also present a second approach to increase the robustness to noise [14]. They propose to amplify abnormal changes via wavelet-filtering the ENF signal, and then extract autoregressive coefficients for tampering detection.

Another line of work models acoustic environmental signatures for splicing detection. Zhao et al. compute features from the acoustic channel impulse response and ambient noise to model such an acoustic environmental signature [37,38]. Rouniyar et al. refine the feature selection and increase performance by using both acoustic channel response and dynamic and static logarithmic spectral characteristics to identify and locate splicing [26].

Recently, Capoferri et al. proposed the reverberation time (RT) as single forensic trace to detect splicing [3]. The RT is assumed to differ in different surroundings. Hence, changes in the RT across different temporal windows of the audio signal are then used to localize splicing.

A shared drawback of all these approaches is that they are restricted by their specific assumptions. This includes specific audio compression formats or the absence of compression [5,34], differing recording devices in the forged audio [6] and changing recording environments, like changing noise [19,24,33], changing acoustic impulse [3,37,38] or indicative ENF patterns [8,13,14].

2.2 Deep Learning Methods

DL methods were successfully applied to various tasks in audio forensics, including double compression detection [16], audio recapture detection [15], speech presentation attack detection [12], and fake speech detection [35]. Surprisingly, the detection of audio splicing received little attention so far. Mao *et al.* [17] target audio tampering (including splicing) with a convolutional neural network (CNN) classifier for detection but without localization. The CNN does not directly operate on the audio samples, but instead on pre-defined ENF features. Zhang *et al.* [36] use an encoder-decoder architecture based on VGG-16 [27] to learn a segmentation mask for spliced audio samples. This method can be seen as a very preliminary splicing detector whose design is dependent on quite restrictive assumptions. Most notably, the architecture only permits the detection of splicings from snippets with 1s duration, where at the same time each snippet is a random crop from a different speaker.

Jadhav *et al.* [10] use the short-term Fourier transform of spliced audio signals directly as input to a shallow CNN architecture. They report that their method is robust under added white Gaussian noise and dynamic range compression. However, this work also does not consider the practically highly relevant case of splices from sources of the same speaker. Additionally, the evaluation of the method is somewhat limited to a relatively small, non-diverse test set.

In this work, we first explore the task of broadly applicable, robust audio splicing detection and localization. We propose a seq2seq Transformer [31] that operates on various representations of audio signals. Transformers excel in various natural language processing tasks [23] and efficiently exploit sequential context information which is also present in audio data. In addition, seq2seq methods have the specific benefit that, differently from CNN based methods [10,36], they can very naturally process sequences of arbitrary input/output lengths.

Contrary to previous approaches [10,36], we validate our method on a challenging, diverse dataset. We include single and multiple splices, as well as various post-processing operations that potentially disguise the splicing, such as multiple MP3 and AMR-NB compressions and added synthetic and real noise. Moreover, we consider forgeries that are created from audios that are recorded in different environments, as well as the more difficult case of identical environments. Additionally, we investigate the very challenging intersplicing scenario, where samples are assumed to be relatively anechoic and stem from the same recording in a static surrounding. With this diversity we also aim at mitigating the application constraints of previous methods that use handcrafted features (Sect. 2.1).

3   Methods

This section consists of four parts. In Sect. 3.1 we describe our setup for data generation, in Sect. 3.2 we formally define our task. Sect. 3.3 summarizes the Transformer design [31] and Sect. 3.4 describes our proposed architecture.

3.1   Data Generation Pipeline

The data for our experiments is generated with base data from the ACE [7] and the Hi-Fi TTS (TTS) [2] datasets. For the ACE dataset, we use the same data split as Capoferri et al. [3], thus 65 speech samples between 1.28 s and 97 s from 5 female and 9 male speakers. For the TTS dataset, we consider all 6 female and 4 male speakers and use the 10 longest utterances per person reading different books. The audio signals vary between 7 s and 20 s. We separate speakers in training, validation and test pools. For ACE, we take 10 speakers for training, 2 for validation, and reserve one female and one male speaker for test. For experiments where we train on ACE, we take all speakers of TTS for testing. When training on the latter, we split it into 7 speakers for training, and for validation and test we use 2 speakers (male and female) each.

For our experiments, we generate training, validation and test inputs from these disjoint speaker pools using our pipeline shown in Fig. 1. The pipeline operates as follows. First, we choose $N \in [1, 5]$ audio signals $a_1(, \ldots, a_N)$ from the same speaker randomly and allow multiple choices of the same sample. Each a_i is convolved with a room impulse response (RIR) randomly sampled from a set of 7 synthetic and 7 real RIRs (step 1) to simulate recordings from environments with various echoic characteristics. Here, we use the same RIRs as Capoferri et al. [3] and allow recordings to stem from equal environments. Note that we skip this step in one experiment without RIR cue (Sect. 4.3). We omit any other individual processing per sample a_i (e.g., added noise or compression) to avoid that our model is accidentally biased to such overly specific features. In the second step, we compute all silent, i.e. non-voice-active, positions for each signal with a voice activation detector. We sample two random silent positions from each a_i and cut the sub-sequence between these points, which we denote as $\tilde{a}_i$. The spliced sample $\tilde{a}$ is then the concatenation of all $\tilde{a}_1, \ldots, \tilde{a}_N$ or equal to $\tilde{a}_1$ if $n = 1$, i.e., no splicing was sampled (step 3). Optionally, post-processing is applied to $\tilde{a}$ which may mask splicing points. To this end, additive noise can first be added with a specified SNR (step 4). Then, compression can be applied once or multiple times with given format and strength (step 5). The length of the resulting audio samples varies between 3 s and 45 s. All specific post-processing parameters for each experiment are stated in Sect. 4.

As a last step, three representations of the resulting signal are computed via torchaudio [30] (step 6). We include the Mel spectrogram and MFCCs as two established features in the speech processing domain and additionally add spectral centroid features which describe the brightness of a sound [18]. Incorporating MFCCs and spectral centroid features additionally to the Mel spectrogram empirically showed to improve the performance in complex settings (Sect. 4).

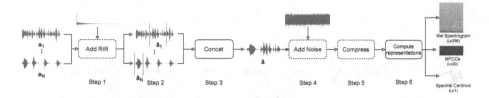

Fig. 1. Adaptive pipeline for generating spliced audio samples. Reverberation of environments is simulated prior to splicing, while additive noise and compression are postprocessing operations that may disguise splicing points. Dotted lines indicate optional operations, allowing for adaptable splicing forgery scenarios.

For computing the spectral features, we use a window size of 500 ms and a sample rate of 16 kHz. For the Mel spectrogram we additionally choose 256 Mel filter banks and then directly compute the MFCCs with `n_mfcc` = 20 from the result. All other parameters are used in their default settings.

3.2   Task Formulation

We model audio splicing detection/localization as a seq2seq task. The Mel Spectrogram of audio signals is our input sequence $\mathbf{S} \in [-1, 1]^{w \times H}$ with fixed H, *i.e.*, fixed frequency resolution and variable width $w \in \mathbb{N}$ depending on the signal length in the time domain. We process $\mathbf{S}$ as a series of slices, $\mathbf{s}_i \in [-1, 1]^H$, *i.e.*, column-by-column, which yields the input series $\tilde{\mathbf{S}} = [\mathbf{s}_1, \mathbf{s}_2, ..., \mathbf{s}_w]$. Our specific task is to translate $\tilde{\mathbf{S}}$ to a series of splicing points $\hat{P} = [\hat{p}_1, \hat{p}_2, ..., \hat{p}_L]$ of variable length L. Each splicing location $\hat{p}_j \in \mathcal{V}$ is provided in seconds from a vocabulary $\mathcal{V}$ of all valid splicing locations.

3.3   Transformers

Transformers [31] are neural network (NN) architectures with a scaled dot-product attention mechanism as core operation. They aim at grasping global dependencies between two sequences $\mathbf{S}_i$, $\mathbf{S}_j$. An important component is self-attention, where $\mathbf{S}_i = \mathbf{S}_j$. The attention function maps a matrix triple $(\mathbf{Q}, \mathbf{V}, \mathbf{K})$ to an output, with $\mathbf{Q}, \mathbf{V}, \mathbf{K}$ being a set of queries $\mathbf{Q}$, values $\mathbf{V}$, and keys $\mathbf{K}$. It is defined as

$$\text{Att}(\mathbf{Q}, \mathbf{V}, \mathbf{K}) = \text{Softmax}\left(\frac{\mathbf{Q}\mathbf{K}^\top}{\sqrt{d_K}}\mathbf{V}\right), \qquad (1)$$

where d_K is the dimension of the queries/keys that normalizes the product. $\mathbf{Q}, \mathbf{K}$ and $\mathbf{V}$ are obtained by projecting input sequences with learnable weight matrices $\mathbf{W}^Q \in \mathbb{R}^{d_m \times d_k}$, $\mathbf{W}^K \in \mathbb{R}^{d_m \times d_k}$ and $\mathbf{W}^V \in \mathbb{R}^{d_m \times d_v}$, where d_m is the model dimension, *i.e.* the output dimension of the model's layers, and d_k, d_v are the keys' and values' dimensions, respectively. Typically, Transformers learn h

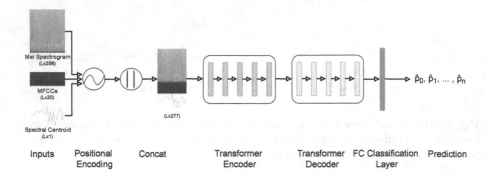

Fig. 2. Proposed network architecture. Different audio representations of length L (dependent on the audio sample length) are concatenated and processed by one encoder, which proved to be superior to separate encoders per representation. The encoded results are fed to the decoder and projected to the vocabulary space to yield the final predicted splicing points.

representations $(\mathbf{Q}, \mathbf{V}, \mathbf{K})$ and compute attention in parallel over those h triples. This is called multi-head attention and formally given by

$$\text{MultiHead}(\mathbf{Q}, \mathbf{V}, \mathbf{K}) = [\text{head}_1 || ... || \text{head}_h]\mathbf{W}^O, \tag{2}$$

where $\mathbf{W}^O \in \mathbb{R}^{hd_v \times d_m}$ and head_i (for $1 \leq i \leq h$) is

$$\text{head}_i = \text{Att}(\mathbf{Q}_i, \mathbf{V}_i, \mathbf{K}_i) . \tag{3}$$

A Transformer for seq2seq tasks consists of a transformer encoder and a transformer decoder network. The input sequence is processed by the encoder, which outputs the encoded result to the decoder. The latter calculates the prediction from that encoder memory and the sequence elements from all previous time steps. Both the encoder and the decoder network consist of several layers. Each encoder layer implements self-attention and fully-connected (FC) sub-layers. Each sub-layer includes layer-normalization as well as a residual connection around itself. The decoder is constructed similarly. However, additionally to self-attention, it also computes the encoder-decoder attention, where $\mathbf{K}$, $\mathbf{V}$ stem from the encoder output, while $\mathbf{Q}$ stems from the decoder. For an in-depth description of the Transformer architecture, we refer to Vaswani *et al.* [31].

3.4   Proposed Network Architecture

Our proposed network architecture is depicted in Fig. 2. It operates on three input representations, the Mel spectrogram, MFCCs and spectral centroid. All inputs are normalized to range $[-1, 1]$ to support training stability. They are then subjected to positional encoding [31], concatenated and fed to the encoder (blue). Fusing the inputs and encoding them empirically showed to perform better than processing each input representation with a separate encoder and fusing the outputs. The encoder and decoder (orange) both consist of 5 layers with 8 heads. The model dimension $d_m = d_k = d_v$ is of size 256 and the dimension of each layer's FC sublayer is 512. The last FC layer (green) projects the output of the decoder to the vocabulary size $|\mathcal{V}|$. Our vocabulary $\mathcal{V} = \{\circ\} \cup \{0.5, ..., 44.5\} \cup \{<\text{pad}>, <\text{bos}>, <\text{eos}>\}$ consists of 93 items representing no splicing ($\circ$), all possible 89 splicing positions $[0.5, ..., 44.5]$ in 500 ms steps as well as 3 special tokens for seq2seq translation.

4 Evaluation

We perform a variety of experiments to show the robustness and general applicability of our method.

For single splicing, we report the top-n accuracy (acc) per sample for $n \in [1, 5]$. Thus, we report the relative frequency that all splicing points are predicted correctly within the n most likely predictions. To provide a more detailed insight on the quality of each prediction, we additionally report the Euclidean distance from the true splicing point d_{sp}. For multisplicing, we compute the Jaccard coefficient J between the predicted splicing points $\hat{P}_{\tilde{\mathbf{S}}}$ and ground truth $P_{\tilde{\mathbf{S}}}$ per sample $\tilde{\mathbf{S}}$. It is calculated as

$$J = \frac{|P_{\tilde{\mathbf{S}}}| \cap |\hat{P}_{\tilde{\mathbf{S}}}|}{|P_{\tilde{\mathbf{S}}}| \cup |\hat{P}_{\tilde{\mathbf{S}}}|}, \tag{4}$$

where 0 means no intersection with the ground truth of (non)-splicing points and 1 is the perfect score. Note that J is independent of the elements' order in $P_{\tilde{\mathbf{S}}}$ and $\hat{P}_{\tilde{\mathbf{S}}}$. We additionally report the recall R. For both metrics, we tolerate time errors for splicing points within a narrow window of size $w = 0.5$ s. We also report softer variants J_w and R_w with larger tolerance windows of $w \in \{1\,\text{s}, 2\,\text{s}, 3\,\text{s}\}$.

4.1 Models and Training Procedures

We consider various baseline methods in our experiments. To the best of our knowledge, the only end-to-end trainable DL method for audio splicing detection was proposed by Jadhav et al. [10]. We do not compare to the method by Zhang et al. [36] due to its very limiting constraints (cf. Sect. 2.2), which are not straightforward to relax to our more general task. We re-implemented the method of Jadhav et al. [10] and filled unspecified network components with plausible settings. This includes the padding strategy, the kernel size k of the convolutional layers and the dimension d of the two FC layers, which we chose as "same" padding, $k = 3$ and $d = 1024$. We additionally compare to state-of-the-art EfficientNet B0 [28] (EffNet-B0) and RegNet-x-400mf [25] (RegNet-400m) recognition models [20]. All models, including our approach, are both evaluated with single-input, which includes only the Mel spectrogram as feature, as well as multi-input, which includes all three representations as shown in Fig. 1.

Among all methods, our model is the most parameter-efficient with $\sim$ 7M, followed by RegNet-400m with $\sim$ 29M, EffNet-B0 with $\sim$ 71M parameters and the work by Jadhav *et al.* with $\sim$ 197M parameters.

We adapt the baseline NNs to our task. Contrary to our model that generalizes naturally to varying lengths, the CNNs expect fixed input/output sizes. We thus pad all inputs to the maximum length of 90 and concatenate all three audio representations along the height. The input layer is thus set to $1 \times 90 \times 277$. For multisplicing, we extend the output FC layer from one to the maximum possible number N of splicing positions, predicting $\hat{p}_i \in [0.5, 1.0, \ldots, 44.5]$ with $i \in [1, N]$ or special token $\hat{p}_{N+1} = \circ$ if no splicing is detected. Given the corresponding ground truth, all models, including ours, are trained using the cross-entropy loss.

Per model, we increase the computational speed by enlarging the training batch size for as long as the training still convergences. We chose a batch size of 512 for our model, 256 for Jadhav *et al.* [10] and RegNet-400m [25], and 64 for EffNet-B0 [28]. Still, the Adam optimizer with learning rate $1e^{-4}$ proved to be most beneficial for all models. We train with early stopping on the validation loss with delta $\delta = 0.2$ and a patience of 10 epochs. Our model is trained with teacher forcing.

We also compare our method to Capoferri *et al.* [3], as a recently proposed method with handcrafted features for single splicing detection. For the first part of the comparative evaluation in Sect. 4.2, we include RIRs in step 1 of our data generation pipeline (cf. Fig. 1). Hence, this feature is present in our data and their analytic approach is applicable in this case. Note, that we consistently allow the same RIR to be sampled for audio sources to model both equal and different environmental sources.

4.2   Basic Single-Splicing Forgery Model

In our first experiments, we consider basic forgery scenarios that only cover single splices. We first conduct a cross-dataset validation (Sect. 4.2), where we omit any post-processing operations. In a second step, the scenario is more difficult with additive synthetic noise and single compression post-processing (Sect. 4.2) as easy mechanisms to disguise splicing.

Cross-Dataset Validation. We perform a cross-dataset validation experiment between data from the ACE [7] and the TTS [2] dataset. For each, we generate a training set of 500000 and multiple test sets of 2000 samples as described in Sect. 3.1. For now, we omit post-processing operations (step 4,5) in the generation pipeline (cf. Fig. 1). This corresponds to the most basic forgery model, where new content is generated from samples of the same speaker with no camouflage operations to disguise the splicing points.

Figure 3 shows the results. The top row reports accuracy, the bottom row the distance d_{sp} to the ground truth splicing point. The four plots in one row show the four combinations of source datasets for training and testing.

Our method (violet) performs best in every case, while Jadhav *et al.* (yellow) is the best baseline. In general, our method in multi-input mode (solid lines)

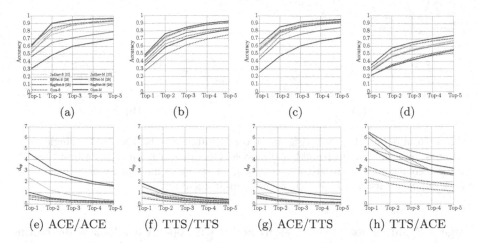

(a)   (b)   (c)   (d)

(e) ACE/ACE   (f) TTS/TTS   (g) ACE/TTS   (h) TTS/ACE

Fig. 3. Results for cross-data validation for the single- (dotted lines) and multi-input (solid lines) variants of the models. Each column portrays one train set/test set run. Top row: top-n accuracies. Bottom row: d_{sp}. We perform best for all combinations. Generalizing from TTS shows to be the most difficult.

achieves an equal (Fig. 3a) or higher accuracy (Fig. 3b–3d) than the single-input variant (dotted lines), even if d_{sp} is slightly larger (Fig. 3e–3h). Contrary, the CNN baselines [10,25,28] mostly perform worse when in multi-input mode. We assume a slight over adaptation due to the additional input representation information, such that training on the single (sparser) representation is beneficial in this case. Concerning the cross-dataset combinations, generalizing from TTS to ACE is the hardest for all models (Fig. 3d, Fig. 3h), while both the ACE/TTS (Fig. 3c, Fig. 3g) and the intra dataset experiment on TTS (Fig. 3b, Fig. 3f) exhibit significantly better results. We thus assume that TTS may contain specific characteristics to which the models adapt to, which results in a decreasing performance when testing on another dataset. For this reason, we take ACE/TTS as training/test combination for all following experiments.

We also run the method by Capoferri et al. [3] on both datasets. By design, it only provides top-1 accuracies. We report an accuracy of 4.9% and 6.8%, as well as a d_{sp} of 4.60 and 2.93 for ACE and TTS, which is below the other methods. We hypothesize that the discrepancy to the reported performances by Capoferri et al. is due to differences in the dataset construction. While Capoferri et al. [3] randomly splice signals, we only splice during silent points, which makes the detection task considerably more difficult.

Influence of Noise and Compression. To disguise splicing points, a forger may take simple measures. Here, we consider additive synthetic noise, MP3 compression, and AMR-NB compression as post-processing operations on the

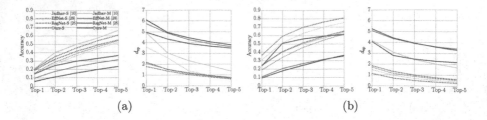

Fig. 4. Results for robustness (Fig. 4a) and adaptability tests (Fig. 4b) for single- (dotted lines) and multi-input (solid lines) models. Overall, our model adapts best (Fig. 4b) and is second best w.r.t robustness (Fig. 4a). Contrary to most other experiments, the single-input accuracy is higher than multi-input accuracy.

forgery. Additive noise may be easily added with openly available audio editing tools [1, 22]. Encoding the audio data in a lossy compression format is even more straightforward. We consider white Gaussian noise as a general noise approximation and MP3 and AMR-NB as two popular lossy compression formats. We generate a test set from the TTS test split (Sect. 3.1) with 30 000 samples and consider weak to strong degradation influence (step 4,5 in Fig. 1). In detail, per sample, we first randomly chose a SNR $\in [-10, 50]$ db for noise. Then, randomly either MP3 or AMR-NB is chosen for compression with random $b_r \in [10, 128] \frac{kb}{s}$ for MP3 and $b_r \in \{4.75, 5.15, 5.9, 6.7, 7.4, 7.95, 10.2, 12.2\} \frac{kb}{s}$ for AMR-NB. In addition, we evaluate the adaptability of the models towards all degradations. For this, we fine-tune all NNs on a ACE training set of 500 000 samples with the same degradation pipeline and rerun on the TTS test set.

The NNs' results are reported in Fig. 4. Figure 4a shows the robustness of the models trained on the clean training set towards the degraded test set. With the exception of Jadhav et al. [10], the single-input models exhibit higher accuracy (Fig. 4a, left). Our single-input model performs second best w.r.t accuracy and has the lowest d_{sp} (Fig. 4a, right). When fine-tuned on the degradations, all models perform better as expected (Fig. 4b). Similar to the CNNs in the cross-dataset setting, the single-input variants are superior, with the difference that also our approach performs better here with single-input. This is, however, a transient effect: the multi-input variant consistently performs better for more complex training and test settings as will be shown in Sect. 4.3.

We also evaluate the handcrafted baseline by Capoferri et al. [3]. Its performance is below the NNs for all experiments with an accuracy of 7% and $d_{\text{sp}} = 2.9$. More in detail, the method achieves a good $d_{\text{sp}} \leq 1.5$ for 30% of the test samples. However, for the remaining 70%, the error is considerably larger.

4.3   Advanced Multi-Splicing Forgery Model

In our following experiments, we extend our forgery model to incorporate various multi-splicing scenarios for evaluating the robustness of the proposed method.

To this end, we generate a training set of 500 000 samples from the ACE training split and fine tune the models previously trained on single splicing on it. We include $n \in [0,5]$ splicing points in equal numbers, and apply all available processing steps, *i.e.*, RIRs, additive white Gaussian noise, and single MP3 or AMR-NB compression with the same SNR and b_r ranges as in Sect. 4.2.

For testing, we now assume a more elaborate forger and hence define several multi-splicing scenarios as they might be expected in the real world. For each scenario, we use test sets with 10 000 samples from the TTS test speaker pool and test the models' generalization ability to the diverse splicing situations that differ from the training setting. The method by Capoferri *et al.* does not support multi splicing, hence we exclude it from this evaluation.

Multi Compression. In this experiment, we consider the difficult case of a forger who not only masks multiple splicing points with noise, but who also compresses the result multiple times afterwards. Note that multi compression may also occur during recurring up- and downloading from the internet.

We consider $n_c \in [0,5]$ compression runs, which also includes uncompressed and single compressed files for reference. We generate 6 test sets, one for each n_c. The full data generation pipeline is applied with the same distortion parameters as for training, which includes RIRs as well as synthetic noise addition. However, the compression step is repeated n_c times with randomly sampled parameters.

The evaluation results are reported in Fig. 5. All baseline CNNs [10,25,28] perform comparably and fluctuate around 13.5% for single-input and 14% for multi-input along all n_c. We note that they show generalization problems towards this task and mostly collapse to predicting the same splicing points for most samples. We ran a series of experiments to tune the hyperparameters of these methods, but were not able to resolve this problem. Since our model did not show such problems, we attribute the advantage to the Transformer seq2seq design which is more naturally suited to the processing of sequential audio information than the per-position baseline classifiers.

As expected, the performance of our model decreases with increasing number of compression runs. Our multi-input method outperforms the single-input method except for the case of no compression, where the latter has a notable advantage of up to 10.0 percentage points (pp) for all metrics. For $w = 1\,\mathrm{s}, 2\,\mathrm{s}$, the multi-input model improves further by 5.7pp for J_{1s} and R_{1s}, and even by 10.7pp for J_{2s} and 10.5pp for R_{2s}.

For the most difficult case with $n_c = 5$ compression runs, our model still achieves $J_{2s} = 43.4\%$ and $R_{2s} = 46.6\%$ which we consider a notable generalization ability towards this difficult setting.

Intersplicing. Intersplicing addresses a particularly difficult scenario, where a forgery is spliced together from a speaker recorded in a static (*i.e.*, unchanging) environment without significant impulse response cues. This can be expected from rather anechoic surroundings like open spaces. We omit RIRs and any further post-processing operations in this experiment and generate one test set

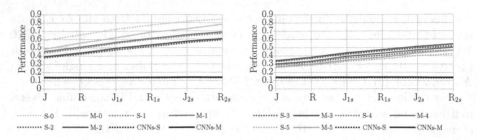

Fig. 5. Performance on $n_c \in [0, 2]$ (left) and $n_c \in [3, 5]$ (right) compression runs for our method trained on single- (dotted lines) and multiple-input (solid lines) representations. All baseline CNNs [10, 25, 28] have difficulties to generalize to the task and perform equally with minimal fluctuations. Our multi-input model exhibits greater robustness than the single-input variant except for $n_c = 0$.

for each number of $n \in [0, 5]$ possible splicing points. Due to little cues and strong deviation from the training set distribution, this experiment requires particularly strong generalization abilities.

In fact, similarly to the phenomenon described in Sect. 4.3, no baseline CNN [10, 25, 28] can meet this requirement. All baseline methods default to a constant performance of 16.7% for J_w and R_w with $w \in \{0.5\,\mathrm{s}, 1\,\mathrm{s}, 2\,\mathrm{s}\}$. Both our single and multi-input model are able to generalize to a certain degree. However, intersplicing proves to be the most challenging of all tested scenarios. The single-input variant achieves a J_w of 17.2%, 19.0% and 21.3% and a R_w of 17.9%, 20.0% and 22.7% for $w \in \{0.5\,\mathrm{s}, 1\,\mathrm{s}, 2\,\mathrm{s}\}$. The multi-input variant performs comparably with a J_w of 16.7%, 17.5% and 18.8%, and a R_w of 17.0%, 18.0% and 19.4% for $w \in \{0.5\,\mathrm{s}, 1\,\mathrm{s}, 2\,\mathrm{s}\}$, respectively.

Overall, we report that our Transformer seq2seq is the only model that generalizes towards this task. However, there is still room for robustness improvements towards data with such large deviations from the training distribution.

Real World Noise. In training, we cover additive white Gaussian noise to approximate background noises. We now evaluate the robustness towards composite samples distorted by a forger with additive real noise to hide splicing points more convincingly. Real noise samples can be easily downloaded from the internet. For our experiments, we chose free ambiance sound samples featuring rain[1], a train passing by[2], an crowded exhibition hall[3], and a crowded boarding gate at the airport[4]. We generate one test set per noise type with SNRs uniformly drawn from the range $[-10, 50]$ db per sample. We also include RIRs and single compression post-processing as described in Sect. 4.3.

---

[1] https://freesound.org/people/straget/sounds/531947/.
[2] https://freesound.org/people/theplax/sounds/615849/.
[3] https://freesound.org/people/BockelSound/sounds/487600/.
[4] https://freesound.org/people/arnaud%20coutancier/sounds/424362/.

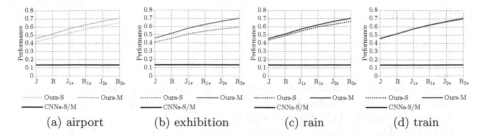

(a) airport   (b) exhibition   (c) rain   (d) train

Fig. 6. Performance on 4 real world noise types. The CNN baselines [10,25,28] are unable to generalize. Our multi-input model (solid lines) is best except for train noise, where the single-input variant (dotted lines) performs comparably.

The results are reported in Fig. 6. As in all previous multi-splice experiments, the tested CNNs [10,25,28] are unable to generalize and yield a performance of 13.5% consistently for all metrics. Our multi-input model outperforms the single-input variant especially for the more complex airport and exhibition background noise (Fig. 6a, Fig. 6b). For the former noise, the average increase over all $w \in \{0.5\,\mathrm{s}, 1\,\mathrm{s}, 2\,\mathrm{s}\}$ is 4.9 and 5.3pp for J_w and R_w, respectively. For the latter noise, the average increase is even 7.1 and 8.2pp, respectively. Averaged over all real world noises, our best performing multi-input model shows satisfying robustness with $J = 45.9\%$ and $R = 51.4\%$ and for the 2 s windows even reaches a performance of $J_{2\mathrm{s}} = 66.7\%$ and $R_{2\mathrm{s}} = 70.3\%$.

5   Conclusion

This work investigates the robust detection and localization of single and multiple splices in audio forgeries under unconstrained settings. We propose a Transformer seq2seq network for this task. We perform extensive evaluations that cover basic and advanced forgery models, including splicing of samples from different/same, echoic/anechoic recording surroundings, and post-processing operations like additive synthetic/real noise and single/multiple compression runs that may disguise splicing. Our method clearly outperforms competing networks and CNN baselines, while requiring the smallest number of parameters. By design, it is also more universally applicable than methods with handcrafted features that exploit specific manipulation characteristics.

The proposed method generalizes well to challenging scenarios with multiple splices that cannot be solved by other CNNs. We hypothesize that this is due to the better suitability of a seq2seq model for processing sequential audio data.

After this first step into the direction of unconstrained audio splicing detection and localization we aim at further improving the robustness of our method. We expect that there is still room for improvement in particularly challenging situations like the generalization to intersplicing (Sec. 4.3) or a large number of post-processing compression steps (Sec. 4.3.)

References

1. Audacity: Audacity ® | Free, open source, cross-platform audio software for multi-track recording and editing. Accessed 12 May 2022. https://www.audacityteam.org/
2. Bakhturina, E., Lavrukhin, V., Ginsburg, B., Zhang, Y.: Hi-Fi multi-speaker English TTS dataset. In: Proceedings of Interspeech, pp. 2776–2780 (2021). https://doi.org/10.21437/Interspeech.2021-1599
3. Capoferri, D., Borrelli, C., Bestagini, P., Antonacci, F., Sarti, A., Tubaro, S.: Speech audio splicing detection and localization exploiting reverberation cues. In: 2020 IEEE International Workshop on Information Forensics and Security (WIFS), pp. 1–6. IEEE (2020)
4. Chen, L., Maddox, R.K., Duan, Z., Xu, C.: Hierarchical cross-modal talking face generation with dynamic pixel-wise loss. In: Proceedings of the IEEE/CVF Conference on Computer Vision and Pattern Recognition, pp. 7832–7841 (2019)
5. Cooper, A.J.: Detecting butt-spliced edits in forensic digital audio recordings. In: Audio Engineering Society Conference: 39th International Conference: Audio Forensics: Practices and Challenges. Audio Engineering Society (2010)
6. Cuccovillo, L., Mann, S., Tagliasacchi, M., Aichroth, P.: Audio tampering detection via microphone classification. In: 2013 IEEE 15th International Workshop on Multimedia Signal Processing (MMSP), pp. 177–182. IEEE (2013)
7. Eaton, J., Gaubitch, N.D., Moore, A.H., Naylor, P.A.: Estimation of room acoustic parameters: the ACE challenge. IEEE/ACM Trans. Audio Speech Lang. Process. **24**(10), 1681–1693 (2016)
8. Esquef, P.A., Apolinário, J.A., Biscainho, L.W.: Improved edit detection in speech via ENF patterns. In: 2015 IEEE International Workshop on Information Forensics and Security (WIFS), pp. 1–6. IEEE (2015)
9. Gao, Y., Singh, R., Raj, B.: Voice impersonation using generative adversarial networks. In: 2018 IEEE International Conference on Acoustics, Speech and Signal Processing (ICASSP), pp. 2506–2510. IEEE (2018)
10. Jadhav, S., Patole, R., Rege, P.: Audio splicing detection using convolutional neural network. In: 2019 10th International Conference on Computing, Communication and Networking Technologies (ICCCNT), pp. 1–5. IEEE (2019)
11. Jia, Y., et al.: Transfer learning from speaker verification to multispeaker text-to-speech synthesis. Adv. Neural Inf. Process. Syst. **31** (2018)
12. Korshunov, P., Gonçalves, A.R., Violato, R.P., Simões, F.O., Marcel, S.: On the use of convolutional neural networks for speech presentation attack detection. In: 2018 IEEE 4th International Conference on Identity, Security, and Behavior Analysis (ISBA), pp. 1–8. IEEE (2018)
13. Lin, X., Kang, X.: Exposing speech tampering via spectral phase analysis. Digital Signal Process. **60**, 63–74 (2017)
14. Lin, X., Kang, X.: Supervised audio tampering detection using an autoregressive model. In: 2017 IEEE International Conference on Acoustics, Speech and Signal Processing (ICASSP), pp. 2142–2146. IEEE (2017)
15. Luo, D., Wu, H., Huang, J.: Audio recapture detection using deep learning. In: 2015 IEEE China Summit and International Conference on Signal and Information Processing (ChinaSIP), pp. 478–482. IEEE (2015)
16. Luo, D., Yang, R., Huang, J.: Detecting double compressed AMR audio using deep learning. In: 2014 IEEE International Conference on Acoustics, Speech and Signal Processing (ICASSP), pp. 2669–2673. IEEE (2014)

17. Mao, M., Xiao, Z., Kang, X., Li, X., Xiao, L.: Electric network frequency based audio forensics using convolutional neural networks. In: DigitalForensics 2020. IAICT, vol. 589, pp. 253–270. Springer, Cham (2020). https://doi.org/10.1007/978-3-030-56223-6_14

18. McKinney, M., Breebaart, J.: Features for Audio and Music Classification (2003)

19. Meng, X., Li, C., Tian, L.: Detecting audio splicing forgery algorithm based on local noise level estimation. In: 2018 5th International Conference on Systems and Informatics (ICSAI), pp. 861–865. IEEE (2018)

20. Models, P.V.: torchvision.models - Torchvision 0.11.0 documentation. Accessed 02 Mar 2022. https://pytorch.org/vision/stable/models.html

21. Nirkin, Y., Keller, Y., Hassner, T.: FSGAN: subject agnostic face swapping and reenactment. In: Proceedings of the IEEE/CVF International Conference on Computer Vision, pp. 7184–7193 (2019)

22. Oceanaudio: ocenaudio. Accessed 12 May 2022. https://www.ocenaudio.com//

23. Otter, D.W., Medina, J.R., Kalita, J.K.: A survey of the usages of deep learning for natural language processing. IEEE Trans. Neural Netw. Learn. Syst. **32**(2), 604–624 (2020)

24. Pan, X., Zhang, X., Lyu, S.: Detecting splicing in digital audios using local noise level estimation. In: 2012 IEEE International Conference on Acoustics, Speech and Signal Processing (ICASSP), pp. 1841–1844. IEEE (2012)

25. Radosavovic, I., Kosaraju, R.P., Girshick, R., He, K., Dollár, P.: Designing network design spaces. In: Proceedings of the IEEE/CVF Conference on Computer Vision and Pattern Recognition, pp. 10428–10436 (2020)

26. Rouniyar, S.K., Yingjuan, Y., Hu, Y.: Channel response based multi-feature audio splicing forgery detection and localization. In: Proceedings of the 2018 International Conference on E-Business, Information Management and Computer Science, pp. 46–53 (2018)

27. Simonyan, K., Zisserman, A.: Very deep convolutional networks for large-scale image recognition. In: International Conference on Learning Representations (2015)

28. Tan, M., Le, Q.: EfficientNet: rethinking model scaling for convolutional neural networks. In: International Conference on Machine Learning, pp. 6105–6114 (2019)

29. Thies, J., Zollhofer, M., Stamminger, M., Theobalt, C., Nießner, M.: Face2Face: real-time face capture and Reenactment of RGB Videos. In: Proceedings of the IEEE Conference on Computer Vision and Pattern Recognition, pp. 2387–2395 (2016)

30. Torchaudio: torchaudio.transforms - Torchaudio 0.10.0 documentation. Accessed 09 Mar 2021. https://pytorch.org/audio/stable/

31. Vaswani, A., et al.: Attention is all you need. In: Advances in Neural Information Processing Systems, pp. 5998–6008 (2017)

32. Viazovetskyi, Y., Ivashkin, V., Kashin, E.: StyleGAN2 distillation for feed-forward image manipulation. In: Vedaldi, A., Bischof, H., Brox, T., Frahm, J.-M. (eds.) ECCV 2020. LNCS, vol. 12367, pp. 170–186. Springer, Cham (2020). https://doi.org/10.1007/978-3-030-58542-6_11

33. Yan, D., Dong, M., Gao, J.: Exposing speech transsplicing forgery with noise level inconsistency. Secur. Commun. Netw. **2021**, 1 6 (2021)

34. Yang, R., Qu, Z., Huang, J.: Detecting digital audio forgeries by checking frame offsets. In: Proceedings of the 10th ACM Workshop on Multimedia and Security, pp. 21–26 (2008)

35. Zhang, Z., Yi, X., Zhao, X.: Fake speech detection using residual network with transformer encoder. In: Proceedings of the 2021 ACM Workshop on Information Hiding and Multimedia Security, pp. 13–22 (2021)
36. Zhang, Z., Zhao, X., Yi, X.: Aslnet: an encoder-decoder architecture for audio splicing detection and localization. Secur. Commun. Netw. **2022** (2022)
37. Zhao, H., Chen, Y., Wang, R., Malik, H.: Audio source authentication and splicing detection using acoustic environmental signature. In: Proceedings of the 2nd ACM Workshop on Information Hiding and Multimedia Security, pp. 159–164 (2014)
38. Zhao, H., Chen, Y., Wang, R., Malik, H.: Audio splicing detection and localization using environmental signature. Multimedia Tools Appl. **76**(12), 13897–13927 (2017)

Comprint: Image Forgery Detection and Localization Using Compression Fingerprints

Hannes Mareen[1]([✉]), Dante Vanden Bussche[1], Fabrizio Guillaro[2],
Davide Cozzolino[2], Glenn Van Wallendael[1], Peter Lambert[1],
and Luisa Verdoliva[2]

[1] imec, IDLab, ELIS, Ghent University, Ghent, Belgium
{hannes.mareen,dante.vandenbussche,glenn.vanwallendael,
peter.lambert}@ugent.be
[2] Università degli Studi di Napoli Federico II, Naples, Italy
{fabrizio.guillaro,davide.cozzolino,verdoliv}@unina.it
https://media.idlab.ugent.be, https://www.grip.unina.it

Abstract. Manipulation tools that realistically edit images are widely
available, making it easy for anyone to create and spread misinformation. In an attempt to fight fake news, forgery detection and localization
methods were designed. However, existing methods struggle to accurately
reveal manipulations found in images on the internet, i.e., in the wild.
That is because the type of forgery is typically unknown, in addition
to the tampering traces being damaged by recompression. This paper
presents Comprint, a novel forgery detection and localization method
based on the compression fingerprint or *comprint*. It is trained on pristine
data only, providing generalization to detect different types of manipulation. Additionally, we propose a fusion of Comprint with the state-of-the-
art Noiseprint, which utilizes a complementary camera model fingerprint.
We carry out an extensive experimental analysis and demonstrate that
Comprint has a high level of accuracy on five evaluation datasets that
represent a wide range of manipulation types, mimicking in-the-wild circumstances. Most notably, the proposed fusion significantly outperforms
state-of-the-art reference methods. As such, Comprint and the fusion
Comprint+Noiseprint represent a promising forensics tool to analyze in-
the-wild tampered images.

Keywords: Image Forensics · Forgery Detection · Forgery
Localization · Deep Learning · In-the-wild Robustness

1 Introduction

Manipulating digital images is both becoming easier and more realistic using
image editing tools and AI-based software. For example, Fig. 1a shows a manipulated image in which the face of Captain Jack Sparrow is replaced with that of

© Springer Nature Switzerland AG 2023
J.-J. Rousseau and B. Kapralos (Eds.): ICPR 2022 Workshops, LNCS 13644, pp. 281–299, 2023.
https://doi.org/10.1007/978-3-031-37742-6_23

another person (original from Pirates of the Caribbean). This forgery was generated in a few seconds using FaceHub.live, a free AI-based tool. Although there are many harmless applications of these powerful tools, manipulated images contribute to problems such as fake news, fake evidence, and fraud. Therefore, it is crucial to investigate forensic methods that can fact check and verify images found on the internet, i.e., *in the wild*.

Forensics forgery detection and localization methods typically look at imperceptible traces of an image's digital history [23]. That is because every step in the camera acquisition and digital editing process leaves a trail of clues. For example, the sensor of the camera introduces a unique noise pattern [16], and compression introduces blocking artifacts [3,4,12,15,27]. Although these traces may be invisible to the human eye, a computer can exploit them. Unfortunately, images found in the wild are often recompressed to a lower quality, which hides these imperceptible traces. As such, successful forgery detection is challenging.

Recent methods that rely on deep Convolutional Neural Networks (CNNs) have shown a higher level of robustness against recompression [22,23]. However, most of them remain intrinsically weak because they can only detect forgeries that were seen during training. Therefore, a promising strategy for forgery detection is using one-class deep-learning methods that are only trained using pristine data. As such, they are not limited to specific types of forgery. For example, the Noiseprint algorithm learns to extract a fingerprint from the camera model using deep learning [7]. Then, inconsistencies in this fingerprint reveal tampering. This is similar to traditional methods using PRNU fingerprints, but does not require images from the camera of the image under investigation. It is trained on images coming from many different cameras, hence being able to detect different sources, but no specific design was made during training to take into account the different JPEG history of such patches.

In this paper, we exploit compression artifacts and extract a different fingerprint, called Comprint. It utilizes compression artifacts, but unlike most of the state-of-the-art works, it does not assume that real regions underwent double compression in contrast to fake regions that underwent single compression. Instead, it simply assumes that the pristine regions have a *different* compression history than the tampered regions. Comprint is based on one-class training with only pristine data: images compressed using a different Quality Factor (QF) or quantization table in the JPEG coding standard. The architecture is based on a Siamese network that is trained to distinguish regions that were compressed differently. As such, the deep-learning method can extract a compression fingerprint or *comprint* from an image under investigation. Then, a localization algorithm segments the distinguished regions into a heatmap. For example, Fig. 1b and Fig. 1c show the extracted comprint and heatmap, respectively, corresponding to the manipulated image of Fig. 1a. We demonstrate that

(a) Manipulated image using free tool FaceHub.live.

(b) Comprint: compression fingerprint.

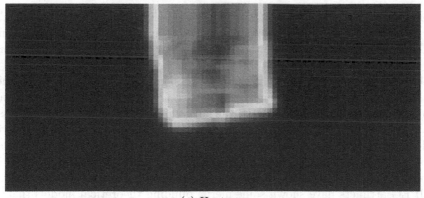

(c) Heatmap.

Fig. 1. Realistically manipulating an image is easier than ever, such as with (a) free AI-based tools. Therefore, we propose (b) Comprint, a forgery detection and localization method based on compression fingerprints. Inconsistencies in the comprint indicate and localize forgeries that can be easily visualized through a (c) heatmap.

Comprint has a high level of robustness to in-the-wild forgeries. Additionally, since Comprint contains characteristics that are complementary to Noiseprint, we propose a fusion of these fingerprints, *Comprint+Noiseprint*. We demonstrate that the fusion results in a an improved performance compared to using each method individually.

2   Related Work

This section briefly discusses the main classes of forgery detection and localization algorithms. More specifically, since this paper proposes a method based on compression artifacts and is inspired by Noiseprint, this section mainly focuses on work related to these aspects.

Conventional Model-Based Methods. Conventional detection methods that were proposed before the emergence of deep learning typically rely on prior assumptions, which limits their applicability in the real world. They build a handcrafted model that describes artifacts left behind by manipulations, and detect anomalies in them. For example, some are based on the photo-response non-uniformity (PRNU) noise, which is a unique noise pattern that sensors introduce, and is used to identify camera models or specific devices. When part of an image does not correlate with the PRNU fingerprint of the camera, it indicates forgery [16]. Although this method is powerful, it requires many images from the same camera that captured the media under investigation. Therefore, it is not always applicable in the wild. Another example is Splicebuster, which extracts expressive features that capture the traces left by in-camera processing, and use those statistics to discover potential inconsistencies caused by splicing [6].

Models Based on JPEG Artifacts. There also exists a large variety of model-based methods that utilize anomalies in JPEG artifacts. For example, a mismatch in JPEG block artifacts, the JPEG grid, or the JPEG block convergence can indicate tampering [12,13,15,27]. Additionally, many methods are based on double quantization or double JPEG compression artifacts [3,4]. That is, these methods assume that the authentic region is compressed twice: once before, and once after manipulation. In contrast, the fake region is assumed to be compressed only once (i.e., only after manipulation). Although these methods work relatively well in the circumstances that they were designed for, they typically perform worse in the wild. For example, images typically undergo multiple compression steps when shared through social networks. In general, although methods based on JPEG artifacts have shown some merit, building theoretical models that are applicable in the wild is very challenging. That is because they are restricted by their assumptions that do not always hold in practice.

Data-Driven Methods. More recent methods are often data driven, in contrast to model-driven conventional methods. As such, the challenge shifts from building a good theoretical model towards building a suitable training dataset which enables good generalisation characteristics for unseen data. In general, data-driven deep-learning methods can be divided into three categories: supervised CNNs looking at specific clues, generic supervised CNNs and one-class training [23].

Supervised CNNs Looking at Specific Clues. An example of the first class of deep-learning-based methods is RRU-Net of Bi *et al.* looks specifically for artifacts left by the splicing manipulation [2]. Another example is the method by Barni *et al.* that looks for traces left behind by double JPEG compression, by training a CNN with pictures that are compressed either once or twice [1]. A disadvantage of such methods is that the generalization is still dependent on the diversity of the training set. As such, in an attempt to improve the in-the-wild performance, Park *et al.* [20] proposed a deep-learning approach that includes a large number of quantization tables in the training set.

Generic Supervised CNNs. Methods using generic supervised CNNs do not look for specific types of manipulations or artifacts, but rather aim to detect any type of manipulation. For example, ManTra-Net [25] and SPAN [10] are trained on 385 different types of manipulations. Another advantage of deep-learning-based methods is that they can capture manipulation clues directly from the raw image data, rather than building handcrafted features, as done in the Constrained Region-based CNN (CR-CNN) of Yang *et al.* [26]. Because of the immense variety in potential manipulations, it is often very challenging to build appropriate training datasets and train these models. As such, they remain intrinsically weak because they can only detect forgeries that were seen during training. In other words, they do not perform well on unseen fakes found in the wild (that may or may not yet exist at the time of training the CNNs).

One-Class Training. The last class of deep-learning methods is one-class training. Instead of trying to build a training set that is representative for all possible manipulations, a one-class training set consists of pristine data only. In this way, the machine-learning model learns the characteristics of a genuine image, anomalies in the extracted characteristics are indications of forgery. For example, the EXIF-SC method by Huh *et al.* detects splicing by analyzing if the image is self consistent (SC), i.e., whether its content could have been produced by a single imaging pipeline [11]. The self consistency is learned by training a Siamese network. Similarly, the Noiseprint method utilized Siamese training to extract a camera model fingerprint or noiseprint [7]. Anomalies in the noiseprint indicate forgeries. This is similar as what is done in conventional PRNU-based methods, yet in a blind fashion and with great generalization to unseen camera models. The idea of partitioning an image into communities of tampered and unaltered regions was further refined by Mayer *et al.* [17,18].

In summary, it is challenging to perform robust forgery detection and localization in the wild. Most interestingly, recent one-class deep-learning strategies are promising because they demonstrated generalization to manipulation types that were not seen during training.

3   Proposed Method: Comprint

The core idea of our proposed method is inspired by two main research directions in the state of the art: exploiting compression artifacts and one-class deep learning.

First, Comprint exploits JPEG compression artifacts, which has been a popular strategy for decades. However, it should be stressed that it is not like conventional double-JPEG-compression methods. That is, instead of assuming that real regions underwent double compression and fake regions single compression, we simply assume that they underwent *different* compression. This is a weaker assumption and therefore should aid generalization in the wild. Additionally, we do not detect which compression and parameters were used exactly. Instead, we only care that the compression is different. This is achieved by extracting the compression fingerprint, and looking for inconsistencies in it.

Second, Comprint uses the advantages of one-class deep learning to create a fingerprint. This is inspired by the fingerprint in Noiseprint [7]. Such fingerprints exhibit great generalization performance and are not trained for specific types of manipulation. As such, Comprint combines the exploitation of compression artifacts with one-class deep learning. More specifically, the aim of our proposed method is to extract a fingerprint of the compression artifacts of an image, i.e., what we name the *comprint*. Then, inconsistencies in the comprint reveal forgeries.

Because Comprint is inspired by the concepts of Noiseprint, we additionally propose to combine these two methods. Because we found that the methods have complementary properties, a fusion is may be able to get better results than each method can get separately.

First, Sect. 3.1 discusses the extraction of the comprint. Subsequently, Sect. 3.2 explains how to convert the comprint into a heatmap of forgery probability, which is used for forgery detection and localization. Finally, Sect. 3.3 explains how the fusion is performed.

3.1   Compression Fingerprint Extraction

Architecture. The proposed system for comprint extraction is inspired by the architecture of Noiseprint [7]. That is, a Siamese architecture is used for training. The Siamese architecture trains a CNN such that image patches that underwent the same compression history should be similar, whereas patches that underwent a different compression should be dissimilar. This is visualized in Fig. 2. During training, pairs of patches are considered that either underwent the same compression history (label -1) or a different compression history (label +1). These patches are converted into fingerprints using the CNN, after which the distance between them is calculated. The distance between each pair of fingerprints is transformed into a loss (using the corresponding label), which is used to update the weights of the CNN. It should be stressed that there is only a single CNN in practice, yet this is visualized as two CNNs with shared weights in Fig. 2. The architecture is described in more detail, later in this section.

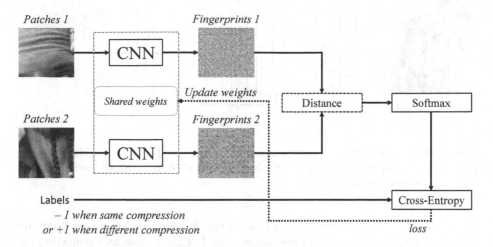

Patches 1   Fingerprints 1

CNN

Shared weights   Update weights   Distance   Softmax

Patches 2   Fingerprints 2

CNN

Labels   Cross-Entropy
 – 1 when same compression
or +1 when different compression   loss

Fig. 2. Siamese architecture used for training the compression fingerprint (i.e., comprint) extraction. Patches with the same compression history are trained to have similar fingerprints, whereas patches with different compression history are trained to have dissimilar fingerprints.

The CNN used in the Siamese network is based on the Denoiser CNN (DnCNN) proposed by Zhang *et al.* for image denoising and JPEG deblocking [28]. That is, the architecture is visualized in Fig. 3, and consists of a depth of d groups of layers (2D convolutional layers, coupled by rectified-linear-unit (ReLu) and batch-normalization layers). For the first and last group of layers, there is no batch-normalization layer, and for the last group, there is no ReLu either. The inputs are zero padded to maintain the same dimensions in the output fingerprint.

This CNN is first pretrained for the task of JPEG-artifact reduction. Then, the weights of this pretrained CNN are used as initialization in the Siamese training step. Finally, after training, any image can be sent through the network to be transformed to a compression fingerprint or *comprint*. As an example, Fig. 1b shows the extracted comprint corresponding to the manipulated image of Fig. 1a.

Implementation Details. First, we pretrain the CNN to directly estimate the JPEG-compression-artifact noise. That is, we provide JPEG-compressed images as input to the CNN, and optimize the CNN to be as close as possible to the corresponding ground-truth noise patch (using the Euclidean distance). Since artifacts appear more in high-frequency than low-frequency spatial content, this estimated compression-noise signal still contains high-level scene content. Therefore, we should not yet use it as a fingerprint. Instead, the weights of this JPEG-artifacts-estimating CNN are used as initialization for the fingerprint-extracting CNN in the subsequent Siamese training process.

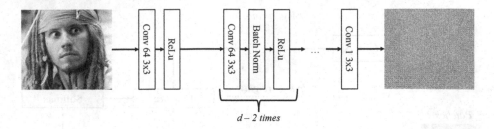

Fig. 3. CNN architecture, used in Siamese architecture of Fig. 2, as well as for the pre-trained JPEG-artifact-reduction CNN that is used to initialize the weights of the CNN in the Siamese architecture.

Ideally, the Siamese training optimizes the fingerprints such that they are orthogonal when different compression was used. This is done by calculating the loss value as schematically presented in Fig. 2, or more detailed in the following manner. If $k_{i,1}$ and $k_{i,2}$ represent two input patches of patch pair i, then the squared Euclidean distance is given by:

$$d_i = ||k_{i,1} - k_{i,2}||^2 \tag{1}$$

This distance has to be calculated for each patch pair inside a batch. Next, the distances are converted into a probability distribution p via softmax processing (with n summing over all pairs inside the batch):

$$p(i) = \frac{e^{-d_i}}{\sum_n e^{-d_n}} \tag{2}$$

This step essentially maps all distances to the interval $[0, 1]$, with large distances going towards 0 and small distances going towards 1. After this operation, we can interpret the resulting values as a probability distribution and use them together with the labels to calculate the cross-entropy loss for each batch, and update the weights accordingly. After training, the weights of the CNN are fixed, and the CNN is used to transform an input image to a comprint.

3.2   Forgery Localization: From Comprint to Heatmap

The comprint that was extracted from an image may visually give some indication of segmentation of regions that underwent different compression. However, on its own, it is not sufficient for pixel-level forgery localization. For this reason, the blind localization algorithm proposed in the Splicebuster-method is applied [6].

A high-level diagram of the localization algorithm is given in Fig. 4. First, the localization algorithm extracts co-occurence-based features [21] from the comprint. For readers familiar with the Splicebuster algorithm, note that we do not apply the high-pass filter that was proposed in Splicebuster. Instead, we simply

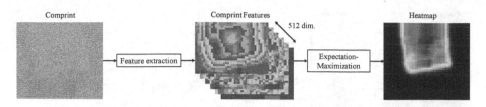

Fig. 4. Forgery localization: a fingerprint is transformed into a heatmap by extracting co-occurence-based features, and clustering these using EM.

apply a normalization to zero mean and unit variance before passing the comprint to the localization algorithm. Then, the multi-dimensional features generated from the comprint are fed to an Expectation-Maximuzation (EM) algorithm. The EM algorithm estimates the model parameters for each segmented region, and allocates pixel locations to each region. This results in a segmentation map with continuous numbers for each pixel, representing the likelihood of the pixel belonging to either the forged or pristine region. These pixel values are represented graphically by the heatmap. As an example, Fig. 1c shows the extracted heatmap corresponding to the comprint of Fig. 1b.

Finally, an image-level forgery detection strategy can be applied to the heatmaps. For example, in our evaluation in Sect. 4.1, we propose to compare the 99.5^{th} percentile highest value of the heatmap to a certain threshold.

3.3 Fusion: Comprint+Noiseprint

Comprint is inspired by Noiseprint's fingerprint-extraction architecture [7], as described in Sect. 3.1. Additionally, both algorithms incorporate the same blind localization algorithm, as described in Sect. 3.2. The main difference between Comprint and Noiseprint is that Comprint exploits noise left by compression artifacts, whereas Noiseprint exploits noise unique to camera models. Since these are complementary strategies, we propose to fuse Comprint with Noiseprint. We define the fused method as *Comprint+Noiseprint*.

A high-level diagram of the fusion algorithm is given in Fig. 5, which adapts the localization process described in Sect. 3.2. More specifically, the co-occurence-based features are additionally calculated from the noiseprint, instead of only from the comprint. Then, the multi-dimensional features from both fingerprints are stacked (in the third dimension). Subsequently, the stacked features are given to the EM algorithm that attempts to segment the features. In general, this stacking of fingerprint features can be used to apply fusion with any fingerprinting-based method. If the fused fingerprint contains complementary characteristics, we expect the performance to increase.

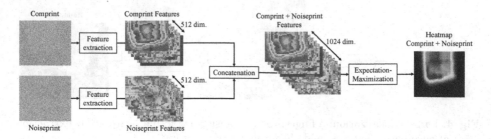

Fig. 5. Fusion diagram. The localization algorithm is adapted by concatenating the features of both Comprint and Noiseprint, and applying EM on the concatenated feature array.

4   Evaluation

This section evaluates the proposed Comprint method for forgery detection and localization, as well as the fusion between Comprint and Noiseprint. First, Sect. 4.1 describes the experimental setup. Then, the results are presented and analysed in Sect. 4.2.

4.1   Experimental Setup

Training Procedure. The training and validation images were obtained from the RAISE dataset [8]. RAISE consists of high-resolution uncompressed images depicting various subjects and scenarios. From this dataset, 1000 images were randomly selected and used for training, and another 100 images were used for validation during training. The images were first converted to grayscale and resized to 200 × 200 pixels, similar to setup used for the DnCNN denoiser upon which our CNN is based [28]. Using training images with a small resolution ensures that patches contain enough variation and information to properly train the network.

After loading the uncompressed images, we additionally apply on-the-fly cropping and JPEG compression during training. That is, for each input pair, the uncompressed input images are randomly cropped to an area of 48 × 48 pixels. The first patch of the pair is compressed with a randomly chosen JPEG Quality Factor (QF) or a randomly chosen quantization table, selected from a predefined list. The JPEG compression was done using python's Pillow library v9.2.0 and using Photoshop CS4 v11.0. With probability $p = 0.5$, the second patch of the pair is compressed using the same QF or quantization table. In the other case, it is compressed with another QF or quantization table from the predefined list. Finally, both patches are subsequently fed to the CNN, in conjunction with the corresponding label that represents if they were compressed with the same (label −1) or a different QF/quantization table (label +1). In other words, in this paper, we limit the scope of the compression history by only utilizing a single compression step using the JPEG encoder with various QFs and quantization tables.

We used 10 different QFs as well as 9 commonly used quantization tables by Adobe Photoshop. That is, the QFs are chosen from the following predefined list: 20, 25, 30, 35, 40, 50, 60, 70, 80, 90, and the quantization tables correspond to Photoshop qualities 4 to 12. For the QF list, a denser quality factor spacing is used at lower QFs because the difference between images compressed with slightly different quality factors is larger at lower QFs, due to the higher amount of noise being introduced. Although only 19 different QFs and quantization tables are used, the training set is augmented to a very large size, because of the random crop and the random pairing of QFs or quantization tables.

The CNN was implemented with $d = 20$ groups of convolutional layers. Moreover, the denoising network that was used as initialization and the Siamese network were trained for 50 epochs, using 4000 batches per epoch, and 200 patch pairs per batch. Furthermore, we used the ADAM optimizer. Future work will explore other, more advanced training setups. For example, we could incorporate other image compression standards.

The code and data have been made available for reproducibility[1].

Reference Methods. We compare the results of our proposed method to 13 reference methods that were proposed in the state of the art. These can be classified in the four classes presented in Sect. 2. First, BLK [15], DCT [27], NADQ [4], ADQ [3], and CAGI [12] are conventional model-driven methods, and they all exploit JPEG artifacts. The implementations of these methods were provided by Iakovidou et al. [12]. Additionally, Splicebuster [6] is also a model-driven method, but exploits traces left by in-camera processing rather than compression artifacts. Second, DJPEG [20] and RRU-Net [2] are supervised CNNs looking at specific clues (being double-JPEG-compression artifacts and splicing artifacts, respectively). Third, ManTraNet [25], SPAN [10], and CR-CNN [26] are generic supervised CNNs that are trained on a large variety of manipulations. Fourth and lastly, EXIF-SC [11] and Noiseprint [7] are one-class deep-learning methods trained on pristine data only, using Siamese networks.

Evaluation Datasets. As we target our method to be applicable in the wild, we selected 9 evaluation datasets that cover a wide variety of manipulations (based on both editing software and AI). These are listed and described in Table 1. The JPEG quality factors that are shown in the table are estimates that give an indication of the quality of the images in the datasets. That is because the QF is undefined when a non-standard quantization tables is used, and we consider the QF of the most similar standard quantization tables.

---

[1] Code available on https://github.com/IDLabMedia/comprint.

Table 1. Datasets used for the forgery detection and localization evaluation.

Dataset		#fake	#real	Format	Description
[9]	VIPP	62	69	JPEG@40-100	Uses double JPEG compression
[5]	DSO-1	100	100	PNG	Only splicing
[29]	FaceSwap	879	1651	JPEG@39-100	Face swaps with FaceSwap-app
[19]	IMD2020	2010	414	PNG & JPEG@45-100	Various forgery types found on the internet, *in the wild*
[14]	OpenForensics	18 895	N/A	JPEG@100	Synthetic face swapping

Forgery Localization Measure. To perform binary pixel-level forgery localization, we can compare each pixel value of the continuous-valued heatmap to a certain threshold. This results in a binary heatmap that can be compared with the ground truth. For example, commonly-used measures such as the True Positive (TP) rate, False Positive (FP) rate and False Negative (FN) rate, precision, and recall can be calculated. In this paper, we combine these measures in the F1 score, calculated as follows:

$$F1 = \frac{1}{\dfrac{1}{\text{precision}} + \dfrac{1}{\text{recall}}} = \frac{2\text{TP}}{2\text{TP} + \text{FN} + \text{FP}} \tag{3}$$

In other words, the F1 score is the harmonic mean of the precision and recall. In the equation, TP, FP and FN represents the number of pixel predictions that are True Positives, False Positives, and False Negatives, respectively. Note that a higher F1 score (i.e., closer to 1) is better than a lower one (i.e., closer to 0).

Two remarks have to be made for this way of evaluating the localization performance. First, to decouple the threshold value from the assessment, the maximum F1 score over all thresholds is taken. Second, the proposed method makes a segmentation of regions that underwent different compression, and hence the choice whether a segment is forged or pristine is arbitrary. Therefore, both the regular and inverted ground truths are considered, and the maximum of the corresponding performance scores is kept.

Forgery Detection Measure. For image-level forgery detection evaluation, we first extract a global statistic from the heatmap. In this paper, we adopt the 99.5^{th} percentile highest value from the heatmap as a global statistic. Next, the global statistic can be compared to a threshold. In order to allow an evaluation that is independent of a certain threshold, we plot the TP rate against the FP rate for a range of thresholds, for each dataset. This plot is the Receiver Operating Characteristic (ROC) curve. Finally, we calculate the Area Under the

ROC Curve (AUC) as a performance measure. Note that a higher AUC score (i.e., closer to 1) is better than a lower one.

Note that other algorithms utilize other global statistics than the 99.5^{th} percentile highest value during image-level forgery detection. For example, ManTraNet [25] and EXIF-SC [11] utilize the average likelihood of the heatmap. However, the average will be significantly lower when the area of forgery is small. Additionally, DCT [27] utilizes the maximum value, which solves the issue of small forgery regions. Nevertheless, the maximum value can be significantly affected by outliers. For this reason, we chose to utilize the 99.5^{th} percentile highest value as a global statistic instead.

In the experiments, we utilized the global statistic that was proposed in the original reference methods [11,25,27]. When not clearly specified [2], we utilized the 99.5^{th} percentile highest value. Additionally, we did not calculate image-level forgery detection results when the reference methods only proposed pixel-level forgery localization [3,4,10,12,15,20,26]. An exception for this are the Splicebuster [6] and Noiseprint [7] methods, for which we did perform image-level forgery detection using the 99.5^{th} percentile highest value. This was done because Comprint is based on these methods and hence an experimental comparison is essential.

4.2   Results

Table 2 and Table 3 summarize the F1 and AUC scores for forgery localization and detection, respectively. In the tables, the three largest values for each dataset are emphasized in bold, underline, and italics, respectively. Note that the AUC metric for forgery detection could not be calculated for OpenForensics since that dataset does not contain real images. This section discusses several interesting observations from the presented results.

Comprint vs. Noiseprint. Comprint and Noiseprint often have similar scores. On average, Noiseprint performs slightly better than Comprint for forgery localization, but Comprint performs slightly better for forgery detection. Their resembling scores can be explained by the fact that they are based on the same architecture and use the same internal localization algorithm. However, it should be stressed that their underlying assumptions are completely different.

Comprint vs. Splicebuster. It is also interesting to compare Comprint with Splicebuster, as they use the same internal localization algorithm, and hence only differ in the input noise residual. In Splicebuster, this residual is obtained by high-pass filtering the input image, in contrast to Comprint which extracts a compression fingerprint. We can observe that, on average, Comprint performs significantly better than Splicebuster for both forgery detection and localization, highlighting its potential.

Table 2. Experimental pixel-level forgery localization results: average F1 score.

Model		VIPP	DSO-1	FaceSwap	IMD2020	OpenFor	Average
[15]	BLK	0.411	0.449	0.097	0.267	0.262	0.297
[27]	DCT	0.416	0.350	0.182	0.328	0.408	0.337
[4]	NADQ	0.248	0.247	0.037	0.170	0.114	0.163
[3]	ADQ	<u>0.572</u>	0.530	**0.426**	<u>0.446</u>	<u>0.675</u>	*0.530*
[12]	CAGI	0.460	0.537	0.172	0.299	0.293	0.352
[6]	Splicebuster	0.447	0.662	0.330	0.326	0.440	0.441
[20]	DJPEG	0.492	0.701	0.334	0.297	0.434	0.452
[2]	RRU-Net	0.349	0.360	0.064	0.336	0.203	0.262
[25]	ManTraNet	0.354	0.538	0.153	0.324	0.653	0.404
[10]	SPAN	0.404	0.390	0.093	0.252	0.173	0.262
[26]	CR-CNN	0.406	0.432	0.128	**0.476**	0.224	0.333
[11]	EXIF-SC	0.424	0.577	0.293	0.323	0.310	0.385
[7]	Noiseprint	*0.556*	<u>0.812</u>	0.309	0.397	*0.672*	<u>0.549</u>
Comprint		0.497	*0.763*	*0.353*	0.388	0.634	0.527
Comprint+Noiseprint		**0.581**	**0.813**	<u>0.417</u>	*0.435*	**0.712**	**0.592**

Table 3. Experimental image-level forgery detection results: AUC score.

Model		VIPP	DSO-1	FaceSwap	IMD2020	Average
[27]	DCT	**0.653**	0.409	**0.569**	*0.600*	0.558
[6]	Splicebuster	0.544	0.775	<u>0.553</u>	0.544	0.604
[2]	RRU-Net	0.512	0.497	0.507	0.565	0.520
[25]	ManTraNet	0.590	*0.874*	0.479	*0.558*	0.625
[11]	EXIF-SC	0.397	0.237	0.453	0.435	0.381
[7]	Noiseprint	0.586	0.848	*0.537*	0.548	*0.630*
Comprint		<u>0.622</u>	**0.940**	0.525	**0.656**	**0.686**
Comprint+Noiseprint		*0.616*	<u>0.930</u>	0.532	<u>0.637</u>	<u>0.679</u>

Double JPEG Compression-Based Methods. For the VIPP dataset, model-based methods using compression artifacts (such as DCT, ADQ, DJPEG and Comprint) are among the best performing methods. This is not a coincidence, as this dataset was built with double compression in mind. In fact, for most datasets, the DCT method [27] performs very well for forgery detection, and ADQ performs very well for forgery localization. However, both methods have a significantly worse performance for DSO-1, which contains images in the losslessly compressed PNG format. In other words, DSO-1 may contain images that did not undergo double compression. This highlights that utilizing only double JPEG compression traces is not sufficient for forgery detection and localization.

Non-standard Quantization Tables. For DSO-1, the model-based methods using compression artifacts perform significantly worse than the other methods. In contrast, the data-driven DJPEG-method which also used compression artifacts performs significantly better. This may be because it is trained using a large variety of non-standard quantization tables, in contrast to the model-based methods that only consider standard QFs. We noticed a similar worse performance when we trained Comprint using only standard QFs, i.e., without non-standard quantization tables. In that case, the F1 and AUC scores were only 0.526 and 0.759, respectively, in contrast to the much higher scores (0.763 and 0.94, respectively) that are established with the final proposed Comprint model that includes Photoshop quantization tables. Future research can analyze more thoroughly how the usage of JPEG implementations or quantization tables unseen during training influences the performance.

Generalization to Unseen Forgeries. The performance on FaceSwap and IMD2020 is relatively low for all methods (i.e., less than 0.5 F1 score), demonstrating that there is still a great need for more in-the-wild forgery localization research. For IMD2020, CR-CNN has the best performance for forgery localization, yet it is among the worst performing methods for the other datasets, indicating its lack of generalization. For OpenForensics, only Noiseprint, Comprint, ManTraNet and ADQ perform relatively well (F1 scores above 0.6). MantraNet exhibits a very poor performance on the other datasets, though. This again demonstrates the lack of generalization for supervised CNNs that include fake images in their dataset. In contrast, Comprint and Noiseprint remain top of the class for all datasets, highlighting the superior generalization capabilities of one-class training methods.

Fusion: Comprint+Noiseprint. For pixel-level forgery localization, the performance of both Comprint (F1 score of 0.527) and Noiseprint (F1 score of 0.549) improves when they are fused (F1 score of 0.592), on average. For image-level forgery detection, Comprint performs slightly better individually (AUC of 0.686) than the fusion (AUC of 0.679), on average. Figure 6 shows an example that highlights the positive effect of fusing Comprint and Noiseprint. Although the individual F1 scores are relatively low and their heatmaps contain false positive detections, the F1 score of the fusion is high and the corresponding heatmap is much more clear.

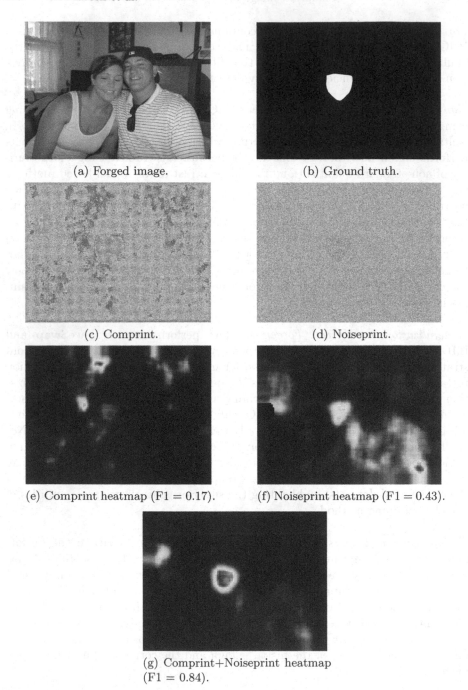

(a) Forged image.

(b) Ground truth.

(c) Comprint.

(d) Noiseprint.

(e) Comprint heatmap (F1 = 0.17).

(f) Noiseprint heatmap (F1 = 0.43).

(g) Comprint+Noiseprint heatmap
(F1 = 0.84).

Fig. 6. Example of (a) image in which faces were manipulated (see (b) for ground truth). The fingerprints of (c) Comprint and (d) Noiseprint both generate (e, f) heatmaps that do not perform very well individually. In contrast, (g) the fusion Comprint+Noiseprint performs outstanding.

Top-Performing Methods. For image-level forgery detection, Comprint (AUC of 0.686) outperforms all methods on average, although it is closely followed by Comprint+Noiseprint, and Noiseprint with average AUC scores of 0.685 and 0.630, respectively. For pixel-level forgery localization, the fusion Comprint+Noiseprint (F1 score of 0.592) outperforms all evaluated methods, and is closely followed by Noiseprint (0.549), and Comprint (0.527).

5 Conclusion

This paper proposed Comprint, a forgery detection and localization method. The main novelty of our proposed method is the usage of the compression fingerprint that represents the compression history. The method is trained using only pristine data, i.e., images compressed in a different way. By detecting and localizing inconsistencies in the compression fingerprint, forgeries are exposed. Additionally, we proposed to fuse Comprint with the complementary Noiseprint.

We demonstrated that Comprint and the fusion of Comprint and Noiseprint exhibit top-notch performance, unmatched by the 13 reference methods. In general, in-the-wild forgery detection and localization is still challenging, though. Therefore, incorporating strategies for improved recompression robustness could be explored [24], as well as fusing more complementary methods. Additionally, Comprint's applicability on (deep)fake videos should be investigated as well. In any case, in its current form, Comprint and the *Comprint+Noiseprint* fusion can already be utilized to aid in-the-wild multimedia forensics.

Acknowledgements. This work was funded in part by the Research Foundation – Flanders (FWO) under Grant V414022N, IDLab (Ghent University – imec), Flanders Innovation & Entrepreneurship (VLAIO), and the European Union. In addition, this material is based on research sponsored by the Defense Advanced Research Projects Agency (DARPA) and the Air Force Research Laboratory (AFRL) under agreement number FA8750-20-2-1004. The U.S. Government is authorized to reproduce and distribute reprints for Governmental purposes notwithstanding any copyright notation thereon. The views and conclusions contained herein are those of the authors and should not be interpreted as necessarily representing the official policies or endorsements, either expressed or implied, of DARPA and AFRL or the U.S. Government. This work is also supported by a Google gift and by the PREMIER project, funded by the Italian Ministry of Education, University, and Research within the PRIN 2017 program.

The computational resources (imec iLabt & STEVIN Supercomputer Infrastructure) and services used in this work were kindly provided by Ghent University, imec, the Flemish Supercomputer Center (VSC), the Hercules Foundation, the Flemish Government department EWI, as well as by University Federico II of Naples.

References

1. Barni, M., et al.: Aligned and non-aligned double JPEG detection using convolutional neural networks. J. Vis. Comun. Image Represent. **49**, 153–163 (2017)
2. Bi, X., Wei, Y., Xiao, B., Li, W.: RRU-Net: the ringed residual U-Net for image splicing forgery detection. In: IEEE/CVF Conference on Computer Vision and Pattern Recognition Workshops (CVPRW), pp. 30–39 (2019)
3. Bianchi, T., De Rosa, A., Piva, A.: Improved DCT coefficient analysis for forgery localization in JPEG images. In: IEEE International Conference on Acoustics, Speech and Signal Processing (ICASSP), pp. 2444–2447 (2011)
4. Bianchi, T., Piva, A.: Image forgery localization via block-grained analysis of JPEG artifacts. IEEE Trans. Inf. Forensics Secur. **7**(3), 1003–1017 (2012)
5. de Carvalho, T.J., Riess, C., Angelopoulou, E., Pedrini, H., de Rezende Rocha, A.: Exposing digital image forgeries by illumination color classification. IEEE Trans. Inf. Forensics Secur. **8**(7), 1182–1194 (2013)
6. Cozzolino, D., Poggi, G., Verdoliva, L.: Splicebuster: a new blind image splicing detector. In: IEEE International Workshop on Information Forensics and Security (WIFS), pp. 1–6 (2015)
7. Cozzolino, D., Verdoliva, L.: Noiseprint: a CNN-based camera model fingerprint. IEEE Trans. Inf. Forensics Secur. **15**, 144–159 (2020)
8. Dang-Nguyen, D.T., Pasquini, C., Conotter, V., Boato, G.: RAISE: a raw images dataset for digital image forensics. In: 6th ACM Multimedia Systems Conference, pp. 219–224 (2015)
9. Fontani, M., Bianchi, T., De Rosa, A., Piva, A., Barni, M.: A framework for decision fusion in image forensics based on Dempster-Shafer theory of evidence. IEEE Trans. Inf. Forensics Secur. **8**(4), 593–607 (2013)
10. Hu, X., Zhang, Z., Jiang, Z., Chaudhuri, S., Yang, Z., Nevatia, R.: SPAN: spatial pyramid attention network for image manipulation localization. In: Vedaldi, A., Bischof, H., Brox, T., Frahm, J.-M. (eds.) ECCV 2020. LNCS, vol. 12366, pp. 312–328. Springer, Cham (2020). https://doi.org/10.1007/978-3-030-58589-1_19
11. Huh, M., Liu, A., Owens, A., Efros, A.A.: Fighting fake news: image splice detection via learned self-consistency. In: Ferrari, V., Hebert, M., Sminchisescu, C., Weiss, Y. (eds.) ECCV 2018. LNCS, vol. 11215, pp. 106–124. Springer, Cham (2018). https://doi.org/10.1007/978-3-030-01252-6_7
12. Iakovidou, C., Zampoglou, M., Papadopoulos, S., Kompatsiaris, Y.: Content-aware detection of JPEG grid inconsistencies for intuitive image forensics. J. Vis. Commun. Image Represent. **54**, 155–170 (2018)
13. Lai, S., Böhme, R.: Block convergence in repeated transform coding: JPEG-100 forensics, carbon dating, and tamper detection. In: 2013 IEEE International Conference on Acoustics, Speech and Signal Processing, pp. 3028–3032 (2013)
14. Le, T.N., Nguyen, H.H., Yamagishi, J., Echizen, I.: OpenForensics: large-scale challenging dataset for multi-face forgery detection and segmentation in-the-wild. In: IEEE/CVF International Conference on Computer Vision (ICCV), pp. 10097–10107 (2021)
15. Li, W., Yuan, Y., Yu, N.: Passive detection of doctored JPEG image via block artifact grid extraction. Sig. Process. **89**(9), 1821–1829 (2009)
16. Lin, X., Li, C.T.: Refining PRNU-based detection of image forgeries. In: 2016 Digital Media Industry Academic Forum (DMIAF), pp. 222–226 (2016)
17. Mayer, O., Stamm, M.C.: Forensic similarity for digital images. IEEE Trans. Inf. Forensics Secur. **15**, 1331–1346 (2019)

18. Mayer, O., Stamm, M.C.: Exposing fake images with forensic similarity graphs. IEEE J. Sel. Top. Sig. Process. **14**(5), 1049–1064 (2020)
19. Novozámský, A., Mahdian, B., Saic, S.: IMD2020: a large-scale annotated dataset tailored for detecting manipulated images. In: IEEE Winter Applications of Computer Vision Workshops (WACVW), pp. 71–80 (2020)
20. Park, J., Cho, D., Ahn, W., Lee, H.-K.: Double JPEG detection in mixed JPEG quality factors using deep convolutional neural network. In: Ferrari, V., Hebert, M., Sminchisescu, C., Weiss, Y. (eds.) ECCV 2018. LNCS, vol. 11209, pp. 656–672. Springer, Cham (2018). https://doi.org/10.1007/978-3-030-01228-1_39
21. Pevny, T., Bas, P., Fridrich, J.: Steganalysis by subtractive pixel adjacency matrix. IEEE Trans. Inf. Forensics Secur. **5**(2), 215–224 (2010)
22. Rössler, A., Cozzolino, D., Verdoliva, L., Riess, C., Thies, J., Niessner, M.: Face-Forensics++: learning to detect manipulated facial images. In: IEEE/CVF International Conference on Computer Vision (ICCV), pp. 1–11 (2019)
23. Verdoliva, L.: Media forensics and deepfakes: an overview. IEEE J. Sel. Top. Sig. Process. **14**(5), 910–932 (2020)
24. Wu, H., Zhou, J., Tian, J., Liu, J., Qiao, Y.: Robust image forgery detection against transmission over online social networks. IEEE Trans. Inf. Forensics Secur. **17**, 443–456 (2022)
25. Wu, Y., AbdAlmageed, W., Natarajan, P.: ManTra-Net: manipulation tracing network for detection and localization of image forgeries with anomalous features. In: IEEE Conference on Computer Vision and Pattern Recognition (CVPR) (2019)
26. Yang, C., Li, H., Lin, F., Jiang, B., Zhao, H.J.: Constrained R-CNN: a general image manipulation detection model. In: IEEE International Conference on Multimedia and Expo (ICME), pp. 1–6 (2020)
27. Ye, S., Sun, Q., Chang, E.C.: Detecting digital image forgeries by measuring inconsistencies of blocking artifact. In: IEEE International Conference on Multimedia and Expo, pp. 12–15 (2007)
28. Zhang, K., Zuo, W., Chen, Y., Meng, D., Zhang, L.: Beyond a Gaussian denoiser: residual learning of deep CNN for image denoising. IEEE Trans. Image Process. **26**(7), 3142–3155 (2017)
29. Zhou, P., Han, X., Morariu, V.I., Davis, L.S.: Two-stream neural networks for tampered face detection. In: IEEE Conference on Computer Vision and Pattern Recognition Workshops (CVPRW), pp. 1831–1839 (2017)

H4VDM: H.264 Video Device Matching

Ziyue Xiang[1]([envelope])[iD], Paolo Bestagini[2][iD], Stefano Tubaro[2][iD],
and Edward J. Delp[1][iD]

[1] Video and Image Processing Lab (VIPER), School of Electrical and Computer
Engineering, Purdue University, West Lafayette, IN, USA
xiang71@purdue.edu, ace@purdue.edu

[2] Dipartimento di Elettronica, Informazione e Bioingegneria, Politecnico di Milano,
Milan, Italy
{paolo.bestagini,stefano.tubaro}@polimi.it

Abstract. Methods that can determine if two given video sequences are
captured by the same device (e.g., mobile telephone or digital camera)
can be used in many forensics tasks. In this paper we refer to this as
"video device matching". In open-set video forensics scenarios it is easier
to determine if two video sequences were captured with the same device
than identifying the specific device. In this paper, we propose a technique
for open-set video device matching. Given two H.264 compressed video
sequences, our method can determine if they are captured by the same
device, even if our method has never encountered the device in training. We denote our proposed technique as H.264 Video Device Matching
(H4VDM). H4VDM uses H.264 compression information extracted from
video sequences to make decisions. It is more robust against artifacts
that alter camera sensor fingerprints, and it can be used to analyze relatively small fragments of the H.264 sequence. We trained and tested our
method on a publicly available video forensics dataset consisting of 35
devices, where our proposed method demonstrated good performance.

Keywords: H.264 Video Compression · Video Device Matching ·
Digital Video Forensics · Deep Learning

1 Introduction

Video Device Identification (VDI) is one of the most important tasks in multimedia forensics [22,25]. A VDI method can associate a video with a specific
source device (e.g., a specific camera). VDI is valuable in forensics investigations
and court defense.

A large amount of VDI techniques rely on the analysis of video camera sensor
fingerprints. For example the Photo Response Non-uniformity (PRNU) pattern is
commonly used in image/video device identification techniques [19,28–30]. Since
PRNU patterns can capture the heterogeneity of the sensor response caused by
imperfections in the sensor manufacturing process, such sensor fingerprints can
attribute a video sequence to one source device uniquely. Despite being powerful

© Springer Nature Switzerland AG 2023
J.-J. Rousseau and B. Kapralos (Eds.): ICPR 2022 Workshops, LNCS 13644, pp. 300–319, 2023.
https://doi.org/10.1007/978-3-031-37742-6_24

in many forensics tasks, the PRNU patterns can be difficult to obtain. The estimation of PRNU patterns usually requires many samples taken by the device under analysis [25]. Obtaining the PRNU patterns from video sequences is more challenging due to the existence of video compression and video stabilization [27]. These challenges limit the application of PRNU patterns in VDI tasks.

H.264 is one of the most popular video compression techniques [18,35]. It offers a wide variety of compression configurations to balance data rate, distortion, and computational complexity. Each configuration will induce a distinct encoding response to the input video sequence. Even for the same compression configuration, the behavior of H.264 encoder implementations used by different device manufacturers may not be identical. Note that the H.264 compression standard only standardizes the decoding but not the encoding [18,35]. In this paper we shall refer to the "encoding pattern" of a H.264 compressed video sequence as the parameters inserted into the compressed bitstream by the encoder and used by the decoder to reconstruct the video sequence. We will show in this paper that these encoding patterns along with the video content can be used to determine the source device of an H.264 video sequence. Since the II.264 encoding pattern tends to be the same for a specific video camera model or firmware version, using it for VDI tasks may only result in a model-level or firmware-level match, which is coarser compared to techniques using video camera sensor fingerprints. However, these H.264 encoding patterns are closely related to the compressed digital video and are less affected by operations that alter the sensor fingerprints such as video stabilization. Compared to metadata forensic methods such as [2,34,49], video forensics methods based on using the video content and encoding parameters can still work even if the metadata information is modified (e.g., when an MP4 video file is converted to an AVI video file without transcoding the video stream). Our proposed method only requires two H.264 Groups of Pictures (GOPs) to make decisions, which allows our approach to work with corrupted or fragmented H.264 data.

In this paper, we focus on open-set Video Device Matching (VDM), which is related to VDI. Open-set classification is the problem of handling classes that are not contained in the training dataset. Traditional classification approaches assume that only known classes appear in the testing environment [36]. In VDI, the video forensics method is asked to identify which device was used to capture the video sequence. In VDM, the video forensics method is asked to determine if two video sequences are captured by the same camera model [1,31,52]. With VDM methods, VDI can be achieved by obtaining a video sequence from a known device and then determining if the video sequence under analysis is captured by the same device. Since VDI methods attribute a given video sequence to a specific source device, these methods require prior knowledge about the devices. As a result, VDI methods are often constrained to closed-set problems, where the video sequence under test comes from a device that is already known to the video forensics method [31]. This tends to have limitations in practice, as forensic investigators are more likely to deal with open-set problems where the video camera model has not been encountered by the method before. Because

VDM methods only analyze if the two video sequences are from the same device, it is possible for these methods to work in open-set scenarios where the devices have never been seen by the VDM methods before [31]. We tested the open-set performance of our proposed VDM technique and verified that it had good performance evaluation metrics for unseen device models. The ability to attain open-set VDM allows our method to be used in a wider range of forensic investigations.

The rest of the paper is organized as follows. In Sect. 2, we show the related work and provide the background knowledge about the H.264 video compression and the machine learning model used in our approach. In Sect. 3, we describe the details of our proposed VDM method. In Sect. 4, we discuss the details of our experiments and present the results. Section 5 concludes the paper and gives insights on open problems and future challenges.

2   Background

In this section we show existing work related to Video Device Identification (VDI), Video Device Matching (VDM), and H.264-based video forensics. Then, we briefly introduce H.264 video compression and transformer neural networks, which are two important concepts for understanding the mechanism of our proposed open-set VDM method.

2.1   Related Work

Video Device Identification (VDI) is an important topic in video forensics. In [38], the authors used the statistics of motion vectors from video codecs for VDI. Yahaya et al. [51] used conditional probability features to achieve VDI. In [2,34,49], the authors used metadata information stored in video container formats for VDI. Most existing work on VDI are based on camera sensor noise fingerprints, which was first studied in [22]. In the seminal work proposed by Chen et al. [6], PRNU analysis was first used for VDI tasks. In [3,11,28,48,52], the authors devised various strategies to improve the performance of PRNU analysis of video, such as selecting key frames, counteracting the effects of video stabilization, using the characteristics of the video codecs, and weighting frames in terms of compression quality. Beyond PRNU patterns, [8,15,41] used deep neural networks to extract features from decoded video frames, which can be used in VDI tasks. Some VDI techniques use multimodal data to improve the performance. Iuliani et al. [19] combined image and video data from the same sensor for better VDI results. Dal Cortivo et al. [9] proposed a VDI approach based on video and audio information.

As described in Sect. 1, Video Device Matching (VDM) is a concept derived from VDI. It is also known as Video Device Verification. In [1,52], the authors improved PRNU analysis for VDM. Mayer et al. [31] addressed the problem of open-set VDM using a deep neural network to extract features from decoded video frames.

There have been a number of video forensics approaches that use the characteristics of H.264 video compression. In [4,13,26,44,45,50,53,54], the authors used information from the H.264 codec to determine if an H.264 video is double compressed. Verde *et al.* [46] used deep neural networks to extract H.264 codec information for video manipulation localization. We believe our proposed technique is the first to use H.264 codec information for open-set VDM problems.

2.2 H.264 Video Compression

The details of the H.264 video compression standard are extremely sophisticated and beyond the scope of this paper. Therefore, we provide a high-level overview of H.264 video compression that is sufficient for understanding our proposed VDM method. More details about H.264 compression can be obtained from [18,35,39].

One important concept that is a part of nearly all video compression standards is the use of both spatial and temporal redundancy in a video sequence to reduce its data rate, particularly the fact that consecutive frames in a small temporal interval can be greatly correlated. The H.264 encoder examines the video frames in a structure known as Group of Pictures (GOP), which is a sequence of consecutive frames. Due to the high temporal correlation, the frames in a GOP can be compressed using motion compensation [35]. The frames in a GOP are divided into I-, P-, and B-frames that are used for the motion compensation. Typically the first frame in a GOP is an I-frame that acts as the reference frame for other frames in the GOP. The I-frame is compressed using intra-frame compression similar to JPEG. The rest of the frames in an H.264 GOP can be P-frames or B-frames, and are compressed with inter-frame compression and motion compensation using the I-frame or a P-frame as a reference frame [35].

In I-, P-, and B-frames, H.264 uses 16×16 frame patches known as macroblocks in each video frame. Each macroblock is associated with a macroblock type, which specifies how the information in the macroblock is compressed. Macroblock-level compression can done by predicting patterns within the macroblock (i.e., intra-coded macroblocks) or using difference information from a similar macroblock in a motion compensated reference frame (i.e., inter-coded macroblocks) [35]. This difference is known as the prediction residual, which is more efficient to compress compared to the original video frame. The pixels in the macroblocks are then transformed and quantized before being entropy coded [35]. The quantization process is controlled by a Quantization Parameter (QP). As the QP increases, the data rate decreases and the quantization distortion increases; as QP decreases, the rate-distortion trade-off goes towards the opposite direction [35]. For inter-coded macroblocks the encoded prediction residuals and the motion vectors from the motion compensation are placed in the compressed bitstream.

H.264 uses the YUV color space, which has one luma (luminance) channel and two chroma (chrominance) channels [35]. Since the human visual system is more sensitive to luminance than chrominance, H.264 prioritizes the compression quality of the luma channel over the chroma channels to reduce data rate. Each color channel has its own QP for rate-distortion control [35].

2.3   Vision Transformers

Our proposed VDM method is based on transformer neural networks [43]. These networks demonstrated outstanding performance in a wide variety of tasks such as language modeling [5], image classification [10], image segmentation [23], video classification [24], audio signal processing [47], and protein structure prediction [20].

Transformers can be used to process sequence data. They possess faster computational speed, higher scalability, and better stability compared to Recurrent Neural Networks such as LSTM [14] and GRU [7,55]. Transformer networks are made up of transformer layers. The output of a transformer layer is used as the input to the next transformer layer. Denote the input to a transformer layer by $Z \in \mathbb{R}^{N \times D}$, where N is the sequence length and D is the dimensionality of the vector at each time step. Transformer layers estimate the relationship between the vectors at each time step in Z based on the Self Attention (SA) mechanism. In SA, the input Z is first linearly projected into three matrices $q, k, v \in \mathbb{R}^{N \times D_h}$ using a matrix $U \in \mathbb{R}^{D \times 3D_h}$ such that $[q|k|v] = ZU$. Then, the SA of Z is computed by $\mathrm{SA}(Z) = \mathrm{softmax}(qk^T/\sqrt{D_h})v$. An extended version of SA known as Multihead Self Attention (MSA) is used in [43], where h different SA values (known as "MSA heads") are computed at the same time. The h different SA values are combined to form the result of MSA using a matrix $V \in \mathbb{R}^{D \times D}$ such that $\mathrm{MSA}(Z) = [\mathrm{SA}_1(Z) \mid \cdots \mid \mathrm{SA}_h(Z)]V$. When choosing the number of MSA heads h, it must hold that h divides D and $D_h = D/h$, which ensures the output of the transformer layer $\mathrm{MSA}(Z)$ has the same dimensionality as the input Z. Since a transformer network consists of a series of such layers, its input and output share the same dimensionality.

Vision Transformer (ViT) [10] uses transformer networks for computer vision tasks. In order to convert image data into the format accepted by transformers, the ViT splits the image into K non-overlapping patches of size $P \times P \times C$, where P is the patch size and C is the number of channels. The patches are flattened to form the matrix $Z' \in \mathbb{R}^{K \times P^2C}$. Since P^2C is usually large, the dimensionality of the flattened vectors from each patch is reduced to D_{ViT} using a linear projection $W \in \mathbb{R}^{P^2C \times D_{\mathrm{ViT}}}$ such that $Z = Z'W$. The original input image can be represented by Z, which is used as the input to the transformer network.

3   Proposed Method

The H.264 Video Device Matching (VDM) problem can be formally defined as follows: given two Groups of Pictures (GOPs) $\mathcal{G}_1$ and $\mathcal{G}_2$ from two video sequences, determine if the two GOPs are from the same device. Note the GOP information includes the decoded frame and the coding parameters. We propose an H.264 Video Device Matching (H4VDM) method for open-set VDM. The block diagram of H4VDM is shown in Fig. 1. This network architecture is commonly used in many open-set digital forensics techniques [29,31,32]. The input to H4VDM is two H.264 GOPs $\mathcal{G}_1$ and $\mathcal{G}_2$. They are then passed to the H4VDM feature extractor separately.

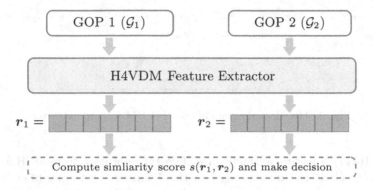

Fig. 1. The block diagram of our proposed H.264 Video Device Matching (H4VDM) method. The details of the H4VDM feature extractor are described in Sect. 3.1. Note the input GOP information includes the decoded frame and the coding parameters.

The H4VDM feature extractor is the key component of our proposed method, which is described extensively in Sect. 3.1. It extracts important information from an H.264 GOP $\mathcal{G}$ and expresses this information in a D_r-dimensional vector representation r known as the GOP feature vector. Let r_1 and r_2 be the corresponding GOP feature vectors of $\mathcal{G}_1$ and $\mathcal{G}_2$, respectively. We compute a similarity score $s(r_1, r_2)$ between the two GOP feature vectors. The similarity score can be used for classification: a higher similarity score indicates that $\mathcal{G}_2$ is more likely to be captured by the same device as $\mathcal{G}_1$. The similarity score used in our proposed method is described in Sect. 3.2.

3.1 H4VDM Feature Extractor

The block diagram of the H4VDM feature extractor is shown in Fig. 2. The feature extractor computes GOP feature vectors using H.264 GOPs containing L frames, where the size of each frame is $H \times W$. If a GOP is longer than L frames, we extract features for the first L frames only without loss of generality. If the frame size of a GOP is larger than $H \times W$, we extract features from an arbitrary $H \times W$ region in the GOP for our analysis. Feature extraction is not possible when the length of GOP is less than L or when the GOP frame size is smaller than $H \times W$. Therefore, it is important to set L, H, and W appropriately so that the H4VDM feature extractor can process GOPs from a wide range of H.264 video sequences.

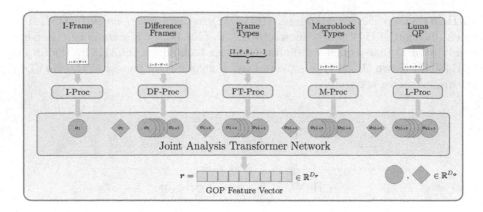

Fig. 2. The block diagram of the H4VDM feature extractor.

The H4VDM feature extractor uses five types of data from an H.264 GOP to generate GOP feature vectors, i.e., the I-frame, the frame differences, the frame types, the macroblock types and the luma QPs. Each type of data is first processed by a specific approach to generate an intermediate output denoted by $o \in \mathbb{R}^{D_o}$. The five processing methods for each data type are known as the I-, DF-, FT-, M-, and L-Proc. Many of these processing methods use Vision Transformers (ViTs) to process image-like information. In total, we use two ViT architectures in our proposed method, i.e., ViT-1 and ViT-2 (as shown in Table 1). ViT-1 is a larger network that processes more complicated data such as I-frames and residual frames. ViT-2 is a smaller network that processes simpler data such as macroblock types and luma Quantization Parameters (QPs). The details of each processing method are described as below.

I-Proc. This processing step extracts feature from the decoded I-frame in the GOP. The I-Proc uses the ViT-1 architecture in Table 1. For each GOP, the input to the I-Proc is an $H \times W \times 3$ vector consisting of the RGB pixel data from the I-frame. The output of the I-Proc is o_1.

DF-Proc. This processing step extracts features from differences of the decoded frames in sequence. The differences we compute are between the decoded frames and the decoded I-frame in the GOP (including the difference between the I-frame and itself, which is all zeros). Using difference frames can better enable the DF-Proc to learn about the characteristics of H.264 compression. The DF-Proc also uses the ViT-1 architecture in Table 1. For each GOP, the input to the DF-Proc is L vectors of dimension $H \times W \times 3$, where each vector is the RGB pixel difference. The L frame difference vectors are processed one by one to generate L outputs $o_3, \ldots, o_{L+2}$.

FT-Proc. This step converts frames types into D_o dimensional vectors. For each input GOP, the frame types are a sequence of L positive integers, each of which represents a valid frame type in H.264 (i.e., I, P, B). The FT-Proc projects each integer to a D_o-dimensional real-valued vector with the widely used embedding technique [33]. In the original integer representation, each integer is an index for a concept (e.g., frame types). The distance between two integer indices is not meaningful. By converting the integer indices into real-valued vectors using a projection learned in the training phase, the vector representation of similar concepts can have smaller distances, which makes learning easier for the machine learning method. The final outputs are L vectors $o_{L+4}, \ldots, o_{2L+3}$.

M-Proc. Here we extract features from the macroblock types. In the original H.264 data stream, a frame is subdivided into macroblocks of size 16×16. Each macroblock in the frame can be compressed with different methods. The compression method used in a macroblock is stored as an integer known as the macroblock type [45]. This macroblock type information is converted into a $H \times W \times 1$ vector by "unpacking" the macroblocks. That is, every pixel in the frame is associated with a macroblock type integer inherited from the macroblock it belongs to. We use the embedding technique to project each macrotype integer into a three dimensional real-valued vector, which is then processed by a ViT-2 network described in Table 1. For the L frames in the GOP, the output is L vectors $o_{2L+5}, \ldots, o_{3L+4}$.

L-Proc. This step extracts features from the luma QPs. The input is an $H \times W \times 1$ vector, where each element is an integer ranging from 0 to 51, i.e., the luma QPs. As the luma QP increases, the H.264 quantization procedure discards more details in the luma channel in exchange for lower data rate [42]. Due to the ordered nature of luma QPs, we process them directly using a ViT-2 network in Table 1. For the L frames in the GOP, the output is L vectors $o_{3L+6}, \ldots, o_{4L+5}$.

Table 1. The hyperparameters of the vision transformers (ViT) [10] used in H4VDM, as discussed in Sect. 4.3.

Hyperparameters	ViT-1	ViT-2
depth	8	4
projection dimension	D_{ViT1}	D_{ViT2}
number of MSA heads	8	4
output dimension	D_o	D_o
patch size	16	16

The intermediate outputs from the five processing networks contain important information about different data types. Similar to [40], we insert special vectors (i.e., o_2, o_{L+3}, o_{2L+4}, o_{3L+5}) to combine the information acquired from various data types. These special vectors can be updated during training. In total, there are $4L + 5$ intermediate output vectors, which are used as the input to the joint analysis network. This network is an 8-layer transformer network [43]. The output of the joint analysis network is linearly projected to a vector $r \in \mathbb{R}^{D_r}$. The vector r is the output of the H4VDM feature extractor (i.e., the GOP feature vector).

Based on the five data types in the input GOP, the H4VDM feature extractor characterizes macroblock type selection, luma QP selection, and other patterns that are specific to the video capturing device. This information is contained in a D_r-dimensional GOP feature vector. By comparing the similarity score between the corresponding GOP feature vectors from two video sequences we can determine if the two video sequences were captured by the same device. Since H4VDM only requires two H.264 GOPs to make decisions, it is able to work in scenarios where data from a test device is scarce, e.g., when the H.264 video sequence is corrupted and only a few GOPs can be recovered.

3.2   Similarity Score and Loss Function

The similarity score between two GOP feature vectors r_1 and r_2 is a real number in the range $[0, 1]$, where 1 indicates the two vectors are the most similar and 0 indicates the two vectors are the most dissimilar. We compute the similarity score using the following function

$$s(r_1, r_2) = 1 - \tanh\left(\|r_1 - r_2\|_2\right),\tag{1}$$

where $\|\cdot\|_2$ denotes L_2-norm. The function $f(x) = 1 - \tanh(x)$ for $x \geq 0$ is shown in Fig. 3. When r_1 and r_2 are more similar, $\|r_1 - r_2\|_2 \to 0$, which indicates $s(r_1, r_2) \to 1$. Conversely, $s(r_1, r_2) \to 0$ when r_1 and r_2 are more dissimilar.

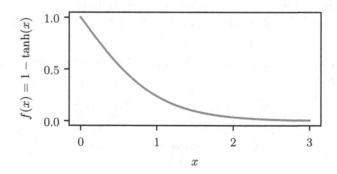

Fig. 3. The similarity score function.

We use binary cross-entropy loss and the similarity score (Eq. (1)) to compute the loss of the H4VDM method during training. Suppose the ground truth label of the GOP feature vector pair (r_1, r_2) is given by y, where $y = 1$ indicates the two GOP features are from the same video capturing device and $y = 0$ indicates the opposite. The loss of the pair is

$$\ell(r_1, r_2, y) = y \log\left[s(r_1, r_2)\right] + (1 - y) \log\left[1 - s(r_1, r_2)\right].\tag{2}$$

4   Experiments and Results

We describe our experiments in this section including the datasets used for training and testing. More details about H4VDM such as hyperparameter selection and training strategy are also discussed. Finally, we present the results from the experiments. We used Area Under the Receiver Operating Characteristic (AUC) score [17], F_1-score [16], and accuracy score to evaluate the performance of H4VDM. Throughout the experiments, we selected the dimensionality of the GOP feature vectors to be 1024, i.e., $D_r = 1024$.

4.1   Dataset Generation

The datasets used in our experiments are generated from the VISION dataset [37]. The VISION dataset contains 648 H.264 video sequences from 35 different video capturing devices. The list of devices in VISION is shown in Table 2.

Table 2. The list of devices contained in the VISION dataset [37].

Device ID	Device Name	Device ID	Device Name
1	Samsung_GalaxyS3Mini	19	Apple_iPhone6Plus (iOS 10.2.1)
2	Apple_iPhone4s (iOS 7.1.2)	20	Apple_iPadMini (iOS 8.4)
3	Huawei_P9	21	Wiko_Ridge4G
4	LG_D290	22	Samsung_GalaxyTrendPlus
5	Apple_iPhone5c (iOS 10.2.1)	23	Asus_Zenfone2Laser
6	Apple_iPhone6 (iOS 8.4)	24	Xiaomi_RedmiNote3
7	Lenovo_P70A	25	OnePlus_A3000
8	Samsung_GalaxyTab3	26	Samsung_GalaxyS3Mini
9	Apple_iPhone4 (iOS 7.1.2)	27	Samsung_GalaxyS5
10	Apple_iPhone4s (iOS 8.4.1)	28	Huawei_P8
11	Samsung_GalaxyS3	29	Apple_iPhone5 (iOS 9.3.3)
12	Sony_XperiaZ1Compact	30	Huawei_Honor5c
13	Apple_iPad2 (iOS 7.1.1)	31	Samsung_GalaxyS4Mini
14	Apple_iPhone5c (iOS 7.0.3)	32	OnePlus_A3003
15	Apple_iPhone6 (iOS 10.1.1)	33	Huawei_Ascend
16	Huawei_P9Lite	34	Apple_iPhone5 (iOS 8.3)
17	Microsoft_Lumia640LTE	35	Samsung_GalaxyTabA
18	Apple_iPhone5c (iOS 8.4.1)		

We decoded the video frames and extracted the GOPs from video sequences in VISION using a customized version of the openh264[1] H.264 decoder, which allows us access to the GOP information. In our analysis, we selected the length

---

[1] https://github.com/cisco/openh264.

of GOP $L = 8$. That is, our method can analyze H.264 GOP with length greater than or equal to 8. The height (H) and width (W) of the frames were set to $H = W = 224$, which is a common size used by popular image or video processing techniques such as [10,12,23,24]. With this choice of H and W, the frame sizes of all video sequences in the VISION dataset are larger than (H, W). Therefore, we cropped a (H, W) region from the center of the frames for analysis. We chose to crop the region at the center because the video content at the center is more likely to change compared to those from the edges or corners. From each video sequence in the VISION dataset, we randomly sampled 15 GOPs whose length is greater than or equal to L. When the length of a sampled GOP is greater than L, only the first L frames in the GOP were used.

We constructed data from the VISION dataset to train and test our method as follows:

1. Provide a set of device indices S, selected from Table 2.
2. Select all pairs of device indices $(i, j) \in S \otimes S$, where $\otimes$ denotes Cartesian product. Denote the set of GOPs from device i and device j by $\mathcal{A}_i$ and $\mathcal{A}_j$, respectively. For each (i, j) do the following:
   (a) If $i \neq j$, randomly sample n_0 unique GOP pairs from the set $\mathcal{A}_i \otimes \mathcal{A}_j$ that are not in the dataset. When determining if a GOP pair is in the dataset, the GOP pair is considered to be unordered. That is, if one swaps the first and the second element, the pair is considered to be the same. These n_0 pairs are assigned label 0 and added to the dataset.
   (b) If $i = j$, randomly sample n_1 unique GOP pairs from the set $\mathcal{A}_i \otimes \mathcal{A}_j$ that are not in the dataset. When determining if a GOP pair is in the dataset, the GOP pair is considered to be unordered. These n_1 pairs are assigned label 1 and added to the dataset.

In our experiments, we chose $n_0 = 15$ and $n_1 = 120$. To better evaluate the performance of H4VDM, we constructed 7 datasets, where each dataset contained a training set and a testing set. For brevity, we refer to these datasets as D1, D2, ..., D7. In each dataset, the set of all device IDs in VISION are split into two disjoint sets S_1 and S_2. They are passed to the dataset construction step to generate the training set and the testing set, respectively. For dataset D1–D4, S_2 contained half of the device IDs that were randomly selected. For dataset D5–D7, the device IDs are split into three disjoint sets and used as S_2 of each dataset. The details of each dataset are shown in Table 3. For the testing set of each dataset, we uniformly sampled 40% of the GOP pairs after dataset generation to reduce its size. In each dataset, we uniformly removed 1/8 of the GOP pairs from the testing set for validation during training. The training process is stopped when the open-set validation performance no longer increases.

We selected $L = 8$ in our experiments based on several factors. Increasing L is likely to improve the quality of GOP feature extraction, because the H4VDM feature extractor is exposed to more information. However, it will increase the complexity of the model and make the training process more computationally intense. Since our method requires the length of the GOP under analysis to be at least L, a larger L value can also reduce the number of valid GOP candidates

Table 3. The details of each dataset. #0 and #1 indicates the number of GOP pairs with class 0 (different device) and class 1 (same device), respectively.

Dataset	Test Device IDs (S_2)	Training		Testing	
		#0	#1	#0	#1
D1	{1, 2, 4, 5, 6, 14, 17, 18, 19, 21, 22, 23, 27, 28, 30, 32, 35}	4590	2160	816	1632
D2	{1, 2, 4, 11, 14, 15, 17, 18, 19, 20, 21, 23, 26, 30, 32, 33, 35}	4590	2160	816	1632
D3	{4, 5, 6, 10, 11, 13, 14, 16, 17, 19, 21, 22, 23, 30, 31, 32, 35}	4590	2160	816	1632
D4	{3, 4, 6, 8, 13, 17, 19, 20, 21, 22, 23, 26, 29, 30, 31, 32, 34}	4590	2160	816	1632
D5	{1, 4, 7, 10, 13, 16, 19, 22, 25, 28, 31, 34}	7590	2760	792	576
D6	{2, 5, 8, 11, 14, 17, 20, 23, 26, 29, 32, 35}	7590	2760	792	576
D7	{3, 6, 9, 12, 15, 18, 21, 24, 27, 30, 33}	8280	2880	660	528

in a video sequence. Note that it is computationally expensive to acquire the decoded frames and GOP information from the H.264 bitstream. In training, since the training data will be used repeatedly in each training epoch, it is more efficient to store the decoded frames and GOP information on disk. Therefore, another factor that affects the choice of L is the storage size of the uncompressed GOPs and decoded frames. With the current dataset configurations, each dataset (training set and testing set) requires approximately 176 GB of disk space. Given such an enormous dataset size, the training process is heavily bounded by the I/O performance of the storage devices, which is much slower compared to other hardware components (e.g., GPUs). In the worst case, the training time can increase linearly with respect to L, which is costly when L is large. We used $L = 8$ as a balance among model performance, model complexity, the usability of our method, training complexity, and training speed. Typical training times were 3–6 h using six 48 GB GPUs.

4.2 Parameter Initialization and Training

From Fig. 3 it can be seen that the gradients of the similarity score function $f(x)$ will saturate when x is large, which can significantly reduce the efficiency of gradient-based learning. Therefore, when initializing the model parameters, we limited the scale of the weights in the output layer to be within $[-0.002, 0.002]$. This reduced the initial scale of $\|r_1 - r_2\|_2$, which can facilitate training.

We trained the H4VDM method using the Adam optimizer [21] with a mini-batch size of 72. We used 5 warm-up epochs, where the learning rate linearly increased from 0 to 8×10^{-6}. After warm-up epochs, we trained the method using an initial learning rate of 8×10^{-6}. An exponential learning rate decay was used with a decay factor of 0.97. During training, we monitored the AUC score on the validation set. The training was stopped when the validation AUC score no longer increased.

4.3 Model Size Selection

We tuned the hyperparameters D_{ViT1} and D_o to control the size of the model. We constructed 3 models of various sizes (i.e., S (small), B (baseline), and L (large)). For each model, we computed the best AUC score on the testing set of Dataset D1. The results are shown in Table 4. Since the H4VDM-B model achieved the best AUC auc score, further experiments were conducted with this model.

Table 4. The best AUC scores of various models on the testing set of Dataset D1.

Model	D_{ViT1}	D_{ViT2}	D_o	Parameters	AUC
H4VDM-S	192	64	192	48.93M	79.8
H4VDM-B	256	64	256	80.10M	80.2
H4VDM-L	320	64	320	118.95M	69.4

4.4 Results

Results on Datasets D1–D4. In Table 5, we show the performance of the H4VDM-B model on datasets D1–D4. When computing the F_1-score, we selected the threshold such that the sum of True Positive Rate (TPR) and True Negative Rate (TNR) is maximized. Our method achieved an overall F_1-score of 67.2 and an average AUC score of 77.4 on datasets D1–D4. Overall, for class 0 (GOP pairs from different devices) the precision is high, which means most retrieved GOP pairs are relevant. For class 1 (GOP pairs from the same device) the recall is high, which means most relevant GOP pairs are retrieved. In Fig. 4, we show the accuracy score matrix of device index pairs of each dataset in testing. From this figure, it can be seen that H4VDM can match devices at a firmware level. For example, device 29 and 34 in dataset D4 are the same device (Apple iPhone5) with different operating system versions. H4VDM was able to distinguish them with high accuracy.

Table 5. The testing performance of the H4VDM-B model on datasets D1–D4.

Dataset	Class 0			Class 1			All Classes			
	Pre.	Rec.	F_1	Pre.	Rec.	F_1	Pre.	Rec.	F_1	AUC
D1	95.9	53.6	68.8	50.6	95.4	66.1	80.8	67.5	67.9	80.2
D2	91.7	49.7	64.5	47.6	91.1	62.5	77.0	63.5	63.8	74.1
D3	89.9	55.4	68.5	49.4	87.5	63.2	76.4	66.1	66.8	78.0
D4	86.0	64.0	73.4	52.3	79.1	63.0	74.8	69.0	69.9	77.3
Overall	90.5	55.7	68.9	49.9	88.3	63.7	76.9	66.5	67.2	77.4

Pre. = Precision   Rec. = Recall

Results on Datasets D5–D7. From the results of H4VDM on datasets D1–D4 (Fig. 4), it can be seen that the performance of H4VDM was low for specific device pairs. This may be caused by the fact that datasets D1–D4 contain only a small number of devices in the training set, which makes it difficult for the method to generalize to a broader scope of devices. To test the performance of H4VDM on datasets with more training devices, we trained and tested H4VDM on datasets D5–D7, whose training sets contain more devices in the VISION dataset. The testing performance of the H4VDM-B model on datasets D5–D7 is shown in Table 6. The accuracy score matrix of device index pairs is shown in Fig. 5. On datasets D5–D7, our method achieved an overall F_1-score of 78.6 and an average AUC score of 85.2. It can be seen that as the number of devices in the training set increases, the performance of H4VDM becomes better. However, since the number of devices in the testing set decreases, the testing performance can vary significantly depending on the choice of the testing devices. Overall, the results on datasets D1–D4 show that H4VDM can learn to achieve open-set VDM given a small number of training devices. The results on datasets D5–D7 show that the performance of H4VDM can improve quickly as more devices are available in training.

Table 6. The testing performance of the H4VDM-B model on datasets D5–D7.

Dataset	Class 0			Class 1			All Classes			
	Pre.	Rec.	F_1	Pre.	Rec.	F_1	Pre.	Rec.	F_1	AUC
D5	85.9	74.5	79.8	75.5	86.5	80.6	80.9	80.2	80.2	87.0
D6	96.1	73.4	83.2	76.9	96.7	85.7	86.9	84.5	84.4	90.0
D7	94.8	48.8	64.4	65.5	97.3	78.3	80.1	73.0	71.3	78.5
Overall	92.3	65.6	75.8	72.6	93.5	81.5	82.6	79.2	78.6	85.2

Pre. = Precision   Rec. = Recall

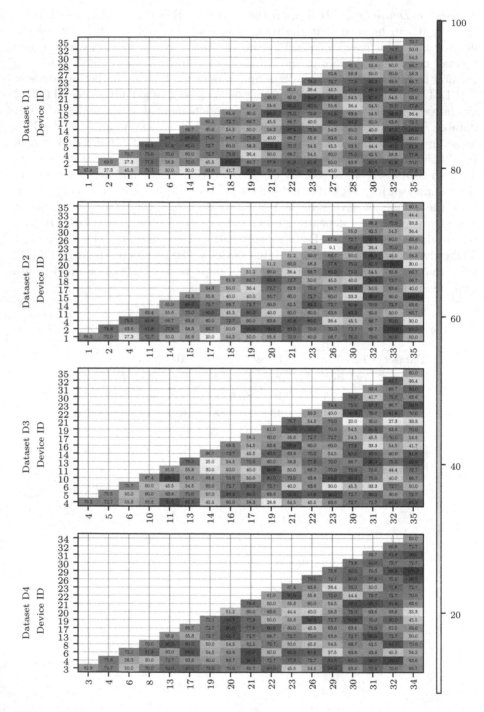

Fig. 4. The testing accuracy score matrix of device index pairs on datasets D1–D4.

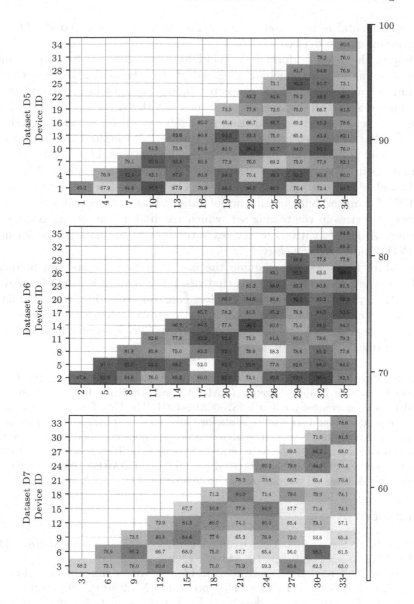

Fig. 5. The testing accuracy score matrix of device index pairs on datasets D5–D7.

5   Conclusion

In this paper we proposed an H.264-based open-set VDM method known as H4VDM. H4VDM uses transformer neural networks to process five types of data from the H.264 decoded frames and the GOPs. We trained and tested the H4VDM-B model on datasets generated from the VISION dataset [37].

The experimental results showed that H4VDM demonstrated good VDM performance on unseen devices.

Despite the good performance, H4VDM has still room for improvement. When selecting hyperparameters, we greedily used the model that had the best performance on Dataset D1. The selected model may not have the best overall performance across all datasets. Some important H.264 codec information such as motion vectors and true prediction residuals were not used in H4VDM. The small number of devices in the VISION dataset also limited the performance evaluation of H4VDM. On datasets D1–D4, less dataset bias is introduced in training/testing split, but the performance of H4VDM is relatively low due to small number of devices in the training set. On datasets D5–D7, the performane of H4VDM is higher, but the influence of dataset bias is stronger due to the small number of devices in the testing set, which resulted in fluctuating testing performamnce. A dataset with more devices is required to evaluate the performance of H4VDM more comprehensively.

In future work, we will examine the use of motion vectors and prediction residuals. We will develop methods that use popular deep learning frameworks efficiently so that the training speed is less constrained by hardware I/O speed. We will collect video data from more video capturing devices for future video forensics research. We are investigating other video compression techniques including H.265, H.266, VP9, and AV1.

Acknowledgments. This material is based on research sponsored by the Defense Advanced Research Projects Agency (DARPA) and Air Force Research Laboratory (AFRL) under agreement number FA8750-20-2-1004. The U.S. Government is authorized to reproduce and distribute reprints for Governmental purposes notwithstanding any copyright notation thereon. The views and conclusions contained herein are those of the authors and should not be interpreted as necessarily representing the official policies or endorsements, either expressed or implied, of DARPA, AFRL or the U.S. Government. Address all correspondence to Edward J. Delp, ace@purdue.edu.

References

1. Altinisik, E., Sencar, H.T.: Source camera verification for strongly stabilized videos. IEEE Trans. Inf. For. Secur. **16**, 643–657 (2021)
2. Altinisik, E., Sencar, H.T.: Camera model identification using container and encoding characteristics of video files. arXiv preprint arXiv:2201.02949 (2022)
3. Altinisik, E., Tasdemir, K., Sencar, H.T.: Mitigation of H.264 and H.265 video compression for reliable PRNU estimation. IEEE Trans. Inf. For. Secur. **15**, 1557–1571 (2020)
4. Bestagini, P., Milani, S., Tagliasacchi, M., Tubaro, S.: Codec and GOP identification in double compressed videos. IEEE Trans. Image Process. **25**(5), 2298–2310 (2016)
5. Brown, T., et al.: Language models are few-shot learners. Adv. Neural Inf. Process. Syst. **33**, 1877–1901 (2020)
6. Chen, M., Fridrich, J., Goljan, M., Lukáš, J.: Source digital camcorder identification using sensor photo response non-uniformity. Proc. Secur. Steganogr. Watermark. Multimedia Cont. IX **6505**, 517–528 (2007)

7. Cho, K., Van Merriënboer, B., Bahdanau, D., Bengio, Y.: On the properties of neural machine translation: encoder-decoder approaches (2014). arXiv preprint arXiv:1409.1259
8. Cozzolino, D., Poggi, G., Verdoliva, L.: Extracting camera-based fingerprints for video forensics. In: Proceedings of the IEEE/CVF Conference on Computer Vision and Pattern Recognition Workshops, Long Beach, CA, USA (2019)
9. Dal Cortivo, D., Mandelli, S., Bestagini, P., Tubaro, S.: CNN-based multi-modal camera model identification on video sequences. J. Imaging **7**(8), 135 (2021)
10. Dosovitskiy, A., et al.: An image is worth 16×16 words: transformers for image recognition at scale. arXiv preprint arXiv:2010.11929 (2020)
11. Ferrara, P., Iuliani, M., Piva, A.: PRNU-based video source attribution: which frames are you using? J. Imag. **8**(3), 57 (2022)
12. He, K., Zhang, X., Ren, S., Sun, J.: Deep residual learning for image recognition. arXiv preprint arXiv:1512.03385 (2015)
13. He, P., Jiang, X., Sun, T., Wang, S., Li, B., Dong, Y.: Frame-wise detection of relocated I-frames in double compressed H.264 videos based on convolutional neural network. J. Vis. Commun. Image Represent. **48**, 149–158 (2017)
14. Hochreiter, S., Schmidhuber, J.: Long short-term memory. Neural Comput. **9**(8), 1735–1780 (1997)
15. Hosler, B., et al.: A video camera model identification system using deep learning and fusion. In: Proceedings of the 2019 IEEE International Conference on Acoustics, Speech and Signal Processing, Brighton, UK, pp. 8271–8275 (2019)
16. Hripcsak, G., Rothschild, A.S.: Agreement, the F-measure, and reliability in information retrieval. J. Am. Med. Inf. Assoc. **12**(3), 296–298 (2005)
17. Huang, J., Ling, C.: Using AUC and accuracy in evaluating learning algorithms. IEEE Trans. Knowl. Data Eng. **17**(3), 299–310 (2005)
18. International Organization for Standardization: ISO/IEC 14496-10:2020 information technology–coding of audio-visual objects–part 10: Advanced video coding. https://www.iso.org/standard/75400.html
19. Iuliani, M., Fontani, M., Shullani, D., Piva, A.: Hybrid reference-based video source identification. Sensors **19**(3), 649 (2019)
20. Jumper, J., et al.: Highly accurate protein structure prediction with alphafold. Nature **596**(7873), 583–589 (2021)
21. Kingma, D.P., Ba, J.: Adam: a method for stochastic optimization. arXiv preprint arXiv:1412.6980 (2014)
22. Kurosawa, K., Kuroki, K., Saitoh, N.: CCD fingerprint method-identification of a video camera from videotaped images. In: Proceedings of the International Conference on Image Processing, Kobe, Japan, vol. 3, pp. 537–540 (1999)
23. Liu, Z., et al.: Swin transformer: hierarchical vision transformer using shifted windows. In: Proceedings of the IEEE/CVF International Conference on Computer Vision, Nashville, CA, USA, pp. 10012–10022 (2021)
24. Liu, Z., et al.: Video swin transformer (2021). arXiv preprint arXiv:2106.13230
25. Lukas, J., Fridrich, J., Goljan, M.: Digital camera identification from sensor pattern noise. IEEE Trans. Inf. For. Secur. **1**(2), 205–214 (2006)
26. Mahfoudi, G., Retraint, F., Morain-Nicolier, F., Pic, M.M.: Statistical H.264 double compression detection method based on dct coefficients. IEEE Access **10**, 4271–4283 (2022)
27. Mandelli, S., Bestagini, P., Tubaro, S., Cozzolino, D., Verdoliva, L.: Blind detection and localization of video temporal splicing exploiting sensor-based footprints. In: Proceedings of the European Signal Processing Conference, Rome, Italy, pp. 1362–1366 (2018)

28. Mandelli, S., Bestagini, P., Verdoliva, L., Tubaro, S.: Facing device attribution problem for stabilized video sequences. IEEE Trans. Inf. For. Secur. **15**, 14–27 (2020)
29. Mandelli, S., Cozzolino, D., Bestagini, P., Verdoliva, L., Tubaro, S.: CNN-based fast source device identification. IEEE Signal Process. Lett. **27**, 1285–1289 (2020)
30. Marra, F., Poggi, G., Sansone, C., Verdoliva, L.: Blind PRNU-based image clustering for source identification. IEEE Trans. Inf. For. Secur. **12**(9), 2197–2211 (2017)
31. Mayer, O., Hosler, B., Stamm, M.C.: Open set video camera model verification. In: Proceedings of the IEEE International Conference on Acoustics, Speech and Signal Processing, Barcelona, Spain, pp. 2962–2966 (2020)
32. Mayer, O., Stamm, M.C.: Forensic similarity for digital images. IEEE Trans. Inf. For. Secur. **15**, 1331–1346 (2020)
33. Mikolov, T., Chen, K., Corrado, G., Dean, J.: Efficient estimation of word representations in vector space. arXiv preprint arXiv:1301.3781 (2013)
34. Ramos López, R., Almaraz Luengo, E., Sandoval Orozco, A.L., Villalba, L.J.G.: Digital video source identification based on container's structure analysis. IEEE Access **8**, 36363–36375 (2020)
35. Richardson, I.E.: The H.264 Advanced Video Compression Standard. John Wiley & Sons, Hoboken (2011)
36. Scheirer, W.J., Rocha, A., Sapkota, A., Boult, T.E.: Towards open set recognition. IEEE Trans. Pattern Anal. Mach. Intell. **35**, 1757–1772 (2013)
37. Shullani, D., Fontani, M., Iuliani, M., Al Shaya, O., Piva, A.: VISION: a video and image dataset for source identification. EURASIP J. Inf. Secur. **15**, 1–16 (2017)
38. Su, Y., Xu, J., Dong, B.: A source video identification algorithm based on motion vectors. In: Proceedings of the Second International Workshop on Computer Science and Engineering, Qingdao, China, vol. 2, pp. 312–316 (2009)
39. Sullivan, G., Wiegand, T.: Video compression - from concepts to the H.264/AVC standard. Proc. IEEE **93**(1), 18–31 (2005)
40. Sun, C., Myers, A., Vondrick, C., Murphy, K., Schmid, C.: VideoBERT: a joint model for video and language representation learning. In: Proceedings of the IEEE/CVF International Conference on Computer Vision, Seoul, Korea, pp. 7463–7472 (2019)
41. Timmerman, D., Bennabhaktula, S., Alegre, E., Azzopardi, G.: Video camera identification from sensor pattern noise with a constrained ConvNet (2020). arXiv preprint arXiv:2012.06277
42. Valenzise, G., Tagliasacchi, M., Tubaro, S.: Estimating QP and motion vectors in H.264/AVC video from decoded pixels. In: Proceedings of the 2nd ACM Workshop on Multimedia in Forensics, Security and Intelligence, Firenze, Italy, pp. 89–92 (2010)
43. Vaswani, A., et al.: Attention is all you need. Adv. Neural Inf. Process. Syst. **30**, 1–11 (2017)
44. Vázquez-Padín, D., Fontani, M., Bianchi, T., Comesana, P., Piva, A., Barni, M.: Detection of video double encoding with GOP size estimation. In: Proceedings of the IEEE International Workshop on Information Forensics and Security, Costa Adeje, Spain, pp. 151–156 (2012)
45. Vázquez-Padín, D., et al.: Video integrity verification and GOP size estimation via generalized variation of prediction footprint. IEEE Trans. Inf. For. Secur. **15**, 1815–1830 (2020)
46. Verde, S., Bondi, L., Bestagini, P., Milani, S., Calvagno, G., Tubaro, S.: Video codec forensics based on convolutional neural networks. In: Proceedings of the

IEEE International Conference on Image Processing, Athens, Greece, pp. 530–534 (2018)

47. Verma, P., Berger, J.: Audio transformers: transformer architectures for large scale audio understanding. adieu convolutions (2021). arXiv preprint arXiv:2105.00335

48. Villalba, L.J.G., Orozco, A.L.S., López, R.R., Castro, J.H.: Identification of smartphone brand and model via forensic video analysis. Expert Syst. Appl. **55**, 59–69 (2016)

49. Xiang, Z., Horváth, J., Baireddy, S., Bestagini, P., Tubaro, S., Delp, E.J.: Forensic analysis of video files using metadata. In: Proceedings of the IEEE/CVF Conference on Computer Vision and Pattern Recognition Workshops, Nashville, TN, USA, pp. 1042–1051 (2021)

50. Xu, Q., Jiang, X., Sun, T., He, P., Wang, S., Li, B.: Relocated I-frames detection in H.264 double compressed videos based on Genetic-CNN. In: The Proceedings of the Asia-Pacific Signal and Information Processing Association Annual Summit and Conference, Honolulu, HI, USA, pp. 710–716 (2018)

51. Yahaya, S., Ho, A.T.S., Wahab, A.A.: Advanced video camera identification using conditional probability features. In: Proceedings of the IET Conference on Image Processing, London, UK, pp. 1–5 (2012)

52. Yang, W.C., Jiang, J., Chen, C.H.: A fast source camera identification and verification method based on PRNU analysis for use in video forensic investigations. Multimedia Tools Appl. **80**(5), 6617–6638 (2021)

53. Yao, H., Ni, R., Zhao, Y.: Double compression detection for H.264 videos with adaptive gop structure. Multimedia Tools Appl. **79**(9), 5789–5806 (2020)

54. Yao, H., Song, S., Qin, C., Tang, Z., Liu, X.: Detection of double-compressed H.264/AVC video incorporating the features of the string of data bits and skip macroblocks. Symmetry **9**(12), 313 (2017)

55. Zeyer, A., Bahar, P., Irie, K., Schlüter, R., Ney, H.: A comparison of transformer and LSTM encoder decoder models for asr. In: Proceedings of the IEEE Automatic Speech Recognition and Understanding Workshop, Sentosa, Singapore, pp. 8–15 (2019)

GBDF: Gender Balanced DeepFake Dataset Towards Fair DeepFake Detection

Aakash Varma Nadimpalli and Ajita Rattani[(✉)]

School of Computing, Wichita State University, Wichita, USA
axnadimpalli@shockers.wichita.edu, ajita.rattani@wichita.edu

Abstract. Facial forgery by deepfakes has raised severe societal concerns. Several solutions have been proposed by the vision community to effectively combat the misinformation on the internet via automated deepfake detection systems. Recent studies have demonstrated that facial analysis-based deep learning models can discriminate based on protected attributes. For the commercial adoption and massive roll-out of the deepfake detection technology, it is vital to evaluate and understand the fairness (the absence of any prejudice or favoritism) of deepfake detectors across demographic variations such as gender and race. As the performance differential of deepfake detectors between demographic sub-groups would impact millions of people of the deprived sub-group. This paper aims to evaluate the fairness of the deepfake detectors across males and females. However, existing deepfake datasets are not annotated with demographic labels to facilitate fairness analysis. To this aim, we manually annotated existing popular deepfake datasets with gender labels and evaluated the performance differential of current deepfake detectors across gender. Our analysis on the gender-labeled version of the datasets suggests (a) current deepfake datasets have skewed distribution across gender, and (b) commonly adopted deepfake detectors obtain unequal performance across gender with mostly males outperforming females. Finally, we contributed a gender-balanced and annotated deepfake dataset, GBDF, to mitigate the performance differential and to promote research and development towards fairness-aware deep fake detectors. The GBDF dataset is publicly available at: https://github.com/aakash4305/GBDF

Keywords: DeepFakes · Fairness and Bias in AI · Facial Analysis

1 Introduction

With the advances in deep generative models, synthetic media have become so realistic that they are often indiscernible from authentic content for human eyes. However, synthetic media generation techniques used by malicious users to deceive pose a severe societal and political threat. In this context, Deepfakes - facial forgery technique that depicts human subjects with altered identities or malicious

© Springer Nature Switzerland AG 2023
J.-J. Rousseau and B. Kapralos (Eds.): ICPR 2022 Workshops, LNCS 13644, pp. 320–337, 2023.
https://doi.org/10.1007/978-3-031-37742-6_25

actions using various deep fake generation techniques- has been flagged as a top AI threat [11,19,26,31,33]. Deep fakes have been used to commit fraud, falsify evidence, manipulate public debates, and destabilize political processes [9,31].

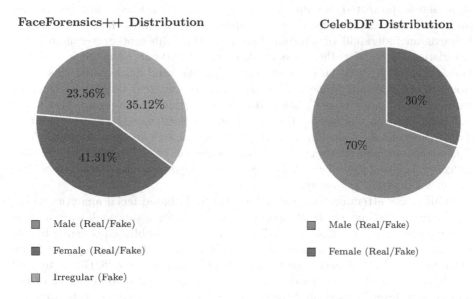

Fig. 1. Illustration of the distribution of videos in Face Forensics++ and Celeb-DF Dataset across gender. The percentage distribution of videos belonging to males (real/fake), females (real/fake) and those classified as irregular swaps is shown.

To mitigate the risk posed by deep fakes, the vision community has developed a series of effective deep fake detection methods [11,26,31] trained on large-scale deepfake datasets. The popular deep fake detection methods include convolutional neural networks (CNN) for detecting visual artifacts [22] and blending boundaries [19], mouth movement analysis [14] and behavioral biometrics [2]. The popular publicly available deep fake datasets include Celeb-DF [21], FaceForensics++ [28], DeeperForensics-1.0 [16] and DFDC [12] for research and development in this field.

Such efforts have been translated into creating **real-world impact** with Microsoft's release of Video Authenticator[1], an automated tool trained on the publicly available FaceForensics++ deepfake dataset, for detection of artificial manipulation in images and videos. Further, Facebook[2] has been advancing its methods to detect and ban AI-generated profiles, along with strengthening its policy on deepfakes and synthetic media. Recently, the Coalition for Content

---

[1] https://blogs.microsoft.com/on-the-issues/2020/09/01/disinformation-deepfakes-newsguard-video-authenticator/.

[2] https://www.wired.com/story/facebook-removes-accounts-ai-generated-photos/.

Provenance and Authenticity (C2PA) has teamed up with Intel, and Adobe to develop new standards targeted at combating the proliferation of deepfakes[3].

While significant advances have been made towards accurate deepfake detection, very little is discussed on the fairness of these deepfake detectors across protected attributes (demographic variations) such as gender and race. Fairness is defined as the absence of any prejudice or favoritism towards an individual or a group based on their inherent or acquired characteristics [5,18]. For the *massive commercial roll-out* of deep fake detection technology, it is vital to examine the bias and fairness of this technology across demographics. This is to avoid any real-world consequences from a biased and flawed system toward a particular sub-group. *As in the common operating scenario, the social media data across gender and race would be audited at the mass level for authenticity via an automated deepfake detection system. Even the small performance differential of deepfake detectors across demographic sub-groups would impact millions of people belonging to the deprived sub-group.*

This draws attention to fairness and bias in AI-based facial analytics where unintended consequences from biased systems call for a thorough examination of the datasets and models [4,5,8,17,18]. Most of the published research in this domain suggests low performance for women, and dark-skinned people for facial attribute-based classification systems such as gender and age [8,17,24,30], and face recognition [4,5]. As biased datasets produce biased models, many of the efforts have been focused on developing gender and race-balanced datasets for various facial-analysis based applications. FairFace [17], a gender and race balanced facial attribute dataset, RFW [34], a racially balanced face recognition dataset, and a gender-balanced dataset developed from existing facial recognition datasets [4] are some of the examples.

This paper aims to examine the **fairness** of deepfake detectors across gender. However, current deepfake detection datasets are not annotated with demographic labels to facilitate the examination of bias. To this aim, deepfake datasets namely FaceForensics++, and Celeb-DF are *manually annotated* with gender labels. The fairness of popular deepfake detectors is evaluated on these datasets across gender. On manual annotation, we found that the gender distribution of the popular deepfake datasets is skewed. The large number of deepfakes in Faceforensics++ are irregular (in conformance with [32])- when a person's face is swapped with the face of another gender or race. This result in the loss of gender-specific information in the fake content. The popular Celeb-DF dataset distribution is heavily skewed towards males (70%).

Figure 1 shows the distribution of videos across gender for the popular Face-Forensics++ [28] and Celeb-DF [21] deepfake datasets. The deepfake detectors evaluated on these skewed datasets along with irregular swaps mostly obtain lower performance for females over males. Finally, we introduced a gender-balanced and annotated deepfake dataset, GBDF, developed from FaceForensics++, Celeb-DF, and DeeperForensics-1.0 and consisting of 10,000 videos. This

---

[3] https://c2pa.org/post/release_1_pr/.

balanced dataset aims to mitigate the performance differential of deepfake detectors due to existing gender unbalanced training sets along with irregular swaps. The dataset information is available to the vision community to promote further research and development in this field. Note that according to ISO/IEC 22116 [7], the term "sex", understood as "the state of being male or female" would be more appropriate instead of "gender" in the context of this study. However, in consistency with the existing studies [4,8], the term gender is used in this paper. To the best of our knowledge, the only study in [32] evaluates the bias of three popular CNN-based deepfake detectors trained on Faceforensics++ across gender and race. The test bed was created using UTKFace and RFW datasets and the deepfakes were generated using the Face X-ray model. The authors reported performance differences for dark-skinned people and emphasized the importance of benchmark representation and auditing for increased demographic transparency.

The main **contributions** of the paper are as follows:

1. Gender label annotation of the popular deepfake datasets namely, FaceForensics++ and Celeb-DF to facilitate analysis of the dataset distribution across gender and the presence of irregular swaps.
2. Evaluation of the fairness of popular deepfake detection algorithms varying in size, architecture, and the methodology, trained and tested on gender annotated versions of the existing datasets.
3. Development of publicly available gender-balanced and annotated deepfake dataset, GBDF, from FaceForensics++ (FF++), Celeb-DF, and Deeper Forensics-1.0 consisting of 10,000 live and fake videos generated using different identity and expression swapping deepfake generation techniques.
4. Cross-comparison of the performance differential of deepfake detectors trained on existing and our gender-balanced GBDF training set, across males and females.

This paper is organized as follows: Section 2 discuss the related work on deepfake detectors and gendered differences in facial analytics. Section 3 discusses the development of the GBDF dataset. Deepfake detection algorithms used in this study are discussed in Sect. 4. Evaluation metrics used for fairness analysis are discussed in Sect. 5. Results and discussion is detailed in Sect. 6. Conclusion and future research directions are discussed in Sect. 7.

2   Related Work

2.1   Deepfake Detection

In this section, we will discuss the existing countermeasure proposed for deep fake detection. Most of the existing methods are CNN-based classification baselines trained for deep fake detection [10,15,25,27].

In [20], Li and Lyu used VGG16, ResNet50, ResNet101, and ResNet152 based CNNs for the detection of the presence of artifacts from the facial regions and the surrounding areas for deep fake detection. Afchar et al. [1] proposed two different CNN architectures composed of only a few layers in order to focus on the mesoscopic properties of the images: (a) a CNN comprised of 4 convolutional layers followed by a fully-connected layer (Meso-4), and (b) a modification of Meso-4 using a variant of the Inception module named MesoInception-4. In [28], an exhaustive analysis of different CNN-based deep fake detection methods by Rosslet et al. suggested efficacy of XceptionNet when evaluated on FaceForensics++. In [19], a face X-ray model has been proposed to detect forgery by detecting the blending boundary of a forged image using a two-class CNN model trained end-to-end.

Apart from the aforementioned CNN-based deep fake detection methods, spatial temporal information using Long Short-term Memory (LSTM) networks [6], facial and behavioral biometrics (i.e., facial expression, head, and body movement), and lipforensics [14] have been used for deep fake detection [2,3,13,27]. In [14], LipForensics that targets high-level semantic irregularities in mouth movements common in many generated deepfake videos, is used for deepfake detection. Studies have also been proposed for improving the performance of deepfake detectors across datasets and deep fake generation methods using techniques such as reinforcement learning [23] and fine-grained multi-attention network [36]. Readers are referred to the published survey in [26,31] for detailed information on deep fake detection methods.

2.2   Gendered Differences in Facial Analytics

There is consensus in the published literature that face analytics-based computer vision applications obtain lower accuracy for females, who often have both a higher false match and a higher false non-match rate over males [4,5,8,17,18]. Examination of the fairness of the gender classification systems using commercial SDKs and deep learning-based CNNs suggest lower accuracy rates for females consistently [8,18]. 2019 Face Recognition Vendor test documents lower female accuracy rates across a broad range of algorithms and datasets[4]. Similarly, lower accuracy rates for females have been obtained for various in-house deep learning-based face recognition systems [4,5,30]. The cause and effect analysis suggests gendered hairstyles resulting in facial occlusion, make-up, and inherent lower variability between different female faces over males to be the factors contributing to lower performance for females [4,5]. The demographic balanced datasets have been proven to mitigate the performance differential of different facial analysis based applications across demographics [4,17,18].

3   GBDF: Gender Balanced DeepFake Dataset

The GBDF dataset is created using FF++($c23$ version), Celeb-DF, Deeper Forensics-1.0 and consist of $10,000$ videos with 5000 each for males and females.

---

[4] https://www.nist.gov/system/files/documents/2019/11/20/ frvt_report_2019_11_19_0.pdf.

The FaceForensics++ [28] (FF++) is an automated benchmark for facial manipulation detection. It consists of several manipulated videos created using two different generation techniques: Identity Swapping (FaceSwap, FaceSwap-Kowalski, FaceShifter, Deep Fakes) and Expression swapping (Face2Face and NeuralTextures). The Celeb-DF [21] deep fake forensic dataset include 590 genuine videos from 59 celebrities as well as 5639 deep fake videos. Celeb-DF, in contrast to other datasets, has essentially no splicing borders, color mismatch, and inconsistencies in face orientation, among other evident deep fake visual artifacts. The deep fake videos in Celeb-DF are created using an encoder-decoder style model which results in better visual quality. The DeeperForensics-1.0 [16] is one of the largest deep fake datasets used for face forgery detection. It consists of 60,000 videos that have around 17.6 million frames with substantial real-world perturbations. The dataset contains videos of 100 consented actors with 35 different perturbations. The real to fake videos ratio is 5:1 and the fake videos are generated by an end-to-end face-swapping framework.

Gender Label Annotation. As none of these existing deepfake datasets contain demographic information, we manually annotated ground truth gender labels for these datasets. To do so, we annotated each subject with the perceived gender male, female. Two graduate annotators were selected for the task of gender label annotation. For each subject, the annotators were presented with an average of 150 frames at various times in the video, which displayed the subject at different light angles and poses. The gender label was assigned to each video based on the consensus between the annotators. With the annotated gender labels, we evaluated the percentage of videos belonging to males, and females and those being irregular face-swaps. Recall that an irregular swap is defined as a swap where a person's face is swapped onto another person's face of a different gender. All the three datasets provided the IDs for pairs of swaps for all the manipulation methods, With the help of the available IDs which are unique for all the identities, we were able to segregate gender labels as well as irregular swaps. FaceForensics++ has 35.12% of irregular deepfakes. Irregular deepfakes were not found in Celeb-DF. DeeperForensics-1.0 dataset has negligible number of irregular swaps. To remain ethnically aware and to maintain demographic information, irregular swaps from FaceForensics++ and deeperforensics-1.0 datasets are not included in the GBDF dataset.

The gender annotated version of the live and deepfake videos (excluding irregular swaps) from these deepfakes datasets are merged to create GBDF dataset. Deepfakes in the GBDF dataset are created using different Identity Swapping (i.e., FaceSwap, FaceSwap-Kowalski, FaceShifter, Encoder-decoder style and End-to-end Face Swapping techniques) and Expression swapping (i.e., Face2Face and NeuralTextures) deepfake generation techniques. The majority of the videos in GBDF are from Caucasians. The ratio of real to fake videos in the GBDF dataset is 1 : 4. The GBDF is further divided into gender-balanced and subject independent training and testing subsets in the ratio of 70 : 30. Figure 2 illustrates the comparison of deepfake videos among existing Deepfake datasets and our GBDF. The number of videos in GBDF is higher than many of the existing deepfake datasets shown on the x axis. The GBDF dataset is publicly available at: https://github.com/aakash4305/GBDF.

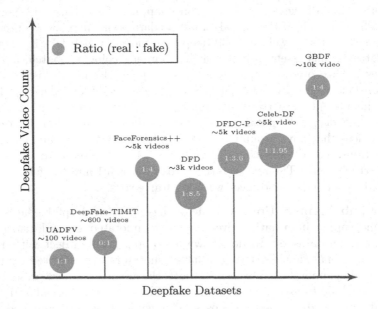

Fig. 2. Illustration of the number of videos in different deepfake datasets along with our proposed GBDF dataset. The figure contains information about the real to fake ratio of videos in the datasets along with deepfake video count. The no. of videos in GBDF is higher than many of the existing deepfake datasets shown on the x-axis.

4   Deepfake Detection Algorithms Used

We investigated fairness of popular deepfake detection models of various sizes, architectures and the underlying concept, across males and females. Specifically, we trained MesoInception4[5], XceptionNet[6], EfficientNet V2-L[7], LipForensics[8] and CNN-LSTM[9] based deepfake detectors.

These models are trained on the popular FF++ dataset(c23 version) and our proposed GBDF training set. We used the sampling approach described in [28] to choose 270 frames per video for training and 150 frames per video for validation and testing of most of the models. The face images were detected and aligned using MTCNN [35] algorithm. MTCNN utilizes a cascaded CNN based

---

[5] https://github.com/HongguLiu/MesoNet-Pytorch.
[6] https://github.com/i3p9/deepfake-detection-with-xception.
[7] https://github.com/d-li14/efficientnetv2.pytorch.
[8] https://github.com/ahaliassos/LipForensics.
[9] https://github.com/oidelima/Deepfake-Detection.

framework for joint face detection and alignment. The images are then resized to 256 × 256 for both training and evaluation.

For all the CNN-based models, we used a batch-normalization layer followed by the last fully connected layer of size 1024 and the final output layer for deep fake classification. The CNN models were trained using an Adam optimizer with an initial learning rate of 0.001 and a weight decay of 1e6. For CNN-LSTM model, we chose EfficientNet V2-L as the backbone CNN model due to its superior performance. The CNN network's output of 2048 feature vector is fed into the LSTM layer for deepfake detection. For LipForensics model, following authors implementation in [14], the network receives 25 grayscale, aligned mouth crops of size 88 × 88 as input for each video. The input is passed through pretrained ResNet-18 (pretrained for lipreading task with an initial 3-D convolutional layer) to obtain output embedding sensitive to mouth motion analysis. A multiscale temporal convolutional network (MS-TCN) was finetuned to detect fake videos based on semantically high-level anomalies in mouth motion, which was also pretrained for lipreading task. All the models were trained on 4 RTX 5000Ti GPUs with a batch size of 64.

5   Evaluation Metrics

Following the standard evaluation metrics adopted for deepfake detectors, we used partial AUC (pAUC) (at 10% False Positive Rate (FPR)) and Equal Error Rate (EER) for the evaluation of performance differences across males and females. Further, as deepfake detection is a binary classification task, we have also analyzed binary classification metrics for fairness evaluation across males and females. Similar to the bias evaluation study on gender classification by Buolamwini et al. [8], we follow the evaluation precedent established by the National Institute of Standards and Technology (NIST) and assessed the overall classification accuracy (ACC), along with the true positive rate (TPR), and false-positive rate (FPR) for males and females.

6   Results and Analysis

In this section, we examine the fairness of the deepfake detectors, discussed in section 4, across males and females on FF++, Celeb-DF, GBDF, and an external DFDC-P [12] test sets. All the **evaluation metrics** (from section 5) are reported in the range [0, 1].

6.1   Performance Differential of Deepfake Detectors on FF++ Test Set

Table 1 shows the performance of the deepfake detectors across males and females when trained on FF++, GBDF, and tested on FF++. Similarly, Table 2 shows the corresponding ACC, TPR, and FPR values of these models. The top

Table 1. Evaluation of the DeepFake Detectors Across Males and Females when trained on FF++, GBDF and tested on **FF++**. The metrics used are AUC, pAUC and EER. The performance differential (P.D) is also calculated as the absolute difference between EER of males and females.

Models	Training Dataset	Overall			Male			Female			P.D↓
		AUC	pAUC	EER	AUC	pAUC	EER	AUC	pAUC	EER	
EfficientNet V2-L	FaceForensics++	**0.991**	**0.979**	**0.024**	**0.995**	**0.986**	**0.019**	0.987	0.972	0.029	0.010
XceptionNet		0.985	0.969	0.037	0.987	0.975	0.029	0.983	0.963	0.045	0.016
MesoInception-4		0.857	0.832	0.229	0.863	0.837	0.221	0.851	0.827	0.237	0.016
CNN-LSTM		0.987	0.972	0.032	0.991	0.979	0.024	0.983	0.967	0.039	0.015
LipForensics		0.990	0.977	0.027	0.987	0.975	0.031	**0.993**	**0.979**	**0.023**	**0.008**
EfficientNet V2-L	GBDF	0.925	0.902	0.136	0.935	0.917	0.121	0.915	0.888	0.140	0.019
XceptionNet		0.906	0.886	0.176	0.912	0.892	0.172	0.899	0.880	0.180	**0.008**
MesoInception-4		0.806	0.785	0.264	0.813	0.794	0.259	0.799	0.775	0.269	0.010
CNN-LSTM		0.918	0.897	0.141	0.910	0.890	0.150	0.926	0.904	0.132	0.018
LipForensics		**0.932**	**0.917**	**0.122**	**0.937**	**0.921**	**0.117**	**0.928**	**0.913**	**0.128**	0.011

performance results are highlighted in bold across various evaluation datasets. EfficientNet V2-L obtained the best results with an overall AUC of 0.991, EER of 0.024, and ACC of 0.975 when trained and tested on FF++.

When trained on FF++, the overall difference in the performance is 0.009 and 0.010 in terms of pAUC and EER, respectively, across males and females. Males outperformed females for the majority of the models despite having a lower percentage than females in FF++ training set. *The reason is 35.12% of the videos in FF++ are irregular deepfakes, it is not certain which gender-group-related features are dominant in irregular facial swaps.* The overall difference in ACC, TPR, and FPR is 0.006, 0.0036, and 0.020, respectively, across males and females (see Table 2). The least performance differential is obtained by LipForensics model when trained and tested on FF++.

When trained on GBDF, the overall difference in the performance is 0.010 and 0.006 in terms of pAUC and EER, respectively, across males and females. The overall difference in ACC, TPR, and FPR was reduced to 0.011, 0.006 and 0.009, respectively, across males and females (see Table 2). XceptionNet model obtained the least performance differential when trained on GBDF and tested on FF++.

Therefore, the overall difference in EER and FPR was reduced to 0.04 and 0.011, respectively, when using GBDF over FF++ as the training set. Using GBDF as the training set, the highest bias mitigation is observed for XceptionNet with the EER difference reduced from 0.016 to 0.008 across gender. Most of the detectors obtained lower error rates when trained on FF++. This is obvious as the test bed is also FF++. The performance of most of the models dropped when trained using GBDF due to domain shift i.e., the data distribution change between the training (GBDF) and testing set (FF++). This is due to change in the image quality of real videos and deep fakes due to advances in sensor technology and the deep fake generation techniques. The GBDF dataset has an additional number of deepfake generation techniques (based on encoder-decoder style and the end-to-end face swapping framework) over FF++.

Table 2. ACC, TPR and FPR of the DeepFake Detectors Across Males and Females when trained on FF++, GBDF and tested on FF++. When trained on GBDF, the drop in the performance of the models is due to domain shift. The GBDF dataset consist of higher number of deepfake generation techniques over FF+.

Models	Training Datasets	Overall			Male			Female		
		ACC	TPR	FPR	ACC	TPR	FPR	ACC	TPR	FPR
EfficientNet V2-L	FaceForensics++	**0.975**	**0.952**	**0.091**	**0.979**	**0.955**	**0.058**	0.971	0.949	0.119
XceptionNet		0.969	0.942	0.128	0.971	0.947	0.109	0.967	0.937	0.139
MesoInception-4		0.825	0.805	0.256	0.834	0.813	0.245	0.816	0.797	0.267
CNN-LSTM		0.971	0.945	0.115	0.976	0.954	0.093	0.966	0.936	0.137
LipForensics		0.972	0.948	0.115	0.967	0.941	0.143	**0.978**	**0.955**	**0.086**
EfficientNet V2-L	GBDF	0.903	0.887	0.182	0.912	0.895	0.175	0.892	0.879	0.187
XceptionNet		0.888	0.869	0.189	0.897	0.876	0.181	0.879	0.862	0.195
MesoInception-4		0.783	0.769	0.284	0.794	0.778	0.276	0.772	0.760	0.292
CNN-LSTM		0.896	0.875	0.185	0.887	0.861	0.189	0.905	0.889	0.178
LipForensics		**0.912**	**0.896**	**0.176**	**0.919**	**0.901**	**0.169**	**0.905**	**0.891**	**0.183**

6.2 Performance Differential of Deepfake Detectors on Celeb-DF Test Set

Table 3. Evaluation of the DeepFake Detectors Across Males and Females when trained on FF++, GBDF and tested on **Celeb-DF**. The metrics used are AUC, pAUC and EER. The performance differential (P.D) is also calculated as the absolute difference between EER of males and females.

Models	Training Dataset	Overall			Male			Female			P.D↓
		AUC	pAUC	EER	AUC	pAUC	EER	AUC	pAUC	EER	
EfficientNet V2-L	FaceForensics++	0.658	0.635	0.379	0.667	0.645	0.372	0.649	0.625	0.386	0.014
XceptionNet		0.651	0.629	0.383	0.657	0.634	0.379	0.645	0.623	0.390	**0.011**
MesoInception-4		0.544	0.519	0.459	0.558	0.528	0.442	0.530	0.510	0.476	0.034
CNN-LSTM		0.675	0.656	0.359	0.686	0.662	0.348	0.664	0.650	0.370	0.022
LipForensics		**0.821**	**0.795**	**0.254**	**0.829**	**0.805**	**0.242**	**0.813**	**0.785**	**0.266**	0.024
EfficientNet V2-L	GBDF	0.861	0.844	0.235	0.869	0.853	0.228	0.853	0.835	0.242	0.014
XceptionNet		0.864	0.847	0.233	0.872	0.855	0.226	0.856	0.839	0.240	0.014
MesoInception-4		0.742	0.725	0.298	0.755	0.735	0.292	0.730	0.715	0.305	0.013
CNN-LSTM		0.887	0.869	0.215	0.898	0.875	0.209	0.876	0.863	0.221	**0.012**
LipForensics		**0.908**	**0.885**	**0.175**	**0.917**	**0.896**	**0.163**	**0.900**	**0.874**	**0.187**	0.024

Table 3 shows the performance differential of the deepfake detectors when trained on FF++, GBDF, and tested on Celeb-DF. Similarly, Table 4 shows the corresponding ACC, TPR, and FPR values for these models. The top performance results are highlighted in bold across various evaluation datasets. The LipForensics model obtained the best results with an overall AUC of 0.908, EER of 0.175, and ACC of 0.889 when trained on GBDF and tested on Celeb-DF.

When trained on FF++, the overall difference in the performance is 0.0162 and 0.021 in terms of pAUC and EER, respectively, across males and females.

The overall difference in ACC, TPR and FPR is 0.019,0.02 and 0.021, respectively, across males and females (see Table 4). The least performance differential is obtained by XceptionNet when trained on FF++ and tested on Celeb-DF.

When trained on GBDF, the overall difference in the performance is 0.017 and 0.015 in terms of pAUC and EER, respectively, across males and females. The overall difference in ACC, TPR and FPR is 0.018, 0.01 and 0.018, respectively, across males and females (see Table 4). The least performance differential is obtained by CNN-LSTM when trained on GBDF and tested on Celeb-DF.

Therefore, the difference in AUC, EER, TPR, and FPR is reduced to 0.001, 0.006, 0.01, and 0.003, respectively, when using GBDF as a training set over FF++. Using GBDF, the highest bias mitigation is observed for MesoInceptionNet-4 model with the EER difference reduced from 0.034 to 0.013 across gender. The overall performance of all the models increased when trained on GBDF over FF++ because of the presence of higher number of deepfake generation techniques. **It is worth noting that the training and testing subset of GBDF and Celeb-DF, respectively, has no subject overlap.** This experiment points out the **merit** of using a demographically balanced dataset for deepfake detection.

Table 4. ACC, TPR and FPR of the DeepFake Detectors Across Males and Females when trained on FF++, GBDF and tested on Celeb-DF.

Models	Training Datasets	Overall			Male			Female		
		ACC	TPR	FPR	ACC	TPR	FPR	ACC	TPR	FPR
EfficientNet V2-L	FaceForensics++	0.637	0.604	0.385	0.650	0.614	0.372	0.626	0.594	0.398
XceptionNet		0.629	0.602	0.395	0.635	0.609	0.383	0.623	0.595	0.402
MesoInception-4		0.525	0.502	0.437	0.534	0.518	0.422	0.516	0.486	0.455
CNN-LSTM		0.652	0.609	0.367	0.664	0.615	0.359	0.640	0.600	0.379
LipForensics		**0.798**	**0.774**	**0.275**	**0.807**	**0.785**	**0.271**	**0.791**	**0.763**	**0.282**
EfficientNet V2-L	GBDF	0.843	0.825	0.242	0.849	0.833	0.239	0.837	0.817	0.246
XceptionNet		0.847	0.825	0.240	0.854	0.834	0.232	0.840	0.816	0.251
MesoInception-4		0.718	0.701	0.324	0.733	0.712	0.309	0.703	0.690	0.340
CNN-LSTM		0.863	0.849	0.225	0.876	0.854	0.211	0.850	0.844	0.235
LipForensics		**0.889**	**0.866**	**0.187**	**0.895**	**0.878**	**0.183**	**0.883**	**0.854**	**0.193**

6.3   Performance Differential of Deepfake Detectors on GBDF and DFDC-P Test Sets

Table 5 shows the performance of the deepfake detectors across males and females when trained on FF++, GBDF, and tested on GBDF subject independent test set. Similarly, Table 6 shows the ACC, TPR, and FPR values associated with these models. The LipForensics model obtained the best results with an overall AUC of 0.978, EER of 0.039, and ACC of 0.967 when trained and tested on GBDF.

Table 5. Evaluation of the DeepFake Detectors Across Males and Females when trained on FF++, GBDF and tested on **GBDF**. The metrics used are AUC, pAUC and EER. The performance differential (P.D) is calculated as the absolute difference between EER of males and females.

Models	Training Dataset	Overall			Male			Female			P.D↓
		AUC	pAUC	EER	AUC	pAUC	EER	AUC	pAUC	EER	
EfficientNet V2-L	FaceForensics++	0.904	0.889	0.179	0.912	0.897	0.171	0.896	0.879	0.187	0.016
XceptionNet		0.889	0.868	0.217	0.902	0.885	0.206	0.876	0.850	0.228	0.022
MesoInception-4		0.769	0.747	0.286	0.759	0.742	0.295	0.779	0.750	0.277	0.018
CNN-LSTM		0.909	0.888	0.177	0.917	0.898	0.161	0.901	0.877	0.192	0.031
LipForensics		**0.942**	**0.926**	**0.109**	**0.938**	**0.922**	**0.113**	**0.947**	**0.929**	**0.105**	**0.008**
EfficientNet V2-L	GBDF	0.967	0.943	0.052	0.972	0.948	0.050	0.962	0.938	0.054	**0.004**
XceptionNet		0.972	0.952	0.046	0.979	0.956	0.043	0.965	0.948	0.049	0.006
MesoInception-4		0.819	0.800	0.256	0.828	0.805	0.250	0.811	0.795	0.264	0.014
CNN-LSTM		0.975	0.957	0.044	0.983	0.964	0.038	0.967	0.950	0.050	0.012
LipForensics		**0.978**	**0.954**	**0.039**	**0.982**	**0.958**	**0.036**	**0.974**	**0.950**	**0.042**	0.006

When trained on FF++, the overall difference in the performance is 0.012 and 0.0092 in terms of pAUC and EER, respectively, across males and females. The overall difference in ACC, TPR and FPR is 0.010, 0.0112 and 0.012, respectively, across males and females (see Table 6). The least performance differential is obtained by EfficientNet V2-L when trained on FF++ and tested on GBDF.

Table 6. ACC, TPR and FPR of the DeepFake Detectors Across Males and Females when trained on FF++, GBDF and tested on GBDF test set.

Models	Training Datasets	Overall			Male			Female		
		ACC	TPR	FPR	ACC	TPR	FPR	ACC	TPR	FPR
EfficientNet V2-L	FaceForensics++	0.880	0.858	0.205	0.895	0.869	0.194	0.865	0.847	0.220
XceptionNet		0.865	0.841	0.222	0.878	0.854	0.209	0.852	0.828	0.235
MesoInception-4		0.745	0.721	0.288	0.735	0.715	0.295	0.754	0.727	0.275
CNN-LSTM		0.883	0.868	0.195	0.894	0.884	0.187	0.872	0.854	0.209
LipForensics		**0.925**	**0.905**	**0.178**	**0.920**	**0.899**	**0.180**	**0.930**	**0.910**	**0.175**
EfficientNet V2-L	GBDF	0.948	0.935	0.154	0.951	0.939	0.149	0.945	0.930	0.159
XceptionNet		0.955	0.941	0.144	0.958	0.947	0.139	0.952	0.935	0.147
MesoInception-4		0.802	0.778	0.282	0.808	0.788	0.275	0.796	0.770	0.287
CNN-LSTM		0.953	0.939	0.148	0.959	0.941	0.144	0.949	0.935	0.154
LipForensics		**0.967**	**0.949**	**0.142**	**0.971**	**0.953**	**0.135**	**0.965**	**0.946**	**0.145**

When trained on GBDF, the overall difference in the performance is 0.010 and 0.008 in terms of pAUC and EER, respectively, across males and females. The overall difference in ACC, TPR and FPR is 0.008,0.010 and 0.009, respectively, across males and females (see Table 6). The least performance differential is obtained by the LipForensics model when trained and tested on GBDF.

Therefore, the difference in ACC, EER, TPR, and FPR decreased by 0.002, 0.001, 0.0012, and 0.003, respectively, when using balanced GBDF as training and testing sets. Using balanced GBDF as a training and testing set, the highest bias mitigation is observed for CNN-LSTM and XceptionNet models. For CNN-LSTM, the difference in EER across gender reduced from 0.031 to 0.012 when trained with FF++ over GBDF as the training set (the test set is GBDF). Similarly, for XceptionNet, the difference in EER across gender reduced from 0.022 to 0.006 when trained with FF++ over GBDF as the training set (the test set is GBDF). Recall that the subjects do not overlap between the training and testing set of GBDF. Further, the samples in the training and testing set of GBDF are from three different deepfake datasets.

Table 7. Evaluation of the DeepFake Detectors Across Males and Females when trained on FF++, GBDF and tested on **DFDC-P**. The metrics used are AUC, pAUC and EER. The performance differential (P.D) is calculated as the absolute difference between EER of males and females.

Models	Training Dataset	Overall			Male			Female			P.D↓
		AUC	pAUC	EER	AUC	pAUC	EER	AUC	pAUC	EER	
EfficientNet V2-L	FaceForensics++	0.659	0.634	0.378	0.665	0.641	0.374	0.653	0.626	0.384	**0.010**
XceptionNet		0.642	0.624	0.391	0.649	0.632	0.384	0.635	0.617	0.398	0.014
MesoInception-4		0.619	0.597	0.421	0.609	0.591	0.432	0.630	0.605	0.410	0.022
CNN-LSTM		0.667	0.648	0.372	0.675	0.661	0.356	0.659	0.635	0.382	0.026
LipForensics		**0.718**	**0.705**	**0.312**	**0.724**	**0.710**	**0.306**	**0.712**	**0.701**	**0.319**	0.013
EfficientNet V2-L	GBDF	0.684	0.662	0.349	0.689	0.665	0.345	0.680	0.661	0.354	**0.009**
XceptionNet		0.668	0.652	0.368	0.675	0.657	0.363	0.663	0.649	0.374	0.011
MesoInception-4		0.615	0.592	0.427	0.621	0.596	0.419	0.608	0.585	0.432	0.013
CNN-LSTM		0.689	0.665	0.343	0.683	0.658	0.350	0.694	0.674	0.334	0.016
LipForensics		**0.732**	**0.721**	**0.299**	**0.736**	**0.724**	**0.292**	**0.727**	**0.716**	**0.307**	0.015

Table 7 shows the performance of the deepfake detectors across males and females when trained on FF++, GBDF, and tested on DFDC-P. **Note that DFDC-P dataset has not been used in the creation of the GBDF dataset.** As the original DFDC-P test set does not contain subject IDs, the subset of DFDC training set is manually annotated with gender labels and used as a test set for this study. Overall, low performance is obtained for all the models on DFDC dataset. This is because DFDC consist of low quality videos that are diverse across gender, skin-tone and age-group. The LipForensics model obtained the best results with an overall AUC of 0.732, EER of 0.299 when tested on DFDC-P.

When trained on FF++, the overall difference in the performance is 0.010 and 0.0082 in terms of pAUC and EER, respectively, across males and females. The least performance differential is obtained by EfficientNet V2-L when trained on FF++ and tested on DFDC-P.

When trained on GBDF, the overall difference in the performance is 0.004 and 0.007 in terms of pAUC and EER, respectively, across males and females. The least performance differential is obtained by EfficientNet V2-L when trained on GBDF and tested on DFDC-P. *These results suggest that using our gender-balanced GBDF training set, bias is mitigated across gender even on an external DFDC-P dataset, not used in the creation of GBDF.*

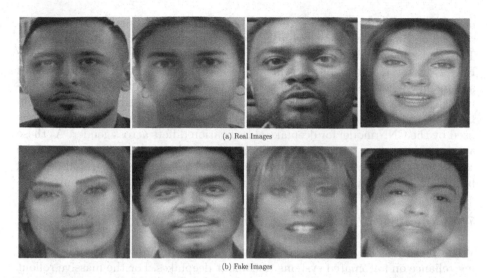

(a) Real Images

(b) Fake Images

Fig. 3. Grad-CAM visualization of the EfficientNet V2-L based deepfake detector on randomly selected live and fake samples from males and females. The distinctive image regions used by the CNN model for deepfake detection differs across gender.

Finally, we also used Explainable AI (XAI) based Gradient weighted Class Activation Mapping (Grad-CAM) [29] visualization to understand the distinctive image regions used by the CNN models in detecting deepfakes across gender. GRAD-CAM uses the gradients of any target concept to generate a coarse localization map that highlights distinctive image regions used for making a decision/prediction [29]. Figure 3 shows the GRAD-CAM visualization of the EfficientNet V2-L-based deepfake detector for live and fake images for males and females. This detector was trained on GBDF dataset. The highly activated region is shown by the red zone on the map, followed by green and blue zones. It can be seen that the highly activated region is the cheek for females and the ocular region for males. For fake images, the mouth and cheek region for males and the complete face region for females are the most activated region. These results were consistent across the datasets depending on the deepfake generation technique. Therefore, different image regions were used by the deepfake detector for live and fake classification across gender.

In **summary**, males outperformed females for most of the models, with the disparity of about 0.034 in terms of EER in the range [0, 1] for MesoInception-4 model. The shallow MesoInception-4 model demonstrated high performance differential across gender for most of the experiments. The LipForensics model, on the other hand, obtained least disparity across gender for most of the experiments. This is because it uses mouth crops for mouth motion analysis. Thus the impact of gendered differences in facial images attributed to bias are mitigated to a major extent. When trained on FF+, males outperformed females for the majority of the models despite having a lower percentage than females. As large number of the videos in FaceForensics++ are irregular deepfakes, it is not certain which gender-group-related features are dominant in irregular facial swaps. The gender-balanced GBDF training set reduced the performance difference over FF++, with the highest being from 0.031 to 0.012 in terms of EER across males and females when tested on GBDF test set. The advantage of using GBDF training set towards gender fair deepfake classification is also noticed for an external DFDC-P set. The grad-CAM visualization suggests the distinctive image regions used by the CNN model for deepfake classification differs across gender. As these automated deepfake detection systems are used at the mass-level for audit of the social media data, even a small reduction in the bias across demographics would positively impact millions of people belonging to the deprived sub-group.

7 Conclusion and Future Research Directions

With the volume of deepfake videos showing staggering growth, there is a growing reliance on automated systems to combat deepfakes. For the massive rollout of this high-impact technology, it becomes vital to understand all the societal aspects including demographic disparities. In this work, we thoroughly examined the fairness of the deepfake detectors on gender-aware deepfake datasets. On manual annotation of gender labels, we found that current deepfake datasets have a highly skewed distribution across gender and contain irregular swaps. The popular deepfake detectors have exhibited disparities in the performance across gender when evaluated on gender-aware datasets, with mostly males outperforming females. This suggest an additional threat imposed by deep fake technology on female subjects, primarily due to the performance differential of SOTA deep fake detectors.

However, using our gender-balanced GBDF dataset, the unequal performance of the deepfake detectors across gender is mitigated to some extent. Our work echoes the importance of benchmarking demographically balanced and labeled deepfake datasets to facilitate intersectional subgroup-based audits of existing deepfake detectors along with the cause and effect analysis. As a part of future work, fairness of the deepfake detectors will also be evaluated across race. Further, the fairness-aware deepfake detectors will be developed for increased demographic transparency and accountability of these high-impact systems.

Acknowledgement. This work is supported in part from National Science Foundation (NSF) award no. 2129173. The research infrastructure used in this study is supported in part from a grant no. 13106715 from the Defense University Research Instrumentation Program (DURIP) from Air Force Office of Scientific Research.

References

1. Afchar, D., Nozick, V., Yamagishi, J., Echizen, I.: MesoNet: a compact facial video forgery detection network. In: 2018 IEEE International Workshop on Information Forensics and Security (WIFS), pp. 1–7 (2018). https://doi.org/10.1109/WIFS.2018.8630761

2. Agarwal, S., Farid, H., El-Gaaly, T., Lim, S.N.: Detecting deep-fake videos from appearance and behavior. In: 2020 IEEE International Workshop on Information Forensics and Security (WIFS), pp. 1–6 (2020). https://doi.org/10.1109/WIFS49906.2020.9360904

3. Agarwal, S., Farid, H., Gu, Y., He, M., Nagano, K., Li, H.: Protecting world leaders against deep fakes. In: CVPR Workshops (2019)

4. Albiero, V., Zhang, K., Bowyer, K.W.: How does gender balance in training data affect face recognition accuracy? In: 2020 IEEE International Joint Conference on Biometrics (IJCB), pp. 1–10. IEEE (2020)

5. Albiero, V., Zhang, K., King, M.C., Bowyer, K.W.: Gendered differences in face recognition accuracy explained by hairstyles, makeup, and facial morphology. Trans. Info. For. Sec. **17**, 127–137 (2022). https://doi.org/10.1109/TIFS.2021.3135750

6. Amerini, I., Caldelli, R.: Exploiting prediction error inconsistencies through LSTM-based classifiers to detect DeepFake videos. In: Proceedings of the 2020 ACM Workshop on Information Hiding and Multimedia Security, IH&MMSec 2020, pp. 97–102. Association for Computing Machinery, New York, NY, USA (2020). https://doi.org/10.1145/3369412.3395070

7. Biometrics, I.J.S.: ISO/IEC WD TR 22116. In: Information Technology - Biometrics - Identifying and Mitigating the Differential Impact of Demographic Factors in Biometric Systems (unpublished)

8. Buolamwini, J., Gebru, T.: Gender shades: intersectional accuracy disparities in commercial gender classification. In: Conference on Fairness, Accountability and Transparency, pp. 77–91. PMLR (2018)

9. Cellan-Jones, R.: DeepFake videos 'double in nine months', October 2019. https://www.bbc.com/news/technology-49961089

10. Chollet, F.: Xception: Deep learning with depthwise separable convolutions. In: 2017 IEEE Conference on Computer Vision and Pattern Recognition (CVPR), pp. 1800–1807. IEEE Computer Society, Los Alamitos, CA, USA, July 2017. https://doi.org/10.1109/CVPR.2017.195. https://doi.ieeecomputersociety.org/10.1109/CVPR.2017.195

11. Citron, D.: How DeepFakes undermine truth and threaten democracy. https://www.ted.com/talks/danielle_citron_how_deepfakes_undermine_truth_and_threaten_democracy?language=en

12. Dolhansky, B., et al.: The DeepFake detection challenge (DFDC) dataset (2020). https://doi.org/10.48550/ARXIV.2006.07397. https://arxiv.org/abs/2006.07397

13. Dong, X., et al.: Identity-driven DeepFake detection. ArXiv abs/2012.03930 (2020)

14. Haliassos, A., Vougioukas, K., Petridis, S., Pantic, M.: Lips don't lie: a generalisable and robust approach to face forgery detection. In: 2021 IEEE/CVF Conference on Computer Vision and Pattern Recognition (CVPR), pp. 5037–5047 (2021). https://doi.org/10.1109/CVPR46437.2021.00500

15. He, K., Zhang, X., Ren, S., Sun, J.: Deep residual learning for image recognition. In: 2016 IEEE Conference on Computer Vision and Pattern Recognition (CVPR), pp. 770–778 (2016)

16. Jiang, L., Li, R., Wu, W., Qian, C., Loy, C.C.: DeeperForensics-1.0: a large-scale dataset for real-world face forgery detection. In: CVPR (2020)

17. Karkkainen, K., Joo, J.: FairFace: face attribute dataset for balanced race, gender, and age for bias measurement and mitigation. In: Proceedings of the IEEE/CVF Winter Conference on Applications of Computer Vision, pp. 1548–1558 (2021)

18. Krishnan, A., Almadan, A., Rattani, A.: Understanding fairness of gender classification algorithms across gender-race groups. In: 2020 19th IEEE International Conference on Machine Learning and Applications (ICMLA), pp. 1028–1035 (2020). https://doi.org/10.1109/ICMLA51294.2020.00167
19. Li, L., et al.: Face x-ray for more general face forgery detection. In: 2020 IEEE/CVF Conference on Computer Vision and Pattern Recognition (CVPR), pp. 5000–5009 (2020). https://doi.org/10.1109/CVPR42600.2020.00505
20. Li, Y., Lyu, S.: Exposing DeepFake videos by detecting face warping artifacts. In: Proceedings of the IEEE/CVF Conference on Computer Vision and Pattern Recognition (CVPR) Workshops, June 2019
21. Li, Y., Yang, X., Sun, P., Qi, H., Lyu, S.: Celeb-DF: a large-scale challenging dataset for DeepFake forensics. In: 2020 IEEE/CVF Conference on Computer Vision and Pattern Recognition (CVPR), pp. 3204–3213 (2020). https://doi.org/10.1109/CVPR42600.2020.00327
22. Matern, F., Riess, C., Stamminger, M.: Exploiting visual artifacts to expose DeepFakes and face manipulations. In: 2019 IEEE Winter Applications of Computer Vision Workshops (WACVW), pp. 83–92 (2019)
23. Nadimpalli, A.V., Rattani, A.: On improving cross-dataset generalization of DeepFake detectors. In: Proceedings of the IEEE/CVF Conference on Computer Vision and Pattern Recognition, pp. 91–99 (2022)
24. Nadimpalli, A.V., Reddy, N., Ramachandran, S., Rattani, A.: Harnessing unlabeled data to improve generalization of biometric gender and age classifiers. In: 2021 IEEE Symposium Series on Computational Intelligence (SSCI), pp. 1–7 (2021)
25. Nguyen, H.H., Fang, F., Yamagishi, J., Echizen, I.: Multi-task learning for detecting and segmenting manipulated facial images and videos. In: 2019 IEEE 10th International Conference on Biometrics Theory, Applications and Systems (BTAS), pp. 1–8 (2019)
26. Nguyen, T.T., Nguyen, C.M., Nguyen, D., Nguyen, D.T., Nahavandi, S.: Deep learning for DeepFakes creation and detection. ArXiv abs/1909.11573 (2019)
27. Ramachandran, S., Nadimpalli, A.V., Rattani, A.: An experimental evaluation on DeepFake detection using deep face recognition. In: 2021 IEEE International Carnahan Conference on Security Technology (ICCST), pp. 1–6 (2021). https://doi.org/10.1109/ICCST49569.2021.9717407
28. Rössler, A., Cozzolino, D., Verdoliva, L., Riess, C., Thies, J., Niessner, M.: FaceForensics++: learning to detect manipulated facial images. In: 2019 IEEE/CVF International Conference on Computer Vision (ICCV), pp. 1–11 (2019). https://doi.org/10.1109/ICCV.2019.00009
29. Selvaraju, R.R., Cogswell, M., Das, A., Vedantam, R., Parikh, D., Batra, D.: Grad-CAM: visual explanations from deep networks via gradient-based localization. In: 2017 IEEE International Conference on Computer Vision (ICCV), pp. 618–626 (2017). https://doi.org/10.1109/ICCV.2017.74
30. Singh, R., Majumdar, P., Mittal, S., Vatsa, M.: Anatomizing bias in facial analysis. arXiv preprint arXiv:2112.06522 (2021)
31. Tolosana, R., Vera-Rodríguez, R., Fierrez, J., Morales, A., Ortega-Garcia, J.: DeepFakes and beyond: a survey of face manipulation and fake detection. Inf. Fusion **64**, 131–148 (2020)
32. Trinh, L., Liu, Y.: An examination of fairness of AI models for DeepFake detection. ArXiv abs/2105.00558 (2021)
33. Verdoliva, L.: Media forensics and DeepFakes: an overview. IEEE J. Sel. Top. Sig. Process. **14**, 910–932 (2020)

34. Wang, M., Deng, W., Hu, J., Tao, X., Huang, Y.: Racial faces in the wild: reducing racial bias by information maximization adaptation network. In: 2019 IEEE/CVF International Conference on Computer Vision (ICCV), pp. 692–702 (2019)
35. Zhang, K., Zhang, Z., Li, Z., Qiao, Y.: Joint face detection and alignment using multitask cascaded convolutional networks. IEEE Signal Process. Lett. **23**(10), 1499–1503 (2016). https://doi.org/10.1109/LSP.2016.2603342
36. Zhao, H., Wei, T., Zhou, W., Zhang, W., Chen, D., Yu, N.: Multi-attentional Deep-Fake detection. In: 2021 IEEE/CVF Conference on Computer Vision and Pattern Recognition (CVPR), pp. 2185–2194 (2021). https://doi.org/10.1109/CVPR46437.2021.00222

Misalignment Estimation in Non-Aligned Double JPEG Scenario Based on AC Histogram Analysis

Giovanni Puglisi[1]([⊠]) [iD] and Sebastiano Battiato[2] [iD]

[1] University of Cagliari, Cagliari, Italy
puglisi@unica.it
[2] University of Catania, Catania, Italy
battiato@dmi.unict.it

Abstract. In forensics investigation, the estimation of the misalignment occurred between consecutive JPEG compressions can be considered an important step to recover the manipulation history of an image under analysis and localize forgeries. Exploiting statistics computed from the AC histograms obtained applying a third compression, an effective method to estimate the misalignment has been designed. Finally, to assess the performance of the proposed approach a series of tests has been conducted considering scenarios involving different patch sizes and quantization matrices, performing also comparisons with state-of-the-art solutions.

Keywords: Non-aligned Double JPEG Compression · Misalignment Estimation

1 Introduction

Today a huge amount of images is acquired by a digital device, edited and uploaded to Social Networks or Instant Messaging platforms. Multiple JPEG compressions ([10,14]) are then applied on the involved image and part of the information contained in the original data is lost. In forensics investigation, the history of an image under analysis needs to be reconstructed ([7,8]), such as example it could be useful to recover information about the camera source device or the camera model ([15,18]) that took the picture. The investigation could start detecting double compression traces [9], retrieving information related to camera model through First Quantization Estimation (FQE) ([1,11]) and identifying the source exploiting Photo Response Non Uniformity (PRNU) analysis ([15,17]).

The typical digital image life-cycle usually involves multiple JPEG compressions. Two scenarios can be found in literature, aligned and non-aligned double JPEG compression based on the presence of misalignment between consecutive quantizations (see Fig. 1). As reported before, the estimation of these horizontal and vertical shifts can be quite useful to localize tempered regions that are usually misaligned with respect to the DCT grid of the background image ([3,20]).

J.-J. Rousseau and B. Kapralos (Eds.): ICPR 2022 Workshops, LNCS 13644, pp. 338–346, 2023.
https://doi.org/10.1007/978-3-031-37742-6_26

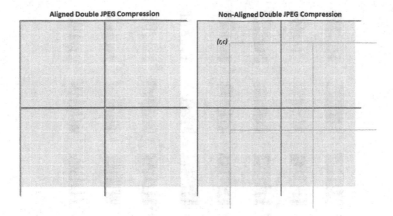

Fig. 1. Aligned (on the left) and non-aligned (on the right) double JPEG compression scenarios. First compression DCT grid is represented in blue whereas the second compression one in orange. (Color figure online)

Moreover, information about misalignment is usually exploited by first quantization matrix estimation methods in NA-DJPEG (non-aligned double JPEG) scenarios ([2,6,21]).

Misalignment estimation in a NA-DJPEG scenario has been usually studied considering pixel domain. In [13] blocking artifact characteristics matrix (BACM) is introduced and the analysis of its symmetry exploited to detect the presence of shifts between consecutive compressions. Moreover, methods based on high-pass filters in pixel domain have been also proposed [4,5] and improved considering homogeneous regions [21]. Finally, DCT coefficient analysis has been also used to design misalignment estimation approaches. In [2], the authors measure the non uniformity of the Integer Periodicity Map (IPM) to perform the estimation of the shift.

In this work we propose a robust and effective solution able to estimate the misalignment occurred between consecutive JPEG compressions also in presence of small patches. To achieve this goal we apply a third compression considering all the possible shifts analysing statistics related to AC histograms obtained in presence of grid alignment or misalignment.

The remainder of this paper is organized as follows: Sects. 2 describes the proposed solution, Sect. 3 reports experimental results and comparisons with state-of-the-art approaches in different scenarios. Finally, Sect. 4 concludes the paper.

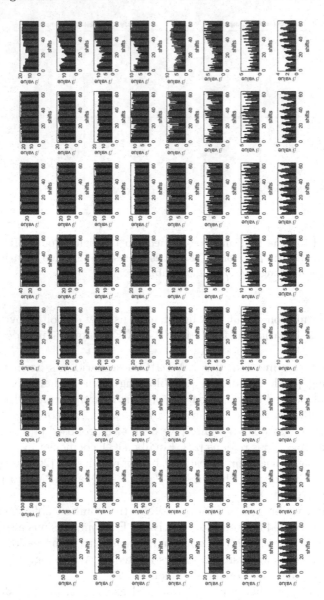

Fig. 2. Histograms of β obtained considering all the possible shifts for each AC location. These histograms are organized to maintain the original structure of the 8×8 block. Minimum values of β usually corresponds to the actual shifts employed between the consecutive compressions ($s = 19$ in the analysed case).

2   Proposed Approach

Given an input raw image I and a 8×8 quantization matrix Q, JPEG compression [19] can be defined as a function $f_Q(I)$ that provides as output a JPEG compressed image I'. At first, RGB image I is converted to YCbCr color space and split in 8×8 non-overlapping blocks. Integer DCT is then applied to each block, divided by Q, rounded and encoded by entropy based engine. Only luminance (i.e., Y channel) will be considered in this paper. Moreover, we denote QF as the quality factor related to standard quantization matrices [19] and QF_i as the quality factor employed in the i-th JPEG compression.

A JPEG double compressed image can be then obtained applying the aforementioned function two times $I'' = f_{Q_2}(f_{Q_1}(I))$, with Q_1 and Q_2 quantization matrices used for the first and the second compression respectively. Depending on the presence of misalignment between DCT grids employed for the two consecutive compressions, two cases are usually considered in literature: A-DJPEG and NA-DJPEG, i.e., aligned and non-aligned scenarios (see Fig. 1).

In order to detect misalignment parameters, a third compression with $Q_3 = Q_2$ tacking into account all the possible shift pairs (r, c) is employed. DCT histograms obtained considering first and third block grids aligned usually have a different shape with respect to the other ones computed with grid misalignment. Statistics computed from DCT coefficients can be then effectively employed to describe the shape of these histograms. Specifically, AC coefficients can be modelled as a zero-centred Laplace distribution [12]:

$$f(x) = \frac{1}{2\beta} \exp\left(-\frac{|x|}{\beta}\right) \tag{1}$$

with β scale parameter computed by maximum likelihood estimation close form solution.

To properly study the behavior of the β values computed at varying of the shifts employed to crop the original image before the third compression, a simple test as been conducted considering a 256×256 double compressed image with $QF_1 = 60$, $QF_2 = 90$ and ground truth misalignment $s = 19$ ($s = r \times 8 + c$, with $r = 2$ and $c = 3$). As can be seen from Fig. 2, for each DCT location (DC is not included), the minimum value of β often corresponds to the real misalignment applied between the consecutive quantizations.

An effective algorithm can be then designed exploiting this simple idea (see Fig. 3). At first, 64 cropped images I_s where $s = r \times 8 + c$ ($r, c \in \{0, 1, \ldots 7\}$) are extracted from the double JPEG compressed input I''. A further compression with Q_2 as third quantization matrix is then performed and 63 AC histograms h_s^{cf} (with s and cf representing shifts and AC location indexes) are obtained. The shape of each AC histogram h_s^{cf} can be then associated to a specific β_s^{cf}. Considering all the AC positions and shifts a 64×63 matrix M_β can be computed. A column-wise minimum computation is then performed, obtaining for each AC location the lowest value of β with respect to all the possible shifts. The final shift $\hat{s}$ is estimated through a simple voting strategy based on a histogram built considering all the shifts related to the minimum vales of β computed before.

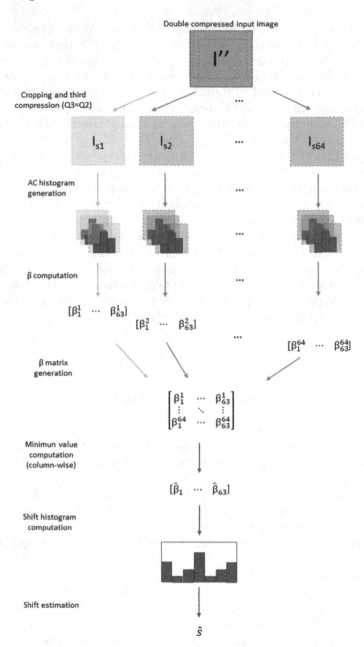

Fig. 3. Overall scheme of the proposed solution. At first, 64 cropped images I_s are extracted from the double JPEG compressed input I''. These images are then compressed again with Q_2 as third quantization matrix and 63 AC histograms h_s^{cf} are obtained. Considering all the AC positions and shifts a 64×63 matrix M_β can be built computing β values from h_s^{cf}. For each AC location the lowest value of β with respect all the possible shifts is selected. Finally the shift $\hat{s}$ is estimated through a simple voting strategy.

3   Experimental Results

To properly assess the performance of the proposed solution, a test dataset D_{test} has been built from UCID collection [16]. Specifically, $d \times d$ patches are cropped from 100 UCID images with $d \in \{64, 128, 256\}$ and double JPEG compressed

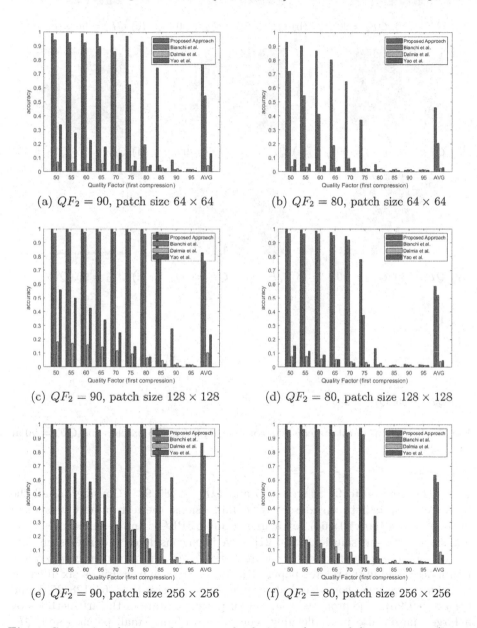

(a) $QF_2 = 90$, patch size 64×64

(b) $QF_2 = 80$, patch size 64×64

(c) $QF_2 = 90$, patch size 128×128

(d) $QF_2 = 80$, patch size 128×128

(e) $QF_2 = 90$, patch size 256×256

(f) $QF_2 = 80$, patch size 256×256

Fig. 4. Comparison between the proposed solution and state-of-the-art approaches at varying of $QF_1 \in \{50, 55, 60, 65, 70, 75, 80, 85, 90, 95\}$, $QF_2 \in \{80, 90\}$, and patch size.

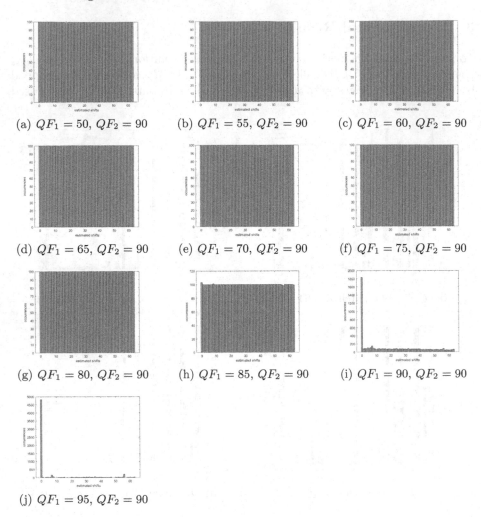

(a) $QF_1 = 50$, $QF_2 = 90$ (b) $QF_1 = 55$, $QF_2 = 90$ (c) $QF_1 = 60$, $QF_2 = 90$

(d) $QF_1 = 65$, $QF_2 = 90$ (e) $QF_1 = 70$, $QF_2 = 90$ (f) $QF_1 = 75$, $QF_2 = 90$

(g) $QF_1 = 80$, $QF_2 = 90$ (h) $QF_1 = 85$, $QF_2 = 90$ (i) $QF_1 = 90$, $QF_2 = 90$

(j) $QF_1 = 95$, $QF_2 = 90$

Fig. 5. Histograms of estimated shifts considering 256×256 patches and $QF_2 = 90$ at varying of QF_1.

with QF_1 from 50 to 95 at step of 5 and $QF_2 \in \{80, 90\}$. Considering all the 64 possible shifts between consecutive compressions, the test dataset consists of 384000 ($3 \times 2 \times 100 \times 10 \times 64$) non-aligned double JPEG compressed patches. Several state-of-the-art solutions ([2,5,21]) have been considered in our tests employing the original code provided by the authors ([2,5]) or reimplementing the algorithm described in the related paper [21]. As can be seen from Fig. 4, six different scenarios have been considered at varying of patch size $d \in \{64, 128, 256\}$ and $QF_2 \in \{80, 90\}$. The proposed solution outperforms state-of-the-art methods by a large margin also in challenging scenarios involving small patches and QF_1 close to QF_2.

The scenario related to 256×256 patches and $QF_2 = 90$ has been further analysed to better understand the relation between the overall accuracy, QF_1 and the actual shift (i.e., the ground truth). Specifically, the histograms of the shifts estimated by the proposed solution have been computed for each QF_1 obtaining quite uniform distributions in the range $[50, 85]$ (see Fig. 5). It is worth noting that in the aforementioned range, aligned scenario is simple considered by the proposed solution as one of the 64 cases. On the contrary, an higher number of estimations $\hat{s} = 0$ can be found for $QF_1 = 90$ (accuracy 0.6152) and $QF_1 = 95$ (accuracy 0.0167). In the last scenario ($QF_1 = 95$), the proposed solution is actually deceived by the grid relate to the strongest compression (i.e., the second one).

4   Conclusions

Typical life-cycles of a digital images often include non-aligned double JPEG compression, hence, estimating the misalignment occurred between consecutive JPEG compressions could be useful for forgery localization and first quantization matrix estimation. Exploiting statistics computed from AC histograms obtained applying a third compression, an effective shift estimation approach has been proposed. To assess the performance of the developed solution a series of tests has been conducted considering scenarios involving various patch sizes, quantization matrices and comparisons with state-of-the-art solutions have been performed. Finally, future works will be devoted to increase the accuracy of the proposed solution also in $QF_1 \geq QF_2$ scenario.

References

1. Battiato, S., Giudice, O., Guarnera, F., Puglisi, G.: First quantization estimation by a robust data exploitation strategy of DCT coefficients. IEEE Access 9, 73110–73120 (2021). https://doi.org/10.1109/ACCESS.2021.3080576
2. Bianchi, T., Piva, A.: Detection of nonaligned double jpeg compression based on integer periodicity maps. IEEE Trans. Inf. Forensics Secur. 7(2), 842–848 (2012). https://doi.org/10.1109/TIFS.2011.2170836
3. Bianchi, T., Piva, A.: Image forgery localization via block-grained analysis of jpeg artifacts. IEEE Trans. Inf. Forensics Secur. 7(3), 1003–1017 (2012). https://doi.org/10.1109/TIFS.2012.2187516
4. Bruna, A.R., Messina, G., Battiato, S.: Crop detection through blocking artefacts analysis. In: Maino, G., Foresti, G.L. (eds.) ICIAP 2011. LNCS, vol. 6978, pp. 650–659. Springer, Heidelberg (2011). https://doi.org/10.1007/978-3-642-24085-0_66
5. Dalmia, N., Okade, M.: A novel technique for misalignment parameter estimation in double compressed jpeg images. In: 2016 Visual Communications and Image Processing (VCIP), pp. 1–4 (2016). https://doi.org/10.1109/VCIP.2016.7805446
6. Dalmia, N., Okade, M.: Robust first quantization matrix estimation based on filtering of recompression artifacts for non-aligned double compressed JPEG images. Signal Process. Image Commun. 61, 9–20 (2018)

7. Fan, Z., De Queiroz, R.: Identification of bitmap compression history: JPEG detection and quantizer estimation. IEEE Trans. on Image Processing **12**(2), 230–235 (2003)
8. Farid, H.: Digital image ballistics from JPEG quantization: A followup study. Department of Computer Science, Dartmouth College, Tech. Rep. TR2008-638 (2008)
9. Giudice, O., Guarnera, F., Paratore, A., Battiato, S.: 1-D DCT domain analysis for JPEG double compression detection. In: Ricci, E., Rota Bulò, S., Snoek, C., Lanz, O., Messelodi, S., Sebe, N. (eds.) ICIAP 2019. LNCS, vol. 11752, pp. 716–726. Springer, Cham (2019). https://doi.org/10.1007/978-3-030-30645-8_65
10. Giudice, O., Paratore, A., Moltisanti, M., Battiato, S.: A classification engine for image ballistics of social data. In: Battiato, S., Gallo, G., Schettini, R., Stanco, F. (eds.) ICIAP 2017. LNCS, vol. 10485, pp. 625–636. Springer, Cham (2017). https://doi.org/10.1007/978-3-319-68548-9_57
11. Kee, E., Johnson, M.K., Farid, H.: Digital image authentication from JPEG headers. IEEE Trans. Inform. Forens. Sec. **6**(3), 1066–1075 (2011)
12. Lam, E.Y., Goodman, J.W.: A mathematical analysis of the DCT coefficient distributions for images. IEEE Trans. on Image Processing **9**(10), 1661–1666 (2000)
13. Luo, W., Qu, Z., Huang, J., Qiu, G.: A novel method for detecting cropped and recompressed image block. In: 2007 IEEE International Conference on Acoustics, Speech and Signal Processing - ICASSP 2007,vol. 2, pp. II-217-II-220 (2007). https://doi.org/10.1109/ICASSP.2007.366211
14. Moltisanti, M., Paratore, A., Battiato, S., Saravo, L.: Image manipulation on facebook for forensics evidence. In: Murino, V., Puppo, E. (eds.) ICIAP 2015. LNCS, vol. 9280, pp. 506–517. Springer, Cham (2015). https://doi.org/10.1007/978-3-319-23234-8_47
15. Piva, A.: An overview on image forensics. ISRN Signal Processing **2013**, 22 (2013). https://doi.org/10.1155/2013/496701
16. Schaefer, G., Stich, M.: UCID: An uncompressed color image database. In: Storage and Retrieval Methods and Applications for Multimedia 2004, vol. 5307, pp. 472–480. International Society for Optics and Photonics (2003)
17. Stamm, M.C., Wu, M., Liu, K.J.R.: Information forensics: An overview of the first decade. IEEE Access **1**, 167–200 (2013). https://doi.org/10.1109/ACCESS.2013.2260814
18. Verdoliva, L.: Media forensics and deepfakes: an overview. IEEE J. Selected Topics Signal Process. **14**(5), 910–932 (2020)
19. Wallace, G.K.: The JPEG still picture compression standard. Commun. ACM **34**(4), 30–44 (1991)
20. Wu, L., Kong, X., Wang, B., Shang, S.: Image tampering localization via estimating the non-aligned double JPEG compression. In: Alattar, A.M., Memon, N.D., Heitzenrater, C.D. (eds.) Media Watermarking, Security, and Forensics 2013, vol. 8665, pp. 260–266. International Society for Optics and Photonics, SPIE (2013). https://doi.org/10.1117/12.2003695
21. Yao, H., Wei, H., Qin, C., Zhang, X.: An improved first quantization matrix estimation for nonaligned double compressed jpeg images. Signal Process. **170**, 107430 (2020). https://doi.org/10.1016/j.sigpro.2019.107430, https://www.sciencedirect.com/science/article/pii/S0165168419304827

Attacking and Defending Printer Source Attribution Classifiers in the Physical Domain

Anselmo Ferreira[✉][iD] and Mauro Barni[iD]

Department of Information Engineering and Mathematics, University of Siena,
53100 Siena, Italy
anselmo.castelo@unisi.it, barni@dii.unisi.it

Abstract. The security of machine learning classifiers has received increasing attention in the last years. In forensic applications, guaranteeing the security of the tools investigators rely on is crucial, since the gathered evidence may be used to decide about the innocence or the guilt of a suspect. Several adversarial attacks were proposed to assess such security, with a few works focusing on transferring such attacks from the digital to the physical domain. In this work, we focus on physical domain attacks against source attribution of printed documents. We first show how a simple reprinting attack may be sufficient to fool a model trained on images that were printed and scanned only once. Then, we propose a hardened version of the classifier trained on the reprinted attacked images. Finally, we attack the hardened classifier with several attacks, including a new attack based on the Expectation Over Transformation approach, which finds the adversarial perturbations by simulating the physical transformations occurring when the image attacked in the digital domain is printed again. The results we got demonstrate a good capability of the hardened classifier to resist attacks carried out in the physical domain.

Keywords: Digital Image Forensics · Printer Source Attribution · Adversarial Attacks

1 Introduction

Printed documents are everywhere. From printed advertisements and contracts to packages and anti-counterfeiting labels, a printer is always involved. However, the cheap access and high demand for new printing technologies raise many concerns about their misuse. For example, documents that could be considered a piece of evidence in a criminal investigation, such as illegal copies of documents, packaging of fake products, and terrorist plans, can be easily produced at anybody's home. Determining the provenance of printed documents, then, may be particularly important in several applications, such as anti-counterfeiting, forensics applications, and authentication of legal documents like statements, contracts, checks, among others. Indeed, according to a forecast from the International Chamber of Commerce, 3.7 trillion dollars and 5.4 million jobs will be

J.-J. Rousseau and B. Kapralos (Eds.): ICPR 2022 Workshops, LNCS 13644, pp. 347–363, 2023.
https://doi.org/10.1007/978-3-031-37742-6_27

lost by 2022 [12] due to piracy. As another example related to piracy, according to the World Health Organization, almost 50% of the Malaria medications in Africa could be fake [37].

Current works on printed document forensics focus on two main tasks: the authentication of printed documents by pinpointing the ownership of a document (source attribution), and the description of copy-proof patterns that are distorted when an illegal copy of a printed authentication element is made (such as 2D barcodes). For the first task, which is the task of interest in this work, several papers have focused on identifying extrinsic artifacts such as noise, texture of printed patterns, banding, among others, and are usually divided in solutions focused on text documents [7,16–18,22,34,36], color documents [5,10,11,20,21, 30,38] or both [3,8,35]. In all of these applications, methodologies based on artificial intelligence through Convolutional Neural Networks (CNNs) showed state-of-the-art performance [3,7,10,11,18].

Despite all these advancements, very little or no attention has been given to the evaluation of printed document forensics in adversarial conditions. A smart counterfeiter could, for example, use the ubiquitous existence of adversarial examples [2,6,23–25,31,32] to generate counterfeited labels that are judged as authentic by a CNN. In the same way, a criminal could modify a printed document to change the result of a source attribution procedure. For the specific domain of interest of this paper, some works have evaluated the transferability of adversarial attacks in the physical domain for computer vision applications. For example, Kurakin et al. [23] showed that printed and recaptured images could fool image classifiers by assuming that the images are presented in a given position. Other works have proven that variations of points of view do not impact the performance of attacks in the physical world [24,25]. In [31], Sharif et al. attacked a face recognition system by proposing the printing of adversarial examples on a pair of eyeglass frames. Such an attack works by interactively looking for a perturbation that can fool the classifier, identified by optimizing a cross-entropy loss over a set of images that have already undergone geometric transformations typical of the recapture process. Athalye et al. [2] proposed an attack done by simulating synthetic transformations that can happen in the printing process of an image several times in the adversarial image construction. This is usually done to minimize the loss of an adversarial or target class (targeted attack) or maximize the loss of the real class (untargeted attack). Eykholt et al. [6] proposed an interesting physical domain attack to mislead stop sign classifiers. To reach their goal, they applied both synthetic and physical transformations and extended their work later to a general object recognition system [32]. Finally, the work by Zhang et al. [39] simulated the distortions a spoofed image is subject to when it is displayed on a smartphone screen to an anti-spoof authentication system. All the above-mentioned works have the same idea of modeling the possible physical world distortions that the image may be subject to during the attack optimization procedure. However, as will be discussed in the rest of this paper, applying such adversarial attacks against source attribution classifiers has some unique peculiarities that do not apply to other settings.

In this paper, we report our findings in fooling and defending printed documents source attribution classifier in the physical domain. To perform such a task, we first propose a simple black-box attack based on re-printing. Then we present a hardened version of the classifier, obtained by fine-tuning the original classifier using the attacked images obtained by reprinting. Finally, we evaluate the effectiveness of the hardened classifier against several white-box attacks, including a newly proposed method based on Expectation Over Transformation [2]. In summary, the contributions of this paper are:

1. We propose two adversarial attacks in the printed domain against source printer attribution classifiers: one of them is based on a simple, yet effective, black-box attack based on reprinting. The other is based on the Expectation Over Transformation strategy applied in a white-box setting.
2. We show how the simple black-box reprint attack can be enough to attack the printer source attribution classifier.
3. We introduce a new version of the source attribution classifier trained on examples attacked with the black-box attack, and demonstrate the effectiveness of such a defense against several white-box attacks, including the newly proposed method based on Expectation Over Transformation.

The rest of this paper is organized as follows: Sect. 2 discusses the threat model and the source attribution system targeted by our attacks. Section 3 presents our white and black-box attacks. Section 4 reports the results we got by attacking the original classifier with a simple rebroadcasting attack. In Sect. 5, we show the results of the experiments we run to validate the security of the hardened classifier. Finally, Sect. 6 concludes our work.

2   Threat Model

In this paper, we adopt the taxonomy introduced by Biggio and Roli [4], and already used in a previous work [39]. Before discussing the goal of the attack, we briefly review the system used for the printer source attribution problem targeted by our attacks.

The source attribution system, the attacks and defenses are based on the analysis and the datasets presented in [9,10]. According to such works, focusing on an 8-class closed set scenario, the best source attribution is achieved by training a RESNET-50 [14] architecture. To apply the RESNET-50 CNN in the laser printer attribution task, the authors adopted classification over regions of interest (with further majority voting for classification), inspired by a previous work on rebroadcasting detection [1]. The source attribution is applied to high-energy regions detected after Canny filtering. Such energy is calculated on the Discrete Wavelet Transform domain and the top-10 highest energy $224 \times 224 \times 3$ patches of the documents are used for training and testing a CNN classifier. For the present work, we added to the dataset used in [9,10] images taken from four new printers (already used in [11]). The images were also used to expand the VIPPrint dataset [9,10] from 8 to 12 printers.

The threat model considered in this paper, which is illustrated in Fig. 1, has two goals: (i) attack the high energy patches in such a way that these attacks remain in the print and scan domain; (ii) modify the patches in such a way to fool the source attribution classifier even after the majority voting scheme. As the classifier works on printed and scanned images, to perform the adversarial attack we print the digital images first, scan the images next and then we apply the adversarial attacks on them. After the attack, the attacked image is printed again, and the classifier is applied after re-scanning.

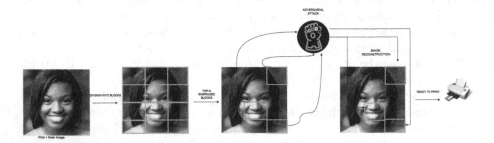

Fig. 1. The threat model considered in our work. We aim at modifying the high-energy patches using adversarial attacks to fool the source attribution system even after that the attacked image is re-printed and re-scanned.

In this work, we assume that the attacker has full access to the attacked system, representing a kind of worst-case assumption for the defender. This means that the attacker has not only access to the weights of the network, but he/she also knows which regions of interest will be used since the attacker also has access to the algorithm used to select the high-energy patches and will try to keep the same high energy patches after the attack. The adversarial replay attack consists of the construction of a scanned image with adversarial high-energy patches that could be scanned even with a scanner other than that used to train the classifier. The goal of the attack is to take an image printed with a certain printer $\mathcal{P}$ and modify it in such a way that the classifier does not recognize anymore that the image had been printed by $\mathcal{P}$. The challenge, here, is that the attack should be effective even after the attacked image has been printed again (by $\mathcal{P}$) and re-scanned. The attack we aim at is a purely exploratory attack [4], meaning that the attacker has no access to the training data used to train the classifier. Moreover, the attack is thought to work against an unattended system without human supervision. Finally, the printer $\mathcal{P}$ we focus our attack on is the Kyocera-ecosysp5021cdn laser printer, which is class #12 of our multiclass classification problem.

3   Proposed Attacks

In this section, we introduce the two attacks used throughout the paper. The first one is a black-box attack based on printing the document after it was already printed and scanned, and will be used to attack and defend the original model. The second attack is a white-box attack aimed at surviving the image distortions occurring between the first and second print. The last attack will be used to attack the hardened classifier fine-tuned with adversarial samples generated by the first method.

3.1   Double Rebroadcast Attack

The first adversarial attack we are considering relies on the experimental observation that a second print and scan process often fools the source attribution classifier with a significant margin. This observation contrasts with some related works, dealing with the effect of rebroadcasting in forensic applications. Zhang *et al.* [39], for example, applies Expectation Over Transformation to add a perturbation p that could fool a spoofing detection method once a spoofed image is displayed on a smartphone screen. The authors state that, without such a perturbation, the second rebroadcasted image could be easily detected as a spoof image by the anti-spoofing CNN. In our case, an image that has been printed and scanned twice can not be classified correctly, and thus a rebroadcasted document can be an adversarial attack against source printer attribution classifiers.

To support our claim, we show in Figs. 2 and 3 some examples of images that are printed and scanned once and twice. We also show, in Fig. 4, how the printing artifacts change in the second print by plotting the HH Discrete Wavelet Transform sub-bands of the first and second print. Such sub-bands were used by the work of Choi et al. [19] for printer attribution. Figure 4 shows that traces of the printer used for the second print are present when the image is printed twice (second and fourth columns of Fig. 4), mixing artifacts and thus causing a classification error.

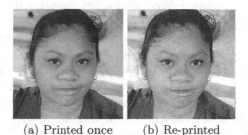

(a) Printed once   (b) Re-printed

Fig. 2. First print (a) and second print (b) of the same image by considering a Kyocera Printer (printer #12) for first and second prints.

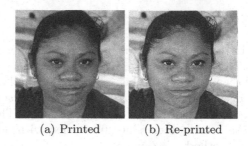

(a) Printed   (b) Re-printed

Fig. 3. First print (a) with Samsung printer (printer #4) and (b) a reprinting of the first print using a Kyocera Printer (printer #12) for the second print.

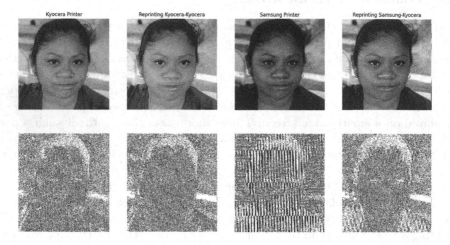

Fig. 4. Discrete Wavelet Transform HH subbands artifacts for images printed twice.

3.2   Expectation over Transformation Attack

In this section, we present a white-box adversarial attack thought to be used against the hardened classifier fine-tuned on the reprinted images obtained by the black-box attack described in the previous subsection.

We start by formalizing the process whereby adversarial examples are generated. We may distinguish between targeted and untargeted attacks first. In the targeted case, given an input image I, we denote the target label of the adversarial example by $l_{adv} \neq l_{true}$, where l_{true} is the true label of the sample. We indicate with S_o the soft output of the neural network under attack. A targeted adversarial white-box attack aims at finding a minimal adversarial perturbation image I_δ solving the following optimization problem [39]:

$$\arg\min_{I_\delta \in \mathcal{I}} L(S_o(I + I_\delta), l_{adv}) + \lambda ||I_\delta||_p, \tag{1}$$

where $\mathcal{I}$ indicates the set of all possible perturbation images, L is the loss function of the neural network, $||\cdot||_p$ denotes the p-norm, and λ controls the strength of the distance penalty term $||I_\delta||_p$.

In the untargeted case, which is what we focus on in this paper, the optimization is rewritten as follows:

$$\arg\max_{I_\delta\in\mathcal{I}} L(S_o(I+I_\delta), l_{true}) + \lambda||I_\delta||_p, \tag{2}$$

In the printed domain setting considered for our source attribution problem, the CNN is not fed directly with the digital image, but with its printed and scanned version. As the CNN works after the printing and scan operation, the attack is applied after the first print and scan process, then the adversarial image is re-printed and re-scanned. As will be discussed later, such an operation makes the source attribution attack scenario unique in terms of attack and defense strategies.

In order to better attack a printer source attribution system, the transformations the image suffers between the first and second print must be modeled during the attack. By denoting with T the set of distortions/transformations the attack must be robust to, the perturbation I_δ is found by optimizing the average loss over T as follows:

$$\arg\max_{I_\delta\in\mathcal{I}} E_{t\sim T}[L(S_o(t(I+I_\delta)), l_{true})] + \lambda||I_\delta||_p, \tag{3}$$

In other words, for an adversarial perturbation I_δ to be successful in the untargeted case, Eq. (3) states that it must maximize the mean loss of a true label after the application of several transformations to the adversarial image. In this way, after the attack, a random class will be given to the attacked image by the classifier (untargeted case). Such transformations are usually defined in such a way to simulate the distortions occurring when the adversarial image is rebroadcasted (in our case, re-printed and re-scanned). This formulation was first introduced by Athalye *et al.* [2] in the context of object recognition and later followed by Zhang *et al.* [39] to attack a face anti-spoofing classifier, and is commonly known as the Expectation Over Transformation (EOT) attack.

In the setting considered in [2], the degradation due to rebroadcasting is mainly due to geometric distortions, different color distributions, light reflections, and printing artifacts. Since in the printer attribution problem the scanning conditions are controlled with a fixed flatbed scanner, geometric distortion artifacts play a minor role. So, we focus on artifacts related to zoom, brightness change, and, most importantly, printing noise. The set of transformations used to implement our attack is listed in Table 1, together with the range of parameters we considered for each of them. For EOT, every t in Eq. (3) is a composite transformation consisting of all the transformations in Table 1 applied randomly. The transformations in Table 1 were defined by visually inspecting the transformations associated with reprinting, since the EOT-based method is expected to be applied in the physical domain, and hence the perturbation will have to survive a second print and scan process. The average loss is then computed over

100 versions of the to-be-attacked image, obtained by applying to it the composite transformations. To solve the minimization problem in Eq. (3), we applied Stochastic Gradient Descent optimization (SGD).

Table 1. Transformations considered to simulate re-printing distortions for the Expectation Over Transformation based adversarial attack. For zoom effect, the interpolation used was bilinear and the values for brightness are the values that are randomly chosen and added to the image pixels in the normalized domain.

Transformation	Range
Zoom	[−0.019,−0.029]
Brightness	[0.1,0.4]
Gaussian Noise (standard deviation)	[0.1,0.3]

Finally, it is worth mentioning that, in our specific attack, we aim at keeping the position of the high energy patches unchanged after the attacked image is printed and scanned for the second time. To accomplish such a goal, a parameter called *strength*, or ϵ, is used to clip the values of the generated adversarial image. This is done by constructing an interval of accepted pixel values, so the original image is not degraded too much and thus the adversarial image will have an acceptable visual aspect. We show an example of the high energy patches in Figs. 5 and 6 when considering a big and a small ϵ respectively. We found that from 70% to 80% of the high energy patches are unchanged in the attacked image when it is printed for the second time if a small ϵ is considered. In the experiments reported in the rest of the paper, we let $\epsilon = 0.01$.

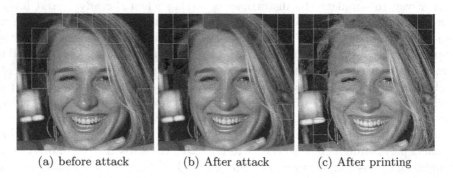

(a) before attack   (b) After attack   (c) After printing

Fig. 5. Effect of a large strength value ϵ on the location of the high energy patches.

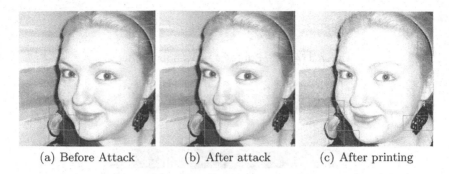

(a) Before Attack   (b) After attack   (c) After printing

Fig. 6. Effect of a small strength value ϵ on the location of high energy patches.

4   Effectiveness of the Black-Box Attack Against the Original Model

In this section, we report the results of the experiments we carried out to test the security of the original source attribution model against the simple black-box attack described in Sect. 3.1.

For the experiments described here and in the next section, we consider the dataset described by Ferreira et al. in [11]. The dataset consists of 200 printed faces, whose top-10 high-energy patches are used for printer attribution. Our attack focuses on one specific printer to which we had full access during our research: the Kyocera-ecosysp5021cdn, which we call printer #12. More specifically, we attack a model trained by considering 10 high-energy patches from 100 printed faces, printed by all 12 printers (10*100*12=12,000 images). For testing, we consider 100 printed faces from printer #12 and their top-10 high-energy patches to generate the adversarial examples.

To highlight the weakness of the original model against a simple reprint attack (hereafter referred to as ReprintingAttack), we considered three versions of the attack, varying the first and second printers as described below:

1. ReprintingAttackv1: we use the same printer (brand and model) for the first and second print: a Kyocera-ecosysp5021cdn.
2. ReprintingAttackv2: we use two different printers with the same brand, but with different models. We use a KyoceraTaskAlfa3551ci for the first print and a Kyocera-ecosysp5021cdn for the second one.
3. ReprintingAttackv3: we use two different printers with different brands and models. We use a Samsung-Multiexpress-X3280NR for the first print and a Kyocera-ecosysp5021cdn for the second one.

Figure 7 summarizes the errors of the classifier after majority voting on the top-10 high-energy patches.

The results reported in Fig. 7 highlight the particularities of the printer source attribution problem in an adversarial setting. Simple black-box attacks

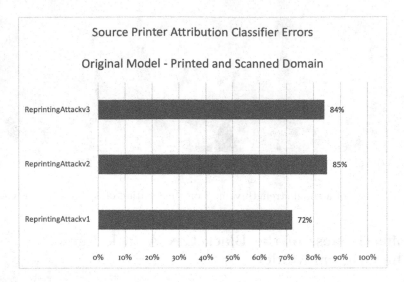

Fig. 7. Effectiveness of `ReprintingAttack` on the original classifier (error probabilities are reported as percentages). The printer used for reprinting is always a Kyocera-ecosysp5021cdn printer. The results are given after majority voting on the high energy patches.

like `ReprintingAttackv1`, `ReprintingAttackv2` and `ReprintingAttackv3` can easily fool the original classifier, with error rates larger than 70%. Results at the patch level, not reported in the figure, confirm the effectiveness of the attack. In particular, `ReprintingAttackv2` and `ReprintingAttackv3`, using different printer sources for the first and second print, results in error rates around 50% and above 90% respectively. The effectiveness of these attacks motivates the development of a hardened classifier, trained on adversarial samples, as will be discussed in the next section.

5   Hardened Source Attribution Model

We used the adversarial images obtained with the `ReprintingAttack` to harden the source attribution classifier. To train the new classifier, we fine-tune the original classifier by loading the original weights (previously found for the original printer source attribution). The fine-tuned classifier is trained on the original data plus the reprinting data (200 training images reprinted, being 100 of them with the same printer in the first and second prints, and the other 100 with different printers for the first and second prints, being the second printer always the Kyocera-ecosysp5021cdn). We establish as the source (or label) of reprinted data the printer that performed the second print. The architecture used to train the hardened model is the same RESNET-50 CNN as the original model, fine-tuned with SGD optimizer under 300 epochs and with a batch size of 32. An initial learning rate of 0.01 is defined and is reduced by a factor of $\sqrt{0.1}$ if there is a plateau in the validation accuracy curve for every 10 epochs. There is an early stopping criterion that stops training if the validation accuracy does not change for 20 epochs. Finally, the best model considering such validation accuracy is saved.

In Table 2, we show the confusion matrix obtained by testing the hardened classifier in the absence of attacks. Not only the fine-tuned RESNET-50 model retains the good performance of the original model, but it also improves the original model's accuracy from 95,83% to 97,08%.

Table 2. Confusion Matrix of a multiclass RESNET-50 source attribution model fine-tuned on reprinted images. The printer that we will focus on for our attack is highlighted in yellow in yellow last row and column.

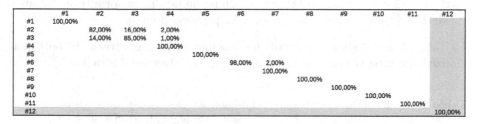

	#1	#2	#3	#4	#5	#6	#7	#8	#9	#10	#11	#12
#1	100,00%											
#2		82,00%	16,00%	2,00%								
#3		14,00%	85,00%	1,00%								
#4				100,00%								
#5					100,00%							
#6						98,00%	2,00%					
#7							100,00%					
#8								100,00%				
#9									100,00%			
#10										100,00%		
#11											100,00%	
#12												100,00%

5.1 Experimental Analysis of the Accuracy of the Hardened Classifier

To show the effectiveness of the hardened classifier against adversarial examples, we start evaluating its performance against adversarial attacks carried out in the digital domain. To do so, we benchmark a number of baseline white-box attacks against the hardened model in terms of performance metrics, selecting the best approaches to be applied in the physical domain. In particular, we focused on adversarial examples that remain effective even when they are converted from the normalized (floating point in the [0,1] range) domain back to the integer domain. Inspired by [33], we rely on the following metrics in both the normalized and integer domains:

1. **Error:** the inverse of accuracy, or the probability that a document is misclassified.
2. **L1 norm:** the mean of absolute pixel-wise differences between the original and the attacked images. Such a value is reported in percentage (0% means no variation, 100% means a variation from 0 to 255 in the pixel values).
3. **Linf norm:** the average maximum pixel-wise difference between the original and the attacked images (this is also given in percentage).
4. **PSNR:** the mean Peak Signal-to-Noise Ratio between the original and attacked images.

5. **%mod:** the average percentage of modified pixels when comparing the original and attacked images.

For the digital domain attacks, we considered the following attacks implemented in the Foolbox 2.0 library [28,29]:

- the white box attack L2FastGradientAttack, also called the Fast Gradient Method (FGM) [13];
- the white box LinfFastGradientAttack, also called the Fast Gradient Sign Method (FGSM) [13];
- the white box DeepfoolAttack attack [27];
- LinfPGDAttack, which is the Projected Gradient Attack [26] using infinity norm;
- the LinfBasicIterativeAttack, which is the L-infinity norm Basic Iterative Method [23] and is built to work in the physical domain.

Tables 3 and 4 show results of the baseline white-box attacks in both normalized and integer domains before printing the adversarial attacks.

Table 3. Results obtained by baseline white-box attacks against the hardened classifier in the digital normalized domain. Best results are highlighted in yellow and metrics are calculated patch-wise (before majority voting).

Approach	Normalized Domain				
	%Error	Norm L1 (%)	Norm Linf (%)	PSNR	%mod
L2FastGradientAttack	7.29	0.15	4.09	53.22	98.83
LinfFastGradientAttack	33.59	48.79	96.22	5.10	98.07
LinfDeepFoolAttack	33.9	10.21	10.60	22.09	96.98
LinfPGDAttack	100	5.41	11.03	24.54	99.26
LinfBasicIterativeAttack	100	1.82	3.64	34.67	99.27

Table 4. Results obtained by baseline white-box attacks against the hardened classifier. Results are given after integer truncation and rounding of the normalized values. Best results are highlighted in yellow and metrics are calculated patch-wise (before majority voting).

Approach	Integer Domain				
	%Error	Norm L1 (%)	Norm Linf (%)	PSNR	%mod
L2FastGradientAttack	6.89	0.12	4.08	53.53	26.73
LinfFastGradientAttack	33.4	48.79	96.22	5.10	98.07
LinfDeepFoolAttack	33.19	10.10	10.47	22.87	94.84
LinfPGDAttack	100	5.41	10.90	24.54	97.50
LinfBasicIterativeAttack	100	1.81	3.57	34.65	92.95

According to Tables 3 and 4, `LinfPGD` and `LinfBasicIterative` are the most effective attacks, reducing the accuracy for printer #12 from 100% to 0%. Both of them generated adversarial samples by considering a small perturbation, highlighted by a small **Norm L1** and **Norm Linf**. For `LinfBasicIterativeAttack`, the mean difference between the adversarial and original images in Table 4 is close to minimum (1.81%), and the maximum difference between them is also very small (3.57%), which means the adversarial perturbations are very small (and weak) in the digital domain. From Table 3 to 4, it can be seen that `LinfPGDAttack` and `LinfBasicIterativeAttack` do not suffer too much when passing from the normalized domain to the integer domain. The only obvious effect is a significant drop in the mean percentage of modified pixels (**%mod** metric), also affected by the truncation and rounding operations. As these approaches were successful in both the normalized and integer digital domains, we decide to also verify their effectiveness when applied in the physical domain (which means, printing the attacked printed images and converting them back in the digital format again).

Now we evaluate the effectiveness of such attacks against the hardened model, and in the presence of a further print and scan process (necessary to implement the attack in the physical domain). To do that, we selected as baseline adversarial attacks the best approaches found in the previous experiments (`LinfPGD` and `LinfBasicIterative`) and we also consider our proposed Expectation of Transformation based adversarial attack. In the sequel, we call our proposed attack as the `EOTReprintingAttack`.

Figure 8 shows the effectiveness of the adversarial attacks against the hardened detector, in the challenging setting imposed by physical domain attacks.

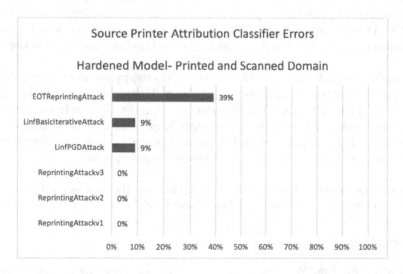

Fig. 8. Success rate of adversarial attacks against the hardened classifier when attacking the top-10 high energy patches. The results are given after majority voting.

To start with, the results in Fig. 8 highlight the effectiveness of the hardened classifier against the simple rebroadcast attacks. For the baseline attacks, their effect drops dramatically due to reprinting and also the adversarial training of the to-be-attacked classifier, with an error rate below 10%. The proposed attack `EOTReprintingAttack`, being explicitly designed to cope with reprinting, exhibits a larger success rate equals to 39%. Still, the hardened classifier retains a good accuracy also in the presence of this powerful attack. We believe that the problem of `EOTReprintingAttack` not surviving the print and scan process is mainly due to the difficulty of simulating the artifact introduced by such a reprinting process,.

6 Conclusion

The security of any machine learning classifier, especially those interfacing directly to the physical domain, has gained importance as they have a substantial impact in several applications such as the reliability of self-driving cars, anti-spoofing systems, physical documents forensics, among many others. In spite of this interest, the security of image forensic tools operating on printed images source attribution has not been sufficiently studied. In this paper, we present some first steps towards this goal. We evaluated the security of a multiclass printer source classifier when it faces adversarial samples in both black box scenarios and white-box scenarios.

As an important finding of the research reported in this paper, we discovered that simple black-box attacks based on reprinting are often enough to attack an original source attribution classifier and thus can be used to harden it through adversarial training. We also proposed an attack based on Expectation Over Transformation to simulate reprinting artifacts in order to attack the hardened classifier. Despite these efforts, when facing the fine-tuned, hardened classifier, the performance of the attacks, including some baselines methods, is not satisfactory.

As future work, we aim to explore better ways to approximate the reprint and re-scan process when using Expectation Over Transformation attacks against protected models. One way that is under investigation is to rely on GANs like pix2pix networks [15] acting together with Expectation Over Transformation for the simulation of second print transformations, thus possibly improving the adversarial performance against adversarially-trained models.

Acknowledgements. This research was funded by the European Union Marie Sklodowska-Curie project PrintOut (grant number 892757).

References

1. Agarwal, S., Fan, W., Farid, H.: A diverse large-scale dataset for evaluating rebroadcast attacks. In: IEEE International Conference on Acoustics, Speech and Signal Processing (ICASSP), pp. 1997–2001 (2018). https://doi.org/10.1109/ICASSP.2018.8462205

2. Athalye, A., Engstrom, L., Ilyas, A., Kwok, K.: Synthesizing robust adversarial examples. In: Dy, J., Krause, A. (eds.) International Conference on Machine Learning. Proceedings of Machine Learning Research, vol. 80, pp. 284–293. PMLR (2018)

3. Bibi, M., Hamid, A., Moetesum, M., Siddiqi, I.: Document forgery detection using printer source identification-a text-independent approach. In: International Conference on Document Analysis and Recognition Workshops, vol. 8, pp. 7–12 (2019)

4. Biggio, B., Roli, F.: Wild patterns: ten years after the rise of adversarial machine learning. Pattern Recogn. **84**, 317–331 (2018). https://doi.org/10.1016/j.patcog.2018.07.023

5. Bulan, O., Mao, J., Sharma, G.: Geometric distortion signatures for printer identification. In: 2009 IEEE International Conference on Acoustics, Speech and Signal Processing, pp. 1401–1404 (2009)

6. Eykholt, K., et al.: Robust physical-world attacks on deep learning visual classification. In: 2018 IEEE/CVF Conference on Computer Vision and Pattern Recognition, pp. 1625–1634 (2018). https://doi.org/10.1109/CVPR.2018.00175

7. Ferreira, A., et al.: Data-driven feature characterization techniques for laser printer attribution. IEEE Trans. Inf. For. Secur. **12**(8), 1860–1873 (2017). https://doi.org/10.1109/TIFS.2017.2692722

8. Ferreira, A., Navarro, L.C., Pinheiro, G., dos Santos, J.A., Rocha, A.: Laser printer attribution: exploring new features and beyond. For. Sci. Int. **247**, 105–125 (2015)

9. Ferreira, A., Nowroozi, E., Barni, M.: VIPPrint: a large scale dataset for colored printed documents authentication and source linking (2021). https://doi.org/10.5281/zenodo.4454971

10. Ferreira, A., Nowroozi, E., Barni, M.: Vipprint: validating synthetic image detection and source linking methods on a large scale dataset of printed documents. MDPI J. Imag. **7**(3) (2021). https://www.mdpi.com/2313-433X/7/3/50

11. Ferreira, A., Purnekar, N., Barni, M.: Ensembling shallow Siamese neural network architectures for printed documents verification in data-scarcity scenarios. IEEE Access **9**, 133924–133939 (2021). https://doi.org/10.1109/ACCESS.2021.3110297

12. Economics, F.: The economic impacts of counterfeiting and piracy. Technical report, Frontier Economics (2016)

13. Goodfellow, I.J., Shlens, J., Szegedy, C.: Explaining and harnessing adversarial examples. In: Bengio, Y., LeCun, Y. (eds.) 3rd International Conference on Learning Representations, ICLR 2015, San Diego, CA, USA, 7–9 May 2015, Conference Track Proceedings (2015). http://arxiv.org/abs/1412.6572

14. He, K., Zhang, X., Ren, S., Sun, J.: Deep residual learning for image recognition. In: IEEE Conference on Computer Vision and Pattern Recognition (CVPR), pp. 770–778 (2016)

15. Isola, P., Zhu, J., Zhou, T., Efros, A.A.: Image-to-image translation with conditional adversarial networks. In: 2017 IEEE Conference on Computer Vision and Pattern Recognition, CVPR 2017, Honolulu, HI, USA, 21–26 July 2017, pp. 5967–5976. IEEE Computer Society (2017). https://doi.org/10.1109/CVPR.2017.632

16. Joshi, S., Khanna, N.: Single classifier-based passive system for source printer classification using local texture features. IEEE Trans. Inf. For. Secur. **13**(7), 1603–1614 (2018)

17. Joshi, S., Khanna, N.: Source printer classification using printer specific local texture descriptor. IEEE Trans. Inf. For. Secur. **15**, 160–171 (2020)

18. Joshi, S., Lomba, M., Goyal, V., Khanna, N.: Augmented data and improved noise residual-based cnn for printer source identification. In: 2018 IEEE International Conference on Acoustics, Speech and Signal Processing (ICASSP), pp. 2002–2006 (2018)

19. Choi, J,H., Im, D.H., Lee, H.Y., Oh, J.T., Ryu, J.H., Lee, H.K.: Color laser printer identification by analyzing statistical features on discrete wavelet transform. In: IEEE International Conference on Image Processing (ICIP), pp. 1505–1508 (2009)
20. Kim, D., Lee, H.: Color laser printer identification using photographed halftone images. In: European Signal Processing Conference (EUSIPCO), pp. 795–799 (2014)
21. Kim, D., Lee, H.: Colour laser printer identification using halftone texture fingerprint. Electron. Lett. **51**(13), 981–983 (2015)
22. Kumar, M., Gupta, S., Mohan, N.: A computational approach for printed document forensics using SURF and ORB features. Soft Comput. **24**(17), 13197–13208 (2020). https://doi.org/10.1007/s00500-020-04733-x
23. Kurakin, A., Goodfellow, I., Bengio, S.: Adversarial examples in the physical world (2016). https://doi.org/10.48550/ARXIV.1607.02533
24. Lu, J., Sibai, H., Fabry, E., Forsyth, D.: No need to worry about adversarial examples in object detection in autonomous vehicles (2017). https://doi.org/10.48550/ARXIV.1707.03501
25. Luo, Y., Boix, X., Roig, G., Poggio, T., Zhao, Q.: Foveation-based mechanisms alleviate adversarial examples (2015). https://doi.org/10.48550/ARXIV.1511.06292
26. Madry, A., Makelov, A., Schmidt, L., Tsipras, D., Vladu, A.: Towards deep learning models resistant to adversarial attacks. In: International Conference on Learning Representations (2018). https://openreview.net/forum?id=rJzIBfZAb
27. Moosavi-Dezfooli, S., Fawzi, A., Frossard, P.: Deepfool: a simple and accurate method to fool deep neural networks. In: 2016 IEEE Conference on Computer Vision and Pattern Recognition, CVPR 2016, Las Vegas, NV, USA, 27–30 June 2016, pp. 2574–2582. IEEE Computer Society (2016). https://doi.org/10.1109/CVPR.2016.282
28. Rauber, J., Brendel, W., Bethge, M.: Foolbox: a python toolbox to benchmark the robustness of machine learning models. In: Reliable Machine Learning in the Wild Workshop, 34th International Conference on Machine Learning (2017). http://arxiv.org/abs/1707.04131
29. Rauber, J., Zimmermann, R., Bethge, M., Brendel, W.: Foolbox native: fast adversarial attacks to benchmark the robustness of machine learning models in pytorch, tensorflow, and jax. J. Open Source Softw. **5**(53), 2607 (2020). https://doi.org/10.21105/joss.02607
30. Ryu, S., Lee, H., Im, D., Choi, J., Lee, H.: Electrophotographic printer identification by halftone texture analysis. In: IEEE International Conference on Acoustics, Speech and Signal Processing, pp. 1846–1849 (2010)
31. Sharif, M., Bhagavatula, S., Bauer, L., Reiter, M.K.: Accessorize to a crime: real and stealthy attacks on state-of-the-art face recognition, pp. 1528–1540. Association for Computing Machinery, New York (2016)
32. Song, D., et al.: Physical adversarial examples for object detectors. In: USENIX Workshop on Offensive Technologies (WOOT 2018). USENIX Association (2018)
33. Tondi, B.: Pixel-domain adversarial examples against cnn-based manipulation detectors. Electron. Lett. **54**, 1220–1222 (2018). https://doi.org/10.1049/el.2018.6469
34. Tsai, M., Hsu, C., Yin, J., Yuadi, I.: Japanese character based printed source identification. In: IEEE International Symposium on Circuits and Systems (ISCAS), pp. 2800–2803 (2015)
35. Tsai, M., Yuadi, M., Tao, Y., Yin, J.: Source identification for printed documents. In: International Conference on Collaboration and Internet Computing (CIC), pp. 54–58 (2017)

36. Tsai, M.J., Yin, J.S., Yuadi, I., Liu, J.: Digital forensics of printed source identification for Chinese characters. Multimedia Tools Appl. **73**(3), 2129–2155 (2014)
37. World Health Organization: A study on public health and socioeconomic impact of substandard and falsified medical products. World Health Organization, Technical report (2017)
38. Wu, H., Kong, X., Shang, S.: A printer forensics method using halftone dot arrangement model. In: IEEE China Summit and International Conference on Signal and Information Processing (ChinaSIP), pp. 861–865 (2015)
39. Zhang, B., Tondi, B., Barni, M.: Adversarial examples for replay attacks against cnn-based face recognition with anti-spoofing capability. Comput. Vision Image Underst. **197–198**, 102988 (2020)

Image Mining: Theory and Applications (IMTA-VIII)

Proceedings of the 8th International Workshop

"Image Mining: Theory and Applications" (IMTA-VIII) (Montreal, Canada, August 21, 2022, within the framework of the 26th International Conference on Pattern Recognition, Montreal, Canada, August 21–25, 2022)

Extended Papers

Current Trends in Automated Image Analysis (the discussing results of the 8th International Workshop "Image Mining: Theory and Applications")

Igor Gurevich[1] ⓘ, Davide Moroni[2] ⓘ, Maria Antonietta Pascali[2] ⓘ, and Vera Yashina[1] ⓘ

[1] Federal Research Center "Computer Science and Control" of the Russian Academy of Sciences, Building 2, 44, Vavilov Str., Moscow 119333, Russian Federation
igourevi@ccas.ru, werayashina@gmail.com

[2] Institute of Information Science and Technologies "A. Faedo", National Research Council of Italy - Research Area of Pisa, I-56124 Pisa National Research Council, Italy
davide.moroni@cnr.it, maria.antonietta.pascali@isti.cnr.it

Abstract. The paper is devoted to discussing of the main scientific results of the 8th International Workshop "Image Mining: Theory and Applications" (August 21, 2022, Montreal, Canada), held within the framework of the 26th International Conference on Pattern Recognition (Montreal, Canada, August 21–25, 2022). The same time it is an introduction to the part of the ICPR-2022 Proceedings including the extended papers based on the talks presented at the IMTA-VIII-2022. It is presented the historical information on this IMTA-series of international workshops, and their significant role in the development of the theory and application of automation of image analysis, pattern recognition, and artificial intelligence is emphasized. The list of the invited and regular papers presented at the IMTA-VIII-2022 is presented as well as the list of the extended papers based on the IMTA-VIII-2022 papers and recommended by the IMTA-VIII-2022 Committee for publishing in The ICPR-2022 Proceedings.

Keywords: IMTA-8-2022 · Image-mining · Image analysis · Mathematical theory of image analysis · Pattern recognition · Artificial intelligence · Automated image analysis · Data mining · Data science · Knowledge engineering · Application problems · Image analysis applications · Pattern recognition applications

1 Introduction

This part of the ICPR-2022 Proceedings is devoted to discussing of the main scientific results of the 8th International Workshop "Image Mining: Theory and Applications" (August 21, 2022, Montreal, Canada), held within the framework of the 26th International Conference on Pattern Recognition (Montreal, Canada, August 21–25, 2022). It includes the extended papers based on the talks presented at the IMTA-VIII-2022. The historical information on this IMTA-series of international workshops is presented, and their significant role in the development of the theory and application of automation of image analysis, pattern recognition, and artificial intelligence is emphasized. The list of the invited and regular papers presented at the IMTA-VIII-2022 is presented as well as the list of the extended papers based on the IMTA-VIII-2022 papers and recommended by the IMTA-VIII-2022 Committee for publishing in the ICPR-2022 Proceedings.

The extended theses of all IMTA-VIII-2022 were published in the Special Issue of the international journal of the Russian Academy of Sciences "Pattern Recognition and Image Analysis: Advances in Mathematical Theory and Applications" (2022, V. 32, No. 3.)

The IMTA-VIII-2022: Proceedings were prepared by the National Committee for Pattern Recognition and Image Analysis of the Russian Academy of Sciences, a collective member of the International Association for Pattern Recognition (IAPR), and by the IAPR Technical Committee No. 16 "Algebraic and Discrete Mathematical Techniques in Pattern Recognition and Image Analysis."

2 Goals and Objectives of IMTA-VIII-2022

The main goal of the IMTA workshop is to provide the integration and joint application of various modern mathematical approaches and methods for image analysis/pattern recognition in accordance with the applied problems to be solved.

This workshop is devoted but not limited to the following subjects:

A. Methodological progress in the field of image analysis and pattern recognition with special emphasis on the following directions:
A.1 Algebra
A.2 Discrete mathematics
A.3 Computational topology
A.4 Machine learning
B. Novel mathematical methods of image mining
B.1 Algebraic approaches

B.2 Image algebras, descriptive image algebras, and lattice algebras

B.3 Lattice-based deep hierarchical representations and neural networks

B.4 Methods of discrete mathematics

B.5 Descriptive image analysis

B.6. Processing and representation of ill-structured data

B.7 Syntactic and structural methods

B.8 Multialgorithmic classifiers and methods for combining the results of individual algorithms

B.9 Pattern recognition methods of knowledge extraction from images

B.10 Other mathematical methods

C. Models, representations, and features of images

C.1 Feature detectors

C.2 Features used in autoencoder networks

C.3 Formalized image models

C.4 Spatial data representation (combinatorial structures of local neighborhoods)

C.5 Dual image representations

D. Automation of intelligent analysis of images and other types of data

D.1 Image analysis and ill-structured data

D.2 Knowledge extraction from images, machine vision, and knowledge-based systems

D.3 Image databases

E. Methods of artificial intelligence in knowledge extraction from images

E.1 Knowledge representation, processing, extracting, and analyzing

E.2 Image knowledge bases

E.3 Linguistic tools for image mining (image ontologies; thesauri of images)

F. Applied image mining problems

F.1 Bioinformatics

F.2 Bioengineering

F.3 Medical applications

F.4 Industry and economics

F.5 Cultural heritage

F.6 Other important complex and interesting applied problems

The basic tasks of IMTA-VIII-2022 are as follows:

1. to provide algebraists, specialists in discrete mathematics, and other mathematically oriented scientists, engineers, researchers, IT specialists in image analysis, pattern recognition, and artificial intelligence with new possibilities to better know and understand each other and to start to communicate on a regular basis;
2. to provide an event for discussing current and promising areas of research and exchanging the latest achievements in algebra, discrete mathematics, and other mathematical methods workable in the field of image analysis and pattern recognition.

IMTA-VIII-2022, just as the previous workshop IMTA-VII-2021, was held within the ICPR (in this case, ICPR-2022) under the auspices of the IAPR.

ICPR is the main scientific event in the field of pattern recognition, image analysis, and applied scientific and technological fields. The methods of intelligent image analysis allow us to extract knowledge and distinguish patterns, which makes it possible to use them in very important applications such as medical diagnostics, precision agriculture, new industries, and many others. Mathematical principles, means and tools are of primary importance for this field of informatics. Actually, mathematical aspects of image analysis, pattern recognition, and, primarily, intelligent image analysis—the leading direction in the modern mathematical theory of image analysis—are the main subjects of interest for IMTA-VIII-2022.

Technological achievements and extended storage capabilities support the emergence of large and detailed, albeit, possibly noisy and damaged, sets of image data. Hence, the subjects of IMTA-VIII-2022 are of primary importance, providing a perfect ground for combining with other new fields, both theoretical and applied.

An example of how the main subject of intelligent image analysis could be profitably combined with other fields such as computational topology, lattice algebra, machine learning, and descriptive image analysis is the emergence of new concepts and trends such as topological features and invariants and their calculation for digital images, representation, and compression of multidimensional images based on topology, learning based on lattices by the images of time series by the intelligent analysis of video images, application of fuzzy lattices in pattern recognition, and many others.

IMTA-VIII-2022 continues the successful series of workshops devoted to new and promising mathematical methods of intelligent image analysis and relevant applications:

- IMTA-I-2008, Funchal, Madeira, Portugal, as part of the 3rd International Conference on the Theory and Applications of Machine Vision (VISAPP 2008);
- IMTA-II-2009, Lisbon, Portugal, within the 4th International Joint Conference on Theory and Applications of Machine Vision, Visualization and Machine Graphics (VISIGRAPP 2009);
- IMTA-III-2010, Anger, France, within the 5th International Joint Conference on Theory and Applications of Machine Vision, Visualization and Machine Graphics (VISIGRAPP 2010);
- IMTA-IV-2013, Barcelona, Spain, within the 8th International Joint Conference on Theory and Applications of Machine Vision, Visualization and Machine Graphics (VISIGRAPP 2013);
- IMTA-V-2015, Berlin, Germany, within the 10th International Joint Conference on Theory and Applications of Machine Vision, Visualization and Machine Graphics (VISIGRAPP 2015);
- IMTA-VI-2018, Montreal, Canada, within the 1st International Conference on Pattern Recognition and Artificial Intelligence (ICPRAI 2018);
- IMTA-VII-2021, Milan, Italy, within the 25th International Conference on Pattern Recognition (ICPR 2020).

3 Scientific Program of the Workshop

The subject of the workshop includes theoretical and applied aspects of a wide class of problems in the following fields:

- extraction, processing, analysis, comparison, clustering, and detection of objects, recognizing and assessing image quality;
- signal recognition, including spectral analysis;
- statistical problems, including development of special metrics;
- studies of the mathematical, including algebraic properties of multimodel image representations;
- methods for constructing, combining, and learning fast multialgorithmic and fuzzy classifiers;
- in-depth study and optimization of convolutional neural networks;
- applied problems of machine vision, artificial intelligence, and machine learning.

The main applied directions of research reported in the workshop are medical problems: histology, machine tomography, ophthalmology, electroencephalogram analysis, laser coagulation, neoplasm detection, diagnostics of neurodegenerative diseases, diagnostics of cardiac diseases, and other automation problems of medical diagnostics, as well as recognition of audiovisual emotions, classification of living natural objects, remote sensing, studies of variability of climate change factors, recognition of texts and symbols, document processing, automation of scientific research, and development of intelligent systems.

Analysis of the scientific contribution of IMTA-VIII-2022 allows us to make the following conclusions:

1. the construction of a unified mathematical theory of image analysis is still under way;
2. the number of contributions devoted to the theoretical aspects of image analysis decreases, which is explained by the commercialization of this direction to the detriment of scientific development; in the future, the organizers of the workshop plan to reduce the number of purely applied presentations and invite authors with theoretical results.
3. problems of artificial intelligence are based on the fundamental results of mathematical theories of pattern recognition, machine leaning, and image analysis;
4. when developing new methods of image analysis and recognition, there is a tendency to expand the mathematical apparatus by involving the areas of mathematics that were not previously used in image analysis (in particular, lattice algebra, Turing machine, and topology);
5. the gap between the capabilities of new mathematical methods of image analysis and recognition, as well as their actual use in solving applied problems, remains significant;
6. there is still an excessive use of neural networks in solving applied problems of image analysis and image recognition, and quite often without proper justification of the solution method and interpretation of the results;

7. technological achievements and extended storage capabilities support the growth of large and detailed, albeit, possibly noisy and damaged, sets of data represented as images;
8. methods of intelligent data analysis allow us to extract valuable knowledge from complex, disaggregated, and ill-structured data, which makes it possible to successfully apply them in quite diverse applied fields: medical diagnostics, robotics, technical diagnostics and nondestructive control, precision agriculture, new computer and information systems for support of industrial and information technologies, remote sensing, anthropogenic and environmental forecasting and monitoring, automation of scientific research, and many others.

The IMTA-VIII-2022 Committee received 44 submissions from 11 countries.

The scientific program of the workshop included 5 invited papers and 23 regular papers of 59 authors from 7 countries. This part of IMTA-VIII-2022 Proceedings includes 19 extended papers.

3.1 The List of Invited Presentations at the IMTA-VIII-2022

1. Viktoriya Evdokimova, Sergey Bibikov, Artem Nikonorov "Meta-Learning Approach in Diffractive Lens Computational Imaging" (Image Processing Systems Institute of the Russian Academy of Sciences – Branch of the Federal Science Research Center "Crystallography and Photonics", Samara, the Russian Federation);
2. Patrizio Frosini "A New Approach to Topological Data Analysis and Geometric Deep Learning through Group Equivariant Non-expansive Operators" (Department of Mathematics, University of Bologna, Bologna, Italy);
3. Igor Gurevich and Vera Yashina "On Modelling of Descriptive Image Analysis Procedures at Specialized Turing Machine" (Federal Research Center "Computer Sciences and Control" of the Russian Academy of Sciences, Moscow, The Russian Federation);
4. Nataly Ilyasova and Nikita Demin "Application of Artificial Intelligence in Ophthalmology for the Diagnosis and Treatment of Eye Diseases" (Samara National Research University, Branch of the Federal Science Research Center "Crystallography and Photonics", Samara, the Russian Federation);
5. Alexander Khvostikov, Andrey Krylov, Ilya Mikhailov and Pavel Malkov "Visualization of whole slide histological images with automatic tissue type recognition" Lomonosov Moscow State University, Moscow, the Russian Federation.

3.2 The List of Contributed Presentations at the IMTA-VIII-2022

1. Nikita Andriyanov «Applying Machine Learning Models to Work with Multimodal Data»
2. Nikita Andriyanov, Vitalii Dementyev and Alexandr Tashlinsky «Optimizing the YOLOv3 Model in the Moving Object Detection»;

3. Viacheslav Antsiperov «Perceptual Compression of Images Based on a System of Receptive Fields»;
4. Antonio Bruno, Massimo Martinelli and Davide Moroni «Exploring Ensembling in Deep Learning»;
5. Vladimir Fursov «Images Recognition with Selection of Informative Subspaces by Conjugacy Criterions»;
6. Alexander Gayer, Daria Ershova and Vladimir Arlazarov «Fast and Accurate Deep Learning Model for Stamps Detection for Embedded Devices»;
7. Igor Gurevich, Vera Yashina and Adil Tleubaev «Research and Development of the Method for Automating the Diagnostic Analysis of Optical Coherent Tomography Angiography Human Fundus Images»;
8. Sathursan Kanagarajah, Thanuja Ambegoda and Ranga Rodrigo «Self Augmenting Task Hallucinal Unified Representation for Generalized Class Incremental Learning";
9. Roopdeep Kaur, Gour Karmakar and Feng Xia «A Reliable Image Quality Assessment Metric: Evaluation using Camera Impacts»;
10. Mikhail Kharinov «An Object in an Image as a Dynamically Structured Pixel Set»;
11. Mikhail Lange and Andrey Lange «Information-Theoretic Lower Bounds to Error Probability for the Models of Noisy Discrete Source Coding and Object Classification»;
12. Liudmila Manilo and Doston Kholmatov «Recognition of congestive heart failure based on a complex correlation measure of the heart rate signal»;
13. Yuanxin Mao, Tianzhuang Zhang, Bo Fu and Dang Ngoc Hoang Thanh «A Self-Attention based WGAN for Single Image Inpainting»;
14. Dmitry Murashov «Application of Combined Quality Measure Based on Information Redundancy and Variation of Information to Image Segmentation»;
15. Evgeny Myasnikov «A Feature Fusion Technique for Dimensionality Reduction»;
16. Andrey Nasonov and Alexandra Nasonova «Linear Blur Parameters Estimation using a Convolutional Neural Network»;
17. Anton Pankratov and Natalia Pankratova «Spectral method for detecting inexact repeats in character sequences»;
18. Vladislav Pyatov and Dmitry Sorokin «Affine Registration of Histological Images Using Transformer-based Feature Matching»;
19. Marco Reggiannini, Oscar Papini and Gabriele Pieri «An automated analysis tool for the classification of Sea Surface Temperature imagery»;
20. Vladimir Ryazanov and Alexander Vinogradov «Multidimensional analogs of image analysis tools in the problems of detecting hidden regularities»;
21. Aleksei Samarin, Alexander Savelev, Aleksei Toropov, Valentin Malykh, Alina Dzestelova, Elena Mikhailova and Alexandr Motyko «One-staged attention-based neoplasms recognition method for single-channel monochrome CT snapshots processing»;
22. Aleksei Samarin, Alexander Savelev, Aleksei Toropov, Alina Dzestelova, Valentin Malykh, Elena Mikhailova and Alexandr Motyko «Trainable agents movement strategies for advertising sign visual descriptors»;

23. Andrey Savchenko and Lyudmila Savchenko «Audio-visual Continuous Recognition of Emotional State in a Multi-user System based on Personalized Representation of Facial Expressions and Voice».

3.3   The List of Extended Papers Based on Presentations at the IMTA-VIII-2022.

The Proceedings includes 16 extended papers:

Invited Papers

1. Igor Gurevich and Vera Yashina "Descriptive Algorithmic Schemes as Image Analysis Machine Programs";
2. Nataly Ilyasova and Nikita Demin "Application of Artificial Intelligence in Ophthalmology for Coagulate Map Formation to Carry out Laser Eye Treatment";
3. Alexander Khvostikov, Andrey Krylov, Ilya Mikhailov and Pavel Malkov "Visualization and analysis of whole slide histological images.

Regular Papers

1. Nikita Andriyanov «Multimodal Data Processing based on Text Classifiers and Image Recognition »
2. Nikita Andriyanov «Optimization of the Computer Vision System for the Detection of Moving Objects»;
3. Viancheslav Antciperov «Neuromorphic Image Coding Based on a Sample of Counts Partition by a System of Receptive Fields»;
4. Antonio Bruno, Massimo Martinelli and Davide Moroni «Revisiting ensembling for improving the performance of deep learning models»;
5. Igor Gurevich, Vera Yashina and Adil Tleubaev «The New Method for Automating the Diagnostic Analysis of Optical Coherent Tomography Angiography Human Fundus Images. Research and Software Kit Realisation»;
6. Vladimir Fursov «Hyperspectral Images Recognition with Selection of Informative Subspaces by Conjugacy Criterions»;
7. Roopdeep Kaur, Gour Karmakar and Feng Xia «Image Quality Assessment Metric fusing Traditional and Dempster-Shafer Theory»;
8. Yuanxin Mao, Tianzhuang Zhang, Bo Fu and Dang Ngoc Hoang Thanh « Single Image Inpainting Method Using Wasserstein Generative Adversarial Networks and Self-Attention»;
9. Dmitry Murashov «Combining Information Measures for Improving Image Segmentation Quality»;
10. Evgeny Myasnikov «A framework for feature fusion with application to hyperspectral images»;

11. Andrey Nasonov and Alexandra Nasonova «Linear Blur Direction Estimation using a Convolutional Neural Network»;
12. Elena Nelyubina, Vladimir Ryazanov and Alexander Vinogradov «Analogs of Image Analysis Tools in the Search of Latent Regularities in Applied Data»;
13. Vladislav Pyatov and Dmitry Sorokin «TAHIR: Transformer-based affine histological image registration»;
14. Marco Reggiannini, Oscar Papini and Gabriele Pieri «Automated image processing for remote sensing data classification»;
15. Aleksei Samarin, Alexander Savelev, Aleksei Toropov, Valentin Malykh, Alina Dzestelova, Elena Mikhailova and Alexandr Motyko «Prior segmentation and attention based approach to neoplasms recognition by single-channel monochrome computer tomography snapshots»;
16. Aleksei Samarin, Alexander Savelev, Aleksei Toropov, Alina Dzestelova, Valentin Malykh, Elena Mikhailova and Alexandr Motyko «The complete study of the movement strategies of trained agents for visual descriptors of advertising signs».

4   Conclusions

There are 2 important remarks concerned with the IMTA-VIII-2022.

It is widely known that image mining, automated image analysis and pattern recognitions are the scientific fields on which the double technologies are based. We are satisfied by the fact that we did not received contributions connected with warfare applications and only a few contributions potentially applicable to human rights violations.

The communication with ICPR-2022 Chairs and Secretariat was not efficient at all. Some requests to them from IMTA-VIII Chairs and participants were ignored or partially satisfied. The questions were mostly related to technical details of ICPR-2022 registration fee payment. Moreover, in the middle of July, 2022, the payment by a bank transfer became impossible without any preliminary notification.

As a result, near a half of IMTA-VIII-2022 contributors were not able to pay a fee and consequently to participate in ICPR-2022 and to submit the extended papers based on their IMTA-VIII-2022 presentations. We hope that this negative experience will be taken into account in the future.

The co-chairmen of IMTA-VIII-2022 would like to thank all the members of the Scientific Committee who helped to peer-review the papers and provided useful comments and remarks that contributed to the success of the workshop.

The National Committee on Pattern Recognition and Image Analysis of the Russian Academy of Sciences and the IAPR TC 16 plan to continue the series of IMTA workshops.

5   Funding

This study was supported in part by the Russian Foundation for Basic Research, project no. 20-07-01031.

Descriptive Algorithmic Schemes as Image Analysis Machine Programs

Igor Gurevich(ID) and Vera Yashina(⊠)(ID)

Federal Research Center "Computer Science and Control" of the Russian Academy of Sciences, Building 2, 44, Vavilov Street, Moscow 119333, Russian Federation
igourevi@ccas.ru, werayashina@gmail.com

Abstract. This article is continued description of an original approach to the definition and description of a Turing machine (TM) for implementing descriptive image analysis methods based on an information structure for generating descriptive algorithmic schemes for automating image analysis. The fundamental problem, to which the subject of the study belongs, is the automation of extracting information from images that is necessary for making intelligent decisions. One of the important and promising areas of research in this problem is the automation of the choice of a method for solving the problem of image analysis. A necessary condition for such automation is a comparative analysis and optimization of the image analysis algorithms, which, in turn, requires estimates of the complexity and efficiency of algorithms and a universal calculator to obtain them. One of the strategic goals for the development of descriptive image analysis is the study of models of image analysis processes. To do this, it is proposed to define and build an "Image Analysis Machine," i.e., TMs specialized for processing spatial information. A method for determining a TM for modeling descriptive algorithmic schemes for image analysis is proposed and described. This machine can also be used to evaluate the mathematical characteristics of image analysis algorithms.

Keywords: image analysis · descriptive image analysis · Turing Machine for Descriptive Image Analysis · mathematical theory of image analysis · image-mining · descriptive algorithmic schemes · mathematical structures · information structures

1 Introduction

The fundamental problem is the automation of the extraction of information from images, which is required to make intelligent decisions. One of the important and promising areas of research in this problem is the automation of the choice of a method for solving the problem of image analysis. A necessary condition for such automation is a comparative analysis and optimization of image analysis algorithms, which, in turn, requires estimates of the complexity and efficiency of algorithms and a universal calculator to obtain them.

As is well known, to automate image analysis, the authors introduced the descriptive analysis (DA) of images, which contains the necessary mathematical and methodological apparatus [5, 7, 9–11].

© Springer Nature Switzerland AG 2023
J.-J. Rousseau and B. Kapralos (Eds.): ICPR 2022 Workshops, LNCS 13644, pp. 375–386, 2023.
https://doi.org/10.1007/978-3-031-37742-6_28

One of the strategic goals of DA development is the study of models of image analysis processes. To do this, it is proposed to define and build an "Image Analysis Machine", i.e., a Turing machine (TM) for the case of processing spatial information, in the generally accepted understanding in mathematical cybernetics of a "machine" as a device that converts information. In this paper, we propose and describe a method for determining a TM for modeling descriptive algorithmic schemes (DASs) for image analysis. This TM can also be used to evaluate the mathematical characteristics of image analysis algorithms.

To regularize the generation of DASs for analysis and image recognition, the authors introduced a mathematical structure [1], so called an information structure for generating a DAS (ISGDAS) for image recognition [10].

We recall the basic concepts and objects of DA, necessary for the definition and construction of TMs for modeling and studying DA procedures: TMDA.

A DA provides for the use of descriptive image algebras (DIAs) [2, 7, 8] to describe a DAS.

This article describes an approach to define and describe a TM [12] for implementing DA imaging methods (TMDA) based on ISGDAS. An example of modeling on a TMDA of information processing procedures implemented on an ISGDAS when solving problems of image analysis is given.

This article consists of an introduction, three sections, a conclusion, and a list of references. Section 2 "Descriptive Image Analysis" describes the basic concepts and objects of DA. Section 3 "TM structure for modeling descriptive image analysis methods" describes the TMDA structure for modeling DAS generation procedures. Section 4 "An example of the realization of a TM for modeling descriptive image analysis methods" presents an example of a TMDA program and its operation during program execution.

2   Descriptive Image Analysis

DA provides the ability to solve both problems related to the construction of formal descriptions of images as recognition objects, and problems of synthesis of recognition procedures and image understanding. The processes of analyzing and evaluating information presented in the form of images (the trajectory of solving the problem) as a whole could be considered as a sequence/combination of transformations and calculations of a set of intermediate and final (determining the solution) estimates. These transformations are defined on the equivalence classes of images and their representations. The latter are defined descriptively, that is, using a basic set of prototypes and corresponding generating transformations that are functionally complete with respect to the equivalence class of permissible transformations. These DA abilities are shown in Fig. 1.

DA provides for the realization of image analysis processes in the image formalization space (IFS) [4], the elements of which are various forms (states, phases) of image representation, which is converted from the original form to a form convenient for recognition (i.e., into a model), and data representation transformation models. The processes of image analysis are considered as sequences of transformations implemented in the phase space and providing the construction of the phase states of the image, which together form the phase trajectory of transferring the image from the original view to the model.

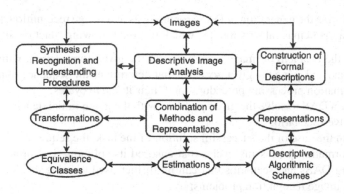

Fig. 1. Descriptive Image Analysis. The Basic Principles

DA considers the set of acceptable representations of images [3, 4, 6] as a set of phase states of an image (original image, image realization, intermediate states of an image, parametric image model, procedural image model, generative image model).

DASs of an image transformation are a key object of DA [9–11].

A DAS is a certain system of transformations applied to the original image that implements mathematical methods for processing, analyzing, and recognizing images, as well as carries out the following tasks:

(a) builds a model or representation of an image that allows the use of classical or spatial recognition algorithms by sequentially transforming the states of the processed image corresponding to the degree of its current formalization;

(b) solves the problem of image recognition by applying recognition algorithms to the model/representation of the image, built in accordance with paragraph (a) of this definition.

It is also assumed that the set of DAS forms a set of "phase states.

The IFS [4] includes states (formal description/representation phases) of an image and a set of states of image transformation schemes (DASs) (see the Fig. 2).

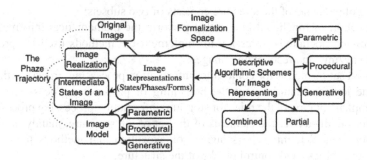

Fig. 2. Image Formalization Space

To regularize the generation of DASs for analysis and image recognition, the authors introduced a mathematical structure [1] which has the following functionality:

(1) solving the problem of image recognition in the given formulation, with the given initial data and using the given scenario that determines the sequence of application of information processing procedures and their iterative cycles;
(2) building a DAS to solve the given problem with the given initial data in the absence of the given scenario;
(3) fixing, in the case of the successful solution of the task, the sequence of procedures and information processing cycles that ensured its solution, determines the corresponding DASs and scenarios that can be further used to solve the corresponding class of image recognition problems;
(4) comparative analysis and optimization of methods for solving image recognition problems by implementing them in the form of DASs and scenarios allowed by the structure.

To determine the structure, relations are specified in which the elements of the set are located (the typical characteristic of the structure) and it is postulated that these relations satisfy the conditions (axioms) of the structure. Since this structure is interpreted in this context as a mathematical model of information processing processes in solving image recognition problems and emulating sequences and combinations of transformations that ensure the implementation of these processes, the introduced structure is functionally interpreted as an information structure for generating a DAS (ISGDAS) for image recognition [10].

The specified ISGDASs are sources of generation of DASs for the recognition of images of an arbitrary type, and these DASs can be set and formed as follows:

a) they can be set by the chosen scenario for solving the image recognition problem; and.
b) they can be formed by determining, selecting, and combining information processing procedures when modeling the processes of solving the recognition problem on an ISGDAS.

The typical characteristic of the introduced ISGDAS is set as follows:

(1) the set of elements of the structure consists of two subsets:
  (a) a subset of functional blocks that perform the mathematical information processing operations necessary to implement the methods used for processing, analyzing, and recognizing images;
  (b) a subset of blocks for controlling information processing processes that check the logical conditions for the branching of processing processes, check the implementation of the rules for stopping information processing processes, etc.;
(2) relations defined over the elements of the set of the structure, mainly partial order relations that determine the sequence of execution and methods for combining functional blocks and control blocks of the structure;
(3) these relations, by definition, must satisfy the axioms of the DA.

DASs constructed in this way can be considered as derivable expressions, which are tree-like figures, including sequences of information processing procedures, sequence branchings, their parallel branches, iterative cycles, and combinations of the indicated modes of implementing information processing procedures when solving problems of image analysis and recognition (see the Fig. 3).

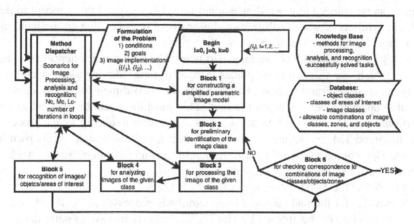

Fig. 3. An Information Structure for Generating Descriptive Algorithmic Schemes

The DAS constructed in this way are convenient for further programming, but they are complex enough for theoretical research. In the Turing machine, the division of the process into simple elementary operations is brought to the limit of possibility. This significantly lengthens the process implemented in the Turing machine, but at the same time the logical structure of the process is greatly simplified and acquires a very convenient standard form for theoretical research.

3   Turing Machine Structure for Modeling Methods of Descriptive Image Analysis

To further describe the specialized TMDA, here are some important remarks about TM.

TM external memory is represented as an unlimited tape on both sides, divided into cells.

By definition, a TM has a finite number of signs (symbols) forming what is called an external alphabet, in which the information supplied to the machine is encoded, as well as those produced in it. Among the signs of the external alphabet there is an empty sign, the entry of which into any memory cell erases the sign that was stored in it and leaves it empty. At any stage of the machine operation, no more than one character can be stored in each cell. The operation of the machine consists of successive cycles, during which the initial information is converted into intermediate ones, and moving along the tape. Moving through the memory tape occurs in two directions: left, right, and you can stay in place.

There are modifications of the external memory of the TMs: multi-storey, multidimensional, multi-tape TMs. Multi-storey TMs contain columns in each cell with a height of n characters and are processed at each clock cycle of the machine in parallel. In fact, this multi-storey TM can be reduced to a single-storey one by programming a parallel composition of several TM. The corresponding theorems are proved [13]. Without limiting generality, if there is not one symbol on each floor, but a vector whose elements are processed independently of each other, then using a parallel composition, such a machine can be reduced to a one-dimensional one. Let's expand this concept to define a TM, the symbols of which will be two-dimensional matrices that are realizations of some image describing a real scene.

To build a specialized TM, we may also need TM with multidimensional external memory, which use n-dimensional planes instead of tape. Moving along such a plane already occurs in several directions. For example, in a two-dimensional TM, movement is possible up, down, left, right, on the spot. This machine could be reduced to a one-dimensional too. This TM configuration seems convenient to use for image processing.

A multitape TM, by definition, contains k tapes, each of which has its own head ($k \in N$). This configuration of the Turing machine is a convenient way to work with different types of information at one time.

Let us define the TMDA structure.

DA provides for the realization of image analysis processes in the IFS. Let us designate all elements of the IFS as Σ. The set Σ consists of two subsets: (a) Σ_I is a subset of image representations [3, 4, 6], which is converted from its original form into a form convenient for recognition (i.e., into a model) and (b) Σ_A is a subset of data representation transformation models [9–11].

The structure of the TMDA will be described in alphabetical order Σ.

A single-tape TM, by definition, consists of two parts: a tape and an automaton:

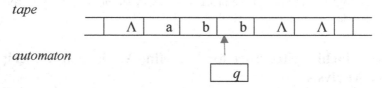

A TMDA contains two tapes: (a) a tape responsible for the current representations of images and (b) a tape responsible for the transformation models of data representations.

The tape is used to store information. It is infinite in both directions and is divided into cells that are not numbered or named in any way. Each cell can contain one character from some given alphabet Σ or nothing is recorded. The contents of the cell can change: another character can be written into it or the character in it can be erased.

We will consider the empty contents of a cell as *empty* and denote them by the sign Λ (lambda).

The automaton is the active part of the TM. At each moment, it is placed under one of the cells of the tape and "sees" its contents; this is a visible cell, and the character in it is a visible character; and the content of neighboring and other cells is not currently visible to the machine. At each moment, the automaton is in one of the states, which will be denoted by symbol q with numbers q_1, q_2, etc.; and Q is the set of all TM states.

Being in a certain state, the automaton performs some operation (for example, it moves to the right along the tape, replacing all symbols b by a); when it is in a different state, it performs another operation.

A pair of the visible character, $S: S \in \Sigma$, , and the current state of automaton (q) will be called a configuration and denoted by $<S, q>$. The configuration of the k-tape TM will be written as $<\{S_i\}_1^k, q>$, where $\{S_i\}_1^k$ is the set of visible symbols on each TM tape in state q.

The TM's operation process is divided into cycles that are performed sequentially. In each cycle, the TM's automaton performs the following three actions; moreover, it has to do so in the order specified below:

(1) it writes some character S' in a visible cell (in particular, the same character can be written as was in it; then the contents of this cell do not change);
(2) it shifts 1 cell to the left (notation: L, left), 1 cell to the right (notation: R, right), or remains motionless (notation: N);
(3) it goes into some state q' (in particular, it may remain in the same state).

Formally, the actions of one cycle will be written as a triple: S', $[L, R, N]$, q', where the set of characters in square brackets means that any of the characters L, R, or N can be written in this place.

A TM works under the control of some program, which is written in the form of a table of the following form:

(a) the names of the rows of the table list all the states in which the automaton can be found;
(b) the column names of the table list all the characters (including Λ) that the machine can see on the tape;
(c) the cells of the table indicate the cycles that the machine must perform when it is in the appropriate state and sees the corresponding symbol on the tape.

In general, the table determines the actions of the TM for all possible configurations and thus completely defines the behavior of the TM. Describing an algorithm in the form of a TM means constructing a table of the specified form.

Let us introduce the concept of a stop cycle. This is a cycle that does not change anything: the automaton writes the same symbol into the visible cell as was in it, does not move, and remains in the same state. Once entering the stop cycle, the TM, by definition, stops, completing its work.

Note that the same algorithm (TM program) can be applicable to some input words (i.e., stop) and inapplicable to others (i.e., loop). Thus, the applicability/inapplicability of the algorithm depends not only on the algorithm itself but also on the input word.

4   An Example of the Realization of a Turing Machine for Modeling Methods of Descriptive Image Analysis

We will assume that, when we start to solve the problem of image recognition, we have the following information [10]:

1. a problem statement, i.e., the goal and the requirements for the solution, as well as the conditions and limitations of the problem;

2. a database (DB) containing contextual information about classes of images/objects/areas of interest for the subject area of the task; and
3. a knowledge base (KB) containing the following information:

   - (a) information about the methods of processing, analyzing, and recognizing images;
   - (b) an archive of successfully solved problems (statements, conditions, restrictions, initial data, and a DAS providing their solution).

The image recognition problem $\Im_1$, $\Im_2$ contains the following information:

1. problem statement, including the purpose of processing, analyzing, and recognizing images in this problem;
2. conditions of the problem:

   - (a) forbidden and impossible order relations, partial order relations, and other conditions and restrictions that reflect the physical and logical organization of the real world—additional information about the original images $\left\{ \tilde{B}_1, \tilde{B}_2, \ldots \right\}$, where $\left\{ \tilde{B}_i \right\} \subseteq \{B_i\}$ for all $i = 1,2,\ldots$;
   - (b) requirements concerning the results of the solution;
   - (c) restrictions on the use of resources necessary to solve the problem (computational and time complexity); and
   - (d) recommendations on the application of the solution methods;
3. realization of the original images $\{I_1\}$, $\{I_2\}$,...

The proposed method for determining the TMDA will be illustrated by the example of modeling on the TM the information processing processes implemented in the ISGDAS when generating the DAS.

A block diagram of the ISGDAS, which represents the logical organization and the main components of the generating structure and the relationships specified on them—the information links that provide the construction of an image recognition DAS, is shown in Fig. 3. The main blocks and information links of the ISGDAS are described in [10].

Let us define a TMDA that simulates the operation of the ISGDAS.

As mentioned earlier, the functioning of the TMDA is determined by a program written in the form of a table. Accordingly, the task of the functional modes of operation of the TMDA begins with the compilation of its program, which provides the desired solution, taking into account the introduced assumptions.

When compiling the program, the following assumptions are introduced:

1. let some algebra, DIA1, describe the set of transformations of realizations into simplified parametric models; then, in general terms, in a table representing the TMDA program, the application of the algorithm to realizations can be described as the application of DIA1 to the initial data;
2. let some algebra, DIA2, describe a set of image classifiers according to their parametric models of the given type; then the application of the algorithm (image classifiers)

from tape 2 will be in the table representing the TMDA program, recorded as the application of DIA2 to the preliminary parametric model of the original image;
3. let some algebra, DIA3, describe the set of transformations of applying image processing algorithms to image realizations; then, in general terms, in a table representing the TMDA program, the application of image processing algorithm can be described as the application of DIA3 to the image realization.

Before starting the TMDA, we should configure it.

In this case, for each image supplied to the input $\Im_t$, $t = 1,2,...$, the following actions need to be taken:

1. write the original realization(s) of the image $\{I_t\}$ in the first cell on tape 1 containing the image representations;
2. write the selected image processing, analysis, and recognition algorithms A_1, A_2,... on tape 2, containing the image transformation models;
3. set the machine to state q_1 (indicated first in the table) and place it under the first character of the input word (original image realizations); if the input word is empty, then the automaton can look at any cell, because they are all empty.

Let us write out the first 3 cycles of the execution of the TMDA program.

Step 1. Construction of a simplified parametric model of the original image [6] *(Block 1, Fig. 3).*

(a) the TMDA's head is located on tape 1 under the cell with the original image realizations; this data is written to the RAM;
(b) the head moves to the empty cell of tape 1 to the right;
(c) the TMDA refers to tape 2 and finds on it an algorithm that allows the input of the realization(s) of the image, and outputs a simplified parametric model at the output;
(d) the result of applying the selected algorithm to the realization(s) of the original image is recorded in the cell on tape 1 $DIA1\{I_t\} = M_{P1}(\{I_t\})$;
(e) The TMDA enters the state q_2.

Step 2 Preliminary determination of the class of the original image according to the parametric model built in step 1 (block 2, Fig. 3).

(a) the automaton is located on tape 1 under the cell containing the description of the simplified parametric model of the original image $M_{P1}(\{I_t\})$; this data is written to the RAM;
(b) the head moves to the empty cell of tape 1 to the right;
(c) the TMDA accesses tape 2 and finds an algorithm on it that allows a simplified parametric image model at the input and outputs a preliminary class identifier to which the original image belongs;
(d) the result of applying the selected algorithm (image classifier) to the parametric model is recorded in the cell on tape 1 as $DIA2(M_{P1}(\{I_t\})) = class$;
(e) The TMDA enters state q_3.

Step 3 Image processing in accordance with a predefined class of the original image (block 3, Fig. 3).

(a) the automaton is located on tape 1 under the cell containing the identifier of a predefined image class; this data is written to the RAM;

(b) the TMDA moves the head on tape 2 to a cell containing an image processing algorithm according to a predetermined class of the original image (i.e., finds an algorithm corresponding to the class);

(c) the automaton moves along tape 1 to the left to the cell containing the realization(s) of the original image; this data is written to the RAM;

(d) the TMDA enters the state q_4;

(e) the head is shifted to an empty cell to the right;

(f) the TMDA refers to tape 2 to the previously selected image processing algorithm applied to the realization of the original image recorded in the RAM;

(g) the result of applying the image processing algorithm from tape 2 to the realization(s) of the original image is recorded in a cell on tape 1 as $DIA3(\{I_t\} = M_{T1}(I_t))$;

(h) the TM goes into state q_5.

Table 1 presents the TMDA program for the first 3 steps of generating a DAS using the ISGDAS.

Table 1. Initial states of the TMDA program.

States	Σ_I is a subset of representations of an image that is converted from its original form into a form convenient for recognition (i.e., into a model): alphabet of tape 1				
	$\{I_t\}$	$M_{P1}(\{I_t\})$	class	$M_{T1}(I_t)$	Λ
q_1	$\{I_t\},R,q_1$	-	–	–	$DIA1\{I_t\},N,q_2$
q_2		$M_{P1}(\{I_t\}), R, q_2$			$DIA2(M_{P1}(\{I_t\}), N, q_3$
q_3	$\{I_t\},R,q_4$	$M_{P1}(\{I_t\}), L, q_3$	$class,L,q_3$		
q_4		$M_{P1}(\{I_t\}), R, q_4$	$class,R,q_4$		$DIA3(\{I_t\},N,q_5$
States	Σ_A is a subset of data representation transformation models: alphabet of tape 2				
	$A_{one} \in DIA1$	$A_2 \in DIA2$	$A_3 \in DIA3$	–	Λ
q_1	A_1,R,q_1	-	-	–	-
q_2	–	A_2, R, q_2	–	–	-
q_3	–	–	A_3,N,q_3		–
q_4	–	–	A_3,R,q_4		–

Note that when building new TM, it is advisable to use previously built programs as separate pieces. To build a complete MFA, it is required, firstly, to accumulate the built programs, and secondly, to develop methods for constructing more complex programs from the existing library of already built ones. The general view of the description of 3 cycles of the execution of the TMDA program, associated with the use of DIA and the assignment of algorithms using another TM tape, opens up opportunities for generalization and unification of individual MTDA programs

5 Conclusions

The fundamental importance of the results of these studies for the development of the mathematical theory of image analysis and their scientific novelty are related to the formulation of problems and the development of methods for modeling the processes of automating image analysis when using poorly formalized image representations as the initial data, including their spatial data: images and their fragments, image models, incompletely formalized representations, and subsets of combinations of these representations.

The idea to use a TM for modeling and studying the complexity of DA algorithmic procedures belongs to the authors of this study and, to the best of their knowledge, has not been discussed in the modern literature on image analysis.

The given example testifies to the productivity of the method for determining the TMDA proposed by the authors, in connection with which the authors plan to continue research in this direction.

The requirements for the TM under construction were formulated in the Fig. 4.

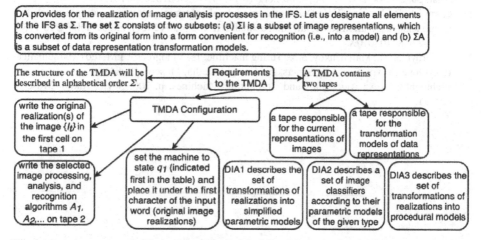

Fig. 4. Requirements to the Turing Machine for Modeling Methods of Descriptive Image Analysis

Funding. This study was partially supported by the Russian Foundation for Basic Research (grant no. 20-07-01031).

References

1. Alekseevskii, D.V.: Structure. In: Vinogradov, I.M. (ed.) Mathematical Encyclopedia, vol. 5. Sovetskaya Entsyklopedia, Moscow, p. 249 (1984)
2. Gurevich, B., Yashina, V.V.: Descriptive image algebras with one ring. Pattern Recognit. Image Anal. **13**, 579–599 (2003)
3. Gurevich, B., Yashina, V.V.: Descriptive approach to image analysis: image models. Pattern Recognit. Image Anal. **18**, 518–541 (2008). https://doi.org/10.1134/S1054661808040020

4. Gurevich, B., Yashina, V.V.: Descriptive approach to image analysis: image formalization space. Pattern Recognit. Image Anal. **22**, 495–518 (2012). https://doi.org/10.1134/S10546 61812040050
5. Gurevich, B., Yashina, V.V.: Descriptive image analysis: genesis and current trends. Pattern Recognit. Image Anal. **27**, 653–674 (2017). https://doi.org/10.1134/S1054661817040071
6. Gurevich, B., Yashina, V.V.: Descriptive image analysis: Part II. Descriptive image models. Pattern Recognit. Image Anal. **29**, 598–612 (2019). https://doi.org/10.1134/S10546618190 40035
7. Gurevich, B., Yashina, V.V.: Descriptive image analysis. foundations and descriptive image algebras. Int. J. Pattern Recognit. Artif. Intell. **33**, 1940018 (2019). https://doi.org/10.1142/ S0218001419400184
8. Gurevich, B., Yashina, V.V.: Algebraic interpretation of image analysis operations. Pattern Recognit. Image Anal. **29**, 389–403 (2019). https://doi.org/10.1134/S105466181903009X
9. Gurevich, B., Yashina, V.V.: Descriptive image analysis: III. Multilevel model for algorithms and initial data combining in pattern recognition. Pattern Recognit. Image Anal. **30**, 328–341 (2020). https://doi.org/10.1134/S1054661820030086
10. Gurevich, B., Yashina, V.V.: Descriptive image analysis: Part IV. Information structure for generating descriptive algorithmic schemes for image recognition. Pattern Recognit. Image Anal. **30**, 649–665 (2020). https://doi.org/10.1134/S1054661820040161
11. Gurevich, B., Yashina, V.V.: Descriptive models of information transformation processes in image analysis. Pattern Recognit. Image Anal. **31**, 402–420 (2021). https://doi.org/10.1134/ S105466182103010X
12. Nagornyi, N.M., Marchenkov, S.S.: Turing machine. In: Vinogradov, I.M. (ed) Mathematical Encyclopedia, vol. 5, p. 456. Sovetskaya Entsyklopedia, Moscow (1984)
13. Trahtenbrot, B.A.: Algorithms and Computing Machines, p. 200. Soviet Radio, Moscow (1974)

Application of Artificial Intelligence in Ophthalmology for Coagulate Map Formation to Carry Out Laser Eye Treatment

Nataly Ilyasova[1,2]([⊠]) [iD] and Nikita Demin[1,2] [iD]

[1] Image Processing Systems Institute of the RAS - Branch of the FSRC "Crystallography and Photonics" RAS, Molodogvardeyskay, 151, 443001 Samara, Russia
ilyasova.nata@gmail.com

[2] Samara National Research University, Moskovskoye Shosse, 34, 443086 Samara, Russia

Abstract. In this paper, we present the main points of artificial intelligence application in ophthalmology for coagulate map formation to carry out laser eye treatment on the example of developing a computer system for personalizing retinal laser photocoagulation. Approaches to the automation of eye disease prediction and treatment based on fundus images are described. The problems of applying the neural network approach are highlighted. Decision support information technology for personalizing laser treatment of diabetic macular edema and identifying prognostic factors of surgical outcome using methods of intellectual analysis of large unstructured data is described. The system allows the doctor to form a plan of optimal coagulation arrangement for retinal laser coagulation for each case, to predict the quality of laser coagulation depending on the initial data on the localization and severity of edema and to improve his skills by comparing the result of coagulation performed and the coagulation plan proposed by the system.

Keywords: Fundus · Laser Coagulation · Diabetic Retinopathy · Image Processing · Segmentation · Artificial Intelligence

1 Introduction

Recently the introduction of artificial intelligence and digital medicine technologies into healthcare practice is rapidly changing the methods of diagnosis and treatment [1, 2]. Increasingly, robotic systems are being used to support the diagnosis and treatment of diseases [3]. According to the Forecast of Scientific and Technological Development of the Russian Federation for the period until 2030, the promising areas of scientific research include the design of intelligent systems to support medical decisions, as well as the provision of services for the analysis of medical data. Ophthalmology is in dire need of a transition to personalized medicine, which would make it possible to make a qualitative leap in the treatment of eye diseases [4]. However, this transition is impossible without the development and implementation of fundamentally new intelligent methods for analyzing patients' biomedical data.

© Springer Nature Switzerland AG 2023
J.-J. Rousseau and B. Kapralos (Eds.): ICPR 2022 Workshops, LNCS 13644, pp. 387–402, 2023.
https://doi.org/10.1007/978-3-031-37742-6_29

Diabetic retinopathy (DR) is often found in diabetes patients, triggering severe complications [5–7]. If timely treatment, vision loss can be prevented in more than 50% of cases [8–12]. A key instrument for treatment of diabetic retinitis is laser photocoagulation, in which a series of well-measured photocoagulates are inflicted on retina areas with pathology [13–16]. Modern systems mainly rely on the use of a preset pattern for generating a photocoagulation map [14–16]. Due to highly variable shapes of the macular edema and vascular system, a uniform photocoagulation map cannot be realized using a standard pattern [14, 15]. However, the ophthalmologist first needs to analyze the retina and eye fundus condition to ensure that the photocoagulates be inflicted in admissible areas. On the one hand, this method provides a more effective laser photocoagulation given a correctly mapped pattern, but on the other hand, it takes the surgeon an extra time to analyze the retina condition.

The aim of the research is to increase the efficiency of retinal laser coagulation by developing information technology that allows implementing a personalized approach to the treatment of diabetic macular edema (DME). To do it, a new technique for applying coagulates was used, which takes into account the various properties of the coagulates totality location. The method of preliminary planning of the coagulates location takes into account the individual features of the anatomical structures location in the area of edema and its shape. To obtain optimal results of laser treatment of DME, a method was used with personalized placement of coagulates at equal distances from each other, taking into account the individual characteristics of anatomical structures and edema boundaries in a particular patient.

2 Methods for Automated Decision Making in the Treatment of Diabetic Retinopathy

Our research focuses on the development of decision automation techniques for the treatment of diabetic retinopathy based on the intelligent analysis of large amounts of unstructured data, including digital biomedical images. Through collaboration with various experts in medical institutions, we are developing new digital technologies for the diagnosis and treatment of eye diseases. On the basis of Samara University, IPSI RAS - a branch of the FSRC "Crystallography and Photonics" RAS and Samara State Medical University, as well as the Ophthalmology Hospital named after Eroshevsky, we are working on the development of new technologies for the diagnosis and treatment of eye diseases. The research is carried out jointly to identify effective ways to diagnose and treat eye diseases. Through collaboration with physicians, work is being done to collect and interpret patient data, for which effective digital methods for diagnosing diseases and supporting decision-making in the treatment process are subsequently determined. Since 2017, research has begun on the treatment of diabetic macular edema using digital image processing, machine learning, and mathematical modeling of biophysical processes.

Diabetes mellitus is recognized as one of the global medical and social problems of modern society. Among its most severe and widespread complications is diabetic retinopathy. This disease has become one of the main causes of visual impairment up to irreversible blindness. As mentioned above, one of the effective treatments for diabetic retinopathy is focal laser surgery - applying multiple dosed microscopic burns (coagulates) in the area of macular edema caused by lesions of the small blood vessels of the retina. The efficiency of this procedure depends on the experience and qualification of the particular ophthalmic surgeon and the accuracy of the placement of the coagulants. In preparation for surgery, the specialist combines data from optical coherence tomography (OCT) and the patient's fundus and uses it to develop a plan for laser photocoagulation of the affected regions of the retina. However, manual placement is not always optimal and accurate enough. Standard templates are used for planning which do not correspond to a variety of edema forms and vessel locations. Uneven placement of cauterization points either creates a risk of increased trauma in areas of excessive coagulation or reduces the effectiveness of treatment in areas where exposure was insufficient. In addition, it takes a long time to plan such an operation.

The use of artificial intelligence makes it possible to accurately segment the retina of a particular patient, ensure uniform planning of coagulates exclusively in the area of the affected area of the eye, and most importantly, dose the power of laser exposure for each cauterization point. Doctors estimate that this will result in a nine-fold decrease in the probability of laser burns beyond the borders of the edema, shorten the time needed to prepare the patient for surgery, and reduce the risk of postoperative complications.

Only one facility in the world uses digital techniques to support laser photocoagulation, the NAVILAS facility [17, 19–22]. We are developing a more advanced technology that will help physicians plan retinal surgeries to prevent blindness in diabetic patients. According to the chief physician of the Samara Regional Clinical Ophthalmologic Hospital named after Eroshevsky Andrei Zolotarev, no laser in the world today is capable of analyzing video data in such a mode, so the doctors suggested creating an intelligent laser coagulation support system that would significantly improve the effectiveness of diabetic macular edema treatment and prevent severe complications after treatment, and, most importantly, that would also individually dose the laser power.

Currently, we are conducting research on semantic segmentation of fundus images to highlight anatomical and pathological zones, separation of retinal layers on optical coherence tomography (OCT) images, mathematical modeling of laser exposure, and developing methods of automatic formation of an effective laser coagulation plan to improve the effectiveness of treatment of diabetic retinopathy.

To solve the problem of semantic segmentation of fundus images we investigated and compared 2 approaches: neural network and texture analysis. The first approach is based on machine learning of deep neural networks to improve the accuracy of detection of pathological and anatomical structures in the edema area.

Recently, most of the data mining tasks are solved by neural network algorithms. The emergence of neural networks has revolutionized image processing tasks. In biomedicine, neural networks have found their frequent application in solving semantic segmentation problems, e.g., to determine the area of lung lesions of the SARS-CoV-2 virus [23], to find human brain tumors, etc. [24].

3 Problems of Applying a Neural Network Approach to the Task of Automating the Analysis of Fundus Images

The application of the neural network approach for solving the problem of semantic segmentation of ocular fundus images is due to a number of reasons. Neural network algorithms have a good generalizing ability; are more accurate (surpassed any other approaches) in many tasks of data mining; are able to take into account the whole context of the image [25]. However, their applicability is limited by the characteristics of the training dataset.

It was found that the application of neural networks in biomedicine involves a number of problems specific to this field.

1. More often than not, due to privacy policies and the laborious nature of the markup procedure, which requires a highly skilled professional, it is extremely difficult to create a sufficiently large set of data of the required quality [26]. The impact of the problem of insufficient data volume can be mitigated through the use of various data augmentation techniques [27]. For example, in tasks related to the processing of biomedical images, especially effective is elastic augmentation [28] of data: random angle rotation, reflections, elastic deformation.
2. Another problem peculiar to biomedical data is the problem of pronounced class imbalance, which is a distinctive feature of our data [29]. The solution of the problem, in the case when a set of classes turn out to be unbalanced, is non-trivial, however, there are algorithms that level this problem [30, 31]. The sample contains classes that do not occur in almost all retinal images, and the relative power of these classes is extremely low. This peculiarity should be taken into account when developing a neural network-based segmentation algorithm. The solution of the problem when many classes are unbalanced is non-trivial, but there are algorithms that neutralize this problem [18].
3. The most complex problem is the poor quality of data labeling [32], which is the most difficult to identify and eliminate at the training stage of the algorithm.

During the development of the intelligent system we solved the following tasks:

1. The applicability of different neural networks for solving the problem of semantic segmentation of eye fundus images was investigated.
2. Factors that must be taken into account to obtain a qualitative segmentation of fundus images were determined.
3. The optimal neural network architecture and hyperparameters were determined.
4. The peculiarities of the data set to be taken into account when developing neural network algorithms were identified.

The peculiarities of our problem are the fact that the original data are unbalanced, the number of images is small, and the labelling does not exactly match the actual location of the objects.

There are a number of works devoted to solving this problem, however, they are mostly highly specialized and consider only the segmentation of images into one class, for example, the class of blood vessels [33] or exudates [34]. In the same paper, the problem of segmentation of fundus images into several classes is considered, which is relevant for creating a decision support technology for a doctor in the diagnosis and treatment of diabetic macular edema [35].

Therefore, for the application of neural network algorithms, the first priority is to prepare the data and level out the problems of unbalanced data and small sample size. The combined use of different data augmentation techniques allowed us to significantly expand the set of available images, bringing the number of images to more than 6000. The images were divided into three sets: training, test, and validation in the ratio of 80%, 10%, and 10%, respectively.

During the research several different neural network architectures were adapted for the task of semantic segmentation [36]. As a result, such architectures as U-NetMobileNetV2, U-NetResNet, U-NetXception were developed and investigated, using pre-trained MobileNetV2, ResNet and Xception networks as a feature extractor, respectively. The average value of the Dice coefficient that was achieved during the experiments was found to be 0.5542. This value was obtained using the U-NetXception architecture, with the error function - FocalLoss with gamma parameter $= 2$. In this research U-Net and ResNet were combined, thus a new architecture for semantic segmentation tasks - U-NetResNet - was obtained. Its advantage over U-Net is that there are weights for ResNet in free access, so we could engage in transfer learning. The decoder structure on U-NetResNet is a mirror image of the encoder. Significant influence on the result had the data balancing algorithm and use of optimization routines, which allowed the neural network based on U-NetXception architecture significantly outperformed the others. In this experiment, class balancing was performed using oversampling and undersampling techniques to obtain a higher frequency of rare classes. The weights of the pre-trained networks were used to initialize the encoder and were fixed for the training time. Neural networks were constructed and trained using the TensorFlow library. The use of pre-trained encoders allows the training of neural networks much faster.

4 Texture Analysis of Fundus Images

The second approach we use to solve the problem of segmentation of fundus images is texture analysis. This is one of the classical methods based on the use of texture features. Studies in which texture features are used for image segmentation are still relevant. Segmentation of images using texture features is performed in several steps [37]:

1. Image fragmentation. The stage at which the image is divided into square areas, for example 12 × 12 pixels.
2. Calculation of texture features for each fragment. At this stage, textural features are calculated for each fragment, for example, using the Mazda software [38]. This stage is the longest, so the calculation of a small set of a couples of tens of features for one image of 1024 × 1024 pixels size can take several hours when using calculations on the central processor of a modern multi-core computer.

3. Classification of fragments based on the calculated values of texture features. At this stage the classification of one pixel of an image fragment by a vector of calculated. Most often, the classifier is built using the decision trees algorithm.

Texture features are well studied and successfully applied to a variety of tasks [37, 39]. However, their use is time-consuming, which makes their implementation in medical practice difficult. In addition, texture features have insufficient generalizability to solve complex problems.

5   A Comparative Study of Different Semantic Segmentation Approaches

For the experiment, we used a dataset consisting of 115 fundus images, which were labeled into 8 classes: optic disk (OD), macula (M), blood vessels (BV), hard exudates (HE), soft exudates (SE), new coagulates (NC), pigmented coagulates (PC), hemorrhage (H). Texture features were also calculated for these images.

When examining this set of images, it was found that the classes of new and pigmented coagulates are rare and are present in less than 10% of the images. Also, a rare class is the class of soft exudates, it is present only in 37% of images. The presence of three rare classes indicates the problem of imbalance in the original data set. The impact of this problem was leveled by using a data balancing algorithm that takes into account the imbalance of many classes [18, 40].

This algorithm does not increase the original data set, but only changes the frequency of selecting images containing a particular class.

The proposed method neither focuses on the feature space for new data generation nor uses undersampling. It performs balancing on a data level via oversampling in a way that increases frequencies of minor classes. In this context, the frequency of a class means the percentage of data samples containing that class. This method allows a better class distribution (frequencies) to be created without making a large number of duplicates or losing any of the data. This makes the proposed method superior in cases where there are little data or if relying on the feature space is impossible, as in the case of images. In the multi-label setting, data imbalance is expressed as some of the labels being significantly more frequent than others. An ideal case would be when all labels have frequencies close to one. The proposed method balances the data, making it as close to the ideal case as possible while keeping the number of duplicates to an acceptable minimum. The proposed method minimizes an objective function that measures the discrepancy of initial class frequencies in the dataset compared to the de-sired ones. Minimization is performed by finding a global minimum in which all partial derivatives with respect to the balancing coefficients are equal to zero.

The problem of a small amount of data was leveled by the use of augmentation: rotation by a random angle, reflections, elastic deformation. As a result of the augmentation, the original data set was expanded 30 times. In addition, a number of errors in data markup were identified.

Neural networks built and trained using the TensorFlow library [41]. The use of pre-trained encoders allows you to train neural networks much faster. The following parameters were used in training:

- Input Size: 1024 × 1024 × 3.
- Number of epochs: 12.
- Loss function: *FocalLoss* [42].
- Optimizer: *Adam* [43].
- Learning rate: 0.003.

Using the full set of texture features for image segmentation is inefficient, so we made a selection of features according to the individual criterion of informativeness of the discriminant analysis [44]. The selection of features according to this criterion is a classical way to find informative features. The choice of this method of feature selection is also due to the properties of the discriminant analysis. Its criteria allow to choose such features that best partition the space of objects. The following metrics have been used to estimate the quality of image segmentation: *precision, recall, f1-score*. The reliability of the results of the experiment was ensured by the use of *k-fold* cross-validation [45]. For neural networks the data set was divided into three parts (k = 3), and for texture features into five (k = 5). The metric values obtained for all parts were averaged.

Table 1 presents the results of the experiment. The TF (Textural features) line corresponds to the results obtained using textural features.

Table 1. Experiment results.

		OD	M	BV	HE	SE	NC	PC	H	avg	w. avg
Precision	Dense-Net	**0.66**	0.53	0.25	0.41	0.33	**0.53**	0.23	0.33	0.41	0.42
	ResNet	0.66	**0.56**	0.26	0.4	**0.72**	0.4	**0.37**	0.37	**0.47**	**0.48**
	Xception	0.6	0.51	**0.27**	0.5	0.54	0.43	0.27	0.33	0.43	0.44
	TF	0.5	0.45	0.52	**0.89**	0	0	0	**0.39**	0.34	0.33
Recall	Dense-Net	0.94	0.81	**0.92**	**0.82**	**0.56**	0.06	0.37	0.85	**0.67**	0.63
	ResNet	0.94	0.81	**0.92**	**0.82**	0.2	0.05	0.28	0.78	0.6	0.56
	Xception	**0.97**	**0.87**	**0.92**	0.71	0.52	**0.13**	**0.4**	**0.83**	**0.67**	**0.64**
	TF	0.79	0.26	0.57	0.59	0	0	0	0.42	0.33	0.31
F1-score	Dense-Net	**0.78**	0.63	0.4	0.54	0.38	0.11	**0.28**	0.47	0.45	0.45
	ResNet	0.77	**0.65**	0.41	0.53	0.27	0.07	0.26	**0.5**	0.43	0.43
	Xception	0.73	0.64	0.41	0.55	**0.48**	**0.15**	**0.28**	0.46	**0.46**	**0.46**
	TF	0.61	0.33	**0.55**	**0.71**	0	0	0	0.41	0.33	0.31

So, according to the precision metric, it is clear that neural networks are superior to textural features in most classes. However, according to precision, textural features are able to separate classes of blood vessels and solid exudates from others better than neural networks. According to the recall metric, neural networks are more sensitive, which may indicate a better generalization ability of neural networks. It is also most likely that neural networks are able to find objects that were skipped during the markup process. The f-score metric shows result similar to the precision metric.

From the analysis of the research results, it was found that neural networks are superior to texture-based features in accuracy (Fig. 1). This fact can be explained by the better generalizing ability of neural networks and their resistance to various fundus shooting conditions. Also, as a result of the experiment, it was noticed that the segmentation of one image, on the CPU, by a neural network takes about a few seconds. In turn, image segmentation using texture features takes much more time (more than an hour).

Moreover, neural networks can be applied for segmentation of fundus images that were obtained under different imaging conditions, in contrast to texture features. The use of pre-trained neural networks and their post-training on a small dataset together with the use of a balancing algorithm and augmentation techniques, allowed to develop sufficiently accurate algorithms for semantic segmentation of fundus images on a small dataset. The fundus image segmentation algorithm based on the use of a neural network with U-NetXception architecture can be used in decision support systems for diagnosticians when they need to work in real time through the use of a user-level graphics card.

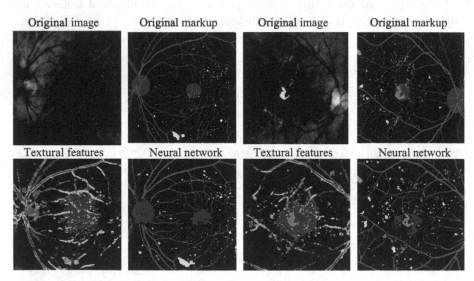

Fig. 1. Examples of fundus image segmentation, obtained as a result of the experiment.

All approaches presented above solve the problem of high-precision recognition of pathological and anatomical structures of the fundus in order to form laser exposure zones and personalized plan of optimal coagulation location in the DME area. This will increase the quality of laser treatment and objective assessment of the volume and localization of pathological structures, allowing predicting treatment results and timely changing the tactics of diabetic retinopathy treatment. Below is a general scheme of technology of coagulation plan formation using the developed methods of fundus images segmentation and coagulation placement (Fig. 2).

6 Technology of Mapping a Photocoagulation Plan of Laser Coagulation

The technology includes original solutions to establish an optimal localization of multitude burns by determining zones exposed to the laser. It also includes the recognition of a large amount of unstructured data on the anatomical and pathological locations' structures in the area of edema and OCT. As a result, a uniform laser application on the pigment epithelium of the affected retina will be ensured. It will increase the treatment safety and its effectiveness.

We offer technology, which is software that takes patient data as input and generates a treatment plan as output. The Diabetic Retinopathy Treatment Plan is used in combination with a laser machine to treat diabetic retinopathy.

The technology is aimed at mapping an effective photocoagulation pattern. The ophthalmologist will be able to correct the processing result for any block in the diagram. For instance, the ophthalmological surgeon can correct the outline of the ROIs for laser treatment if in their opinion the ROIs have not all been automatically marked off.

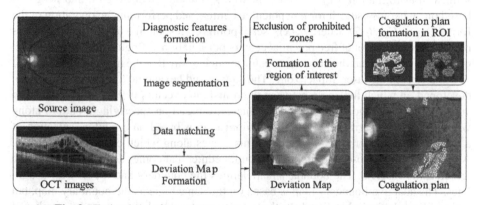

Fig. 2. Technology of mapping a photocoagulation plan of laser coagulation.

For the pathological zone to be extracted, one needs to have information on deviations of the retina thickness from the normal values. By performing preprocessing, the software builds a map of deviations of a particular retina from the norm. Enhanced deviations indicate that the given zone has a pathology.

A fundus image reconstructed from OCT data needs to be aligned with a fundus-camera-aided retinal image. The technology proposed herein suggests that key points should be marked in the reconstructed retinal image and fundus image, followed by marking off a pathological zone, which is then aligned with the fundus image. The zone of laser exposure, which is generated automatically based on the segmentation result and the pathological zone, can be corrected manually if necessary. At the final step, a photocoagulation pattern is mapped, for which quality characteristics are calculated and the probability of the successful outcome of laser treatment is evaluated.

Automatic formation of a preliminary coagulation plan in the laser exposure zone includes the stage of identifying potential centers of circles and the stage of arranging centers with a specified minimum distance (Fig. 3).

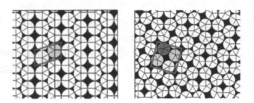

Fig. 3. The problem of packing circles.

9 algorithms for the formation of a plan of coagulates have been developed. Among them, regular algorithms based on the construction of a translation mesh given by the translation vectors $\bar{a}$ и $\bar{b}$ and described by the multitude $Y_{\varphi\bar{s}}^{\overline{a}\overline{b}} = \left\{\bar{y} = \Phi_{\varphi\bar{s}}\left[i\bar{a} + j\bar{b}\right] : i, j \in \mathbb{Z}, \bar{y} \in Q\right\}$, where Q – laser impact zone, $\Phi_{\varphi\bar{s}}[\bar{x}] = M_{\varphi}\bar{x} + \bar{s}$ – linear transformation, M_{φ} – rotation matrix, $\bar{s}$ – displacement vector, and irregular, based on an iterative search for free potential centers and performing an operation of the form $C_{k+1} = C_k \setminus B_r(\bar{x})$, where $B_r(\bar{x})$ – set of points corresponding to a circle with radius r and center $\bar{x}$, C_k – set of free potential centers per iteration k. Regular algorithms select the rotation matrix and displacement vector in such a way that the maximum number of coagulates is in the laser impact zone. The square and hexagonal algorithms have been developed, in which the angle between the translation vectors is 90° for a square map and 120° for a hexagonal one. Irregular maps are based on specifying a pattern along which iteration is carried out. Thus, a random map is based on a random selection of a free potential center. The wave map forms waves along which coagulates are filled. An ordered map chooses the first free potential center that comes across as a result of a left-to-right traversal. The boundary map defines the boundary and fills it with coagulates. The adaptive-boundary map is based on the same logic as the boundary map, but before filling the boundary, it selects the arrangement at which the maximum number of coagulates will fill the boundary. Algorithms were also proposed that combine regular maps with a boundary map: the boundaries of local areas are distinguished, which are filled with regular maps [46–48].

All the developed algorithms and methods formed the basis of the system for the automatic formation of a coagulation plan (Fig. 4).

The effectiveness of a photocoagulation pattern can be estimated by calculating a number of features relating to the mutual position of coagulates. The majority of the features can be best described in terms of the inter-coagulate distance. The sampling of distances can be formed in a variety of ways, for instance, by conducting a Delaunay triangulation relative to marked points.

Each of the proposed algorithms offers its own photocoagulation plan, for which characteristics such as variance, a median, and the number of coagulates need primarily to be analyzed (Table 2).

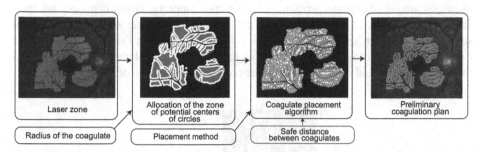

| Laser zone | Allocation of the zone of potential centers of circles | Coagulate placement algorithm | Preliminary coagulation plan |

| Radius of the coagulate | Placement method | Safe distance between coagulates |

Fig. 4. Scheme of automatic formation of the coagulation plan.

As far as a minimal inter-coagulate distance is observed, mapping a photocoagulation pattern within a pathological zone guarantees safe photocoagulation because such an approach enables one to exclude two possible problems: exposure of prohibited areas to the laser light and excessive retina damage due to a very small distance between neighboring coagulates. Nonetheless, even if the laser parameters are chosen correctly, minor damage to the retina due to micro burns cannot be ruled out. Although the damage is usually insignificant but it should be possibly avoided.

Table 2. Feature values for various algorithms for mapping a coagulation plan.

Algorithm	Variance	Median	Number
Random map	6.32	31.62	223
Square map	6.09	30.00	220
Hexagonal map	7.68	30.00	248
Wave map	0.95	30.08	311
Boundary map	0.90	30.08	305
Boundary-adaptive map	0.70	30.07	315
Ordered map	0.19	30.08	312

An important problem is analyzing the mutual arrangement of photocoagulates as a result of planning. Characteristics of the photocoagulation plan are able to provide a prognosis of the laser coagulation outcome. In any case, to be able to estimate its various properties, the preliminary plan needs to be described quantitatively. We note that the preliminary plan can be mapped using an arbitrary technique, including a manual one. A photocoagulation plan comprises an array of points each of which is characterized by certain parameters. The parameters affect the degree of burn at the exposed points and can be evaluated using a technique described in [49, 50]. The laser treatment parameters can be fitted in an optimal way at any layout of points given that the minimal distance is observed. With all the points known to be located in the ROI that needs to be exposed to laser treatment, inter-point distances come to the forefront.

For a distance sampling to be generated, a point-connecting technique needs to be chosen based on some rule. Next, using a standard Euclidean measure, values of the distances are calculated and written into a general sampling. Noise distances are then excluded and statistical characteristics are calculated, before being written in the general set of features. Such an approach is schematically depicted in Fig. 5. Based on their expertise, ophthalmologists [14, 15, 46] suggest using statistical characteristics such as the variance of mutual distances, the mathematical mean, and so on.

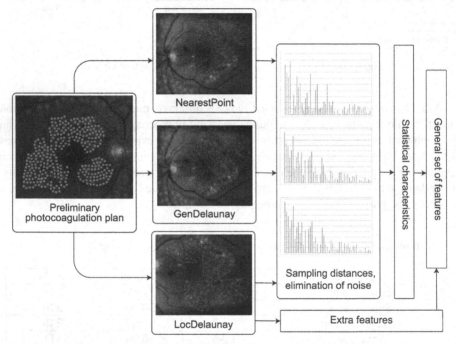

Fig. 5. Flowchart of feature calculation based on a preliminary photocoagulation pattern.

Medical doctors used to analyze the uniformity of the photocoagulation pattern primarily based on the variance. The features used include various statistical characteristics of the inter-coagulate distance (a mutual location feature) and features corresponding to the coagulation pattern volume and the area covered (general features). The triangulation distances are written into the general sampling, from which distances disobeying a three-sigma rule are then excluded. Among statistical characteristics, the following were chosen: a mean arithmetic, variance, a root-mean-square deviation, median, asymmetry, kurtosis, a minimal value, and a maximal value [47]. These characteristics form a basis for evaluating the uniformity and balance of the photocoagulation pattern. Alongside statistical characteristics, an important feature is the number of points in the photocoagulation plan. As an extra feature, the number of local regions in the coagulation pattern may be used.

7 Conclusion

The paper considers the application of artificial intelligence methods in ophthalmology for the treatment of eye diseases on the example of a computer system for retinal laser photocoagulation personalization. The main problems of using the neural network approach in the tasks of biomedical image analysis are described. To solve the problem of semantic segmentation of images to highlight anatomical and pathological areas of the fundus two approaches were investigated and compared: neural network analysis and texture analysis. The disadvantages and advantages of each approach were highlighted. The results of the application of neural network algorithms for solving the problem of semantic segmentation of fundus images with a pronounced class imbalance are presented. The studies showed that neural networks are superior to texture-based features in accuracy. Moreover, neural networks can be used to segment fundus images that were obtained under various shooting conditions, in contrast to textural features. The use of pre-trained neural networks and their additional training on a small data set, together with the use of a balancing algorithm and augmentation techniques, made it possible to develop fairly accurate algorithms for the semantic segmentation of fundus images based on a small data set.

The fundus image segmentation algorithm based on the use of a neural network with the XceptionUnet architecture can be used in decision support systems for diagnosticians if it is necessary to work in real time through the use of a user-level graphics accelerator. Decision support information technology for personalization of laser treatment of diabetic macular edema and identification of prognostic factors of surgical outcomes using methods of intellectual analysis of large unstructured data is presented.

We have proposed a software complex for mapping and analyzing a preliminary photocoagulation plan for laser treatment of diabetic retinopathy. The software is aimed at automatically mapping a recommended photo-coagulation plan and provides for the correction of interim results. The feasibility of introducing corrections at any interim stage of data processing in the computerized system makes for a safe treatment. A key module of the proposed software architecture is the system for the intelligent analysis of the photocoagulation pattern, allowing the proposed plan to be analyzed and the treatment outcome to be prognosticated.

Acknowledgments. This work was performed within the State assignment of Federal Scientific Research Center "Crystallography and Photonics" of Russian Academy of Sciences.

References

1. Rottier, J.B.: Artificial intelligence: reinforcing the place of humans in our healthcare system. Rev. Prat. **68**(10), 1150–1151 (2018)
2. Fourcade, A., Khonsari, R.H.: Deep learning in medical image analysis: a third eye for doctors. J. Stomatology Oral Maxillofacial Surg. **120**(4), 279–288 (2019)
3. Gao, A., et al.: Progress in robotics for combating infectious diseases. Sci. Robot. **6**(52), 1–17 (2021)
4. Trinh, M., Ghassibi, M., Lieberman, R.: Artificial Intelligence in retina. Adv. Ophthalmol. Optometry **6**, 175–185 (2021)

5. Vorobieva, I.V., Merkushenkova, D.A.: Diabetic retinopathy in patients with type 2 Diabetes Mellitus. Epidemiology, a modern view of pathogenesis. Ophthalmology **9**(4), 18–21 (2012)
6. Dedov, I.I., Shestakova, M.V., Galstyan, G.R.: The prevalence of type 2 diabetes mellitus in the adult population of Russia (nation study). Diab. Mellitus **19**(2), 104–112 (2016)
7. Tan, G.S., Cheung, N., Simo, R.: Diabetic macular edema. Lancet Diab. Endoc. **5**, 143–155 (2017)
8. Amirov, A.N., Abdulaeva, E.A., Minkhuzina, E.L.: Diabetic macular edema. epidemiology, pathogenesis, diagnosis, clinical features, treatment. Kazan Med. J. **96**(1), 70–76 (2015)
9. Doga, A.V., Kachalina, G.F., Pedanova, E.K., Buryakov, D.A.: Modern diagnostic and treatment aspects of diabetic macular edema. Diab. Mellitus **17**, 51–59 (2014)
10. Bratko, G.V., Chernykh, V.V., Sazonova, O.V.: On early diagnostics and the occurrence rate of diabetic macular edema and identification of diabetes risk groups. Siberian Sci. Med. J. **35**(1), 33–36 (2015)
11. Wong, T.Y., et al.: Relation between fasting glucose and retinopathy for diagnosis of diabetes: three population-based cross-sectional studies. Lancet **371**(9614), 736–743 (2008)
12. Acharya, U.R., Ng, E.Y., Tan, J.-H., Sree, S.V., Ng, K.-H.: An integrated index for the identification of diabetic retinopathy stages using texture parameters. J. Med. Syst. **36**(3), 2011–2020 (2011)
13. Astakhov, Y., Shadrichev, F.E., Krasavina, M.I., Grigorieva, N.N.: Modern approaches to the treatment of diabetic macular edema. Ophthalmol. Statements **4**, 59–69 (2009)
14. Zamytsky, E.A., Zolotarev, A.V., Karlova, E.V., Zamytsky, P.A.: Analysis of the coagulates intensity in laser treatment of diabetic macular edema in a Navilas robotic laser system. Saratov J. Med. Sci. Res. **13**(2), 375–378 (2017)
15. Zamytskiy, E.A., Zolotarev, A.V., Karlova, E.V., Il'yasova, N.Y., Shirokanev, A.S.: Comparative quantitative assessment of the placement and intensity of laser spots for treating diabetic macular edema. Russ. J. Clin. Ophthalmol. **21**(2), 58–62 (2021)
16. Kotsur, T.V., Izmaylov, A.S.: Comparative estimation of laser coagulation efficiency in macular and microphotocoagulation of high density in diabetic maculopathy treatment. Ophthalmol. J. **9**(4), 43–45 (2016)
17. Chhablani, J., El-Emam, S., Kozak, I., Barteselli, G.: A novel navigated laser system brings new efficacy to the treatment of retinovascular disorders. Oman J. Ophthalmol. **6**(1), 18 (2013)
18. Mukhin, A., Kilbas, I., Paringer, R., Ilyasova, N.: Application of the gradient descent for data balancing in diagnostic image analysis problems. IEEE Xplore, pp. 1–4 (2020)
19. Kozak, I., Luttrull, J.K.: Modern retinal laser therapy. Saudi J. Ophthalmol. **29**(2), 137–146 (2015)
20. Kernt, M., Cheuteu, R., Liegl, R.: Navigated focal retinal laser therapy using the NAVILAS® system for diabetic macula edema. Ophthalmologe **109**, 692–700 (2012)
21. Ober, M.D.: Time required for navigated macular laser photo coagulation treatment with the Navilas®. Graefes Arch. Clin. Exp. Ophthalmol. **251**(4), 1049–1053 (2013)
22. Syed, A.M., Hassan, T., Akram, M.U., Naz, S., Khalid, S.: Automated diagnosis of macular edema and central serous retinopathy through robust reconstruction of 3D retinal surfaces. Comput. Methods Programs Biomed. **137**, 1–10 (2016)
23. Apostolopoulos, I.D., Mpesiana, T.A.: COVID-19: automatic detection from X-ray images utilizing transfer learning with Convolutional Neural Networks. Phys. Eng. Sci. Med. **43**(2), 635–640 (2020)
24. Abdelaziz Ismael, S.A., Mohammed, A., Hefny, H.: An enhanced deep learning approach for brain cancer MRI images classification using residual networks. Artif. Intell. Med. **102**, 101779 (2020)
25. Gabbasov, R., Paringer, R.: Influence of the receptive field size on accuracy and performance of a Convolutional Neural Network. IEEE Xplore, pp. 1–4 (2020)

26. Arellano, A.M., Dai, W., Wang, S., Jiang, X., Ohno-Machado, L.: Privacy policy and technology in biomedical data science. Annu. Rev. Biomed. Data Sci. **1**, 115–129 (2018)
27. Shorten, C., Khoshgoftaar, T.M.: A survey on image data augmentation for Deep Learning. J. Big Data **6**(1), 1–48 (2019)
28. Castro, E., Cardoso, J.S., Pereira, J.C.: Elastic deformations for data augmentation in breast cancer mass detection. In: 2018 IEEE EMBS International Conference on Biomedical & Health Informatics (BHI), pp. 230–234 (2018)
29. Ishwaran, H., O'Brien, R.: Commentary: the problem of class imbalance in biomedical data. J. Thorac. Cardiovasc. Surg. **161**(6), 1940–1941 (2021)
30. Charte, F., Rivera, A.J., del Jesus, M.J., Herrera, F.: MLSMOTE: approaching imbalanced multilabel learning through synthetic instance generation. Knowl.-Based Syst. **89**, 385–397 (2015)
31. Pereira, R.M., Costa, Y.M.G., Silla, C.N., Jr.: MLTL: a multi-label approach for the Tomek link undersampling algorithm. Neurocomputing **383**, 95–105 (2020)
32. Hao, D., Zhang, L., Sumkin, J., Mohamed, A., Wu, S.: Inaccurate labels in weakly-supervised deep learning: automatic identification and correction and their impact on classification performance. IEEE J. Biomed. Health Inform. **24**(9), 2701–2710 (2020)
33. Tian, C., Fang, T., Fan, Y., Wu, W.: Multi-path convolutional neural network in fundus segmentation of blood vessels. Biocybern. Biomed. Eng. **40**(2), 583–595 (2020)
34. Kaur, J., Mittal, D.: A generalized method for the segmentation of exudates from pathological retinal fundus images. Biocybern. Biomed. Eng. **38**(1), 27–53 (2018)
35. Bhagat, N., Grigorian, R.A., Tutela, A., Zarbin, M.A.: Diabetic macular edema: pathogenesis and treatment. Surv. Ophthalmol. **54**(1), 1–32 (2009)
36. Ilyasova, N.Y., Paringer, R.A., Shirokanev, A.S., Demin, N.S.: An approach to semantic segmentation of retinal images using deep neural networks for mapping laser exposure zones for the treatment of diabetic macular edema. In: Kovalev, S., Tarassov, V., Snasel, V., Sukhanov, A. (eds.) Proceedings of the Fifth International Scientific Conference "Intelligent Information Technologies for Industry" (IITI' 2021). IITI 2021. LNNS, vol. 330, pp. 106–116. Springer, Cham (2021). https://doi.org/10.1007/978-3-030-87178-9_11
37. Ilyasova, N., Paringer, R., Kupriyanov, A., Kirsh, D.: Intelligent feature selection technique for segmentation of fundus images. In: 2017 Seventh International Conference on Innovative Computing Technology (INTECH), pp. 138–143 (2017)
38. MaZda Web Site. http://www.eletel.p.lodz.pl/programy/mazda/index.php. Accessed 1 May 2021
39. Wu, J., Poehlman, S., Noseworthy, M.D., Kamath, M.V.: Texture feature based automated seeded region growing in abdominal MRI segmentation. In: 2008 International Conference on BioMedical Engineering and Informatics, vol. 2, pp. 263–267 (2008)
40. Mukhin, A.V., Kilbas, I.A., Paringer, R.A., Ilyasova, N.Y., Kupriyanov, A.V.: A method for balancing a multi-labeled biomedical dataset. Integr. Comput.-Aided Eng. **29**(2), 209–225 (2022)
41. TensorFlow. https://www.tensorflow.org. Accessed 1 May 2021
42. Lin, T.-Y., Goyal, P., Girshick, R., He, K., Dollar, P.: Focal loss for dense object detection. In: 2017 IEEE International Conference on Computer Vision (ICCV), pp. 2980–2988 (2017)
43. Kingma, D.P.: Adam: a method for stochastic optimization. arXiv. 1412.6980 (2014)
44. Tang, H., Maitre, H., Boujemaa, N., Jiang, W.: On the relevance of linear discriminative features. Inf. Sci. **180**(18), 3422–3433 (2010)
45. Stone, M.: Cross-validatory choice and assessment of statistical predictions. J. Roy. Stat. Soc.: Ser. B (Methodol.) **36**(2), 111–133 (1974)
46. Ilyasova, N., Kirsh, D., Paringer, R., Kupriyanov, A., Shirokanev, A., Zamycky, E.: Coagulate map formation algorithms for Laser Eye treatment. In: 2017 3rd International Conference on Frontiers of Signal Processing (ICFSP), pp. 120–124 (2017)

47. Shirokanev, A., Kirsh, D., Ilyasova, N., Kupriyanov, A.: The study of algorithms for the placement of coagulates on the image of the fundus. Comput. Opt. **42**(4), 712–721 (2018)
48. Ilyasova, N., Shirokanev, A., Kirsh, D., Paringer, R., Kupriyanov, A., Zamycky, E.: Development of coagulate map formation algorithms to carry out treatment by laser coagulation. Procedia Eng. **201**, 271–279 (2017)
49. Shirokanev, A., Ilyasova, N., Andriyanov, N., Zamytskiy, E., Zolotarev, A., Kirsh, D.: Modeling of Fundus Laser Exposure for estimating safe laser coagulation parameters in the treatment of diabetic retinopathy. Mathematics **9**, 967 (2021)
50. Ilyasova, N., et al.: Identification of prognostic factors and predicting the therapeutic effect of laser photocoagulation for DME treatment. Electronics **10**, 1420 (2021)

Visualization and Analysis of Whole Slide Histological Images

Alexander Khvostikov[1](✉)[iD], Andrey Krylov[1][iD], Ilya Mikhailov[2][iD],
and Pavel Malkov[3][iD]

[1] Faculty of Computational Mathematics and Cybernetics,
Lomonosov Moscow State University, Moscow, Russia
{khvostikov,kryl}@cs.msu.ru
[2] Faculty of Medicine, Lomonosov Moscow State University, Moscow, Russia
imikhailov@mc.msu.ru
[3] Medical Research and Educational Center, Lomonosov Moscow State University,
Moscow, Russia
pmalkov@mc.msu.ru

Abstract. The use of modern approaches based on convolutional neural networks (CNNs) for segmentation of whole slide images (WSIs) helps pathologists obtain more stable and quantitative analysis results and improve diagnosis objectivity. But working with WSIs is extremely difficult due to their resolution, size and the presence of a large number of incompatible image storage formats from equipment manufacturers. In addition, the use of modern CNN-based image analysis methods is complicated by the need to use a set of tools with a low level of internal integration.

In order to facilitate the interaction of histologists with whole slide images and modern image analysis methods we implemented PathScribe – a new universal cross-platform cloud-based tool for comfortable viewing and manipulating large collections of WSIs on almost any device, including tablets and smartphones.

We also consider the important problem of automatic tissue type recognition on WSIs and propose a new CNN-based method of automatic tissue type recognition on WSIs with a 2 subsets of PATH-DT-MSU dataset which contain high-quality whole slide images of digestive tract tumors with tissue type area annotations.

The proposed method achieved 0.929 accuracy on CRC-VAL-HE-7K dataset (9 classes) and 0.97 accuracy on PATH-DT-MSU-WSS1, WSS2 datasets (5 classes). The developed method allows to classify the areas corresponding to the gastric own mucous glands in the lamina propria and distinguish the tubular structures of a highly differentiated gastric adenocarcinoma with normal glands.

Keywords: Histology · Digital Pathology · Segmentation ·
Histological Image Viewer · Whole Slide Images · Segmentation ·
Convolutional Neural Networks

Supported by RSCF and Non-commercial Foundation for the Advancement of Science and Education INTELLECT.

J.-J. Rousseau and B. Kapralos (Eds.): ICPR 2022 Workshops, LNCS 13644, pp. 403–413, 2023.
https://doi.org/10.1007/978-3-031-37742-6_30

1   Introduction

This work expands on our previous publication [9] with more detailed description of PathScribe project [1].

The complexity and variety of histological structures that histologists have to work with, makes a variety of approaches and methods of automatic processing and analysis of histological images in demand. These include histological structure segmentation methods, methods of histological images registration that allow histologists to efficiently analyze differently stained adjacent sections, content-based image retrieval systems that allow quickly find similar tissue fragments, methods to improve the quality of histological images and many more [13].

A distinctive feature of modern digital pathology is the ability to obtain whole slide images (WSIs) by scanning a complete microscope slide and creating a single high-resolution digital file [10]. This is commonly achieved by capturing many small high-resolution image tiles or strips and then montaging them to create a full image of a histological section. This kind of images definitely amaze with their quality and detail but have a pile of drawbacks. The first drawback is the size of these images. Since the typical resolution of WSIs if scanned with 40X magnification is 100000×100000 pixels, the size of these images is around 2-4 gigabytes [12]. Moreover, modern histological scanners can produce images of even higher resolution, with the image size of tens of gigabytes. Another drawback of dealing with WSIs is that each scanner manufacturer has its own format of storing whole slide images incompatible with others and requires special software provided by this manufacturer.

In addition, the development of the mentioned above tasks of analyzing histological images in the case of WSIs seems to be extremely difficult due to their resolution and size. The more demanded become the methods of automatic analysis of whole slide histological images. One of these problems is recognition of tumors and layers of the stomach wall as well as tumors and wall layers of other organs of the digestive tract.

Analysis of WSIs in gastric cancer using deep learning algorithms is used to estimate the density of infiltration by various types of immune cells [4]. Existing algorithms make it possible to identify lymphoid tissue and tumor area, and then to determine the ratio of tumor area to lymphoid tissue area in order to find lymphogenous metastases in gastric cancer [15]. Nevertheless, the existing algorithms based on deep learning are so far aimed only to solve specific narrow problems in relation to histological images of gastric cancer. While there are already quite effective algorithms for recognizing the depth of invasion and the layers of the intestinal wall in colorectal cancer [7], but there are no similar algorithms for gastric cancer. That can be explained by the higher frequency of diffuse type tumors and tumors with a discohesive component among gastric tumors.

2   Segmentation of Whole Slide Images

Since the full-fledged segmentation of whole slide images is difficult because of their resolution and the necessity of high quality and very detailed annotation, the most common way is to perform rough segmentation by splitting image into small patches and predicting a tissue class for each patch [10]. In this paper we implement exactly this way.

2.1   Used Data

In this work we use three different image datasets that are developed for the purpose of WSI segmentation and tissue type recognition. NCT-CRC-HE-100K and CRC-VAL-HE-7K [6] consists of 100.000 and 7180 non-overlapping image patches from hematoxylin & eosin (H&E) stained histological images of human colorectal cancer and normal tissue. Each patch has a resolution of 224×224 pixels and is matched with one of the 9 class labels according to the specific tissue type or background: adipose (ADI), background (BACK), debris (DEB), lymphocytes (LYM), mucus (MUC), smooth muscle (MUS), normal colon mucosa (NORM), cancer-associated stroma (STR), colorectal adenocarcinoma epithelium (TUM).

The third dataset is represented by WSS1 and WSS2 subsets of PATH-DT-MSU dataset [11], containing in total 20 *H&E* whole slide histological images of digestive tract tumors. Each WSI image is a full-thickness fragment of the stomach wall, cut from the surgical material, and includes areas of adenocarcinoma, adjacent areas of visually unchanged lamina propria and the underlying layers of the stomach wall. Each image (Fig. 1) is accompanied with polygonal annotations of tissue areas corresponding to 5 classes: areas of gastric adenocarcinoma (TUM), unchanged areas of the lamina propria (LP), unchanged areas of the muscularis mucosae (MM), areas of the submucosa, the own muscle layer of the stomach and subserous areas in one class (AT), background (BG). In order to train the patch classification model and make WSIs from PATH-DT-MSU dataset compatible with NCT-CRC-HE-100K and CRC-VAL-HE-7K we extract patches from the images in accordance with annotations.

2.2   Segmentation Through Patch Classification

In this work we use a CNN-based model for automatic tissue type recognition of whole slide histological images based on the patch classification approach. Since the amount of data in the obtained datasets is limited, we chose the DenseNet architecture [5] as it tends to perform well in the case of relatively small number of training samples. We use the transfer learning principle gradually tuning the DenseNet model to be able to classify patches from the target PATH-DT-MSU whole slide images within 3 steps.

At first, we fine tune the DenseNet-121 model that is pretrained on the ImageNet dataset. We replace the last fully-connected layer with the new one

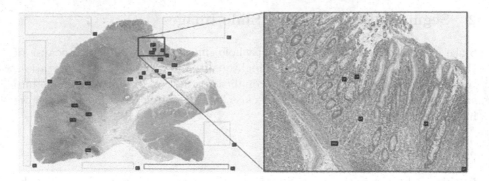

Fig. 1. Sample image from WSS1 subset of PATH-DT-MSU dataset with annotation of tissue types.

with 9 outputs in correspondence with the number of classes in NCT-CRC-HE-100K dataset, freeze all head layers and train the obtained modified DenseNet for 20 epochs with the initial learning rate of $2*10^{-5}$. The validation is performed on CRC-VAL-HE-7K dataset. We reached the accuracy value of 0.919 and balanced accuracy of 0.8816 at this step.

Secondly, in order to better adapt it for working with histological images we unfreeze all layers in the model and further train it with the same NCT-CRC-HE-100K dataset for 30 epochs with the initial learning rate of 10^{-4}. At this step we reached the accuracy value of 0.929 and balanced accuracy of 0.903.

Finally, we fine tune the model on patches from whole slide images of PATH-DTMSU dataset. We replace the last fully-connected layer with the new one with 5 outputs in correspondence with the number of classes in PATH-DT-MSU dataset, freeze all head layers and train the model for 8 epochs with the initial learning rate of 10^{-5}. The validation is performed on the test set of patches extracted from WSS1 and WSS2 subsets of PATH-DT-MSU. At this step we finally achieved the accuracy value of 0.97 and balanced accuracy of 0.935.

2.3   Results of Tissue Type Recognition

To use the trained CNN model in the task of automatic tissue type recognition we apply it to the whole slide images from test sets of PATH-DT-MSU WSS1 and WSS2. Each WSI image is split into patches of size 224×224 pixels without overlap, for each patch the trained model predicts the class label, after that all the predictions are combined into a matrix, which is then visualized as a semi-transparent layer on the source WSI. The visualization of the proposed method of tissue type recognition is shown in Fig. 2.

2.4   Implementation Details

The proposed CNN-based method for automatic tissue type recognition in whole slide histological images was implemented using Python 3 programming language

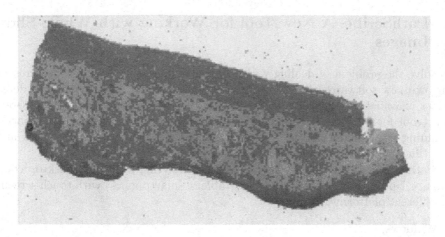

Fig. 2. Resulting visualization of the proposed method of tissues type recognition. Recognized tissues are highlighted with different colors: AT with orange, BG with cyan, LP with green, MM with red, TUM with purple. (Color figure online)

and open-source software library for machine learning Tensorflow 2. Processing of WSIs was done using slideio library, shapely library was used for geometric calculations during patch extraction.

3 Whole Slide Image Treatment Problems

As it can be seen from the above mentioned example of whole slide images segmentation, the typical pipeline which is performed by pathologists, includes the steps of collecting images, annotating them, exporting data, transfer the really impressive amounts of data, applying the trained model and visualizing the results. In the case of more complicated tasks of digital pathology, such as determination of tumor invasion depth [2,14] or whole slide image registration [3] the number of steps included in these pipelines is even more and the steps itself are more challenging.

Unfortunately, at the current moment almost every step of these typical pipelines is performed using different software solutions. The situation is especially aggravated by the presence of different histological data storage formats and different markup tools available in software solutions of individual scanner manufacturers. All this complicates the work of a pathologist who wants to apply modern AI-based methods for a more detailed analysis of histological material.

Having experienced all these problems first hand, we decided to implement a new software solution that is applicable in described situations and facilitates the interaction of histologists with whole slide images and modern image analysis methods.

4   PathScribe–A New Tool for Working with Whole Slide Images

To solve the problem of dealing with whole slide histological images we present our own new software called PathScribe [1]. Its detailed description with demo videos is available at https://pathscribe.ru. PathScribe is a cross-platform software tool for viewing and managing large collections of histological images, including whole slide images. It is aimed to be used for both educational and scientific purposes.

PathScribe allows to comfortably work with WSIs, both on a desktop computer or laptop, and on mobile devices (tablets, smartphones) with touch screens on different platforms:

- Windows,
- Android,
- MacOS (coming soon),
- Linux (coming soon).

PathScribe has an adaptive interface and can work with a large range of display's resolution and aspect ratios.

The main screen of PathScribe for Windows and Android versions is shown in Fig. 3. At the moment of writing this paper PathScribe is under active development and its user interface is likely to be changed.

For its work PathScribe requires an active Internet connection, the bandwidth requirements are minimal. Even mobile Internet can be used which makes possible to use PathScribe on mobile devices practically everywhere.

PathScribe implements client-server architecture and consists of a server (written in Python 3, consists of several microservices), client (flutter app) and image converter (written in Python 3).

4.1   Images Formats and Converter

In order to work with WSIs obtained from scanners of different manufacturers PathScribe in its backend part implements an own universal format for storing histological images with .*psi* extension, as well as a converter that allows to convert popular image formats to *psi* for comfortable viewing and working inside PathScribe.

The developed image format stores image in tiles within a pyramid of scales. The efficiency of the proposed format is ensured with a set of histological image-oriented algorithms that analyze the content of tiles at different scales and can detect the background areas that a not stored in the image container. We also use a more efficient compression algorithms to encode tiles compared to the conventional histological image formats. All this allows to sufficiently reduce the amount of storage for WSIs stored on the server, reduces storage requirement and speeds up the client part of the PathScribe. For example, a set of 3 image obtained with Leica Aperio AT2 scanner in *svs* format after converting to *psi*

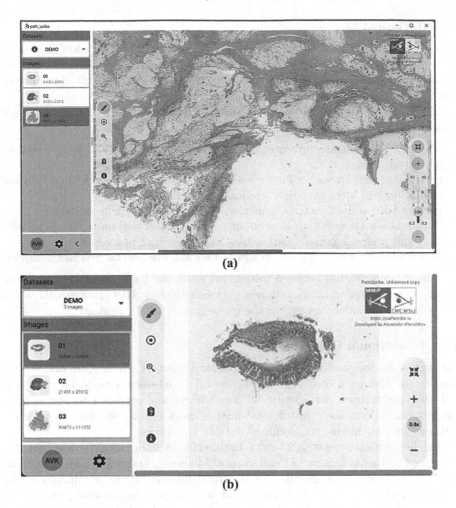

Fig. 3. Screenshot of main screen of PathScribe graphical user interface: 3a windows client, 3b android client.

format reduced in size from 3.3 GB to 771 MB (4.38x compression). And a set of 281 images obtained with PANNORAMIC 250 Flash III DX scanner in *mrxs* format after converting to *psi* format reduced in size from 232 GB to 96 GB (2.41x compression). Moreover, we continue optimizing the developed histological image format and will soon release an updated version with ∼ 20% more effective compression.

The converter currently supports popular general-purpose image formats (*jpg, png, bmp, tif*) and formats used to store WSIs (*svs, mrxs*). The number of supported formats will be increased during development.

4.2 Technical Details

PathScribe is designed for quick and easy working with whole slide images. It allows to fluently switch between hundreds of WSIs, zoom in and view any part of the selected image in real time using even mobile internet (all video demos can be found at https://pathscribe.ru).

The obtained image loading speed of PathScribe is achieved through a few tricks:

- only the tiles that are currently needed to render the area which is viewed by user are loaded;
- for a faster and smoother image loading the tiles are first preloaded in a low resolution and after that they are loaded in full resolution;
- loading tiles and all meta information is performed asynchronously;
- PathScribe makes assumptions about where the user will move the viewfinder next and preloads corresponding tiles in background processes;
- tiles are loaded with a few parallel processes and are also cached on the device.

The communication between microservices at the backend of PathScribe as well as client-server communication is performed using gRPC framework, which also is more efficient compared to the conventional REST protocol.

4.3 Educational Opportunities

PathScribe is designed not only as universal viewer of whole slide histological images but also as a tool that can be useful in education to teach pathological anatomy courses. PathScribe allows teachers and students to access large educational collections of histological images quickly and conveniently over the Internet without having to download data to the device.

In the academic year 2022-2023 PathScribe will be used in teaching the pathology course at faculty of Fundamental Medicine, Lomonosov Moscow State University. The course includes 28 practical lessons (10 to 30 images each), 6 staged colloquia (sum of all images of several practice lessons), exam (100 images), which makes all-together 281 WSIs in total. All these images form a separate dataset, which is accessible inside PathScribe for all students and teachers registered for the course.

Embedding PathScribe into the pathology teaching system will increasing the efficiency of students' assimilation of the material of the course of pathology by providing a constant opportunity of access to educational images.

4.4 Additional Features

Security. To prevent accidental access to PathScribe we implemented user registration and authorization features. User is verified with his email and with an easy password recovery option. For user convenience PathScribe uses jwt tokens for repeated authorization. This allows to avoid entering login credentials after restarting the application in case of successfull login. In order to make the data transfer secure all communication channels between client and server and between microservices are encrypted with SSL.

Image Attributes. Since PathScribe is aimed to work with very big collections of images we have also implemented several features that make the application more convenient for finding the required image. This is implemented as follows. Different image collections are stored in PathScribe as separate datasets. Each dataset can be assigned with attributes, that can be of 2 types:

- fields, which are text descriptions of some properties,
- tags, which are fixed text values that can be assigned to an image, wherein tags are united into tag families.

For example, the user can create a dataset, then add fields "description" and "comments", create tag family "organ" with corresponding tags "lung", "liver", "colon", etc., and a tag family "theme" with corresponding tags "lesson 1", "lesson 2", "exam", etc. After this text values for "description" and "comments" fields can be filled for every image in the dataset. And each image in the dataset can be tagged with zero, one or more tags for each tag family.

The developed mechanism of attributes can be used to store description of images and to filter images by tags (e.g. show only images of chosen organ or stain, or with some special disease) without the need to scroll through hundreds of images.

The key factor of the developed image attribute system is that it is totally customizable and dataset-independent. This means that for each dataset users can create its own set of fields, tags and tag families depending on the tasks for which the dataset is intended.

Administration Tool. In order to administrate all processes related to PathScribe project we made a telegram-bot which allows to manage access of registered users to the existing datasets (mainly is used in education), configure attributes for the datasets (create tag families, tags, fields), edit values of attributes for individual images, manage access to the bot itself and manage PathScribe versioning.

The developed telegram-bot is planned as a temporary solution, in the future it's functionality will be moved to PathScribe app.

4.5   Collab Mode

One more thing that is currently developed in PathScribe is collab mode. It is designed for simultaneous work with images by several users at once. One user within a PathScribe app creates a virtual room and becomes a host, while all other users enter this virtual room (they input room ID and PIN) and become listeners. After this all actions that are performed by the host (select image, zoom it, move it and so on), are straightaway performed inside a PathScribe instance of each listener until he leaves the room.

Collab mode in PathScribe makes collaboration of users much easier and can be used for teaching. It also enables the software to be effectively used in telemedicine.

5 Conclusion

In this paper we presented a detailed description of PathScribe - a new universal cross-platform cloud-based tool for comfortable viewing and manipulating large collections of WSIs on almost any device, including tablets and smartphones.

We also proposed a new CNN-based method of automatic tissue type recognition on WSIs. It achieved 0.929 accuracy on CRC-VAL-HE-7K dataset and 0.97 accuracy on WSS1 and WSS2 subsets of PATH-DT-MSU dataset (5 classes).

6 Further Development

PathScribe is designed to be used for academic and research purposes. In the nearest future we plan to develop it further in both educational and scientific directions.

The scientific part of PathScribe development will consist in integrating a bunch of modern algorithms developed by our team for CNN assisted accelerated annotating [8], classification, segmentation, analysis, and content-based search.

The educational part of PathScribe development will include extending and improving of the collab mode and implementing interactive test system for students.

This will help PathScribe to become a universal assistant for histologists, significantly speeding up and automating the ways of how they work with histological images.

Acknowledgements. The scientific part of the work was supported by Russian Science Foundation grant 22-41-02002, the PathScribe development as the educational tool is funded by Non-commercial Foundation for the Advancement of Science and Education INTELLECT.

References

1. Pathscribe - a new cross-platform software tool for viewing, annotation and automatic analysis of whole slide histological images (2022). https://pathscribe.ru
2. Ali, L., et al.: Digital assessment of depth of invasion in melanoma using different immunohistochemical stains. Archives of the Balkan Medical Union **55**(2), 290–297 (2020)
3. Borovec, J., et al.: Anhir: automatic non-rigid histological image registration challenge. IEEE Trans. Med. Imaging **39**(10), 3042–3052 (2020)
4. Chen, Y., et al.: The immune subtypes and landscape of gastric cancer and to predict based on the whole-slide images using deep learning. Front. immunol. **12** (2021)
5. Huang, G., Liu, Z., Van Der Maaten, L., Weinberger, K.Q.: Densely connected convolutional networks. In: Proceedings of the IEEE Conference on Computer Vision and Pattern Recognition, pp. 4700–4708 (2017)
6. Kather, J.N., Halama, N., Marx, A.: 100,000 histological images of human colorectal cancer and healthy tissue (v0.1) (2018). https://doi.org/10.5281/zenodo.1214456

7. Kather, J.N., et al.: Predicting survival from colorectal cancer histology slides using deep learning: A retrospective multicenter study. PLoS Med. **16**(1), e1002730 (2019)
8. Khvostikov, A., Krylov, A.S., Mikhailov, I., Malkov, P.: CNN assisted hybrid algorithm for medical images segmentation. In: Proceedings of the 2020 5th International Conference on Biomedical Signal and Image Processing, pp. 14–19 (2020)
9. Khvostikov, A., Krylov, A.S., Mikhailov, I., Malkov, P.: Visualization of whole slide histological images with automatic tissue type recognition. Pattern Recognit Image Anal. **32**(3), 483–488 (2022)
10. Kumar, N., Gupta, R., Gupta, S.: Whole slide imaging (wsi) in pathology: current perspectives and future directions. J. Digit. Imaging **33**(4), 1034–1040 (2020)
11. Mikhailov, I., Khvostikov, A., Krylov, A., Malkov, P., Danilova, N., Oleynikova, N.: Development of cnn-based algorithm for automatic recognition of the layers of the wall of the stomach and colon. In: Virchows Archiv, vol. 479, pp. S36–S37. Springer One New York Plaza, Suite 4600, New York, Ny, United States (2021)
12. Patel, A.: Contemporary whole slide imaging devices and their applications within the modern pathology department: A selected hardware review. J. Pathology Inform. **12**(1), 50 (2021)
13. Salvi, M., Acharya, U.R., Molinari, F., Meiburger, K.M.: The impact of pre-and post-image processing techniques on deep learning frameworks: A comprehensive review for digital pathology image analysis. Comput. Biol. Med. **128**, 104129 (2021)
14. Song, J.H., Hong, Y., Kim, E.R., Kim, S.H., Sohn, I.: Utility of artificial intelligence with deep learning of hematoxylin and eosin-stained whole slide images to predict lymph node metastasis in t1 colorectal cancer using endoscopically resected specimens; prediction of lymph node metastasis in t1 colorectal cancer. J. Gastroenterol., 1–13 (2022)
15. Wang, X., et al.: Predicting gastric cancer outcome from resected lymph node histopathology images using deep learning. Nat. Commun. **12**(1), 1–13 (2021)

Multimodal Data Processing Based on Text Classifiers and Image Recognition

Nikita Andriyanov[(✉)] [iD]

Financial University under the Government of the Russian Federation, Leningradsky pr-t 49/2, 125167 Moscow, Russian Federation
naandriyanov@fa.ru

Abstract. A rapid growth of using special intelligent systems in applied tasks has recently been observed in such an area of artificial intelligence as the joint processing of data from different modalities. In other words, in order to obtain more accurate predictions in artificial general intelligence, multimodal processing must be present. The study is devoted to solving the problem of classifying images containing data with text. A complex analysis model is proposed, which includes such steps as text extraction, image processing, text preprocessing, text processing, prediction integration. An important advantage of the multimodal model was an increase in classification efficiency by 5–8% compared to homogeneous information processing approaches. The problem of partitioning into 3 classes is considered, for which an accuracy metric of 86% was achieved.

Keywords: Natural Language Processing · Image Recognition · Complex Data Processing · Multimodal Approach · Efficiency Improvement · Machine Learning

1 Introduction

Some papers note the need to create an artificial general intelligence (AGI) [1–3]. The creation of such a highly intelligent system is not possible without the analysis of completely heterogeneous information, as is the case with a human who has several senses. A human lives in a multimodal world [4–6], in which person processes what person sees, hears, reads, etc. An increase in the number of data sources will also improve the quality of solving a number of applied problems of artificial intelligence. In particular, in the case of classifying images subjected to visual attacks [7, 8], the main component is changed to bypass the system. However, if characteristics of a non-visual nature are additionally taken into account in such a system, then the probability of successfully countering such attacks potentially increases.

The trend of research in 2022, in addition to increasing the number of modalities of processed data, is the development and training of large models consisting of billions of parameters. At the same time, this is explained, among other things, by the need to complicate the models due to the complexity of the data. An example of large models is the development of Megatron-Turing Natural Language Generator (MT NLG) [9]. This

J.-J. Rousseau and B. Kapralos (Eds.): ICPR 2022 Workshops, LNCS 13644, pp. 414–423, 2023.
https://doi.org/10.1007/978-3-031-37742-6_31

model includes 530 billion parameters and is able to extract features from heterogeneous data.

At the same time, the interest of researchers in deep learning methods related to the tasks of computer vision and natural language processing is understandable [10]. Currently, they are the most popular, since they cover a large layer of applied tasks.

Thus, our study is aimed, on the one hand, at image recognition, but, on the other hand, it is necessary to improve the quality of such recognition using text analysis. Because the input object is a ".jpeg" format image (the text is just present in the image itself), the text data must be extracted separately. The study used the PyTesseract [11] library for this. Unfortunately, it did not provide very high accuracy (100% accuracy) extraction of texts, so the base of textual information in the final version was corrected and replenished by a person manually.

The second section is devoted to a detailed description of the source data used in the study. In the next section, special attention is paid to algorithms for processing multimodal and unimodal information. Next, a comparative analysis of the results of classification by various metrics is performed.

2   Data Collection and Pre-processing

The main idea was that it is necessary to process such images, inside which there are text inserts. To collect a database of images, a specialized program was developed that parses web pages. Nevertheless, the results of classification of such images are of the greatest interest, and not the processes of their assembly, despite the fact that the dataset under study is not trivial enough. It was planned that the data would correspond to 10 different classes, but the analysis of the collected images showed that their labeling (manual classification) into 10 categories causes a number of difficulties. Thus, it was decided to conduct a study based on 3 classes of images. It should be noted that all texts on images were in English.

Memes are one of the most common types of images with texts, which is why they are included in the first class. Often, the textual information in such images can be more class-defining than the image itself. This, in turn, increases the chances of a successful multimodal classification.

Figure 1 shows one of the images from the meme base.

The second group of images are pictures that contain advertising information. Usually texts and slogans inside such images agitate for action or call for a purchase. In addition, they may contain the names of advertised products. Thus, there is potential to improve the quality of the classification of such data.

Figure 2 illustrates an example image from the sample for the second class.

The third group consisted of greeting cards images. While memes and ads may stand out with text, they can have a deeper message. At the same time, greeting cards are characterized by the presence in the text of the names of holidays and directly congratulatory words and phrases.

Figure 3 shows an example of a greeting card.

It is important to note that a specially balanced dataset was prepared, since this greatly simplifies the learning process [12]. Therefore, there were the same number of

Fig. 1. Meme class image.

Fig. 2. Advertising class image.

Fig. 3. Greeting card class image.

examples of each class in the training set. Table 1 shows the distribution of initial data by class and sample.

Table 1. Original dataset.

Class	Train Sample	Test Sample
Memes	90	49
Advertisements	90	31
Greeting cards	90	20

From the presented distribution, it can be seen that the test sample is not balanced, therefore, precision and recall metrics will be important in further analysis.

At the next stage, after dataset splitting, a block of textual information was selected as preprocessing, which made it possible to proceed to multimodal data. Extraction of texts is done with the free tool PyTesseract. Figure 4 shows an example of how PyTesseract works in one of the images.

The presented example allows to conclude that the method does not always work perfectly. However, its preliminary application before manual processing can significantly reduce labor costs. At the output, PyTesseract provide images marked up in 3 folders, as well as string data tables with a set class. Next, consider the process of training models.

```
Out[3]:  'Meviu Chusjmas & NAPPY NEW YEAR'
```

Fig. 4. Extracting text from an image.

3 Development of Algorithms for Multimodal and Unimodal Data Classification

Earlier it was noted that based on images with texts, it was possible to obtain two related samples: the first is a set of images in the ".jpeg" format itself, the second is text inserts extracted from images. Accordingly, each sample can be processed separately. For example, for images, it is possible to use computer vision models, and for texts, it is possible to use vectorization and text classification models.

By means of a manual check, all texts were brought into the correct state. This process took some time (around 2 h), but will provide better classification results.

Consider the methods of processing textual information used in this study. First, to train the classifier, it was necessary to vectorize the texts. The output of any text must be a matrix of a given dimension. Moreover, before vectorization, well-known text preprocessing methods were previously applied, such as tokenization, lemmatization, removing stop words. Tokenization means highlighting words, lemmatization is highlighting the stems of words. Some examples of stop words are not useful words as "or", "then", "but". At the output after preprocessing, the body of texts was already more compact, and the content itself was more essential. Then vectorization was used based on the term frequency – inverse document frequency (TF-IDF) model [13]. Such a model takes into account the direct relationship between the frequency of using a word in a particular text and the frequency of using a word in the entire corpus of texts. Indeed, if a word occurs frequently in texts of one class, it can probably be its indicator. However, if it is also frequently used in other classes, then its contribution to the definition of the class is reduced. In essence, the output matrix is a set of weights for words from a corpus of texts. To process new text, vectorization should always be performed only under the given structure. And after vectorization, the next processing step can be any classification model. In the current study, the support vector machine (SVM) [14] was used. Thus, the text classification block is fully described.

For image processing, it makes no sense to do a similar vectorization. Images are usually represented by brightness matrices. However, as a preprocessing, it is not bad to perform normalization so that the maximum brightness value is 1 and the minimum value is 0. Convolutional neural networks (CNNs) have proven themselves well for pattern recognition from images. The research will based on a ready-made pre-trained model and for such model only transfer learning will be performed. A network of 16 layers called VGG-16 [15] was used as computer vision model. Figure 5 shows the architecture of this network.

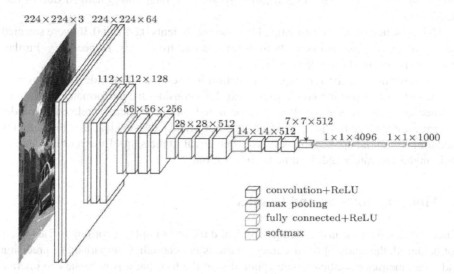

Fig. 5. VGG-16 Convolutional Network Architecture.

The initial structure of the network allows to say that the image is convolving over several cores. However, the last layer is flatten and has 1000 outlets. In our case, instead of 1000 there will be 3 outputs corresponding to the selected classes. The layer is activated using softmax function. In other words, the output has a vector of three values normalized so that they add up to one. Then each value separately can be interpreted as the probability of belonging to one of the classes. The SVM chosen for working with texts also allows, in addition to hard class predictions, to obtain soft membership probabilities. This allows to build a complex solution.

Let us write an expression (1) for estimating the resulting probability of belonging to one of the classes.

$$\max_{p_i} \overline{p} = \max[i_1 p_{i1} + t_1 p_{t1}; i_2 p_{i2} + t_2 p_{t2}; i_3 p_{i3} + t_3 p_{t3}] \tag{1}$$

where (i_j, t_j) are weights of the contributions of the probabilities of assignment to the j-th class based on the image and based on the text respectively, (pi_j, pt_j) are estimates of the probabilities of assignment to the j-th class based on the image and on the basis of the text.

From expression (1) it is clear that developed algorithm always provide a vector of three numbers, on the basis of which the class is selected by the maximum value. Let's take a closer look at an example. Let there be two probability vectors after unimodal processing. The first is from the computer vision model, the second is from the natural language processing model. For example, at the output of the VGG-16 network, there is a vector of the form $(0.4\ 0.3\ 0.3)$, and there is the vector $(0.4\ 0.6\ 0)$ at the output of the SVM algorithm. Let's assume that the contribution of each modality is the same. Then the weight coefficient for each will be equal to 0.5. So, after calculations vector $(0.4\ 0.45\ 0.15)$ will be obtained. The maximum value is 0.45 and it corresponds to the second class. From the presented example, it can be seen that the multimodal model refined the results of image classification so that the final class changed due to text classification.

Using pseudo-gradient estimation [16], the coefficients 0.64 and 0.36 were selected for the vector of class assessments from images and from texts, respectively. Further results were obtained for given coefficients.

Thus, methods for performing classification in one modality are described, as well as a model for complexing predictions. Next, let's consider the performance of various approaches on a test sample. It should be noted that only metrics related to model accuracy are analyzed, while performance is not evaluated. It is clear that the complex model in sequential application will take time equal to the sum of the running time of each model separately and the time for integration.

4 Model Evaluation and Results

Since the classification task is being solved, and the test sample, according to Table 1, is not balanced, the study of the accuracy metric is not enough. Comparison of precision and recall metrics complicates perception due to the fact that it is necessary to operate with two values, so it was decided to use F1-score as the main metric. Its advantage lies in the ability to combine recall and precision scores. Table 2 presents the calculated F1-score results for various models.

Table 2. Comparison of different approaches.

Modality	F1-score
Image	0.8235
Text	0.7968
Image + Text	0.8767

Table 2 shows that multimodal processing provides a gain of 5–8% compared to unimodal approaches. An interesting result is also that the image classification is slightly better than the text classification.

For a deeper analysis, it is appropriate to consider what mistakes the multimodal model makes. Table 3 shows the confusion matrix for the best approach. It uses short forms of class names.

Table 3. Confusion matrix.

	mem_predicted	adv_predicted	card_predicted
mem	42	7	0
adv	4	25	2
card	0	0	20

An analysis of the results presented in Table 3 shows that the developed model correctly selected all 20 greeting cards, but made 2 errors when predicting the "greeting card" class for the image of the "advertisement" class. Most of the mistakes are made when recognizing advertising images and memes. This can be easily explained by the fact that textual information on greeting cards is more specific. Advertising images, like memes, allow for humorous text.

Let us represent the confusion matrix in the form of precision and recall characteristics. Metrics for the multimodal model only are presented in Table 4.

Table 4. Precision and recall analysis.

Class	Precision	Recall
Memes	0.913043	0.857143
Advertisements	0.78125	0.806452
Greeting cards	0.909091	1

From the results of Table 4, it is clear that the hypothesis about the best quality of work with greeting cards turned out to be only partially correct. Indeed, the recall of this class is 1, but the accuracy is slightly worse than that of memes. The worst metrics are obtained when working with the "Advertisement" class.

5 Conclusions

The article presents the results of a study of various approaches to image processing with text inserts. The database of images, including 3 classes of images, is described in detail. Known models for pattern recognition in images, as well as for processing texts in natural language, are considered. On the basis of such models, an algorithm for complexing predictions is proposed and optimal weight values for unimodal models are selected. The study showed that taking into account the multimodality of data allows achieving the best results in terms of the F1-score metric. Additional metrics for the developed model are especially deeply considered. It is shown that the precision and recall metrics for all classes are about 80% and higher. The completeness for greeting cards was 100%. In general, the results are acceptable, and the model can be used to solve such problems.

References

1. Fjelland, R.: Why general artificial intelligence will not be realized. Humanit. Soc. Sci. Commun. **7**, 10 (2020). https://doi.org/10.1057/s41599-020-0494-4
2. Hsu, W.N., Bolte, B., Hubert, Y.H., Lakhotia, K., Salakhutdinov R., Mohamed, A.: HuBERT: Self-supervised Speech Representation Learning by Masked Prediction of Hidden Units. https://arxiv.org/abs/2106.07447. Accessed 30 Aug 2023
3. Ramesh, V., Kolonin, A.: Unsupervised context-driven question answering based on link grammar. In: Goertzel, B., Iklé, M., Potapov, A. (eds.) AGI 2021. LNCS (LNAI), vol. 13154, pp. 210–220. Springer, Cham (2022). https://doi.org/10.1007/978-3-030-93758-4_22
4. Remesh, A., et al.: Zero-Shot text-to-image generation. https://arxiv.org/abs/2102.12092. Accessed 28 Aug 2023
5. Radford, A., et al.: Learning Transferable Visual Models From Natural Language Supervision. https://arxiv.org/abs/2103.00020. Accessed 30 Aug 2023
6. Andriyanov, N.A., Dementiev, V.E., Tashlinskii, A.G.: Detection of objects in the images: from likelihood relationships towards scalable and efficient neural networks. Comput. Opt. **46**(1), 139–159 (2022). https://doi.org/10.18287/2412-6179-CO-922
7. Andriyanov, N.: Methods for preventing visual attacks in convolutional neural networks based on data discard and dimensionality reduction. Appl. Sci. **11**, 5235 (2021). https://doi.org/10.3390/app11115235
8. Vizilter, Y.V., Vygolov, O.V., Zheltov, S.Y.: Morphological analysis of mosaic shapes with directed relationships based on attribute and relational model representations. Comput. Opt. **45**(5), 756–766 (2021). https://doi.org/10.18287/2412-6179-CO-843
9. Tompson, A.: AI: Megatron the Transformer, and its related language models. https://lifearchitect.ai/megatron/. Accessed 31 Aug 2023
10. Fuentes, J.: How deep learning is transforming design: NLP and CV applications. https://towardsdatascience.com/how-deep-learning-is-transforming-design-cv-and-nlp-applications-4518c50690e6. Accessed 31 Aug 2023
11. PyTesseract, https://pypi.org/project/pytesseract/. Accessed 31 Aug 2023
12. Bae, S.Y., Lee, J., Jeong, J., Lim, C., Choi, J.: Effective data-balancing methods for class-imbalanced genotoxicity datasets using machine learning algorithms and molecular fingerprints. Comput. Toxicol. **20**, 10–22 (2021). https://doi.org/10.1016/j.comtox.2021.100178
13. Salton, G., Buckley, C.: Term-weighting approaches in automatic text retrieval. Inf. Process. Manage. **24**(5), 513–523 (1988)
14. Corinna, C., Vapnik, V.N.: Support-vector networks. Mach. Learn. **20**(3), 273–297 (1995). https://doi.org/10.1007/BF00994018.S2CID206787478

15. Andriyanov, N.A., Dementev, V.E., Vasiliev, K.K., Tashlinskii, A.G.: Investigation of methods for increasing the efficiency of convolutional neural networks in identifying tennis players. Pattern Recognit. Image Anal. **31**(3), 496–505 (2021). https://doi.org/10.1134/S1054661821030032

16. Vasil'ev, K.K., Dement'ev, V.E., Andriyanov, N.A.: Application of mixed models for solving the problem on restoring and estimating image parameters. Pattern Recognit. Image Anal. **26**, 240–247 (2016). https://doi.org/10.1134/S1054661816010284

Optimization of the Computer Vision System for the Detection of Moving Objects

Nikita Andriyanov[1]([envelope]) [ID], Vitaly Dementiev[2] [ID], and Alexandr Tashlinskiy[2] [ID]

[1] Financial University Under the Government of the Russian Federation, Leningradsky Pr-T 49/2 125167, Moscow, Russian Federation
naandriyanov@fa.ru
[2] Ulyanovsk State Technical University, Ul. Severny Venets, 32 432027, Ulyanovsk, Russian Federation

Abstract. The main goal of the presented work is to optimize the developed intelligent system for recognizing and detecting vehicles on video data using the YOLOv3 convolutional neural network. Basic results are obtained for real work conditions with the use of graphic processors. In addition, a special performance study was made for the Intel Core i5–8500 CPU. Optimization is based not only on classical neural network methods, such as model pruning, but also modified procedures have been proposed for efficient processing of video information, in particular, optical flow and motion prediction. After the optimization, the data processing speed increased by 4 times when using the NVIDIA RTX 2080 Super GPU and amounted to about 30 frames per second. CPU acceleration was achieved using the Intel OpenVINO toolkit. Performance on the CPU reached almost the same values as on the video card, and the acceleration was almost 30 times from slowest model to fastest. It is important to note that the implementation of optical flow and motion extrapolation was not required on the CPU.

Keywords: Pruning · Fine-Tuning · Inference · High Performance Algorithms · Optical Flow · Motion Extrapolation · YOLOv3

1 Introduction

Recently, technologies for automatic photo and video processing are increasingly penetrating various industries. In transport monitoring, the main task is operational control over the traffic situation in order to prevent accidents or detect violations of traffic rules. Recordings from Closed Circuit Television (CCTV) cameras can be used as a source for information analysis and control. However, there is a significant increase in the number of drivers and the volume of recorded information. A person in manual mode is no longer able to monitor the traffic situation with high efficiency for the allotted time. Either an increase in regular operators performing monitoring is required, or the development of automatic algorithms for tracking vehicles.

The second way involves solving the problem of automating the task of processing video information [1–3]. And this approach has a number of advantages compared to

© Springer Nature Switzerland AG 2023
J.-J. Rousseau and B. Kapralos (Eds.): ICPR 2022 Workshops, LNCS 13644, pp. 424–431, 2023.
https://doi.org/10.1007/978-3-031-37742-6_32

attracting additional staff, in addition to saving material or financial resources. First of all, the advantages lie in the possibility of continuous operation without loss of quality. The intelligent system does not lose concentration and attention, can be adapted to changing lighting conditions, and is also capable of monitoring tens and hundreds of vehicles on a single image frame at a much faster rate.

However, the automation option also has its drawbacks. The main one is that even with modern computing power, the use of deep models is very demanding on resources. True optimization in production conditions requires that the specified processing characteristics be achieved with the minimum cost of equipment. For this, it is not enough to simply perform transfer learning of known architectures of neural networks [4–6] on a large amount of data. This will solve the quality problem, but not the processing speed. For algorithms to be efficient in terms of speed, optimization is required. The easiest way involves optimizing the equipment, which will lead to an increase in material costs. This study is devoted to the development of an optimization method based on software (algorithmic) solutions.

Thus, from the traditional accuracy metrics in this work, there is a shift towards model performance metrics. It is clear that performance improvements cannot allow accuracy to fall below a given threshold. Recently, solutions have been actively proposed in the literature to speed up the logical inference of neural networks [7–12]. Despite the convenience and prevalence of the Python language, which implements most of the deep learning models in computer vision, the models provided in its libraries are not optimal in terms of performance. Code optimization methods were used by Intel, and studies [7, 8] have shown that for processors of this family in the Inference Engine with implementation in OpenVINO, there is a significant increase in inference characteristics. In [9], an increase in the processing speed is provided by the use of information compression methods, such as the principal component analysis (PCA) and singular value decomposition (SVD). The approach from [9] is not particularly novel, and the compression itself can lead to a serious deterioration in the quality metrics of detection and recognition. As an alternative, a compression model with quantization was proposed [10], but the approach was not further developed. In artificial neural networks, the idea of dimensionality reduction has also been widely used. Thus, in [11], weight quantization methods are proposed, which in a number of problems significantly increase the speed of neural networks without significant loss in quality. Another acceleration approach is the use of numerical methods, including on two-dimensional and three-dimensional grids [12]. The proposed methods can be effectively applied directly on video cards and CPUs of the Intel family.

However, a number of methods are not applicable to the problem considered in the article. First, dimensionality reduction cannot be used because many vehicles occupy a very small area in the image. Secondly, quantization was rejected because studies have shown that it does not always work, and often even leads to large losses in quality. But taking into account the structure of the video sequence of frames, it was decided to add classical methods for taking into account the connection of images in the sequence [13, 14]. It is shown that the use of an optical flow [15], which makes it possible not to repeatedly detect an object by tracing its key points from the previous frame, provides a significant increase in the processing speed. Unfortunately, after a certain number of frames, the algorithm stops working, and model have to search for objects again. Finally, motion vector prediction [16] also simplifies detection calculations in practice. But with strong motion prediction errors, it also leads to the accumulation of errors, so it is necessary to carry out detection from scratch every 3–4 frames.

So, in the ongoing study, a combination of classical methods of working with video images and neural network optimization approaches in the form of pruning is proposed, and specialized code optimization software will also be used. Discovery will be performed using the well-established YOLOv3 model, which will be discussed in more detail in the next section. It should be noted right away that the choice of this architecture is explained by the convenience of data markup, and it is also easier to implement than new versions of the model. Another factor in favor of this network is the results of a review of object detection algorithms [17]. After describing the architecture, the next section will be devoted to describing the optimization technique. Finally, after evaluating all algorithms with optimizations, a comparative analysis of the results in terms of average precision and processing speed will be performed.

2 Architecture of YOLOv3

A convolutional neural network of the YOLO architecture has received a very wide application in the problem of detecting objects in images. The abbreviation YOLO stands for "You Only Look Once". This explains how the network works. Unlike the first neural network detectors, only one pass is performed in the YOLO network, after which the object is localized and recognized in the image.

Single-pass networks are much more productive than two-pass detectors, such as the R-CNN family [18], however, acceptable processing speed results appear in the third version of the YOLO model [19]. In a simple approximation, the network divides the original image into square areas of different sizes, where the recognition problem is solved. The pretrained model is able to detect 80 object classes from the COCO dataset. Also, the bounding box and its coordinates are refined in order to maximize the Intersection over Union (IoU) parameter, which characterizes how close the object frame is to the one that the expert would draw.

The transfer learning procedure in the case of YOLOv3 is a standard procedure that allows, instead of the objects specified in COCO, to train the network to detect objects of interest in a new task. The rest of the network will work the same way as in the basic version of YOLOv3, i.e. feature extraction, square region formation, etc. Training is performed only for the last layer with the number of outputs in accordance with the number of classes. Note that the task of monitoring vehicles presented in the article does not provide for division into categories and brands of vehicles. Thus, it is possible to consider the task of binary detection: either there is a vehicle (or several) on the image or its section, or not. The task is to find all vehicles, i.e. their coordinates in the image.

Figure 1 shows the block architecture of the YOLO version 3 convolutional network.

It should be noted that the DarkNet model is used for classification, for which it is necessary to provide certain sizes of the specified areas. Equally important parts of the network are convolution and pooling layers with different parameters.

Next, let's implement transfer learning of such a network and perform its optimization.

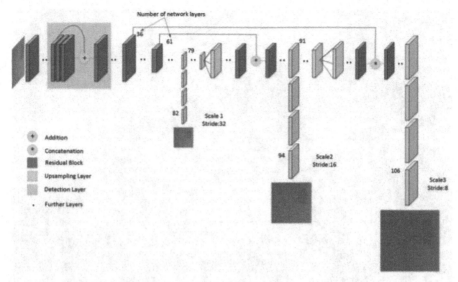

Fig. 1. YOLOv3 architecture.

3   Training and Optimization of the Developed Model

Despite the fact that video material is being processed, detection is performed on its individual frames. In this regard, the training took place on a large sample, which included 4,000 images. And the total number of vehicles in the sample was more than 70,000. The training period was set to 40 epochs, the optimization was implemented by the ADAM method, the learning rate was adaptive. During training, the NVIDIA RTX 2080 Super GPU is used, which is also used for inference.

Basic transfer learning with the parameters noted above was successful. It should be noted that image augmentation technologies were additionally used [20, 21]. It's expedient to estimate the quality of the model according to the classical metric of mean average precision (mAP). When checking on a test sample of 500 images (with more than 5000 vehicles), the mAP value reached 0.9702. The number of frames processed per second was 3.4.

The next step is fine-tuning the model. The following optimal parameters were selected: input image size is 608x608 px, batch size is 3. Thus, fine-tuning managed to achieve a 2.3 times speedup of the neural network. The number of processed frames per second approached 7.5. Losses on the mAP metric were negligible.

Figure 2 shows an example of how the algorithm works on one of the frames. Figure 2 shows that the algorithm works confidently and detects all vehicles in the presented image.

However, the resulting acceleration was not enough to work in the processing mode of 25 frames per second, even when using a video card. To increase the processing speed, the weights of the trained model were pruned. A cyclic operation was performed, during which weights were incriminated, including up to a complete reset, as long as the weights of the model exceeded the specified threshold value. Due to pruning, a reduction

Fig. 2. An example of the operation of a neural network after training.

in connections within the neural network is achieved, which leads to a reduction in calculations. After optimization, it was possible to achieve a processing speed of 10 frames per second, while the mAP loss was about 0.3%.

Quantization could become a new optimization step, but due to the reasons described earlier, quantization was not implemented. But the optical flow was implemented. The next step was to use the optical flow using the tools of the Python programming language. Optical flow is not often used in modern video information processing tasks, although it can be used to estimate the movement of key points in an optical image. The disadvantage of this method is the inability to accurately calculate the optical flow over a long period of time. In the current study, errors increased significantly after processing three frames. However, the rejection of the inference of the neural network during the intermediate frames made it possible to increase the speed by another 2 times.

Figure 3 shows an example of how optical flow technology works. The figure shows how the key points of the truck move based on the sparse optical flow.

The use of optical flow resulted in a performance of 20 frames per second. This is not enough to achieve the goal. The last optimization step was to use the motion extrapolation method. The new position of the vehicle was predicted based on the estimated speed. To do this, the motion vector is estimated along the image axes and a prediction is made. Based on this approach, there is no necessarily to perform vehicle detection from scratch, which provides acceleration.

Figure 4 shows an example of new position prediction and velocity vector estimation.

Fig. 3. Sparse optical flow technology example.

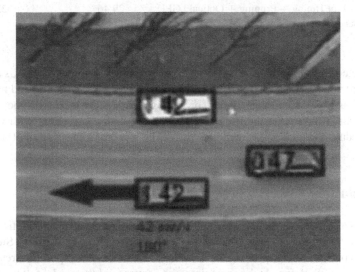

Fig. 4. Motion extrapolation example.

Thus, the step-by-step procedures guarantee the required frame processing speed. The final performance was 29.5 frames per second. It is important to note that there is no loss in the quality of the neural network after applying the optical flow and motion extrapolation, since no changes are made to the neural network itself.

Finally, it also should be noted that also interesting acceleration results were obtained using the Intel OpenVINO toolkit, which, firstly, does not lead to quality losses, and secondly, accelerates the neural network obtained as a result of fine tuning by 2.5 times. This is because OpenVINO optimizes the code for the Intel processor.

4   Comparison of Optimization Results

As noted earlier, mAP was used as the quality metric, and fps was used as the performance metric. Table 1 presents the results for various models.

Table 1. Comparison of performance and precision.

Methods	Hardware	Performance, FPS	Precision, mAP
YOLOv3	CPU	1.1	0.9702
YOLOv3 + FineTuning	CPU	2.85	0.9656
YOLOv3 + FineTuning + OpenVINO	CPU	7.42	0.9656
YOLOv3	GPU	3.42	0.9702
YOLOv3 + FineTuning	GPU	7.56	0.9656
YOLOv3 + FineTuning + Pruning	GPU	10.92	0.9622
YOLOv3 + FineTuning + Pruning + Optical Flow	GPU	20.04	0.9622
YOLOv3 + FineTuning + Pruning + Optical Flow + Speed Extrapolation	GPU	29.46	0.9622

From the results presented in Table 1, it is possible to conclude that GPUs are somewhat faster than the OpenVINO-optimized CPU detector. Also, pruning and fine-tuning reduce the quality of the model slightly, providing a significant increase in performance. It is important to note that the use of traditional methods of working with video data does not reduce the quality of the model, providing a processing speed of 30 frames per second.

5   Conclusions

Algorithms and methods that provide optimization of the YOLOv3 convolutional neural network model in the problem of vehicle detection and tracking are studied. Step by step application of fine tuning, pruning, optical flow and motion extrapolation resulted in a performance of 29.46 fps. At the same time, the accuracy of the model fell by only 0.8% according to the mAP metric. In the future, it is planned to conduct similar studies for the YOLOv4 and YOLOv5 versions, as well as perform weight quantization.

References

1. Andriyanov, N., Dementiev, V., Kondratiev, D.: Tracking of Objects in Video Sequences. In: Czarnowski, I., Howlett, R.J., Jain, L.C. (eds.) Intelligent Decision Technologies. SIST, vol. 238, pp. 253–262. Springer, Singapore (2021). https://doi.org/10.1007/978-981-16-2765-1_21
2. Li, G., Zhang, D., Zeng, J., Chen, S.: Vehicle monitor system for public transport management based on embedded technology. Phys. Procedia **24**(2), 953–960 (2012). https://doi.org/10.1016/j.phpro.2012.02.143
3. Khan, S.U., Alam, N., Jan, S.U., Koo, I.S.: IoT-Enabled vehicle speed monitoring system. Electronics **11**, 614 (2022). https://doi.org/10.3390/electronics11040614
4. Cai, Z., Vasconcelos N.: Cascade R-CNN: High Quality Object Detection and Instance Segmentation, https://arxiv.org/abs/1906.09756, Accessed 27 Aug 2022

5. Carion, N., Massa, F., Synnaeve, G., Usunier, N., Kirillov, A., Zagoruyko, S.: End-to-End Object Detection with Transformers, https://arxiv.org/abs/2005.12872, Accessed 27 Aug 2022
6. Song, X., Gu, W.: Multi-objective real-time vehicle detection method based on yolov5. In: 2021 International Symposium on Artificial Intelligence and its Application on Media (ISAIAM) Proceedings, pp. 142–145 (2021). https://doi.org/10.1109/ISAIAM53259.2021.00037
7. Andriyanov, N.: Analysis of the acceleration of neural networks inference on Intel processors based on OpenVINO Toolkit. In: Proceedings of 2020 Systems of Signal Synchronization, Generating and Processing in Telecommunications, SYNCHROINFO, pp. 1–6 (2020). https://doi.org/10.1109/SYNCHROINFO49631.2020.9166067
8. Arnautović, A., Teskeredzic, E.: Evaluation of artificial neural network inference speed and energy consumption on embedded systems. INFOTEH 1, 1–5 (2021). https://doi.org/10.1109/INFOTEH51037.2021.9400658
9. Zhang, X., Zou, J., He, K., Sun, J.: Accelerating very deep convolutional networks for classification and detection, https://arxiv.org/pdf/1505.06798.pdf, Accessed 28 Aug 2022
10. Xiao, B., Shi, W., Lu, G.: An optimized quantization technique for image compression using discrete tchebichef transform. Pattern Recognit. Image Anal. 28, 371–378 (2018). https://doi.org/10.1134/S1054661818030021
11. Novac, P.E., Boukli, G.H., Pegatoquet, A., Miramond, B., Gripon, V.: Quantization and deployment of deep neural networks on microcontrollers. Sensors 21, 2984 (2021). https://doi.org/10.3390/s21092984
12. Shirokanev, A.S., Andriyanov, N.A., Ilyasova, N.Y.: Development of vector algorithm using CUDA technology for three-dimensional retinal laser coagulation process modeling. Comput. Opt. 45(3), 427–437 (2021). https://doi.org/10.18287/2412-6179-CO-828
13. Andriyanov, N.A., Vasil'ev, K.K.; Dement'ev, V.E.: Investigation of filtering and objects detection algorithms for a multizone image sequence. International Archives of the Photogrammetry, Remote Sensing and Spatial Information Sciences - ISPRS Archives 42, is. 2/W12, 7–10 (2019). https://doi.org/10.5194/isprs-archives-XLII-2-W12-7-2019
14. Borman, S., Stevenson, R.: Image Sequence Processing. University of Notre Dame, Paris (2002)
15. Anitha, E., Jiji, C.V.: Optical acceleration for motion description in videos. In: CVPR 2017 Proceedings, pp. 1–9 (2017)
16. Flynn, J., Neulander, I., Philbin, J., Snavely, N.: Deepstereo: Learning to predict new views from the world's imagery. In: Proceedings of the IEEE Conference on Computer Vision and Pattern Recognition, pp. 5515–5524 (2016)
17. Andriyanov, N.A., Dementiev, V.E., Tashlinskii, A.G.: Detection of objects in the images: from likelihood relationships towards scalable and efficient neural networks. Comput. Opt. 46(1), 139–159 (2022). https://doi.org/10.18287/2412-6179-CO-922
18. Girshick, R.: Fast R-CNN. In: Proceedings of International Conference on Computer Vision (ICCV), vol. 1, pp. 1440–1448 (2015). https://doi.org/10.1109/ICCV.2015.169
19. Redmon, J., Farhadi, A.: YOLOv3: An incremental improvement, https://arxiv.org/abs/1804.02767 Accessed 30 Aug 2022
20. Dementyiev, V.E., Andriyanov, N.A., Vasilyiev, K.K.: Use of images augmentation and implementation of doubly stochastic models for improving accuracy of recognition algorithms based on convolutional neural networks. In: Proceedings of 2020 Systems of Signal Synchronization, Generating and Processing in Telecommunications, SYNCHROINFO, pp. 1–4 (2020). https://doi.org/10.1109/SYNCHROINFO49631.2020.9166000
21. Buslaev, A., Iglovikov, V.I., Khvedchenya, E., Parinov, A., Druzhinin, M., Kalinin, A.A.: Albumentations: fast and flexible image augmentations. Information 11, 125 (2020). https://doi.org/10.3390/info11020125

Neuromorphic Image Coding Based on a Sample of Counts Partition by a System of Receptive Fields

Viacheslav Antsiperov[(✉)] [iD]

Kotelnikov Institute of Radioengineering and Electronics of RAS, Mokhovaya 11-7, Moscow,
Russian Federation
antciperov@cplire.ru

Abstract. The problem of synthesis of image encoding methods based on the
data of the images themselves is considered. The proposed approach is based on
the previously developed special representation of images by samples of counts
(sampling representations). Since sampling representations are essentially random
constructions, the synthesis of encoding methods is carried out strictly within the
generative approach. Within the framework of this approach, the image coding
procedure is treated as a special case of statistical parametric estimation of the
probability distribution density. The choice of a parametric family of possible distributions is limited in work by a model of a mixture of predefined components.
Accordingly, a set of estimates of the weights of the mixture components, calculated from a sampling representation, considered as input data, is interpreted
as the output of the image encoding procedure. In this context, the natural criterion for optimal coding is the maximum likelihood criterion. For the algorithmic
implementation of the coding procedure, the mixture model is equipped with a
structure of receptive fields, known in neurophysiology as the basic principle of
organizing human retinal receptors. On this basis, a relatively simple recurrent
coding algorithm is synthesized, close to the popular EM algorithm in machine
learning. The article presents an interpretation of some features of the algorithm
from the point of view of known facts about image processing in the periphery of
the visual system, discusses options for implementing the algorithm, and presents
some results of numerical simulation.

Keywords: Neuromorphic Coding · Sampling representations · Receptive Fields

1 Introduction

Image compression methods, due to the explosive development of multimedia technologies initiated by the ongoing progress of Internet communications, are currently
extremely in demand and are the subject of extensive research [1]. In this regard, recent
research related to advances in deep learning and its application to image processing
should be highlighted [2]. At the same time, we note that despite the novelty of this
direction, it is still based on the fundamental ideas of Claude Shannon, outlined half a
century ago in his famous work [3], devoted to the rate-distortion theory.

© Springer Nature Switzerland AG 2023
J.-J. Rousseau and B. Kapralos (Eds.): ICPR 2022 Workshops, LNCS 13644, pp. 432–444, 2023.
https://doi.org/10.1007/978-3-031-37742-6_33

The rate-distortion theory in essence analyzes the fundamental trade-off between the bit rate used to transfer some encoded representation of data and the distortion that occurs in the decoding/recovering process. Initially, it was believed that the main goal of this theory, especially in the field of image compression, is to find ways to reduce the distortion of the recovered data as much as possible (for a given rate). However, it has recently been shown that minimizing the distortion itself does not necessarily result in the good perceptual quality of the recovered images. For example, it has been shown that the use of coding methods in generative adversarial networks can lead to a notable improvement in the quality of image perception, although the distortion of the original image may be not minimal [2]. Considering these facts, it would be natural to correct the traditional rate-distortion theory for factors related to human perception of images. It is extremely important to find out how the best achievable bit rate / compression ratio depends not only on distortion, but also on the quality of perception of the result. Recently, several attempts have been made to include characteristics related to the quality of perception into the rate-distortion theory [4, 5]. Unfortunately, there is still neither good theoretical concept, nor even convincing practical recommendations on the influence of this factor on the trade-off between rate and distortion.

In the classical Shannon's theory objective image quality measures are usually calculated using the distortion function, a quantitative metric, representing the absolute or quadratic difference between the recovered version of the image and it's original. However, it is well known that the image distortion perceived by a human viewer cannot be adequately described by such simple mathematical means. Since visual perception is very complex, subject to many distortion factors and difficult to model, building a quantitative metric of perceptual quality is one of the most difficult tasks in the field of image processing. It is for these reasons that, until recently, the characteristics of the perceptual quality of images were assessed, as a rule, only with the help of categorical scales associated with subjective assessments in groups of viewers. To somehow correct the existing situation, significant efforts have recently been made to find objective features related to visual quality. The main requirement for these features was the need for their high correlation with known categorical quality assessments and with subjective opinions. The most promising feature-based metrics proposed until now are structural similarity image metric (SSIM) [6]/multiscale structural similarity image metric (MS-SSIM) [7], visual information fidelity (VIF) [8], spatial and temporal most apparent distortion (MAD) [9], perception-based video metric (PVM) [10] etc. Also noteworthy is the machine learning-based video multimethod assessment fusion (VMAF) [11] developed by researchers at Netflix, which evaluates subjective image quality by combining a regression model score and several other metrics – detail loss metric (DLM), VIF (at four different scales) etc.

This work is also devoted to issues declaring the perceptual quality [5] of images after compression/recovery as the main factor in image encoding. However, in contrast to the approaches listed above, we have chosen a fundamentally different way - the way of perceptual coding synthesis based on the most adequate for human perception representations of images, and not on the most appropriate perceptual metrics. Namely, we base our approach on the previously developed biologically motivated representation of images by controlled size samples of counts (sampling representations) [12] which are discussed in Sect. 1 below. Since the sampling representations are essentially random, the proposed approach differs noticeably from the others in its fundamentally statistical orientation. In this respect, our approach is much closer to the generative model-based approaches currently popular in machine learning, such as Generative Adversarial Networks (GANs) [13], Variational Autoencoders (VAEs) [14], Deep Belief Networks (DBNs) [15] etc. The basic scheme of the proposed approach focused on generative image models in the form of sampling representations, is described in Sect. 2.

Since within the framework of generative models the main objects are the probability distributions of input/output data [16], the focus of our approach is also on the probability distributions of sampling representation counts. Having in mind that the specific feature of sampling representations is the fact that their complete statistical description has the form of a product of the distribution densities of individual counts, the goal of the proposed approach is, in essence, to estimate these densities. Within the scheme of the proposed approach, such estimates are the parameters of the densities chosen from a certain parametric family of probability distributions. In this regard, the choice of the model of the parametric family that is adequate to the features of visual perception is extremely important, both from the point of view of the features of perceptual encoding of images and from the point of view of the perceptual quality of their recovered versions. Section 3 discusses in detail the choice of a parametric family in the form of a system of receptive fields. We specifically emphasize that the main criterion for the adequacy of human perception of images in the approach concerns modeling the mechanisms of human visual system (HVS) [17], and not the maximum correlation with known categorical quality scales.

The theoretical aspects of the proposed approach are supported in Sect. 4 by the discussion of a possible algorithmic implementation of perceptual image compression and by the results of computer simulation.

2 The Essence of the Sampling Representation

In several previous papers [18, 19] we proposed the representation of images by the samples of random counts (representation by counting statistics [20]). The proposed representations imply the well-known principles of the interaction of radiation with matter at the microlevel and are associated with the resulting flow of random events related to registration of photons of incident radiation. These events, depending on the substance of the photodetector, can be of different physical nature. For example, they may represent changes in the conformation of the rhodopsin molecules in the retina photoreceptor, which ultimately leads to the generation of neuro-impulses in the optic nerve. From a statistical point of view, the nature of these events, in the terminology of [20] - counts, is not important. They are regarded simply as random events in the sense of classical probability theory and are given by random coordinates $\vec{x}$. In the semiclassical approximation [21], the probability of occurrence of n events (n counts) $X = (\vec{x}_1, \ldots, \vec{x}_n)$ when radiation intensity $I(\vec{x})$ is registered by a detector with a photosensitive surface Ω is given by the statistics of a two-dimensional inhomogeneous point Poisson process with the intensity function $\lambda(\vec{x}) = \alpha I(\vec{x})$, where α is a constant coefficient depending on the average photon energy, detector quantum efficiency and time of registration.

Unfortunately, under normal conditions of light perception, the number of counts n is too large (the photon flux from the sun through $\Omega \sim 1\,cm^2$ for 1 ms is $\sim 10^{12}-10^{14}$ [22]), so the direct use of the representation X in the form of point Poisson process is practically unrealizable. To solve this problem, i.e., to reduce the size of representations, some time ago we proposed the following approach [1]. From the very beginning, we fix some acceptable value of the representation size in k counts and, considering the entire set X of the image counts as some general population, we choose a random sample $X_k = (\vec{x}_{i_1}, \ldots, \vec{x}_{i_k})$ of k counts from it. Obviously, such a sample, in full accordance with the principles of classical statistical theory, will still represent an image. Such X_k, as the image representation we name a sample of random counts or, in short, a sampling representation. The statistical description of the sampling representation X_k easily follows from the Poisson statistics for X and has an extremely simple form:

$$
\begin{aligned}
&\rho(X_k|I(\vec{x})) = \prod_{j=1}^{k} \rho(\vec{x}_j|I(\vec{x})), \\
&\rho(\vec{x}_j|I(\vec{x})) = \frac{1}{W}I(\vec{x}_j), \\
&W = \iint_{\Omega} I(\vec{x})ds,
\end{aligned}
\tag{1}
$$

Note that the statistical description of the sampling representation (1) has several remarkable properties. First, distribution $\rho(X_k|I(\vec{x}))$ fixes the conditional independence (for a given intensity $I(\vec{x})$) and the same distribution (iid property) of all k counts $\vec{x}_j$. Secondly, the distribution density of each of the counts $\rho(\vec{x}_j|I(\vec{x}))$ is related to the intensity of the detected radiation $I(\vec{x})$ in the simplest way – it is equal to its normalized version (W is the total radiation energy at the surface Ω). And, thirdly, description (1) is in a certain sense universal - it does not depend on the coefficient α (the energy of photons, the quantum efficiency of the detector), nor on the registration time, nor on the intensity units $I(\vec{x})$.

In view of the proportionality $\rho(\vec{x}|I(\vec{x})) \sim I(\vec{x})$ (1), digital images, traditionally interpreted as the values of the registered intensity $I(\vec{x})$, digitized with a certain reso-lution $Q = \Delta I$, can now be interpreted (up to the value of the total illumination W) as probability distributions of individual iid count $\vec{x}$. This allows the treatment of images as probabilistic models and opens the way to generative modeling and immersion of image perceptual compression problems in the context of machine learning research.

As an example, consider the application of the Monte Carlo technique [23] to the problem of generating a sampling representation of a bitmap image given by pixels $\{n_i\}$, $i = 1, \ldots, N$, where n_i are the digitization levels of the registered intensity $I(\vec{x})$, $n_i \approx I(\vec{x}_i)/Q$, $\vec{x}_i$ are the locations of pixels in the image field Ω. In accordance with (1), this bitmap specifies the following approximation of the probability distribution of individual count:

$$
\hat{\rho}(\vec{x}_j|I(\vec{x})) \approx \frac{n_i}{\sum_{k=1}^{N}n_k},
\tag{2}
$$

where the count $\vec{x}_j$ belongs to the site of the pixel $\vec{x}_i$. Thus, the problem of generating a sampling representation is essentially reduced to the problem of choosing a sample of k random counts from distribution (2). To solve the problem in the field of machine learning, there are many methods for sampling counts - Monte Carlo methods [6]. Some methods, for example, the rejection sampling [23], do not even require preliminary normalization of pixels - it is enough to know the maximum possible pixel values $n_{max} = I_{max}/Q = 2^{\nu}$, where ν denotes the bit depth of the bitmap image. To illustrate, consider generating sampling representations of the standard "Mandril" image (see Fig. 1) using the rejection sampling [23]. The algorithm is executed iteratively, at each iteration a random vector $\vec{x} \in \Omega$ with floating point coordinates x_1, x_2 is formed. Each coordinate is generated by a standard generator of random numbers uniformly distributed on $[0, L)$, where L is the linear size of the (square) image. Based on $\vec{x}$, a pixel n_i is determined in the $int(x_1)$ row and $int(x_2)$ column of the image map, where $int()$ is the rounding operation. Then an auxiliary standard random value $y \in [0, n_{max})$ is generated and the value of n_i is compared with the value y. If the pixel value n_i is less than y, the $\vec{x}$ vector is added to the X sample, if not, it is rejected. When the number of selected random counts in X becomes equal to the given k, the algorithm ends, and the generated sample is declared to be a sampling representation X_k. Figure 1 shows examples of the original "Mandril" image and its representations by samples of sizes 100,000 and 1,000,000 counts.

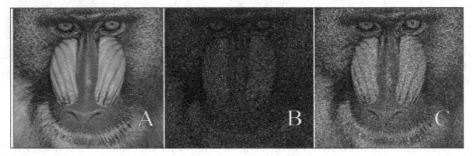

Fig. 1. Representation of the "Mandril" image by samples of random counts: A) original image in TIF format, B), C) representation by samples of sizes, respectively, 100.000 and 1.000.000 counts

3 General Image Encoding Scheme Based on Selective Sampling Representation

Returning to the statistical description of the sampling representation (1), let us emphasize once again that as soon as the probabilistic image model $\rho(\vec{x}|I(\vec{x}))$, which up to normalization W coincides with the intensity distribution $I(\vec{x})$ on Ω, is given, the sample X_k is completely statistically determined and, in particular, its random realization can be generated, for example, in the manner described above. Since the sample size k is a controllable parameter, the sampling representation X_k can also be viewed as some controlled compression of the original large population X of counts, representing the image $\sim I(\vec{x})$ (see above). In other words, the sampling representation X_k can be interpreted as a "compressed" image, and the compression procedure, as noted above, most adequately simulates the mechanisms of visual perception in the retina (a more detailed discussion of these issues can be found in [24]).

In connection with the interpretation of the sampling representation X_k as a compressed image, the question immediately arises of how it is possible to recover the original image from X_k with a lack or absence of information about it. Within the framework of the statistical formulation of the problem, the formalization of this question leads to a well-known problem in the field of generative approaches in machine learning – the restoration of the probabilistic distribution $\rho(\vec{x}|I(\vec{x}))$ using the set of observations–counts $X_k = \{\vec{x}_j\} - \hat{\rho}(\vec{x}|X_k)$, with incomplete or missing information about $I(\vec{x})$ [25].

The simplest solution to the problem of restoring a probability distribution is a nonparametric estimate of the distribution density - an empirical probability density function (epdf) [26]:

$$\hat{\rho}(\vec{x}|X_k = \{\vec{x}_j\}) = \frac{1}{k}\sum\nolimits_{j=1}^{k}\delta(\vec{x} - \vec{x}_j), \tag{3}$$

where $\delta(\vec{x})$ is the Dirac delta function. The density estimates of the form (3) have been widely used as the sampling density for the bootstrap [27]. With its help, you can get simple estimates of the average values of arbitrary functions on images, for example, the moments:

$$\begin{aligned} E(\vec{x}) &= \iint_\Omega \vec{x}\hat{\rho}(\vec{x}|X_k = \{\vec{x}_j\})ds = \frac{1}{k}\sum\nolimits_{j=1}^{k}\vec{x}_j \\ E(\vec{x}\vec{x}^T) &= \iint_\Omega \vec{x}\vec{x}^T\hat{\rho}(\vec{x}|X_k = \{\vec{x}_j\})ds = \frac{1}{k}\sum\nolimits_{j=1}^{k}\vec{x}_j\vec{x}_j^T \end{aligned}, \tag{4}$$

etc., however, from the point of view of perception, recovered images of the form (3) are of very low quality, especially for small k. To verify this, it is sufficient to refer to Fig. 1. Unfortunately, numerous generalizations of (3) in the form of kernel density estimators and even adaptive kernel density estimators [26] do not solve the problem either. As applied directly to the problems of recovering images from sampling representations, the corresponding results (concerning the Parzen-Rosenblatt windows) can be found in [24].

The problem with the low perceptual quality of recovered images by classical density estimation methods, as noted in the introduction, is associated with the use of non-perceptual metrics as distortion functions. Recently, however, a search for alternative approaches to the issues of perceptual image recovering has intensified. A remarkable result here was the discovery of the fact that human perception is more focused not on distortions understood in the classical (metric) sense, but on the information similarity of the corresponding images [5]. Note that within the framework of our approach, in which images are interpreted as distributions of probabilities of counts, it is easy to formally write down the proper measure of informational similarity of images as the relative information (Kullback-Leibler divergence) of corresponding distributions [28]:

$$D_{KL}(\rho_1(\vec{x})|\rho_2(\vec{x})) = -\iint_\Omega \rho_1(\vec{x})\ln\frac{\rho_2(\vec{x})}{\rho_1(\vec{x})}ds, \tag{5}$$

where $\rho_1(\vec{x})$ and $\rho_2(\vec{x})$ are the probability densities of counts, corresponding to images. Note, by the way, the well-known fact that the measure D_KL (5) is not a metric [28].

If we take as $\rho_1(\vec{x})$ the epdf (3), and as $\rho_2(\vec{x})$ a density from some family of densities $\mathcal{R} = \{\rho_a(\vec{x})\}$ that can be accepted for recovering, then the based on (5) procedure of perceptual image recovering will take the form:

$$\begin{aligned} \rho_2(\vec{x}) &= arg\min_{\rho_a(\vec{x})\in\mathcal{R}} D_{KL}(\hat{\rho}(\vec{x}|X_k = \{\vec{x}_j\})|\rho_2(\vec{x})) \\ &= -arg\min_{\rho_a(\vec{x})\in\mathcal{R}}\sum\nolimits_{j=1}^{k}\ln\rho_a(\vec{x}_j) = arg\max_{\rho_a(\vec{x})\in\mathcal{R}}\ln\rho_a(X_k = \{\vec{x}_j\}), \end{aligned} \tag{6}$$

where, in accordance with (1) $\rho_a(X_k = \{\vec{x}_j\}) = \prod_{j=1}^{k} \rho_a(\vec{x}_j)$ is the likelihood function of sampling representation X_k. If the family of densities $\mathcal{R}$ is parametric $\mathcal{R} = \{\rho(\vec{x}; \vec{\theta})\}, \vec{\theta} \in \Theta$, then the recovery procedure (6) turns exactly into R. Fisher's maximum likelihood parameter estimation [29]:

$$\rho_{ML}(\vec{x}) = arg \max_{\vec{\theta} \in \Theta} \ln \rho\left(X_k; \vec{\theta}\right)$$
$$\rho\left(X_k; \vec{\theta}\right) = \prod_{j=1}^{k} \rho\left(\vec{x}_j; \vec{\theta}\right) \quad (7)$$

Since the maximum likelihood approach has existed for more than a hundred years, it has a huge number of methods of solving the problem (7). So, the last difficult task for the proposed approach is the choice of definite parametric family $\mathcal{R} = \{\rho(\vec{x}; \vec{\theta})\}$.

4 Equipping an Image Encoding Scheme with a System of Receptive Fields

Since the work of Hubel and Wiesel [30], it has been known that the visual neurons of the inner retinal layer do not respond to the signals of individual photoreceptors, but to the cooperative activation of groups of receptors located in small areas of the outer retinal layer. The small area of the retina, the activation of which leads to the excitation of some output neuron, is called the receptive field of this neuron. Some neighboring on/off-center pairs of neurons have completely overlapped fields, while the receptive fields for other neurons do not overlap them. The size and arrangement of the receptive fields is such that they form a complete mosaic map of the visual field Ω on the retina. Considering these facts, we choose a parametric model of the desired probability distribution density $\rho(\vec{x}; \vec{\theta})$ in the form of a mixture of K pairs of components $\{C_i(\vec{x}), E_i(\vec{x})\}, i = 1, \ldots, K$, located in nodes $\{\vec{\mu}_i\}$ of some imaginary regular grid covering Ω entirely:

$$\rho\left(\vec{x}; \vec{\theta}\right) = \sum_{i=1}^{K} w_i C_i(\vec{x}) + v_i E_i(\vec{x}) \quad (8)$$

where $\vec{\theta} = \{w_i, v_i\}$ are positive mixture weights, model parameters. Components $C_i(\vec{x})$ and $E_i(\vec{x})$ represent a compact center and a concentric antagonistic environment of the i-th receptive field and are given by positive probability distribution densities with a common compact support Δ_i, which is a neighborhood of the node $\vec{\mu}_i$. The set of carriers of receptive fields $\{\Delta_i\}$ constitutes a partition of the overall field of view - they do not intersect with each other, but their union densely covers Ω.

Take as components $C_i(\vec{x})$ and $E_i(\vec{x})$ copies of some base center $C(\vec{x}) \geq 0$ and base environment $E(\vec{x}) \geq 0, \vec{x} \in \Delta \subset \mathbb{R}^2$ moved to the grid nodes $\{\vec{\mu}_i\}$. The region Δ in which $C(\vec{x}), E(\vec{x}) \neq 0$ will be called the base support. The support Δ is assumed to be symmetric so that it contains origin $\vec{0} \in \Delta$ and together with each $\vec{x} \in \Delta$ contains its opposite $-\vec{x}$.

The simplest example of component geometry is the base center $C(\vec{x})$ supported by a circular region $\Delta_C \subset \Delta$ and its base environment $E(\vec{x})$ supported by the complement

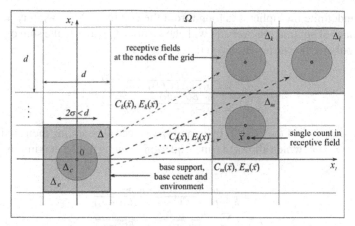

Fig. 2. The simplest geometry of the arrangement of receptive fields $C_i(\vec{x})$ and $E_i(\vec{x})$ at the nodes $\vec{\mu}_i$ of the grid, covering Ω with step d

$\Delta_E = \Delta - \Delta_C$, where Δ is a square base support with side d, coinciding with the grid step. This geometry is shown in Fig. 2.

Considering the assumptions made, model (8) can be written as:

$$\rho\left(\vec{x}; \vec{\theta}\right) = \sum_{i=1}^{K} w_i C(\vec{x} - \vec{\mu}_i) + v_i E(\vec{x} - \vec{\mu}_i). \tag{9}$$

From the normalization conditions for $\rho\left(\vec{x}; \vec{\theta}\right)$, $C(\vec{x})$ and $E(\vec{x})$ it follows:

$$\sum_{i=1}^{K} w_i + v_i = 1. \tag{10}$$

Assuming the independence of the counts $\{\vec{x}_j\}$ and considering that each sample $\vec{x}_j$ can belong to only one carrier Δ_{i_j} for some $i_j \in \{1, \ldots, K\}$, we write the likelihood function of the sampling representation X_n in the form:

$$\rho\left(\{\vec{x}_j\}|\vec{\theta}\right) = \prod_{j=1}^{k} \left[w_{i_j} C(\vec{x}_j - \vec{\mu}_{i_j}) + v_{i_j} E(\vec{x}_j - \vec{\mu}_{i_j})\right]. \tag{11}$$

Since further it is convenient to work with the logarithmic likelihood function $\Lambda_{X_n}\left(\vec{\theta}\right) = \ln\rho\left(\{\vec{x}_j\}|\vec{\theta}\right)$, we rewrite (11) explicitly for $\Lambda_{X_n}\left(\vec{\theta}\right)$ as:

$$\Lambda_{X_n}\left(\vec{\theta}\right) = \sum_{j=1}^{k} \ln\left[w_{i_j} C(\vec{x}_j - \vec{\mu}_{i_j}) + v_{i_j} E(\vec{x}_j - \vec{\mu}_{i_j})\right]. \tag{12}$$

The maximum-likelihood parameters $\vec{\theta} = \{w_i, v_i\}$ corresponding to $\Lambda_{X_n}\left(\vec{\theta}\right)$ (12) can be found by applying the Lagrange multipliers method under constraint (10). As a result, the following system of equations is obtained:

$$\begin{cases} \dfrac{\partial \Lambda_{X_n}\left(\vec{\theta}\right)}{\partial w_i} = \sum_{j=1}^{k} \dfrac{C(\vec{x}_j - \vec{\mu}_{i_j})}{w_{i_j} C(\vec{x}_j - \vec{\mu}_{i_j}) + v_{i_j} E(\vec{x}_j - \vec{\mu}_{i_j})} \delta_{i_j, i} = \lambda \\[4mm] \dfrac{\partial \Lambda_{X_n}\left(\vec{\theta}\right)}{\partial v_i} = \sum_{j=1}^{k} \dfrac{E(\vec{x}_j - \vec{\mu}_{i_j})}{w_{i_j} C(\vec{x}_j - \vec{\mu}_{i_j}) + v_{i_j} E(\vec{x}_j - \vec{\mu}_{i_j})} \delta_{i_j, i} = \lambda \end{cases}. \tag{13}$$

where the indefinite multiplier λ is found from the condition $\sum_{i=1}^{K} w_i + v_i = 1$ (10).

If the place of summation over all j with the symbol $\delta_{ij,i}$ goes to the sum over samples belonging only to the carrier Δ_i, we get:

$$\sum_{j}^{ij=i} \frac{C(\vec{x}_j - \vec{\mu}_i)}{w_i C(\vec{x}_j - \vec{\mu}_i) + v_i E(\vec{x}_j - \vec{\mu}_i)} = \lambda$$
$$\sum_{j}^{ij=i} \frac{E(\vec{x}_j - \vec{\mu}_i)}{w_i C(\vec{x}_j - \vec{\mu}_i) + v_i E(\vec{x}_j - \vec{\mu}_i)} = \lambda \quad . \tag{14}$$

Multiplying each of the Eqs. (7) by w_i and v_i, respectively, adding them and summing over i, we get $\lambda = k$, which allows the final equations to hang for the maximum-likelihood parameters:

$$w_i = \frac{1}{k} \sum_{j}^{ij=i} \frac{C(\vec{x}_j - \vec{\mu}_i) w_i}{w_i C(\vec{x}_j - \vec{\mu}_i) + v_i E(\vec{x}_j - \vec{\mu}_i)}$$
$$v_i = \frac{1}{k} \sum_{j}^{ij=i} \frac{E(\vec{x}_j - \vec{\mu}_i) v_i}{w_i C(\vec{x}_j - \vec{\mu}_i) + v_i E(\vec{x}_j - \vec{\mu}_i)} \quad . \tag{15}$$

The system of Eqs. (15) is a relatively simple nonlinear system that expresses the required parameters $\vec{\theta} = \{w_i, v_i\}$ through the function $\vec{G}$ of themselves and of the samples $\{\vec{x}_j\}$ (sampling representation X_k): $\vec{\theta} = \vec{G}(\vec{\theta}; X_k)$. A well-known method for solving such equations is the method of successive approximations [31], which iteratively finds the next approximation $\vec{\theta}^{(\tau+1)} = \vec{G}(\vec{\theta}^{(\tau)}; X_k)$. There are many algorithmic implementations of the method [32], the specifics of each of the algorithm are determined by the features of the iterating function $\vec{G}$.

In the case of system (15), a feature of the function $\vec{G}(\vec{\theta}; X_k)$ is that it depends on $\vec{\theta}$ only through the likelihood ratios $L_i(\vec{\theta}; \vec{x}_j) = v_i E(\vec{x}_j - \vec{\mu}_i) / C(\vec{x}_j - \vec{\mu}_i) w_i$. Therefore, it is natural to split the calculations of each iteration into two steps: at the first, calculate all the ratios $L_i(w_i^{(\tau)}, v_i^{(\tau)}; \vec{x}_j)$, and already at the second step recalculate the current approximation $w_i^{(\tau+1)}, v_i^{(\tau+1)}$:

$$\textit{for} \quad i = 1, \ldots, K :$$
$$I : \quad \textit{for all } j : \; ij = i : L_i\left(w_i^{(\tau)}, v_i^{(\tau)}; \vec{x}_j\right) = \frac{v_i E(\vec{x}_j - \vec{\mu}_i)}{C(\vec{x}_j - \vec{\mu}_i) w_i},$$
$$II : \quad w_i^{(\tau+1)} = \frac{1}{k} \sum_{j}^{ij=i} \frac{1}{1 + L_i\left(w_i^{(\tau)}, v_i^{(\tau)}; \vec{x}_j\right)}, \quad v_i^{(\tau+1)} = \frac{1}{k} \sum_{j}^{ij=i} \frac{L_i\left(w_i^{(\tau)}, v_i^{(\tau)}; \vec{x}_j\right)}{1 + L_i\left(w_i^{(\tau)}, v_i^{(\tau)}; \vec{x}_j\right)}. \tag{16}$$

Note that adding the equations at the step II in (16), we get at each iteration (τ) $w_i^{(\tau+1)} + v_i^{(\tau+1)} = k_i/k$, where k_i is the number of counts in X_k belonging to i–th receptive field, independent of iteration. This implies that it is sufficient to calculate only one of the current approximations $w_i^{(\tau+1)}$ or $v_i^{(\tau+1)}$, the second one will be determined automatically.

The iterative scheme (16) can be significantly simplified if we accept the following approximation. Let the ratio $L_i\left(w_i^{(\tau)}, v_i^{(\tau)}; \vec{x}_j\right)$ equal to zero if $L_i\left(w_i^{(\tau)}, v_i^{(\tau)}; \vec{x}_j\right) < 1$, i.e. the joint probability of the given $\vec{x}_j$ and its belonging to the center of the receptive field $\Delta_i C(\vec{x}_j - \vec{\mu}_i) w_i$ is greater than the corresponding probability $v_i E(\vec{x}_j - \vec{\mu}_i)$ for the environment. Within this approximation, the equations at the step II in (16) are simplified to $w_i^{(\tau+1)} = k_{i,C}^{(\tau+1)}/k$ and $v_i^{(\tau+1)} = k_{i,E}^{(\tau+1)}/k$, where $k_{i,C}^{(\tau+1)}$ is the estimate of the number of compact center counts and $k_{i,E}^{(\tau+1)}$ is the estimate of the number of antagonistic environment counts of the i–th receptive field.

The above approximation at each iteration (τ) leads to a one-to-one association of each count $\vec{x}_j$ in the i–th receptive field with the center or with the environment. Equally it implies the partition of the counts $\{\vec{x}_j | i_j = i\}$ in two non-overlapping groups $X_{i,C}^{(\tau+1)}$ and $X_{i,E}^{(\tau+1)}$, containing $k_{i,C}^{(\tau+1)}$ and $k_{i,E}^{(\tau+1)}$ counts. So, the general iterative scheme (16) can be approximately implemented as follows:

$$
\begin{aligned}
&for \quad i = 1, \ldots, K : X_{i,C}^{(\tau+1)} = \emptyset = X_{i,E}^{(\tau+1)}, \\
&I : for \ all \ j : i_j = i : if \left(\frac{v_i E(\vec{x}_j - \vec{\mu}_i)}{C(\vec{x}_j - \vec{\mu}_i) w_i} < 1 \right) : X_{i,C}^{(\tau+1)} = X_{i,C}^{(\tau+1)} \cup \vec{x}_j, \\
&II : k_{i,C}^{(\tau+1)} = \left| X_{i,C}^{(\tau+1)} \right| w_i^{(\tau+1)} = \frac{k_{i,C}^{(\tau+1)}}{k}, k_{i,E}^{(\tau+1)} = k_i - k_{i,C}^{(\tau+1)}, v_i^{(\tau+1)} = \frac{k_{i,E}^{(\tau+1)}}{k}.
\end{aligned}
\tag{17}
$$

In the iterative scheme (17) steps I and II correspond to steps E and M of the well-known EM-algorithm for mixtures in its hard implementation (also known as the K-means algorithm). It is known that the EM-algorithm, when the number of components K is relatively small ($\sim$10–100), is quite stable and allows finding maximum-likelihood solutions of (7) in the foreseeable time. Unfortunately, with large amounts k of data, for example, for standard digital images, the use of the traditional EM algorithm is problematic. These problems are associated with high memory requirements, as well as with a low (linear) convergence rate of the EM algorithm. In the proposed receptive fields model, due to the reduction in the required amount of memory to $2k$ (for $k_{i,C}^{(\tau+1)}$ and $k_{i,E}^{(\tau+1)}$) and reducing the amount of computation due to limited summation over j-counts in I (17), the resource requirements are much less than for the EM algorithm.

As a final note, we note that a method analogous to (17), associated with lattice partitions of sample counts has already arisen in a slightly different context and was analyzed in [19].

5 Results of Numerical Simulation

To illustrate the above theoretical aspects, special software was developed for generating sampling representations of bitmap images and perceptual recovering based on the receptive fields model (formulas (17)) of the originals. Below are the results of recovering the sampling representations of the image "Mandril" shown in Fig. 1. Restoration was carried out with various combinations of the following parameters: the shape of the center of the receptive fields - square, circle and diamond, different ratios $r = \sigma/d$ of the center size σ to the size d of the receptive field and for a different number K of lattice nodes (Figs. 3, 4 and 5).

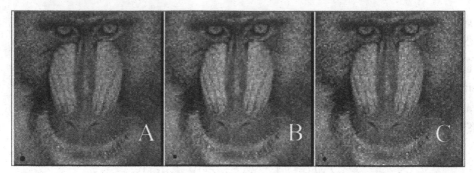

Fig. 3. Recovering of the image "Mandril" (Fig. 1.A) by sampling representation of 1 000 000 counts (Fig. 1.C) for different shapes of the receptive field center: A – square, B – circle, C –diamond; $r = 0.6$; $K = 10^4$;

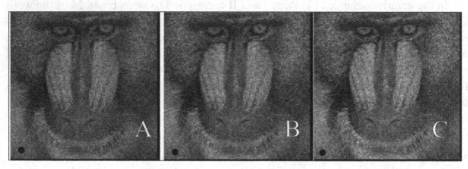

Fig. 4. Recovering of the image "Mandril" (Fig. 1.A) by sampling representation of 1 000 000 counts (Fig. 1.C) for different ratios center/field: A – $r = 0.4$, B – $r = 0.6$, C – $r = 0.9$; center as circle; $K = 10^4$;

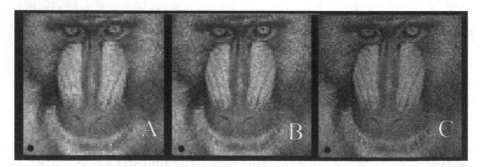

Fig. 5. Recovering of the image "Mandril" (Fig. 1.A) by sampling representation of 1 000 000 counts (Fig. 1.C) for different number K of nodes: A – $K = 0.36 * 10^3$, B – $K = 0.64 * 10^3$, C – $K = 10^4$; center as circle; $r = 0.6$;

6 Conclusions

The paper demonstrates, that basing on the specifics of sampling representations, it is possible to form a generative (generative) approach to the synthesis of neuromorphic (perceptual) image coding methods, which automatically introduces the problem under consideration into the range of machine learning problems and into the field of iterative algorithms like the EM algorithm.

In particular, the paper presents one of the possible iterative schemes for encoding–images of varying complexity. A feature of the proposed schemes is the concept of receptive fields. It effectively overcomes the well-known difficulties of iterative algorithms that process mixtures with many components, for example, 10^4–10^6 components in the case of the EM algorithm.

In general, according to the results obtained in the work and in the experiments performed, we can express a cautious hope that the approach proposed in the work will find both its further theoretical development and effective use in numerous applied problems.

References

1. Bull, D. R., Zhang, F.: Intelligent Image and Video Compression: Communicating Pictures, 2nd edn. Academic Press, London (2021). https://doi.org/10.1016/C2019-0-00641-3
2. Tschannen, M., Agustsson, E., Lucic, M.: Deep generative models for distribution-preserving lossy compression. In: Proceedings of the 32nd International Conference on Neural Information Processing Systems (NIPS), pp. 5933–5944 (2018)
3. Shannon, C.E.: Coding Theorems for a Discrete Source with a Fidelity Criterion - Institute of Radio Engineers, International Convention Record, vol. 7, 1959. In: Claude E. Shannon: Collected Papers, pp. 325–350. IEEE (1993). https://doi.org/10.1109/9780470544242.ch21
4. Matsumoto, R.: Introducing the perception-distortion tradeoff into the rate-distortion theory of general information sources. IEICE Commun. Exp. 7(11), 427–431 (2018). https://doi.org/10.1587/comex.2018XBL0109
5. Blau, Y., Michaeli, T.: Rethinking lossy compression: the rate-distortion-perception tradeoff. In: Proceedings of the 36th International Conference on Machine Learning, PMLR 97, pp. 675–685 (2019)
6. Wang, Z., Bovik, A., Sheikh, H., Simoncelli, E.: Image quality assessment: from error visibility to structural similarity. IEEE Trans. Image Process. 13(4), 600–612 (2004). https://doi.org/10.1109/TIP.2003.819861
7. Wang, Z., Lu, L., Bovik, A.: Video quality assessment based on structural distortion measurement. Sig. Process. Image Commun. 19(2), 121–132 (2004). https://doi.org/10.1016/S0923-5965(03)00076-6
8. Sheikh, H., Bovik, A., de Veciana, G.: An information fidelity criterion for image quality assessment using natural scene statistics. IEEE Trans. Image Process. 14(12), 2117–2128 (2005). https://doi.org/10.1109/TIP.2005.859389
9. Larson, E.C., Chandler, D.M.: Most apparent distortion: full-reference image quality assessment and the role of strategy. J. Electron. Imaging 19(1), 011006 (2010). https://doi.org/10.1117/1.3267105
10. Zhang, F., Bull, D.R.: A perception-based hybrid model for video quality assessment. IEEE Trans. Circuits Syst. Video Technol. 26(6), 1017–1028 (2016). https://doi.org/10.1109/TCSVT.2015.2428551

11. Li, Z.: Toward a practical perceptual video quality metric. Netflix Tech Blog (2016). https:// netflixtechblog.com/toward-a-practical-perceptual-video-quality-metric-653f208b9652

12. Antsiperov, V.: Maximum similarity method for image mining. In: Del Bimbo, A., et al. (eds.) ICPR 2021. LNCS, vol. 12665, pp. 301–313. Springer, Cham (2021). https://doi.org/10.1007/ 978-3-030-68821-9_28

13. Goodfellow, I., et al.: Generative adversarial networks. Commun. ACM **63**(11), 139–144 (2020). https://doi.org/10.1145/3422622

14. Kingma D. P., Welling, M.: Auto-encoding variational Bayes. In: Proceedings of the 2nd International Conference on Learning Representations, ICLR 2014 (2014). https://arxiv.org/ abs/1312.6114

15. Hinton, G.E., Osindero, S., Teh, Y.-W.: A fast learning algorithm for deep belief nets. Neural Comput. **18**(7), 1527–1554 (2006). https://doi.org/10.1162/neco.2006.18.7.1527

16. Bishop, C.M., Lasserre, J.: Generative or discriminative? Getting the best of both worlds. In: Bayesian Statistics, vol. 8, pp. 3–24. Oxford University Press, London (2007)

17. Schiller, P.H., Tehovnik, E.J.: Vision and the Visual System. Oxford University Press (2015). https://doi.org/10.1093/acprof:oso/9780199936533.001.0001

18. Antsiperov, V.: Generative model for autoencoders learning by image sampling representations. In: Proceedings of the 11th International Conference on Pattern Recognition Applications and Methods, ICPRAM, pp. 354–361 (2022). https://doi.org/10.5220/001091520000 3122

19. Antsiperov, V.E.: Representation of images by the optimal lattice partitions of random counts. Pattern Recogn. Image Anal. **31**(3), 381–393 (2021). https://doi.org/10.1134/S10546618210 30044

20. Barrett, H.H., Myers, K. J.: Foundations of Image Science. Wiley, Hoboken, New Jersey (2004)

21. Goodman, J.W.: Statistical Optics, 2nd edn. Wiley, Hoboken; New Jersey (2015)

22. Rodieck, R.W.: The First Steps in Seeing. Sinauer, Sunderland, MA (1998)

23. Robert, C.P., Casella, G.: Monte Carlo Statistical Methods, 2nd edn. Springer, New York (2004). https://doi.org/10.1007/978-1-4757-4145-2

24. Antsiperov, V.E., Kershner, V.A.: Image coding by count sample, motivated by the mechanisms of light perception in the visual system. Commun. Comput. Inf. Sci. **1534**, 715–729 (2022). https://doi.org/10.1007/978-3-030-96040-7_54

25. Liu, Q., Xu, J., Jiang, R., Wong, W. H.: Density estimation using deep generative neural networks. Proc. Natl. Acad. Sci. (PNAS) **118**(15), 1 (2021). https://doi.org/10.1073/pnas.210 1344118

26. Scott, D.W.: Multivariate Density Estimation. Wiley, Somerset (2015)

27. Efron, B.: The Jackknife, The Bootstrap, and Other Resampling Plans. Society for Industrial and Applied Mathematics (1982)

28. van Erven, T.T., Harremoes, P.: Rényi divergence and Kullback-Leibler divergence. IEEE Trans. Inf. Theor. **60**(7), 3797–3820 (2014). https://doi.org/10.1109/TIT.2014.2320500

29. Aldrich, J.: R. A. Fisher and the making of maximum likelihood 1912-1922. Stat. Sci. **12**(3), 162–176 (1997)

30. Hubel, D.H., Wiesel, T.N.: Brain and Visual Perception: The Story of a 25-year Collaboration. Oxford University Press, New York (2004). https://doi.org/10.1093/acprof:oso/978019517 6186.001.0001

31. Rheinboldt, W.C.: Methods for Solving Systems of Nonlinear Equations, 2nd edn. Soceity for Applied Mathematics (1998)

32. Ortega, J.M., Rheinboldt, W.C.: Iterative Solution of Nonlinear Equations in Several Variables. Soceity for Industrial and Applied Mathematics (2000)

Revisiting Ensembling for Improving the Performance of Deep Learning Models

Antonio Bruno[ID], Davide Moroni[✉][ID], and Massimo Martinelli[ID]

Institute of Information Science and Technologies, National Research Council
of Italy, Via Moruzzi, 1, 56124 Pisa, (IT), Italy
{antonio.bruno,davide.moroni,massimo.martinelli}@isti.cnr.it
https://www.isti.cnr.it

Abstract. Ensembling is a very well-known strategy consisting in fusing several different models to achieve a new model for classification or regression tasks. Over the years, ensembling has been proven to provide superior performance in various contexts related to pattern recognition and artificial intelligence. Moreover, the basic ideas that are at the basis of ensembling have been a source of inspiration for the design of the most recent deep learning architectures. Indeed, a close analysis of those architectures shows that some connections among layers and groups of layers achieve effects similar to those obtainable by bagging, boosting and stacking, which are the well-known three basic approaches to ensembling. However, we argue that research has not fully leveraged the potential offered by ensembling. Indeed, this paper investigates some possible approaches to the combination of weak learners, or sub-components of weak learners, in the context of bagging. Based on previous results obtained in specific domains, we extend the approach to a reference dataset obtaining encouraging results.

Keywords: Ensembling · bagging · machine learning · deep learning · image classification · convolutional neural networks

1 Introduction

Representation learning and deep learning have achieved amazing results in the last decades, obtaining unparalleled performance under challenging tasks such as image classification and object detection [13]. After the first impressive leap, many works have been of incremental nature in the previous years, often focused on architecture engineering for achieving minor improvements over a sensible increase in complexity. Indeed, the performance gain versus the computational increment ratio has become less attractive. Therefore, research has moved to find optimal tradeoffs between accuracy and computational load [17]. This is also motivated by the widespread adoption of deep learning paradigms that calls for the sustainable use of artificial intelligence (AI). AI has operational costs than can be directly measurable in energy consumption, having therefore a relevant

J.-J. Rousseau and B. Kapralos (Eds.): ICPR 2022 Workshops, LNCS 13644, pp. 445–452, 2023.
https://doi.org/10.1007/978-3-031-37742-6_34

environmental footprint [16]. Ensembling is a well-known approach that enables using a collection of different models (e.g., classifiers or regressors) to obtain a new model having other (and generally superior) performance with respect to predefined metrics. Ensembling has a long history that dates back even before the birth of machine learning. Indeed, it is customary to state that the first application of Ensembling is majority voting in statistics as in the claim of the theorem by Marquis de Condorcet: in 1785 he proved that if the probability of each voter being correct is more than one-half and the voters are independent, then the addition of more voters increases the likelihood of the majority vote being correct (see, e.g., [2]). Long after that, Ensembling has been used to turn weak models into superior models showing encouraging results in several domains. It has been reported that ensemble models often become in the first place in public competitions such as those promoted by Kaggle [1]. The relationship between deep learning and Ensembling is at least twofold. From one side, basic constructions of Ensembling known as bagging, boosting and stacking have somehow influenced architectures commonly used in deep learning and the way they are trained. For instance, residual networks behave like ensembles of relatively shallow networks [18]. On the other side, thanks to Ensembling strategies, deep learning models can be used as basic models to build more complex models. This paper focuses on this second aspect by recapping Ensembling and its role in deep learning, exploring several directions. Based on previous results obtained in a specific domain, preliminary results are then reported on a benchmark dataset. This paper extends the short paper [3].

2   Related Works

Ensembling generally refers to machine learning approaches in which a set of *weak learners* (or *basic models*) is turned into a *strong learner* (or *ensemble model*). The set of weak learners might consist of homogenous models (i.e., they are all from the same family or architecture) or might be heterogeneous, i.e., the basic models belong to different machine learning paradigms. The basic example is to put together multiple models trained for solving the same classification or regression task and then combine them together in some fashion, e.g., by performing majority voting in the case of classification or averaging in the case of regression. The scope of performing Ensembling is generally related to the desire to reduce the bias or variance that affects a machine learning task [7]. As it is well known, a very simple model might have a great error in achieving good performance on a dataset, even during training. This is generally linked to the low representation capabilities of simple models that cannot capture all the complex patterns in the training datasets. Such error during training is referred to as the bias of the model. By converse, very complex models have many degrees of freedom to adhere to the training dataset completely and obtain excellent performance during training. However, they capture not only the relevant features of the problem but also learn insignificant features of the training dataset. This results in relatively poor performance during test and validation: the model is overfitted to the training dataset and does not reach good general results, having scarce generalization capabilities. We refer to this issue, as saying that the model has high variance. The three basic approaches to performing Ensembling are bagging, boosting, and stacking. In general, bagging reduces the variance among the base classifiers, while boosting-based ensembles lead to bias and variance reduction. Stacking is commonly used as a bias-reducing technique. In more detail, bagging is performed by subdividing the training datasets into different subsets according to some criteria, e.g., balancing class distributions inside each subset or other forms of equalization. Then, each subset of the training set is used to train a weak classifier. Any such classifier ideally has a low bias on the training set but possibly high variance. Using a fusion layer, the outputs of the single classifiers are combined by performing (weighted) voting or performing a weighted average. The model given by the fusion of the weak classifiers is called a strong classifier, and it potentially exhibits lower variance. Notice that the weak classifiers might be trained independently and in parallel. Very often, such classifiers share the same architecture. In boosting instead, weak classifiers are very simple and low complexity but are trained cleverly, for example, using cascading. Adaboost [15] is one of the most popular approaches in which each classifier is trained so as to properly deal with the examples in the training set on which previous weak classifiers have failed. The boosting concept is also known to be the backbone behind well-known architectures like Deep Residual networks [10]. Finally, stacking often considers heterogeneous weak learners. Training is performed in parallel, while a final combination is obtained by training a meta-model to output a prediction based on the different weak models' predictions. Deep convex nets (DCN) [6] are recognized to be a deep learning architecture composed of a variable number of modules stacked together to form the deep architecture. In general, all of these approaches have been used in conjunction with deep learning models. The review [9] presents some recent literature on the subject systematically.

3 Methodology

As seen in the previous section, ensemble and deep learning have a twofold relationship. This section aims to briefly report some experiments on Ensembling that is worthwhile exploring for optimising deep learning models.

1. Varying the number of classifiers. After having fixed a deep learning architecture, such architecture can be regarded as a weak model. Different training runs starting with random weights might result in different classifiers. Majority voting can be applied in this case as shown in Fig. 1. The dependence of the performance with respect to the number of classifiers might be studied.
2. Sampling strategies and balancing. Besides performing training of all the weak learners on the full training set as described before, procedures for sampling can be applied. For instance, using disjoint datasets for each weak classifier helps have a set of independent classifiers. In addition, stratification can be applied to keep the same class frequencies in each subset; conversely, it might

be interesting to explore the possibilities given by training each classifier to make it specialised in addressing a special class.

3. Control size and model complexity. The ensembling approaches can be performed by keeping track of the model size and model complexity; this can help understand the heuristics for the optimal choice of the weak learners' dimensions and the ensemble size.

4. Stacking at the deep feature levels. In many cases, the first layers of a deep network perform feature extraction, while the final layers, usually fully connected, perform classification/regression. A possibility in ensembling is given by stacking weak models by removing the final classification layers from each one and training an ad hoc meta classifier as shown in Fig. 2.

5. Learning strategies. Given the trained ensemble, it is still possible to fine-tune the model parameters by properly training the model, freezing or not some of the overall network layers.

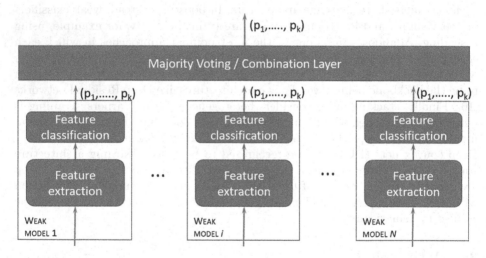

Fig. 1. Majority voting can be applied to fuse the output of multiple weak learners and obtain a strong one. In the figure, we consider a variable number of N weak classifiers (trained for instance using special partitions of the training data), each one producing in output a confidence level vector for k classes. Majority voting or other schemes for combination might be used and the dependence of the performance with respect to the number N of weak classifiers might be studied.

4   Experimental Results

In this section, we report preliminary experimental results obtained by following the methodology discussed in Sect. 3. In all the experiments we used as a basic weak learner a convolutional neural network belonging to the EfficientNet family [17]. This is a family of eight neural networks named b0, b1,..., b7 featuring different complexity, where b0 is the most simple model ($5, 5M$ parameters)

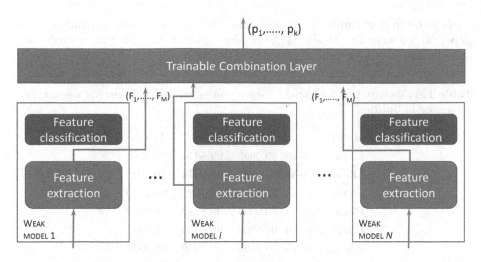

Fig. 2. A different and innovative approach to ensembling of deep weak classifier is reported pictorially in the figure. After having trained each weak classifier independently, only the convolutional layers are kept while the final decision layers of each classifier are disregarded. In summary, we keep a sequence of N *weak feature extractor* modules, each one producing a M-dimensional deep feature vector. These modules can be turned into an ensemble by adding a trainable final decision layer, e.g. made of fully-connected networks, having an input size equal to $N \cdot M$.

while b7 ($66, 7M$ parameters) is the most complex. Such networks are obtained through a process of aggregate scaling across depth, width and resolution dimensions starting from an archetype based on the inverted bottleneck MBConv, first introduced in MobileNet [14]. The aggregate scaling is performed in a uniform way so as to optimise according to some heuristics the performance of the network. For this characteristic, EfficientNet is an excellent building block to study ensembling strategies. Notice that in our experiments we use transfer learning. In more detail, all the EfficientNet models we used as weak classifiers share the weights of pre-trained models from ImageNet [5].

To show concretely some possibilities, we report two examples. The first regards an application to a specific dataset for precision agriculture, i.e. the PlantVillage dataset [12], which contains images of plants, either healthy or with a wide range of diseases. The dataset has been analyzed in a recent study [4], which we recap here. A second example is given by a popular benchmark dataset, i.e. the CIFAR-100 dataset [11], which consists of 60000 32×32 colour images divided in 100 classes, with 600 images per class. The 100 classes in the CIFAR-100 are grouped into 20 superclasses. Each image comes with a "fine" (the class it belongss to) and a "coarse" label (the superclass to which it belongs). In the experiments, the fine-grained version with 100 classes has been used.

For the first example, using particular and ad hoc tricks explained in the paper [4], we were able to obtain the results reported in Table 1 for a single *weak* model trained end-to-end.

Table 1. Table with best Weighted F1-score results, for each EfficientNet variant. Best values are in **bold**.

Model	Test	Valid	Train
EfficientNet-b0	99.6995	99.8454	99.9960
EfficientNet-b1	99.5793	99.8454	100.000
EfficientNet-b2	99.5192	99.7681	99.9140
EfficientNet-b3	99.6394	99.8712	99.9860
EfficientNet-b4	99.6995	99.8454	99.9980
EfficientNet-b5	99.7596	99.7939	99.9920
EfficientNet-b6	**99.7596**	**99.8712**	**99.9880**
EfficientNet-b7	99.5192	99.8454	99.9960

Then ensembling was applied using the methodology depicted in Fig. 2. Given the generally good performance of the models reported in Table 1 and aiming at reduced complexity, we restricted to performing ensembling (i) only on b0 models and (ii) using the minimum number of weak learners, i.e. only two learners. As a combination layer for the ensemble, we used the final layer of the weak learners scaled to accommodate the input of two learners. Five runs of training were conducted to train the combination layers keeping frozen the deep feature extractor module of each weak classifier. The results demonstrate a 100% F1-score in training and test for all the five runs, while in validation four runs achieved 100% performance but one, which featured a 99.998% performance.

Similar tests were conducted on the more challenging CIFAR-100 dataset, where the ensemble model was able to reach a 96.808% with an improvement of 0.728% over the previous state-of-the-art [8]. We notice that the proposed ensemble has $\approx 11M$ parameters with respect to the previous state-of-the-art model which had $\approx 480M$ parameters. For what regards floating point operations, the proposed ensemble features $\approx 0.9G$ FLOPS by contrast with the $\approx 299G$ FLOPS required by the previous model. This shows that the proposed methodology is effective in producing accurate models with lower complexity in the CIFAR-100 case.

5   Conclusions

This short paper has explored several directions for introducing Ensembling in the deep learning context. The approaches and the involved ideas are well-grounded in previous knowledge and guarantees connected to Ensembling in machine learning, yet there are many possible pathways and combinations to explore. In some preliminary experiments, we studied an adaptive ensembling based on bagging, making it possible to achieve 100% accuracy on a known dataset in agricultural applications [12]. Other experiments on a well know benchmark dataset have shown a significant boost in performance over the state-of-the-art coupled with a reduction of complexity. Further experiments are underway to show the applicability range of the proposed method and the results will be reported in the next future.

References

1. Bojer, C.S., Meldgaard, J.P.: Kaggle forecasting competitions: An overlooked learning opportunity. Int. J. Forecast. **37**(2), 587–603 (2021)
2. Boland, P.J.: Majority systems and the condorcet jury theorem. J. Royal Statist. Soc. Ser. D (The Statistician) **38**(3), 181–189 (1989)
3. Bruno, A., Martinelli, M., Moroni, D.: Exploring ensembling in deep learning. Pattern Recognit Image Anal. **32**(3), 519–521 (2022). https://doi.org/10.1134/S1054661822030087
4. Bruno, A., et al.: Improving plant disease classification by adaptive minimal ensembling. Front. Artifi. Intell. (2022). https://doi.org/10.3389/frai.2022.868926
5. Deng, J., Dong, W., Socher, R., Li, L., Kai Li, Li Fei-Fei: Imagenet: A large-scale hierarchical image database. In: 2009 IEEE Conference on Computer Vision and Pattern Recognition, pp. 248–255 (2009). https://doi.org/10.1109/CVPR.2009.5206848
6. Deng, L., Yu, D.: Deep convex net: A scalable architecture for speech pattern classification. In: Twelfth Annual Conference of the International Speech Communication Association (2011)
7. Dong, X., Yu, Z., Cao, W., Shi, Y., Ma, Q.: A survey on ensemble learning. Front. Comp. Sci. **14**(2), 241–258 (2020)
8. Foret, P., Kleiner, A., Mobahi, H., Neyshabur, B.: Sharpness-aware minimization for efficiently improving generalization. In: 9th International Conference on Learning Representations, ICLR 2021, Virtual Event, Austria, 3–7 May (2021)
9. Ganaie, M.A., Hu, M., et al.: Ensemble deep learning: A review. arXiv preprint arXiv:2104.02395 (2021)
10. He, K., Zhang, X., Ren, S., Sun, J.: Deep residual learning for image recognition. In: Proceedings of the IEEE Conference on Computer Vision and Pattern Recognition, pp. 770–778 (2016)
11. Krizhevsky, A., Nair, V., Hinton, G.: Cifar-10 (canadian institute for advanced research). http://www.cs.toronto.edu/kriz/cifar.html
12. Mohanty, S.P., Hughes, D.P., Salathé, M.: Using deep learning for image-based plant disease detection. Front. Plant Sci. **7**, 1419 (2016)
13. Pouyanfar, S., et al.: A survey on deep learning: Algorithms, techniques, and applications. ACM Comput. Surv. (CSUR) **51**(5), 1–36 (2018)
14. Sandler, M., Howard, A., Zhu, M., Zhmoginov, A., Chen, L.C.: Mobilenetv 2: Inverted residuals and linear bottlenecks. In: Proceedings of the IEEE Conference on Computer Vision and Pattern Recognition, pp. 4510–4520 (2018)
15. Schapire, R.E.: Explaining AdaBoost. In: Schölkopf, B., Luo, Z., Vovk, V. (eds.) Empirical Inference, pp. 37–52. Springer, Heidelberg (2013). https://doi.org/10.1007/978-3-642-41136-6_5

16. Schwartz, R., Dodge, J., Smith, N.A., Etzioni, O.: Green AI. Commun. ACM **63**(12), 54–63 (2020)
17. Tan, M., Le, Q.: Efficientnet: Rethinking model scaling for convolutional neural networks. In: International Conference on Machine Learning, pp. 6105–6114. PMLR (2019)
18. Veit, A., Wilber, M.J., Belongie, S.: Residual networks behave like ensembles of relatively shallow networks. In: Advances in Neural Information Processing Systems 29 (2016)

Hyperspectral Image Recognition with Selection of Informative Observations by Conjugacy Criterion

Vladimir Fursov[1,2]([email]) [iD]

[1] Image Processing Systems Institute of the RAS - Branch of the FSRC "Crystallography and Photonics" RAS, Molodogvardeyskaya, 151, 443001 Samara, Russia
fursov@ssau.ru
[2] Samara National Research University, Moskovskoye Shosse, 34, 443086 Samara, Russia

Abstract. The article proposes a method for hyperspectral image recognition, in whichthe conjugacy with subspaces formed by training class vectors is used as a measure of proximity. The geometric interpretation of the proximity measure used is given in a space formed by eigenvectors. An algorithm for hyperspectral image recognition is built with sequential selection of the most informative subspaces according to the criterion of maximum conjugacy. The results of vegetation recognition experiments on the test hyperspectral image «Indian Pines» that had been obtained within the project AVIRIS (Airborne Visible/Infrared Imaging Spectrometer) are presented. The experiment showed the possibility of achieving higher recognition quality in comparison with known methods.

Keywords: Digital image processing · Hyperspectral image recognition · Conjugacy criterion

1 Introduction

Digital images are one of the most common ways to represent information about various phenomena. Therefore, determining the characteristics of various objects and studying their properties is often reduced to classification and pattern recognition tasks. Classification methods based on the calculation of indicators of proximity between images were among the first approaches to solving problems of pattern recognition [11]. This approach has not lost its relevance and is widely used in modern automatic systems, as well as in artificial intelligence systems. Classification of hyperspectral images often uses the spectral angle criterion [2, 12]. Euclidean distance is most commonly used as a criterion for the proximity of images. The Euclidean metric is the basis for constructing a large number of recognition methods. In particular, using this metric, such popular approaches were implemented: the support vector machine [6], the maximum likelihood method [13], the spectral angle method [9], etc.

Currently, a large number of practical tasks are associated with the hyperspectral image recognition. Hyperspectral images contain hundreds of continuous spectral bands which can provide a large amount of information for different types of applications,

© Springer Nature Switzerland AG 2023
J.-J. Rousseau and B. Kapralos (Eds.): ICPR 2022 Workshops, LNCS 13644, pp. 453–463, 2023.
https://doi.org/10.1007/978-3-031-37742-6_35

such as mineral identification, agriculture, natural resources survey, and so on. These applications usually solve the problems of classifying sections of the earth surface and objects. Since these images have a large number of spectral components, the use of traditional methods of forming a feature space is a laborious task. To overcome these difficulties, various methods and algorithms for dimension reduction [8, 3], as well as linear and nonlinear transformations of components [6, 9] are used.

In previous works [4, 14], we introduced the term"conjugacy index". This index is a generalization of the cosine measure and characterizes the proximity of the vector to the subspace formed by the set of support vectors. In one of the recent papers [5], as an example of using the conjugacy index, we gave a solution to the problem of vegetation type recognition in the «Indian Pines» hyperspectral image from the open Multispec package.

The peculiarity of this test is that class differences are observed only in small spectral ranges. Taking into account this feature, in [1] methods of increasing the efficiency of hyperspectral images classification by highlighting the most informative data were considered. In particular, the effectiveness of a method that takes into account spatial information at various processing stages was investigated on a test hyperspectral image. In [1], the authors showed that the best results are obtained by combining spatial preliminary processing of initial data and pixel-by-pixel spectral classification procedures.

In this work, we are developing the ideas of the work [1] and offer a technology for hyperspectral image recognition which combines preliminary spatial processing and a classification method based on the use of a conjugacy criterion [5]. In particular, after preprocessing all spectral levels with a median filter, it is proposed to implement an iterative algorithm in which conjugacy indices are calculated sequentially with subspaces of decreasing dimension. At each step, we search for a subspace for which the proximity measure defined in form of conjugacy criterion is maximized. The partition of the original space of features into subspaces is carried out both by spatial and spectral component. Thus, the decision which class will be chosen is made by taking into account the most informative components of the feature vectors. The proposed technology allows us to implement automatic search for the most informative data.

2 Recognition Problem Formulation

Mathematical formulation of the image recognition problem is a standard problem of a pattern recognition. Let M be a number of available images of the same size for some object. Each image can be transformed to $N \times 1$-vector $\mathbf{x} = [x_1, x_2, ..., x_N]^T$, where $x_1, x_2, ..., x_N$ are the components of the feature vector, N is the total number of pixels/features. We assume that the set of feature vectors corresponding to the images of one object forms the class. These M vectors can be used as a training data set in a form of $N \times M$-matrix of the class:

$$\mathbf{X} = [\mathbf{x}_1, \mathbf{x}_2, ..., \mathbf{x}_M] \tag{1}$$

Suppose K various objects and M_K training vectors for each object is given (for simplicity, we assume that equal number M of training vectors is given for each object). Thus, matrices $\mathbf{X}_k$, $k = \overline{1, K}$ can be formed for K classes.

Let $\mathbf{x}$ be the feature vector for the object of some class. The problem of the classifier creation consists in definition of a decision function $f(\mathbf{x})$ which determines a class number which vector $\mathbf{x}$ belongs to. Let $\mathbf{X}_k$ be $N \times M$-matrix of a k-th class (1.1). We define a proximity measure of vector $\mathbf{x}$ to k-th class as a conjugation index of $\mathbf{x}$ with the subspace formed by vectors of the matrix $\mathbf{X}_k$:

$$R_k = \left(\mathbf{x}^T \mathbf{X}_k \left[\mathbf{X}_k^T \mathbf{X}_k\right]^{-1} \mathbf{X}_k^T \mathbf{x}\right)\left(\mathbf{x}^T \mathbf{x}\right)^{-1} \tag{2}$$

Along with the conjugation index (2) we consider a conjugation index with zero space of the matrix $\mathbf{X}_k$:

$$S_k = \left(\mathbf{x}^T \mathbf{T}_{k,0} \mathbf{T}_{k,0}^T \mathbf{x}\right)\left(\mathbf{x}^T \mathbf{x}\right)^{-1} \tag{3}$$

Here $\mathbf{T}_{k,0}$ is the $N \times (N - M)$-matrix made of eigenvectors corresponding to zero eigenvalues of a $N \times N$-matrix $\mathbf{X}_k \mathbf{X}_k^T$.

Now, we can formulate the rule on the use of conjugation indices (2) as proximity measures for decision function creation. We assume that for each k-th class one of the following $N \times N$- matrixes is created

$$\mathbf{Q}_{k,R} = \mathbf{X}_k \left[\mathbf{X}_k^T \mathbf{X}_k\right]^{-1} \mathbf{X}_k^T \tag{4}$$

Then, decision function $f(\mathbf{x})$ can be constructed as follows. The vector $\mathbf{x}$ belongs to m- th class, i.e. $f(\mathbf{x}) = m$, $m = 1, 2, ...K$, if

$$R_\mathrm{m} = \max_k R_k \; where \, R_k = \left(\mathbf{x}^T \mathbf{Q}_{k,R} \mathbf{x}\right)\left(\mathbf{x}^T \mathbf{x}\right)^{-1} \tag{5}$$

It should be noted that the use of the conjugation index (2) as a proximity measure is possible only in the case when the training vectors are independent, and their dimension exceeds the number of the training vectors in each class, since matrix $\mathbf{X}_k^T \mathbf{X}_k$ must be none-singular. Otherwise, it is necessary to carry out the selection of some number of training vectors.

Let us denote as *support subspaces* the subspaces formed by the training sets ($N \times M$- matrix $\mathbf{X}_k$) of each class. At the same time, it is necessary to answer two questions: how many vectors should be included in matrixes $\mathbf{X}_k$ and what the selection rule is. This article proposes an algorithm for the formation of informative reference subspaces, the use of which improves the quality of recognition.

3 Geometric Interpretation of the Conjugation Indices

To answer the above questions, it is useful to consider geometric interpretation of the conjugation indices. We consider the conjugation index determined by formula (2). We use approach based on orthogonal transformations of the $\mathbf{Q}_{k,R}$ matrix (4).

Formula (4) of matrix $\mathbf{Q}_{k,R}$ (hereinafter matrices have no indices, for simplicity) can be rewritten as

$$\mathbf{Q}_{k,R} = \mathbf{X}\mathbf{F}\mathbf{F}^T \left[\mathbf{X}^T \mathbf{X}\right]^{-1} \mathbf{F}\mathbf{F}^T \mathbf{X}^T \tag{6}$$

where $\mathbf{F}$ is $M \times M$–matrix such that

$$\mathbf{X}^T\mathbf{X} = \mathbf{F}\Lambda\mathbf{F}^T$$

where diagonal matrix $\Lambda = diag(\lambda_1, \lambda_1, ..., \lambda_M)$ is composed of M eigenvalues $\lambda_i > 0$, $i = \overline{1, M}$, and columns of matrix $\mathbf{F}$ are corresponding eigenvectors. Representation (5) is equivalent to (3) because of the following equations

$$\mathbf{FF}^T = \mathbf{F}^T\mathbf{F} = \mathbf{E}, \mathbf{F}^{-1} = \mathbf{F}^T, \quad \left[\mathbf{F}^T\right]^T = \mathbf{F}, [\mathbf{ABC}]^{-1} = \mathbf{C}^{-1}\mathbf{B}^{-1}\mathbf{A}^{-1}.$$

and

$$\mathbf{F}^T\left[\mathbf{X}^T\mathbf{X}\right]^{-1}\mathbf{F} = \mathbf{F}^{-1}\left[\mathbf{X}^T\mathbf{X}\right]^{-1}\left[\mathbf{F}^T\right]^{-1} = \left[\mathbf{F}^T\mathbf{X}^T\mathbf{XF}\right]^{-1} = \Lambda^{-1} \qquad (7)$$

Formula (6) can be rewritten by using equalities (7) as follows:

$$\mathbf{Q}_{k,R} = \mathbf{XF}\Lambda^{-1}\mathbf{F}^T\mathbf{X}^T = \mathbf{XF}\Lambda^{-1/2}\Lambda^{-1/2}\mathbf{F}^T\mathbf{X}^T \qquad (8)$$

Let us consider a matrix

$$\mathbf{T}_\lambda = \mathbf{XF}\Lambda^{-\frac{1}{2}} \qquad (9)$$

It is possible to show that columns $\mathbf{t}_{\lambda,i}$, $i = \overline{1, M}$ of matrixes $\mathbf{T}_\lambda$ are eigenvectors corresponding to nonzero eigenvalues of the matrix $\mathbf{XX}^T$. With the use of equality (9), formula (8) can be rewritten as

$$\mathbf{Q}_{k,R} = \mathbf{T}_\lambda\mathbf{T}_\lambda^T \qquad (10)$$

In (2), we can use normalized vector $\overline{\mathbf{x}} : \|\overline{\mathbf{x}}\| = 1$ instead of $\mathbf{x}$ to disregard the denominator $\mathbf{x}^T\mathbf{x}$. Thus, in accordance with the formula (10), the conjugation index (2) for vector $\overline{\mathbf{x}}$ can be presented as

$$R(\overline{\mathbf{x}}) = \mathbf{V}_\lambda^T\mathbf{V}_\lambda \qquad (11)$$

where $\mathbf{V}_\lambda$ is $M \times 1$-vector:

$$\mathbf{V}_\lambda = \mathbf{T}_\lambda^T\overline{\mathbf{x}} = \left[\cos\left(\widehat{\mathbf{t}_{\lambda,1}, \mathbf{x}}\right), \cos\left(\widehat{\mathbf{t}_{\lambda,2}, \mathbf{x}}\right), ..., \cos\left(\widehat{\mathbf{t}_{\lambda,M}, \mathbf{x}}\right)\right]^T \qquad (12)$$

Taking into account (11) and (12), we can write

$$R(\mathbf{x}) = \sum_{i=1}^{M} \cos^2\left(\widehat{\mathbf{t}_{\lambda,i}, \mathbf{x}}\right) \qquad (13)$$

Thus, the conjugation index (2) is the sum of the squared cosines of the angles between a vector $\mathbf{x}$ and eigenvectors $\mathbf{t}_{\lambda,i}$ corresponding to nonzero eigenvalues of the matrix $\mathbf{XX}^T$. It can be seen from formula (13) that the greater the value of the conjugacy index, the greater (in the sense of angular measure) the proximity to the corresponding subspace.

When constructing a decision rule using the zero-space conjugacy index (3), the class matrix $\mathbf{Q}_{k,S}$ is represented in the same form as in formula (10):

$$\mathbf{Q}_{k,S} = \mathbf{T}_{k,0}\mathbf{T}_{k,0}^T \tag{14}$$

In this case, the decision rule is formulated as follows: the vector x belongs to m-th class, if

$$S_m = \min_k R_k, \text{ where, } S_k = \left(\mathbf{x}^T\mathbf{Q}_{k,S}\mathbf{x}\right)\left(\mathbf{x}^T\mathbf{x}\right)^{-1} \tag{15}$$

Using (14), it is easy to deduce similar representation for conjugation index $S_k(\mathbf{x})$ of the vector x using zero space of the matrix $\mathbf{X}$. Unlike formulas (13) and (12), we use eigenvectors $\mathbf{t}_{0,i}$, $i = \overline{1, N - M}$ corresponding to zero eigenvalues of the matrix $\mathbf{XX}^T$ instead of $\mathbf{t}_{\lambda,i}$:

$$S(\mathbf{x}) = \sum_{i=1}^{N-M} \cos^2\left(\widehat{\mathbf{t}_{0,i}, \mathbf{x}}\right) \tag{16}$$

In conclusion, it should be noted that conjugation indices (2) and (3) are related as follows:

$$R(\mathbf{x}) = 1 - S(\mathbf{x}) \tag{17}$$

Let us prove it. First, we are going to show the correctness of the equality

$$\mathbf{E}_N - \mathbf{X}\left[\mathbf{X}^T\mathbf{X}\right]^{-1}\mathbf{X}_k^T = \mathbf{T}_0\mathbf{T}_0^T \tag{18}$$

where $\mathbf{E}_N$ is the unity $N \times N$-matrix and $\mathbf{T}_0$ is identical to matrix $\mathbf{T}_{k,0}$ in (14). Equality (18) can be proven by multiplication of its both parts on the left by $\mathbf{T}_0^T$ and on the right by $\mathbf{T}_0$ with use of properties

$$\mathbf{T}_0^T\mathbf{X} = 0 \quad \left(\mathbf{X}^T\mathbf{T}_0 = 0\right), \quad \mathbf{T}_0^T\mathbf{T}_0 = \mathbf{E}_{N-M} \tag{19}$$

Further, according to definition (2), it is possible to write down:

$$1 - R(\mathbf{x}) = \frac{\mathbf{x}^T\mathbf{x}}{\mathbf{x}^T\mathbf{x}} - \frac{\mathbf{x}^T\mathbf{X}[\mathbf{X}^T\mathbf{X}]^{-1}\mathbf{X}^T\mathbf{x}}{\mathbf{x}^T\mathbf{x}} = \frac{\mathbf{x}^T\left[\mathbf{E}_N - \mathbf{X}[\mathbf{X}^T\mathbf{X}]^{-1}\mathbf{X}^T\right]\mathbf{x}}{\mathbf{x}^T\mathbf{x}} \tag{20}$$

Finally, using substitution $\mathbf{T}_0\mathbf{T}_0^T$ from (18) to the right part of expression (20) in accordance with (3) we obtain equality (17). Thus, indices (2) and (3) for given x and $\mathbf{X}$ are equivalent and interchangeable (see (17). Therefore, the decision of using particular one of two conjugation indices (2) or (3) is made for each specific case based on computational difficulty.

4 Recognition Algorithm with Selection of Informative Subspaces

From formulas (13), (16) it follows that the contribution to the criterion of some variables of the orthogonal decomposition can be more noticeable. The subspaces formed by such sets of vectors are more informative. Our goal is to find the most informative subspace in the original space formed by these vectors. The decision to assign a vector to a class is then based on the criterion of proximity to the correspondent subspace. Next, we describe the algorithm that implements this idea.

The algorithm for selecting informative subspaces is implemented in two stages. At the first stage, a subset of the most informative vectors is selected, for which the conjugation index with the current vector is maximum. At the second stage, the matrix composed of these vectors is sequentially divided into submatrices with a decreasing number of spectral components. The decision which class to choose is made according to the maximum value of the conjugation index with one of the obtained subspaces. The block diagram of the algorithm is shown in Fig. 1.

Thus, as a result of the implementation of the algorithm, we determine the components for which the differences between the classes, both in the spatial and spectral regions, are maximum. As a result, this algorithm automatically searches for the most informative observations in the sense of the conjugacy criterion. Further we provide an outline of the functions of its main blocks.

In block 1, observation data dimension thresholds are defined and hyperspectral images are preprocessed (if necessary). In this work, preprocessing is carried out only in experiment # 2. In this experiment, we will process all the spectral layers of the hyperspectral image with a median filter to eliminate pulsed interference. In block 2, an arbitrary vector $\mathbf{x}(k)$ is selected from the test set of vectors. Blocks 3–7 implement the first stage of the technology: choosing the most informative subset of a given dimension from the training set of vectors. To do this, the following steps re sequentially implemented.

Block 3 selects M vectors from an available set of training vectors and forms an $N \times M$ matrix $\mathbf{X}$. Next, in block 4, the conjugation index $R(k + 1)$ of vector x with the space of matrix $\mathbf{X}(k + 1)$ is calculated. If the value of $R(k + 1)$ is greater than that obtained earlier ($R(0) = 0$ is set when the algorithm is started), the matrix $\mathbf{X}(k + 1)$ and the obtained $R(k + 1)$ are stored (see blocks 5 and 6). At the same time the matrix and the indicator $R(k)$ stored earlier are removed from memory. Block 7 checks whether there are any training vectors that have not yet been used. If the number of the remaining training vectors is greater than M, return to block 3. Otherwise, the last stored $N \times M$-matrix $\mathbf{X}$ and the index R are passed to the second step of the technology to block 8.

In block 8, the matrix is divided into two submatrices ($\mathbf{X}1, \mathbf{X}2$) of dimension $N/2 \times M$ (in the case of an odd N, one row is added or removed). Block 9 calculates the conjugacy index of vector x with subspaces of both matrices. Only one of the matrices for which the conjugacy index was higher is stored in memory (see blocks 10, 11, 12). Block 13 checks that the obtained matrix can be split again. If the size of the last submatrix has reached a given threshold value and it cannot be further split, the stored conjugacy index value is added to the value obtained at the first step of the technology. The algorithm is then repeated (starting from block 3) for the training vectors of the subsequent classes. To decide whether the vector $\mathbf{x}(m)$ belongs to a certain class, the obtained conjugacy indicators with informative subspaces of the classes are compared

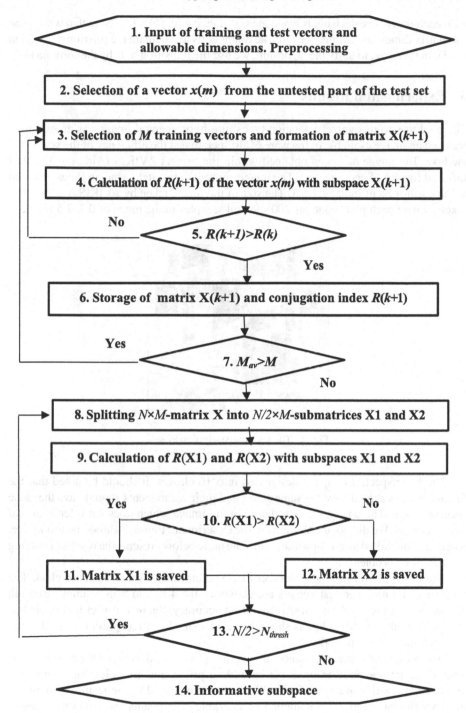

Fig. 1. Block diagram of the algorithm

with each other. The decision is made in accordance with (5), (15). Note that with some submatrix dimensions, it may be more advantageous to calculate the proximity criterion as (3). In this case, to unify the algorithm, we use the transition to R by the formula (17).

5   Experimental Results

The goal was to recognize vegetation types in a hyperspectral image. As an example, we used an image available in freeware MultiSpec to test the efficiency of the suggested method. The image had been obtained within the project AVIRIS (Airborne Visible / Infrared Imaging Spectrometer). The image shows the test field «Indian Pines» located in the north-west of Indiana, USA. The size of the image taken by AVIRIS is 145 × 145 pixels, where each pixel contains 200 spectral samples in the range of 0.4–2.5 mkm.

Fig. 2. The test image «Indian Pines»

The hyperspectral image is designated into 16 classes. It should be noted that the feature vectors should have the same sizes, and their components should have the same spectral range. There is an unmarked area in the image which does not refer to any of the 16 classes. We did not use this area in the experiment. Figure 2 shows the test image, where the unmarked area is of white color. The table below presents the results of solving the described problem.

The third column shows the number of 200-dimensional vectors in each class. The number of training and test vectors are shown in the 4-th and 5-th columns. The 6th column shows the results of class recognition accuracy obtained earlier and published in [5]. The 7th and 8th columns show the results (in %) of recognition of each class obtained in the present work.

We carried out two experiments. In experiment # 1, we developed the classification algorithm that was used in work (4) by adding procedures for selecting informative observations, which are given in the block diagram (Fig. 1). The results obtained in this experiment are given in column 7 of the table. The results show that the average classification accuracy can be improved by 15% only by selecting the most informative observations.

Table 1. Experimental results.

#	Classes	Number of counts			Results (%)		
		Total	Train	Testing	In [5]	Exp#1	Exp#2
1	2	3	4	5	6	7	
1	Alfalfa	46	23	23	41.0	**86.96**	100.00
2	Corn-notill	854	140	714	68.8	**89.78**	93.98
3	Corn-mintill	555	140	415	72.2	**89.64**	96.87
4	Corn	237	118	119	45.7	**98.31**	97.46
5	Grass-pasture	381	140	241	87.0	**100.0**	100.00
6	Grass-trees	505	140	365	91.9	**99.18**	100.00
7	Grass-pasture-mowed	28	14	14	68.8	**85.71**	100.00
8	Hay-windrower	379	140	239	98.3	**100.0**	100.00
9	Oats	20	10	10	24.7	**100.0**	100.00
10	Soybean-notill	626	140	486	73.4	**79.22**	96.71
11	Soybean-mintill	1367	140	1227	60.1	**85.09**	89.24
12	Soybean-clean	436	140	296	79.1	**98.65**	96.28
13	Wheat	205	102	103	91.2	**100.0**	100.00
14	Woods	772	140	632	92.1	**100.0**	100.00
15	Buildings-Grass-Trees-Drives	333	140	193	69.5	**93.26**	99.48
16	Stone-Steel-Towers	93	46	47	75.7	**100.0**	100.00
	Average recognition accuracy				76.6	**91.66**	95.72

In experiment # 2, we additionally introduced preprocessing of all spectral levels of the hyperspectral image with a median filter. This preprocessing ensured that the number of gross errors (pulse interference) was significantly reduced. Due to this, it was possible to further increase the average classification accuracy by more than 4% (see column # 8).

Thus, the proposed technology made it possible to significantly improve the results obtained earlier.

6   Conclusion

A new algorithm for vegetation classification in hyperspectral images has been proposed.It is based on the use of the conjugation index as a measure of proximity. The idea of the algorithm is to divide the total space of training vectors into smaller subspaces and select the most informative ones among them. The key idea is the search for spectral components for which the differences between classes are maximum. A two-stage algorithm implementing this idea has been built. At the first stage, a subset of the most informative training vectors in the sense of the maximum conjugacy criterion is selected. At the second stage, the most informative spectral components of these vectors are chosen. An important advantage of the algorithm is the automatic search for such fragments.

Two experiments were carried out that confirmed the high efficiency of the proposed algorithm. The use of the developed classification algorithm with the choice of informative subspaces made it possible to increase the recognition accuracy compared to previous results obtained using the method of reference subspaces by more than 15%. In the second experiment, due to the preprocessing of the hyperspectral image by the median filter, the classification accuracy was further increased by more than 4%. Thus, the overall increase in classification accuracy, compared to the results of the previous solution, was more than 19%.

Acknowledgments. This work was financially supported by the Ministry of Science and Higher Education of the Russian Federation under the FSRC "Crystallography and Photonics" of the Russian Academy of Sciences (the state task No. 007-GZ/Ch3363/26).

References

1. Borzov, S.M., Potaturkin, O.I.: Increasing the classification efficiency of hyperspectral images due to multi-scale spatial processing. Comput. Opt. **44**(6), 937–943 (2020). https://doi.org/10.18287/2412-6179-CO-779
2. Carvalho, O.A., Meneses, P.R.: Spectral correlation mapper: an improvement on the spectral angle mapper (SAM). Summaries of the 9th JPL Airborne Earth Science Workshop, JPL Publication 00–18, vol. 9, p. 9. JPL Publication, Pasadena (2000)
3. Fodor, I.: A survey of dimension reduction techniques: Technical Report UCRL-ID-148494, p. 26. University of California, Oakland (2002)
4. Fursov, V.A., Minaev, E.Y., Zherdev, D.A., Kazanskiy. N.L.: Support subspaces method for recognition of the synthetic aperture radar images using fractal compression. Int. J. Adv. Robotic Syst., 1–8 (2017). : https://doi.org/10.1177/1729881417733952
5. Fursov, V.A., Bibikov, S.A., Zherdev, D.A., Kazanskiy, N.L.: Thematic classification with support subspaces in hyperspectral images. Int. J. Eng. Syst. Modelling Simulat. **11**(4), 186–193 (2020)
6. Gualtieri, J.A., Cromp, R.F.: Support vector machines for hyperspectral remote sensing classification. In: Proceedings of 27th AIPR Workshop: Advances in Computer-Assisted Recognition, p. 221–232 (1999)
7. Lavanya, A., Sanjeevi, S.: An improved band selection technique for hyperspectral data using factor analysis. J. Indian Soc. Remote Sensing. **41**(2), 199–211 (2013)
8. Martinez-Uso, A., Pla, F., Sotoca, J.M., Garcia-Sevilla, P.: Clustering based band selection for hyperspectral images. IEEE Trans. Geosci. Remote Sens. **45**(12), 4158–4171 (2007)
9. Meer, F.: The effectiveness of spectral similarity measures for the analysis of hyperspectral imagery. Intern. J. Appl. Earth Obs. Geoinf. **8**(1), 3–17 (2006)
10. Ratle, F., Weston, J.: Semisupervised neural networks for efficient hyperspectral image classification. IEEE Trans. Geosci, Remote Sensing **48**(5), 2271–2282 (2010)
11. Soifer, V.A.: Computer Image Processing, Part II: Methods and algorithms, p. 584 . VDM Verlag (2010)
12. Shafri, M., Affendi, S., Shattri, M.: The performance of maximum likelihood, spectral angle mapper, neural network and decision tree classifiers in hyperspectral image analysis. J. Comput. Sci. **3**(6), 419–423 (2007)

13. Xiuping, J.: Simplified maximum likelihood classification for hyperspectral data in cluster space. In: IEEE Geoscience and Remote Sensing Symposium, vol. 5, pp. 2578–2580 (2002)
14. Zherdev, D.: Object recognition of real targets using modelled SAR images. J. Phys. Conf. Ser. **936** (2017)

New Method for Automating the Diagnostic Analysis of Human Fundus Images Produced by Optical Coherent Tomography Angiography. Research and Software Kit Realization

I. B. Gurevich⬤, V. V. Yashina⁽✉⁾ ⬤, and A. T. Tleubaev⬤

Federal Research Center "Computer Science and Control" Russian Academy of Sciences, Building 2, 44, Vavilov street, Moscow 119333, Russian Federation
igourevi@ccas.ru, werayashina@gmail.com

Abstract. This article presents the results of the joint work of specialists in the field of image analysis and ophthalmologists on the task of analyzing images obtained by the method of optical coherence tomography angiography. A descriptive algorithmic scheme for analyzing images obtained using optical coherence tomography angiography is built to automate the detection of pathological changes in the morphometric characteristics of the fundus. The algorithmic scheme is based on the methods of image processing, analysis, and recognition. The previously developed feature space is supplemented and modified, based on which it is possible to identify pathological changes in the structure of the choroid plexuses of the human retina. It was possible to improve the accuracy of classifying images of healthy and pathological eyes, as well as significantly increasing the accuracy of classification of borderline cases. Software is created that makes it possible to accurately carry out differential diagnostics of the normal state of vessels from the pathological one in the offline mode, which increases its diagnostic value. It is planned to achieve higher classification accuracy results for all three cases.

Keywords: image analysis · automated image analysis · mathematical morphology · automation of scientific research · biomedical images · segmentation · ophthalmology · automated diagnostics · intermarginal space of human eyelids · angiogram · vascular detection · extraction of ischemia zones · human fundus images

1 Introduction

At present, the development of the field of image processing and analysis has reached a high level, which makes it possible to apply these developments in various tasks that were previously either unsolvable or resource-intensive. The use of image processing tools for medical purposes, as a means of presenting the results of biological and clinical research in the main sections of medical science and practical medicine, allows us to more accurately and quickly diagnose various pathologies, or the beginning of the development of these pathologies. Vessels and vascular tissues are important objects

© Springer Nature Switzerland AG 2023
J.-J. Rousseau and B. Kapralos (Eds.): ICPR 2022 Workshops, LNCS 13644, pp. 464–481, 2023.
https://doi.org/10.1007/978-3-031-37742-6_36

of analysis on ophthalmic images. The human visual system is good at assessing the qualitative characteristics of objects, but the quantitative description of the same objects in most cases is quite subjective. Automation of characterization of objects (counting the number and measurement of their parameters) allows us not only to increase the accuracy of objects' estimation but also allows us to save images and the results of their processing in a large-capacity database, and therefore use large amounts of training, control, and test data in diagnostics, which, together with the unification of measurements, makes it possible to carry out diagnostics quite objectively [7].

Automation of scientific research allows significant progress in solving a large number of diverse and multifaceted problems. Over the years, the authors of the article have been developing and experimentally researching new methods for automating image analysis for processing, analyzing, and interpreting the results of biomedical research [6–10, 12, 16]. This study is a direct continuation of the work on solving the problem of automating the diagnostic analysis of images of a human's eye fundus.

Manual analysis and calculation of the characteristics of medical ophthalmological images require the involvement of several specialists and the investment of time and material costs. Automation of this process, through the development and implementation of digital image analysis, can significantly reduce all costs [7].

The article consists of an introduction, problem statement, description of the method, experiments, software implementation and conclusions.

In the "Problem statement" section, a description of the medical problem for which the automation method is being developed is provided. The section "A method for the automated detection of pathological changes in the morphometric characteristics of the eye fundus" describes the method implemented in the previous article [12]. A description of new features that modify the previously implemented method is also given. The section "Experimental study of the proposed method" describes the results of testing the new developed features. The section "Software implementation" describes the developed user interface.

2 Problem Statement

Intravital examination of the retinal and choroidal vascular beds is widely used by the medical community for the diagnosis of vascular and nonvascular pathology. Examination of the retinal vasculature can reveal a wide range of diseases such as hypertension, diabetes mellitus (DM), atherosclerosis, cardiovascular disease, and stroke.

The early assessment of pathological changes in the vessels of the microvasculature due to diabetic retinopathy will allow timely and high-quality screening and monitoring of diabetic retinopathy (DR) and starting therapy in the early stages of the disease, which will lead to a decrease in severe and proliferative forms of the disease, as well as in the number of complications.

DR is a chronic, progressive disease that affects retinal microvessels and develops in patients with DM. Diabetic macular edema (DME) is the leading cause of vision loss in DR among the working population [1].

Starting the treatment of DR in the early stages of the disease is more effective than at the stage of proliferative DR and when clinically significant macular edema occurs. That is why early detection of DR is relevant for prescribing timely treatment and minimizing its complications, which lead to blindness and low vision in the working population [4, 20, 26].

The method of optical coherent tomography angiography (OCT-A) makes it possible to visualize and study microcirculatory changes by a layer-by-layer study of the vascular plexuses of the retina [5, 12].

OCT-A is a noninvasive method for visualizing retinal and choroidal blood vessels, which is used to study changes in blood vessels in patients with diabetes mellitus [22]. The method provides high-resolution cross-sectional images of the neurosensory retina and choroid.

Currently, based on the image (Fig. 1) obtained using the Spectralis HRA + OCT device with the Heidelberg Engineering OCT Angiography module, the researcher makes a subjective assessment of the state of the retinal choroid plexuses and their qualitative characteristics, for example, the presence of ischemic zones and the density of the vascular pattern. The availability of software that allows evaluating the indicated parameters of the obtained images will allow obtaining an objective assessment of the state of the vascular plexuses of the retina and monitoring its changes over time. In particular, the assessment of vascular density is of greatest interest. The presence of software capabilities for detecting changes in this indicator will make it possible to objectively judge the development of neovascularization processes and the degree of retinal ischemia.

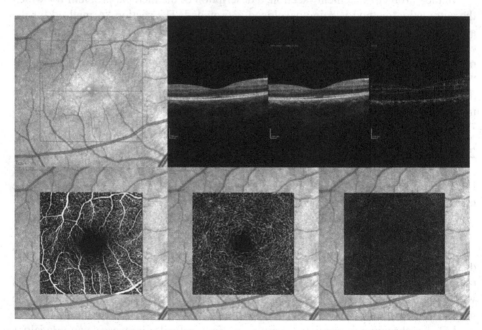

Fig. 1 Image obtained by optical coherent tomography angiography.

The parameters required to assess the state of the vascular bed: (1) localization of the foveolar avascular zone (FAZ) on OCT angiograms; (2) quantitative assessment of the area of the FAZ (the area of the FAZ in dynamics makes it possible to judge the development of ischemia of the macular zone of the retina); (3) visualization of the complex of vessels that make up the choroid plexuses of the retina; (4) quantitative assessment of vascular density (defined as the ratio of the area of the vascular complex to the area of the entire image; the value of vascular density is directly related to the process of neovascularization and the severity of retinal ischemia); (5) visualization of the components of the vascular frame (areas in which there are vessels that make up the choroid plexuses of the retina); and (6) quantitative assessment of the curvature of the vessels.

The original images were provided by the Research Institute of Eye Diseases; they are color images of retinal tissues, divided into several layers. The spectralis HRA + OCT device with the Heidelberg Engineering OCT Angiography module provides high-resolution OCT angiograms with a lateral resolution of 5.7 μm/pixel. The TruTrack Active Eye Tracking module improves the accuracy of the OCTA module, allowing fine visualization of fine capillary networks. An axial resolution of 3.9 μm/pixel allows segmentation of all four histologically confirmed retinal choroid plexuses. Using the built-in software, the device selects 3 layers of the retina, for which it shows the corresponding vascular patterns: the layer from the inner limiting membrane (ILM) to the inner plexiform layer (IPL) is the superficial capillary plexus (SCP); the layer from the IPL to the outer plexiform layer (OPL) is a deep capillary plexus (DCP); and the layer from the OPL to the Bruch membrane (BM) constitutes the avascular zone (AZ).

Microaneurysms (MAs) are small sac-like bulges in the wall of the retinal blood vessel (Fig. 2), most often observed in patients with underlying systemic diseases such as diabetes mellitus, hypertension, and atherosclerosis. They appear on the retina as a small, round, red spot. MAs are typically 10 to 125 μm in size and are visually threatening if they occur in the macula. MAs are one of the first signs of DR, and their quantity indicates the progression of DR. Therefore, the detection of MAs is critical for diagnosing and monitoring DR.

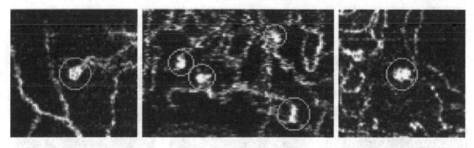

Fig. 2 Examples of MAs

OCT biomarkers such as the central retinal thickness (CRT), disorganization of the inner layers of the retina and destruction of the ellipsoidal zone, the presence of subretinal fluid (SRF) or cystic macular edema (CME) can serve as excellent signals of the changes occurring during DR. The thickness of the choroid differs in patients at the proliferative stage of DR, and there is also a significant decrease in the choroid in patients with DME.

Retinal hyperreflective 4 points are small, sometimes punctated, hyperreflective areas seen on OCT B-scans both internally and externally of the outer layers of the retina (Fig. 3).

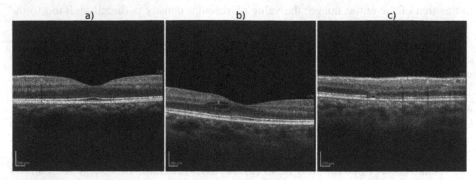

Fig. 3 Examples of images of the inner and outer layers of the retina: (a) healthy image; (b) cystic macular edema (CME); (c) disorganization of the inner layers of the retina, hyperreflexive points of the retina

The main task, which is solved in this study, is to modify the method of automatic calculation of morphological characteristics, by making changes to the image processing method and adding new features, based on which it is possible to assess pathological changes in blood vessels.

The image database consists of two parts: the first part is images of the eyes of completely healthy people, without vascular disorders, etc.; the second group contains images of the eyes of people with a confirmed diagnosis of diabetes. The last group is divided into 3 subgroups: (1) images of eyes with a healthy vascular bed, with characteristics very close to healthy eyes (Fig. 4a); (2) images of eyes with the onset of pathological changes, an increase in FAZ, a decrease in vascular density, the so-called borderline case (Fig. 4b); (3) images of eyes with obvious pathologies (Fig. 4c).

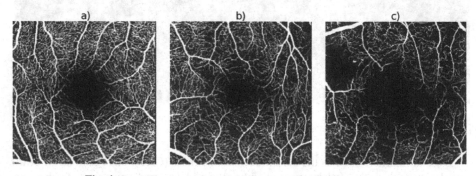

Fig. 4 (a–c) The state of the vascular network of different groups

3 A Method for the Automated Detection of Pathological Changes in the Morphometric Characteristics of the Eye Fundus

3.1 Description of the Previous Method

The previous work [12] described a method for automating the detection of pathological changes in the morphometric characteristics of the eye fundus; the method consisted of the following stages of image processing and analysis.

The purpose of the image processing stage is to improve the image quality, filter and reduce the influence of various noises and artifacts, and prepare the image for the calculation of morphological features. This stage consisted of the following steps: selection of images of different layers of the retina (Fig. 5.); image binarization, i.e., the application of the Gaussian filter [21], Sauvol's adaptive binarization [19], cleaning of small noise components; and obtaining images of the skeleton of the vessels and images of the boundaries of the vessels (perimeter).

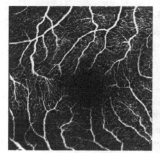

Fig. 5 Three layers of the retina

The purpose of the image analysis stage is to calculate the features based on the processed image and further classify the images. Table 1 shows list of features.

For each selected image of the retinal layer, the features, based on which the classification was carried out, were calculated. The random forest algorithm was used as the classifier, the work was carried out on two (conditionally healthy, pathology) and three classes (conditionally healthy, borderline case, pathology).

3.2 Modification of the Image Processing Step

Work has been done to modify the image processing stage to improve the quality of the resulting images and eliminate the noise that was allowed in the previous method.

Two variants of image binarization have been developed.

Option 1. A filter in the form of a cylinder (top-hat filter) [24] is applied to the image to smooth out the background and remove small objects, then a Gaussian filter [21] is also applied to reduce noise. Further, the image is binarized in two ways: Sauwol's adaptive binarization [19] and Otsu's global threshold binarization [18]. The final binarized image is obtained by crossing the two received binarizations, in which the pixel is considered

Table 1. Features

Features	Unit	Description	Meaning
Features based on the grouping of pixels with different brightnesses			
Bright vessels	%	The ratio of all white pixels in the binary image with brightness higher than the threshold in the initial image to the total number of pixels	Percentage ratio of bright vessel pixels to image area
Dull vessels	%	The ratio of all white pixels in the binary image with brightness less than the threshold in the initial image to the total number of pixels	Percentage ratio of dull vessel pixels to image area
Not vessels	%	The ratio of all black pixels in the binary image to the total number of pixels	Percentage ratio of nonvessels pixels to image area
Features based on the localization of the FAZ and ischemic zone			
Dark zone	%	The ratio of all black pixels in the binary image, related to large areas of FAZ and ischemic zones, to the total number of pixels	Percentage ratio of FAZ and ischemic zones to image area
Features based on quantitative analysis [2]			
Vessel area density VAD	%	The ratio of all white pixels in the binary image to the total number of pixels	Provides an estimate of the actual density of the vascular plexuses, since it takes into account both the length and diameter of the vessels
Vessel skeleton density VSD	%	The ratio of all white pixels in the skeleton image to the total number of pixels	Provides an estimate of the density of the vascular plexuses, takes into account only the very existence of the vessel, since only the length of the vessel is estimated, regardless of its diameter
Vessel diameter index VDI	pixel	The ratio of all white pixels in the binary image to all white pixels in the skeleton image	Allows calculates the mean vessel diameter in the image, but it does not show a change in vessel density
Vessel perimeter index VPI	%	The ratio of all white pixels in the perimeter image to the total number of pixels	Provides an assessment of the density of the vascular plexuses, taking into account the perimeter of the vessels
Vessel complexity index VCI	-	The ratio of all white pixels in the perimeter image to the total number of pixels	Provides an assessment of the complexity of the vascular plexuses

white only if it is white in each of the received binarizations. In the next step, the binarized image is also cleared of small noise components.

Option 2. This option almost completely corresponds to Option 1, except that not the intersection of two binarized images is chosen as the final binarized image but the result of Sauvola's adaptive binarization [19].

In the course of experiments with binarization 1, it was determined that modifying the method by adding a filter in the form of a cylinder and using the intersection of two binarizations gives better results in filtering out noise, artifacts, and debris (Fig. 6c). It also allows us to better highlight large vessels. However, at the stage of image analysis, it was found that such modifications adversely affect the signs and further classification, due to the fact that a lot of information is lost regarding small, dim vessels. As a result, a second variant of binarization was developed, in which only a filter in the form of a cylinder is added to the old method, which also allows us to eliminate additional noise and has a positive effect on the further classification (Fig. 6d).

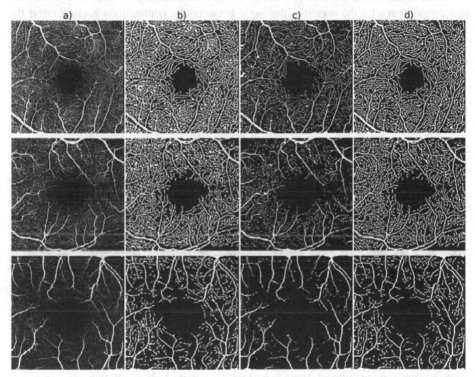

Fig. 6 Examples of binarization options: (a) original image; (b) binarized image by the old method; (c) binarized image by method Option 1; (d) binarized image by method Option 2;

3.3 Addition of New Features Based on the Microaneurysm Count

A method for searching for objects that are potentially microaneurysms has been developed, which makes it possible to calculate the sign of the density of potential MAs.

Together with the experts, a number of rules were drawn up, according to which it is possible to select potential MAs; these rules include the allowable sizes of the objects found, their shape, and location relative to the vessels.

To select objects, an algorithm for searching for local maximums is used, then the found maximums are combined into objects that are filtered.

Filter by size: all objects smaller than 4 and larger than 100 pixels are discarded.

Filtering by form: overly elongated objects are removed based on the aspect ratio and eccentricity characteristics.

Filtering based on the intersection with the binarized image: if less than 70% of the object's pixels intersect with the binarized image, then this object is filtered out and considered garbage.

Filtering based on location relative to vessels: for all the remaining objects, the connection with the vessels is checked; for this, the image of the skeleton is used. If the object is not connected to the skeleton or is connected to only one branch of the skeleton, then this object is considered a potential MA. For all other objects that have more than one connection with the skeleton, the angle between the connections is checked; if the angle between the connections is not more than 85 degrees, then this object is also considered a potential MA, and all other objects are filtered out. An 85-degree angle for a vessel means a kink, and the appearance of a bright object at the kink in most cases means the occurrence of MA.

The attribute of the potential MA density is calculated by the ratio of the total number of pixels of potential MA objects (Fig. 7) to the total number of white pixels in the binary image.

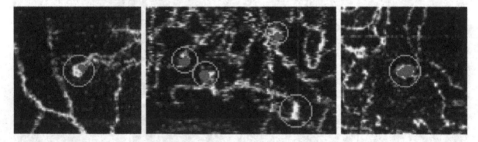

Fig. 7 Found objects of potential MA (marked in red);

For healthy images, all the objects found are mostly small and are in small quantities, and due to the high density of vessels and their area, the value of the feature tends to zero. For patients, in contrast, there is a greater number of objects with a large area, and the overall density of the vessels is degraded.

3.4 Adding a New Feature Based on Skeleton Branch Point Density

The feature is based on the calculation of the number of branch points. The points on the skeleton image, where one vessel divides into several others, are considered branching points (Fig. 8). The biological significance of vascular branching means the degree of blockage and the diversity of vessels. In order to search for branching points in the skeleton image, 3 × 3 pixel windows are selected, the number of outgoing branches from the central pixel is counted, and pixels with more than two outgoing branches are sought.

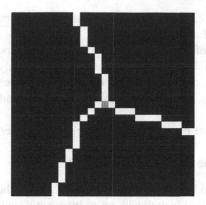

Fig. 8 Vessel branch point.

Analysis of all 3 × 3 pixel windows for a 512 × 512 pixel image is a lengthy operation; thus, the following simplifying approach is applied. For a 3 × 3 pixel window, there are a limited number of combinations in which there are more than two outgoing branches for the central pixel (Table 2).

Table 2. Examples of windows with vascular branch points

0	1	1		1	0	1		0	1	1		1	0	1		0	1	0
0	1	0		0	1	1		1	1	0		0	1	0		1	1	1
1	0	1		1	0	1		1	0	1		1	0	1		0	0	0

The intersection of these windows with the image of the skeleton gives the image of the branch points. In this case, the ratio of the total number of branch points to the total number of skeleton points is selected as a sign.

3.5 Addition of New Features Based on the Cross-Sectional Processing of Retinal Layers

Analysis of the cross-sectional images of the layers was added to the image processing of individual retinal layers (Fig. 3). The morphological features were analyzed based on the brightness and shape of the layers.

When forming an image with the software complex of the microscope, the cross section of the retinal layers was already analyzed by visually separating the layers with a dotted line; thus, the cross section of the retina was divided into the following layers: the inner and outer retinas. This division is sufficient for the analysis of layers and formation of features. The following features were generated:

1. Sign of layer density, calculated by the ratio of the total number of pixels in the layer to the total number of pixels in the image;
2. Signs of brightness of the pixels of the upper layer (inner retina) are calculated as follows: (a) the ratio of the total number of excessively dark pixels, below the threshold, to the total number of pixels of this layer; (b) the ratio of the total number of overly bright pixels, above the threshold, to the total number of pixels of the given layer;
3. The layer width feature is calculated by calculating the average layer width.

3.6 Modification of the Vessel Complexity Index Feature

The vessel complexity index (VCI) feature was replaced by the fractal dimension (FD) feature [27], as an improved feature with more informative content. This feature is calculated based on the Minkowski box-counting dimension, within which the relationship between the number of blocks of a certain resolution that completely cover the image skeleton and the resolution is calculated.

This feature is calculated by the formula

$$FD = \frac{\log N_r}{\log r^{-1}} \tag{1}$$

where N_r is the number of boxes, with scale r, covering the image skeleton pattern. This feature allows us to reflect the complexity of vascular branching: the more complex and branched the vascular bed the higher values the feature will take.

4   Experimental Study of the Proposed Method

4.1   Analysis of Characteristic Values

An image database was provided for the work: 70 images of the eyes of healthy people and 370 images of the eyes of people with confirmed diabetes. In turn, the patient base was divided into three subgroups: 100 images close to the norm, 150 images with pathology, and 120 with the so-called borderline cases.

The values of the features included in the parametric model of the images of the OCT angiograms were analyzed on the original images. Tables 3. shows the mean values of the signs and the standard deviations for different groups of patients and layers of the retina. The columns correspond to the trait values, and the rows indicate the group of patients and the retinal layer for which it is determined. Each cell of the table shows the mean value of the feature in the first row and the standard deviation in the second row. The analysis of the obtained values showed the distinguishability of the presented groups according to the selected features.

Table 3. Statistical values of features of layer density, pixel brightness and retinal layer width

	Inner Retinal Layer Density	Outer Retinal Layer Density	Dark Pixels Inner Retinal	White Pixels Inner Retinal	Width Inner Retinal	Width Outer Retinal
Healthy	0.0698	0.0898	0.0416	0.0155	35.77	45.00
	0.0069	0.0054	0.0101	0.0113	3.56	2.79
Normal	0.0706	0.0888	0.0413	0.0094	36.15	44.51
	0.0077	0.0048	0.0082	0.0069	3.90	2.46
Borderline	0.6826	0.0892	0.0408	0.0091	34.95	44.67
	0.0066	0.0040	0.0095	0.0096	3.42	2.05
Pathology	0.0746	0.0855	0.0539	0.0108	38.21	42.79
	0.0217	0.0103	0.0341	0.0139	11.11	5.30

4.2 Image Classification

Two experiments were conducted with two and three class approaches. In the first experiment, OCT angiogram images were classified into two classes: those related to apparently healthy patients and those containing pathological changes. For training, images of healthy patients, patients close to the norm, and those with pathology were used. The sample was divided into two parts: training and testing, with equal shares of each class. In the second experiment, OCT angiogram images were classified into three classes: those related to apparently healthy patients, borderline cases, and those containing pathological changes. The sample was also divided into two parts, with equal shares of each class.

Table 4. shows the results for two experiments with different image processing and different feature sets.

Comparisons were made between several variants of approaches and with a previously implemented method. The use of binarization modification 1 gave worse results for the two class approach, but the results in the three class approach turned out to be at the same level; only the distribution of accuracy over classes changed. The use of binarization modification 2 gave a slight improvement in both types of classification, which indicates the positive results of changing the approach with binarization.

Updating the feature space significantly improves the classification accuracy, by 3% and 6% for the two and three-class approaches, respectively.

Table 4. Results of two and three class classification experiments with different processing approaches: (A) the original approach from [12]; (B) modified version with binarization 1; (C) modified version with binarization 2; (D) modified version with binarization 2 with the addition of new features;

	A	B	C	D
Two class classifiers				
Accuracy	92%	87%	93%	95%
Pathology	89%	85%	90%	95%
Healthy/close to normal	94%	89%	95%	95%
Three class classifiers				
Accuracy	71%	71%	73%	78%
Pathology	78%	76%	79%	80%
Healthy/close to normal	81%	69%	74%	82%
Borderline	40%	60%	45%	59%

5   Software Implementation

As part of the developed method for the automated detection of pathological changes in the morphometric characteristics of the eye fundus, a user interface has been developed.

The user interface is designed to be used by ophthalmologists to analyze OCT-A images. To do this, in addition to detecting pathological changes, the interface implements various visualizations of calculated features. The processed image displays bright vessels, dull vessels and the background in separate colors, and also visualizes FAZ and ischemic zones. Separately, information is displayed regarding some other features, with the possibility of comparison with each other for different layers and different images.

5.1   Description of the User Interface

The implemented interface (Fig. 9) is a window with several sub-windows:

1. The main menu on top with the buttons necessary for work;
2. The main image window on the top left is a means of interacting with the image;
3. Window for numerical display of features and classification result on the top right;
4. Window of graphical display of signs from below.

Button description:

1. Opening an image - button ➕, works in two modes: the first is the opening of a single image, the second is the opening of several images (multi-image mode);
2. Image analysis - button 🔍, the analysis of the image and further visualization of the results are carried out in the windows of numerical and graphical displays of features (Fig. 9). Also, in the mode of opening a single image, visualization of bright and dull

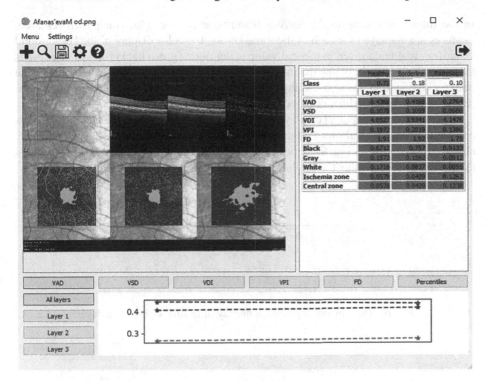

Fig. 9 User interface

vessels, background, FAZ and ischemic zones is carried out on this image. As a result of the analysis of the image/images, the results obtained, such as numerical signs and classification results, are recorded in the database for storing information about all processed images;

3. Save results – button 🖫, the results of the feature calculation are saved in a Microsoft Excel file, in the multi-image mode all data will be saved in one file, the image of vessels is also saved in monochrome, with color separation into bright and dull vessels, background, FAZ and ischemic zones, in addition, images of the skeleton and perimeter for each of the three layers are saved. In multi-image mode, the results for each image are saved separately;

4. Setting - button ⚙, allows to configure the minimum and maximum values of features within which a numeric value is considered the norm;

5. Help – button ❷, opens a window with additional information about the operation of the program;

6. Exit – button ➡, close program button.

The main image window displays one or more images that you can interact with. The main window, among other things, is a means of displaying vessels of different brightness and FAZ.

The window for the numerical display of features (Fig. 9) is used to display the numerical value of the counted features that are significant for experts ophthalmologists.

In the future, according to the derived features, experts conduct their own research. Features are displayed for each of the three layers, the color display of the background visualizes whether a given numerical value is the norm (green background), or exceeds the maximum value or below the minimum value (red background). The results of the image classification are also displayed as a probability of being related to one of the classes: healthy, borderline, or pathological.

The window of graphical display of features is designed to analyze changes in signs on a time series, which allows analyzing various changes for one patient based on images taken at different times Fig. 9. In the single-layer operation mode, Fig. 10 also displays the norm zone. To display the brightness of pixels, histograms are used in Fig. 11.

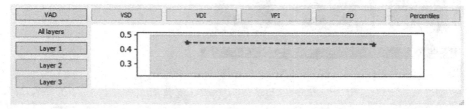

Fig. 10 The window of graphical display of feature VAD for one layer

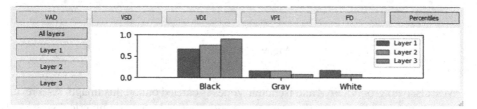

Fig. 11 The window of graphical display of feature brightness of pixels for three layers

5.2 Further Plans for the Development of the User Interface

As part of the work on the further development of the user interface, work is underway to develop functionality for automatic retraining of the classification model. Automatic retraining of the model will make the programming interface a self-sufficient software package that does not require intervention from developers.

As part of this work, it is planned to develop a number of rules according to which new images will be selected for analysis to enrich the existing training set, which will allow ophthalmologists to independently train the image classification model to improve its accuracy.

6 Conclusions

In this study, methods of image processing and analysis were used in the problem of image analysis of OCT angiograms. The developed feature space was supplemented and the approach to image processing was modified, based on which it became possible to identify pathological changes in the structure of the vascular plexuses of the human retina more accurately.

It was possible to improve the accuracy of the classification of borderline cases, without losing the accuracy of classification of healthy and pathological eyes.

In the future, work will be carried out to expand the feature space, improve the operation of algorithms, and obtain more detailed labeling of images of patients with a confirmed diagnosis of diabetes. Other classification methods will be tested, and new approaches to the use of features both separately and in combinations will be developed.

For the developed method of OCT angiogram image analysis, a user interface was developed and handed over to expert ophthalmologists for work.

The uneven flow of patients during DR screening and the need to analyze tomograms by an experienced ophthalmologist-retinologist, and in borderline conditions the need to convene a panel, create an overload in the work of doctors, which makes it extremely important to create an automated system for identifying pathological changes on tomograms. Replacing one doctor-retinologist with a diagnostic system will help relieve the work of medical ophthalmological centers through prompt advisory assistance, reducing the psychological burden on patients and doctors. The visual analysis of the tomogram image may not always make it possible to determine the exact diagnosis of the patient's condition; therefore, methods and algorithms are needed to intelligently support image analysis and make a final diagnosis.

To date, a large number of works are underway to create automated systems for analyzing color images of the fundus in patients with DM [16]; however, OCT angiography is the only method that allows us to evaluate all three vascular plexuses of the eye fundus. Violation of retinal hemodynamics in DM manifests itself in a deep choroid plexus.

In our study, a program was created that allows us to accurately carry out differential diagnostics of the normal state of the vessels from the pathological one, which increases its diagnostic value. In the future, more detailed work is planned with borderline conditions, which are the main problem in screening patients with DM.

References

1. Cheung, N., Mitchell, P., Wong, T.Y.: Diabetic retinopathy. Lancet **376**, 124–146 (2010). https://doi.org/10.1016/S0140-6736(09)62124-3
2. Chu, Z.: Quantitative assessment of the retinal microvasculature using optical coherence tomography angiography. J. Biomed. Opt. **21**, 066008 (2016). https://doi.org/10.1117/1.JBO.21.6.066008
3. Dedov, I., Shestakova, M., Vikulova, O.: Epidemiology of diabetes mellitus in russian federation: clinical and statistical report according to the federal diabetes registry. Diabetes Mellitus **20**(1), 13–41 (2017). https://doi.org/10.14341/DM8664
4. Fong, D.S., Gottlieb, J., Ferris, F.L., Klein, R.: Understanding the value of diabetic retinopathy screening. Arch. Ophthalmol. **119**, 758–760 (2001). https://doi.org/10.1001/archopht.15.758
5. Gildea, D.: The diagnostic value of optical coherence tomography angiography in diabetic retinopathy: a systematic review. Int. Ophthalmol. **39**(10), 2413–2433 (2018). https://doi.org/10.1007/s10792-018-1034-8
6. Gurevich, I.B., Harazishvili, D.V., Salvetti, O., Trykova, A.A., Vorob'ev, I.A.: Elements of the information technology of cytological specimens analysis: Taxonomy and factor analysis.

Pattern Recognit. Image Anal. **16**, 114–116 (2006). https://doi.org/10.1134/S10546618060 10366

7. Gurevich, I.B., et al.: Development and experimental investigation of mathematical methods for automating the diagnostics and analysis of ophthalmological images. Pattern Recognit. Image Anal. **28**, 612–636 (2018). https://doi.org/10.1134/S1054661818040120

8. Gurevich, I.B., Yashina, V.V., Fedorov, A.A., Nedzved, A.M., Tleubaev, A.T.: Development, investigation, and software implementation of a new mathematical method for automatizing analysis of corneal endothelium images. Pattern Recognit. Image Anal. **27**, 550–559 (2017). https://doi.org/10.1134/S1054661817030130

9. Gurevich, I.B., Yashina, V.V., Fedorov, A.A., Nedzved, A.M., Ospanov, A.M.: Development, investigation, and software implementation of a new mathematical method for automated identification of the lipid layer state by the images of eyelid intermarginal space. Pattern Recognit. Image Anal. **27**, 538–549 (2017). https://doi.org/10.1134/S1054661817030129

10. Gurevich, I.B., Zhuravlev, Y., Myagkov, A.A., Trusova, Y., Yashina, V.V.: On basic problems of image recognition in neurosciences and heuristic methods for their solution. Pattern Recognit. Image Anal. **25**, 132–160 (2015). https://doi.org/10.1134/S105466181501006X

11. Gurevich, I., Yashina, V.: Basic models of descriptive image analysis. In: Del Bimbo, A., et al. (eds.) ICPR 2021. LNCS, vol. 12665, pp. 275–288. Springer, Cham (2021). https://doi. org/10.1007/978-3-030-68821-9_26

12. Gurevich, I.B., et al.: A new method for automating the diagnostic analysis of human fundus images obtained using optical coherent tomography angiography. Pattern Recognit. Image Anal. **31**, 513–528 (2021). https://doi.org/10.1134/S1054661821030111

13. Hirano, T., et al.: Vitreoretinal interface slab in OCT angiography for detecting diabetic retinal neovascularization. Ophthalmol. Retina **4**, 588–594 (2020). https://doi.org/10.1016/j. oret.2020.01.004

14. Hirano, T., Kitahara, J., Toriyama, Y., Kasamatsu, H., Murata, T., Sadda, S.: Quantifying vascular density and morphology using different swept-source optical coherence tomography angiographic scan patterns in diabetic retinopathy. Br. J. Ophthalmol. **103**, 216–221 (2019). https://doi.org/10.1136/bjophthalmol-2018-311942

15. Soares, J.V.B., Leandro, J.J.G., Cesar, R.M., Jelinek, H.F., Cree, M.J.: Retinal vessel segmentation using the 2-D Gabor wavelet and supervised classification. IEEE Trans. Med. Imaging **25**, 1214–1222 (2006). https://doi.org/10.1109/TMI.2006.879967

16. Nedzvedz, O.V., Ablameyko, S.V., Gurevich, I.B., Yashina, V.V.: A new method for automazing of stem cell populations investigation based on the integral optical flow of a video sequence analysis. Pattern Recognit. Image Anal. **27**, 599–609 (2017). https://doi.org/10.1134/S10546 61817030221

17. Olvera-Barrios, A., et al.: Diagnostic accuracy of diabetic retinopathy grading by an artificial intelligence-enabled algorithm compared with a human standard for wide-field truecolour confocal scanning and standard digital retinal images. Br. J. Ophthalmol. **105**, 265–270 (2020). https://doi.org/10.1136/bjophthalmol-2019-315394

18. Otsu, N.: A threshold selection method from gray-level histograms. IEEE Trans. Syst., Man, Cybern. **9**, 62– 66 (1979). https://doi.org/10.1109/TSMC.1979.4310076

19. Sauvola, J., Pietikäinen, M.: Adaptive document image binarization. Pattern Recognit. **33**, 225–236 (2000). https://doi.org/10.1016/S0031-3203(99)00055-2

20. Sinclair, S.H., Delvecchio, C.: The internist's role in managing diabetic retinopathy: Screening for early detection. Cleveland Clin. J. Med. **71**, 151–159 (2004). https://doi.org/10.3949/ccjm. 71.2.151

21. Zha, H., Chen, X., Wang, L., Miao, Q. (eds.): CCCV 2015. CCIS, vol. 546. Springer, Heidelberg (2015). https://doi.org/10.1007/978-3-662-48558-3

22. Spaide, R.F., Fujimoto, J.G., Waheed, N.K., Sadda, S.R., Staurenghi, G.: Optical coherence tomography angiography. Prog. Retinal Eye Res. **64**, 1–55 (2018). https://doi.org/10.1016/j.preteyeres.2017.11.003

23. Spaide, R.F.: Volume-rendered optical coherence tomography of diabetic retinopathy pilot study. Am. J. Ophthalmol. **160**, 1200–1210 (2015). https://doi.org/10.1016/j.ajo.2015.09.010

24. Untracht, G.R., et al.: OCTAVA: An open-source toolbox for quantitative analysis of optical coherence tomography angiography images. PLoS ONE **16**, e0261052 (2021). https://doi.org/10.1371/journal.pone.0261052

25. Vermeer, K.A., Vos, F.M., Lemij, H.G., Vossepoel, A.M.: A model based method for retinal blood vessel detection. Comput. Biol. Med. **34**, 209–219 (2004). https://doi.org/10.1016/S0010-4825(03)00055-6

26. Vujosevic, S., et al.: Screening for diabetic retinopathy: New perspectives and challenges. Lancet Diabetes Endocrinol. **8**, 337–347 (2020). https://doi.org/10.1016/S2213-8587(19)30411-5

27. Yao, X., Alam, M.N., Le, D., Toslak, D.: Quantitative optical coherence tomography angiography: A review. Exp. Biol. Med. **245**, 301–312 (2020). https://doi.org/10.1177/1535370219899893

28. Zhang, B., Zhang, L., Zhang, L., Karray, F.: Retinal vessel extraction by matched filter with first-order derivative of Gaussian. Comput. Biol. Med. **40**, 438–445 (2010). https://doi.org/10.1016/j.compbiomed.2010.02.008

Image Quality Assessment Metric Fusing Traditional and Dempster-Shafer Theory

Roopdeep Kaur[✉][iD] and Gour Karmakar[iD]

Institute of Innovation, Science and Sustainability, Federation University Australia, Ballarat, Australia
roopdeepkaur@students.federation.edu.au, gour.karmakar@federation.edu.au

Abstract. Image analysis is being applied in many applications including industrial automation with the Industrial Internet of Things and machine vision. The images captured by cameras, from the outdoor environment are impacted by various parameters such as lens blur, dirty lens and lens distortion (barrel distortion). There exist many approaches that assess the impact of camera parameters on the quality of the images. However, most of these techniques do not use important quality assessment metrics such as Oriented FAST and Rotated BRIEF and Structural Content. None of these techniques objectively evaluate the impact of barrel distortion on the image quality using quality assessment metrics such as Mean Square Error, Peak signal-to-noise ratio, Structural Content, Oriented FAST and Rotated BRIEF and Structural Similarity Index. In this paper, besides lens dirtiness and blurring, we also examine the impact of barrel distortion using various types of dataset having different levels of barrel distortion. Analysis shows none of the existing metrics produces quality values consistent with intuitively defined impact levels for lens blur, dirtiness and barrel distortion. To address the loopholes of existing metrics and make the quality assessment metric more reliable, we present two new image quality assessment metrics. For our combined metric, results show that the maximum values of impact level created by barrel distortion, blurriness and dirtiness are 66.6%, 87.9% and 94.4%, respectively. These results demonstrate the effectiveness of our metric to assess the impact level more accurately. The second approach fuses the quality values obtained from different metrics using a decision fusion technique known as the Dempster-Shafer (DS) theory. Our metric produces quality values that are more consistent and conform with the perceptually defined camera parameter impact levels. For all above-mentioned camera impacts, our metric DS exhibits 100% assessment reliability, which includes an enormous improvement over other metrics.

Keywords: Camera lens distortion · Image quality assessment · Quality assessment metrics · Dempster-Shafer theory

© Springer Nature Switzerland AG 2023
J.-J. Rousseau and B. Kapralos (Eds.): ICPR 2022 Workshops, LNCS 13644, pp. 482–497, 2023.
https://doi.org/10.1007/978-3-031-37742-6_37

1 Introduction

In real-world and industrial applications, digital image processing plays a vital role majorly in the Industrial Internet of Things (IIoT) and computer vision. There are a lot of applications like smart transportation, agriculture, and homes. Most of these applications require images captured by the traditional camera or Internet of Things (IoT) vision sensors. These captured images can be mainly impacted by blurring of the lens, dirtiness of the lens and various distortions of lenses such as barrel distortion. Lens blur leads to a change in the size of the image and also results in noise and interference [7]. However, lens blur is not the only problem while capturing images. Lens dirtiness is also one of the major parameters which lead to image degradation. For example, a camera lens with dirt can produce low-quality images for which we are unable to detect some criminal activities and also for other object detection applications [3]. Another camera parameter impact is barrel distortion which brings some non-linear changes. IoT images generally possess barrel distortion. As a result, the outer area of the image becomes smaller as compared to the actual one. It can also lead to corrupted features of an image [6].

The existing works assess the effect of lens blur and lens dirtiness in terms of image quality metrics such as Mean Squared Error (MSE), Peak signal-to-noise ratio (PSNR) and Structural Similarity Index (SSIM) [17] but no other metrics such as Structural Content (SC) [18] and Oriented FAST and Rotated BRIEF (ORB) [15]. Also, some algorithms and deep neural network techniques are there to remove the lens blurriness [16]. However, to the best of our knowledge, no techniques exist which can assess the quality of images having barrel distortion in terms of image quality metrics such as MSE, PSNR, SSIM, SC and ORB. None of the quality assessment metrics (e.g., MSE, PSNR, SC, ORB, SSIM) shows perceived and consistent image quality values for all camera impacts. To address this issue, we present reliable image quality assessment metrics by leveraging a combined and decision fusion technique, which is equally applicable to assessing both IoT and non-IoT images. The major contributions of the paper are as follows:

1. We present two new image quality assessment metrics that can produce consistent values conforming with the different impact levels estimated by the people.
   (a) For the first image quality assessment metric combined (COM), we combine ORB, SSIM and normalized PSNR. Since all three quality assessment metrics are equally important, we use their product to present a new image quality assessment metric.
   (b) From our research experience in analysing image quality values, we perceive that there exist some uncertainties in quality values produced by existing assessment metrics. For this reason, we use the renowned decision fusion and reasoning technique named Dempster-Shafer (DS) theory to fuse the quality assessment values produced by PSNR, ORB and SSIM by leveraging their uncertainty values. For the fusion, we estimate the

uncertainty associated with the quality assessment performed by a particular metric and automatically select the metrics that will participate in the decision fusion.

2. We present a new approach for assessing the impact of camera parameters such as lens blur, lens dirtiness, and barrel distortion on the quality of images. We use image metrics such as SC and ORB which were not used earlier to assess the image quality.

3. We assess the impact of barrel distortion in terms of image quality metrics such as MSE, PSNR, SSIM, SC and ORB which were also not assessed earlier.

4. We evaluate our metric using real-world image data comprising lens blurriness, lens dirtiness and simulated barrel distortion compared with the existing image quality assessment metrics.

   (a) Results show that the maximum values of impact level created by barrel distortion, blurriness and dirtiness are 66.6%, 87.9% and 94.4%, respectively for our first COM metric.

   (b) The assessment reliability of our second metric DS is 100% for all above-mentioned camera impacts and thus, our proposed metrics outperforms others by a considerable margin.

The organisation of the paper is as follows: The assessment of camera parameter impacts is summarised in Sect. 2. Our approaches for assessing the image quality is mentioned in Sect. 3. Section 4 explains the results. The conclusion is presented in Sect. 5.

2   Assessment of Camera Parameter Impacts

Various camera parameters lead to the degradation of images such as lens blurriness, lens dirtiness and lens distortion. The impact assessment approaches can be broadly classified into four groups - (i) blurring, (ii) dirtiness, (iii) barrel distortion and (iv) other parameter impact assessment techniques. They are presented as follows:

In [11], the authors explored the use of autonomous mobile robots for the identification of different species of plants. They used deep neural networks to test the accuracy of systems in many environments. For the camera parameter, the impact of variations in camera distance is analysed. However, this approach does not cover other camera parameters such as lens blur, lens dirtiness and lens distortion. In an outdoor environment, pictures are changed by the outdoor environmental parameters and thus, there is a reduction in the contrast and gradient information. However, by contrast, for better computer vision performance, clear visibility is required for the precise detection of image features that are captured from the dynamic environment. This approach [14] describes the enhancement of visibility techniques in computer vision applications and considers environmental parameters such as fog, haze and mist. But it does not consider lens parameters such as lens blur, lens dirtiness and barrel distortion. One of the most common image degradations is image blurring. The method presented in [5] compares the traditional iterative approach with the AI method to improve the quality of images with significant blurring not anticipated in conventional test images. However, the results for blurring are not shown.

Bachoo [2] did real-time blur level assessment using Haar wavelet, but other camera parameters such as lens dirty and lens distortion are neglected in both approaches presented in [2,5]. Temel et al. [17] demonstrated that the performance of Application Programming Interfaces (APIs) - Amazon Rekognition and Microsoft Azure Computer Vision decline when challenging conditions such as exposure and dirty lens are present. They assessed the quality with two image quality assessment metrics such as PSNR and SSIM, but other important metrics such as ORB and SC are not used. Moreover, they considered camera parameters such as lens blur and lens dirtiness, but not lens distortion such as barrel distortion, which also plays a crucial role while assessing the image quality.

In [16], the authors explored the reliability of traffic sign recognition algorithms under complex weather conditions and camera parameters such as lens blur and lens dirtiness. The database used in the experiment contains over two million traffic sign photographs which are real-world images. The authors compared the performance of current technologies and examined how the approach responds to difficult circumstances. The conclusion states that daunting environments would dramatically reduce the efficiency of baseline approaches. Techniques such as Support Vector Machines (SVMs) were used to classify traffic sign pictures. A Convolutional Neural Network (CNN) was employed and the robustness of their algorithms is checked with PSNR and SSIM but the comparison of the quality of images with image metrics such as PSNR, SSIM, SC, and ORB is not done. Also, they proved that lens blur has more impact on the quality of images compared with lens dirtiness. But the impact of barrel distortion on the camera lens is not covered. Similarly, to convert the traditional parking system into the smart one, Optical Character Recognition (OCR) was used by [13] to ensure that an employee is a legitimate employee. After the algorithm is based on image processing, there is the retrieval of numbers from the number plate and forwarded to the server for the verification of the employee. This method saves time as well but while recognizing the number plates, the challenging conditions such as lens blur, lens dirtiness and lens distortion will be there which leads to misunderstanding of the numbers on the plate.

Wang et al. [19] used PSNR and SSIM for image quality assessment for the analysis of the blurred images, JPEG compressed images and others. However, camera parameters such as lens dirtiness and lens distortion are neglected in this analysis. Also, another subjective analysis is done in which images are blurred first and then compressed with the help of a JPEG encoder. The investigation of various kinds of distortions affecting the quality judgment of humans and objective algorithms is done. However, the authors just considered camera parameters such as lens blurriness but other parameters such as lens distortion and lens dirtiness are ignored [8].

In [12], Liedlgruber et al. did barrel-type distortion correction, but they did not analyze the effect of barrel distortion on the quality of images through subjective and objective methods. They checked the robustness of their proposed method in terms of PSNR and SSIM, but the assessment of image quality with metrics such as PSNR, SSIM, ORB and SC is not done [9]. Overall, none of the methods consider all camera parameters. Also, the results of all these methods show that the values of these quality assessment metrics are not consistent for the images having all possible camera parameter impacts.

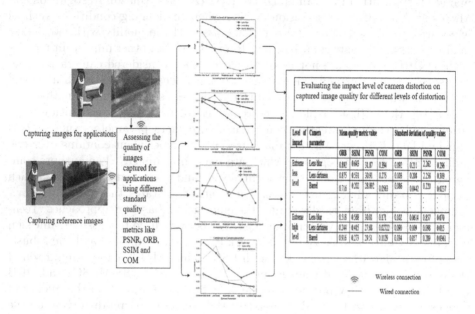

Fig. 1. Block diagram of our COM approach.

3   Our Models for Camera Parameter Impact Analysis

In this section, we first assess the quality of images that are captured with different camera parameters such as lens blur, lens dirtiness and barrel distortion at different levels with the image quality metrics such as PSNR, MSE, ORB, SC and SSIM. As per our experimental results, we noticed that PSNR and SSIM would not decrease consistently with an increase in the level of camera parameter impacts. For example, ORB generally decreases in barrel distortion and lens blur. However, it increases at extreme less level rather than to decrease. Also, PSNR increases at extreme high level of all impacted parameters, but as expected it should have decreased as shown in Fig. 6(b). So, to overcome the random variations of these assessment metrics, there is a need to present image quality assessment metrics that gives us more intuitive and consistent results. One of the possible ways to achieve this is to present new metrics that exploits the merits of these image quality assessment metrics.

The overview of our impact analysis and proposed metrics are given in the following sections.

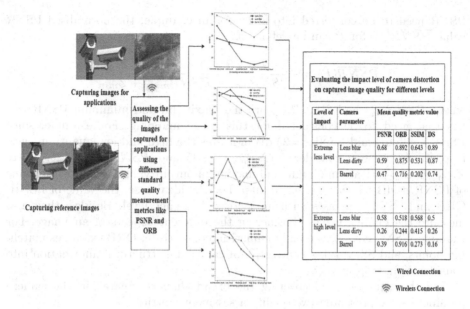

Fig. 2. Block diagram of our DS approach.

3.1 Overview of Our Image Quality Assessment

The overview of the image quality assessment is shown in Fig. 1 and Fig. 2. The figure shows both original and observed images are captured using traditional cameras or IoT image devices. After having an observed image, the image quality is calculated using the popular and widely used quality assessment metrics including our metrics. For the performance analysis and testing the efficacy of our metrics, the quality values produced by it are compared and contrasted with the other quality assessment metric values. An example of such comparison is presented in a tabular manner in Fig. 1 and Fig. 2.

3.2 Our Proposed Quality Measurement Metrics

For consistent quality measure, as alluded to before, we need to fuse multiple quality metrics and thus, define a new metric based on their merits. This is because, as mentioned before, all of the quality measurement metrics do not produce consistent/expected results for different camera impact levels. For example, even though, PSNR consistently decreases with the level of camera parameter increase, however, at extremely high levels, it increases which is not expected. Also, SSIM varies randomly in the dirty lens. The new metrics can include any quality metrics. For treating equally all metrics in the combination, we need to map the value of all quality metrics into an equal range like [0 1]. Although the values of some metrics like ORB and SSIM are in the range of 0 to 1, others such as PSNR values are not in the range [0 1]. For this reason, other parameters like

PSNR need to be converted into [0 1]. As an example, the normalised PSNR value $\overline{PSNR}(\bar{P})$ for $\bar{P}$ can be defined as

$$\overline{PSNR}(\bar{P}) = \frac{(\bar{P} - PSNR_{min}) \times (Z_{max} - Z_{min})}{(PSNR_{max} - PSNR_{min}) + Z_{min}} \tag{1}$$

where $PSNR_{max}$ and $PSNR_{min}$ are the maximum and minimum PSNR values that need to be considered for this range mapping. For example, since PSNR>=35 dB and PSNR<=25 dB indicates the high and low-quality images, respectively, we can consider $PSNR_{max} = 35$ and $PSNR_{min} = 25$. where $Z_{min}=0$, $Z_{max}=1$ are minimum and maximum output values and $\bar{P}$ is the value of PSNR in dB which we need to map. For the ideal case, the value of PSNR, ORB and SSIM decreases with an increased impact level. Besides, they also measure the quality values considering the different aspects of an image. For example, PSNR considers mainly numerical comparison, ORB examines matching points, and SSIM takes contrast, luminance and structural information into consideration, respectively.

For these reasons and covering the broad changes created in the camera parameters, we presented two quality assessment metrics.

3.2.1   Our First Image Quality Assessment Metric
Combined metric $COM(x,y)$ approach is as follows:

$$COM(x,y) = \overline{PSNR}(\bar{P}) \times ORB(x,y) \times SSIM(x,y) \tag{2}$$

Note, SC is not considered in the combined metric because its values are quite random in nature and not varying consistently with different levels of environmental parameters.

3.2.2   Our Second Image Quality Assessment Metric
We define our metric DS which combines the assessment values produced by different assessment metrics based on Dempster-Shafer decision fusion theory.

1. The finite nonempty set $\chi = \{A, \overline{A}\}$ of possible outcomes of an assessment metric is known as a discernment frame. A and $\overline{A}$ are the propositions that support and oppose the quality value produced by a metric, respectively.
2. A set of all observable outcomes is known as the focal set X, i.e., $X \in 2^{\chi}$, where $X \neq \emptyset$ and $2^{\chi}=\{\Lambda, \overline{\Lambda}, (\Lambda \cup \overline{\Lambda}), (\Lambda \cap \overline{\Lambda})\}$ is the power set of χ. Here, proposition $(\Lambda \cup \overline{\Lambda})$ denotes the uncertainty measure, whereas $(\Lambda \cap \overline{\Lambda})=\Phi$ represents the null hypothesis [10]. The Standard Deviation (SD) represents uncertainty. Therefore, the SD, σ of all historical assessment values over a time window is used to determine the amount of uncertainty associated with a mass value m(X), referring to evidence that supports X, where $m(X) : 2^{\chi} \longrightarrow [0,1]$ [1]. For ensuring σ is calculated using the most recent historical values i.e., current impact level, the time window is successively updated by

adding the previous assessed value. To make sure $\sum_{X_i \in 2^X} m(X_i) = 1$, we define uncertainty $m(\Lambda \cup \overline{\Lambda})$ as:

$$m(\Lambda \cup \overline{\Lambda}) = min(1 - m(X), \sigma). \tag{3}$$

3. For increasing assessment reliability, the set of assessment metrics to be used in the fusion is selected,

$$\tau = \{i | (1 \leq i \leq n) \wedge (\Gamma \oplus (\neg \Gamma \wedge (\sigma_i \leq \overline{\sigma})))\} \tag{4}$$

where, a logical expression $\Gamma = ((\hat{\sigma}_i \in \zeta) \wedge (0.12 \leq \overline{\sigma}_i \leq 0.15))$; n is the number of assessment metrics considered in the fusion; σ_i is the standard deviation for i^{th} metric; ζ represents a set comprising majority metrics with $\hat{\sigma}_i \leq 0.05$; $\overline{\sigma}_i \notin \zeta$; $\overline{\sigma}$ denotes the mean for all assessment metrics and $\oplus$ represents the XOR operation. In (4), for improving reliability, when uncertainty is low for all metrics i.e., $\hat{\sigma}_i \leq 0.05$ for majority of metrics and the $\overline{\sigma}_i \in [0.12, 0.15]$ for other metrics is used to set metrics for the fusion. Otherwise, average $\overline{\sigma}$ is applied for the selection of the metrics.

4. Independent bodies (metrics) of evidence (assessed quality values) can be combined using the Dempster's rule. For the selected mass functions (metrics) by (4), belief function b : $2^X \longrightarrow [0, 1]$ explains the degree of belief i.e., the assessed quality value by our metric DS, is defined as,

$$b(X) = 1/(1 - k) \sum_{\cap_i X_j} \prod_{i \in \tau} m_i(X_j). \tag{5}$$

where, $m_i()$ represents i^{th} mass function i.e., the function representing i^{th} metric. A measure of conflict between different bodies of evidence which is also called as the sets of mass functions is represented by k and defined as

$$k = \sum_{\cap_i X_j = \phi} \prod_{i \in \tau} m_i(X_j). \tag{6}$$

(a) Original image (b) Extreme less level (c)   Less level (d) Moder-ate level (e)   High level (f) Extreme high level

Fig. 3. Images with lens blur.

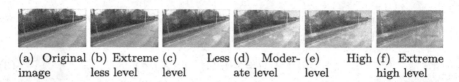

| (a) Original | (b) Extreme | (c)   Less | (d) Moder- | (e)   High | (f) Extreme |
| image | less level | level | ate level | level | high level |

Fig. 4. Images with lens dirtiness.

| (a) Original | (b) Extreme | (c)   Less | (d) Moder- | (e)   High | (f) Extreme |
| image | less level | level | ate level | level | high level |

Fig. 5. Images with lens barrel distortion.

4   Results and Discussions

We investigate the image quality based on the widely used quality assessment metrics such as PSNR, MSE, SC, ORB and SSIM. The Standard Deviation (SD) of the values produced by a particular metric for a specific impact level is calculated to analyze their consistency and deviation from the mean value. We used a sliding time window to calculate SD and the size of the time window used to calculate SD was 50. Using (3), uncertainty is measured. We also compare the quality values yielded by our metrics with those produced with other existing metrics as mentioned above.

4.1   Datasets

We used challenging Unreal and Real Environments for Traffic Sign Recognition (CURE-TSR) dataset for the analysis of image quality in terms of quality assessment metrics such as PSNR, SC, ORB, MSE and SSIM and our approach DS. This dataset has one original image and five distorted images with different levels of camera parameter impacts such as extreme less level, less level, moderate level, high level and extreme high level of lens blur, lens dirtiness and lens barrel distortion as seen in Fig. 3, 4 and 5, respectively. We utilised 250 images for each camera impact (lens blur, dirtiness and barrel distortion) in which 50 images per camera impact level (such as extreme less level, less level and others) were used.

4.2   Performance Analysis of Image Quality with Different Existing Metrics

The image quality values for the different impacts of camera parameters in terms of MSE are shown in Fig. 6(a). In general, the values of MSE increase with the rise in the impact level of camera parameter but it decreases at the extremely

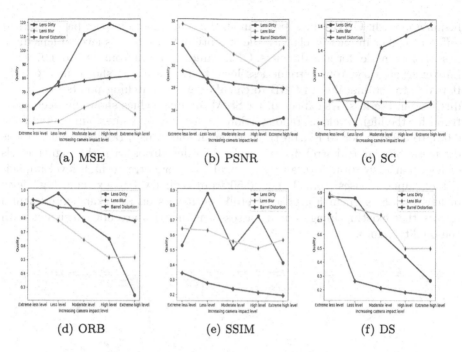

Fig. 6. Image quality with MSE, PSNR, SC, ORB, SSIM and our metric DS for different levels of lens blur, dirtiness and barrel distortion.

high level of camera impact in lens blur and lens dirtiness. At this level, MSE cannot determine the perceived difference between the pixels of the original and distorted images. For example, it increases from 47.7 to 67.2 as the impact of the camera parameter increases from extreme less level to a high level of lens blur. However, it decreases from 67.2 to 54.8 at extreme high levels of lens blur. Also, in lens dirtiness, it decreases from 118.8 to 110.9 at extreme high levels as shown in Fig. 6(a).

Similarly for PSNR, generally, it decreases from 31.8 to 29.8 dB in lens blur but increases from 29.8 to 30.8 dB at extreme high level of camera parameter impact as it can be seen in Fig. 6(b). As with MSE, for barrel distortion, PSNR consistently decreases as the level of camera impact parameter increases. For example, it decreases from 29.2 to 28.6 dB as the level of barrel distortion increases from extreme less level to extreme high level because, in barrel distortion, PSNR can capture the intuitive difference between the original and the distorted image as it is seen in the Fig. 6(b).

As expected, SC increases from 1.1 to 1.59 as the level of barrel distortion rises from extreme less level to extreme high level as seen in Fig. 6(c). However, by contrast, it decreases from 0.98 to 0.97 in lens blur and randomly varies between 0.98 to 0.96 in the dirty lens. This decrease and random variations do not conform with the expected results. So, as alluded to before, this randomness of SC values indicates that it is not exactly the right parameter for our decision fusion approach. ORB values reduce in all types of camera impact parameters at different higher impact levels with the exceptional case at less level of lens dirtiness. For example, for lens dirtiness, ORB values increase from 0.87 to 0.97 while impact levels vary from extreme less level to less levels as shown in Fig. 6(d). It is due to the inability of ORB to calculate good matching points because of dirtiness in the less. As expected, for SSIM, quality values show the decreasing trend for the high levels barrel distortion impact having values plummeted from 0.037 to 0.026 (refer to Fig. 6(e)). However, it shows us a random trend in lens dirtiness. Similar to barrel distortion, SSIM value drops with the higher levels of lens blur distortion with an exceptional case for extreme high level impact. For example, it rises from 0.51 to 0.56 from high level to extreme high level of lens blur as seen in Fig. 6(e). Overall, we have seen from our experimental results that existing image quality assessment metrics are not consistent with the quality values.

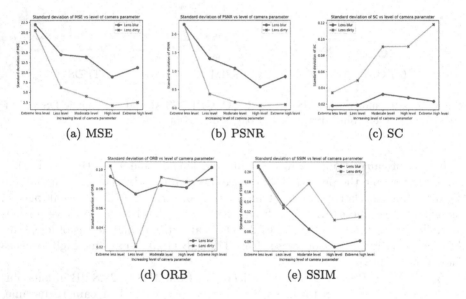

Fig. 7. Standard deviation of image metrics with different levels of lens blur and dirtiness.

4.3   Performance Analysis of Our First Proposed Metric COM

For our combined approach COM, we obtain better results which are more consistent with human percept impact levels as compared with the quality values produced by other metrics. We have a consistent decrease in the value as the level of camera impact increases from extreme less level to extreme high levels in lens blur, lens dirtiness and barrel distortion. For example, the value consistently decreases from 0.15 to 0.06 as the level of barrel distortion increases

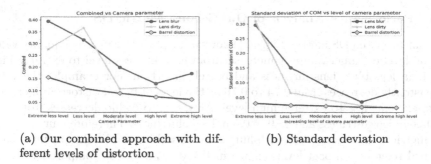

(a) Our combined approach with different levels of distortion

(b) Standard deviation

Fig. 8. Our combined approach results and their SD.

from extreme less to extreme high level as seen in Fig. 8(a). Also, it decreases from 0.27 to 0.02 with only one exceptional case at less level of lens dirty where it increases from 0.27 to 0.36 as it is depicted in Fig. 8(a). Similarly, the value consistently decreases from 0.39 to 0.17 as the level of lens blur increases from extreme less to extreme high level with one exceptional case at extreme high level where it is increasing from 0.12 to 0.17. So, the efficacy of image quality analysis with this combined approach is highly improved. In terms of various camera impact levels, the impact of barrel distortion is more in comparison with the effect of lens blur and lens dirty. For example, in Fig. 8(a), the quality value is less i.e., 0.15 at extreme less levels of barrel distortion in comparison with lens blur and lens dirty which are 0.39 and 0.27 respectively.

4.4 Standard Deviation of Different Quality Assessment Metrics

For showing how the image quality values vary for a specific camera impact level, we also analyze the standard deviation of different image quality metrics such as MSE, PSNR, SSIM, SC, ORB and COM. For PSNR and MSE, SD decreases consistently as the level of camera impact parameter increases from extreme less level to extreme high level. However, it varies randomly for SC, ORB and SSIM. For instance, in SC, SD increases from 0.01 to 0.03 when lens blur level increases from extreme less to a moderate level and then again decreases to 0.02 at extreme high level of lens blur as can be seen in Fig. 7(c). Similarly for SSIM, it increases from 0.12 to 0.17 at fewer levels of lens dirtiness and then decreases to 0.10 at high levels of lens dirtiness as shown in Fig. 7(e). In our method, for all camera impacts, SD decreases as the level of camera parameter increases from extreme less to extreme high level with only an exceptional case of lens blurriness at extreme high level where it is increasing from 0.05 to 0.09 as seen in Fig. 8(b). This confirms that our proposed metric COM is more reliable than the other existing quality assessment metrics.

4.5   Performance Analysis of Our Second Metric DS

For our proposed DS metric, Fig. 6(f) shows a consistent decrease in quality value as the level of camera impact increases from extreme less level to extreme high levels in lens blur, lens dirtiness and barrel distortion. For example, the value consistently decreases from 0.74 to 0.16 as the level of barrel distortion increases from extreme less to extreme high level. Also, quality value decreases from 0.87 to 0.26 in lens dirtiness and 0.89 to 0.5 in lens blurriness. Therefore, our proposed DS metric is more consistent with human perceived impact levels (the intuitively defined reference impact levels shown in Fig. 3, 4 and 5) as compared with the quality values produced by other metrics.

Table 1. Comparison of reliability percentage among PSNR, ORB, SSIM and our proposed DS approach.

Method	Impact			
	Dirty(%)	**Blur(%)**	**Barrel(%)**	**Overall(%)**
DS	100	100	100	100
PSNR	75	75	100	83.3
ORB	75	75	100	83.3
SSIM	50	75	100	75

Also, we measured the Inter-rater reliability (IRR) [4] of the image quality assessment metrics (PSNR, ORB and SSIM) and our metric DS.

Inter-rater reliability is defined as:

$$IRR = s/S \qquad (7)$$

where, s = number of metrics satisfy decision fusion criterion as per equation (4) and S = total number of image quality assessment metrics Note, from PSNR, ORB and SSIM, a set of metrics is selected by (4) for the decision fusion. As depicted from Table 1, the reliability of our metric is maximum (100%) in comparison with PSNR, ORB and SSIM. Consequently, the efficacy of image quality analysis with this decision fusion approach (DS) is highly improved.

4.6   Comparative Performance Between COM and DS

As per results and discussions, it is clear that our COM and DS metrics are more reliable in comparison with existing image quality assessment metrics.

In comparison to each other, DS approach is more reliable as it is vividly depicted from Table 2. Table 2 represents the percentage of reliability for our COM and DS metric.

↓ represents that the quality of image is decreasing when the level of camera impacts is increasing. Similarly, ↑ signifies that when the level of camera impact

Table 2. Reliability percentage for our proposed COM metric among different levels of lens blur, lens dirty and barrel distortion.

Level of impact	Impact							
	Dirty(%)		Blur(%)		Barrel(%)		Overall(%)	
	COM	DS	COM	DS	COM	DS	COM	DS
Extreme less level to Less level	↑	↓	↓	↓	↓	↓	75	100
Less level to moderate level	↓	↓	↓	↓	↓	↓	100	100
Moderate level to high level	↓	↓	↓	↓	↓	↓	100	100
High level to extreme high level	↓	↓	↑	↓	↓	↓	75	100
Overall(%)	75	100	75	100	100	100	83.3	100

is increasing, the quality of image is also increasing which is not consistent. We can perceive inconsistencies in Table 2 shown by red ↑ for our first COM metric. Consequently, the reliability of COM metric is 83.3% and the reliability of DS metric is 100%.

The DS metric is better in comparison with COM because:

1. DS considers uncertainty exploiting mass values and standard deviation. However, COM considers only standard deviation as uncertainty. For this reason, DS does not only produce high quality values, but also provides more accurate quality.
2. DS fuses the quality metrics using the mass values and the uncertainty involved with those mass values. These mass values are calculated from the images which represents the quality values of the metrics.

5   Conclusion

We present new image quality assessment metrics based on COM and the decision fusion approach. We evaluate it to assess the impact of camera parameters (lens blur, lens dirtiness and barrel distortion) on image quality. There is a consistent decrease in the quality of an image with an increase in the camera impact level in case of our metric DS. Therefore, experimental results show our image quality assessment metric DS is more consistent with intuitively defined impact levels (human perception). Because DS fuses the quality assessment metrics with the help of mass values and uncertainties associated with it. The quality values and consistency among the values indicate that our metric DS is more reliable and can be utilized in many images and computer vision applications.

References

1. Altig, D., et al.: Economic uncertainty before and during the covid-19 pandemic. J. Public Econ. **191**, 104274 (2020)
2. Bachoo, A.: Blind assessment of image blur using the haar wavelet. In: Proceedings of the 2010 Annual Research Conference of the South African Institute of Computer Scientists and Information Technologists, pp. 341–345 (2010)
3. Fujii, Y., Ohta, N., Ito, T., Saitoh, S., Matsuura, T., Yamamoto, T.: Image restoration for security cameras with dirty lens under oblique illumination. In: Proceedings of the 2006 IEEE International Workshop on Imagining Systems and Techniques (IST 2006), pp. 100–103. IEEE (2006)
4. Glen, S.: Inter-rater reliability irr: Definition, calculation. https://www.statisticshowto.com/inter-rater-reliability/ (2016)
5. Goto, M., Goto, T.: Accuracy comparison between learning method and signal processing method using iteration for severely blur images. In: 2020 3rd International Conference on Digital Medicine and Image Processing, pp. 68–73 (2020)
6. Haneishi, H., Yagihashi, Y., Miyake, Y.: A new method for distortion correction of electronic endoscope images. IEEE Trans. Med. Imaging **14**(3), 548–555 (1995)
7. Hassan, N.B., et al.: Impact of camera lens aperture and the light source size on optical camera communications. In: 2018 11th International Symposium on Communication Systems, Networks & Digital Signal Processing (CSNDSP), pp. 1–5. IEEE (2018)
8. Jayaraman, D., Mittal, A., Moorthy, A.K., Bovik, A.C.: Objective quality assessment of multiply distorted images. In: 2012 Conference Record of the Forty Sixth Asilomar Conference on Signals, Systems and Computers (ASILOMAR), pp. 1693–1697. IEEE (2012)
9. Kakani, V., Kim, H.: Adaptive self-calibration of fisheye and wide-angle cameras. In: TENCON 2019–2019 IEEE Region 10 Conference (TENCON), pp. 976–981. IEEE (2019)
10. Karmakar, G.C., Das, R., Kamruzzaman, J.: Iot sensor numerical data trust model using temporal correlation. IEEE Internet Things J. **7**(4), 2573–2581 (2019)
11. Kazerouni, M.F., Saeed, N.T.M., Kuhnert, K.D.: Exploration of autonomous mobile robots through challenging outdoor environments for natural plant recognition using deep neural network. In: 2019 IEEE 15th International Conference on Intelligent Computer Communication and Processing (ICCP), pp. 279–285. IEEE (2019)
12. Liedlgruber, M., Uhl, A., Vécsei, A.: Statistical analysis of the impact of distortion (correction) on an automated classification of celiac disease. In: 2011 17th International Conference on Digital Signal Processing (DSP), pp. 1–6. IEEE (2011)
13. Rane, S., Dubey, A., Parida, T.: Design of iot based intelligent parking system using image processing algorithms. In: 2017 International Conference on Computing Methodologies and Communication (ICCMC), pp. 1049–1053. IEEE (2017)
14. Roy, S.D., Bhowmik, M.K.: A survey on visibility enhancement techniques in degraded atmospheric outdoor scenes. In: 2017 IEEE Region 10 Humanitarian Technology Conference (R10-HTC), pp. 349–352. IEEE (2017)
15. Rublee, E., Rabaud, V., Konolige, K., Bradski, G.: Orb: An efficient alternative to sift or surf. In: 2011 International Conference on Computer Vision, pp. 2564–2571. IEEE (2011)
16. Temel, D., Kwon, G., Prabhushankar, M., AlRegib, G.: Cure-tsr: Challenging unreal and real environments for traffic sign recognition. arXiv preprint arXiv:1712.02463 (2017)

17. Temel, D., Lee, J., AlRegib, G.: Cure-or: Challenging unreal and real environments for object recognition. In: 2018 17th IEEE International Conference on Machine Learning and Applications (ICMLA), pp. 137–144. IEEE (2018)
18. Vora, V., Suthar, A., Makwana, Y., Davda, S.: Analysis of compressed image quality assessments, m. Tech Student in E & C Dept, CCET, Wadhwan-Gujarat (2010)
19. Wang, Z., Bovik, A.C., Sheikh, H.R., Simoncelli, E.P.: Image quality assessment: from error visibility to structural similarity. IEEE Trans. Image Process. **13**(4), 600–612 (2004)

Combining Information Measures
for Improving Image Segmentation Quality

D. M. Murashov[(✉)] [ID]

Federal Research Center "Computer Science and Control, Russian Academy of Sciences,
Moscow, Russia
d_murashov@mail.ru

Abstract. In this work, we present a new combined measure for improving the quality of digital image segmentation. The measure has two components. The first is information redundancy, and the second is variation of information. The new measure makes it possible to obtain an image partition that provides a compromise between the conflicting objectives of minimizing the number of information-important segments and minimizing the information dissimilarity between the original and segmented images. We found the conditions for the minimum of the combined measure. The conducted computational experiment showed an improvement in segmentation results when using the proposed combined measure in comparison with the previously used information redundancy measure.

Keywords: Image Segmentation · Segmentation Quality · Information Redundancy Measure · Variation of Information · Combined Measure

1 Introduction

This work is devoted to solving the problem related to providing the quality of digital image segmentation.

One of the well-known approaches is to select such a partition from the ensemble of partitions of the input image that would provide the optimal value of a certain quality index. The quality can be characterized by one of the well-known measures that describe the boundary localization error, segment consistency, segment overlap coefficient, etc. [1–4]. These measures allow one to compare different partitions of images into non-overlapping segments. In a number of papers, the segmentation problem is formulated as a multiobjective optimization problem. In such a problem, the improvement of one of the criteria can lead to the deterioration of others. Therefore, when optimizing, it is necessary to look for a compromise solution.

One of the approaches to solving multicriteria problems is related to the search for Pareto-optimal solutions. In a number of papers, researchers propose methods for multi-level threshold segmentation of color images that combine traditional thresholding algorithms and multiobjective swarm intelligence algorithms, such as NSGA-II, MOPSO, MOGWO, and MOEA (Multi-objective Evolutionary Algorithm) [5]. For example, in [6], the authors constructed a quality functional as a combination of the Kapur's entropy

© Springer Nature Switzerland AG 2023
J.-J. Rousseau and B. Kapralos (Eds.): ICPR 2022 Workshops, LNCS 13644, pp. 498–508, 2023.
https://doi.org/10.1007/978-3-031-37742-6_38

and a function for calculating thresholds using the Otsu method. To search for Pareto-optimal threshold values, they used the MOGWO (Multiobjective Grey Wolf Optimizer) method [7]. In [8], Ripon et al. proposed a multi-objective segmentation technique for color images. The technique found Pareto-front by simultaneous optimization of three objectives. The overall deviation, edge value, and connectivity measure were optimized using the Strength Pareto Evolutionary Algorithm-2 (SPEA-2) [9].

Another approach to solving multicriteria problems is to compose a quality functional as a combination of several quality measures. A complex functional can be formed, for example, using a weighted sum of simple functionals. In [10], the authors solved the problem of fusing roughly segmented images as a multiobjective optimization problem. To evaluate the result of combining segments, they used the mean variation of information, and to evaluate the accuracy of segment boundaries, they used the F-measure. The problem of multicriteria optimization was solved using an optimization procedure based on superpixels and derived from the iterative conditional mode algorithm (ICM). The applied multicriteria approach improved the result of image segmentation in comparison with the basic method involved the criterion of minimum mean variation of information between the combined image and each of the coarse segmentation maps [11].

In the present work, we propose to use a functional in the problem of image segmentation that combines two information-theoretic quality measures. In [12, 13], the criterion of the minimum of information redundancy measure was applied to find the best image partition in an ensemble of partitions obtained at different values of the segmentation parameter. The informational dissimilarity between the original image and the resulting partition, which is used as one of the segmentation quality indicators, was estimated by the values of variation of information [14, 15]. In this case, small values of variation of information are achieved on partitions with a large number of segments and a relatively large value of information redundancy. In order to improve the segmentation quality, we propose to choose a partition minimizing a functional that combines a measure of information redundancy and variation of information. Such a quality functional will provide an opportunity to find a compromise between two conflicting criteria.

2 A New Segmentation Quality Measure

In [12, 13], it was proposed to use an information channel model to describe the segmentation operation. We assume that the original and segmented images are the input and output of the stochastic information system. The grayscale levels of the input and output images are described by discrete random variables U and V with values u and v, $0 \leq u \leq 256$, $0 \leq v \leq 256$. Then we can represent the segmentation operation as follows:

$$V = F(U + \eta, t), \tag{1}$$

where U is the signal at the channel input, V is the channel output, F is the transformation function, t is a parameter; η is the channel noise.

In [12, 13], the segmentation problem was formulated as follows. Given input image U segmentation algorithm (1) generates a set of Q images $\mathfrak{V} = \{V_1, V_2, ..., V_q, ..., V_Q\}$

obtained at different values of parameter t. It is necessary to choose a partition $V_{q\,\text{min}}$ that minimizes the quality measure $M(U, V_q)$:

$$V_{q\,\text{min}} = \arg\min_{V_q}\left[M(U, V_q)\right], \quad q = 1, 2, ..., Q. \tag{2}$$

The measure of quality was chosen to be equal to the measure of information redundancy:

$$R(U, V_q) = \frac{H(V_q|U)}{H(V_q)}, \tag{3}$$

where $H(V_q|U)$ is the conditional entropy of the channel output given input U, $H(V_q)$ is the entropy of the channel output.

To estimate the informational difference between the original image and the resulting partition, in [15] a variation of the information [14] was used:

$$VI(U, V) = 2H(U, V) - H(U) - H(V), \tag{4}$$

where $VI(U, V)$ is the variation of information, $H(U)$ and $H(V)$ are the entropies of the compared images (U and V), and $H(U, V)$ is the joint entropy of the images U and V. In this work, we use the normalized variation of information:

$$VI_n(U, V) = \frac{VI(U, V)}{H(U, V)}. \tag{5}$$

The best segmentation result corresponds to a partition $V_{q\,\text{min}}$ with small values of the redundancy measure $R(U, V_{q\,\text{min}})$ and a relatively small number of segments $K = K_{\text{min}}$. A small information dissimilarity $VI_n(U, V_q)$ between the original image U and the partition V_q can be obtained with a sufficiently large number of segments K. As noted above, these two objectives are conflicting.

In [12, 13], we also evaluated the informational dissimilarity $VI_n(V^{GT}, V_q)$ between the obtained partitions $V_q \in \mathfrak{V}$ and the ground truth partitions V^{GT} made by experts. The evaluation results showed that for a large group of test images, the minimum measure $R(U, V_q)$ and the minimum $VI_n(V^{GT}, V_q)$ are achieved on the partition $V_{q\,\text{min}}$ with the number of segments $K = K_{\text{min}}$. This means that the greatest similarity in terms of measure (5) between partitions $V_q \in \mathfrak{V}$ and ground truth partitions is achieved when information redundancy (3) is minimal. However, there is a group of images for which the minimum $VI_n(V^{GT}, V_q)$ holds for a partition V_q with the number of segments $K \neq K_{\text{min}}$. Therefore, the problem arises to correct the measure of quality in such a way as to reduce the dissimilarity measures $VI_n(U, V_{q\,\text{min}})$ and $VI_n(V^{GT}, V_{q\,\text{min}})$.

To improve the segmentation result, we propose to combine information redundancy and the normalized variation of information in a new measure of quality:

$$M(U, V_q) = \frac{1}{2}\left[R(U, V_q) + \gamma VI_n(U, V_q)\right], \tag{6}$$

where γ is a weighting factor that regulates the proportion of measures, $0 \leq \gamma \leq 1$. This combined measure of quality could increase the information similarity between the original and segmented images with a slight increase in information redundancy. Then the problem will be to find the image V_q^* that provides the minimum of the measure (6).

We find the optimal solution in the following way. For the original image U and each of the partitions $V_q, q = 1, 2, ..., Q$ obtained with different values of the segmentation algorithm parameter, we compute the values of the functional (6). From the set of partitions V_q, we choose the partition V_q^* corresponding to the global minimum of the quality measure (6).

In the next section, some properties of the proposed combined measure will be considered.

3 Properties of the Combined Measure of Quality

The proposed combined measure of quality has the following main properties.

First, the measure (6) is not symmetric, since the redundancy $R(U, V))$ is not symmetric.

Secondly, measure (6) takes values from 0 to 1, since $0 \leq R(U, V) \leq 1, 0 \leq VI_n(U, V) \leq 1$ and $0 \leq \gamma \leq 1$.

The next property to note is that the combined measure has a minimum. In [13], a simplified information model of the segmentation system was developed. It was shown that the redundancy measure R depends on the number of segments K and has a minimum at $K = K_{\min}$ corresponding to the partition $V_{q\min}$. It was also shown that in the neighborhood of the minimum of $R(K)$, the variation of information $VI_n(K)$ decreases. For $K > K_{\min}$, the rate of decrease in $VI_n(K)$ decelerates, while $R(K)$ increases. Therefore, for $K > K_{\min}$ and some values of γ, measure (6) will have a minimum at $K = K^* > K_{\min}$. Let us find the condition for the extremum of the measure $M(U, V_q)$. To analyze the function $M(U, V_q)$, as in [13], we assume that in formulas (3)-(6) the entropies and redundancy R are functions not of the discrete variable K, but of the real variable z. Then the minimum of $R(z)$ corresponds to the value of $z = z_{\min}$. Let's differentiate the expression (6) with respect to z:

$$M'(U, V_q) = \tfrac{1}{2}\left[R'(U, V_q) + \gamma VI_n'(U, V_q)\right].$$

Taking into account equalities (3) - (5), we get:

$$M'(U, V_q) = \frac{\gamma[R(z) - 1]H'(V(z))H(U)}{2[H(U) + R(z)H(V(z))]^2}$$
$$+R'(z)\frac{[H(U) + R(K)H(V(z))]^2 + \gamma H(V(z))[H(U) + H(V(z))]}{2[H(U) + R(z)H(V(z))]^2}. \tag{7}$$

The denominators of the fractions on the right side of (7) are positive. Then the extremum of the measure (6) at the point $z = z^*$ exists if:

$$R'(z^*) + \frac{\gamma[R(z^*) - 1]H'(V(z^*))H(U)}{[H(U) + R(z^*)H(V(z^*))]^2 + \gamma H(V(z^*))[H(U) + H(V(z^*))]} = 0. \tag{8}$$

For the segmentation system model proposed in [13], the first term in (8) is zero for $z = z_{\min}$ and positive for $z > z_{\min}$. The second term in (8) is negative. The minimum of measure $M(U, V)$ exists if the following inequality holds for $z > z^*$:

$$R'(z) > \frac{\gamma[1 - R(z)]H'(V(z))H(U)}{[H(U) + R(z)H(V(z))]^2 + \gamma H(V(z))[H(U) + H(V(z))]}.$$

The next section will describe a computational experiment conducted to confirm the effectiveness of the proposed combined functional in the segmentation problem (1–3).

4 Computational Experiment

To illustrate the proposed method, we used the set of images from the Berkeley BSDS500 database [15].

In the computational experiment, we performed the following tasks. First, using a test image, we demonstrate the selection of a partition that minimizes the proposed two-objective quality functional. Secondly, we compared the obtained optimal partition of the test image with the ground truth partitions from the BSDS500 dataset. Third, we evaluated the performance of the proposed combined functional on a set of 54 images from the BSDS 500 dataset and 270 ground truth segmentations.

In the first part of the experiment, each of the studied images was segmented using a modified SLIC algorithm [16] with different values of the parameter of the post-processing procedure [12]. As a result of segmenting the original image U, we have obtained a set of Q partitions $\mathfrak{V} = \{V_1, V_2, ..., V_Q\}$. For the image U and each of the images $V_q, q = 1, 2, ..., Q$, we computed the values of the quality measure $M(U, V_q)$ (6), and found the partition V_q^* corresponding to the global minimum of $M(U, V_q)$.

To take into account all the color channels of the image U, when calculating the functional (6), we used a weighted redundancy measure and a normalized weighted variation of information. The weighted redundancy measure is defined as

$$R_w(U, V_q) = \frac{R_L H_L(U) + R_a H_a(U) + R_b H_b(U)}{H_L(U) + H_a(U) + H_b(U)} \tag{9}$$

where R_i is the redundancy measure computed in the $i \in \{L, a, b\}$ channel of the CIE Lab color space of U and V_q images; H_i is the entropy of the color channel i of the image U. The weighted normalized variation of information is defined by the formula:

$$VI_w(U, V_q) = \frac{VI_{nL} H_L(U) + VI_{na} H_a(U) + VI_{nb} H_b(U)}{H_L(U) + H_a(U) + H_b(U)}, \tag{10}$$

where

$$VI_{ni}(U, V_q) = \frac{2H_i(U, V_q) - H_i(U) - H_i(V_q)}{H_i(U, V_q)}. \tag{11}$$

Here, $VI_w(U, V_q)$ is the weighted variation of information; VI_{ni} is the normalized variation of information between color channels i of U and V_q images; $H_i(U, V_q)$ is the joint entropy in the i-th color channel.

We select an image V_q^* minimizing the measure M (6, 9–11):

$$M_w(U, V_q) = R_w(U, V_q) + \gamma VI_w(U, V_q). \tag{12}$$

The results of the first part of the experiment are illustrated in the color version of the 8068.jpg image shown in Fig. 1. Figure 1 (a) shows the original image, Fig. 1(b) and Fig. 1(c) show the partitions into 8 and 48 segments. The minimum of the weighted redundancy measure is reached on the partition Fig. 1 (b), and the minimum of the measure (12) is reached on the partition Fig. 1 (c).

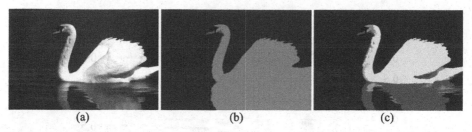

(a)   (b)   (c)

Fig. 1. Image 8068.jpg from the BSDS500 dataset and its partitions: (a) original image; (b) partition into 8 segments; (c) partition into 48 segments.

The obtained dependences of the weighted redundancy measure $R_w(U, V_q)$ (9) on the number of segments K in the partitions V_q for this image are plotted in Fig. 2 by a solid line, and the values of variation of information $VI_w(U, V_q)$ (10, 11) are shown by a dotted line. Graphs of the composite measure $M_w(U, V_q)$ (12) for different values of γ are shown in Fig. 3. In this figure, one can see that the extremum of the quality functional shifts from the point $K = 8$ to the point $K = 48$ at $\gamma = 0.1$. Figure 2 shows that for a partition with $K = 8$ segments, the value of variation of information $VI_w(U, V_q)$ decreases, while the redundancy $R_w(U, V_q)$ increases slightly.

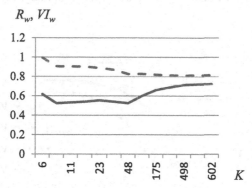

Fig. 2. Plots of the weighted redundancy measure R_w (solid line) and weighted normalized variation of information $VI_w(U, V_q)$ (dashed line).

The next task of the experiment was to compare five ground truth segmentations V_s^{GT} of the studied image with the number of segments K_{GT} equal to 9, 2, 8, 10, and 9 with a series of partitions V_q obtained using the superpixel SLIC algorithm [16] with the post-processing procedure [12] for threshold values $0 \leq \Delta_1 \leq 2.1$. The result of the comparison is shown in Fig. 4. All ground truth segmentations give a minimum distance in measure (10–11) (which means the greatest similarity) with a partition of original image into 48 segments, which produces a minimum of the measure $M_w(U, V_q)$ calculated by formula (12).

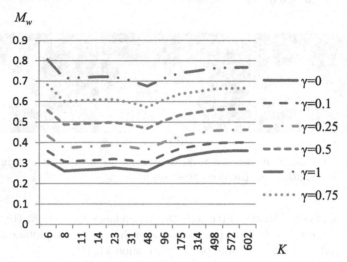

Fig. 3. Plots of the combined measure of quality $M_w(U, V_q)$ at different values of the weighting factor γ.

At the third stage of the computational experiment, for a set of images from the BSDS500 database, we evaluated the quality of the partitions obtained using the proposed two-objective quality functional. To evaluate the quality of image segmentation, we used the relative difference.

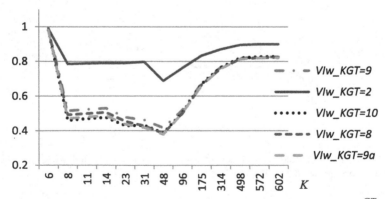

Fig. 4. Graphs of dependences of the normalized variation of information $VI_w(V_s^{GT}, V_q)$, $s = 1, 2, ..., 5$ on the number of segments K, obtained by comparing segmented images V_q with ground truth partitions V_s^{GT} from the BSDS500 dataset.

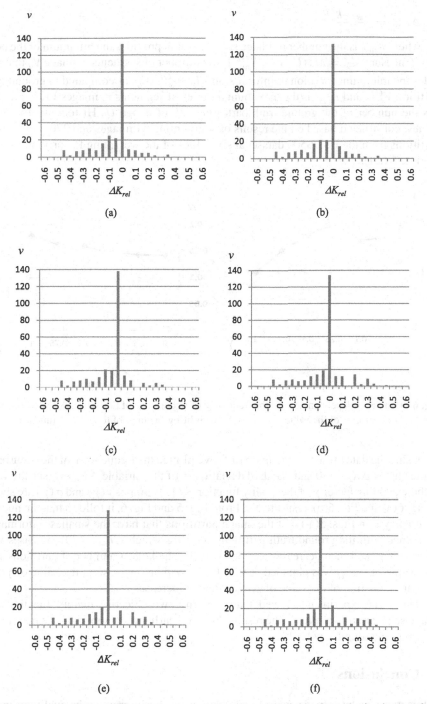

Fig. 5. Histogram of the ΔK_{rel} values computed based on the results of segmenting images from the BSDS500 dataset at the values of the weight coefficient of the quality measure (12): (a) $\gamma = 0$; (b) $\gamma = 0.1$; (c) $\gamma = 0.25$; (d) $\gamma = 0.5$; (e) $\gamma = 0.75$; (f) $\gamma = 1$; here v is the frequency of occurrence of a particular ΔK_{rel} value.

$$\Delta K_{rel} = \frac{K_{min} - K_{min}^{GT}}{K_{max}},$$

where K_{min} is the number of image segments that provides the minimum of the combined measure $M_w^* = M_w(U, V_q^*)$, K_{min}^{GT} is the number of segments in image V_q that provides the minimum variation of information $VI_w(V_s^{GT}, V_q)$ as compared to ground truth partition V_s^{GT}, and K_{max} is the maximum number of segments in images $V_1, V_2, ..., V_Q$, s is the number of the ground truth partition V_s^{GT} of image U. Histograms for ΔK_{rel} values, constructed based on the results of segmenting 54 images and 270 ground truth partitions from the BSDS500 dataset at six values of the weighting factor γ, are shown in Figs. 5 (a-f).

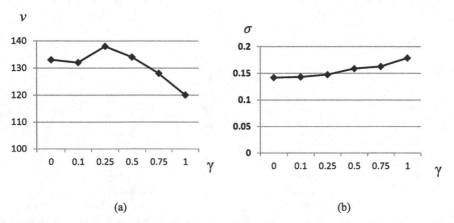

(a)   (b)

Fig. 6. Graphs of dependencies: (a) the frequency of occurrence of the values $\Delta K_{rel} = 0$; (b) the standard deviation σ of the value ΔK_{rel} on the weighting factor γ of the quality functional.

Using the data presented in Figs. 5 (a-f), we plotted the frequency v of the occurrence of the values $\Delta K_{rel} = 0$ and standard deviation σ of the variable ΔK_{rel} versus the value of the weighting factor γ of the quality functional (12). Graphs $v(\gamma)$ and $\sigma(\gamma)$ are shown in Fig. 6(a) and Fig. 6(b), respectively. From Fig. 5 and Fig. 6, it follows that the number (frequency v in Figs. 5(a-f)) of the image partitions that have the smallest information difference with the ground truth partitions (i.e., for which $\Delta K_{rel} = 0$) increases with growth of γ, and then decreases as γ tends to 1. The largest number of partitions with zero value of ΔK_{rel} was obtained at $\gamma = 0.25$. With an increase in the value of γ, the standard deviation of the value of ΔK_{rel} slightly increases.

Thus, the experiment showed that applying two-objective quality functional in image segmentation improves the results obtained earlier by minimizing the measure of information redundancy [13].

5   Conclusions

In this work, we proposed a new combined measure for improving the quality of image segmentation. This measure includes two components. The first is a measure of information redundancy, and the second is variation of information. Such a measure makes it possible to obtain an image partition that provides a compromise between the requirements to minimize the information redundancy (or the number of segments in image partition) and to minimize the informational dissimilarity between the original image and the obtained partition. Conditions for the minimum of the combined measure are found. Computational experiment on a set of test images from the BSDS500 database showed that application of two-objective quality functional improves the segmentation results obtained earlier using the criterion of minimum of information redundancy measure. The future research will be aimed at applying the proposed combined measure to the problem of improving the segmentation quality by combining several image partitions.

References

1. Martin, D., Fowlkes, C., Tal, D., Malik J.: A database of human segmented natural images and its application to evaluating segmentation algorithms and measuring ecological statistics, In: Proceedings of the Eighth IEEE International Conference on Computer Vision (ICCV 2001), vol. 2, pp. 416–423. IEEE (2001). doi: https://doi.org/10.1109/ICCV.2001.937655
2. Strehl, A., Ghosh, J.: Cluster ensembles - a knowledge reuse framework for combining multiple partitions. J. Mach. Learn. Res. **3**, 583–617 (2002)
3. Unnikrishnan, R., Pantofaru, C., Hebert, M.: A measure for objective evaluation of image segmentation algorithms In: Proceedings of the 2005 IEEE Computer Society Conference on Computer Vision and Pattern Recognition (CVPR 2005), vol. 03, pp. 34–41. IEEE (2005). DOI https://doi.org/10.1109/CVPR.2005.390. URL http://dx.doi.org/10
4. Zhang, H., Fritts, J.E., Goldman, S.A.: Image segmentation evaluation: A survey of unsupervised methods. Comput. Vis. Image Underst. **110**(2), 260–280 (2008)
5. De, S., Bhattacharyya, S., Chakraborty, S., Dutta, P.: Image segmentation: a review. In: Hybrid Soft Computing for Multilevel Image and Data Segmentation. CIMA, pp. 29–40. Springer, Cham (2016). https://doi.org/10.1007/978-3-319-47524-0_2
6. Oliva, D., Abd Elaziz, M., Hinojosa, S.: Image segmentation as a multiobjective optimization problem. In: Metaheuristic Algorithms for Image Segmentation: Theory and Applications. SCI, vol. 825, pp. 157–179. Springer, Cham (2019). https://doi.org/10.1007/978-3-030-12931-6_13
7. Mirjalili, S., Saremi, S., Mirjalili, S.M., Coelho, L.S.: Multi-objective grey wolf optimizer: a novel algorithm for multi-criterion optimization. Expert Syst Appl. **47**(C), 106–119 (2016). DOI:https://doi.org/10.1016/j.eswa.2015.10.039
8. Ripon, K.S.N., Ali, L.E., Newaz, S., Ma, J.: A Multi-objective evolutionary algorithm for color image segmentation. In: Ghosh, A., Pal, R., Prasath, R. (eds.) MIKE 2017. LNCS (LNAI), vol. 10682, pp. 168–177. Springer, Cham (2017). https://doi.org/10.1007/978-3-319-71928-3_17
9. Zitzler, E., Laumanns, M., Thiele, L.: SPEA2: Improving the strength Pareto evolutionary algorithm for multiobjective optimization. In: Evolutionary Methods for Design Optimization and Control with Applications to Industrial Problems, ETH Zurich, pp. 95–100 (2001). DOI:https://doi.org/10.3929/ethz-a-004284029
10. Khelifi, L., Mignotte, M.: EFA-BMFM: A Multi-criteria framework for the fusion of colour image segmentation. Information Fusion **38**, 104–121 (2017). https://doi.org/10.1016/j.inffus.2017.03.001
11. Mignotte, M.: A label field fusion model with a variation of information estimator for image segmentation. Inform. Fusion **20**, 7–20 (2014). https://doi.org/10.1016/j.inffus.2013.10.012
12. Murashov, D.: Theoretical-information quality model for image segmentation. Procedia Engineering **201**, 239–248 (2017). https://doi.org/10.1016/j.proeng.2017.09.603

13. Murashov, D.M.: An Information model for digital image segmentation. Pattern Recognit. Image Anal. **31**, 632–645 (2021). https://doi.org/10.1134/S1054661821040179
14. Meilă, M.: Comparing clusterings: an axiomatic view. In: Proceedings of the 22nd international conference on Machine learning 2005, pp. 577–584. ACM (2005)
15. Arbelaez, P., Maire, M., Fowlkes, C., Malik, J.: Contour detection and hierarchical image segmentation. IEEE Trans. Pattern Anal. Mach. Intell. **33**(5), 898–916 (2011). https://doi.org/10.1109/TPAMI.2010.161
16. Achanta, R., Shaji, A., Smith, K., Lucchi, A., Fua, P., Süsstrunk, S.: SLIC superpixels compared to state-of-the-art superpixel methods. IEEE Trans. Pattern Anal. Mach. Intell. **34**(11), 2274–2282 (2012). https://doi.org/10.1109/tpami.2012.120

A Framework for Feature Fusion with Application to Hyperspectral Images

Evgeny Myasnikov$^{(\boxtimes)}$ (iD)

Samara National Research University, Moskovskoe Shosse 34A, Samara 443086, Russia
mevg@geosamara.ru

Abstract. The fusion of different features is necessary when it is advisable to use several different feature systems to solve applied problems. Such a problem arises, for example, in hyperspectral image classification, when the combination of spectral and texture features significantly improves the quality of the solution. Likewise, several modalities can be used to identify a person, such as facial and hand features.

The most commonly used feature merging method can be considered a simple concatenation. The problem with such a merger may be the different nature of the features, the need to use different dissimilarity measures, etc. To solve these problems, this paper proposes a framework for feature fusion based on the transition of the features to intermediate forms of data representation with the subsequent dimensionality reduction. A special case is considered when a space with the Euclidean metric is used as the intermediate representation.

To demonstrate the proposed framework, we consider the per pixel classification problem for two known hyperspectral scenes.

Keywords: Feature Fusion · Dimensionality Reduction · Nonlinear Mapping · Hyperspectral Images

1 Introduction

The fusion of different features is necessary when it is advisable to use several different feature systems to solve applied problems. Such a problem arises, for example, in hyperspectral image classification, when the combination of spectral and texture features significantly improves the quality of the solution [8]. Likewise, several modalities can be used to identify a person, such as facial and hand features [7].

The most commonly used feature merging method is a simple concatenation. Unfortunately combining feature systems may not be entirely obvious for the following reasons [2]:

- the explicit relationship between feature systems may not be known,
- feature systems may be incompatible (for example, features of variable and fixed dimensions),

© Springer Nature Switzerland AG 2023
J.-J. Rousseau and B. Kapralos (Eds.): ICPR 2022 Workshops, LNCS 13644, pp. 509–518, 2023.
https://doi.org/10.1007/978-3-031-37742-6_39

– a simple concatenation of features can lead to a very high dimensional space and unsatisfactory results in solving applied problems (for example, when learning from a small number of examples).

Additional problems may be caused by the need to use different metrics or similarity measures to compare objects in different feature systems.

Some of the problems can be partially eliminated by normalizing and applying feature selection or dimensionality reduction techniques (see [7], for example). However, the different nature of features or the need to use different metrics or similarity measures can still introduce considerable complexity. In this paper, we propose a framework for feature fusion based on the transition of the features to intermediate forms of data representation with the subsequent dimensionality reduction. It is shown that this transition can be done implicitly in the case when Euclidean metric is used in the intermediate space.

The paper is organized as follows. The next section describes the proposed approach in general terms. Then a special case of a space with Euclidean metric is considered as an intermediate representation. The experimental part describes the application of the proposed framework to the problem of per pixel classification of hyperspectral images using the spectral and texture features. The paper ends up with the conclusion and the list of references.

2 Proposed Technique

The approach proposed in this paper to the fusion of features is based on the transition of the original features to homogeneous (in the sense of the properties of the corresponding spaces) intermediate representations, followed by the merging of these representations with the subsequent dimensionality reduction. The general scheme of the approach is shown in Fig. 1.

As can be seen from this diagram, the inputs are two sets of feature vectors presented in two different spaces of possibly different dimensions. In each input space there can be defined different dissimilarity measures. An important element in the considered approach is the choice of parameters of the internal form of representation, namely the dimension of the intermediate space and the metric defined on it.

Since the main task of the intermediate representation is to coordinate the input data presented in different spaces, it seems appropriate to form spaces with the same metric. We consider that the most important requirement for the generated internal representations is to preserve pairwise differences (measured by the given measures in the input spaces and by the chosen metric in the intermediate representations) between vectors. Another important requirement is the computational efficiency of the procedure for generating the internal representation. In the case when the scale of the generated representations is different, the procedure for generating the internal representation should provide for the normalization of the generated representations in one way or another.

The procedure for merging internal representations, taking into account the coordination of internal representations, can be implemented, for example, by the concatenation of feature representations.

The dimensionality of the result formed as a result of merging intermediate representations may turn out to be excessive, which leads to the need to reduce the dimensionality.

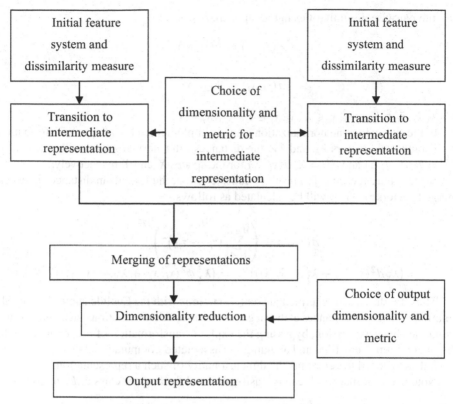

Fig. 1. Scheme of the proposed framework for feature fusion with subsequent dimensionality reduction.

Here we again come to the need to choose the dimensionality of the output space and the metric. It is advisable to make such a choice based on the efficiency of solving the required applied problems.

It is worth noting that the techniques based on the preserving of pair wise dissimilarity measures or the techniques based on the approximation of given pair wise dissimilarities by Euclidean distances can be exploited in the considered approach to perform a transformation to intermediate representations or dimensionality reduction (see [4, 5] for example).

3 Space with Euclidean Metric as Intermediate Representation

Since the most commonly used is the Euclidean metric, let's consider this particular case. Let some dissimilarity measures $\varphi(x_i, x_j)$ and $\psi(y_i, y_j)$ be given in the input spaces $X \subset R^M$ and $Y \subset R^K$, where $x_i, x_j \in X$, $y_i, y_j \in Y$. Suppose there is a way to map the input spaces X and Y into the intermediate spaces $\tilde{X} \subset R^{\tilde{M}}$ and $\tilde{Y} \subset R^{\tilde{K}}$, of dimensions $\tilde{M}$ and $\tilde{K}$ respectively, providing an exact correspondence between the Euclidean distances and the pairwise dissimilarities in the input spaces:

$$d(\tilde{x}_i, \tilde{x}_j) = \phi(x_i, x_j),$$

$$d(\tilde{y}_i, \tilde{y}_j) = \psi(y_i, y_j),$$

where $\tilde{x}_i, \tilde{x}_j \in \tilde{X}$, $x_i, x_j \in X$, $\tilde{y}_i, \tilde{y}_j \in \tilde{Y}$, $y_i, y_j \in Y$.

In the case when the normalization stage is implemented by a linear transformation with some scale factors λ_X and λ_Y, the distances after normalization will be equal to $\tilde{d}_{ij}^X = \lambda_X d(\tilde{x}_i, \tilde{x}_j)$ and $\tilde{d}_{ij}^Y = \lambda_Y d(\tilde{y}_i, \tilde{y}_j)$ for the spaces $\tilde{X}$ and $\tilde{Y}$ respectively.

After feature merging as a result of concatenation, the Euclidean distances between merged vectors z_i and z_j will be calculated as follows:

$$d(z_i, z_j) = \left(\sum_{k=1}^{\tilde{M}+\tilde{K}} (z_{ik} - z_{jk})^2 \right)^{1/2}$$
$$= \left(\lambda_X^2 d^2(\tilde{x}_i, \tilde{x}_j) + \lambda_Y^2 d^2(\tilde{y}_i, \tilde{y}_j) \right)^{1/2} = \left(\lambda_X^2 \phi^2(x_i, x_j) + \lambda_Y^2 \psi^2(y_i, y_j) \right)^{1/2}.$$

Thus, for the case of intermediate representations with the Euclidean metric, the calculation of pairwise distances at the stage of dimensionality reduction can be performed using the above expression, bypassing the explicit transformation of the input data into the internal representation, and avoiding the associated computational costs and errors as well as the need to determine the dimensionality of such a representation.

Note that a similar result can be easily obtained for a wider class of L^p metrics:

$$d(z_i, z_j) = \left(\sum_{k=1}^{\tilde{M}+\tilde{K}} (z_{ik} - z_{jk})^p \right)^{1/p}$$
$$= \left(\lambda_X^p d^p(\tilde{x}_i, \tilde{x}_j) + \lambda_Y^p d^p(\tilde{y}_i, \tilde{y}_j) \right)^{1/p} = \left(\lambda_X^p \phi^p(x_i, x_j) + \lambda_Y^p \psi^p(y_i, y_j) \right)^{1/p}$$

We can draw a parallel between the idea of the proposed approach and the composite kernels for SVM classification [8] where fusion of different features is performed at the SVM kernel level. The key difference here is that the proposed approach can be used in solving problems other than classification (for example, clustering, visualization, etc.), and does not limit the choice of the classifier to the SVM.

4   Experimental Results

To demonstrate the proposed approach, let's consider the problem of dimensionality reduction of hyperspectral images with the subsequent per pixel classification.

According to the proposed scheme, we combine both spectral and textural image features. We use image pixels directly as spectral features after normalization step. To compare spectral features, we utilize the Spectral Angle Mapper (SAM) measure.

$$\theta(x_i, x_j) = \arccos \left(\frac{x_i^T x_j}{\|x_i\| \, \|x_j\|} \right)$$

as well as and Hellinger divergence (HD).

$$HD(x_i, x_j) = \sqrt{1 - \sum_{k}^{M} \sqrt{p_k(x_i)p_k(x_j)}}$$

Recently, it has been shown [6] that the latter allows one to efficiently solve classification problems, while possessing the properties of a true metric.

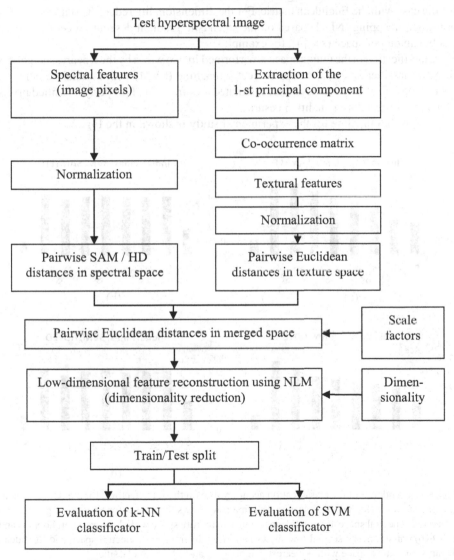

Fig. 2. Computational pipeline for the experimental study.

As textural features, we utilize a widely used set of features calculated on the basis of the pixel co-occurrence matrix [3]: Contrast, Correlation, Energy, and Homogeneity. The co-occurrence matrix is calculated using a single channel image obtained as a projection of the initial hyperspectral data onto the first principal component. The co-occurrence matrices are formed for four different offsets ([0, 1], [−1, 1], [−1, 0], [−1, −1]) and 64 level quantization. We calculate the averaged textural features and normalize them by standard deviations. We use the Euclidean distance as a distance measure for textural features.

We perform feature merging according to the scheme given in the previous section for the case with the Euclidean metric. For the dimensionality reduction step, we use the non-linear mapping (NLM) based on the stochastic gradient descent procedure for the Euclidean output space (see [4], for example).

Classification in the output space is performed in two ways: by the k nearest neighbors (k-NN) classifier and by the support vector machine (SVM) with a radial kernel. The overall classification accuracy (Acc) calculated as a fraction of properly classified pixels of a test set is used as a quality measure.

The overall pipeline for the experimental study is shown in the Fig. 2.

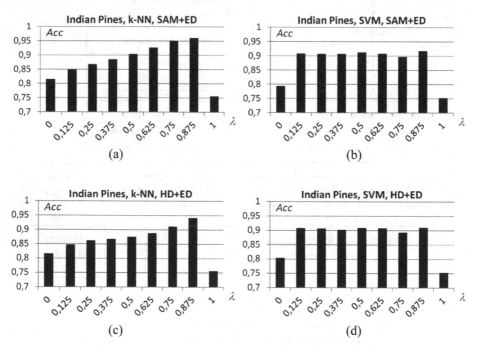

Fig. 3. Dependence of the classification accuracy Acc on the scale factor λ for the output dimensionality $D = 10$ (Indian Pines scene). The first row shows the results for Spectral angle mapper measure in spectral space and Euclidean distance in texture space with: k-nearest neighbor (a) and SVM (b) classifier. The second row shows Hellinger divergence in spectral space and Euclidean distance in texture space with: k-nearest neighbor (c) and SVM (d) classifier.

In the first group of experiments, we use the Indian Pines [1, 9] image recorded by the AVIRIS sensor as a test hyperspectral scene. The test image has a size of 145 × 145 pixels in 220 spectral bands. We use a version with 200 spectral channels, in which some channels were excluded due to noise and water absorption.

Some results showing the dependence of the classification quality on the scale factor are shown in Fig. 3. Here the scale factor λ defines the impact of the spectral features and $(1 - λ)$ stands for the impact of texture features. As can be seen from the results, the textural features play an important role in the quality of classification for the considered test scene. The combination of both spectral and texture features makes it possible to significantly improve the quality of classification.

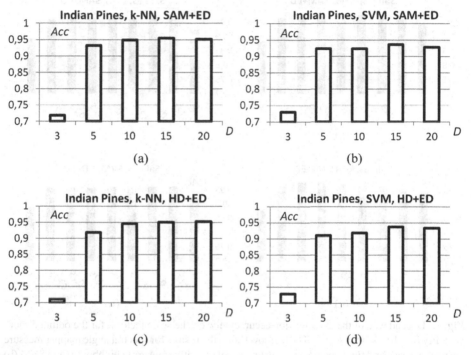

Fig. 4. Dependence of the classification accuracy *Acc* on the dimensionality *D* of the output space (Indian Pines scene). The first row shows the results for spectral angle mapper measure in spectral space and Euclidean distance in texture space with: k-nearest neighbor (a) and SVM (b) classifier. The second row shows Hellinger divergence in spectral space and Euclidean distance in texture space with: k-nearest neighbor (c) and SVM (d) classifier.

Figure 4 shows the dependence of the classification quality *Acc* on the dimensionality *D* of the generated output representation. As you can see, the merging of spectral and textural features makes it possible to form spaces of a relatively small dimensionality $(D = 10, 15, 20)$, the classification quality in which is much higher than that for each of the feature systems separately.

Similar results for another hyperspectral scene Salinas [9] are shown in Fig. 5, 6. This scene was also recorded by the AVIRIS sensor, has a size of 512 × 217 pixels in 224

516   E. Myasnikov

spectral bands, which was reduced to 204 channels image. To reduce the computational load, we applied a spatial thinning with step 3 to the image.

Figure 5 shows the dependence of the classification quality on the scale factor for the Salinas image. Figure 6 shows the dependence of the classification quality on the dimensionality of the output space. In general, the results presented confirm what was written above.

It is worth noting that the results presented can probably be further improved by more careful selection of parameters. The main goal of these experiments is to demonstrate the possibility of merging heterogeneous feature systems within the developed framework.

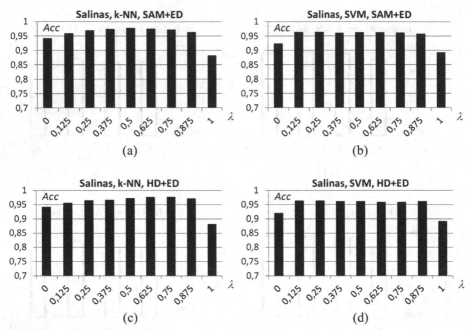

Fig. 5. Dependence of the classification accuracy Acc on the scale factor λ for the output dimensionality $D = 10$ (Salinas scene). The first row shows the results for spectral angle mapper measure in spectral space and Euclidean distance in texture space with: k-nearest neighbor (a) and SVM (b) classifier. The second row shows Hellinger divergence in spectral space and Euclidean distance in texture space with: k-nearest neighbor (c) and SVM (d) classifier.

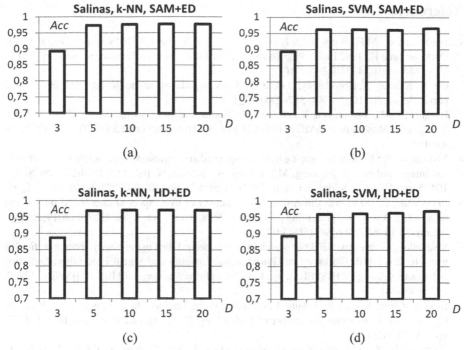

Fig. 6. Dependence of the classification accuracy *Acc* on the dimensionality *D* of the output space (Salinas scene). The first row shows the results for: Spectral angle mapper measure in spectral space and Euclidean distance in texture space with: k-nearest neighbor (a) and SVM (b) classifier. The second row shows Hellinger divergence in spectral space and Euclidean distance in texture space with: k-nearest neighbor (c) and SVM (d) classifier.

5   Conclusions

In this paper, we propose a framework for fusion of feature systems with data dimensionality reduction. The proposed method is based on the transition to an intermediate data representation and allows one to merge heterogeneous features in cases when different dissimilarity measures are used to measure the mismatch between features. A special case is considered when a space with the Euclidean metric is used as such a representation.

The application of the proposed framework to the task of per pixel hyperspectral image classification is considered. In the considered case, the spectral angle mapper and Hellinger divergence were used to measure the mismatch in the spectral space, and the features based on the co-occurrence matrix were used as textural features. The results of the study showed that the proposed method makes it possible to form spaces of a relatively small dimension, the classification quality in which significantly exceeds that for the base feature systems.

In the future, we plan to apply the developed framework to solve other problems, in particular, the problem of automatic segmentation of hyperspectral images.

References

1. Baumgardner, M.F., Biehl, L.L., Landgrebe, D.A.: 220 Band AVIRIS Hyperspectral Image Data Set: June 12, 1992 Indian Pine Test Site 3, Purdue University Research Repository (2015). https://doi.org/10.4231/R7RX991C
2. Gu, L., Kanade, T., Gorodnichy, D.O., et al.: Encyclopedia of Biometrics, pp. 597–602 (2009). https://doi.org/10.1007/978-0-387-73003-5_157
3. Haralick, R.M., Shanmugan, K., Dinstein, I.: Textural features for image classification. IEEE Trans. Syst. Man Cybern. SMC **3**, 610–621 (1973). https://doi.org/10.1109/TSMC.1973.4309314
4. Myasnikov, E.: Nonlinear mapping based on spectral angle preserving principle for hyperspectral image analysis. In: Felsberg, M., Heyden, A., Krüger, N. (eds.) CAIP 2017. LNCS, vol. 10425, pp. 416–427. Springer, Cham (2017). https://doi.org/10.1007/978-3-319-64698-5_35
5. Myasnikov, E.: Nonlinear dimensionality reduction of hyperspectral data based on spectral information divergence preserving principle. J. Phys.: Conf. Ser. **1368**, 032030 (2019). https://doi.org/10.1088/1742-6596/1368/3/032030
6. Myasnikov, E.: Nearest neighbor search in hyperspectral data using binary space partitioning trees. In: 2021 11th Workshop on Hyperspectral Imaging and Signal Processing: Evolution in Remote Sensing (WHISPERS), pp. 1–4 (2021).https://doi.org/10.1109/WHISPERS52202.2021.9484041
7. Ross A., Govindarajan, R.: Feature Level fusion using hand and face biometrics. In: Proceedings of SPIE Conference on Biometric Technology for Human Identification II, vol. 5779, pp. 196–204 (2005)
8. Camps-Valls, G., Gomez-Chova, L., Munoz-Mari, J., Vila-Frances, J., Calpe-Maravilla, J.: Composite kernels for hyperspectral image classification. IEEE Geosci. Remote Sens. Lett. **3**(1), 93–97 (2006). https://doi.org/10.1109/LGRS.2005.857031
9. Hyperspectral Remote Sensing Scenes. http://www.ehu.eus/ccwintco/index.php/Hyperspectral_Remote_Sensing_Scenes

Linear Blur Direction Estimation Using a Convolutional Neural Network

Andrey Nasonov$^{(\boxtimes)}$ ⓘ and Alexandra Nasonova

Laboratory of Mathematical Methods of Image Processing, Faculty of Computational Mathematics and Cybernetics, Lomonosov Moscow State University, GSP -1, Leninskie Gory, Moscow 119991, Russian Federation
nasonov@cs.msu.ru

Abstract. The paper is focused on the estimation of the parameters of motion blur produced by unintended camera motion. We consider a scenario when a photo is taken using a handheld camera with relatively fast shutter speed, and motion vectors have little time to change significantly. We use linear model for the motion and propose a deep learning approach for linear blur parameter estimation at patch level using a convolutional neural network. We also introduce an aperture criterion and propose a method for constructing the training dataset by choosing the patches that meet this criterion.

Keywords: Linear blur estimation · Convolutional neural network · Motion blur

1 Introduction

Photographs obtained with handheld cameras represent a significant category of digital images. The resolution of an image is measured in megapixels, which influences the amount of details that can be captured in an image, but a higher megapixel count does not always equate to a better picture. The amount of noise is directly related to the overall amount of light captured in an image, and the factor that contributes a lot to image quality is the size of the camera's sensor.

A sure way to increase the amount of light the sensor receives is prolonging the exposure time, but that inevitably leads to blurring from even the slightest motions of a camera. Especially in low-light conditions, it is impossible to acquire both sharp and noise-free images using hand-held cameras.

Reconstructing a sharp image from a blurry one is an ill-posed problem, with various additional constraints used to regularize the solution. While numerous blind deconvolution algorithms have shown decent performance in certain cases [11], they typically do not perform well in more complex yet common scenarios such as images with strong motion blur.

Some modern approaches for image enhancement are based on reconstructing a high-quality image from a series of images. For example, the algorithm [5] utilizes a pair of images that can be easily acquired in low-light conditions: a

J.-J. Rousseau and B. Kapralos (Eds.): ICPR 2022 Workshops, LNCS 13644, pp. 519–528, 2023.
https://doi.org/10.1007/978-3-031-37742-6_40

blurred image taken with low shutter speed and low ISO value, and a noisy image captured with high shutter speed and high ISO value. Both images are sliced into patches, and the authors extend the Gaussian mixture model to model the underlying intensity distribution of each patch using the corresponding patches in the noisy image.

The algorithm [9] makes use of natural hand tremor, which is typical in hand-held photography, to acquire a burst of raw frames. These frames are then aligned and merged to form a single image.

The increase of the resolution of modern hand-held cameras makes the blur more prominent, and even with a shorter exposure time some blurring still remains. This supports the demand for high-quality image deblurring algorithms. During a short exposure, there is little time for the motion vector to change direction, so the motion blur can be approximated with linear blur, which is much easier to model.

Many state-of-the-art deblurring algorithms are based on the deep learning approach [12]. In [2], a neural network is trained to estimate a set of image-adaptive basis motion kernels with weight coefficients for each pixel, which produces a per-pixel motion blur field.

Gong et al. [4] use a Fully Convolutional Network (FCN) for the estimation of a dense linear motion flow parameterized by the horizontal and vertical components. For FCN training they generate synthetic pairs of blurred images and corresponding motion flow.

Sun et al. [8] consider a set of predefined linear motion kernels parameterized by their lengths and orientations. They split the image into patches and use a CNN to predict probabilistic distribution of the kernel parameters for each patch. The sparse patch-level distribution is then converted to a dense motion field using a Markov random field that ensures its smoothness.

The existing deep learning solutions to image deblurring usually present a pipeline with an image at the input and an enhanced image at the output, yet there are cases when some parts of an image remain blurry. This commonly happens due to inaccurate estimation of the blur parameters as the neural network solves the problem as a whole and does not provide the capability to control the parameters of the blur.

It is our belief that refining the parameters of the deblurring process warrants improvement of the overall performance of existing algorithms. We dedicate our research to the assessment of the non-uniform linear motion blur instead of developing yet another deblurring pipeline. In this article we focus on the estimation of the direction of linear blur.

The paper extends our previous work in [1] with more detailed description and evaluation of the method.

2   Linear Blur Model

We use the following model of a linear blur kernel with direction θ and length l:

$$h[\theta, l] = h[l](x \cos \theta + y \sin \theta, -x \sin \theta + y \cos \theta),$$

$$h[l](x,y) = \frac{1}{l}\int_{-l/2}^{l/2} G_\sigma(x-p,y)dp, \quad G_\sigma(x,y) = \frac{1}{2\pi\sigma^2}e^{-\frac{x^2+y^2}{2\sigma^2}}.$$

Here $h[l]$ is the linear blur kernel along x-axis with the length l and G_σ is Gaussian filter kernel which is used to prevent aliasing, we use $\sigma = 0.3$. Examples of the modeled linear blur kernels are shown in Fig. 1.

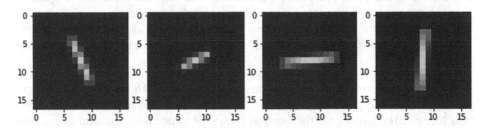

Fig. 1. Examples of linear blur kernels with different parameters.

3 CNN Model

In order to keep the computational complexity low, we do not process the entire image at once. Instead of this, we split the images into patches and develop an algorithm that infers the parameters of the linear motion blur for each patch. The resulting sparse motion vector field can be interpolated to a dense motion vector field using various methods: simple averaging [3], fine-tuning [10] or more sophisticated methods like Markov random field for ensuring the motion smoothness [8].

We use a convolution neural network (CNN) to solve the problem of assessing the parameters of linear blur. The structure of the CNN is shown in Fig. 2.

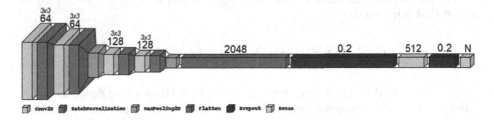

Fig. 2. Structure of the proposed CNN for the estimation of the parameters of a linear blur kernel.

We have explored several options for the output vector of the CNN:

1. Indicator vector. Consider a discrete set of linear blur parameters

$$\{\theta_i, l_j\}, \quad i = 1,\ldots,N, \quad j = 1,\ldots,M,$$

where θ is the direction of the blur and l represents its length. In this case, the output of the CNN is a vector which characterizes the probabilistic distribution of motion kernels [8]. The disadvantage of this approach is that different blur kernels may produce similar blurred patches, which would impair the learning process. In this case constructing an adequate training dataset becomes an overly complicated problem.

2. Pairs of values $\{\theta, l\}$. The main problem here is that the direction wraps over π, and it cannot be handled by a common CNN model.
3. A vector $\{\sin^2 \theta, \cos^2 \theta, l\}$. Here we calculate $\sin^2$ and $\cos^2$ values instead of the direction θ itself. The values belong to the interval $[0, 1]$ and change smoothly.

We have observed that simultaneous estimation of both direction and length parameters fails to produce an accurate estimation of the length since the direction has greater impact on the blurred image. Further investigation has shown that using two independently trained CNNs for finding direction and length gives the the most accurate results.

During the follow-up investigation we have observed a higher error rate with directions close to $\pi/4$ and $3\pi/4$, when the values of $(\sin^2 \theta, \cos^2 \theta)$ are farthest from both 0 and 1. In order to overcome this problem, we have increased the number of values in the output vector $\{v_0, \ldots, v_{N-1}\}$:

$$v_n = \sin^2 \left(\theta + \frac{\pi n}{N}\right).$$

We have compared the distributions of absolute error for the estimated direction θ on the test part of the training dataset for different N. The histograms are shown in Fig. 3. It can be seen that adding two more values ($N = 4$) drastically decreases the amount of patches with absolute error greater than 15°C. Further increasing N leads to better accuracy but increases computational complexity. We have chosen $N = 6$.

In order to find the angle θ from the vector output $v = \{v_n\}$ of the CNN, we find θ that minimizes

$$\theta_{opt} = \arg\min_{\theta} F(v, \theta), \quad F(v, \theta) = \sum_{n=0}^{N-1} \left(v_n - \sin^2 \left(\theta + \frac{\pi n}{N}\right)\right)^2.$$

The value $F(v, \theta_{opt})$ for a given vector v can be used as a *confidence level*: low values $F(v, \theta_{opt})$ corresponds to blocks that likely contains pronounced motion blur. We eliminate the patches with $F(v, \theta_{opt}) > 0.02$. The threshold has been set experimentally.

4   Dataset Preparation

For the creation of the training dataset, we use the images from the KonIQ-10k dataset [6] that contains about 10 thousand images of diverse content. Each image is split into 32×32-pixel patches with 16-pixel overlap.

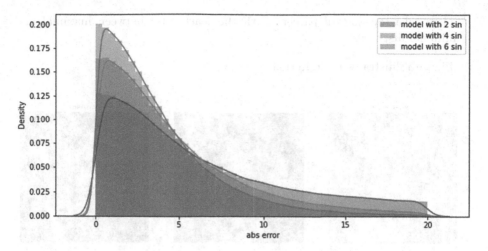

Fig. 3. Histograms of erroneously predicted blur directions using CNN models with different output vector length N.

4.1 Aperture Problem

A blurred patch can be obtained from the corresponding reference patch using different blur kernels (see Fig. 4). This results in uncertainty in blur vector estimation.

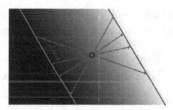

Fig. 4. Aperture problem: multiple blur directions match the blurred image fragment.

Therefore, we introduce an *aperture criterion* — a condition that a blurred patch can be constructed from the reference patch using only one blur kernel, and construct the dataset only of patches that meet this criterion using the following algorithm:

1. Each reference image is blurred with linear blur with fixed $l = 5$ and a set of directions $\{\theta_i\}$, $\theta_i = \frac{\pi i}{K}$, we use $K = 6$.
2. For every patch from the reference image we calculate the minimal and the maximal mean squared distance between corresponding blurred patches over all the pairs (θ_i, θ_j), $i \neq j$.
3. Take top 10% of patches with the highest minimal distance.

4. Then take top 50% of patches with the least ratio between maximal and minimal distances.

Figure 5 illustrates the criterion.

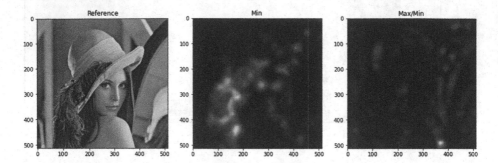

Fig. 5. Visualization of the minimal mean squared distances between blurred patches and the ratio between maximal and minimal distances.

4.2   Blurred-Reference Pair Generation

For each patch passed the aperture criterion we add random impairments:

1. Apply patch-wise centering, subtracting the mean intensity value from each patch.
2. Apply linear blur kernel with random parameters (θ, l), $\theta \in [0, \pi]$, $l \in [0, 10]$.
3. Add Gaussian noise with random standard deviation $\sigma \in [0, 8]$.

The dataset is split randomly into train/test sets with 80%/20% ratio.
An example of patches from the training dataset is shown in Fig. 6.

5   Additional Mask

The proposed CNN has been trained using 'good' patches — the patches with clearly identifiable blur direction. When applied to real images, the CNN may produce unpredictable results for 'bad' patches — the patches that does not meet aperture criterion or that are not suitable for blur estimation, for example, flat areas.

Although the confidence level $F(\boldsymbol{v}, \theta_{opt})$ can be used to identify the majority of patches with clearly estimated blur direction, it does not eliminate all the 'bad' patches. In order to improve the results, we have developed another CNN that estimates the patch quality and constructs a mask of 'good' patches. This CNN has the same model as in Fig. 2 and outputs a single value within $[0, 1]$ range. It is trained using both patches that meet the aperture criterion and that do not meet it (see Fig. 6 for example).

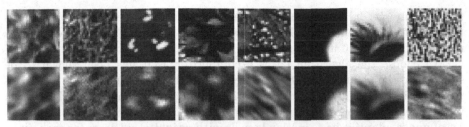

a) Patches that have passed the aperture criterion. Top row: patches from reference
images. Bottom row: corresponding blurred patches with random linear blur.

b) Patches that do not match the aperture criterion and are not included in the
training dataset.

Fig. 6. An example of patches in the training dataset.

An example of the result produced by this algorithm is shown in Fig. 7. It
can be seen that only textured and detailed patches are marked as 'good' (yellow
area).

Finally, we intersect the mask produced by this algorithm with the confidence
level threshold to find the patches with reliably estimated motion vectors.

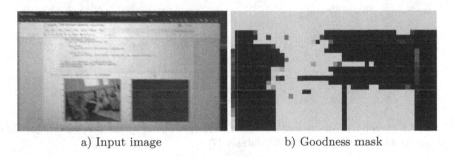

a) Input image   b) Goodness mask

Fig. 7. An example of finding the mask containing 'good' patches.

6   Experiments and Results

We evaluate the proposed method using images with real and synthetic motion
blur corresponding to handheld camera movement. The blur is modeled by

translation (dx, dy) and rotation α around image center. The parameters (dx, dy, α) are chosen randomly such that the length of motion blur vector does not exceed $l_{max} = 10$ in each pixel.

We choose the algorithm [2] as a competitor as it has been shown to be superior to the algorithms [4, 8] specially designed for the linear blur. The algorithm [2] is a blind deconvolution algorithm with the estimation of the motion blur kernel as the core part. It uses a convolutional neural network to estimate a set of image-adaptive basis motion kernels with weight coefficients for each pixel, which produces a per-pixel motion blur field. We approximate the blur kernels obtained by this algorithm with linear kernels.

Figure 8 demonstrates the application of the proposed algorithm to images with real blur from the GOPRO dataset [7]. It can be seen that the proposed algorithm produces sparse vector field with reliable motion information.

Figure 9 shows the comparison of the proposed algorithm with the competitor algorithm on the images with synthetic blur from the KonIQ-10k dataset [6]. Although the proposed method cannot produce dense motion field, it tends to be less error-prone.

The average processing time for an image with 1024×768 size is about 0.2 seconds on NVIDIA GTX 3080Ti.

Source code and data are available at
https://imaging.cs.msu.ru/en/research/motiondeblur

Fig. 8. An example of sparse motion vector fields produced by the proposed algorithm. Images are taken from the GOPRO dataset [7].

Blurred images

Reference motion field

Carbajal et al [2]

Proposed method

Fig. 9. Visual comparison of the proposed method with the state-of-the-art algorithm.

7   Conclusion

An algorithm for linear blur parameters estimation using a convolution neural network has been proposed. It produces sparse direction field for the motion blur. Interpolation of the sparse field into dense field and incorporation of the proposed algorithm into the deblurring pipeline will be part of the future work.

Acknowledgements. The work was supported by Russian Science Foundation Grant 22-41-02002.

References

1. Nasonov, A.V., Nasonova, A.A.: Linear blur parameters estimation using a convolutional neural network. Pattern Recognit Image Anal. **22**(3), 611–615 (2022)
2. Carbajal, G., Vitoria, P., Delbracio, M., Musé, P., Lezama, J.: Non-uniform blur kernel estimation via adaptive basis decomposition. arXiv preprint arXiv:2102.01026 (2021)
3. Chakrabarti, A.: A neural approach to blind motion deblurring. In: European Conference on Computer Vision, pp. 221–235 (2016)
4. Gong, D., et al.: From motion blur to motion flow: A deep learning solution for removing heterogeneous motion blur. In: Proceedings of the IEEE Conference on Computer Vision and Pattern Recognition, pp. 2319–2328 (2017)
5. Gu, C., Lu, X., He, Y., Zhang, C.: Blur removal via blurred-noisy image pair. IEEE Trans. Image Process. **30**, 345–359 (2020)
6. Hosu, V., Lin, H., Sziranyi, T., Saupe, D.: Koniq-10k: an ecologically valid database for deep learning of blind image quality assessment. IEEE Trans. Image Process. **29**, 4041–4056 (2020)
7. Nah, S., Hyun Kim, T., Mu Lee, K.: Deep multi-scale convolutional neural network for dynamic scene deblurring. In: Proceedings of the IEEE Conference on Computer Vision and Pattern Recognition, pp. 3883–3891 (2017)
8. Sun, J., Cao, W., Xu, Z., Ponce, J.: Learning a convolutional neural network for non-uniform motion blur removal. In: Proceedings of the IEEE Conference on Computer Vision and Pattern Recognition, pp. 769–777 (2015)
9. Wronski, B., et al.: Handheld multi-frame super-resolution. ACM Trans. Graph. (TOG) **38**(4), 1–18 (2019)
10. Xu, X., Pan, J., Zhang, Y.J., Yang, M.H.: Motion blur kernel estimation via deep learning. IEEE Trans. Image Process. **27**(1), 194–205 (2017)
11. Xu, Z., Chen, H., Li, Z.: Fast blind deconvolution using a deeper sparse patch-wise maximum gradient prior. Signal Process.: Image Commun. **90**, 116050 (2021)
12. Zhang, K., et al.: Deep image deblurring: A survey. International Journal of Computer Vision, pp. 1–28 (2022)

Analogs of Image Analysis Tools in the Search of Latent Regularities in Applied Data

Elena Nelyubina[1], Vladimir Ryazanov[2], and Alexander Vinogradov[2(✉)]

[1] Kaliningrad State Technical University, Kaliningrad, Russia
[2] Federal Research Center, "Computer Science and Control" of the Russian Academy of Sciences, Vavilova St., 44-2, 119333 Moscow, Russia
vngrccas@mail.ru

Abstract. The problem of detecting hidden latent regularities in large-scale applied data is investigated. A new approach is presented, where the possibilities of using multidimensional analogs of image processing and understanding methods adapted for higher dimensions are studied. Several promising options for combining practical competencies while solving applied problems from these positions are presented, and some prospects for further development of the approach are outlined.

Keywords: Regularity · Cluster · Parametric Space · Generalized Precedent · Wavelet · Algebraic Hypersurface · Hough Transform

1 Introduction

Nowadays, a characteristic feature of research in various applied fields is the possibility of automatic accumulation and efficient storage of large amounts of data in digital form [1, 3, 6, 14]. Potentially, these volumes contain manifestations of intrinsic regularities that rule the behavior of the data in general [2, 4, 7, 15, 23]. Knowledge of such regularities can play a decisive role in many problems of data analysis: in explaining nature of data, in making decisions, in predicting similar situations, and so on [11, 16, 19, 20, 24, 26, 27]. Since the data volumes are large, some sets of occurrences are representative in statistical sense, which opens up the possibility of reliably detecting these regularities and reconstructing them explicitly. From this point of view, one of the main priorities of the search is to provide the repeatability of the studied regularity, i.e., the multiplicity of its recorded manifestations in the sample.

So, at present we have a new situation in the world, which has arisen in concern with the development and penetration of digital infrastructure and methods everywhere. If earlier the central place in data technologies was occupied by the efficient placement, transfer and extraction of the necessary records, now the analysis of sample data themselves from various points of view, that is, Data Mining in an expanded sense comes to the fore, moreover, in a rapidly expanding sense. The input data can be of any nature, not necessarily in numerical form, but for them it is also possible to count the number of matches, repetitions, and similar exact characteristics. We show that in the construction

© Springer Nature Switzerland AG 2023
J.-J. Rousseau and B. Kapralos (Eds.): ICPR 2022 Workshops, LNCS 13644, pp. 529–540, 2023.
https://doi.org/10.1007/978-3-031-37742-6_41

of numerical models, including hypotheses about potentially present regularities, there are some common features that can be combined in the form of a regular computational toolkit. The central place in this respect will be occupied by the concept of generalized precedent (GP), as a parametric description of some typical particular regularity.

Generalized precedents provide a wider range of possibilities. The fractioning of the sample into operable structural elements acts in this case as analogues of spatial differentiation in the classical Hough scheme and can be subject to certain requirements of the researcher in advance. We consider a separate objects tuple of an implementation of the desired regularity as a structural element of this kind.

In view of the extended possibilities, filling the scheme of generalized precedents requires the use of many a priori assumptions and professional intuition of experts. At the same time, competencies of two types are involved simultaneously. The specialist in the subject area formulates the most probable properties and the general form of the expected regularity. On the other hand, the knowledge of IT specialists is also needed to help optimize calculations and represent the results adequately for the needs of applications. In case of detecting complicated latent regularities the two types of competence are used bound, for instance, in numerical search of those indirect and/or integrated parameters that provide the most efficient evidences of the desired phenomenon.

As is known, the concept of regularity in the general setting is very complicated. The discovery of a new, previously unknown regularity is a good result for any field of knowledge. We will not delve into this topic and further rely only on hypotheses about specific regularity that are based on the skill and experience of specialists in the subject area and in IT. Namely, further we consider the following model of regularity, the specific content of which will be supported by practical experience, various indirect confirmations, or simply intuitive guesses of specialists.

Let X, $X \subset R^N$ be a sample of digitized applied data of a large volume. The main object will be a tuple of points $x = \{x^1, \ldots, x^M\}$, $x^m \in X$, $m = 1, \ldots, M$, for which the following conditions are formulated by the expert:

$$P_1(x^1, \ldots, x^M) = P_1(x_1^1, \ldots, x_N^1, \ldots, x_1^M, \ldots, x_N^M),$$
$$P_2(x^1, \ldots, x^M) = P_2(x_1^1, \ldots, x_N^1, \ldots, x_1^M, \ldots, x_N^M),$$
$$\ldots$$
$$P_L(x^1, \ldots, x^M) = P_L(x_1^1, \ldots, x_N^1, \ldots, x_1^M, \ldots, x_N^M).$$

The set of conditions $P = \{P_1, \ldots, P_L\}$ is a formulation of some hypothesis about the presence of a regularity. To check it, we need to consider all the inclusions $x \subset X$, if we want to find the maximum number of confirmations of the hypothesis. The task in this formulation seems to be computationally time-consuming, so, with a sample size $|X| = 10^6$ and $M = 5$ about 10^{30} checks must be done. In addition, not all possible complications were named above:

- each element $P_l(x^1, \ldots, x^M) \in P$, $l = 1, \ldots, L$, can describe the mutual dependence of random variables, and in this case, instead of X, it is required to explore M times the entire accessible area in R^N and use (instead of integer numbers of coincidences) the sum of values of some probabilistic proximity measure for sets of the form x;

- the hypothesis can also be parameterized if the set of conditions is additionally loaded with some list of options w or internal parameters $P = P(w)$, which the expert would like to compare with each other.

Below we show how some methods originally developed in the field of IP and IA can be adapted to the case of multidimensional data of an arbitrary nature, which allows us to eliminate or significantly reduce some of the noted difficulties.

2 Ways to Simplify the Model

We note first that in the case of $M = 1$, the desired regularity should be checked simply at points of the sample $X \subset R^N$. The regularity is global from this point of view, and the multiplicity of its manifestations is determined by the size of the sample X. Let us describe an example of an idealized situation when the behavior of a regularity can be presented to an expert practitioner friendly, for example, in the form of a 2-dimensional array on the screen. Let $L = N - 2$, and $P = \{P_1, ..., P_L\}$ is a system of polynomial equations proposed by an expert:

$$f_1(x^1) = f_1(x_1^1, ..., x_N^1) = 0,$$
$$f_2(x^1) = f_2(x_1^1, ..., x_N^1) = 0,$$
$$\cdots$$
$$f_{N-2}(x^1) = f_{N-2}(x_1^1, ..., x_N^1) = 0.$$

Thus, a two-dimensional smooth algebraic hypersurface R, $R \subset R^N$, is defined in the feature space, and the manifestation of the sought regularity at the point $x \in X$ corresponds to the condition $x \in R$. We will calculate the total for the sample X of manifestations of the regularity, taking into account all random deviations, $S(X) = \sum_X \rho(x, R)$, where $\rho(x, R) \geq 1$ in case $x \in X$, and $\rho(x, R)$ decreases rapidly with increasing distance from point x to the surface R. From now on, to designate any regularity under study, we also use the letter R.

Suppose the expert pays attention to parameters $x^1{}_1$, $x^1{}_2$. If the system of N-2 equations can be reduced to the form

$$x_3 = F_3(x_1^1, x_2^1),$$
$$x_4 = F_4(x_1^1, x_2^1),$$
$$\cdots$$
$$x_N = F_N(x_1^1, x_2^1),$$

and the functions $F_3, ..., F_N$ have no singularities, then the projection of the sample X onto the hypersurface R can be one-to-one mapped onto the coordinate plane $(x^1{}_1, x^1{}_2)$, in particular, onto the monitor screen. If, in this case, the sum of manifestations of the regularity $S(X)$ is large and makes up a significant proportion of the sample size $|X|$, the resulting sweep of the sample according to the regularity R can be very valuable for the visual and professional intuition of the expert practitioner. It is easy to take another step in the same direction by replacing in the visualization all images of the projections of points x with the values $\rho(x, R)$. Then the contributions of outlayers will be weakened, and the expert will see on the screen the behavior of the regularity R in a "distilled" form, however, only in terms of (x^1_1, x^1_2).

To reiterate, the above is an idealized situation that is unlikely to be often implemented in practice. At the same time, we consider the advantages achieved here as a goal to which we should strive.

Let now $M > 1$, the list w is not empty, and the conditions $P(w)$ have a more complicated form than just a polynomial system of equations. We seek to identify in the sample the maximum number of manifestations of the regularity R that satisfy these conditions. Let's try to reduce the dimension of the problem due to the probabilistic components of the set $P(w)$. In principle, an expert can formulate the conditional distributions of the form $p(x_n | x \backslash x_n)$ assumed in his hypothesis. But, with an increase in the number M of simultaneously taken into account and interacting sample points, the formulation of such hypotheses quickly turns into an overwhelming task. Moreover, the effort may lose its meaning if the measurements of the parameters $x_1, ..., x_N$ themselves are not accurate. Let's try to shift the expert's difficulties to the capabilities of the computer. We will require the presence in the model of regularity only of expert estimates for average values, in the hope of restoring in the process of calculations all the probabilistic components in the form of empirical distributions over the sample X, which will include inaccuracy components as well.

In the model simplified in this way, all the conditions P are deterministic, and to take into account those manifestations $x \subset X$ of the regularity R that only slightly deviate from the conditions P, we will use some version of the proximity measure $\rho(x, R)$ described above, which now looks like $\rho(x, R)$. Let us give an example of a search problem, where the expert hypothesis contains the binding condition P, which presumably operates within an essential share of tuples $x \subset X$, where the length M of the tuple x is greater 1, $M > 1$.

Now let $X \subset R^N$ be a sample of records of biological parameters of individuals in a large population, for example, anthropometric indicators for residents of a country, city, etc. If a practitioner is interested in demographics, then most likely he will be interested in the behavior of the parent-child relationship for various pairs of objects $x^1 \in X$, $x^2 \in X$, $x^1 \neq x^2$. Therefore, lets first consider the case $M = 2$ and define the proximity measure as follows: $\rho(x, R) = \sum_1^N \sigma_n, \sigma_n = \begin{cases} 1, |x_n^1 - x_n^2| \leq \varepsilon_n \\ 0, |x_n^1 - x_n^2| > \varepsilon_n \end{cases}$, where all ε_n belong to some set of threshold values that define the boundaries on the scales of anthropometric indicators.

Among other possible ones, we include the condition $x^1 \neq x^2$ to the list P, and will display marks about the presence of regularity with points on the plane $(\rho, \varkappa)$, where $\varkappa = |x_{n\prime}^1 - x_{n\prime}^2|$, $n\prime$ - age parameter.

Then in a neighborhood of the point $(\rho = b, \varkappa \approx 25)$, $1 < b < N$, on this plane, a pronounced cluster with an increased density of marks will be observed, since many anthropometric indicators in the parent-child pair often turn out to be close. In this setting, it is easy to increase the length of the tuple x to $M = 5$ or more, assuming that both ancestors and at least 3 descendants are present in the sample. Such condition options may correspond to various alternatives that are considered in the list w and reflect the requests of the expert practitioner. Thus, the location and shape of the cluster will depend on the region of study, and when testing, say, military or school students, the content of this cluster will be insignificant, etc.

Implicitly, in this example, another, more radical way of simplifying the setting is presented. Simultaneously it is the most common and developed in the field of data analysis. In the expression for $\sigma_n = \begin{cases} 1, |x_n^1 - x_n^2| \leq \varepsilon_n \\ 0, |x_n^1 - x_n^2| > \varepsilon_n \end{cases}$ coordinate constraints are applied. In fact, only one (and any) point x of the tuple $\boldsymbol{x}$ is important, the rest of $\boldsymbol{x}$ form a non-zero contribution to the final sum $S(X) = \sum_X \rho(\boldsymbol{x}, R)$ if and only if they are in some neighborhood V of this point. As a result, the amount of $|X|^M$ calculations is reduced to M-1 neighborhoods: $|X||V|^{M-1}$, $|X| > > |V|$, which is much simpler. In what follows, we will only point out the possibility of using any highly sparse or spatially extended in R^N tuples of the form $\boldsymbol{x}$.

3 Analogs of the Hough Transform, Wavelets, and Generalized Precedents in Higher Dimensions

As is known, cluster analysis is one of the main tools that allow to endow an abstract sample with an operable structure [10, 24, 25]. Motives for choosing a clustering method vary. In some cases, it is necessary to provide computational advantages or efficient access: elementary logical regularities [18] of the 1st and 2nd kind (ELR-1, ELR-2), multidimensional analogs of a quadtree, in particular, hypercubes of positional representation [21], etc. In others, the goal is to reveal an objectively existing internal structure in the sample based on a study of the nature and behavior of the data themselves, for example, an approximation of the empirical distribution by a mixture of kernels with a known distribution function, if it is assumed that all observed objects are distorted versions of a limited number of central ones.

These goals are not antagonistic, the approaches of the two types overlap to a large extent. Note that the proximity factor works in both the first and second cases: for example, only densely filled segments of a quadtree or ELR-1 hyperparallelepipeds are important, a subsample with an increased density of implementations is combined into a cluster (a cloud with a known distribution of distortions of the central object). In both cases, this means that the internal distances are small or that the cluster is compact in some sense. Recall, however, that we want to put in a single scheme sparse tuples of the form $\boldsymbol{x}$, too. Such tuples can also represent latent regularities in the sample X, and then the proximity measure should be used for them in a different form.

We will rely on the geometric features of those types of clusters that are best suited for structuring purposes. The degree of cluster filling in the cluster structure can be considered as a reinforcement of the presence of the regularity. At the same time, the relation of proximity of objects in the sample, in particular, the form of the function $\rho(\boldsymbol{x}, R)$, comes to the fore. The presence of a wide variety of clustering methods can help in the task of detecting the expected regularity and even solve the problem as a whole, if the type of cluster is chosen correctly. In this matter, an expert practitioner or a specialist in the applied field can rely on the competence of IT specialists. Let $\boldsymbol{B}_s$, $s = 1, 2, ..., S$, is a set of parametric descriptions of various types of clusters. Let's fix the list of criteria $Q_z(s)$, $z = 1, 2, ..., Z$, which give numerical estimates of the quality of representation of the sample X when using clusters of the type B_s. Having carried out the necessary calculations, we obtain a matrix q_{sz} of quality estimates, which can serve as the basis for choosing certain forms of clusters B_{s*}, $s* = 1, 2, ..., S*$, as the best. We call such clusters basic and will count their occurrences in the sample X. The solution obtained of the optimization problem generally gives a more objective vision of the problem and narrows the initial diversity assumed by the expert B_s, $s = 1, 2, ..., S$.

We will work further with just one of the basic clusters $B*$. For example, this happens in a situation when the only type of cluster $B*$ is specified by the expert in advance as a non-alternative one. We further assume that the clustering of the sample X using clusters of type $B*$ has been completed, and the set of clusters $C^T = \{c^t\}$, $t \in T$, that has arisen in R^N is available to us. It was noted above that spatial constraints actually bring us back to the $M = 1$ situation. This means that the geometric properties of $B*$ can be placed in the list $P(w)$. Moreover, if the necessary pass on X was carried out, then the degrees of filling of clusters in the structure $C^T = \{c^t\}$, $t \in T$, are known, and then this information can be used in various ways at our discretion.

We will strive for the goal presented in the first example. One can simply calculate the sum $S(X)$ of confirmations of the hypothesis, for example, in the form $S(X) = \sum_T |c^t|$, but many opportunities will be missed. Indeed, the expert is interested in the behavior of the regularity in terms of certain important parameters. In particular, the list w may contain a list of alternatives of the hypothesis to be compared during the verification process. We choose a limited number of such parameters $(Y_1,...,Y_D)$ on the assumption that the information presented with their help will be convenient for the expert to perceive, in particular, for visualization in the form of graphs, diagrams, 2- or 3-dimensional distributions, etc. Note that, in principle, any limited group of variables in the list of conditions $P(w)$ is suitable for these purposes. Each fact of manifestation of the regularity $B*$ in one or another cluster $c^t \epsilon C^T$ is called generalized precedent (GP), i.e. precedent of the regularity, and we will map it to the corresponding point in the D-dimensional parametric space Y [9, 13, 17]. For points $Y = (Y_1, ..., Y_D) \epsilon Y$ we will also use the term GP.

This scheme was used to solve several applied problems. Thus, in [20], lineament was considered as $B*$, the role of $(Y_1, Y_2) \epsilon Y$ was played by the length and orientation angle, while the lineament textures formed isolated clusters in space Y, which served as a separating feature for classes in the sample. In [22], the coefficients of the normals to the ELR-2 faces were placed in the Y space, and the detected clusters of close normals were used to unify the directions of the normals and reduce calculations. In [5, 28], a large sample of records about purchases in a trading network was studied. The focus was on the nature of the law that determines the preferences of buyers in relation to certain brands. In the role of informative parameters (Y_1, Y_2) the coefficients of repetition (B_i, P_i) of product names and brands in one purchase were used, and by this some new knowledge was obtained (Fig. 1).

In this case, a different behavior of the parameter of duplication of product and brand names in checks was found for these two subsamples. The problem of identifying the causes of such situation was investigated, and the discovered effect was confirmed, thou before not assumed by retailers in any way.

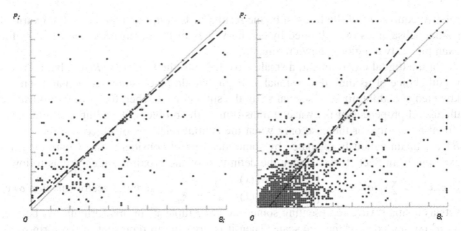

Fig. 1. Linear regression of the ratio of prevailing repetition rates of brands B_i and products P_i for the subsample with constraints $C^{min} = 1$, $C^{max} = 125$ (left) and $C^{min} = 126$, $C^{max} = 1000$ (right), where C - the average price of a product in the purchase.

It is easy to see the similarity of this scheme with the main elements of the Hough transform [9, 12, 13]. The role of spatial differentiation here is played by the clustering process, a limited set of parameters $(Y_1, ..., Y_D)$ corresponds to the geometric characteristics of the desired object (line, circle, polyhedron, etc.), object detection leads to the filling of the cluster c^t in corresponding parametric space Y. Parallels can be traced not only in terms of advantages, but also limitations: the way of interacting with the initial data is limited by options for spatial differentiation, only part of the available information is concentrated in the parametric space. So, in the usual Hough algorithm for lines, the position of the gradient point on the line is ignored and only the number of such points is counted. Similarly, in our consideration, we also restrict ourselves to standard methods at the clustering stage and take into account only certain local parameters of the basic cluster B^*. In both cases, additional effort is required when considering the spatial arrangement of both ordinary and generalized precedents.

Let's try to improve our model in the indicated direction. As is known, a number of variants and specializations have been developed for the gradient operator of the Hough scheme. The models of GP and basic cluster are even richer - one or another type of spatial arrangement of objects in the cluster can itself be an object of interest and enter the definition of the cluster B^*. Actually, we have already encountered such a situation in the second example for $M > 1$. The limiting case arises when the spatial arrangement of objects in the x tuple is not parametrized in any way, and the hypothesis is confirmed by the fact that tested cluster is close to the etalon only in spatial form [8]. Let us pay attention to the similar properties of the wavelet transform, where also cross-correlation plays the role of spatial differentiation. A 'small wave' can have, generally speaking, an arbitrary shape, which is represented by some reference tuple x^*, and the task is now to search for similar objects in certain spatial regions. Let's note the differences, too. The proximity measure $\rho(x, R)$ need to be defined here for two tuples $\rho(x, x^*)$. The wavelet coefficients preserve the spatial arrangement. In multidimensional case, the relative equivalent of the last can be the results of testing the hypothesis R on various spatial subsamples of X, limited by certain values of the parameters $(Y_1, ..., Y_D)$, for example, as two regions shown in Fig. 1.

In the digital environment, a small wave fits into the model $(x, P(w))$, but a meaningful choice of its multidimensional analogue would place increased demands on the knowledge and intuition of specialists in the subject area. Therefore, we will illustrate the useful properties of the wavelet transform in the problem of finding a multidimensional regularity for the case only when the spatial relations of objects in the cluster B^* are unambiguously regulated by some meaningful considerations. Continuing the example from Sect. 1, we change the definition of the proximity measure as follows:

$$\rho(x, x^*) = \sum_1^N \sigma_n, \sigma_n = \begin{cases} 1, |x_n^1 + \alpha_n(x) - x_n^2| \le \varepsilon_n \\ 0, |x_n^1 + \alpha_n(x) - x_n^2| > \varepsilon_n \end{cases} \text{, where the vector function } \alpha(x)$$

acts as a small wave representing some reference tuple x^* in this formula. As before, let n' be the index of the age scale. Then it is possible to represent in the form $\alpha(x)$, for example, the age aspects of similarity in the pair "ancestor-descendant", that depend both on the difference in age $\varkappa = |x_{n'}^1 - x_{n'}^2|$ and its absolute value $x_{n'}^1$. The original setting without the function $\alpha(x)$ corresponded to the zero version of such small wave, i.e., the situation of the ideal similarity of the ancestor and descendant. Note that x contains absolute coordinates in the feature space R^N, and they can be used to form Y as a suitable parametric space that describes certain 'coordinate' aspects of the behavior of this GP.

4   Choosing Observable Parameters and Prospects of the Toolkit

Let's point out some promising directions for the further research that also fit into the GP scheme. It's about looking for regularities that are really hidden from observation. Let $F = (F_1, ..., F_N)$ be a list of objects with complex behavior, not necessarily digitized. Let's use the expert's applied competencies and form a vector of numerical dependencies $f = (f_1, ..., f_N)$, which represents a limited list of options for the behavior of objects F. Let's consider the problem of reconstructing the vector f in a situation where only some indirect or integral parameters of the form $z(F)$ are available for immediate observation, while the vector f acts as GP. If there are more than just one indirect or integral parameter, we deal with a vector of values $z(F)$ that potentially can be represented by numerical dependencies $z(f)$. It is required to reconstruct the distribution of the GP according to the available statistics of readings $z(F)$. The resulting cluster structure $C^T = \{c^t\}$, $t \in T$, contains certain information about the correctness of the expert's understanding of the behavior of objects $F_1, ..., F_N$, as well as about the most common values of the corresponding parameters $f_1, ..., f_N$.

This setting was studied in [11], list F included patterns of runoff in several regions of the river basin, when direct measurement of local runoffs $f_1, ..., f_N$ is difficult or impossible. In this case, an expert practitioner can only set numerical models for each f_i, and further try to fit them to available statistics, Fig. 2.

Of course, it is necessary to model numerically the dependencies $z(f)$, too. Here the main assumption was that the river runoff is the sum of regional runoffs at the moment.

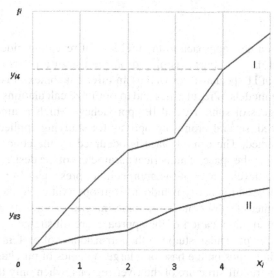

Fig. 2. Local runoff functions f_i modeled by its values y_{ij} in few points on the axis of regional moisture level x_i. Non-square matrix y_{ij} corresponds to a point of GP in $5N$-dimensional parametric space.

The sample was a time series $x(t) = (z(t), x_1(t), ..., x_N(t))$, the feature space R^{N+1} contained readings of the moisture levels calculated from precipitation in the regions $(x_1(t), ..., x_N(t))$, as well as the observed total river runoff $z(t)$ as the only observable integral parameter.

Figure 2 shows one of the lot of ways to parameterize functions $f_1, ..., f_N$. We checked the correspondence $z(t) = \sum_i^N f_i(x_i(t))$ and put all variants of acceptable values y_{ij} in the GP space. Adequate matrices y_{ij} appears close to each other in the GP space for different moments t, and the resulting cluster structure C^T allows the expert to identify in this case the regions of the basin, for example, dangerous of floods (Fig. 2,I) or, on the contrary, prone to moisture accumulation (Fig. 2,II), depending on the interpretation of the GP distribution that he needs.

If the vector $z(f)$ has more than one component, a question arises which of them is better, or is it of worth to use them simultaneously? In some cases, as above mentioned sum $z(t) = \sum_i^N f_i(x_i(t))$, the IT specialists can answer and give an analytical assessment or verify possibilities numerically. Taking into account applied experience too, one can achieve unexpected improvements. For instance, let the water quality is analyzed along with total runoff measurements. If one of the regions differs from others by presence of some unique ingredient, i.e. mineral, biological, anthropogenic, then dimensionality of GP can be reduced since corresponding input to the total runoff is determined by the share of this ingredient found in the runoff water.

5 Conclusion

The paper presents a new approach to the problem of revealing hidden regularities in large-scale applied data. Emphasis is placed on the use of a priori expert knowledge and competencies of IT specialists, as well as an informal context, in order to meaningfully fill numerical models of regularities and to optimize calculations. The possibilities of applying analogues of some IA and IP approaches to higher-dimensional data are systematically traced, several promising options for studying applied data from these positions are presented. The central place is occupied by the concept of generalized precedent as a point in the space of numerical parameters of the desired regularity. Some perspectives for the development of the approach are presented. In particular, for situations where the desired regularity is hidden from observation in the full sense of the word, and only numerous observations of some integral parameters are available. The examples of successful application of the approach are illustrated by several modeled and practical tasks, in particular, studying the intrinsic law of preferences that are paid by buyers to certain brands on the base of a large statistics of purchases in some retail group, restoring the runoff structure of the river regions, when only the integral runoff is directly observed. Some prospects for further development are outlined, in particular, the theme of usage integral and/or indirect parameters.

Acknowledgment. This work was supported in part by project 20-01-00609 of the Russian Foundation for Basic Research.

References

1. Binos, T., Adamopoulos, A., Vince, B.: Decision support research in warehousing and distribution: a systematic literature review. Int. J. Inf. Technol. Decis. Mak. **19**(03), 653–693 (2020)
2. Coleman, S.Y., Kenett, R.S.: The information quality framework for evaluating data science programs. In: Encyclopedia with Semantic Computing and Robotic Intelligence, vol. 02, no. 02 (2018)
3. De Mauro, A., Greco, M., Grimaldi, M.: Understanding Big Data through a systematic literature review: the ITMI model. Int. J. Inf. Technol. Decis. Making **18**(04), 1433–1461 (2019)
4. Dokukin, A.: Classless logical regularities and outliers detection. In: Krasnoproshin, V., Ablameyko, S. (eds.) Pattern Recognition and Information Processing, PRIP 2016. Communications in Computer and Information Science, vol. 673, pp. 44–52. Springer, Cham (20217). https://doi.org/10.1007/978-3-319-54220-1_5
5. Dokukin, A., Zhuravlev, Yu., Senko, O., Stefanovskiy, D.: Matematicheskaya model' vydeleniya grupp soputstvuyushchikh tovarov v roznichnoy torgovle po cyfrovym sledam. Ekonomicheskie strategii **2**, 116–124 (2019)
6. Ren, F., Bao, Y.: A Review on Human-Computer Interaction and Intelligent Robots. Int. J. Inf. Technol. Decis. Mak. **19**(01), 5–47 (2020)
7. Ko, A., Gillani, S.: A research review and taxonomy development for decision support and business analytics using semantic text mining. Int. J. Inf. Technol. Decis. Mak. **19**(01), 97–126 (2020)

8. Kuznetsova, A.V., Kostomarova, I.V., Senko, O.V.: Modification of the method of optimal valid partitioning for comparison of patterns related to the occurence of ischemic stroke in two groups of patients. Pattern Recognit. Image Anal. **22**(4), 10–25 (2013)
9. Laptin, Y., Nelyubina, E.A., Ryazanov, V.V., Vinogradov, A.P.: Shape of basic clusters: using analogues of hough transform in higher dimensions. Pattern Recognit. Image Anal. **28**(4), 653–658 (2018)
10. Naouali, S., Ben Salem, S., Chtourou, Z.: Clustering categorical data: a survey. Int. J. Inf. Technol. Decis. Mak. **19**(01), 49–96 (2020)
11. Naumov, V.A., Nelyubina, E.A., Ryazanov, V.V., Vinogradov, A.P.: Analysis and prediction of hydrological series based on generalized precedents. In: Book of abstracts of the 12th International Conference on Intelligent Data Processing, IDP-12, Gaeta, Italy, pp. 178–179 (2018)
12. Nelyubina, E., Ryazanov, V., Vinogradov, A.: Shape of basic clusters: finding coherent ELR-2s via Hough- type transform. In: Proceedings of ICPRAI 2018 - International Conference on Pattern Recognition and Artificial Intelligence, Montréal, Canada, 14–17 May, pp. 702–706. CENPARMI, Concordia University (2018)
13. Nelyubina, E., Ryazanov, V., Vinogradov, A.: Transforms of Hough type in abstract feature space: generalized precedents. In: Proceedings of the 12th International Joint Conference on Computer Vision, Imaging and Computer Graphics Theory and Applications, VISIGRAPP 2017, Porto, Portugal, vol. 4, pp. 651–656 (2017)
14. Pace, A.: Technologies for large data management in scientific computing. Int. J. Mod. Phys. C **25**(02), 1430001 (2014)
15. Pesarin, F., Salmaso, L.: Permutation Tests for Complex Data. Theory, Applications and Software. Wiley (2010)
16. Rahmati, B., Sohrabi, M.K.: A systematic survey on high utility itemset mining. Int. J. Inf. Technol. Decis. Mak. **18**(04), 1113–1185 (2019)
17. Ryazanov, V., Vinogradov, A.: Dealing with realizations of hidden regularities in data as independent generalized precedents. In: IEEE Xplore Proceedings of 2021 International Conference on Information Technology and Nanotechnology, ITNT-2021, pp. 1–3 (2021)
18. Ryazanov, V.V.: Logicheskie zakonomernosti v zagachakh raspoznavayiya (parametricheskiy podkhod). Zhurnal Vychislitelnoy Matematiki i Matematicheskoy Fiziki **47**(10), 1793–1808 (2007)
19. Ryazanov, V.V., Vinogradov, A.P., Laptin, Y.: Using generalized precedents for big data sample compression at learning. J. Mach. Learn. Data Anal. **1**(1), 1910–1918 (2015)
20. Ryazanov, V., Vinogradov, A., Laptin, Y.: Assembling decision rule on the base of generalized precedents. Inf. Theor. Appl. **23**(3), 264–272 (2016)
21. Vinogradov, A., Laptin, Yu.: Using bit representation for generalized precedents. In: Proceedings of International Workshop OGRW-9, Koblenz, Germany, December 2014, pp. 281–283 (2015)
22. Vinogradov, A., Laptin, Yu.: Mining coherent logical regularities of type 2 via positional preprocessing. In: Proceedings of the 4th International Workshop on Image Mining: Theory and Applications, Barcelona, pp. 56–62. INSTICC Press, Portugal (2013)
23. Zhang, C., Chen, Y.: A review of research relevant to the emerging industry trends: Industry 4.0, IoT, Blockchain, and Business Analytics. J. Ind. Integr. Manage. **05**(01), 165–180 (2020)
24. Zhuravlev, Yu.I., Ryazanov, V.V., Senko, O.V.: RASPOZNAVANIE. Matematicheskie metody. Programmnaya sistema. Prakticheskie primeneniya. Izdatelstvo "FAZIS", Moscow, 168 str. (2006)
25. Zhuravlev, Yu., Dokukin, A., Senko, O., Stefanovskiy, D.: Use of clasterization technique to highlight groups of related goods by digital traces in retail trade. In: Proceedings of 9th International Conference on Advanced Computer Information Technologies, ACIT-2019, pp. 84–88 (2019)

26. Zhuravlev, Yu.I., Sen'ko, O.V., Bondarenko, N.N., Ryazanov, V.V., Dokukin, A.A., Vinogradov, A.P.: A method for predicting rare events by multidimensional time series with the use of collective methods. Pattern Recogn. Image Anal. **29**(4), 763–768 (2019)

27. Zhuravlev, Y.I., Sen'ko, O.V., Bondarenko, N.N., Ryazanov, V.V., Dokukin, A. A., Vinogradov, A.P.: Issledovanie vozmozhnosti prognozirovaniya izmeneniy finansovogo sostoyaniya kreditnoy organizacii na osnove publikuemoy otchetnosti. Informatika i eyo primeneniya **13**(4), 32–37 (2019)

28. Zhuravlev, Yu.I., et al.: Using Hough-like transforms for extracting relevant regularities from big applied data. Pattern Recogn. Image Anal. **31**(4), 699–709 (2021)

TAHIR: Transformer-Based Affine Histological Image Registration

Vladislav A. Pyatov⬤ and Dmitry V. Sorokin$^{(\boxtimes)}$⬤

Laboratory of Mathematical Methods of Image Processing, Faculty of Computational
Mathematics and Cybernetics, Lomonosov Moscow State University, Moscow, Russia
dsorokin@cs.msu.ru
https://imaging.cs.msu.ru

Abstract. In medical practice it is often necessary to jointly analyze differently stained histological sections. However, when slides are being prepared tissues are subjected to deformations and registration is highly required. Although the transformation between images is generally non-rigid, one of the most challenging subproblems is to calculate the initial affine transformation. Existing learning-based approaches adopt convolutional architectures that are usually limited in receptive field, while global context should be considered. Coupled with small datasets and unsupervised learning paradigm, this results in overfitting and adjusting the structure only locally. We introduce transformer-based affine histological image registration (TAHIR) approach. It successfully aggregates global information, requires no histological data to learn and is based on knowledge transfer from nature domain. The experiments show that TAHIR outperforms existing methods by a large margin on most-commonly used histological image registration benchmark in terms of target registration error, being more robust at the same time. The code is available at https://github.com/VladPyatov/ImgRegWithTransformers.

Keywords: Image registration · Affine transformation · Histology · Transformer · Deep Learning

1 Introduction

In histopathology it is frequently necessary to analyze several images of the examined tissue by scanning the slices independently (see Fig. 1) and visually compare them afterwards. This approach is used in rapidly growing area of histological Whole Slide Images (WSI) analysis [14,19] as well as in 3D reconstruction from 2D images [21], fusing information from differently stained slides [20] or methods [7], and stain marker segmentation with information from adjacent tissue slides [13]. Image registration is a crucial step in these tasks being at the same time challenging problem due to complex tissue deformations and different staining.

The work was supported by Russian Science Foundation grant 22-41-02002.

J.-J. Rousseau and B. Kapralos (Eds.): ICPR 2022 Workshops, LNCS 13644, pp. 541–552, 2023.
https://doi.org/10.1007/978-3-031-37742-6_42

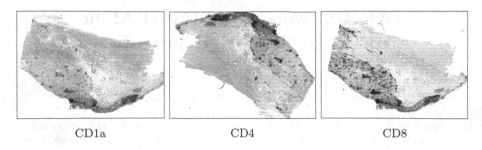

CD1a   CD4   CD8

Fig. 1. Illustration of differently stained consecutive histological sections (dyes are signed below the images)

Although the transformation between different histological images is usually non-rigid, one of the most challenging subproblems of histological image registration is calculating the initial affine transformation. There are several approaches to this problem. Among classic algorithms, most prominent are intensity-based [3], Fourier-based [2] and feature-based [9,25].

Deep learning-based image registration methods can be divided into two main categories. Supervised approaches [8] take advantage of known transformations or ground truth points, but usually suffers from overfitting when the dataset is small. In contrast, unsupervised solutions [11], where predefined similarity metric with task-specific regularization is being optimized, are not so susceptible to overfitting and generalize well. However, similarity metric should be differentiable and must be properly defined for the task at hand.

Another approach is indirect registration through feature matching. Given two images to be matched, most existing matching methods perform image feature detection, description, and matching pipeline [18,24]. However, when dealing with histological images, detectors usually fail to extract representative set of keypoints due to repetitive texture patterns, loss of contextual information, multiple staining, and presence of noise and artifacts [1]. Even if there are enough points to match, a significant part of keypoint pair candidates will be rejected during the matching phase for the same reason. Recent works have attempted to avoid feature detection by establishing pixel-wise dense matches [15,23]. However, the receptive field of the features extracted by convolutional neural networks is limited. When it comes to histological images, correspondences are being established with both local and global context, so large receptive field is an important factor to consider.

Transformers [28] can capture long-range dependencies with the attention mechanism and have been extensively adopted in main computer vision tasks over the past few years, such as image classification [17], object detection [6], etc. Moreover, transformer-based feature matching approach LoFTR [26] have recently proven itself as the model of choice for visual localization tasks.

In this work we introduce transformer-based affine histological image registration (TAHIR) framework, an approach that combines Transformer-based feature matching with classic optimization of affine transformation parameters.

We show that transformer model pretrained on the general nature outdoor dataset MegaDepth [16] generalizes well to biomedical images from open dataset provided for the Automatic Non-rigid Histological Image Registration (ANHIR) challenge [5], thus no additional training is required. The proposed method is suitable for small datasets, works well for images with different resolution and outperforms existing affine histological image registration methods by a large margin. The paper extends our previous work in [22] with more thorough evaluation, method description and several ablation experiments to demonstrate the improvement of each of the proposed approach components.

2   Method

Let $I_S(x)$ be the source image defined over 2D spatial domain $\Omega_S \subset \mathbb{R}^2$ and $I_T(x)$ be the target image defined over 2D spatial domain $\Omega_T \subset \mathbb{R}^2$.

Affine image registration is the problem of finding an affine transformation matrix $\hat{A} = (a_{i,j}) \in \mathbb{R}^{2 \times 3}$, such that:

$$\hat{A} = \underset{A}{\operatorname{argmin}} \mathcal{L}(A; I_T; I_S) = \underset{A}{\operatorname{argmin}} \mathcal{L}(I_T; I_S \circ A),$$

where $I_S \circ A$ represents I_S warped by A

In our approach we use negative global normalized cross correlation (NCC) as the loss function $\mathcal{L}$.

When the transformation is found, resulting registered image $I_R(x)$ can be estimated as:

$$I_R(x) = I_S \circ \hat{A}.$$

2.1   Preprocessing

In this work we follow the preprocessing algorithm proposed in [29], which includes: (i) converting the images to grayscale, (ii) intensity normalization, (iii) smoothing and resampling images to lower resolution, (iv) intensity inversion, (v) padding to the same size. Downsampling the images to 512 pixels in the biggest dimension is sufficient to produce satisfactory quality, but we choose to downsample the images to 1024 pixels and save more fine-level details as it enables to obtain better results, being less memory efficient, though. Preprocessed images are presented in Fig. 2.

2.2   Feature Matching

As a Transformers can capture long-range dependencies, we propose to use LoFTR [26] for the feature matching stage. LoFTR adopts Transformer with self and cross attention layers to process the dense local features extracted from the convolutional backbone. First, dense matches are extracted between the two sets of transformed features at a low resolution (1/8 of the image dimension). Then matches with high confidence are refined to a subpixel level with a

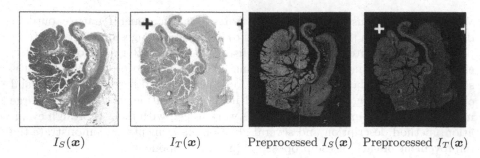

$I_S(\boldsymbol{x})$ $I_T(\boldsymbol{x})$ Preprocessed $I_S(\boldsymbol{x})$ Preprocessed $I_T(\boldsymbol{x})$

Fig. 2. Source and target images after preprocessing.

correlation-based algorithm. More importantly, the global receptive field provided by Transformer enables LoFTR to produce dense matches in areas with repetitive texture patterns, where feature detectors usually struggle to produce reliable interest points. The results of feature matching are represented in Fig. 3. In this example clearly, Transformers' large receptive field is well suited for regions with low and repetitive texture, where global context should be considered.

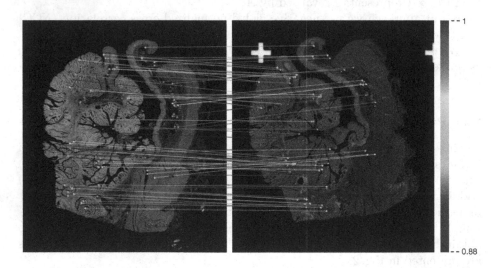

Fig. 3. QuadTree LoFTR feature matching visualization. Only top 100 matches out of 879 are depicted. Color reflects confidence (red - most confident). (Color figure online)

As mentioned above, we downsample the images to 1024 pixels rather than 512 pixels in the biggest dimension to save fine-level details. This brings two problems for LoFTR. The first is computational complexity. Although in LoFTR it is solved with linear attention it still compromises the quality. The second problem is that in low-textured regions there still can be mismatches on a coarse level of LoFTR. To solve these problems, we use QuadTree attention [27], which builds 3-level token pyramid and computes attention in a coarse-to-fine manner, keeping only top K regions with the highest attention scores at each level (K equals 16, 8 and 8). This approach helps to skip irrelevant regions on coarse quadtree level, and does not attend on fine quadtree level, as it would be difficult in parts of the tissue with repetitive patterns. It also adopts standard attention computation, while keeping linear computational complexity.

Moreover, we found that LoFTR's confidence threshold θ_c should be tuned for histological images due to their specific nature. Experiments showed that threshold value of 0.5 is the best choice for the data. It will be further discussed in Sect. 3.2.

The ANHIR [5] dataset is relatively small to be used for training and produce relevant results, so we decided to adopt knowledge transfer from nature domain. Namely, we use MegaDepth [16] pretrained model by QuadTree [27] authors, as its content is most similar to ANHIR data. No additional data was used for training.

2.3 Transformation Estimation

After the features are matched, we compute affine transformation using RANSAC [12] as the robust estimator. The registration results are presented in Fig. 4.

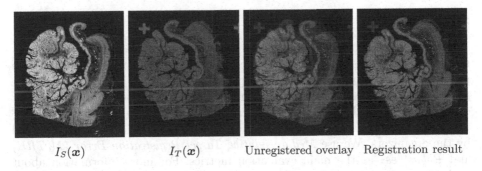

$I_S(\boldsymbol{x})$ $\qquad$ $I_T(\boldsymbol{x})$ $\qquad$ Unregistered overlay $\quad$ Registration result

Fig. 4. Affine registration results. Source and target images are depicted in yellow and purple colorscale respectively for better visualization clarity. (Color figure online)

LoFTR is not rotation invariant, so to avoid registration errors we apply feature matching to the rotated $I_S(\boldsymbol{x})$ image (by 0°, 90°, 180° and 270°), estimate transformation and select the result with the best NCC metric. If there is no result better than the initial NCC similarity, then the rotated image with the best NCC metric is selected. In addition, four angles can be checked simultaneously if memory is not a problem. Algorithm 1 summarizes the proposed registration pipeline.

Input: $I_S(\boldsymbol{x})$, $I_T(\boldsymbol{x})$

```
/* initialization */
```

$ncc_{best} = NCC(I_S(\boldsymbol{x}), I_T(\boldsymbol{x}))$

$I_R(\boldsymbol{x}) = I_S(\boldsymbol{x})$

$\hat{A} = Id$ `// Identity transform`

for $angle$ **in** $[0, 90, 180, 270]$:

  $I_S^\circ(\boldsymbol{x}) = rotate(I_S(\boldsymbol{x}), angle)$ `// rotate source image`

  $P_S, P_T = LoFTR(I_S^\circ(\boldsymbol{x}), I_T(\boldsymbol{x}))$ `// compute matches`

  $A = RANSAC(P_S, P_T)$ `// compute transformation`

  $I_W(\boldsymbol{x}) = warp(I_S^\circ(\boldsymbol{x}), A)$

  if $ncc > ncc_{best}$:

    $ncc_{best} = ncc$

    $I_R(\boldsymbol{x}) = I_W(\boldsymbol{x})$

    $\hat{A} = compose(angle, A)$

Output: $\hat{A}$, $I_R(\boldsymbol{x})$

Algorithm 1. Image registration pseudocode.

3   Results

3.1   Comparison

The proposed method was evaluated on the open dataset provided for the Automatic Non-rigid Histological Image Registration (ANHIR) challenge [5]. The provided dataset consists of 8 tissue types with 481 image pairs of varying size - 230 annotated by experts training pairs and 251 evaluation pairs. Full dataset description is available at https://anhir.grand-challenge.org/.

All the results were produced with server-side evaluation system provided by the organizers. We use *Median relative Target Registration Error* (*MrTRE*) and *Robustness* as the main evaluation metrics. For more information about evaluation metrics, we refer to [5].

For comparison, we have reproduced the results of two learning-based methods that directly predict transformation matrix. The first is *Learning-Based Affine Registration of Histological Images* (LBARHI) [29] based on patch-wise feature extraction and convolution attention mechanisms. The second is affine part of *DeepHistReg* (AffineDHR) [30] framework, which is ResNet-like convolutional neural network. Please note that our reproduced results are slightly worse than the numbers reported in [29] as we used the same deformation field composition operation implementation for all the evaluated methods, which differs from [29] and is based on widely adopted VoxelMorph [4] implementation. Despite that, our algorithm still outperforms the numbers reported by the authors in

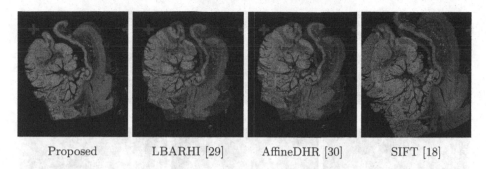

| Proposed | LBARHI [29] | AffineDHR [30] | SIFT [18] |

Fig. 5. Visualization of the evaluated methods for the source and target images in Fig. 4. The proposed algorithm works well, while SIFT fails to establish reliable correspondences. Learning-based methods unable to identify global structure and adjust shape locally, as they were trained in unsupervised fashion with NCC loss function.

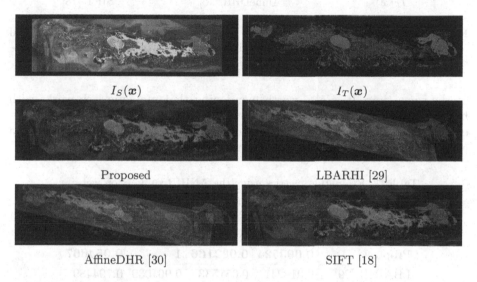

$I_S(\boldsymbol{x})$	$I_T(\boldsymbol{x})$
Proposed	LBARHI [29]
AffineDHR [30]	SIFT [18]

Fig. 6. Registration comparison where source and target images are quite different in terms of the structure. Despite it, the proposed method works surprisingly well, while learning-based methods struggle to estimate transformation. SIFT works well only on the right side of the image where the structure is sharp, while the left side with complex patterns remains unregistered.

[29]. We also compare the proposed approach to the classic SIFT descriptors [18]. We summarize the obtained results in Table 1 and show the comparison visualization with other methods in Fig. 5. More complex registration cases related to structure variation and repetitive patterns depicted in Fig. 6 and Fig. 7, respectively.

The results show that the proposed method attains excellent quality in terms of target registration error and outperforms other approaches, being more robust

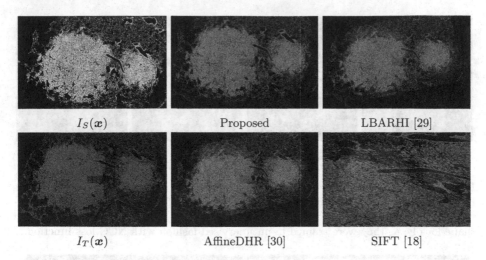

Fig. 7. Registration case with noticeable repetitive patterns. Transformer's global receptive field enables TAHIR to perform high-quality registration, while limited receptive field of the convolutional methods considers the local structure as well as SIFT.

at the same time. It is also worth mentioning that our approach works with histological images in zero-shot mode, which undoubtedly proves its strong generalization ability. We can confidently say, that proposed method can serve as a good starting point prior to nonrigid registration.

Table 1. Evaluation metrics using the ANHIR submission website.

	MrTRE		*Robustness*	
	Median	Average	Median	Average
Proposed	**0.003524**	**0.022166**	1	**0.954067**
LBARHI [29]	0.016241	0.051533	0.961039	0.794489
AffineDHR [30]	0.014216	0.050248	0.961039	0.807963
SIFT [18]	0.037986	0.113356	0.931818	0.652211

We also report an extended performance evaluation of our method on both train (230 pairs) and evaluation (251 pairs) parts of ANHIR dataset (see. Table 2). It demonstrates, that the proposed algorithm works equally well on both subsets and there is no bias in results as the numbers on the train and evaluation parts are comparable.

3.2   Ablation Study

We perform a set of various ablation experiments to show the relative importance of each detail of our approach. The results of the ablations are shown in Table 3.

Table 2. Extended metrics for the train and evaluation ANHIR data subsets.

	MrTRE		Robustness	
	Median	Average	Median	Average
Train	0.003360	0.017691	1	0.955928
Evaluation	0.003559	0.026266	1	0.952361

Below we describe each of the experiments and give explanations for better understanding of TAHIR.

Table 3. Ablation experiments.

	MrTRE		Robustness	
	Median	Average	Median	Average
Reference model	0.003524	0.022166	1	0.954067
Lower $\theta_c = 0.2$	0.003531	0.019604	1	0.959715
Higher $\theta_c = 0.8$	0.003574	0.021823	1	0.947237
512px images	0.004018	0.026458	1	0.949525
ScanNet [10] dataset	0.040302	0.077918	0.763158	0.665405
w/o QuadTree attention	0.003897	0.035739	0.992126	0.930078

Confidence Threshold: In LoFTR, the matches with confidence above the threshold θ_c are selected from the coarse matches and later refined to a sub-pixel level. When $\theta_c = 0.2$ the method produces less outliers (in terms of Average MrTRE and Robustness), but works slightly worse in terms of the main challenge criteria (Median MrTRE). With higher θ_c the method performs slightly worse in terms of Robustness and Median MrTRE because reliable matches are sometimes occur on repetitive tissue patterns and thus are not confident enough.

Image Size: The original size of ANHIR images varies from 2000 to 19000 pixels in the biggest dimension. To reduce the computational cost and to save as much fine-level details as possible, we downsample the images to 1024 pixels in the biggest dimension. Downsampling to lower resolution leads to the loss of structure and a subsequent increase of the registration error.

Dataset: We use model pretrained on MegaDepth [16] outdoor dataset. Our experiments showed, that pretraining on indoor scenes of ScanNet [10] is not suitable for histological images. This gives an interesting observation that important is not the pretraining itself but the data used for it.

Attention Module: We test the importance of skipping irrelevant tissue regions on quadtree pyramid levels by evaluating the model without QuadTree attention. Results show, that it has profound effect on registration error, and considering only top K regions with the highest attention scores at each level in important.

4   Conclusion

In this work, we presented TAHIR – Transformer-based Affine Histological Image Registration framework. It combines learnable feature matching with classic optimization of transformation parameters and demonstrates high level of performance. TAHIR significantly outperforms other methods, creates new opportunities for histological image registration and looks promising for further extension to non-rigid registration approaches and applications in other domains.

References

1. Abdelsamea, M.M., Zidan, U., Senousy, Z., Gaber, M.M., Rakha, E., Ilyas, M.: A survey on artificial intelligence in histopathology image analysis. Wiley Interdisc. Rev. Data Min. Knowl. Discovery, e1474 (2022)
2. Anoshina, N.A., Krylov, A.S., Sorokin, D.V.: Correlation-based 2D registration method for single particle cryo-EM images. In: Proceedings of the IEEE International Conference on Image Processing Theory, Tools and Applications (IPTA), pp. 1–6 (2017)
3. Arganda-Carreras, I., Fernandez-Gonzalez, R., Ortiz-de Solorzano, C.: Automatic registration of serial mammary gland sections. In: The 26th Annual International Conference of the IEEE Engineering in Medicine and Biology Society, vol. 1, pp. 1691–1694 (2004)
4. Balakrishnan, G., Zhao, A., Sabuncu, M.R., Guttag, J., Dalca, A.V.: VoxelMorph: a learning framework for deformable medical image registration. IEEE Trans. Med. Imaging **38**(8), 1788–1800 (2019)
5. Borovec, J., et al.: ANHIR: automatic non-rigid histological image registration challenge. IEEE Trans. Med. Imaging **39**(10), 3042–3052 (2020)
6. Carion, N., Massa, F., Synnaeve, G., Usunier, N., Kirillov, A., Zagoruyko, S.: End-to-end object detection with transformers. In: Vedaldi, A., Bischof, H., Brox, T., Frahm, J.-M. (eds.) ECCV 2020. LNCS, vol. 12346, pp. 213–229. Springer, Cham (2020). https://doi.org/10.1007/978-3-030-58452-8_13
7. Ceritoglu, C., Wang, L., Selemon, L.D., Csernansky, J.G., Miller, M.I., Ratnanather, J.T.: Large deformation diffeomorphic metric mapping registration of reconstructed 3D histological section images and in vivo MR images. Frontiers Hum. Neurosci., 43 (2010)
8. Chee, E., Wu, Z.: AIRNet: self-supervised affine registration for 3D medical images using neural networks. arXiv preprint arXiv:1810.02583 (2018)
9. Cooper, L., Sertel, O., Kong, J., Lozanski, G., Huang, K., Gurcan, M.: Feature-based registration of histopathology images with different stains: an application for computerized follicular lymphoma prognosis. Comput. Methods Programs Biomed. **96**(3), 182–192 (2009)

10. Dai, A., Chang, A.X., Savva, M., Halber, M., Funkhouser, T., Nießner, M.: Scan-Net: richly-annotated 3D reconstructions of indoor scenes. In: Proceedings of the IEEE Conference on Computer Vision and Pattern Recognition (CVPR), pp. 5828–5839 (2017)

11. De Vos, B.D., Berendsen, F.F., Viergever, M.A., Sokooti, H., Staring, M., Išgum, I.: A deep learning framework for unsupervised affine and deformable image registration. Med. Image Anal. **52**, 128–143 (2019)

12. Fischler, M.A., Bolles, R.C.: Random sample consensus: a paradigm for model fitting with applications to image analysis and automated cartography. Commun. ACM **24**(6), 381–395 (1981)

13. Gupta, L., Klinkhammer, B.M., Boor, P., Merhof, D., Gadermayr, M.: Stain independent segmentation of whole slide images: a case study in renal histology. In: IEEE 15th International Symposium on Biomedical Imaging (ISBI 2018), pp. 1360–1364 (2018)

14. Khvostikov, A., Krylov, A., Mikhailov, I., Malkov, P., Danilova, N.: Tissue type recognition in whole slide histological images. CEUR Workshop Proc. **3027**, 50 (2021). https://doi.org/10.20948/graphicon-2021-3027-496-507

15. Li, X., Han, K., Li, S., Prisacariu, V.: Dual-resolution correspondence networks. Adv. Neural. Inf. Process. Syst. **33**, 17346–17357 (2020)

16. Li, Z., Snavely, N.: MegaDepth: learning single-view depth prediction from internet photos. In: Proceedings of the IEEE Conference on Computer Vision and Pattern Recognition (CVPR), pp. 2041–2050 (2018)

17. Liu, Z., et al.: Swin transformer: hierarchical vision transformer using shifted windows. In: Proceedings of the IEEE/CVF International Conference on Computer Vision (ICCV), pp. 10012–10022 (2021)

18. Lowe, D.G.: Distinctive image features from scale-invariant keypoints. Int. J. Comput. Vision **60**(2), 91–110 (2004)

19. Mikhailov, I., Khvostikov, A., Krylov, A.S., Malkov, P., Danilova, N., Oleynikova, N.: Development of CNN-based algorithm for automatic recognition of the layers of the wall of the stomach and colon. Virchows Arch. **479**(Suppl 1), OFP-15-004 (2021). https://doi.org/10.1007/s00428-021-03157-8

20. Obando, D.F.G., Frafjord, A., Øynebråten, I., Corthay, A., Olivo-Marin, J.C., Meas-Yedid, V.: Multi-staining registration of large histology images. In: 2017 IEEE 14th International Symposium on Biomedical Imaging (ISBI 2017), pp. 345–348 (2017)

21. Pichat, J., Iglesias, J.E., Yousry, T., Ourselin, S., Modat, M.: A survey of methods for 3D histology reconstruction. Med. Image Anal. **46**, 73–105 (2018)

22. Pyatov, V., Sorokin, D.: Affine registration of histological images using transformer-based feature matching. Pattern Recogn. Image Anal. **32**(3), 626–630 (2022). https://doi.org/10.1134/S1054661822030324

23. Rocco, I., Arandjelović, R., Sivic, J.: Efficient neighbourhood consensus networks via submanifold sparse convolutions. In: Vedaldi, A., Bischof, H., Brox, T., Frahm, J.-M. (eds.) ECCV 2020. LNCS, vol. 12354, pp. 605–621. Springer, Cham (2020). https://doi.org/10.1007/978-3-030-58545-7_35

24. Sarlin, P.E., DeTone, D., Malisiewicz, T., Rabinovich, A.: SuperGlue: learning feature matching with graph neural networks. In: Proceedings of the IEEE/CVF Conference on Computer Vision and Pattern Recognition (CVPR), pp. 4938–4947 (2020)

25. Sorokin, D.V., Tektonidis, M., Rohr, K., Matula, P.: Non-rigid contour-based temporal registration of 2D cell nuclei images using the Navier equation. In: IEEE 11th International Symposium on Biomedical Imaging (ISBI 2014), pp. 746–749 (2014)

26. Sun, J., Shen, Z., Wang, Y., Bao, H., Zhou, X.: LoFTR: detector-free local feature matching with transformers. In: Proceedings of the IEEE/CVF Conference on Computer Vision and Pattern Recognition (CVPR), pp. 8922–8931 (2021)
27. Tang, S., Zhang, J., Zhu, S., Tan, P.: Quadtree attention for vision transformers. arXiv preprint arXiv:2201.02767 (2022)
28. Vaswani, A., et al.: Attention is all you need. In: Advances in Neural Information Processing Systems, vol. 30 (2017)
29. Wodzinski, M., Müller, H.: Learning-based affine registration of histological images. In: International Workshop on Biomedical Image Registration, pp. 12–22 (2020)
30. Wodzinski, M., Müller, H.: DeepHistReg: unsupervised deep learning registration framework for differently stained histology samples. Comput. Methods Programs Biomed. **198**, 105799 (2021)

Automated Image Processing for Remote Sensing Data Classification

Marco Reggiannini[✉][iD], Oscar Papini[iD], and Gabriele Pieri[iD]

Institute of Information Science and Technologies, National Research Council
of Italy, Via G. Moruzzi 1, 56124 Pisa, Italy
{marco.reggiannini,oscar.papini,gabriele.pieri}@isti.cnr.it

Abstract. Remote sensing technologies allow for continuous and valuable monitoring of the Earth's various environments. In particular, coastal and ocean monitoring presents an intrinsic complexity that makes such monitoring the main source of information available. Oceans, being the largest but least observed habitat, have many different factors affecting theirs faunal variations. Enhancing the capabilities to monitor and understand the changes occurring allows us to perform predictions and adopt proper decisions. This paper proposes an automated classification tool to recognise specific marine mesoscale events. Typically, human experts monitor and analyse these events visually through remote sensing imagery, specifically addressing Sea Surface Temperature data. The extended availability of this kind of remote sensing data transforms this activity into a time-consuming and subjective interpretation of the information. For this reason, there is an increased need for automated or at least semi-automated tools to perform this task. The results presented in this work have been obtained by applying the proposed approach to images captured over the southwestern region of the Iberian Peninsula.

Keywords: Image Processing · Remote Sensing · Mesoscale Patterns · Sea Surface Temperature · Machine Learning · Climate change

1 Introduction

To achieve a broader understanding and evaluation of the sea environment, an improvement in marine observation is required. Among all the relevant underlying processes in such a differentiated biological system, mesoscale events such as upwelling, countercurrents and filaments are of particular interest and constitute the subject of our analysis. These events, which transport deeper, colder and nutrient-rich waters to the surface, and affect the biological parameters of the habitat, enhancing the local biodiversity [7], can be observed by analysing Sea Surface Temperature (SST) recorded in remote sensing imagery.

Identifying and categorising upwelling regimes occurring in a marine ecosystem is an essential achievement for its characterisation. The main objective of this paper is to propose a method for performing an automatic classification of

© Springer Nature Switzerland AG 2023
J.-J. Rousseau and B. Kapralos (Eds.): ICPR 2022 Workshops, LNCS 13644, pp. 553–560, 2023.
https://doi.org/10.1007/978-3-031-37742-6_43

images in place of the usual manual one completed by experts. When the number of images approaches the thousands, i.e. the typical order of magnitude having the goal to investigate long term and climate-related changes, the manual procedure is not manageable anymore. The method is applied to the Iberia/Canary Current System (ICCS), one of the least studied among the upwelling ecosystems [1]. Despite a general circulation similar to others, in ICCS we have diverse factors having a profound impact on the whole region.

The method proposed in this work is based on implementing an automatic procedure for classifying large datasets of images according to the different regimes of observable upwelling patterns. Such classification consists of several stages: starting from the extraction of quantitative features from a region of interest in the SST maps, proceeding to the characterisation of specific temperature patterns, which are correlated with the water flows between geographical points at different temperatures. The latter stage is performed by applying a set of rules to the computed features, which enable the assignment of a final class label to the considered region.

This paper follows a preliminary presentation given in [5] and represents a further extension of the work in [6]. It is arranged as follows: Section 2 provides a description of the employed dataset and the related ground truth classification; Sect. 3 reports on the pipeline used in our methods and describes a study case; Sect. 4 concludes the paper by discussing the outcomes of this work and providing a few considerations about future perspectives.

2   Materials

For the purposes of this work, SST data captured by Metop-A/B (EUMETSAT) and Aqua (NASA) have been collected and processed. Only data covering the region of interest were downloaded for each source (whose respective details are reported in Table 1). In particular, points with latitude between 35° and 40° N and longitude between 12° and 6° W were considered, resulting in 2–3 images per day at most.

Table 1. Data specifications

Satellite	Sensor Type	Spatial Resolution (km)	Temperature Resolution (°C)
Metop-A/B [3]	AVHRR	1	10^{-2}
Aqua [2]	MODIS	1	$5 \cdot 10^{-3}$

Expert oceanographers have preliminarily inspected the collected data to identify recurring SST patterns based on the detection of relevant mesoscale features (water filaments, upwelling jets and countercurrents). This way, it was possible to identify four prevailing patterns, named E1–E4 (see [5] for a detailed description). Furthermore, each image was labelled according to the observed pattern, returning a ground truth dataset that could be used as a reference for the classifier implementation.

3   SST Analysis

In order to better analyse the different types of upwelling patterns, SST data are retrieved from the sources described in the previous section and arranged in a *spaghetti plot*, which is a simultaneous representation of the different SST trends for a given geographical area and a time interval. It is obtained by first dividing the considered area into a grid of small squares (whose size may be equal to or larger than the image spatial resolution). Then, for each square, the SST spatial average value is computed for each time sample in the dataset falling within the considered time window. Finally, the obtained ensemble of averaged SSTs is plotted versus time within the same diagram.

Figure 1 shows an example of an event classified as E4 in the ground truth and the spaghetti plots corresponding to the selected areas. Events of type E4 are characterised by the presence of a warm countercurrent originating in the Gulf of Cádiz and running along the southern Iberian coast, eventually reaching Cape St. Vincent (see Fig. 1c). A cold water filament going westwards is also recognisable (see Fig. 1b), which is a pattern typical for events of type E1. In this case, the squares' size and the time interval are 0.25° and 15 days respectively (notice that the ground truth event occurs at the end of the time window). After several tests, these specific values have been chosen since they return a better agreement between the results and the ground truth.

A spaghetti plot is then processed to extract statistical features, which depend on the SST signal in each square and its neighbourhood. These features are later used to classify the considered area, which is then associated with one of the four mesoscale patterns.

Let a be a square in the grid. As said, we have a temporal series of spatial SST averages in a, say μ_i, computed at times t_i, $i = 1, \ldots, n$. Notice that n may change from square to square, since it depends on the number of SST values captured by the sensor. In fact, the SST recording may fail for some parts of the area of interest (e.g. due to interfering clouds disturbances). Because of these considerations, the number of samples n can be considered as an index of reliability for the classification of the square a. The statistics features computed for a are:

1. the temporal mean $\mu(a)$, defined as the mean of the values μ_i;
2. the standard deviation $\sigma(a)$, defined as the standard deviation of the values μ_i;
3. the linear regression coefficient $\theta(a)$, defined as the slope of the straight line that better interpolates the values (t_i, μ_i).

The values μ, σ and θ are computed for every square in the grid. Figure 2 shows these values for our case study (event of 7 October 2017; see Fig. 1).

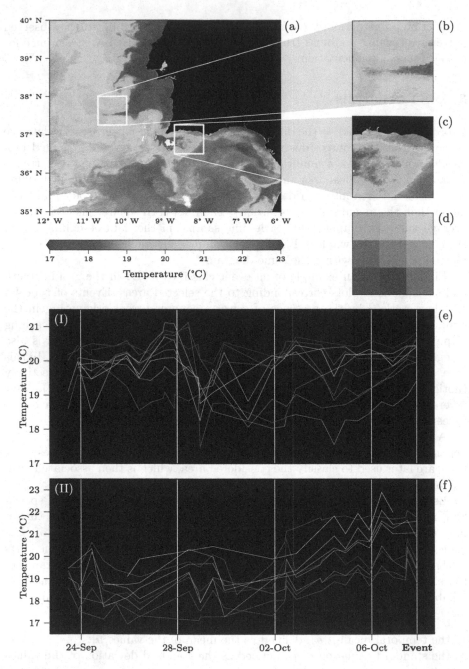

Fig. 1. Event of 7 October 2017 at around 21:00 UTC. (a) SST map at the date of the event; (b) detail of the SST in the reference area for spaghetti plot I (latitude between 37.25° and 38° N, longitude between 10.75° and 10° W); (c) detail of the SST in the reference area for spaghetti plot II (latitude between 36.5° and 37.25° N, longitude between 8.75° and 8° W); (d) reference grid for both plots (dimension of squares 0.25°); (e, f) generated spaghetti plots.

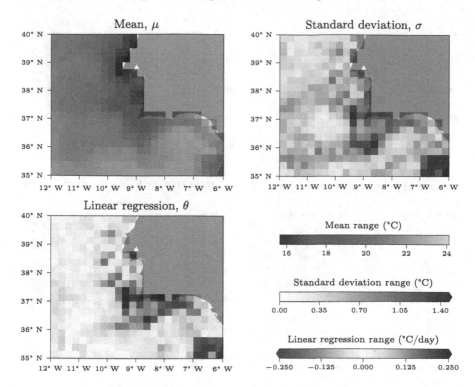

Fig. 2. Maps representing the values of the statistics for each square, computed for the event of 7 October 2017 using data from the period between 23 September and 7 October.

The next step is to apply a set of rules to obtain, for each square a, an array of four scores (e_1, e_2, e_3, e_4), with $e_j \in [0, 1]$. The value e_j represents a belief index for the event of type Ej to have occurred inside a at the end of the considered time interval. The implementation of the rules is a crucial component for the classifier. Indeed, they are handcrafted so that the score e_j is boosted only if the behaviour of the features μ, σ and θ, inside and in the neighbourhood of the square a, matches the one observed in the case of an Ej pattern. Figure 3 shows the scores for each square of the grid for the event of Fig. 1, computed using the values of the statistics depicted in Fig. 2.

The classification of a square is finally completed by considering the maximum score $e_m = \max\{e_1, e_2, e_3, e_4\}$: if e_m is above a certain threshold, empirically defined, then the square is labelled "Em"; otherwise no label is assigned. Figure 4 represents a heatmap with the classification results applied to the event of Fig. 1 using the scores of Fig. 3, with each square coloured with the corresponding classification label. Also, each square is labelled with the numerical percentage of the related SST data, which is proportional to the n value as discussed above.

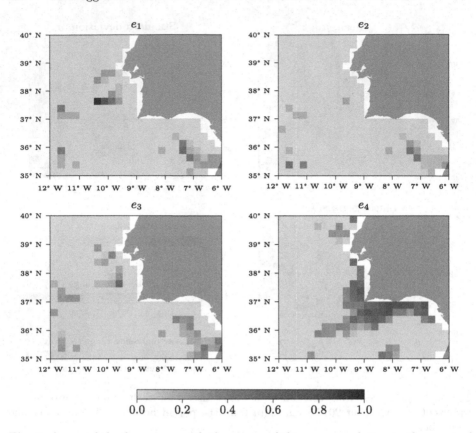

Fig. 3. Array of the four maps with the scores of the squares relative to the event of 7 October 2017.

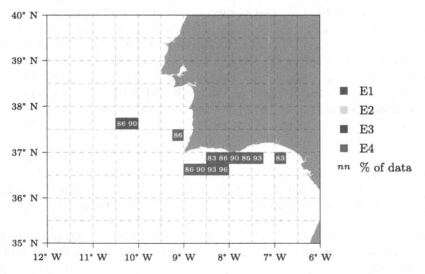

Fig. 4. Labels given to each square of the grid, depending on their scores.

4   Discussion and Conclusion

In this work, a methodology for classifying upwelling events based on the analysis of SST time series has been proposed. Preliminary tests proved that the proposed method succeeds in classifying different mesoscale events. A few considerations can be pointed out concerning the presented case study (Fig. 1). First, it is worth noticing that the labelling returned by the classifier agrees with the ground truth: among the squares located in the area where E4 events usually occur, those that fulfilled the previously mentioned data abundance constraints have been correctly labelled (Fig. 4). Second, it is to remark that the occurrence of a mesoscale event is a phenomenon that depends on both space and time. In this work, the criterion adopted to formulate the classification rules is to estimate how much an SST pattern, observed within a given spatial and temporal neighbourhood, is close to a theoretical one. For the presented case study, these rules have been applied to the computed SST statistics (see Fig. 2), eventually yielding the score maps in Fig. 3. Each score map represents the closeness between the SST signal and each possible mesoscale event. Moreover, the extracted features take into account not only the SST final observation, corresponding to the ground truth label, but also the SST variations captured in the preceding time window. This is the reason behind the presence of squares classified differently from E4, in apparent conflict with the ground truth. Since the proposed approach takes into consideration the SST signal over an extended range of time, it is reasonable that more than one label is assigned, in agreement with the multiple observed mesoscale events. It is even more so considering that inside the presented case study's dataset, different ground truth labels have been assigned to images captured very close in time. For example, on 6 October, two distinct events are observed: one classified as E1 in the ground truth approximately at 10:00 UTC, and a second one around 21:20 UTC classified as E4.

The test and validation of the proposed algorithm are carried out and will continue as part of the activities of the EU H2020 project NAUTILOS [4].

Acknowledgements. The authors express gratitude to Prof. Flávio Martins and Dr João Janeiro from the University of Algarve, Centre for Marine and Environmental Research, for their support.

Funding Information. This paper is part of a project that has received funding from the European Union's Horizon 2020 research and innovation programme under grant agreement No. 101000825 (NAUTILOS).

Conflict of Interests. The process of writing and the content of the article does not give grounds for raising the issue of a conflict of interest.

References

1. Chavez, F.P., Messié, M.: A comparison of eastern boundary upwelling ecosystems. Prog. Oceanogr. **83**(1), 80–96 (2009). https://doi.org/10.1016/j.pocean.2009.07.032
2. NASA/JPL: GHRSST level 2P global sea surface skin temperature from the moderate resolution imaging spectroradiometer (MODIS) on the NASA aqua satellite (GDS2) (2020)
3. OSI SAF: Full resolution L2P AVHRR sea surface temperature metagranules (GHRSST) - Metop (2011)
4. Pieri, G., et al.: New technology improves our understanding of changes in the marine environment. In: Proceedings of the 9th EuroGOOS International Conference. EuroGOOS (2021)
5. Reggiannini, M., Janeiro, J., Martins, F., Papini, O., Pieri, G.: Mesoscale patterns identification through SST image processing. In: Proceedings of the 2nd International Conference on Robotics, Computer Vision and Intelligent Systems – ROBOVIS, pp. 165–172. SciTePress (2021). https://doi.org/10.5220/0010714600003061
6. Reggiannini, M., Papini, O., Pieri, G.: An automated analysis tool for the classification of sea surface temperature imagery. Pattern Recogn. Image Anal. **32**(3) (2022). https://doi.org/10.1134/S1054661822030336
7. Varela, R., Lima, F.P., Seabra, R., Meneghesso, C., Gómez-Gesteira, M.: Coastal warming and wind-driven upwelling: a global analysis. Sci. Total Environ. **639**, 1501–1511 (2018). https://doi.org/10.1016/j.scitotenv.2018.05.273

Prior Segmentation and Attention Based Approach to Neoplasms Recognition by Single-Channel Monochrome Computer Tomography Snapshots

Aleksei Samarin[1], Alexander Savelev[1], Aleksei Toropov[1], Alina Dzestelova[1], Valentin Malykh[1], Elena Mikhailova[1], and Alexandr Motyko[2]([⊠])

[1] ITMO University, St. Petersburg 197101, Russia
[2] St. Petersburg Electrotechnical University "LETI", St. Petersburg 197022, Russia
motyko.alexandr@yandex.ru

Abstract. Computer tomography is most commonly used for diagnosing lung cancer, which is one of the deadliest cancers in the world. Online services that allow users to share their single-channel monochrome images, in particular computer tomography scans, in order to receive independent medical advice are becoming wide-spread these days. In this paper, we propose an optimization for the previously known two-staged architecture for detecting cvancerous tumors in computer tomography scans that demonstrates the state-of-the-art results on Open Joint Monochrome Lungs Computer Tomography (OJLMCT - Open Joint Monochrome Lungs Computer Tomography dataset firstly proposed in Samarin et al. [14]) dataset. Modernized architecture allows to reduce the number of weights of the neural network based model (*4,920,073* parameters vs. *26,468,315* in the original model) and its inference time (*0.38* s vs. *2.15* s in the original model) without loss of neoplasms recognition quality (*0.996* F_1 score). The proposed results were obtained using heavyweight encoder elimination, special combined loss function and watershed based method for the automated dataset markup and a Consistency Regularization approach adaptation that are described in the current paper.

Keywords: Biomedical images processing · Neoplasms recognition · Computer tomography snapshots classification

1 Introduction

Lung cancer is one of the most frequently diagnosed cancers and the leading cause of cancer-related deaths worldwide, with an estimated 2 million new cases and 1.76 million deaths per year [19]. One way to recognize this disease is with the help of computer tomography (CT). A CT scan allows examination in detailed snapshots of human organs layer-by-layer.

© Springer Nature Switzerland AG 2023
J.-J. Rousseau and B. Kapralos (Eds.): ICPR 2022 Workshops, LNCS 13644, pp. 561–570, 2023.
https://doi.org/10.1007/978-3-031-37742-6_44

At the same time, within online services of medical consultation, fast processing of monochrome CT images is required, which is due to the requirements of the load and ease of use. Such online medical services[1] becomes increasingly popular for obtaining an independent opinion on a CT image. Using that services, patients can get advice from real medical specialists, as well as process their image using machine learning algorithms.

Over the past decade, a number of approaches have been proposed to recognize lung cancer using CT scans and machine learning techniques. Unfortunately, most of them are either too heavyweight [8,10,15] for usage in the context of Internet services or do not support monochrome image processing at all [5,21].

However, one of the contemporary methods for recognizing neoplasms on single-channel monochrome images demonstrated excellent performance (0.99 in F1 score) on OJMLCT dataset proposed in the article "Two-Staged Self-Attention Based Neural Model For Lung Cancer Recognition" [14]. That approach used a two-staged model for cancerous neoplasms presence detection. The first stage of the proposed model is responsible for detecting cavities in the lungs and the second stage is responsible for classifying the detected cavities. Despite the advantages of that solution (such as high performance and interpretable neural network architecture), it has several significant disadvantages. The first drawback is non-optimal inference time which is due to the presence of two strictly consecutive stages and a quite heavyweight DNN based classifier with the self-attention module. The second drawback is the difficult training process that requires independent training of detector and classifier.

In this paper, we focus on optimising approach that was originally proposed by Samarin et al. [14]. So we introduce special OJLMCT dataset markup and model training pipeline that allows using a lightweight one-staged classifier in the context of the problem under consideration. We also propose a special loss function and improve the quality metrics with consistency regularisation principles adaptation.

2   Proposed Solution

2.1   Neoplasm Segmentation Approach for a Prior Dataset Markup

As an alternative for a prior lung cavity detection step, we took advantage of the U-Net [13] model ability to use segmentation information. In order to provide prior segmentation markup for succeeding I-Net training, we investigated several approaches described below.

The first considered approach uses SLIC [1] superpixelization that steps are given below:

1. Initialize cluster centers $C_k = [l_k, a_k, b_k, x_k, y_k]^T$ by sampling pixels at regular grid steps S.

---

[1] Online medical consultation services: betterhelp (https://www.betterhelp.com/), amwell (https://amwell.com/cm/), Yandex Health (https://health.yandex.ru/), Sber Med AI (https://sbermed.ai/).

2. Perturb cluster centers in an $n \times n$ neighborhood, to the lowest gradient position.
3. **repeat**
4.   **for** each cluster center C_k **do**
5.   Assign the best matching pixels from a $2S \times 2S$ square neighborhood around the cluster center according to the distance measure
6.   **end for**
7.   Compute new cluster centers and residual error E $L1$ distance between previous centers and recomputed centers
8. **until** $E \leq threshold$
9. Enforce connectivity.

Where N stands for a number of pixels in the input image. K stands for a number of superpixels. S denotes grid interval. It also should be noted that we used $[labxy]$ space, where $[lab]$ is the pixel color vector in CIELAB color space as described in the original paper [1].

The visualization of such superpixelization results is shown in Fig. 1. However its usage for prior markup did not demonstrate appropriate efficiency. So we focused our attention on watershed-based algorithms.

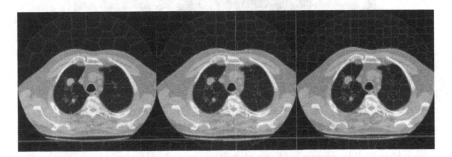

Fig. 1. The example of the SLIC superpixelization algorithm output with different clusters number.

A simple and computationally effective algorithm for obtaining a lung cavity segmentation map is based on the well-known Otsu method for image binarization. It is known from practice, that the Otsu method, which relies on the idea that maximization of interclass variance is equivalent to minimization of intraclass variance, provides good results for images where object and background classes are comparable in area and, in addition, objects have clear localization.

Looking at the target images (Fig. 2), it is clear that they just potentially fit the described case. Indeed, the dark lung cavities and the background around the image are roughly comparable in area to the tissue image (lighter tones). At the same time, the cavities are quite clearly localized inside the light area.

In addition, there is some a priori information about the cavities we are looking for (specificity of initial data): maximal and minimal area, mutual location, and so on. Thus, the structure of the algorithm is as follows:

1. Low-pass image filtering to suppress noise
2. Binarization by Otsu method
3. Finding closed inner contours in a binarized image
4. The selection from the set of resulting candidate contours the two most corresponding to the a priori information about the target objects.

The example of the algorithm performance is shown in Fig. 2.

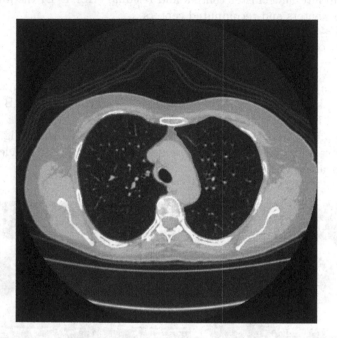

Fig. 2. The example of the algorithm based on Otsu binarization

Nevertheless, practice has shown that the algorithm demonstrates satisfactory results for databases containing images with similar characteristics (scale, signal-to-noise ratio), in other words obtained by the same devices. However, the images obtained from different scanners may differ significantly. And in this case, the algorithm requires some adjustment for the other type of images. For machine learning, where unsorted data from dozens of different scanners can be used, this is a significant disadvantage. This algorithm lacks adaptivity. In this sense, the watershed algorithm is much more promising for the given task.

So we apply a segmentation algorithm based on the watershed [7, 9] method to OJLMCT dataset in order to obtain lung cavity segmentation maps that are suitable for U-Net training (Fig. 3).

The watershed method is a mathematical morphology algorithm. An input image is treated as some map of terrain, where brightness values represent elevation values relative to some level (Fig. 4).

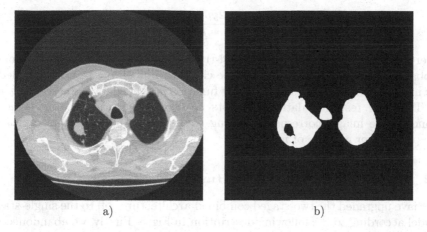

Fig. 3. Examples of lungs CT scan with neoplasm from the OJLMCT dataset: (a) before watershed method; (b) after watershed method

As far as that terrain is filled with water the pools are formed. If the water level exceeds the level of the partitions between the pools, that pools are merged. The barriers where that pools are separated are marked as watershed lines (Fig. 3).

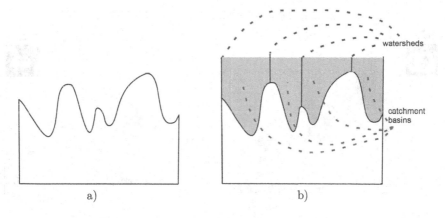

Fig. 4. Illustration of the watershed algorithm: (a) before watershed method; (b) after watershed method

We chose the thresholds for the watershed based segmentation algorithm according to the idea of maximizing the Dice [6, 17] coefficient value between the output of our segmentation method and the ground truth lung cavity areas from the patch of our combined dataset where segmentation markup is presented [3]. The Dice coefficient, also known as the overlapping index, is determined with the formula:

$$1 - \frac{2y\hat{p} + 1}{y + \hat{p} + 1}$$

where $y \in \{1, 0\}$ specifies the ground-truth class, $\hat{p} \in [0, 1]$ is the estimated probability of model predictions for the class with label $y = 1$ and 1 is added in the numerator and denominator so that function is defined for the case $y = \hat{p} = 0$.

Thus the resulting dataset consists of triads: the original single-channel monochrome image, corresponding lung cavity mask and the label indicating the presence or absence of neoplasms.

2.2   U-Net Based DNN Architecture

We have upgraded the two-staged combined architecture [14] to the single-staged model according to the following description in Fig. 5. Firstly, we abandoned the concept of the prior lung cavity detection and trained our U-net based model using prior lung cavities segmentation information instead of that. It should be noted that we use only L-Net (encoder patch of the whole U-Net DNN architecture) for classification purposes (Fig. 5). To do this, we used the self-attention mechanism in the L-Net output stage to help machine learning models focus on individual parts. Its extended Multi-head Self-Attention architecture, which replaces a single self-attention mechanism with a multi-head version of this mechanism, was taken from the improved two-staged model [14].

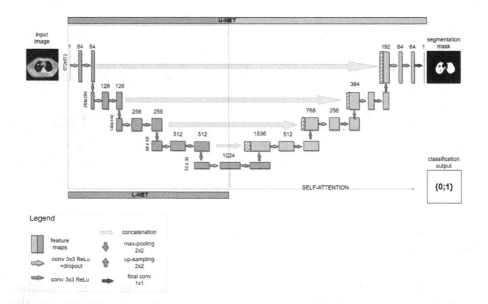

Fig. 5. U-Net based DNN model for neoplasms presence recognition.

So the inference uses only L-Net (encoder part of the U-Net architecture) for neoplasms presence recognition. The segmentation head of U-Net model, which outputs lung cavities mask, is only used for training with the special loss function. Thus we implicitly highlighted segmentation information and used a lightweight form of neural network encoder without segmentation patch in inference. Using that approach, we were able to significantly reduce the inference time and the number of parameters (Sect. 3).

2.3   Consistency Regularization

Furthermore, in addition to using a prior segmentation information, we have adapted consistency regularisation techniques to improve the quality of the classification. Consistency Regularisation (CR) is an approach that is actively used in semi-supervised learning [2,11,16,20]. The basic idea behind this method that successfully applied in computer vision (for example in such problems as image enhancement [18]) is to impose additional constraints on the loss function for similar images using the formula:

$$L_{CR} = L_{segmentation} + L_{classification} + \alpha \times f(I, aug(I)),$$

where α is an error control coefficient, I is the original image, aug() stands for an augmentation function.

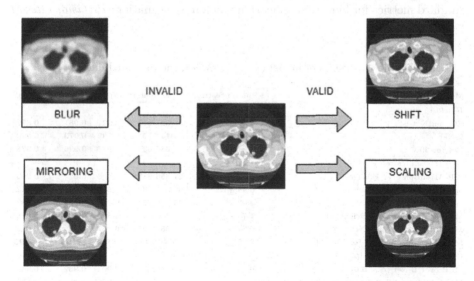

Fig. 6. Valid and invaild CR image transformation examples.

Minor transformations, i.e. the difference between the images before and after applying which is sufficiently small, we considered random shift (by only several pixels along four directions) and random insignificant upscaling and downscaling.

It should also be noted that not all augmentation techniques (blur, mirroring) are applicable for that problem due to anatomical features of the human body, such as a heart location (Fig. 6).

3   Evaluation

3.1   Dataset

The dataset for training, validation and testing consists of 10052 single-channel monochrome images, which were separated in the ratio 7196:1428:1428 respectively. It was obtained from a combination of publicly available datasets from Radiology Moscow [12] and The Cancer Imaging Archive [3]. Each image is classified according to the presence of a neoplasm. In this way, the dataset is divided into 2 equally sized classes sets, each of that was split into the training, test and validation groups according to mentioned above ratio. In addition to the classification markup, we generated a segmentation mask for each dataset sample according to watershed based method described in Sect. 2. The segmentation result is a binary set where 0 is the background and 1 lung cavities area (Fig. 3).

3.2   Experimental Results

According to the above, the dataset is divided into two classes. So we use the standard metrics for binary classification efficiency estimation: *Precision, Recall, and F1-score* [4].

Table 1. Results of model experiments on the proposed dataset

Model	Inference time	#parameters	F_1	Precision	Recall
Baseline					
EfficientNet-b4	1.68 s	21 521 217	0.921	0.981	0.877
L-Net	0.46 s	5 914 577	0.882	0.973	0.820
ResNet-50	2.01 s	25 687 633	0.987	0.996	0.978
Two-staged architectures [14]					
Self-Attention over EfficientNet-b4	1.70 s	21 656 913	0.938	0.979	0.905
Self-Attention over L-Net	0.48 s	6 050 073	0.891	0.937	0.872
Self-Attention over ResNet-50	2.02 s	25 823 329	0.991	0.996	0.982
MultiAttention over EfficientNet-b4	1.76 s	22 301 899	0.943	0.969	0.918
MultiAttention over L-Net	0.61 s	6 695 259	0.967	0.986	0.953
MultiAttention over ResNet-50	2.15 s	**26 468 315**	**0.996**	**0.999**	**0.993**
One-staged architectures (ours)					
MLP over L-Net ($\alpha = 0.0$)	0.50 s	7 105 239	0.904	0.962	0.853
Multi-Attention X 1 over L-Net ($\alpha = 0.0$)	0.38 s	4 920 073	0.928	0.975	0.886
Multi-Attention X 3 over L-Net ($\alpha = 0.0$)	0.40 s	5 520 125	0.959	0.984	0.936
MLP over L-Net ($\alpha = 0.75$)	0.50 s	7 105 239	0.938	0.984	0.897
Multi-Attention X 1 over L-Net ($\alpha = 0.75$)	0.38 s	**4 920 073**	**0.996**	**0.999**	**0.993**
Multi-Attention X 3 over L-Net ($\alpha = 0.75$)	0.40 s	5 520 125	0.996	0.999	0.993

In addition to the classification quality estimation, we provide a comparison of inference time using our[2] hardware configuration and model parameters number of investigated neural network based architectures. The results obtained using the test set are presented in Table 1.

The presented results demonstrated that the use of additional segmentation markup, Consistency Regularization practices and combined loss allowed us to train the one-staged lightweight classifier architecture that significantly surpasses the counterparts in terms of inference time and the number of trainable parameters. Moreover obtained classification quality results are similar to the state-of-the-art heavyweight two-staged architecture proposed by Samarin et al. [14].

4   Conclusion

In this paper, we presented a lightweight version of neoplasms recognition neural network based model that demonstrates the state-of-the-art results ($F_1 - score = 0.996$) on the OJLMCT dataset. The original architecture was optimized using heavyweight encoder elimination, special combined loss function and watershed based method for the automated dataset markup and a Consistency Regularization approach adaptation that were described above in the current paper.

The proposed approach allows to provide tumor recognition in CT monochrome snapshots that is extremely helpful for online medical consultation services.

The further research can be focused on our method application for differential diagnostic by the monochrome CT snapshots.

References

1. Achanta, R., Shaji, A., Smith, K., Lucchi, A., Fua, P., Süsstrunk, S.: SLIC superpixels. Technical report, EPFL (2010)
2. Bachman, P., Alsharif, O., Precup, D.: Learning with pseudo-ensembles. In: Advances in Neural Information Processing Systems, vol. 27, pp. 3365–3373 (2014)
3. Clark, K., et al.: The Cancer Imaging Archive (TCIA): maintaining and operating a public information repository. J. Digit. Imaging **26**(6), 1045–1057 (2013). https://doi.org/10.1007/s10278-013-9622-7
4. Goutte, C., Gaussier, E.: A probabilistic interpretation of precision, recall and F-score, with implication for evaluation. In: Losada, D.E., Fernández-Luna, J.M. (eds.) ECIR 2005. LNCS, vol. 3408, pp. 345–359. Springer, Heidelberg (2005). https://doi.org/10.1007/978-3-540-31865-1_25
5. Heuvelmans, M.A., et al.: Lung cancer prediction by deep learning to identify benign lung nodules. Lung Cancer **154**, 1–4 (2021). https://doi.org/10.1016/j.lungcan.2021.01.027. https://www.sciencedirect.com/science/article/pii/S0169500221000453
6. Jadon, S.: A survey of loss functions for semantic segmentation, pp. 1–7 (2020). https://doi.org/10.1109/CIBCB48159.2020.9277638

---

[2] GPU: NVIDIA GeForce RTX 3060; CPU: Intel(R) Core(TM) i5-10400 CPU @ 2.90 GHz 2.90 GHz; RAM: 16 GB.

7. Lalitha, K.V., Amrutha, R., Michahial, S., Shivakumar, M.: Implementation of watershed segmentation. IJARCCE **5**, 196–199 (2016). https://doi.org/10.17148/IJARCCE.2016.51243

8. Kasinathan, G., Jayakumar, S.: Cloud-based lung tumor detection and stage classification using deep learning techniques. BioMed Res. Int. **2022** (2022)

9. Kaur, A.: Image segmentation using watershed transform (2014)

10. Kobylińska, K., Orlowski, T., Adamek, M., Biecek, P.: Explainable machine learning for lung cancer screening models. Appl. Sci. **12**, 1926 (2022). https://doi.org/10.3390/app12041926

11. Kuo, C.-W., Ma, C.-Y., Huang, J.-B., Kira, Z.: FeatMatch: feature-based augmentation for semi-supervised learning. In: Vedaldi, A., Bischof, H., Brox, T., Frahm, J.-M. (eds.) ECCV 2020. LNCS, vol. 12363, pp. 479–495. Springer, Cham (2020). https://doi.org/10.1007/978-3-030-58523-5_28

12. Morozov, C., Kul'berg, H., Gombolevskij, B.: Tagged lung computer tomography results, March 2018

13. Ronneberger, O., Fischer, P., Brox, T.: U-net: convolutional networks for biomedical image segmentation. In: Navab, N., Hornegger, J., Wells, W.M., Frangi, A.F. (eds.) MICCAI 2015. LNCS, vol. 9351, pp. 234–241. Springer, Cham (2015). https://doi.org/10.1007/978-3-319-24574-4_28

14. Samarin, A., Savelev, A., Malykh, V.: Two-staged self-attention based neural model for lung cancer recognition. In: 2020 Science and Artificial Intelligence Conference (SAI ence), pp. 50–53. IEEE (2020)

15. Shimazaki, A., et al.: Deep learning-based algorithm for lung cancer detection on chest radiographs using the segmentation method (2022). https://doi.org/10.1038/s41598-021-04667-w

16. Sohn, K., et al.: FixMatch: simplifying semi-supervised learning with consistency and confidence. arXiv preprint arXiv:2001.07685 (2020)

17. Sudre, C.H., Li, W., Vercauteren, T., Ourselin, S., Jorge Cardoso, M.: Generalised dice overlap as a deep learning loss function for highly unbalanced segmentations. In: Cardoso, M.J., et al. (eds.) DLMIA/ML-CDS -2017. LNCS, vol. 10553, pp. 240–248. Springer, Cham (2017). https://doi.org/10.1007/978-3-319-67558-9_28

18. Tatanov, O., Samarin, A.: LFIEM: lightweight filter-based image enhancement model. In: 2020 25th International Conference on Pattern Recognition (ICPR), pp. 873–878 (2021). https://doi.org/10.1109/ICPR48806.2021.9413138

19. Thai, A.A., Solomon, B.J., Sequist, L.V., Gainor, J.F., Heist, R.S.: Lung cancer. Lancet **398**(10299), 535–554 (2021)

20. Xie, Q., Dai, Z., Hovy, E., Luong, M.T., Le, Q.V.: Unsupervised data augmentation for consistency training. arXiv preprint arXiv:1904.12848 (2019)

21. Yang, H., et al.: Deep learning-based six-type classifier for lung cancer and mimics from histopathological whole slide images: a retrospective study. BMC Med. (2021). https://doi.org/10.1186/s12916-021-01953-2

The Complete Study of the Movement Strategies of Trained Agents for Visual Descriptors of Advertising Signs

Aleksei Samarin[1], Alexander Savelev[1], Aleksei Toropov[1], Alina Dzestelova[1], Valentin Malykh[1], Elena Mikhailova[1], and Alexandr Motyko[2(✉)]

[1] ITMO University, St. Petersburg 197101, Russia
[2] St. Petersburg Electrotechnical University "LETI", St. Petersburg 197022, Russia
motyko.alexandr@yandex.ru

Abstract. We provide a complete description of our investigation into specialized visual descriptors application as a part of combined classifier architecture for advertising signboards photographs classification problem. We propose novel types of descriptors (pure convolutional neural networks based and based on trainable parametrized agent movement strategies) showing the state of the art results in the extraction of visual characteristics and related semantics of text fonts presented on a sign. To provide comparisons of developed approaches and its effectiveness examination we used two datasets of commercial building facade photographs grouped by the type of presented business.

Keywords: Combined classifier · Visual and textual features · Optical character recognition · Specialized image descriptor

1 Introduction

At the present time, some applied marketing problems are related with computer vision [1–4, 9, 12–16, 24–26]. We consider the problem of commercial building facades photographs classification by the type of provided services [12, 14–16, 24]. That issue becomes urgent in the process of business segment analysis by snapshots and video fragments of considered locations. However, that problem is extremely difficult due to the presence of the following factors. Advertising signs text often contains a wide variety of fonts and colors. The background of the text area of a plate under consideration can contain elements of irregular shapes and often has a non-uniform color scheme. Another significant classification complicating circumstance is various shooting conditions and capture devices configurations that affect the resulting images.

An essential feature of the considered classification problem is the possibility of making a decision based on several heterogeneous features at once [12, 14–16]. Among the sources of such information can be noted the text presented on the advertising sign, its design, as well as the background of the whole scene.

© Springer Nature Switzerland AG 2023
J.-J. Rousseau and B. Kapralos (Eds.): ICPR 2022 Workshops, LNCS 13644, pp. 571–585, 2023.
https://doi.org/10.1007/978-3-031-37742-6_45

In order to take into account all the listed sources of information, it is convenient to use a combined classification architecture [12,14–16]. It should also be noted the low efficiency of the general image classification methods [6,7,20] for solving the problems of classifying the facades of commercial buildings by the type of services provided [12,14–16].

This circumstance is explained by the significant difference between heterogeneous images [5,10] from photographs of facades of commercial buildings with advertising signs. This difference is determined both by the monotony of the background against which the largest central object is a commercial building and by the specificity of the form of advertising posters. It should also be noted that there is a slight difference in the forms of posters among advertisements of various types of business, which requires fine tuning of the visual features encoders.

In addition to a purely visual component, to make a target decision, it is possible to use a semantic component extracted from the text presented on the poster. Such approaches solve the problem of optical character recognition using special engines [19,23,27]. Unfortunately, one cannot fail to note the low accuracy of text recognition in the context of the problem under consideration. This circumstance is due to various shapes, sizes, angles of shooting an advertising poster, as well as intrinsic camera calibration parameters and distortions of various nature (Fig. 1). Moreover, the text classification itself does not show high results in determining the type of services provided by the text on the advertising signboard due to the lack of sufficient context and inaccuracies in the process of text recognition [12,15]. Thus, the idea of building the architecture of a combined classifier arose, allowing to take into account all available sources of information for the most complete coverage of the context presented on the scene [12,14–16]. That type of approaches demonstrated the best efficiency in the solving problem under consideration.

In the study of combined classifiers for solving the problem of determining the type of services provided by photographs of facades of commercial buildings with advertising signs, a high significance of features based on the visual style of the text was established [14,16]. To take into account these features, a number of special descriptors of the visual style of the text presented on the advertising signboards were developed [14,16]. The current article contains the complete research of descriptors presented in [14,16] and its comparative analysis with two new types of advertising signboards descriptors firstly proposed in the current article as a part of the combined classifier model. The first type of introduced descriptors are pure CNN-based visual descriptors. And the second type is presented with a trace of special agents movement. The strategy of agents movement is based on trainable rules that maximize the performance of the resulting classifier.

2   Problem Statement

According to the above, in the current article, we present the complex comparative analysis on special types of image descriptors usage for implicit signboard information extraction. Our comparative study is presented in the context of the following problem.

A commercial building's facade photograph under investigation has to contain a signboard with text. We use such a photograph as an input for our model. As an output we expect a number $C = C_i$, where $i \in [0, N]$. The obtained number denotes one of N types of provided services that have to be recognized by an input image.

It should also be noted that input images are captured in various shooting conditions by different devices, hence: a) may contain such visual defects as sun glare, noise, including those that greatly impede optical text recognition and visual features of input image; b) angle, framing, lighting and colour balance are unknown and can vary significantly from snapshot to snapshot; c) position of a signboard in frame can also vary greatly.

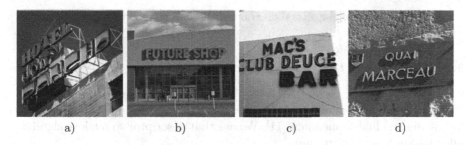

a)   b)   c)   d)

Fig. 1. Considered dataset illustration: a) photograph of a hotel; b) photograph of a store facade; c) image of a restaurant signboard; d) photograph of a signboard that does not belong to categories listed above.

3 Proposed Method

In order to establish a fixed environment for our experiments, we use a similar combined classifier scheme, as described in [12,15]. The proposed architecture contains several modules: a visual features extraction module, a text detection one, and the special image descriptor module (Fig. 2). It is remarkable that the proposed modular architecture does not require any special preprocessing stage since we use fairly stable and noise resistant approaches for significant information retrieval and we also make a decision based on an analysis of a wide range of features. We use the CNN-based module for visual features extraction, since CNN-based image features extractors are effective in solving problems of general images classification [6,7,20,22]. Unfortunately, general images classifiers that are based only on CNN extracted features demonstrate poor results in advertising posters photographs classification [12,15]. In order to increase the performance of our classifier, we introduce another special image descriptor that is obtained from original photo regions that contain text. Then we add some post-processing to prepare general visual features and our special descriptor for concatenation. Then we project the result of the concatenation onto a space of dimension 4 (according to the number of classes). After that, we apply SoftMax function to the obtained vector and interpret result values as the probabilities of target classes.

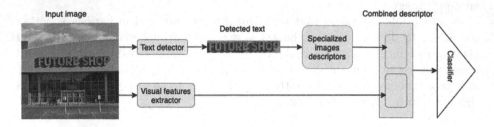

Fig. 2. General architectural diagram of the proposed combined classifier.

3.1   CNN-Based Feature Extractors

According to [12,15], we use MobileNet [6] for a whole image features extraction. Thus a visual features extractor is a sequence of convolutional, fully connected layers and residual connections [11]. We use that descriptor to retrieve significant information from background.

We also use CNN-based EAST [27] architecture for text detection on an input image. Advantages of using this method are its speed and resistance to an angle varying.

3.2   Special Image Descriptors

We present special types of descriptors for images containing textual information. The procedure for calculating proposed descriptors is parallelized naturally and does not require significant computing resources.

The considered descriptors (including our newly presented) are based on the idea of obtaining the maximal information from the mutual arrangement of regions with the maximum brightness variation. We also intend to retrieve information from different locations simultaneously. Thus image descriptors could be considered as traces of a certain number of agents moving from given initial positions on the image according to predefined strategies.

Image descriptor type A originally presented in [16] and implies the special strategy for agent movement. At each step agent select movement type according to the following rule:

$$m_{i+1}^v = \arg\max_{m \in M_p}(|R_1^i - R_2^i| + c_p * \mathbb{1}_{\{p\}}(m)),$$

$$(R_1^i, R_2^i) = \begin{cases} (R_{up}^i, R_{down}^i), & \text{if } |R_{up}^i - R_{down}^i| > |R_{left}^i - R_{right}^i| \\ (R_{left}^i, R_{right}^i), & \text{otherwise,} \end{cases}$$

$$R_{up}^i = I[x_i - s/2 : x_i + s/2; y_i - s : y_i],$$

$$R_{down}^i = I[x_i - s/2 : x_i + s/2; y_i : y_i + s],$$

$$R_{left}^i = I[x_i - s : x_i; y_i - s/2 : y_i + s/2],$$

$$R_{right}^i = I[x_i : x_i + s; y_i - s/2 : y_i + s/2],$$

where m_i^v stands for a movement direction, i stands for a step number, I denotes an input image, and (x, y) denotes position of a pixel on the input image, p stands for priority movement direction, M_p is a subset of $\{up, down, left, right\}$ that denotes allowed movements according to priority direction p, c_p denotes bonus for movement along the priority direction and s stands for a step size in pixels.

The trace of each agent with predefined movement direction can be formalized as follows:

$$T^p(x_0, y_0) = (m_1(x_0, y_0), ..., m_N(x_0, y_0)),$$

where $T^p(x_0, y_0)$—trace of an agent with priority movement direction p and initial position (x_0, y_0), $m_i(x_0, y_0)$ stands for chosen agents movement at step i with predefined initial position and priority direction and N denotes the length of each trajectory (if an edge of the image achieved before making N steps then trace is padded with a special value). Thus trajectories of that descriptor type tends to be placed along contours of an input image.

All of trajectories are grouped by priority directions and initial positions:

$$T^{up} = (T^{up}(x_0, H), ..., T^{up}(x_A, H)),$$

$$T^{down} = (T^{down}(x_0, 0), ..., T^{down}(x_A, 0)),$$

$$T^{left} = (T^{left}(W, y_0), ..., T^{left}(W, y_B)),$$

$$T^{right} = (T^{right}(0, y_0), ..., T^{right}(0, y_B)),$$

where A and B stands for horizontal-oriented and vertical-oriented agents number, W denotes an input image width and H denotes image height. Finally we merge groups of trajectories for each direction into the complete image descriptor that can be described as follows:

$$T = (T^{up}, T^{down}, T^{left}, T^{right}).$$

From the above description, it is easy to construct a procedure that calculates the proposed descriptor for the number of steps that linearly depend on the number of pixels of an input image. It should also be noted that the algorithm for calculating this descriptor is parallelized with a small effort.

Image descriptor type B (firstly presented in [16]) differs from type A only with movement direction rule:

$$m_{i+1}^v = \arg\max_{m \in M_p}(|R_1^i - R_2^i| + \alpha * c_p * \mathbb{1}_{\{p\}}(m)),$$

where α equals 1 if movement direction was changed at least once and 0 otherwise. That modification allows agent to avoid priority direction influence if significant element was found during agents movement.

Image descriptor type C (presented in [14]) is also based on agents trace concept. However Each movement type is selected according to the following expression:

$$m_{i+1}^v = \arg\max_{m \in M}(\mathrm{Var}[I[x, y]] + c(m, v)),$$

where

$$(x, y) \in P((x_i, y_i), s), \ v \in \{up, down, left, right\}.$$

Image descriptor type D is a novel approach we introduce in the context of the combined schema under consideration. Following [15] we use the combined two-fold feature extractor engine as image descriptor for the minimum size area containing the text presented on the advertising poster. We use two Efficient-Net [22] variants simultaneously to get image embeddings. We concatenate and project these embeddings to fit the classifier input. Therefore this approach is not agent-based and uses well-known building blocks, simplifying the overall architecture.

Final scheme of our background feature extractor presented in Fig. 3. We use EfficientNet B2 and EfficientNet B3 as two branches of our image descriptor, as this combination showed the best performance in feature extraction task. The details are presented in Sect. 4.3. Interestingly, this combination is also outperformed its counterparts in [15].

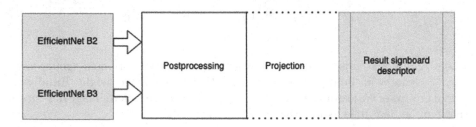

Fig. 3. CNN based signboard descriptor generation scheme.

We also tried to use ensembles of CNN-based features encoders as presented in Fig. 4. However, we did not achieve significant performance boost. So we stop

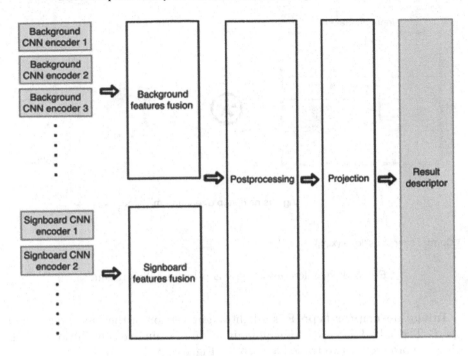

Fig. 4. CNN based signboard descriptor generation scheme with encoder ensembles.

our investigation of image descriptor type D on configuration that is demonstrated in Fig. 3.

Image descriptor type E is based on trainable image descriptor extraction procedure (similar to *image descriptor type D*). However instead of training CNN we use gradient descent optimization for movement strategies parameters tuning. We use the same agents trace based descriptor building approach as for *image descriptors types A, B* and *C* with modified trainable step direction selection rule:

$$m_{i+1}^v = \arg\max_{m \in M_p}(SoftMax(\mathbb{1}_{M_p}(up) * Patch(I, (x_i, y_i), d) \circledast Kernel_{up},$$

$$\mathbb{1}_{M_p}(down) * Patch(I, (x_i, y_i), d) \circledast Kernel_{down},$$

$$\mathbb{1}_{M_p}(left) * Patch(I, (x_i, y_i), d) \circledast Kernel_{left},$$

$$\mathbb{1}_{M_p}(right) * Patch(I, (x_i, y_i), d) \circledast Kernel_{right})), where$$

$$Patch(I, (x_i, y_i), d) = I[x_i - d/2 : x_i + d/2; y_i - -d/2 : y_i + d/2],$$

$Kernel_{up}$, $Kernel_{down}$, $Kernel_{left}$, $Kernel_{right}$—a set of trainable kernels of size d. Convolutions with presented kernels stand for usefulness of movement along corresponding direction (Fig. 5). It should be noted that kernel values are trained as a part of the resulting NN based classifier using gradient descent weights optimization.

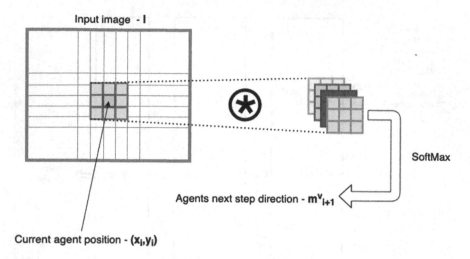

Fig. 5. Image descriptor Type E principles illustration.

Image descriptor type F is a lightweight version of the *image descriptor type E*. The only difference is the approximation of trainable convolution kernels using the product of two trainable vectors (Fig. 6):

$$Kernel_{direction} = Vector^1_{direction} * Vector^2_{direction},$$

where

$$direction \in \{up, down, left, right\}.$$

$Kernel_{direction}$ ($d * d$ elements)—product of trainable vectors $Vector^1_{direction}$ ($d * 1$ elements) and $Vector^2_{direction}$ ($1 * d$ elements).

The main motivation for creating this type of descriptor was to reduce the number of trainable parameters for the *image descriptor type E*. However, as shown in the experiments Sect. 4, such a decomposition of the convolution did not bring an increase in quality as part of our classification pipeline.

Image descriptor type G is a modification of *image descriptor type E* that introduces a combined kernels construction. We used a liner combination of a trainable kernel and Sobel operator (Fig. 7):

$$Kernel_{direction} = kernel^{trainable}_{direction} + A_{direction} * Sobel_X + B_{direction} * Sobel_Y,$$

where

$$direction \in \{up, down, left, right\}.$$

$Kernel_{direction}$ ($d * d$ elements)—for every direction is a linear combination of trainable $kernel^{trainable}_{direction}$ ($d * d$ elements) and directed *Sobel* kernels of corresponding size ($d * d$ elements) with trainable coefficients A and B.

Such combined directed kernels construction was introduced in order to amplify sensitivity to difference in the intensity of the image pixels along the

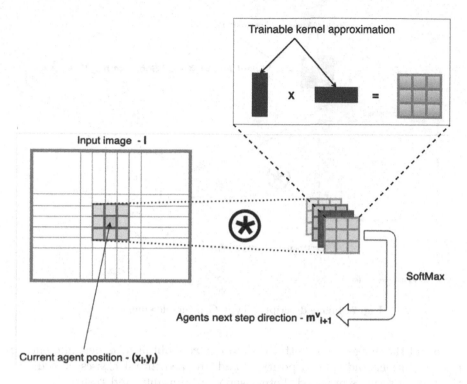

Fig. 6. Image descriptor Type F principles illustration.

horizontal and vertical directions due to the use of the corresponding kernels of Sobel operator. However, the use of this type of descriptor did not allow us to increase the performance of our combined classifier model (Sect. 4).

4   Experiments

4.1   Datasets

We investigated performance of the proposed model and its variations using two datasets. The first Google Street View (GSV) dataset was presented in [12]. It contains snapshots from Google Street View service captured mostly in the U.S. The dataset contains only 357 images roughly uniformly split into four classes.

The second one is Signboard Classification Dataset (SCD) introduced in [16]. It was collected from publicly available sources, namely from Flickr. This dataset contains photos from different authors who made their work available for research purposes. The number of images in the dataset is 1000. The class distribution is uniform. The dataset is publicly available[1].

---

[1] https://github.com/madrugado/signboard-classification-dataset.

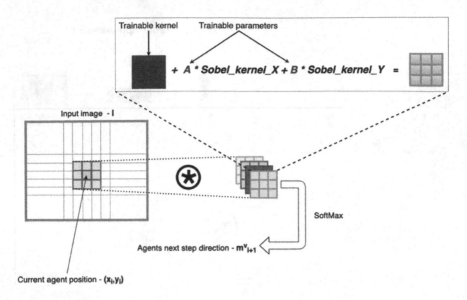

Fig. 7. Image descriptor Type G principles illustration.

All of the images from both the datasets were obtained under different capture conditions and camera positions and grouped into 4 classes according to the type of services provided (hotels, shops, restaurants, and "other").

4.2   Performance Comparison

We used an macro-averaged F_1 as a quality metric in all experiments are given in Table 1. As one can see our proposed image descriptor allows the model to reach new state of the art performance on SCD dataset, while being close to state of the art on GSV one.

4.3   Ablation Study

As a signboard descriptors we investigated intermediate representation of several CNN architectures: VGG [18], Inception [20], ResNet [7], MobileNet [17], EfficientNet [22], DenseNet [8], InceptionResNet [21] in order to achieve the best performance using **image descriptor type D**. We selected these network architectures due to remarkable results demonstrated by them in general images classification problems. We also noticed that combined descriptors allow to obtain better performance in our pipeline. In order to find the best configuration of our model we investigated all of the possible combinations of mentioned CNN encoders. Below we provide top 5 results of an ablation study for our modular architecture with different CNN based signboard descriptors (see Table 2).

We also investigated performance of our combined classifier configured with **image descriptor type E** and different kernel sizes (from 3 to 27). Top 5 results of that ablation study are presented in Table 3.

Table 1. Performance investigation results. **Best** result is given in bold, *second* best – in italic.

Model	Dataset	
	GSV [12]	SCD [16]
Malykh & Samarin, 2019 [12]	0.24	0.47
ours with descriptor type A	0.38	0.59
ours with descriptor type B	0.35	*0.63*
ours with descriptor type C	0.27	0.51
ours with descriptor type D	*0.40*	0.62
ours with descriptor type E	**0.55**	**0.76**
ours with descriptor type F	0.31	0.44
ours with descriptor type G	0.47	0.60

Table 2. F-measure for our system configured with different CNN-based signboard descriptors (**image descriptor type D**) (top-5 results) on SCD dataset.

CNN based signboard descriptor type	F_1 score
EfficientNet B4 + EfficientNet B2	0.57
EfficientNet B4 + InceptionResNet	0.59
EfficientNet B4 + EfficientNet B3	0.60
EfficientNet B3 + InceptionResNet	0.60
EfficientNet B2 + EfficientNet B3	**0.62**

Table 3. F-measure for our system configured with **image descriptor type E** and different kernel sizes - **d** (top-5 results) on SCD dataset.

d	F_1 **score**
11	0.7
19	0.71
17	0.71
13	0.75
15	**0.76**

Table 4. F-measure for our system configured with **image descriptor type F** and different length of trainable parameter vectors (**d**) on SCD GSV datasets.

d	GSV [12]	SCD [16]
3	0.21	0.28
5	0.21	0.29
7	0.20	0.29
9	0.22	0.29
11	0.23	0.34
19	0.25	0.33
17	0.23	0.37
13	0.26	0.40
15	0.27	0.39
17	0.31	0.42
19	0.31	**0.44**
21	0.32	0.44
23	0.35	0.44
25	0.35	0.43
27	0.36	0.42
29	0.34	0.43
31	0.35	0.42
33	0.36	0.41
35	0.36	0.41
37	**0.37**	0.40
39	0.30	0.36
41	0.32	0.36
43	0.32	0.35
45	0.32	0.30
47	0.32	0.28
49	0.31	0.23
51	0.29	0.20
53	0.29	0.21

We were unable to achieve the expected performance metrics from the **image descriptor type F** as part of our combined classification model. A detailed analysis of the hyperparameters (lengths of trainable vectors) of this type of descriptor was carried out. The results of this study are shown in Table 4.

Below we present the results of a study of the effectiveness of using **image descriptor type G** with different kernel sizes (from 3 to 27) as part of our combined classifier. Top 5 results of that ablation study are presented in Table 5.

Table 5. F-measure for our system configured with **image descriptor type G** and different kernel sizes - d (top-5 results) on SCD dataset.

d	F_1 score
7	0.54
13	0.55
9	0.57
15	0.53
11	**0.60**

5 Conclusion

In the article, we provide a detailed description and comparative analysis of all specialized descriptors types that were used within the combined classification model in comparison with general visual descriptors and textual embeddings. Also we introduced two new types of special trainable descriptors (pure CNN based and trainable agents movement strategy based). We used an experimental environment that is based on two specialized datasets, namely GSV and SCD. The performance of newly proposed types of descriptors as a part of a combined classifier demonstrated the state of the art performance (0.55 and 0.76 in $F_1 score$ on GSV and SCD datasets respectively). According to obtained results, further research could be focused on the study of new descriptors in order to further improve achieved results.

References

1. Ballan, L., Bertini, M., Bimbo, A.D., Jain, A.: Automatic trademark detection and recognition in sport videos. In: 2008 IEEE International Conference on Multimedia and Expo, pp. 901–904, June 2008. https://doi.org/10.1109/ICME.2008.4607581
2. Chacra, D.A., Zelek, J.: Road segmentation in street view images using texture information. In: 2016 13th Conference on Computer and Robot Vision (CRV), pp. 424–431, June 2016. https://doi.org/10.1109/CRV.2016.47
3. Chattopadhyay, T., Sinha, A.: Recognition of trademarks from sports videos for channel hyperlinking in consumer end. In: 2009 IEEE 13th International Symposium on Consumer Electronics, pp. 943–947, May 2009. https://doi.org/10.1109/ISCE.2009.5156881
4. Clavelli, A., Karatzas, D.: Text segmentation in colour posters from the Spanish civil war era. In: 2009 10th International Conference on Document Analysis and Recognition, pp. 181–185, July 2009. https://doi.org/10.1109/ICDAR.2009.32
5. Deng, J., Dong, W., Socher, R., Li, L., Li, K., Fei-Fei, L.: ImageNet: a large-scale hierarchical image database. In: 2009 IEEE Conference on Computer Vision and Pattern Recognition, pp. 248–255, June 2009. https://doi.org/10.1109/CVPR.2009.5206848
6. Howard, A.G., et al.: MobileNets: efficient convolutional neural networks for mobile vision applications (2017)

7. He, K., Zhang, X., Ren, S., Sun, J.: Deep residual learning for image recognition. In: 2016 IEEE Conference on Computer Vision and Pattern Recognition (CVPR), pp. 770–778, June 2016. https://doi.org/10.1109/CVPR.2016.90
8. Huang, G., Liu, Z., Van Der Maaten, L., Weinberger, K.Q.: Densely connected convolutional networks. In: 2017 IEEE Conference on Computer Vision and Pattern Recognition (CVPR), pp. 2261–2269 (2017)
9. Intasuwan, T., Kaewthong, J., Vittayakorn, S.: Text and object detection on billboards. In: 2018 10th International Conference on Information Technology and Electrical Engineering (ICITEE), pp. 6–11, July 2018. https://doi.org/10.1109/ICITEED.2018.8534879
10. Lin, T.-Y., et al.: Microsoft COCO: common objects in context. In: Fleet, D., Pajdla, T., Schiele, B., Tuytelaars, T. (eds.) ECCV 2014. LNCS, vol. 8693, pp. 740–755. Springer, Cham (2014). https://doi.org/10.1007/978-3-319-10602-1_48
11. Liu, T., Fang, S., Zhao, Y., Wang, P., Zhang, J.: Implementation of training convolutional neural networks. CoRR abs/1506.01195 (2015)
12. Malykh, V., Samarin, A.: Combined advertising sign classifier. In: van der Aalst, W.M.P., et al. (eds.) AIST 2019. LNCS, vol. 11832, pp. 179–185. Springer, Cham (2019). https://doi.org/10.1007/978-3-030-37334-4_16
13. Romberg, S., Pueyo, L.G., Lienhart, R., van Zwol, R.: Scalable logo recognition in real-world images. In: Proceedings of the 1st ACM International Conference on Multimedia Retrieval, ICMR 2011, pp. 25:1–25:8. ACM, New York, NY, USA (2011). http://doi.acm.org/10.1145/1991996.1992021. http://www.multimedia-computing.de/flickrlogos/
14. Samarin, A., Malykh, V.: Worm-like image descriptor for signboard classification. In: Proceedings of The Fifth Conference on Software Engineering and Information Management (SEIM-2020) (2020)
15. Samarin, A., Malykh, V.: Ensemble-based commercial buildings facades photographs classifier. In: van der Aalst, W.M.P., et al. (eds.) AIST 2020. LNCS, vol. 12602, pp. 257–265. Springer, Cham (2021). https://doi.org/10.1007/978-3-030-72610-2_19
16. Samarin, A., Malykh, V., Muravyov, S.: Specialized image descriptors for signboard photographs classification. In: Robal, T., Haav, H.-M., Penjam, J., Matulevičius, R. (eds.) DB&IS 2020. CCIS, vol. 1243, pp. 122–129. Springer, Cham (2020). https://doi.org/10.1007/978-3-030-57672-1_10
17. Sandler, M., Howard, A., Zhu, M., Zhmoginov, A., Chen, L.: MobileNetV2: inverted residuals and linear bottlenecks. In: 2018 IEEE/CVF Conference on Computer Vision and Pattern Recognition, pp. 4510–4520 (2018)
18. Simonyan, K., Zisserman, A.: Very deep convolutional networks for large-scale image recognition. CoRR abs/1409.1556 (2014)
19. Smith, R.: An overview of the tesseract OCR engine. In: Ninth International Conference on Document Analysis and Recognition (ICDAR 2007), vol. 2, pp. 629–633, September 2007. https://doi.org/10.1109/ICDAR.2007.4376991
20. Szegedy, C., et al.: Going deeper with convolutions. In: 2015 IEEE Conference on Computer Vision and Pattern Recognition (CVPR), pp. 1–9, June 2015. https://doi.org/10.1109/CVPR.2015.7298594
21. Szegedy, C., Ioffe, S., Vanhoucke, V., Alemi, A.: Inception-v4, inception-ResNet and the impact of residual connections on learning. In: AAAI Conference on Artificial Intelligence (2016)
22. Tan, M., Le, Q.: EfficientNet: rethinking model scaling for convolutional neural networks. In: International Conference on Machine Learning, pp. 6105–6114. PMLR (2019)

23. Tian, Z., Huang, W., He, T., He, P., Qiao, Yu.: Detecting text in natural image with connectionist text proposal network. In: Leibe, B., Matas, J., Sebe, N., Welling, M. (eds.) ECCV 2016. LNCS, vol. 9912, pp. 56–72. Springer, Cham (2016). https://doi.org/10.1007/978-3-319-46484-8_4
24. Tsai, T., Cheng, W., You, C., Hu, M., Tsui, A.W., Chi, H.: Learning and recognition of on-premise signs from weakly labeled street view images. IEEE Trans. Image Process. **23**(3), 1047–1059 (2014). https://doi.org/10.1109/TIP.2014.2298982
25. Watve, A., Sural, S.: Soccer video processing for the detection of advertisement billboards. Pattern Recogn. Lett. **29**(7), 994–1006 (2008). https://doi.org/10.1016/j.patrec.2008.01.022
26. Zhou, J., McGuinness, K., O'Connor, N.E.: A text recognition and retrieval system for e-business image management. In: Schoeffmann, K., et al. (eds.) MMM 2018. LNCS, vol. 10705, pp. 23–35. Springer, Cham (2018). https://doi.org/10.1007/978-3-319-73600-6_3
27. Zhou, X., et al.: East: an efficient and accurate scene text detector. In: 2017 IEEE Conference on Computer Vision and Pattern Recognition (CVPR), pp. 2642–2651, July 2017. https://doi.org/10.1109/CVPR.2017.283

Single Image Inpainting Method Using Wasserstein Generative Adversarial Networks and Self-attention

Yuanxin Mao[1], Tianzhuang Zhang[1], Bo Fu[1], and Dang N. H. Thanh[2(✉)]

[1] School of Computer and Information Technology, Liaoning Normal University, Dalian 116081, China
[2] College of Technology and Design, University of Economics Ho Chi Minh City, Ho Chi Minh City, Vietnam
thanhdnh@ueh.edu.vn

Abstract. Due to various factors, some parts of images can be lost. Recovering the damaged regions of images is essential. In this paper, a single image inpainting method using Wasserstein Generative Adversarial Networks (WGAN) and self-attention is proposed. The global consistency of the inpainting region is established and the Wasserstein distance is used to measure the similarity of the two distributions. Finally, self-attention is embedded to exploit the self-similarity of local features. The experiments confirm that the proposed method can recover the global correlation of corrupted images better than similar methods.

Keywords: Image Inpainting · Generative Adversarial Networks · Wasserstein distance · Kullback–Leibler divergence · Jensen–Shannon divergence

1 Introduction

In image processing and analysis, the image inpainting problem has many important applications in practice. It can be used for image reconstruction, object elimination, image expansion, image denoising, image dehazing, image deblurring, image super-resolution, and style transfer. Basically, image inpainting is to fill in the missing areas of an image or generate a complete image by using the information of the undamaged areas of the image. Image inpainting techniques can be extended for the image extension (also known as image outpainting).

In recent years, with the development of the convolution neural networks (CNN), image inpainting methods use a large amount of training data to optimize the parameters of the network. However, CNN-based methods do not perform well in understanding global structure or supporting multivariate completion due to some inherent properties, e.g., local induction priors, and no consideration of feature continuity.

Generative Adversarial Network (GAN) is a generative model with the generator (G), and the discriminator (D). The inpainting result data obtained by the generative network will become more and more perfect, approaching the real data. The desired data can be generated. However, the GAN-based inpainting method also has some limitations. First of all, its training procedure is difficult. For some data, it is impossible to make the generator learn in the correct direction. In addition, the image inpainting performance of the GAN-based methods mainly depends on the generator part of GAN implemented by CNN, so the GAN-based methods also face the drawback of the CNN-based methods: misunderstanding the global structure.

In response to the above drawbacks, we propose the self-attention-based WGAN for image inpainting. We use Convolutional Block Attention Module (CBAM) as the self-attention module. For conducting experiments, we use the Place2 dataset.

2 Related Works

2.1 Image Inpainting

Approaches for image inpainting can be divided into traditional methods and deep-learning-based methods. For traditional approaches, there are some notable works. The image extension-based methods try to extend the texture of the valid parts to corrupted parts. Bertalmio et al. proposed the BSCB (Bertalmio-Sapiro-Casells-Ballester) algorithm [2]. Then, Bertalmio et al. proposed an optimized BSCB algorithm [4] focused on improving the propagation rate. However, this algorithm is mainly aimed at narrow or small missing areas. The patching-based image inpainting methods focus on maintaining the image structure such as texture and edges. Efros et al. proposed a texture synthesis repair algorithm [9]. Then, this algorithm was improved by Efros et al. [8]. They divided the effective areas of an image into many independent small blocks and process the missing areas on these blocks. A sample-based image inpainting model was proposed by Criminisi et al. [6]. Holding a similar idea, Bames et al. proposed the PatchMatch algorithm [3], which uses the fast nearest-neighbor field algorithm to perform matching calculations based on the continuity of the images, reducing the range of similarity calculations, thereby coming out with improved efficiency.

Deep learning-based methods not only utilize the shallow texture information of the image but also utilize the deep semantic features of an image [13]. Pathak proposed the Context Encoder method based on GAN [24], using the encoder-decoder structure with reconstruction loss. Iizuka et al. proposed local and global discriminators [16] to ensure the consistency of image local and image global, and used dilated convolution to improve the receptive field, resulting in higher resolution results. Yang et al. used a pre-trained VGG model based on the encoder-decoder structure to improve the final output result [30], but the model is computationally expensive. The Contextual Attention (CA) model adopts a two-stage encoder-decoder network from rough to detail. The first stage gets rough repair results, and the second stage strengthens the network to perform texture matching through an attention module. However, these methods are mainly aimed at the rectangular missing areas, and the filling in irregular shapes cannot achieve the desired effect. Liu et al. proposed a special convolution layer called Partial Convolution [20], which updates the mask in each layer of convolution operation to limit the weight, reduce the influence of the shape of the masks, and force the convolution process to pay more attention to the effective parts. Therefore, Partial Convolution improved the image inpainting performance for various shapes of missing parts. Yu et al. adopted

Gated Convolution [31] to automatically learn the distribution of the masks, which further improved the inpainting effect. The Edge Connect model of Nazeri et al. adopts a two-stage structure [16]: repair the edge information of the image, and then the edge information is used to repair the image. The Edge Connect model also reduces the blurry details. However, the above methods do not perform well with large missing areas. To deal with this issue, Jingyuan Li et al. proposed a recursive feature inference model [19]. However, the model still cannot solve the issue of the complicated structure.

2.2 Generative Adversarial Network

Comparing with supervised learning, the accuracy rate of unsupervised learning is often lower. Therefore, it is necessary to improve the performance of unsupervised learning and reduce the dependence on supervised learning. Generative adversarial networks (GAN) [10] are a key direction to improving the performance of unsupervised learning. Structure of GAN is presented in Fig. 1.

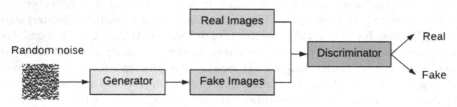

Fig. 1. GAN's network Structure

GAN is a new framework for estimating generative models through an adversarial process. Radford and Metz improved GAN and proposed DCGAN [25]. DCGAN uses the convolution layer instead of the fully connected layer, and uses the convolution with stride instead of upsampling to better extract image features. The discriminator and the generator exist symmetrically, which greatly improves the stability of the GAN training and the generation results. Arjovsky et al. proposed Wasserstein GAN (WGAN) [1]. WGAN mainly improves GAN from the perspective of the loss function. Gulrajani et al. [11] proposed WGAN-GP based on WGAN. WGAN-GP is slightly better than WGAN in terms of training speed and quality of generated samples.

2.3 Attention Mechanism

The human visual system employs attention to effectively comprehend complicated scenes [12] and is prone to pay more attention to vital regions while ignoring unnecessary ones. Attention processes have aided a variety of visual tasks, including image classification [14, 15, 32], objection detection [5, 18, 21], and few-shot learning. Self-attention is now the mainstream due to its ease of implementation and reusability, except for early works on forecasting attention using RNN [22] or sub-networks [17].

Self-attention was initially introduced in the field of natural language processing (NLP) [26], and it has made major contributions. Wang et al. quickly draw attention [27]. According to the different domains involved, self-attention can be divided into four categories: channel attention, spatial attention, temporal attention, and mixed attention.

SENet with SE-block was proposed by Hu et al. [15], to adaptively recalibrate channel-wise feature responses by explicitly modeling channel interdependencies. Woo et al. [29] offer the convolutional block attention module (CBAM) to enhance informative channels as well as critical regions by stacking channel and spatial attention. ViT was first developed by Dosovitskiy et al. [7], who proved the enormous potential for transformer-based models. ViT is a pure attention-based model that delivers better outcomes than CNN by stacking several multi-head attention layers with fully connected layers.

3 Method

There are two main approaches to current deep learning based image restoration:

(1) Train a deep regression network (GAN, VAE - Variational Autoencoder) in the form of a codec using the original and masked images, and tune the parameters using adversarial training.
(2) Mapping an implicit prior (Latent Prior) onto the original image by a generative model, and then reconstructing the image by selecting the best matching prior during the forward derivation.

The second approach is difficult to find a suitable implicit prior, so this paper focuses on image restoration based on the first approach. It mostly uses generative adversarial networks for image generation, using coding and decoding for feature extraction and upsampling of images, while the multi-layer feature discriminator and jump connection modules are also helpful for generating more realistic images in order to obtain information about each feature level of the images. Meanwhile, the perception module can obtain effective contextual semantic information, which not only allows the network model to learn the feature information of the image, but also relates the image context for restoration. For the image restoration results, reasonable extraction of multi-scale features will play a very effective role; therefore, reasonable setting of the network multi-scale extraction feature structure has significantly improved the results. In addition, the focus varies for different restoration tasks. For the image extension task, because of the area to be restored at larger edges, the image features utilized in the convolution process are not sufficient, which often leads to confusion and strong non-consistency in the results, therefore, improving the perceptual field, is the focus of image extension. Also, the additional setting of different loss functions to reduce the confusion and chromatic aberration improves the texture richness.

3.1 Model Framework

Since the original Context-Encoder model has a low performance for image inpainting, we will add a convolutional self-attention module to the Context-Encoder model. In the original network model, due to the existence of GAN, the model is prone to gradient disappearance and mode collapse during training. To solve the issue, we will utilize WGAN and CBAM [5]. CBAM is used for better image restoration.

The network structure context encoder in this paper is improved based on the generator and the discriminator. The generator consists of two parts: encoding and decoding. The encoding stage uses an encoder composed of a convolutional network to extract the features of an image, and then the extracted features are input into the decoder to generate the missing parts of the image. The discriminator compares the image generated by the generator with the real image to determine whether the generated image is real or fake. The training process of the overall network: first, fix the generator to train the discriminator and then input the corrupted image to the generator to generate the missing parts of the image, and then input the generated image and the corrupted image to the discriminator to train. Next, fix the discriminator after training to train the generator, and the occluded image is input to the generator. The generator extracts the features through the encoder and then generates the missing parts through the decoder.

CBAM structured is presented in Fig. 2, is a simple and effective attention module that contains two submodules, the Channel Attention Module and the Spatial Attention Module. CBAM module multiplies the feature maps generated by the convolutional neural network with the attention maps generated by the Channel Attention Module and the Spatial Attention Module and performs optimization. CBAM has a low overhead in practical applications, so it can be applied to any CNN framework.

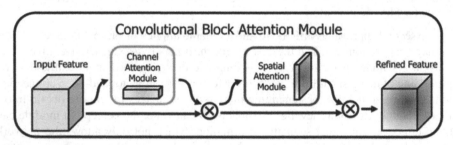

Fig. 2. The structure of CBAM module

Channel Attention Module (Fig. 3) is to compress the features generated by convolutional neural in spatial dimension. The compression of the channel attention is Average Pooling plus Max Pooling. Average Pooling and Max Pooling collect spatial information of the feature map, and then the collected information is passed through a specific network to compress the spatial dimension of the input feature map, and then summed and merged element by element to produce a channel attention map. When performing gradient backpropagation computation, Average Pooling provides feedback for each pixel point on the feature map, while Max Pooling provides gradient feedback only for the most responsive points in the feature map.

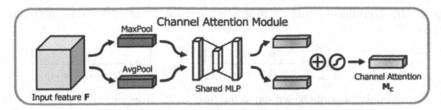

Fig. 3. The structure of channel attention module

The Spatial Attention Module (Fig. 4) compresses the channels by pooling the mean and maximum values of the channel dimensions, MaxPooling extracts the maximum values in the channels by multiplying the height by the width, and AvgPooling extracts the mean values in the channels by multiplying the height by the width. Then, the previously extracted feature maps (both with channel number 1) are combined to obtain a two-channel feature map.

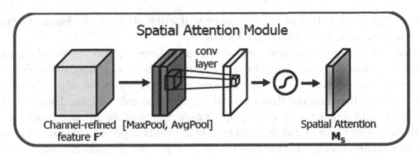

Fig. 4. The structure of Spatial attention module

In the process of training GAN, a phenomenon often occurs: when the discriminator is trained effectively, the performance of the generator is difficult to improve. The reason for this phenomenon is the defect of the basic theory of GAN. The earliest form of the objective function of GAN is as follows:

$$\min_{\theta_g} \max_{\theta_d} E_{x \sim p_{data}}\big[\log D_{\theta_d}(x)\big] + E_{z \sim p(z)}\big[\log\big(1 - D_{\theta_d}\big(G_{\theta_g}(z)\big)\big)\big], \qquad (1)$$

where x is real data, y is fake data, z is noisy data, θ_d is the parameters of the discriminator D, θ_g is the parameters of the generator G, p_z is the probability distribution of z, p_{data} is the probability distribution of x.

It shows that when we fix the generator, the optimal discriminator is:

$$D_G^*(x) = \frac{p_{data}(x)}{p_{data}(x) + p_g(x)}, \qquad (2)$$

where p_g is the probability distribution of generated data. But when the discriminator is optimal, the optimization objective of the generator becomes:

$$C(G) = \max_D V(G, D),$$

where $V(G, D)$ is the objective function of a generator G and a discriminator D, and we obtain:

$$C(G) = E_{x \sim p_{data}}\left[\log \frac{p_{data}(x)}{p_{data}(x) + p_g(x)}\right] + E_{x \sim p_g}\left[\log \frac{p_g(x)}{p_{data}(x) + p_g(x)}\right] \quad (3)$$

The above formula can be written in the form of JS divergence:

$$W(p_r, p_g) = \inf_{y \sim \prod(p_r, p_z)} E_{(x,y)-y}\left[\|x - y\|_2\right], \quad (4)$$

where p_r is the probability distribution of real samples, $\prod(p_r, p_z)$ is the set of all possible joint distributions of both p_r, p_z.

It can also be said that when we train the discriminator effectively, the training goal of the entire GAN becomes the JS divergence between real data and synthetic data:

$$W(p_r, p_g) = \inf_{y \sim \prod(p_r, p_g)} E_{(x,y)-y}\left[x - y_2\right]. \quad (5)$$

The objective function of JS divergence will bring about the problem of gradient disappearance. It will be difficult to train GANs.

Based on the above problems, the Wasserstein distance, also known as the Earth-Mover (EM) distance, emerged. For the two distributions of p_r and p_g, their joint distribution set is expressed as $\prod(p_r, p_g)$. Any joint distribution γ in the set can be sampled from $(x, y) - y$ to obtain real data x and fake data y, and calculate the distance of their distribution, and then we can get the sample's expectation of the distance under the joint distribution. The lower bound that can be taken on this expected value in all possible joint distributions is defined as the Wasserstein distance. Wasserstein distance represents the minimum cost of transferring between two distributions. Compared with JS and KL divergence, Wasserstein distance can reflect their distance even if overlap does not occur between two distributions. Wasserstein GAN is optimized with an objective function. Since the EM distance is difficult to solve directly, the problem is transformed into:

$$W(p_r, p_\theta) = \sup_{\|f\|_L \leq 1} E_{x \sim p_\theta}\left[f(x)\right], \quad (6)$$

where p_θ is probability distribution of generated data.

It takes the upper bound for functions f satisfying the l-$Lipschitz$ restriction on $E_{x \sim p_r}\left[f(x)\right] - E_{x \sim p_\theta}\left[f(x)\right]$. Among them, the Lipschitz limit specifies the maximum local variation of a continuous function, and K-$Lipschitz$ is $|f(x_1) - f(x_2)| \leq K|x_1 - x_2|$. After satisfying the l-$Lipschitz$ limit, optimize the neural network parameters to solve:

$$\max_{\omega \in W} E_{x \sim p_t}\left[f_\omega(x)\right] - E_{z \sim f(z)}\left[f_\omega(g_\theta(z))\right], \quad (7)$$

where g_θ is data generated from the generator, $f_\omega(x)$ is the parameter to be optimized by the evaluator.

The discriminator has also been changed and has been given a new name, Critic. Critic has abandoned the last layer of sigmoid, and no longer outputs the probability like the discriminator, but instead outputs the score in the general sense. The objective

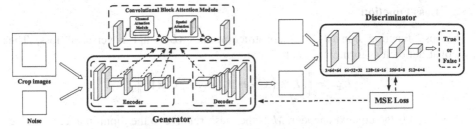

Fig. 5. The Overall framework of the Self-Attention based WGAN

function of Critic has also changed, as shown in Eq. (7). At the same time, after each update, the parameters must be truncated to a certain range, that is, weight clipping, to ensure the Lipschitz limit. The better the Critic is trained, the easier the generator is to improve, overcoming the vanishing gradient of the original GAN. The training of the whole network is further stabilized, and the problems of vanishing gradient and mode collapse are solved.

Table 1. Parameters of the Generator

	Kernel	Strides	Padding	Activate
Conv (1, 2, 3, 4, 5)	4	2	1	LeakyReLU
Conve6	4	0	0	LeakyReLU
Conve7	4	1	0	ReLU
Convenience (8, 9, 10, 11)	4	2	1	ReLu

The network model of the generator is shown in Fig. 5 (the left side). It consists of an encoder and a decoder. The encoder consists of five convolutional layers plus three convolutional attention modules. The convolutional attention module is in the second, third, and four. After four convolutional layers, the encoder pays more attention to the features of the incomplete image when extracting features. Hence, the generated image is closer to the real image. The decoder part is five successive upsampling layers using ReLu as an activation function, i.e., a series of upsampling and non-linear weighted upsampling including features produced by the encoder until we roughly reach the original target size.

The convolutional layer of the generator part uses a convolution kernel size of 4, each sliding step size is 2, and the activation function uses the LeakyReLU function. Its specific parameters are as in Table 1.

The main function of the discriminator is to judge the authenticity of the image generated by the generator network. The network structure of the discriminator is composed of five consecutive convolutional layers. The convolutional kernel size used in the convolutional layer is 4 × 4 and the sliding step size is 2. The specific network structure of the discriminator is shown in Fig. 5 (the right side).

3.2 Loss Function

The loss function consists of reconstruction loss (L_2) and adversarial loss. The reconstruction loss formular is as follows:

$$L_{rec} = \left\| \hat{M} \otimes \left(x - F\left(\left(1 - \hat{M} \right) \otimes x \right) \right) \right\|_2, \tag{8}$$

where $F(\cdot)$ is the context encoder, $\hat{M}$ is the mask relative to the input image, the value of the missing parts is 1, while the value of the valid parts is 0.

The adversarial loss is calculated through the expected value of the sample pair distance under the joint distribution γ:

$$E(x, y) \sim \gamma \left[\|x - y\| \right]. \tag{9}$$

3.3 Image Evaluation Metrics

Image evaluation metrics are used to assess the strengths and weaknesses of image processing algorithms, as well as to highlight the strengths and weaknesses of algorithms by comparing them with other algorithms. The more evaluation metrics are used by most people, the more convincing the results will be. For image peak signal-to-noise ratio (PSNR) [34] and structural similarity index (SSIM) [34] are the most common evaluation metrics, so we also use peak signal-to-noise ratio (PSNR) and structural similarity index (SSIM) in this paper as the evaluation metrics for image quality in this paper.

4 Experiments

4.1 Datasets and Pre-processing

Places2 is a scene image dataset containing more than 10 million images, more than 400 different types of scene environments, the data will be divided into 8 million images for training, 36 thousand images for validation, and 328 thousand images from 365 scene categories are used for testing, often used for visual cognitive tasks with scene and environment as application content. We selected 10 thousand images cropped to 256 × 256 for experiments. 8 thousand images of them are used for the training set and 2 thousand remaining images are used for the test set.

When feeding data to the network model, 64 missing images are fed into the network model at the same time. All images have the same input size. The network model requires the input size of 256 × 256, the number of dimensions is 3 (RGB color images), and the pixel value range is [0, 1]. For generating the corrupted image, a rectangle with the value of 1 with a size of 64 × 64 was added at the center of the image. It is denoted for the mask M.

4.2   Experiment Details

The proposed model is implemented using PyTorch 1.10.2, all experiments are conducted on a laptop with Nvidia GeForce RTX 1050Ti on Windows 10. We use *Adam Optimizer*, *the learning-rate* is 0.0002, *beta* is 0.5, *eps* is 10^{-8} and *weight-decay* is 0, to optimize the generator, and *RMSprop*, *learning-rate* is 0.01, *alpha* is 0.99, *eps* is 10^{-8}, *weight_decay* is 0, and *momentum* is 0, to optimize the discriminator.

4.3   Experiments

We use PSNR, SSIM to evaluate model performance and objectively evaluate the model effect. Here, we present extensive comparison with several state-of-the-art models: Context-Encoder [24], Edge-Connect [23], GMCNN [28], PICNet [33], and GC [16]. In this paper, 2 thousand images in the test set are used for calculating PSNR and SSIM, and the average results are shown in Table 2. It can be seen that the proposed model achieved the best scores in PSNR and was slightly lower than GMCNN model in SSIM.

Figure 6 present some image inpainting results by the proposed method. As we can see that the proposed method recovers missing regions effectively.

Table 2. PSNR and SSIM Comparison on Places2

	PSNR	SSIM
Context-Encoder	28.05600	0.78604
Edge-Connect	29.8162	0.8339
PICNet	24.96	0.837
GC	23.94	0.849
GMCNN	25.84	**0.8844**
Ours	**30.4232**	0.8626

Fig. 6. Generated Image Comparison on Places2: First column – Corrupted images, Second column – Inpainted results, and Third column – the ground truth

5   Conclusions

In this paper, we have proposed a single image inpainting method using WGAN and self-attention. The proposed model measures the similarity of the two distributions using the Wasserstein distance. When compared to the KL and JS divergences, the Wasserstein distance can still indicate the distance between the two distributions even if the support sets of the two distributions do not overlap or overlap very little, which is beneficial to GAN stability. Experiments showed that the proposed method recover corrupted images impressively.

Funding.   This research was funded by University of Economics Ho Chi Minh City (UEH), Vietnam.

References

1. Arjovsky, M., Chintala, S., Bottou, L.: Wasserstein generative adversarial networks. In: Proceedings of 2017 International Conference on Machine Learning, Sydney (2017)

2. Ballester, C., Bertalmio, M., et al.: Filling-in by joint interpolation of vector fields and gray levels. IEEE Trans. Image Process. **10**(8), 1200–1211 (2001)
3. Barnes, C., Shechtman, E., et al.: PatchMatch: a randomized correspondence algorithm for structural image editing. ACM Trans. Graph. **28**(3), 1–11 (2009)
4. Bertalmio, M., Sapiro, G., et al.: Image inpainting. In: Proceedings of the 27th Annual Conference on Computer Graphics and Interactive Techniques, New Orleans (2000)
5. Carion, N., Massa, F., Synnaeve, G., et al.: End-to-end object detection with transformers. In: Vedaldi, A., Bischof, H., Brox, T., Frahm, J.M. (eds.) Computer Vision – ECCV 2020, vol. 12346, pp. 213–229. Springer, Cham (2020). https://doi.org/10.1007/978-3-030-58452-8_13
6. Criminisi, A., Patrick, P., Kentaro, T.: Region filling and object removal by exemplar-based image inpainting. IEEE Trans. Image Process. **13**(9), 1200–1212 (2004)
7. Dosovitskiy, A., Beyer, L., Kolesnikov, A., et al.: An image is worth 16×16 words: transformers for image recognition at scale (2020). arXiv:2010.11929
8. Efros, A.A., Freeman, W.T.: Image quilting for texture synthesis and transfer. In: Proceedings of the 28th Annual Conference on Computer Graphics and Interactive Techniques, Los Angeles (2001)
9. Efros, A.A., Leung, T.K.: Texture synthesis by non-parametric sampling. In: Proceedings of the Seventh IEEE International Conference on Computer Vision, Corfu (1999)
10. Goodfellow, I., et al.: Generative adversarial nets. In: Advances in Neural Information Processing Systems, vol. 27 (2014)
11. Gulrajani, I., et al.: Improved training of Wasserstein GANS. In: Advances in Neural Information Processing Systems, vol. 30 (2017)
12. Guo, M.H., Xu, T.X., et al.: Attention mechanisms in computer vision: a survey (2021). arXiv: 2111.07624
13. He, K., Zhang, X., Ren, S., et al.: Deep residual learning for image recognition. In: Proceedings of the IEEE Conference on Computer Vision and Pattern Recognition, Las Vegas (2016)
14. Hou, Q., Zhou, D., Feng, J.: Coordinate attention for efficient mobile network design (2021). arXiv:2103.02907
15. Hu, J., Shen, L., Albanie, S., et al.: Squeeze-and-excitation networks (2017). arXiv:1709. 01507
16. Iizuka, S., Simo-Serra, E., Ishikawa, H.: Globally and locally consistent image completion. ACM Trans. Graph. (ToG) **36**(4), 1–14 (2017)
17. Jaderberg, V., Simonyan, K., Zisserman, A., et al.: Spatial transformer networks (2015). arXiv: 1506.02025
18. Kechaou, A., Martinez, M., Haurilet, M., et al.: Detective: an attentive recurrent model for sparse object detection. In: Proceedings of 25th International Conference on Pattern Recognition (ICPR), Milan (2021)
19. Li, J., et al.: Recurrent feature reasoning for image inpainting. In: Proceedings of the 2020 IEEE/CVF Conference on Computer Vision and Pattern Recognition, Washington (2020)
20. Liu, G., Reda, F.A., Shih, K.J., Wang, T.-C., Tao, A., Catanzaro, B.: Image inpainting for irregular holes using partial convolutions. In: Ferrari, V., Hebert, M., Sminchisescu, C., Weiss, Y. (eds.) ECCV 2018. LNCS, vol. 11215, pp. 89–105. Springer, Cham (2018). https://doi. org/10.1007/978-3-030-01252-6_6
21. Mao, J., Niu, M., Bai, H., et al.: Pyramid R-CNN: towards better performance and adaptability for 3D object detection (2021). arXiv:2109.02499
22. Mnih, V., Heess, N., Graves, A., et al.: Recurrent models of visual attention (2014). arXiv: 1406.6247
23. Nazeri, K., Ng, E., Joseph, T., et al.: EdgeConnect: generative image inpainting with adversarial edge learning (2019). arXiv:1901.00212

24. Pathak, D., Krahenbuhl, P., et al.: Context encoders: feature learning by inpainting. In: Proceedings of the 2016 IEEE Conference on Computer Vision and Pattern Recognition, Las Vegas (2016)

25. Radford, A., Metz, L., Chintala, S.: Unsupervised representation learning with deep convolutional generative adversarial networks (2015). arXiv:1511.06434

26. Vaswani, A., Shazeer, N., Parmar, N., et al.: Attention is all you need (2017). arXiv:1706.03762

27. Wang, X., Girshick, R., Gupta, A., et al.: Non-local Neural Networks. In: Proceedings of 2018 IEEE/CVF Conference on Computer Vision and Pattern Recognition, Salt Lake City (2018)

28. Wang, Y., Tao, X., et al.: Image inpainting via generative multi-column convolutional neural networks. In: Proceedings of the 32nd International Conference on Neural Information Processing Systems, Montreal (2018)

29. Woo, S., Park, J., Lee, J.Y., et al.: CBAM: convolutional block attention module (2018). arXiv:1807.06521

30. Yang, C., et al.: High-resolution image inpainting using multi-scale neural patch synthesis. In: Proceedings of the 2017 IEEE Conference on Computer Vision and Pattern Recognition, Washington (2017)

31. Yu, J., et al.: Free-form image inpainting with gated convolution. In: Proceedings of the 2019 IEEE/CVF International Conference on Computer Vision, Seoul (2019)

32. Zhao, H., Jia, J., Koltun, V.: Exploring self-attention for image recognition. In: Proceedings of 2020 IEEE/CVF Conference on Computer Vision and Pattern Recognition (CVPR), Seattle (2020)

33. Zheng, C., Tat-Jen, C., Cai, J.: Pluralistic image completion. In: Proceedings of the 2019 IEEE/CVF Conference on Computer Vision and Pattern Recognition, Long Beach (2019)

34. Thanh, D.N.H., Dvoenko, S.D.: A denoising of biomedical images. Int. Arch. Photogramm. Remote Sens. Spatial Inf. Sci. **XL-5/W6**, 73–78 (2015), https://doi.org/10.5194/isprsarch ives-XL-5-W6-73-2015

International Workshop on Pattern Recognition in Healthcare Analytics (PRHA 2022)

PRHA

International Workshop on Pattern Recognition in Healthcare Analytics was held in conjunction with the 26th International Conference on Pattern Recognition on August 21, 2022. This workshop aimed to present some of the latest developments in pattern recognition for healthcare analytics, an interdisciplinary domain aiming to assist physicians using computational techniques and digital health data. Pattern recognition offers essential tools for various healthcare tasks posing numerous challenges. These challenges inspire the pattern recognition domain to explore new ideas to help solve specific problems in the healthcare domain. The following papers address some healthcare-related challenges and showcase innovative ideas to solve them using pattern recognition techniques.

Healthcare data comes with multiple modalities and types. For instance, an electrocardiogram (ECG) signal is one of the critical discriminators for diagnosing cardiovascular diseases. Therefore, developing predictive models for cardiovascular diagnoses based on ECG datasets is ubiquitous. On the other hand, noisy ECG signals commonly encountered in public and private datasets hinder the accuracy of data-driven models and clinicians' manual examination. Dua *et al.* present a deep learning framework to automatically detect noisy ECG signals for more reliable clinical decision-making in their study titled Automatic Detection of Noisy Electrocardiogram Signals without Explicit Noise Labels. Medical image is another modality facilitating the diagnosis and detection of various diseases. Developing pattern recognition models based on medical images requires large-scale datasets with annotations. However, obtaining such a dataset with proper annotations is not always possible such as annotations for segmentation of medical images with ambiguous boundaries. Felfeliyan *et al.* address this challenge by proposing to train deep learning-based segmentation frameworks with probabilistic labels and a noise-robust loss for MRI scans in their study titled Weakly Supervised Medical Image Segmentation with Soft Labels and Noise Robust Loss. As we can see from these examples, we may pose healthcare tasks as well-known pattern recognition problems such as time series classification and image segmentation. We may directly apply familiar feature extraction techniques in pattern recognition to solve healthcare tasks in such cases. On the other hand, some healthcare problems require innovation in the feature extraction stage when the patient data is not a type commonly tackled in pattern recognition problems. For instance, Kim *et al.* designed a method to extract tremor features that can be used as a biomarker to classify vocal diseases in their Tremor Feature Extraction for Enhanced Interpretability of Vocal Disease Classification study.

As we, the organizing committee of PRHA 2022, present you with these studies, we hope to inspire the researchers in the pattern recognition community to join forces for creative and innovative solutions to healthcare problems that might eventually help improve the life quality of people around the world.

ICPR 2022 PRHA Organizing Committee

Ayşe Başar
Arzucan Özgür
Edward Choi
İnci M. Baytaş

Weakly Supervised Medical Image Segmentation with Soft Labels and Noise Robust Loss

Banafshe Felfeliyan[1,2]([✉]), Abhilash Hareendranathan[3][iD], Gregor Kuntze[2][iD],
Stephanie Wichuk[3], Nils D. Forkert[1][iD], Jacob L. Jaremko[3,4],
and Janet L. Ronsky[1,2,5][iD]

[1] Department of Biomedical Engineering, University of Calgary, Calgary,
AB, Canada
banafshe.felfeliyan@ucalgary.ca
[2] McCaig Institute for Bone and Joint Health University of Calgary, Calgary,
AB, Canada
[3] Department of Radiology and Diagnostic Imaging, University of Alberta,
Edmonton, AB, Canada
[4] Alberta Machine Intelligence Institute (AMII), University of Alberta, Edmonton,
AB, Canada
[5] Mechanical and Manufacturing Engineering, University of Calgary,
Calgary, AB, Canada

Abstract. Recent advances in deep learning algorithms have led to significant benefits for solving many medical image analysis problems. Training deep learning models commonly requires large datasets with expert-labeled annotations. However, acquiring expert-labeled annotation is not only expensive but also is subjective, error-prone, and inter-/intra- observer variability introduces noise to labels. This is particularly a problem when using deep learning models for segmenting medical images due to the ambiguous anatomical boundaries. Image-based medical diagnosis tools using deep learning models trained with incorrect segmentation labels can lead to false diagnoses and treatment suggestions. Multi-rater annotations might be better suited to train deep learning models with small training sets compared to single-rater annotations. The aim of this paper was to develop and evaluate a method to generate probabilistic labels based on multi-rater annotations and anatomical knowledge of the lesion features in MRI and a method to train segmentation models using probabilistic labels using normalized active-passive loss as a "noise-tolerant loss" function. The model was evaluated by comparing it to binary ground truth for 17 knees MRI scans for clinical segmentation and detection of bone marrow lesions (BML). The proposed method successfully improved precision 14, recall 22, and Dice score 8 percent compared to a binary cross-entropy loss function. Overall, the

Jacob L. Jaremko—Supported by a Canada CIFAR AI Chair.
Banafshe Felfeliyan—Supported by an Alberta Innovates Graduate Student Scholarship for Data-Enabled Innovation.

© Springer Nature Switzerland AG 2023
J.-J. Rousseau and B. Kapralos (Eds.): ICPR 2022 Workshops, LNCS 13644, pp. 603–617, 2023.
https://doi.org/10.1007/978-3-031-37742-6_47

results of this work suggest that the proposed normalized active-passive loss using soft labels successfully mitigated the effects of noisy labels.

Keywords: Weak Label · Soft Label · Noise-tolerant Loss · Segmentation

1   Introduction

Automatic or semi-automatic clinical features and biomarker measurements based on deep learning (DL) are useful for longitudinal assessment of medical images. DL-based techniques using Convolutional Neural Networks (CNN) have shown great success in tissue and pathology detection and segmentation [3,26]. The accuracy of deep learning methods is highly dependent on the quality of the training data and corresponding ground truth labels. For sensitive applications like medical image segmentation, it is particularly important to use anatomically accurate labels for training of DL models. However, acquiring "ground truth" (GT) labels in the medical domain can be challenging because pixel-wise labeling is expensive, subjective, and error-prone. Inter-reader variability combined with the presence of ambiguous anatomical boundaries between tissues (*e.g.*, due to partial volume effects) makes labels uncertain [6]. Furthermore, the presence of lesions and pathologies in unexpected locations increases the chance of inattentional blindness [2]. Consequently, medical image datasets are likely to contain sub-optimal, inaccurate and noisy labels [15].

A DL model trained on weak/noisy annotations may have biases and overfit to incorrect annotations [36]. Therefore, different approaches have been investigated to reduce the effects of noise and imperfect labels in medical image analysis, including label smoothing and label correction [11,29]. Despite the efforts to develop noise-resistant learning approaches, many aspects have remained unexplored, particularly for medical image segmentation tasks. Therefore, for medical image segmentation task, there is a high demand for robust and reliable methods for training DL models based on noisy and suboptimal labels (*e.g.*, annotations that are not pixel-wise or partial labels).

In this work, we proposed to train an instance segmentation model with soft labels obtained from noisy/partial region of interest (ROI) labels using a noise resistance loss function. We assume that partial ROI labels as highly noisy labels and attempt to perform weakly supervised instance segmentation under this assumption. Our key contributions are:

1. Exploration of training of an improved version of MaskRCNN [3] using probabilistic partial labels.
2. Creation of probabilistic labels based on multi-rater scoring, MRI spatial redundancy, and tissue/lesion characteristics, as well as considering image contextual information.
3. Proposal of combining a noise-tolerant loss function (active passive loss) and soft ground truth for training DL models.

As a practical application, we focus on bone marrow lesion (BML) detection and segmentation, which is one of the inflammatory components of osteoarthritis (OA). Accurate quantification of features related to OA inflammation can provide a basis for effective clinical management and a target for therapy [13]. This task is challenging as BMLs do not have distinctive edges and it is challenging to create binary labels. Furthermore, it is hard to generate precise clean annotations for BMLs, since they may appear in multiple locations, and humans are susceptible to inattentional blindness (missing BMLs in plain sight) [2].

2   Related Work

2.1   Learning with Noisy Labels

To mitigate the effect of noisy labels, different approaches like label correction, noise-robust loss, robust regularization, and loss correction have been deployed, which are briefly described in the following.

Label Correction. Label correction aims to improve the quality of raw labels. Different methods have been proposed to estimate label noise distribution, correct corrupted labels [35], or separate the noise from the data using properties of learned representations [19,21]. Even though the label correction methods are effective, they usually require additional precise annotated data or an expensive process of noise detection and correction [10,23].

Noise-Robust Loss. One approach for noise-robust learning is using loss functions that are inherently noise-tolerant or losses that created by using regularization terms or modifying well-known loss functions to make them noise-tolerant.

Ghosh et al. theoretically proved that symmetric losses perform significantly better in case of learning with noisy labels [4]. The Mean Absolute Error (MAE) loss is symmetric and noise-tolerant for uniform noise and class-conditional label noise and satisfies the symmetry condition. In contrast to that, cross-entropy (CE) is not symmetric and does not perform well in the presence of noise [4]. Therefore, training with CE in addition to complementary losses robust to noise to achieve learning sufficiency and robustness has been suggested [32,33]. Wang et al. demonstrated that the Reverse Cross-Entropy (RCE) [4] loss, which is robust to label noise, can be used as the complementary robust loss term [33]. They proposed the so-called Symmetric Cross-Entropy (SCE) loss, which is defined as $l_{SCE} = \alpha l_{ce} + \beta l_{Rrce}$, where l_{ce} is the CE loss and l_{Rrce} is the RCE loss. Using the SCE idea, Ma et al. recently addressed the learning under label noise by characterizing existing loss functions into two types Active vs. Passive [23]. Based on their characterization the active loss is a loss that maximizes $p(k = y|x)$ and the passive loss is a loss that minimizes $p(k \neq y|x)$. Then they proposed the Active and Passive Loss (APL), which combines an active loss and a passive loss in order to maximize the probability of belonging to a given class and minimize the likelihood of belonging to another class [23]. The APL loss was shown to be noise-tolerant if both active loss and passive loss have been chosen from noise-tolerant losses [23]. In the same work, Ma et al. proved that any loss can be noise-tolerant if normalization is applied to it [23]. Their results showed that APL addresses the underfitting problem and can leverage both robustness and convergence advantages.

Robust Regularization. Regularization methods have been widely used to increase robustness of deep learning models against label noise by preventing overfitting. These methods perform well in the presence of moderate noise, and are mostly used in combination with other techniques [28]. Different regularization techniques include explicit regularization like weight decay and dropout or implicit regularization like label smoothing.

Loss Correction. Most of loss correction methods estimate noise-transition matrices to adjust the labels during training. These techniques aim to minimize global risk with respect to the probability distribution. The backward and forward correction involves modifying two losses based on the noise transition matrix [25]. Some loss correction methods assume the availability of trusted data with clean labels for validation and to estimate the matrix of corruption probabilities [9] or they may require complex modifications to the training process.

Recently, Lukasik et al. [22] have shown that label smoothing is related to loss-correction techniques and is effective in coping with label noise by assuming smoothing as a form of shrinkage regularization. To mitigate noise, Label smoothing may require a simple modification to the training process and does not require additional labels and offers loss correction benefits.

2.2 Label Smoothing and Soft Labels

Traditionally, the label (y) of each pixel is encoded binary (or as a one-hot vector). In binary labeling, one instance belongs to either one or the other class. This hard labeling assigns all probability mass to one class, resulting in large differences between the largest logit and the rest of the logits in networks using the sigmoid (or soft-max) activation function in the output layer [31]. Consequently, in applications such as medical imaging, in case of partial volume effects or disagreement between readers, hard labels may cause overfitting and reduce the adaptability of the network in these situations [31]. In contrast, soft labels encode the label of each instance as a real value probability, whose k-th entry represents $p(Y = k|X = x) \in [0, 1]$. For example, the soft label $x1 = [0.3, 0.7]$ indicates that $p(Y = 1|X = x_i) = 0.7$, whereas hard labels only have 0/1 values. Soft labels can provide additional information to the learning algorithm, which was shown to reduce the number of instances required to train a model [31].

Label smoothing techniques can be considered as utilization of probabilistic labels (soft labels). These approaches have been shown to give a better generalization, faster learning speed, better calibration, and mitigation of network over-confidence [24]. Label smoothing has been deployed and examined in different applications including image classification [31], model network uncertainty [27], and recognition [30]. Probabilistic labels have been used to mitigate reader variability and human assessment noise for classification problems [34].

While methods based on uniform label smoothing techniques may improve the network calibration, they do not necessarily improve classification accuracy. As a solution, Vega et al. proposed to compute probabilistic labels from relevant features$(Z(X))$ in the raw images (X) for a classification task [31]. In that work, a method is trained to estimate $p(Y|Z(X))$, which is used as a probabilistic labels' classification task. This probabilistic labeling approach was shown to provide better calibration and improved classification accuracy than uniform label smoothing.

Soft Labels for Medical Image Segmentation. Smoothing labels and probabilistic labels have only been investigated recently in segmentation tasks. This is because earlier developed methods of label smoothing were originally proposed for image classification, in which the hard labels were flattened by assigning a uniform distribution overall to all classes to prevent model overconfidence. However, this is likely problematic in segmentation tasks, since this approach assigns a probability greater than zero to pixels, even those that one can be confident about not belonging to a certain class (*e.g.*, background outside the body).

Islam et al. addressed this problem by proposing a Spatially Varying Label Smoothing (SVLS) to capture expert annotation uncertainty [11]. SVLS considers the likelihood with neighboring pixels for determining the probability of each class. Li et al. proposed super-pixel label softening to encounter descriptive contextual information for soft labeling. Using super-pixel soft labels and KL (Kullback-Leibler divergence) loss improved Dice coefficient and volumetric similarity [20].

The high uncertainty in defining lesion borders was investigated by Kats et al. who developed a model that uses soft labels (generated by morphological dilation of binary labels) with the soft-Dice loss to segment multiple-sclerosis lesions in MRI data to account for the high uncertainty in defining lesion borders [16]. However, further analysis revealed that the soft-Dice may introduce a volumetric bias for tasks with high inherent uncertainty [1]. Gross et al. used soft labels obtained through data augmentation for the segmentation task [6]. They assumed that using soft labels is analogous to a regression problem, and they used the NormReLU activation and a regression loss function for medical image segmentation [6]. However, using NormReLU as the last layer has two main drawbacks. First, it is not highly effective when the maximum is an outlier. Second, it only uses one image to normalize ReLU, which may cause the algorithm to not converge to a good solution since a single image may not be a good representation of the entire data set distributions.

In some studies, soft labels were generated by fusing multiple manual annotations. One of the best methods to obtain a consensus mask from multi-reader annotation is the Therefore, Kats et al. proposed a soft version of the STAPLE algorithm [17], which showed superior results compared to morphological dilation used in the aforementioned soft Dice loss approach [16].

3   Method

Ma et al. [23] and Lukasik et al. [22] showed that a normalized loss function and label smoothing are both effective ways to mitigate noise effects. In this paper, we are investigating whether the combination of label smoothing, and a normalized loss function leads to quantitative benefits.

3.1   Problem Formulation

The aim of supervised learning for classification problems is to learn the function $f(x; \theta)$. This function maps the input x to the output y using a deep neural network parametrized by θ. f approximates the underlying conditional distribution $p(y|x; \theta)$ to minimize the loss function. We can define a strongly labeled dataset with correct annotation as $D_S = \{(x, y_S)_m\}_{1 \leq m \leq |D|}$, where $y_S \in 0, 1$. In addition, the weakly soft labeled set (noisy labeled) can be defined as $D_W = \{(x, \bar{y})_n\}_{1 \leq n \leq |D|}$, $\bar{y} \in [0, 1]$, where $x^{(i)} \in \Re^{n_x}$ denotes input MRI image (feature space), $y_s^{(i)} \in \Re^{m_y}$ is the distribution correct strong labels, and $\bar{y}^{(i)} \in \Re^{n_y}$ is the distribution of observed labels (weak soft labels), K the number of segmentation classes, and $\hat{y}_i = f(x_i)$ the output of the model given pixel i. Consequently, $p(\hat{y}_{i,k} = k|x_i; \theta)$ is the probability that pixel i is assigned to class $k \in K$ (denoted as $\hat{p}_{i,k}$).

The problem with weak labels (poor, noisy, and partial) is that the probability distribution of the observed label is not equal to the correct labels $P(\bar{Y}_W|X) \neq P(Y_S|X)$, which is typically caused by (a) partial instance segmentations or (b) missing object instances in the observed labels.

In classification problems, the aim is to minimize the risk of f, defined as $R(f) = E_{p(x,y)}[l(Y, f(X))]$ where $l(Y, f(X))$ is the loss function. The goal of classification with weak labels continues to minimize the classification risk, defined as $\bar{R}(f) = E_{p(X,\bar{Y})}[\bar{l}(\bar{Y}, f(X))]$, where $\bar{l}(\bar{Y}, f(X))$ is a proper loss function for learning noisy labels. Using a noise-tolerant loss, assuming that f^* that minimizes $\bar{R}(f)$ can be determined, would be a global minimizer of $R(f)$ as well. In contrast, DL models using loss functions without robustness to noisy labels tend to memorize the noisy samples to minimize the $\hat{R}(f)$ risk. Therefore, in this paper, we are using soft labels and a noise-robust loss function to combat weak label problem and to determine f^* to minimize $\hat{R}(f)$, which is also a global minimizer of $R(f)$.

3.2   Model

We used the IMaskRCNN [3] as the baseline deep learning model for training and evaluation of the proposed extensions. The IMaskRCNN model is an improved version of the well-known instance segmentation model Mask RCNN [8] that improves the segmentation accuracy around object boundaries by adding a skip connection and an extra encoder layer to the mask segmentation head (inspired by U-net architecture) [8]. Similar to the original Mask RCNN, the IMaskR-CNN is constructed from a backbone (ResNet), which is responsible for feature extraction, a region proposal network (RPN) for extracting the ROI bounding box, and two heads: one for mask segmentation (Mask Head), and the other for classifying the extracted bounding boxes (Classification Head).

3.3 Loss

Similar to the Mask RCNN, the IMaskRCNN has a multi-task learning loss (L) for each sampled ROI, which is the result of the classification loss, the bounding-box loss, and the mask-loss accumulation $L = L_{cls} + L_{bbox} + L_{mask}$.

Mask-Loss for Pixel-Level Noise. In Mask RCNN, the mask-head is performing binary segmentation of the detected ROI and L_{mask} is only defined on the k_{th} mask (other mask outputs do not contribute to the loss). Therefore, binary CE (BCE) has been chosen as L_{mask} in Mask R-CNN [8].

Assuming the segmentation error to be the major source of error in comparison with the classification error, we aimed to modify L_{mask} to mitigate the effect of pixel-level noise. Therefore, we propose to replace the BCE loss used as Mask-loss with the APL loss [23] and adapt the APL loss for soft labels. APL loss is constructed from an active loss term and a passive loss term as:

$$L_{APL} = \alpha.L_{active} + \beta.L_{passive} \tag{1}$$

where α and β are parameters to balance two terms.

Ma et al. [23] have shown that normalized losses guarantee robustness against noise. Thus, we use normalized losses (L_{norm}):

$$L_{norm} = \frac{L(f(x), y)}{\sum_{j=1}^{K}(f(x), j)} \tag{2}$$

In this paper, we considered Normalized BCE (NBCE) and Normalized RCE (NRCE) for the combination of active and passive losses.

The cross-entropy loss for two distributions, q (GT distribution) and p (predicted distribution), is defined as $H(q, p)$ (Eq. 3) and RCE is defined as $H(p, q)$ (Eq. 4). By applying the CE and RCE losses to soft labels ($\bar{y}$), it follows that:

$$l_{sce} = H(q, p) = -[\bar{y} \log \hat{y} - (1 - \bar{y}) \log(1 - \hat{y})] \tag{3}$$

$$l_{srce} = H(p, q) = -[\hat{y} \log \bar{y} - (1 - \hat{y}) \log(1 - \bar{y})] \tag{4}$$

and then the normalized soft CE and normalized soft RCE can be defined using Eq. 2.

As $log0$ is undefined, the following constraint is applied to probabilities. For $H(a, b) = H(a, b^*)$, where b^* is the probability clipped between two values $b^* \in [P_{min}, 1 - P_{min}]$ and $P_{min} = 1e-20$:

$$b^* = \begin{cases} P_{min} & b < P_{min} \\ b & P_{min} \leq b \leq 1 - P_{min} \\ 1 - P_{min} & b > 1 - P_{min} \end{cases} \tag{5}$$

4 Experiments and Results

4.1 Data and Labels

In this study, we used the publicly available multicenter Osteoarthritis Initiative (OAI, https://nda.nih.gov/oai/) dataset. OAI contains the demographic and imaging information from 4796 subjects aged 45–79 years who underwent annual knee assessments, including MRIs. A total of 126 knee MRI scans (sagittal intermediate-weighted fat suppressed (IWFS) 444×448 imaging matrix, slice thickness 3 mm, field-of-view 159×160 mm) were selected and scored by experts (2 to 7 readers musculoskeletal radiologists and rheumatologists) for the presence of BML (BML; bright spots in bone) at the tibia, femur, and patella using the Inflammation MRI Scoring System (KIMRISS) [12]. In this work, we used the BML annotations obtained from KIMRISS along with proxy labels of bones (femur and tibia) obtained from automatic segmentation using the IMaskRCNN trained on registered data from our previous work [3]. In the following, we explain how we prepared BML annotations for training.

Leverage Informative Labels from Rectangular Annotations. KIMRISS is a granular semi-quantitative scoring system, which measures inflammation in patients with knee osteoarthritis (OA) [12]. In the KIMRISS [12], by overlaying a transparent grid template on top of the bones (tibia, femur, and patella), the reader specifies regions in slices that contain BML to determine an estimate for BML volume by multiplying granular regions identified as BML [12]. Using this scoring system and regions specified to have BML it is possible to obtain rectangular ROIs from specified areas on the KIMRISS granular template. In the following, we attempt to first provide cleaner labels and produce soft labels by using scoring results from different raters, spatial redundancy in MRI scans, and BML characteristics in IWFS scans. The following steps were taken to create soft labels from multiple annotations after data cleaning and fixing major errors (Fig. 1).

1. Scoring results of raters were aggregated and normalized based on the number of raters who rated the scan.
2. Bone proxy mask areas of the overlayed grid template outside bone were excluded.

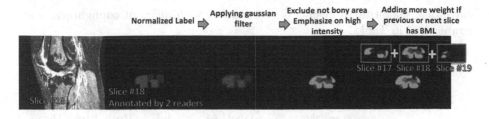

Fig. 1. Generating soft pseudo-GT for BML pipeline

3. BML is described as the presence of ill-defined hyperintense areas within trabecular bone on IWFS images. Given this knowledge, we consider areas with greater intensity than other areas of the bone in the trabecular bone more likely to be BML. Therefore, if areas are selected in step 3, we would consider their probability equal to one.

4. We improved labels by adding labeling information from the previous and next MRI slices, based on the likelihood with neighboring voxels as shown in Fig. 1 (i.e., if the previous/next slices of the slice A contains BML, the slice A is more likely to contain BML as well).

We divided the dataset into 108 scans (from 54 subjects, 1280 slices contain BML) for training, 4 scans (from 2 subjects, 66 slices) for validation, and 17 scans (from 9 subjects, 650 slices) for testing. Furthermore, the validation and test data were segmented manually pixel by pixel by two experts using ITK-snap [7]. The input images were cropped to 320×320 pixels. To receive more spatial information, we used 2.5D MRI slices (three sequential slices as RGB channels). Furthermore, we have used mirroring as data augmentation to increase number of training data.

4.2 Implementation

All models were trained on one NVIDIA V100 GPU for 200 epochs and 200 iterations using an Adam optimizer and a learning rate of 0.001. The complete DL model was implemented in Keras using the TensorFlow 2 backbone.

4.3 Evaluation Criteria

For evaluation, the metrics used included precision $(= TP/(TP + FP))$, recall $(= TP/(TP + FN))$, Intersection of over Union (IoU) $(= (GT \cap Pred)/(GT \cup Pred))$, and average precision (AP), as well as the Dice similarity score $(= 2 \times TP/(2 \times TP + FP + FN))$ for segmentation. For all of these metrics, higher values indicate better performance.

4.4 Ablation Study

Multiple experiments were performed to evaluate the effect of using soft labels and noise resistance loss on BML detection and segmentation with hard and soft labels. Quantitative results of the training with different configurations are summarized in Table 1.

Table 1. RESULTS OF DIFFERENT CONFIGURATIONS (FOR BML)

Method	Configuration				Detection						Seg.
	Loss weight			label	AP		IoU%	Rec.	Prec.	Dice
	BCE	*SCE*	*RCE*		*50*	*75*				
Baseline	1	0	0	bin	12	4	31	0.46	0.52	0.27
APL binary	1	0	1	bin	8	3	29	0.43	0.47	0.21
	2	0	1	bin	8	1	27	0.26	0.40	0.20
Soft Baseline	0	1	0	soft	14	11	37	0.63	0.60	0.28
APL + soft lbl	0	1	1	soft	**19**	**17**	**35**	**0.64**	**0.64**	**0.31**
	0	2	1	soft	12	10	33	0.54	0.55	0.36
	1	1	1	soft	**20**	**15**	**38**	**0.68**	**0.66**	**0.35**
	2	2	1	soft	14	10	30	0.50	0.56	0.30

Soft Labels vs. Hard Labels. We investigated two types of labeling methods, binary labels and soft labels. In conventional label smoothing, the labels are smeared based on a α where $p(Y = k|X = x) \in (\alpha, 1 - \alpha)$. Conventional label smoothing takes binary $(0, 1)$ labels and changes its value uniformly. While in our soft labeling approach the $p(Y = k|X = x)$ can have any value between 0 to 1, and label confidence is adjusted using other information like the intensity of pathology, its location and neighboring voxels. The results are shown in Table 1 demonstrate that using soft labels and a noise resistance loss separately has a positive effect on precision and recall for detecting BML. Comparing the results from BCE (baseline) and soft BCE (soft baseline), shows 4% improvement in recall and 2% improvement in precision and Dice similarity metric. Based on Fig. 2 (a and d), it can be observed that using soft labels is effective in preventing overconfidence (as we expected under noisy labels [22]).

APL Loss vs. BCE Loss. We tested different combinations of active loss $(\alpha_1.NBCE + \alpha_2.NSCE)$ and passive loss $(\beta.NRCE)$ and compared it to the baseline using the BCE loss. For the active loss, we considered using a combination of the Binary CE and soft CE together. Using APL for binary labels does not seem to be effective. Comparing results from the baseline and APL binary in Table 1 shows using APL for binary labels is not improving the metric. Further, as shown in Fig. 2(c, d) binary APL also failed to detect patella's BML in the patella.

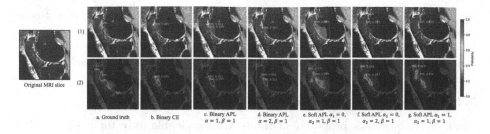

Fig. 2. Results of different configurations for BML detection

APL + SoftLabels. The combination of APL + softLabels has improved the recall and precision 10% in comparison to the baseline method. As mentioned above, soft labels decrease results confidence. Adding the BCE term ($\alpha_1.NBCE$) to the active loss increases confidence mostly on the true positive labels (Fig. 2e, g) and increased recall 22%, precision 14%, and dice 8%. Further, the probability distribution of active loss with BCE term is visually closer to the ground truth.

5   Discussion

In this paper, we proposed a noise-resistance deep learning pipeline using soft labels and an active-passive learning loss. The proposed method primarily addresses the problem of training a CNN using partially annotated data. This simple yet effective method has improved the detection rate of BML. Furthermore, we have generated soft labels that conformed to anatomic structures by combining features directly obtained from the images (pixel intensity and anatomy) with the ROI highlighting general areas of pathology, by using medical scores provided by human readers that can be used for semi-supervised learning.

The results using the OAI dataset for BML segmentation show that using a noise-resistant loss in combination with soft labels improves performance in both detection and segmentation tasks, compared to using noise-sensitive losses like CE or noise-robust losses such as MAE, SCE, or APL. Moreover, the proposed combination of active and passive losses for APL improved sensitivity on labeled areas without additional punishment for missed-labeled regions.

5.1   Effect of Segmentation Loss on Detection Task

Changes in segmentation loss function improved the result of the segmentation task (Dice score) and detection results (recall, precision, and IoU). This improvement can be attributed to the multi-tasking nature of the Mask RCNN approach. Mask RCNN learning tasks aim to concurrently identify instances, classify instances, and segment instances. Multi-task learning is proven to improve learning efficiency and prediction accuracy compared with training separate models for each task [5, 18]. In multi-task learning, generic parameters are softly constrained. Moreover, during back-propagation, the loss of one task has an impact on the concurrent tasks as well. Therefore, in IMaskRCNN, adding noise resistance loss to the mask-head contributes to regularization in other tasks as well.

5.2 Multi-label Data with Label Noise

Most of the previous proposed methods are applicable only for a single-label multi-class segmentation problem, where each data example is assumed to have only one true label. However, most medical image applications require the segmentation of multiple labels, for example, some pixels could be associated with multiple true class labels. However, methods that are developed based on MaskR-CNN are suitable for multi-label applications since in MaskRCNN the L_{mask} is defined only on positive ROIs and other mask outputs do not contribute to the loss. This constraint leads to no competition among classes for generating masks, which is suitable for identifying lesions in tissues multi-label data with weak labels.

5.3 Challenges and Limitations of the Data

Using KIMRISS annotation for training a network is challenging since we can only obtain weak labels. The reason is that KIMRISS objectives has not been providing pixelwise BML annotation and exact BML volume. Thus, some discrepancy exists between raters in the exact location and size of the templates. Furthermore, ROIs obtained from KIMRISS are rectangular shapes and do not provide pixel or shape information. In addition, labeling uncertainty (uncertainty of disagreement and uncertainty of single-target label [14]), which is common in medical images annotations, introduces another noise to these partial labels. Due to varying thresholds between readers for defining positive lesions, disagreement uncertainty exists for the KIMRISS annotation, which is measured as inter-observer reliability for the BML volume. Although the measured reliability suggests an acceptable confidence interval for clinical decisions [12], these kinds of discrepancy affect model training.

Other sources of noise labeling were investigated through close observation and follow-up reading. The follow-up reading suggests that approximately 50% of areas with BML were missed or underestimated in the consensus labels and more than 60% of areas with BML had been underestimated (or missed) by single readers (mainly due to inattentional error and tunnel vision). It is possible to consider a part of these annotation errors as a random variable, since the same annotator may not make the same errors when annotating the same scan, a second time (after a period of time). Furthermore, our visual observation shows smaller or dimmer BML, BMLs in starting slices, and difficult slices were more likely to be missed by readers.

Moreover, we had much less data (only 1280 slices for training) compared to similar works who aimed to solve segmentation using weak label problem. To mitigate the effect of low number of annotations, we can use self-supervised or knowledge distillation training. However, in this paper, our focus was only to investigate the effect of using soft-labeling and normalized APL loss.

6 Conclusion and Future Work

Combination of soft labeling and noise tolerant loss is an effective method for weakly supervised segmentation of medical images. It provides a convenient approach for improving the performance of DL models with minimal intervention to the existing methods, while revealing a novel way to design noise-robust loss functions for segmentation. The proposed method has the flexibility to quickly adapt to the state-of-the-art architectures and learning algorithms, unlike most of the current approaches that require changing the learning process to estimate correct labels of the training examples and learn under label noise. This method is suitable for knowledge distillation as it gives more information when compared to hard labels and is effective for one stage training. It does not suffer from class imbalance and, unlike U-net based architectures developed to be robust against noise, it is able to perform multi-class segmentation problem.

The research result is designed to integrate with the KIMRISS scoring online platform [12] for identifying BMLs and its volume in the clinical domain. Therefore, we need to investigate the effect of our method on network calibration and confidence in future work, and also measure the reader's uncertainty.

Acknowledgment. Academic time for JJ, is made available by Medical Imaging Consultants (MIC), Edmonton, Canada. We thank the members of the OMERACT MRI in Arthritis Working Group for their participation and support in this project.

References

1. Bertels, J., Robben, D., Vandermeulen, D., Suetens, P.: Optimization with soft dice can lead to a volumetric bias. In: Crimi, A., Bakas, S. (eds.) BrainLes 2019. LNCS, vol. 11992, pp. 89–97. Springer, Cham (2020). https://doi.org/10.1007/978-3-030-46640-4_9

2. Busby, L.P., Courtier, J.L., Glastonbury, C.M.: Bias in radiology: the how and why of misses and misinterpretations. Radiographics **38**(1), 236–247 (2018)

3. Felfeliyan, B., Hareendranathan, A., Kuntze, G., Jaremko, J.L., Ronsky, J.L.: Improved-mask R-CNN: towards an accurate generic MSK MRI instance segmentation platform (data from the osteoarthritis initiative). Comput. Med. Imaging Graph. **97**, 102056 (2022)

4. Ghosh, A., Kumar, H., Sastry, P.S.: Robust loss functions under label noise for deep neural networks. In: Proceedings of the AAAI Conference on Artificial Intelligence, vol. 31 (2017)

5. Goodfellow, I., Bengio, Y., Courville, A.: Deep Learning. MIT Press (2016)

6. Gros, C., Lemay, A., Cohen-Adad, J.: SoftSeg: advantages of soft versus binary training for image segmentation. Med. Image Anal. **71**, 102038 (2021)

7. Yushkevich, P.A., et al.: User-guided 3D active contour segmentation of anatomical structures: significantly improved efficiency and reliability. Neuroimage **31**(3), 1116–1128 (2006)

8. He, K., Gkioxari, G., Dollár, P., Girshick, R.: Mask R-CNN. IEEE Trans. Pattern Anal. Mach. Intell. **42**(2), 386–397 (2020). https://doi.org/10.1109/TPAMI.2018. 2844175

9. Hendrycks, D., Mazeika, M., Wilson, D., Gimpel, K.: Using trusted data to train deep networks on labels corrupted by severe noise. In: Advances in Neural Information Processing Systems, vol. 31 (2018)

10. Ibrahim, M.S., Vahdat, A., Ranjbar, M., Macready, W.G.: Semi-supervised semantic image segmentation with self-correcting networks. In: Proceedings of the IEEE/CVF Conference on Computer Vision and Pattern Recognition, pp. 12715–12725 (2020)

11. Islam, M., Glocker, B.: Spatially varying label smoothing: capturing uncertainty from expert annotations. In: Feragen, A., Sommer, S., Schnabel, J., Nielsen, M. (eds.) IPMI 2021. LNCS, vol. 12729, pp. 677–688. Springer, Cham (2021). https://doi.org/10.1007/978-3-030-78191-0_52

12. Jaremko, J.L., et al.: Validation of a knowledge transfer tool for the knee inflammation MRI scoring system for bone marrow lesions according to the OMERACT filter: data from the osteoarthritis initiative. J. Rheumatol. **44**(11), 1718–1722 (2017)

13. Jaremko, J.L., et al.: Preliminary validation of the knee inflammation MRI scoring system (KIMRISS) for grading bone marrow lesions in osteoarthritis of the knee: data from the osteoarthritis initiative. RMD Open **3**(1), e000355 (2017)

14. Ju, L., et al.: Improving medical images classification with label noise using dual-uncertainty estimation. IEEE Trans. Med. Imaging **41**, 1533–1546 (2022)

15. Karimi, D., Dou, H., Warfield, S.K., Gholipour, A.: Deep learning with noisy labels: exploring techniques and remedies in medical image analysis. Med. Image Anal. **65**, 101759 (2020). https://doi.org/10.1016/j.media.2020.101759

16. Kats, E., Goldberger, J., Greenspan, H.: Soft labeling by distilling anatomical knowledge for improved MS lesion segmentation. In: 2019 IEEE 16th International Symposium on Biomedical Imaging, ISBI 2019, pp. 1563–1566. IEEE (2019)

17. Kats, E., Goldberger, J., Greenspan, H.: A soft STAPLE algorithm combined with anatomical knowledge. In: Shen, D., et al. (eds.) MICCAI 2019. LNCS, vol. 11766, pp. 510–517. Springer, Cham (2019). https://doi.org/10.1007/978-3-030-32248-9_57

18. Kendall, A., Gal, Y., Cipolla, R.: Multi-task learning using uncertainty to weigh losses for scene geometry and semantics. In: Proceedings of the IEEE Conference on Computer Vision and Pattern Recognition, pp. 7482–7491 (2018)

19. Kim, T., Ko, J., Choi, J., Yun, S.Y., et al.: Fine samples for learning with noisy labels. In: Advances in Neural Information Processing Systems, vol. 34 (2021)

20. Li, H., Wei, D., Cao, S., Ma, K., Wang, L., Zheng, Y.: Superpixel-guided label softening for medical image segmentation. In: Martel, A.L., et al. (eds.) MICCAI 2020. LNCS, vol. 12264, pp. 227–237. Springer, Cham (2020). https://doi.org/10.1007/978-3-030-59719-1_23

21. Liu, S., Zhu, Z., Qu, Q., You, C.: Robust training under label noise by over-parameterization. arXiv preprint arXiv:2202.14026 (2022)

22. Lukasik, M., Bhojanapalli, S., Menon, A., Kumar, S.: Does label smoothing mitigate label noise? In: International Conference on Machine Learning, pp. 6448–6458. PMLR (2020)

23. Ma, X., Huang, H., Wang, Y., Romano, S., Erfani, S., Bailey, J.: Normalized loss functions for deep learning with noisy labels. In: International Conference on Machine Learning, pp. 6543–6553. PMLR (2020)

24. Müller, R., Kornblith, S., Hinton, G.E.: When does label smoothing help? In: Advances in Neural Information Processing Systems, vol. 32 (2019)
25. Patrini, G., Rozza, A., Krishna Menon, A., Nock, R., Qu, L.: Making deep neural networks robust to label noise: a loss correction approach. In: Proceedings of the IEEE Conference on Computer Vision and Pattern Recognition, pp. 1944–1952 (2017)
26. Pedoia, V., Norman, B., Mehany, S.N., Bucknor, M.D., Link, T.M., Majumdar, S.: 3D convolutional neural networks for detection and severity staging of meniscus and PFJ cartilage morphological degenerative changes in osteoarthritis and anterior cruciate ligament subjects. J. Magn. Reson. Imaging **49**(2), 400–410 (2019)
27. Silva, J.L., Oliveira, A.L.: Using soft labels to model uncertainty in medical image segmentation. arXiv preprint arXiv:2109.12622 (2021)
28. Song, H., Kim, M., Park, D., Shin, Y., Lee, J.G.: Learning from noisy labels with deep neural networks: A survey. IEEE Trans. Neural Netw. Learn. Syst. (2022)
29. To, M.N.N., et al.: Coarse label refinement for improving prostate cancer detection in ultrasound imaging. Int. J. Comput. Assist. Radiol. Surg. **17**, 841–847 (2022)
30. Vaswani, A., et al.: Attention is all you need. In: Advances in Neural Information Processing Systems, vol. 30. Curran Associates, Inc. (2017)
31. Vega, R., et al.: Sample efficient learning of image-based diagnostic classifiers using probabilistic labels. arXiv preprint arXiv:2102.06164 (2021)
32. Wang, D.B., Wen, Y., Pan, L., Zhang, M.L.: Learning from noisy labels with complementary loss functions. In: Proceedings of the AAAI Conference on Artificial Intelligence, vol. 35, pp. 10111–10119 (2021)
33. Wang, Y., Ma, X., Chen, Z., Luo, Y., Yi, J., Bailey, J.: Symmetric cross entropy for robust learning with noisy labels. In: Proceedings of the IEEE/CVF International Conference on Computer Vision, pp. 322–330 (2019)
34. Xue, Y., Hauskrecht, M.: Efficient learning of classification models from soft-label information by binning and ranking. In: The 30th International Flairs Conference (2017)
35. Yi, R., Huang, Y., Guan, Q., Pu, M., Zhang, R.: Learning from pixel-level label noise: a new perspective for semi-supervised semantic segmentation. IEEE Trans. Image Process. **31**, 623–635 (2021)
36. Zhang, C., Bengio, S., Hardt, M., Recht, B., Vinyals, O.: Understanding deep learning (still) requires rethinking generalization. Commun. ACM **64**(3), 107–115 (2021)

Tremor Feature Extraction for Enhanced Interpretability of Vocal Disease Classification

Changhyun Kim$^{(\boxtimes)}$, Sangjae Lee , and Kwangseok Lee

SKTelecom, Seongnam-si, Gyeonggi-do 13487, South Korea
changhyk@sktair.com

Abstract. Recently, attempts to solve various biomedical problems using AI technology have been made in the fields of radiology, diagnostic medicine, and pharmaceuticals. Due to the nature of the bio field, reliable medical services will be possible only when the causal relationship of diseases is clearly explained. In this paper, based on this necessity, we developed Tremor Feature Extraction voice disease biomarker as a voice visualization technology by applying edge detection technology used in computer vision, and verified its effectiveness by using the Pretrained VGG16 Deep Learning model mainly used in images. We proposed the Tremor feature and Tremor Residual feature, which can better represent the X-Y-axis movement of the spectral unstable harmonics and the noise components interposed therebetween. Its performance was verified by applying the traditional Machine Learning (ML) method and the Deep Learning (DL) method. In fact, when the Tremor feature and the Tremor Residual feature were used at the same time, there was a performance improvement of about 0.48% compared to the Log-Mel feature alone. When using LogMel Feature together with the proposed Tremor Residual Feature as a model input of the traditional ML Ensemble classifier, the precision was improved by 11% compared to using only LogMel feature, which was confirmed to be 73%. To the best of our knowledge, it is the first vocal disease bio-marker originated from the computer vision research methodology such as edge detection, and especially, also successfully analyzed the vocal diseases through Grad-CAM explainable AI technology.

Keywords: Voice disease biomarker · Tremor feature · Tremor residual feature · Grad-CAM · Explainable AI

1 Introduction

The number of patients with geriatric voice disorders is increasing due to the aging of the population. In addition, the demand for voice medical services is increasing due to professional voice users such as teachers, singers, and announcers and social and economic changes. In order to accurately diagnose voice diseases and diseases of the larynx, invasive tests such as a stroboscope are required. However, studies using voice data for diagnosing voice diseases in a non-invasive way have been introduced. Recently, several studies have attempted to use a machine learning-based classifier to classify normal and abnormal voices using deep learning [10–12].

© Springer Nature Switzerland AG 2023
J.-J. Rousseau and B. Kapralos (Eds.): ICPR 2022 Workshops, LNCS 13644, pp. 618–633, 2023.
https://doi.org/10.1007/978-3-031-37742-6_48

1.1 Challenges of Vocal Diseases

Due to differences in the severity of symptoms for each disease and differences in voice and tone between individuals, diagnosis accuracy of vocal diseases by medical doctors is even less than 60% [8]. Also, the amount of benchmark data set for developing a recognizer is small (6–2000 person samples). In other words, it is too small to generalize [13–16]. To supplement this, a disease-specific feature extraction technique that is distinct from the conventional features must be developed as an embedding technique to enable more accurate voice disease recognition.

In the case of voice diseases, the human experts are 2 laryngologist and 2 general otolaryngologists each [8]. For a total of 4 target diseases, the average accuracy was 58.1% and 47.3%, confirming that the classification accuracy was more than 8% lower than that of the ML model 66.9%. Here, the reason for the low absolute value is the interpretation that it is difficult to classify, if the characteristics of the target disease are less revealed according to the severity.

It is difficult to find features that effectively explain the presence or absence of voice disorder. In particular, this is because some phenomena associated with voice diseases (e.g. periodicity, noise component) also appear in non-pathological conditions due to perturbations inherent in the vocalization process. Proposed tremor feature is a feature extraction technique that is optimized for periodic shaking of the X-Y axes of harmonic edges. Therefore, it is optimized for spasmodic dysphonia disease. Conversely, tremor residual feature is sensitive to black dot noise components scattered on the spectrum between harmonics. For this reason, it is a feature extraction technique optimized for VFPolyp disease.

As seen in previous studies, it is difficult to find a prior thesis that extracts the characteristics of a specific voice disease by looking at the audio signal itself as an image. However, through this voice disease recognition and analysis work, this paper has the following three contributions:

- Proposal of tremor (residual) feature extraction method optimized for recognition of specific voice disease and successful verification of the effectiveness
- Applying visually explainable AI technology (Grad-CAM) for tremor (residual) feature engineering technique to verify the focused part of each disease recognized by the model
- Successfully developed a novel and general vocal disease feature extraction method applicable to not only DL models but also ML models.

2 Related Work

In order to recognize voice disease better, both various voice signal processing techniques and deep learning classifiers have been studied for many years.

2.1 Feature Extraction and Feature Engineering Method

A voice signal has a mixture of periodic and aperiodic components. A periodic element such as vocal cord vibration may be characterized by a fundamental frequency or pitch

[1], and aperiodic element such as noise may be characterized by an NHR(noise to harmonic ratio) [2]. In the case of pathological voice, vocal cord vibration is severely irregular or there is almost no vocal cord vibration. It is hard to analyze the voice because it is difficult to find the periodicity of the vocal cord vibrations. Phonation features measured from vocal cord vibrations include pitch (Fundamental frequency) [1], jitter(pitch perturbation), shimmer(amplitude perturbation) [3], and NHR(noise to harmonic ratio) [2]. Articulation features that make up the voice through the vocal tract tunnel include MFCC [4] and Formant [5]. Pitch detection is performed using the autocorrelation method widely adopted in the existing speech analysis tools such as Praat [6] and MDVP [7]. The pitch is considered normal in the range of 75–110 Hz for males and 120–220 Hz for females, and it can be regarded as an abnormal finding if it is outside the range. The frequency perturbation rate (jitter local) is 1.04%, and the amplitude perturbation rate (shimmer local) is 3.81%, which is known as a voice pathological threshold. In speech recognition applications, it is common to reduce noise and use dominant features, however in voice disease identification, noise removal should not be considered as phenomena such as irregularities during vocal cord vibrations or additional noises are inherent in pathological conditions [8]. CPP (Cepstral Peak Prominence) is also known as a feature extraction method based on pathological knowledge to classify speech diseases [9].

2.2 Image Classification and End2End Classification

It can be divided into a method of using an image classifier by converting a Waveform into a Spectrum Image, and a model that uses the Waveform as a 1D signal input as it is for speech disease recognition. A model that can hierarchically select local/global features from input images of various scales shows the best performance in object detection and segmentation [17]. Multi-modality of image, text, and audio also can be used to train a more general model in the target audio domain [18, 19]. In this way, there is an advantage that various image classifier models can be introduced and used as they are, and in particular, recognition performance can be improved from a pre-learning model that has already been trained with other modality data. On the other hand, the syncnet series of studies successfully introduced the concept of band pass filter to the waveform input and applied contrastive loss to increase the discrimination power [20–22].

3   Proposed Approach

3.1   Yonsei Severance Dataset

For patients who came to Yonsei Severance Hospital (South Korea) with a voice abnormality, a sustained voice of "ah ~" (/ah ~ /) was recorded for the past 20 years. Data were collected to evaluate the voice state of the diseased compared to that of a normal person by analyzing the fundamental frequency, vibration, and regularity of voices that appear during vowel utterance. (Non-vowel voice disorder index questionnaire (K-VAPP), speech therapy (GRBAS), and EGG signals were additionally collected, but were excluded from the scope of this paper).

As for the collected data, 12,261 vowel vocalization data were collected, including the normal control group and the negatively ill patients. It mainly includes 12 diseases including unilateral benign lesion (VFPolyp), unilateral/bilateral paralysis (VFP), and spasmodic dysphonia. However, there is a significant difference in the number of patients who visited for each disease, and the data collected accordingly also has a large variance in the number of patients depending on the type of disease. In addition, the types of diseases that occur according to gender and age appear differently. In particular, it is often found that the types of diseases that occur according to gender are completely different. For example, there are 736 cases of spasmodic dysphonia in women, and less than 100 cases in men. Conversely, more than 300 cases of LaryngealCa were collected for men, while a low number of cases were collected for women with 18 cases. Table 1. shows the amount of data collected by disease type. Gender M and F indicate Male and Female respectively.

One of the representative characteristics of patients with voice disorders is noise, such as noise mixed with the voice. In general speech recognition task, a denoising technique that removes noise is used, but when noise is removed for the classification of speech diseases and disorders, there is a risk that disease characteristics may be simultaneously removed. Therefore, the noise signal for each frequency domain included in the voice should be treated as important information. These characteristics are also important factors in gender differences. Figure 1 shows the male and female spectrograms. In the case of men, the space between the harmonic regions where disease characteristics are expressed is relatively narrow. Due to this, the disease characteristics expressed as a noisy signal among harmonics cannot be expressed relatively well, or when background noise / input noise is included, it may be difficult to distinguish them.

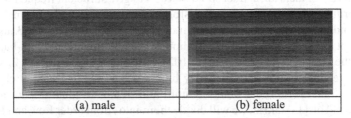

| | (a) male | (b) female |

Fig. 1. Quantity of data collected Differences in spectrograms between men and women

In this paper, four types of diseases were targeted by giving priority to the quantity of disease data among female data. In addition, since it is advantageous as the number of data collected for machine learning increases, major diseases were selected with priority based on the number of diseases. Among them, VFNodules and VFPolyp are known to be difficult to distinguish with the naked eye/endoscope in terms of pathology/medical diagnosis, and almost impossible to distinguish with the voice itself [23, 24]. Other includes all other diseases including the normal control group. Therefore, in this paper, except for VFNodules, four types of Other, VFPolyp, SpasmodicDysphonia, and VFP were tested in the order of the largest number of patients' data.

Table 1. Quantity of data collected by disease type

Pathologies	Male	Female
Other	2076	2481
VFPolyp	976	917
VFNodules	165	788
SpasmodicDysphonia	100	736
VFP	592	679
IntracordalCyst	184	332
ReinkesEdema	150	236
SulcusVocalis	577	239
Papilloma	181	78
Granuloma	163	49
LaryngealCa	302	18
VFLeukoplakia	77	8

3.2 Preprocessing Parameter Setting

In order to extract Log Mel Spectrum from Fig. 2 below, several signal processing coefficients should be set as hyperparameters. In particular, since the male (~700 Hz) and female (~1100 Hz) voice frequency bands are different, select 11.025 kHz, a frequency band that can cover them all, and set NFFT = 1024 to give sufficient frequency resolution when performing Short Time Fourier Transform. When extracting the log mel-spectrum, 256 mel-bands were used. By doing this, it can be confirmed from Fig. 3 above that it has sufficient sharpness of harmonics. Although the aforementioned mel-bands are set to 256, in the case of the tremor feature, 1024 NFFT is mapped to fs = 22.05 kHz as a physical frequency, so if 512 frequency bins are used, 11.025 kHz is obtained. As a result, since the 512th order tremor feature and tremor residual feature represent a frequency band of 11.025kHz, we will divide them into 256th order Low and Hi features that are the same as logMelspectrum, respectively, and use it as a two separated channel input.

3.3 Tremor (Residual) Feature Extraction

Tremor Feature Extraction Process. Tremor is caused by a change in pitch, called Tremolo, in music. This phenomenon is often observed in people with voice disorders. Therefore, it is intended to extract the spectrum-based characteristics of specific vocal diseases by understanding the X-Y axis change periodicity of vocal harmonics. In other words, the most important process is to apply 2D FFT to the spectrum to measure the period of spectrum harmonics once again and recalculate it. This is the 2D FFT/FFT shift operation processed in the third block of Fig. 3, and cross filtering is applied through the X-Y axis where harmonics exist to extract only harmonic components (the rest are

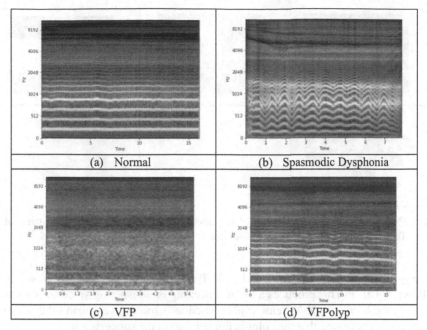

Fig. 2. LogMel Spectrogram of targeted four diseases

noise components). (Cross Pass Filter) Finally, the 2D IFFT operation is processed in order to pass the spectrum of the spectrum that has been passed through this way back to the spectral domain (Fig. 3). Conceptually, to do this, in order to do edge detection in the field of computer vision research, the technique of extracting the part with a large amount of change between pixels (large gradient value) is applied. That is, the contour of harmonics can be found more clearly through the 2D FFT/IFFT process (Fig. 4).

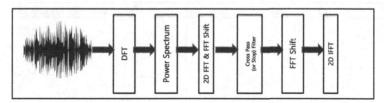

Fig. 3. Tremor Feature Extraction Process Block diagram

Tremor Features of Vocal Diseases. In the case of convulsive dysphonia, a tense sound characterized by a strong pronunciation corresponds to this case. Compared to other diseases, if harmonics are clearly visible, involuntary convulsive internal abduction (or spasm) of the vocal cords during vocalization is the cause, and the "tremor" phenomenon, which shakes along the X-Y axis, tends to be observed more than other diseases. Appear

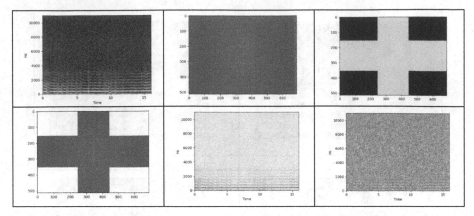

Fig. 4. Power Spectrum, 2D Spectrum of the Spectrum, Cross-pass filter, Cross-pass-filtered output, Tremor Feature, Tremor Residual Feature

in the order of (Tremor tendency: SD > VFP (harmonics are frequently observed) > VFPolyp > Other) This produces a lot of squeezing or whispering voices. As shown in Fig. 5(e), the harmonic X-Y tremolo phenomenon is more severe than other diseases, and it can be confirmed that the color is thicker due to the squeezing sound.

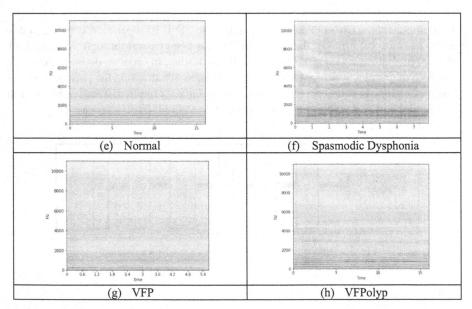

Fig. 5. Tremor Features of Three Vocal Disease patient and Normal person

Tremor Residual Features of Vocal Diseases. In the case of VFP or VFPolyp, a parasitic voice (hoarse phlegm voice) or a breathy voice is an important point. As a result, the vocalization time decreased, and a monotonous pitch or pitch deviation appeared as shown in Fig. 6. It is observed that sparse black dot noises with large particles between harmonics on the rest of the spectrum except for harmonics tend to exist in Tremor Residual Features.

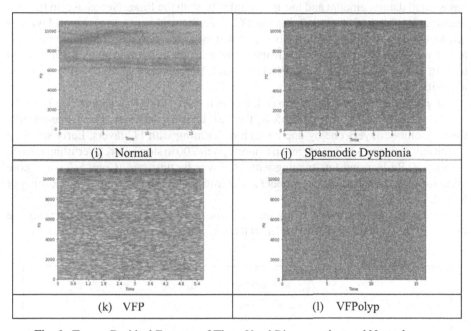

Fig. 6. Tremor Residual Features of Three Vocal Disease patient and Normal person

4 Experiment for Classification

In order to verify the effectiveness of the tremor (residual) feature, the following two disease recognizer experiments are conducted. In this experiment, female voice recording files of the Yonsei Severance Dataset were used. Among thirteen vocal diseases, four diseases of interest (Other, SpasmodicDysponia, VFP, VFPolyp) were targeted for a total of 4160 samples (Train + Validation: 3328/Test:832). In particular, by observing the class activation map for each layer of CNN bottleneck blocks, it is possible to explain what parts on the map are focused on using the Grad-CAM technique. For testing, we randomly sampled the data set into train + validation:test with the ratio of 8:2, while maintaining the ratio of the number of class samples. The train + validation set was augmented with the SMOTE method. The best model and parameter sets were firstly selected by performing standard 5-fold cross validation with the train + validation set. Then fine-tunning on all train + validation set was performed followed by testing.

4.1 Transfer Learning Using Pretrained CNN Model

Layer-wise Step-by-Step Fine-tunning Method. A classification experiment was conducted using the ImageNet 1000 class pretrained VGG16 model as a CNN bottleneck network. Due to the characteristics of bio-medical data such as voice disease, since it has a small dataset amount and low task similarity with the ImageNet dataset in transfer learning, the method of fine-tuning the FC classifier and some convolution layers is sequentially applied to achieve the best performance. The purpose of this experiment is to see whether the Tremor residual feature is helpful for performance improvement and to train a large model such as the VGG16 model. For this reason, we did only train and test without validation.

Step 1. Learn only FC layer (Conv. Layer is fixed in VGG16 state) in Fig. 7.

Step 2. Unfreezing from Conv5–3, the last layer of VGG16. Then, fine-tunning the convolution layers one by one through re-learning with FC layers. Early stopping condition: patience 3 or 7, perform up to max epoch 200 to stop before overfitting occurs.

Step 3. Re-learning fine-tunning with FC layer by unfrozen (Conv 5–2) one more layer using the best performance model as the initial model as a result of the learning of Step 2.

Step 4. In this way, fine-tunning learning continues until Step 18. At this time, the input conversion CNN 2D layer under VGG16 is always fine-tunned.

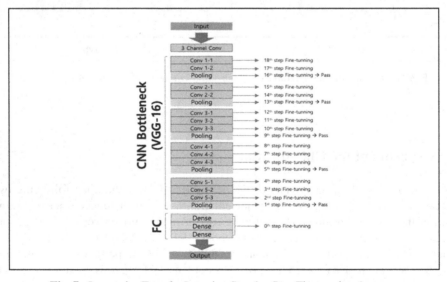

Fig. 7. Layerwise Transfer Learning Step-by-Step Finetunning Accuracy

Hyper Parameter Settings with Meta Learner. As Table 2. shows, there are four different hypter parameters; learning rate, optimizer, patience, and multichannel input kinds. Eash hyper parameters have attribute values as in the value columns.

As shown in Fig. 8, the best performance as a result of training is 5 channel input case (LogMel (1ch) + Tremor Low (1ch) + Tremor Hi (1ch) + Tremor Residual Low

Table 2. Hyper-Parameter Kinds.

Hyperparameter	Values
Learning rate	0:5e-6 (slow), 1:5e-5 (mid), 2:5e-4 (fast)
Optimizer	0:SGD, 1:Adam
Patience	3 or 7
Multi-channel Input Kinds	0:logmel256, 1:logmel256 + SpectLow256 + SpectHi256, 2:logmel256 + TremorLow256 + TremorHi256, 3:lowmel256 + TremorResidualLow256 + TremorResidualHi256 4:logmel256 + TremorLow256 + TremorResidualLow256 5:logmel256 + TremorLow256 + TremorHi256 + TremorResidualLow256 + TremorResidualHi256

(1ch) + Tremor Residual Hi (1ch)) for all 256 dimentional features. When this input channel setup is used, the accuracy is confirmed as 59.01% in the 15th fine-tunning step. The second order indicates when Tremor (2ch) feature or Spectrum (2ch) feature is added (58.77%), then when Tremor Low (1ch) + Tremor Residual Low (1ch) feature is used (58.65%). Finally, LogMel alone or LogMel with TremorResidual feature have the accuracy of 58.53%.

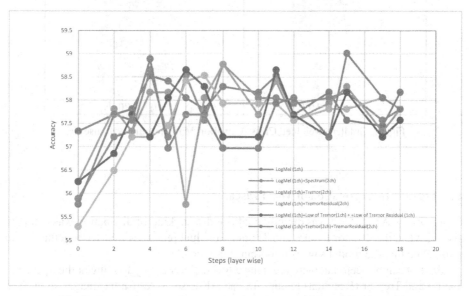

Fig. 8. Layerwise Transfer Learning Step-by-Step Finetunning Accuracy

Based on the above results, it is confirmed that using both Tremor feature and Tremor Residual feature together with LogMel feature helps to improve performance in vocal disease classification. The additional use of only the Tremor feature can be expected to have the same effect as the additional use of the spectrum feature.

When fine-tunning the pretrained VGG16 CNN layers through step-by-step layer-wise learning, in the case of 5-channel input, the 15th step shows the best performance, as Fig. 8 shows. In the case of the next order, it was also confirmed that the next higher performance was obtained only when unfrozen fine learning was performed up to the fourth step using all five features. That is, it was experimentally proved that it is insufficient to perform fine-tunning only on the FC layers.

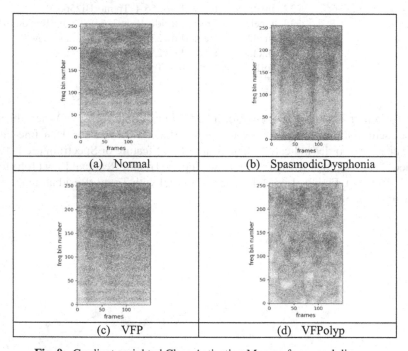

Fig. 9. Gradient-weighted Class Activation Map on four vocal diseases

4.2 Feature Interpretation of Vocal Diseases

Using Grad-CAM [25], it was directly confirmed what kind of distinction was made by disease when the Tremor feature and Tremor Residual feature were used together in the visual area that the model saw as important for each class.

First, it can be seen that there are quite a few differences by looking at the Spectrum feature and Tremor (Residual) feature for each disease as Appendix images show. The structure of harmonics and the distribution of noises therebetween are quite different between diseases. In the case of Grad-CAM images, the correlation between visually activated regions and features in the Grad-CAM images up to the Block3 pooling layer for each disease or the connection with the voice features of the voice disease itself could be found as follows.

As Fig. 9 (a) shows, the onset part of the class activation map (CAM) on the CNN block 2 and 3 is activated at low frequency and x-axis harmonic line below frequency bin number 50 is also activated. In particular, it was experimentally observed that the harmonics structure on the CAM gradually increased as the number of channel inputs increased (Appendix:a-1 ~ a-5). However, in the case CAM images of Blocks 4 and 5 (Appendix: b-3-b-5), it was difficult to find a correlation with input channel images. In the case of SpasmodicDysphonia, a squeezing sound or a tremor-like sound comes. If you look at the input feature harmonics structure (Appendix:c-1, c-2, c-4), you can see the tremor in the Y-axis. It can be checked evenly throughout the entire time zone.In the case of the Block3 pooling layer, it was observed that the activated line on the y frequency axis occurred at around tenth frame. This can be understood as the activation of disease characteristics as the model responds to the vibration of harmonics in the frequency axis direction. However, it is not easy to find features matching the input features in the Block4 and Block5 pooling layer activation maps (Appendix: d-3–d-5).

In the case of VFP disease, a monotonous pitch sound is dissolved as an air-suffocated voice. On Fig. 9 (c), it can be seen that activation appears on the entire x-axis. This characteristic can be understood as an important part for disease recognition in VFP. The airy noise sound exists everywhere. Lastly, in the case of VFPolyp, activation dots appear everywhere on the low frequency spectrum rather than harmonics due to a rough and hoarse voice on Fig. 9 (d). This can be confirmed more clearly as the number of channels is increased, and it can be confirmed that R (Roughness) and B (Breathy) scores in GRABAS evaluation also show high values. However, it still is not easy to find the input features matching with the Block4 and Block5 pooling layer activation maps (Appendix: f-3–f-5, h-3–h-5) for both VFP and VFPolyp diseases. This makes it possible to infer that if there are three VGG16 block layers, it will be sufficient for a vocal disease recognizer, and in the next section C, we will try to check whether the performance is maintained or improved by conducting a traditional ML ensemble classifier experiment by simplifying the recognizer model.

4.3 ML (Machine Learning) Ensemble Classifier

In a simpler, general ML classifier, we conduct an experiment to verify the effectiveness of Tremor (Residual) features. In order to perform detailed validation experiments for each feature by class, ensemble classification experiments were performed with Decision Tree, Random Forest, XGBoost, Extra Tree, Logistic Regression, and Stochastic Gradient Decent used in Machine Learning. Unlike the CNN classifier, the ML classifier experiments show Meta data such as sex, age group, formant peak information, noise to harmonics ratio, fundamental frequency are additionally used by late fusion. Specifically, a low dimensional feature vector passed through a pretrained VGG network for LogMel, Spectrum, Tremor feature or Tremor Residual feature was first extracted, then meta data vectorized again, and concatenated to put more information as a recognizer input. Table 3 results shows following result.

- In the case of Spasmodic Dysphonia, when Tremor Residual Feature was used, precision was improved by 10–11% (62% → 73%) compared to when Tremor Residual Feature was not used or when General Spectrum was used, and F1 score was also improved by 2% (59% → 61%) to experimentally confirm

- For the four diseases of interest, on average, when Tremor Residual Feature is used, the precision is improved by 3–4% compared to when not using or using the general spectrum (52.6% → 56.5%), and in the case of Accuracy, it is 2 to 2.7% (55.5% → 58.2%) experimentally confirmed.

Accordingly, the effectiveness of Tremor Feature and Tremor Residual Feature also was verified in ML classifier Ensemble model, which is simpler than CNN.

Table 3. ML Ensemble Classifier Result

Features	LogMel				LogMel+ Spectrum				LogMel+ Tremor				LogMel+ Tremor- Residual			
Acc.	0.555				0.562				0.543				0.582			
Prec.	0.526				0.539				0.508				0.566			
Classwise Acc. 0 : Normal		Prec.	Recall	F1-score		Prec.	Recall	F1-score		Prec	Recall	F1-score		Prec.	Recall	F1-score
1:Spasemodic-Dysphonia	0	0.58	0.75	0.65	0	0.59	0.76	0.67	0	0.57	0.74	0.65	0	0.58	0.84	0.68
2: VFP	1	0.63	0.56	0.59	1	0.62	0.57	0.59	1	0.57	0.58	0.58	1	0.73	0.52	0.61
3. VFPolyp	2	0.50	0.47	0.48	2	0.45	0.46	0.46	2	0.45	0.45	0.45	2	0.51	0.43	0.47
	3	0.33	0.13	0.19	3	0.41	0.14	0.21	3	0.33	0.09	0.14	3	0.44	0.10	0.17

5 Conclusion

In this paper, it was experimentally proved that the target disease can be recognized more accurately by using the proposed Tremor (Residual) feature that distinguishes harmonics from other noises as a bio-marker.

To this end, the Tremor (Residual) feature engineering is processed and used for vocal disease classification using the VGG16 pretrained model through the transfer learning method, which is widely used in deep learning.

In particular, using the Grad-CAM technology, it was visually explained that the recognizer model also focused on a point similar to the point at which a person recognizes a disease from the activation map of the VGG16 model with proposed Tremor (Residual) feature for each vocal disease. Moreover, it was inferred that a simple ML recognizer rather than a deep learning model such as VGG16 is experimentally proven that it could be a good competitive classifier for vocal disease CNN pretrained classifiers.

In the future, to improve the absolute classification performance, it will be possible to apply the Tremor (Residual) feature to the currently available Transformer-based or self-supervised learning based SOTA algorithms [22, 26, 27].

Acknowledgment. This work was supported by the Korea Medical Device Development Fund grant funded by the Korea government (the Ministry of Science and ICT, the Ministry of Trade, Industry and Energy, the Ministry of Health & Welfare, the Ministry of Food and Drug Safety) (Project Number: KMDF_PR_20200901_0093).

Appendix. Feature and Grad-CAM Images

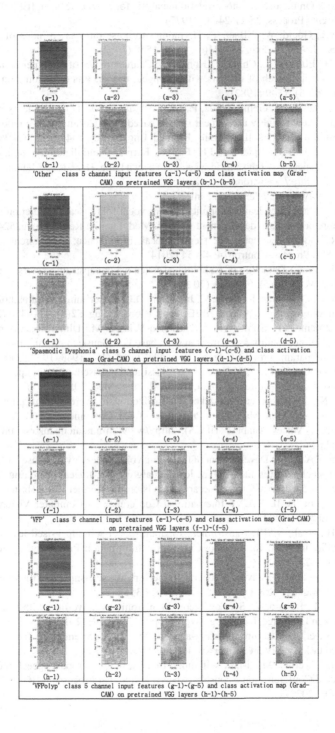

'Other' class 5 channel input features (a-1)~(a-5) and class activation map (Grad-CAM) on pretrained VGG layers (b-1)~(b-5)

'Spasmodic Dysphonia' class 5 channel input features (c-1)~(c-5) and class activation map (Grad-CAM) on pretrained VGG layers (d-1)~(d-5)

'VFP' class 5 channel input features (e-1)~(e-5) and class activation map (Grad-CAM) on pretrained VGG layers (f-1)~(f-5)

'VFPolyp' class 5 channel input features (g-1)~(g-5) and class activation map (Grad-CAM) on pretrained VGG layers (h-1)~(h-5)

References

1. Rabiner, L.: On the use of autocorrelation analysis for pitch detection. IEEE Trans. Acoust. Speech Signal Process. **25**(1), 24–33 (1977)
2. Yumoto, E., Gould, W.J., Baer, T.: Harmonics-to-noise ratio as an index of the degree of hoarseness. J. Acoust. Soc. Am. **71**(6), 1544–1550 (1982)
3. Kasuya, H., Ebihara, S., Chiba, T., Konno, T.: Characteristics of pitch period and amplitude perturbations in speech of patients with laryngeal cancer. Electron Commun. Jpn. (Part I: Commun.) **65**(5), 11–9 (1982)
4. Godino-Llorente, J.I., Gomez-Vilda, P., Blanco-Velasco, M.: Dimensionality reduction of a pathological voice quality assessment system based on gaussian mixture models and short-term cepstral parameters. IEEE Trans. Biomed. Eng. **53**(10), 1943–1953 (2006)
5. Sapir, S., Ramig, L.O., Spielman, J.L., Fox, C.: Formant centralization ratio: a proposal for a new acoustic measure of dysarthric speech. J. Speech Lang. Hear. Res. **53**(1), 114–125 (2010)
6. Praatmanual. http://www.fon.hum.uva.nl/praat/
7. MDVP. http://www.kayelemetrics.com
8. Hu, H.-C., et al.: Deep learning application for vocal fold disease prediction through voice recognition: preliminary development study. J. Med. Internet Res. **23**(6), e25247 (2021)
9. Fraile, R., Godino-Llorente, J.I.: Cepstral peak prominence: a comprehensive analysis. Biomed. Sig. Process. Control **14**, 42–54 (2014)
10. Fang, S.H., et al.: Detection of pathological voice using cepstrum vectors: a deep learning approach. J. Voice **33**(5), 634–641 (2019)
11. Umapathy, K., Krishnan, S., Parsa, V., Jamieson, D.G.: Discrimination of pathological voices using a time-frequency approach. IEEE Trans. Biomed. Eng. **52**(3), 421–430 (2005)
12. Godino-Llorente, J.I., Gómez-Vilda, P., Blanco-Velasco, M.: Dimensionality reduction of a pathological voice quality assessment system based on Gaussian mixture models and short-term cepstral parameters. IEEE Trans. Biomed. Eng. **53**(10), 1943–1953 (2006)
13. Eskidere, Ö., Gürhanlı, A.: Voice disorder classification based on multitaper mel frequency cepstral coefficients features. Comput. Math. Methods Med. **2015** (2015)
14. Maor, E.: Noninvasive vocal biomarker is associated with severe acute respiratory syndrome coronavirus 2 infection. Mayo Clin. Proc. Innov. Qual. Outcomes **5**(3) (2021)
15. Saarbruecken Voice Database (IPUS). http://www.stimmdatenbank.coli.uni-saarland.de/help_en.php4
16. Mesallam, T.A., et al.: Development of the arabic voice pathology database and its evaluation by using speech features and machine learning algorithms. J. Healthcare Eng. **2017** (2017)
17. Liu, Z., et al.: Swin transformer: hierarchical vision transformer using shifted windows. In: Proceedings of the IEEE/CVF International Conference on Computer Vision, pp. 10012–10022. IEEE/CVF (2021)
18. Akbari, H., et al.: VATT: transformers for multimodal self-supervised learning from raw video, audio and text. In: Advances in Neural Information Processing Systems, vol. 34, pp. 24206–24221 (2021)
19. Baevski, A., et al.: Data2vec: a general framework for self-supervised learning in speech, vision and language. arXiv preprint arXiv:2202.03555 (2022)
20. Ravanelli, M., Bengio, Y.: Speaker recognition from raw waveform with sincnet. In: 2018 IEEE Spoken Language Technology Workshop (SLT). IEEE (2018)
21. Pascual, S., et al.: Learning problem-agnostic speech representations from multiple self-supervised tasks. arXiv preprint arXiv:1904.03416 (2019)
22. Ravanelli, M., et al.: Multi-task self-supervised learning for robust speech recognition. In: International Conference on Acoustics, Speech and Signal Processing (ICASSP), pp. 6989–6993. IEEE (2020)

23. Wallis, L., et al.: Vocal fold nodule vs. vocal fold polyp: answer from surgical pathologist and voice pathologist point of view. J. Voice **18**(1), 125–129 (2004)
24. "Vocal Cord Nodules and Polyps": The American Speech-Language-Hearing Association (ASHA) (1997–2022). https://www.asha.org/public/speech/disorders/vocal-cord-nodules-and-polyps/
25. Selvaraju, R.R., et al.: Grad-CAM: visual explanations from deep networks via gradient-based localization. In: Proceedings of the IEEE International Conference on Computer Vision, pp. 618–626. IEEE (2017)
26. Gong, Y., et al.: SSAST: self-supervised audio spectrogram transformer. arXiv preprint arXiv: 2110.09784 (2021)
27. Dutta, S., Ganapathy, S.: Multimodal transformer with learnable frontend and self attention for emotion recognition. In: IEEE International Conference on Acoustics, Speech and Signal Processing (ICASSP), pp. 6917–6921. IEEE (2022)

Automatic Detection of Noisy Electrocardiogram Signals Without Explicit Noise Labels

Radhika Dua[1] , Jiyoung Lee[1] , Joon-myoung Kwon[2] ,
and Edward Choi[1(✉)]

[1] KAIST, Daejeon, Republic of Korea
{radhikadua,jiyounglee0523,edwardchoi}@kaist.ac.kr
[2] Medical AI Inc., Daejeon, Republic of Korea
cto@medicalai.com

Abstract. Electrocardiogram (ECG) signals are beneficial in diagnosing cardiovascular diseases, which are one of the leading causes of death. However, they are often contaminated by noise artifacts and affect the automatic and manual diagnosis process. Automatic deep learning-based examination of ECG signals can lead to inaccurate diagnosis, and manual analysis involves rejection of noisy ECG samples by clinicians, which might cost extra time. To address this limitation, we present a two-stage deep learning-based framework to automatically detect the noisy ECG samples. Through extensive experiments and analysis on two different datasets, we observe that the deep learning-based framework can detect slightly and highly noisy ECG samples effectively. We also study the transfer of the model learned on one dataset to another dataset and observe that the framework effectively detects noisy ECG samples.

Keywords: ECG · Noisy ECG Signals Detection · Noisy ECG · Electrocardiogram

1 Introduction

Electrocardiogram (ECG) signals provide useful information to clinicians in examining a patient's health status. However, ECG signals are often corrupted by various kinds of noise artifacts, including baseline wander, power line interference, muscle artifact, and instrument noise [18,19]. They are generally categorized into Level 1 (clean samples), Level 2 (slightly noisy samples), and Level 3 (very noisy samples). The presence of these noises in ECG signals are obstacles in diagnosing a patient's status and sometimes makes it impossible to distinguish the basic information such as from which lead the given ECG signal was measured. Moreover, these noise artifacts degenerate the performance of deep learning models employed on ECG signals because the noise impedes the models in learning key features from the given data [1]. Therefore, it is essential to detect and remove noisy ECG signals before they flow into deep learning models or to clinicians [16].

© Springer Nature Switzerland AG 2023
J.-J. Rousseau and B. Kapralos (Eds.): ICPR 2022 Workshops, LNCS 13644, pp. 634–643, 2023.
https://doi.org/10.1007/978-3-031-37742-6_49

Despite the significance of the automatic detection of noisy ECG signals, not much research has been conducted to tackle this issue. Previous research mainly focused on classifying the type of noise that exists in the given signal [15,17]. These work generate a synthetic dataset in which specific noise types are injected into clean ECG signals which is unnatural and rare in the real-world [9]. In the very early stage, statistical analysis from the data, such as extracted features from QRS peaks, pulse portions, and RR intervals, has been used to detect noisy signals [11]. Some work relies on decomposition techniques, like Independent Component Analysis (ICA) and Empirical Mode Decomposition (EMD) [5,6,24]. However, there has not been much research done on detecting noisy ECG signals using deep learning models [13].

To this end, we present a two-stage deep learning-based framework to automatically detect the noisy ECG signals, which includes the detection of Level 2 and Level 3 ECG samples. First, we train a Convolutional Auto-encoder (CAE) model only on clean ECG signals that learns to reconstruct the signal. Then we obtain the feature representation of ECG samples from the latent space of the CAE and use a cluster-conditioned method in the feature space based on Mahalanobis distance [7] to detect the noisy ECG samples.

We conduct a suite of experiments on two datasets that show the promise of the presented approach for the detection of noisy ECG signals. We also conducted extensive experiments to study whether the presented approach, trained on a dataset, can be used to detect noisy samples in other datasets for which we have limited clean (Level 1) samples. We observe that the learned model well transfers to another challenging dataset by finetuning on a small subset of the dataset. To the best of our knowledge, this is the first such effort to use a deep learning-based method to automatically detect noisy ECG samples.

2   Related Work

In the very early stage of detecting noisy signals, statistical analysis based on the given data, such as extracted features from QRS peaks, RR intervals, has been widely used [11]. Also, some works implement frequency and time domain filters, *e.g.*, wavelet thresholding technique, to detect noisy ECG signals [2,3,20].

Recently, decomposition techniques, like Independent Component Analysis (ICA) and Empirical Mode Decomposition (EMD), emerge as a new method to detect noisy ECG signals [5,6,24]. Adaptive filters, which apply Least Mean Square [8,22], Bayesian Filters [12,14], are also employed to detect noisy signals. These adaptive filters have shortcoming in that they need prior training of the data to acquire the best parameters to reconstruct ECG from noisy data.

Although deep learning is gaining popularity, there is limited research related to denoising or removing noisy ECG signals [13]. In this paper, we implement a deep learning model to automatically detect noisy signals.

3   Noisy ECG Signals Detection

ECG signals are often corrupted by different types of noise artifacts. We refer to such samples as Noisy samples and the task of detecting such samples as

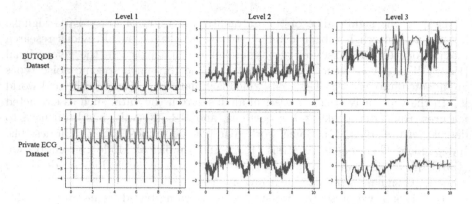

Fig. 1. Examples of clean (Level 1) and noisy (Level 2 and Level 3) samples from BUTQDB and Private ECG datasets. Level 3 samples look much different from Level 1 samples compared to the Level 2 samples.

Noisy ECG signals detection. These noisy samples are divided into two broad categories, Level 2 and Level 3, based on the amount of noise present in the ECG sample (refer to Sect. 5 for more details on datasets). Noisy ECG signals detection task solves two purposes: (i) it enhances the reliability of real-world decision making systems by detecting such noisy samples instead of producing incorrect diagnoses; (ii) it reduces clinicians' efforts as they can focus on clean samples for examining a patient's health status.

We now formally define the task. We consider a dataset composed of clean ECG samples drawn i.i.d. from some underlying data distribution $P_{\mathbf{X}}$ and train an auto-encoder $g(\mathbf{x})$ on $P_{\mathbf{X}}$. Let $f : \mathbf{x} \to \mathcal{Z}$, where $\mathcal{Z} \in \mathbb{R}^m$, denote the feature extractor parameterized by the encoder of the auto-encoder model g, which maps a sample, $\mathbf{x}$, from the input space to the m-dimensional latent space $\mathcal{Z}$. Our objective is to extract the features of the input sample $\mathbf{x}$ using f and design an approach to detect whether the input sample is noisy or clean.

4   Methodology

We present a two-stage framework for the detection of noisy ECG signals.

Stage 1. We train a one-dimensional convolutional auto-encoder (CAE) model g on a training dataset $P_{\mathbf{X}}$ composed of clean ECG samples. The encoder is composed of one-dimensional convolutional neural networks (1D CNNs), and it extracts the latent features smaller than the input sample $\mathbf{x}$. The decoder comprises of transposed 1D CNNs, and it reconstructs output similar to the input sample using the latent features extracted from the encoder. The CAE model is trained to minimize the reconstruction error between the input sample and the reconstructed output generated by the decoder.

Stage 2. Following [4,21,23], we employ a cluster-conditioned detection method in the feature space to detect the noisy samples. Given the training dataset $P_{\mathbf{X}}$ composed of clean ECG samples, we obtain their features using the feature extractor f (parameterized by the encoder of the convolutional auto-encoder g) that extracts the latent features of an input sample $\mathbf{x}$ from the CAE model g trained on $P_{\mathbf{X}}$. Then, we split the features of the training data $P_{\mathbf{X}}$ into m clusters using Gaussian Mixture Model (GMM). Next, we model features in each cluster independently as multivariate gaussian distribution and use the Mahalanobis distance to calculate the Noise detection score $s(\mathbf{x}_{test})$ of a test sample $\mathbf{x}_{test}$ as follows:

$$s(\mathbf{x}_{test}) = -\min_{m}(f(\mathbf{x}_{test}) - \mu_m)^T \Sigma_m^{-1}(f(\mathbf{x}_{test}) - \mu_m), \qquad (1)$$

where $f(\mathbf{x}_{test})$ denotes the features of a test sample $\mathbf{x}_{test}$. μ_m and Σ_m denote the sample mean and sample covariance of the features of the mth cluster. Note that we negate the sign to align with the conventional notion that $s(\mathbf{x}_{test})$ is higher for samples from training distribution and lower for samples from other distributions (noisy samples). Essentially, we use the Noise detection score $s(\mathbf{x}_{test})$ to detect the samples located away from the training data (Level 1 samples) in the latent space as noisy.

Ensembling. We also present an ensembling approach in which we obtain Noise detection score $s(\mathbf{x}_{test})$ for different values of $m \in [m_1, m_2, m_3, ..., m_n]$ and average them to obtain a final score, $s_{\text{ensemble}}(\mathbf{x}_{test})$. More specifically, we run the GMM model multiple times with different values of the number of clusters to split the features of the training dataset into clusters. For each run, we use Mahalanobis distance to calculate the Noise detection score. Then, we obtain the aggregated score by averaging the noise detection scores obtained from different runs. This approach ensures a sample is detected as Noisy only if the majority of the participants in the ensemble agree with one another.

5 Experiments and Results

5.1 Datasets

We evaluate the performance of the presented approach on two datasets.

BUTQDB Dataset. Brno University of Technology ECG Quality Database (BUTQDB) [10] is a publicly available dataset for evaluating the ECG quality provided by Physionet. The samples are measured by using a mobile ECG recorder from 15 subjects in balanced gender and age. Each sample has a noise level annotated by ECG experts.

Private ECG Dataset. This dataset is collected in Asia from 2927 subjects. The data covers a wide range of ages, 18 at the youngest and 102 at the oldest. This data also has a balanced gender ratio.

Both datasets follow the same criteria in annotating the noise level as described below [10]:

1. Level 1 : All significant waveforms (P wave, T wave, and QRS complex) are clearly visible, and the onsets and offsets of these waveforms can be detected reliably.
2. Level 2 : The noise level is increased, and significant points in the ECG are unclear (for example, PR interval and/or QRS duration cannot be measured reliably), but QRS complexes are clearly visible, and the signal enables reliable QRS detection.
3. Level 3 : QRS complexes cannot be detected reliably, and the signal is unsuitable for any analysis.

Fig. 1 presents ECG samples from Level 1 , 2 , and 3 from the BUTQDB and Private ECG datasets. Level 2 and Level 3 samples looks much different from Level 1 samples. Further, Level 3 samples are more shifted away from Level 1 samples relative to Level 2 samples.

Level 1 in BUTQDB and Private ECG datasets are composed of 22, 828 and 1, 314 samples, respectively. We randomly split the Level 1 dataset to make a 80/10/10% train/val/test split. Note that the data of the same samples could be present in multiple splits. We use the BUTQDB dataset and form Level 2 and Level 3 noisy datasets containing 4568 and 1150 ECG samples, respectively. Further, we use the Private ECG dataset and form Level 2 and Level 3 noisy datasets, each containing 172 ECG samples. All these noisy datasets are balanced and comprises of equal number of noisy and clean samples.

5.2   Experimental Setup

Baselines.   We compare our proposed method with two baselines.

– **Convolutional Auto-encoder (CAE) + reconstruction error (AE + recons).**   We determine the noisy samples based on the reconstruction loss produced by the trained Convolution Auto Encoder. The less the reconstruction loss, the more probability the given sample is a clean sample.
– **Convolutional Variational Auto-encoder + log probability (CVAE + log prob).**   We determine the noisy samples based on the log probability calculated by the trained Convolutional Variational Auto-Encoder. The higher the log probability, the more likely the given sample is a clean sample.

Evaluation Metrics.   We evaluate the effectiveness of our method for noisy ECG signals detection using two metrics, namely AUROC and AUPRC.

– **AUROC.**   It measures the Area Under the Receiver Operating Characteristic curve, in which the true positive rate is plotted as a function of false positive rate for different threshold settings.
– **AUPRC-Out.**   It measures the Area Under the Precision-Recall (PR) curve. In a PR curve, the precision is plotted as a function of recall for different threshold settings. For the AUPRC-Out metric, the noisy samples are specified as positive.

Training Details. We stacked two Convolutional layers for each encoder and decoder in CAE with latent hidden channel size of 64. All experiments are conducted with one 3090 RTX GPU. We trained our model using AdamW optimizer with a learning rate of $1e - 4$.

Table 1. Noisy ECG signals detection performance of our approach on BUTQDB and Private ECG datasets measured by AUROC and AUPRC. The models are trained on Level 1 samples and evaluated for Noisy ECG signals detection on Level 2 and 3 of the respective datasets. The results are averaged across 5 seeds. We compare the Noisy ECG signals detection performance of Ours (Ensemble) with the baselines (CAE + recons, VAE + log prob) and observe that our approach obtains superior results (indicated by **bold** numbers).

Method	BUTQDB Dataset				Private ECG Dataset			
	Level 2		Level 3		Level 2		Level 3	
	AUROC	AUPRC	AUROC	AUPRC	AUROC	AUPRC	AUROC	AUPRC
CAE + recons	73.25 ± 0.20	**75.46 ± 0.50**	84.43 ± 0.40	86.06 ± 0.30	67.78 ± 3.31	60.28 ± 2.54	79.96 ± 0.78	66.62 ± 0.86
CVAE + log prob	57.63 ± 1.50	59.26 ± 0.50	67.85 ± 1.50	81.10 ± 0.60	54.13 ± 0.74	52.91 ± 1.06	**82.00 ± 0.09**	72.62 ± 0.07
Ours (m = 1)	80.52 ± 1.35	76.96 ± 1.68	94.02 ± 0.71	91.84 ± 1.28	68.23 ± 1.40	62.84 ± 1.39	67.30 ± 0.81	57.61 ± 0.62
Ours (m = 2)	81.40 ± 1.45	77.28 ± 1.63	96.13 ± 0.39	94.42 ± 0.89	71.19 ± 3.75	66.44 ± 5.62	73.91 ± 4.96	66.45 ± 7.02
Ours (m = 3)	77.88 ± 0.96	73.55 ± 1.92	96.57 ± 0.53	95.05 ± 1.17	72.47 ± 2.71	67.72 ± 3.99	77.11 ± 5.51	68.61 ± 8.32
Ours (m = 4)	77.03 ± 1.38	73.31 ± 1.61	95.98 ± 0.67	94.60 ± 1.07	73.88 ± 2.80	71.23 ± 3.69	79.31 ± 5.86	74.29 ± 10.93
Ours (m = 5)	76.63 ± 1.16	72.93 ± 1.41	95.59 ± 0.94	94.20 ± 1.28	73.93 ± 2.71	70.49 ± 3.40	80.05 ± 4.69	76.61 ± 8.48
Ours (m = 6)	75.56 ± 1.33	70.92 ± 0.95	95.59 ± 1.21	94.03 ± 1.45	74.48 ± 2.88	72.12 ± 3.96	81.43 ± 5.09	77.48 ± 9.28
Ours (m = 7)	73.87 ± 2.72	69.04 ± 3.13	94.97 ± 2.26	93.10 ± 3.16	73.79 ± 2.61	71.28 ± 4.04	82.22 ± 4.66	78.71 ± 9.25
Ours (m = 8)	73.22 ± 0.85	68.38 ± 0.83	94.55 ± 0.64	92.78 ± 0.89	75.55 ± 2.55	74.11 ± 4.07	81.51 ± 5.02	77.88 ± 9.58
Ours (m = 9)	73.98 ± 1.06	69.36 ± 1.63	95.33 ± 1.09	93.78 ± 1.58	74.75 ± 3.48	73.47 ± 5.39	81.89 ± 5.33	78.98 ± 10.17
Ours (m = 10)	73.31 ± 1.96	68.22 ± 2.55	94.83 ± 2.42	92.85 ± 3.71	74.82 ± 3.19	72.96 ± 4.92	81.46 ± 5.26	78.26 ± 9.85
Ours (Ensemble)	77.82 ± 1.05	73.49 ± 1.31	**95.84 ± 0.70**	**94.25 ± 1.13**	**74.28 ± 2.18**	**72.09 ± 3.09**	80.25 ± 4.92	**76.60 ± 9.84**

5.3   Results

Quantitative Results Table 1 presents the noisy ECG signals detection performance of our presented method on BUTQDB and Private ECG datasets. We observe that our approach with different values of the number of clusters and ensembling approach outperforms the baselines for detecting Level 2 and Level 3 noisy samples across the two datasets. Although detecting the Level 2 samples is challenging, the presented framework effectively detects them and outperforms the baselines. We also observe that all the methods, including baselines and our approach, obtain higher scores for Level 3 samples than Level 2 samples. This indicates that all methods detect samples from Level 3 as noisier than samples from Level 2, which aligns with the description of Level 2 and Level 3 samples.

PCA Analysis. We analyze the PCA visualizations of the clean and noisy samples. As shown in Fig. 2, we apply principal component analysis (PCA) on the feature representations obtained from the latent space of the convolutional auto-encoder (CAE) model to visualize the location of clean samples (Level 1 samples) and noisy samples (Level 2 and Level 3). We observe that Level 2 samples are located close to the clean (Level 1) samples whereas Level 3 samples are located away from the clean (Level 1) samples. Since the Level 3 samples are more shifted from the Level 1 samples compared to Level 2 samples, our approach obtains higher AUROC and AUPRC scores for Level 3 samples.

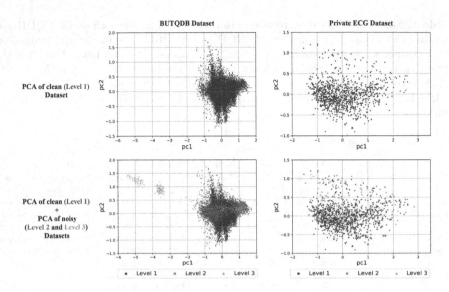

Fig. 2. *(top)* PCA visualization of clean (Level 1) samples from BUTQDB and Private ECG datasets to demonstrate the location of clean samples. *(bottom)* PCA visualization of clean (Level 1) samples overlapped by PCA visualization of noisy samples (Level 2 and Level 3) from BUTQDB and Private ECG datasets to demonstrate the location of Level 2 and Level 3 samples relative to Level 1 samples. In both the datasets, Level 3 samples are more shifted from the Level 1 samples compared to Level 2 samples.

Transfer to Private ECG Dataset. In the real-world, it is time-consuming and requires clinicians' effort to collect large datasets with annotations of Level 1, 2, and 3 . To this end, we also studied whether the presented approach, trained on the BUTQDB dataset, can be used to detect noisy samples in other datasets for which we have limited clean (Level 1) samples. We use the convolutional auto-encoder (CAE) model trained on the BUTQDB dataset and finetune it on different percentages of Level 1 samples from the Private ECG dataset. We finetune the model on 20%, 40%, 60%, 80%, and 100% of the total Level 1 samples in Private ECG dataset. Then, we evaluate the finetuned model for noisy ECG signals detection on Level 2 and Level 3 samples from the Private ECG dataset. Note that we do not test the generalization ability of our framework by training the model on the BUTQDB dataset and evaluating it on the Private ECG dataset (i.e., zero-shot test). This is because the Level 1 samples of the two datasets might have different distributions due to diverse factors such as different dataset collection setup, ethnicity, etc. Due to this, Level 1 samples of the Private ECG dataset might also be detected as noisy. Table 2 shows the noisy signals detection performance of the model finetuned on different amounts of Level 1 samples from the Private ECG dataset. We observe that finetuning the model on a very small dataset hurts performance. In our experiments, finetuning on more than 40% of dataset demonstrates decent noise detection performance of Level 2 and Level 3 noisy samples. Our finetuned model outperforms the baselines finetuned on BUTQDB. Further, from Table 1 and Table 2, we observe that finetuning the model pretrained on BUTQDB helps in better detection of Level 2 and 3 samples compared to training from scratch on Private ECG dataset.

Table 2. Noisy ECG signals detection performance of our approach on Private ECG dataset measured by AUROC and AUPRC. The models pretrained on Level 1 samples of BUTQDB dataset are finetuned on different amount of Level 1 samples of private dataset and evaluated for Noisy ECG signals detection on Level 2 and 3 of the private dataset. We compare the Noisy ECG signals detection performance of Ours (Ensemble) with the baselines (CAE + recons, VAE + log prob) and observe that our approach obtains superior results (indicated by **bold** numbers).

	Method	Level 2					Level 3				
		Dataset Amount					Dataset Amount				
		20	40	60	80	100	20	40	60	80	100
AUROC	CAE + recons	68.23	66.75	67.46	68.56	71.14	**80.91**	80.76	80.52	80.67	81.19
	CVAE + log prob	53.66	47.70	52.03	51.66	54.99	78.42	77.92	79.57	79.22	81.88
	Ours ($m = 1$)	71.34	71.24	71.01	70.98	69.12	69.94	68.85	68.85	68.65	67.70
	Ours ($m = 2$)	70.89	72.26	73.70	73.40	73.00	68.66	73.32	75.08	76.20	76.28
	Ours ($m = 3$)	70.82	74.96	76.28	74.82	72.01	68.48	80.67	78.87	77.27	79.34
	Ours ($m = 4$)	70.80	77.11	77.39	77.11	75.38	68.66	86.78	81.96	81.72	82.95
	Ours ($m = 5$)	74.81	78.22	77.58	76.95	75.53	77.53	88.72	86.11	81.52	85.24
	Ours ($m = 6$)	74.85	78.37	79.26	79.41	75.70	78.02	89.02	86.83	84.46	84.90
	Ours ($m = 7$)	74.50	76.81	77.58	79.75	77.81	78.41	85.88	84.55	85.32	88.30
	Ours ($m = 8$)	75.28	78.26	81.14	79.91	75.69	78.98	91.25	90.82	89.41	88.03
	Ours ($m = 9$)	69.74	78.26	81.58	79.42	76.46	71.34	91.25	89.82	86.47	87.11
	Ours ($m = 10$)	71.67	78.26	81.15	78.46	78.42	70.66	91.25	91.08	84.63	90.27
	Ours (Ensemble)	**72.05**	**78.91**	**79.85**	**78.5**	**76.31**	72.47	**89.43**	**88.05**	**84.11**	**86.24**
AUPRC	CAE + recons	59.69	58.72	59.44	60.49	62.93	67.79	67.75	67.45	67.61	68.07
	CVAE + log prob	53.23	47.08	51.19	48.81	54.06	70.81	67.19	71.93	72.52	75.66
	Ours ($m = 1$)	67.45	65.45	64.74	63.35	63.53	62.81	59.44	58.80	57.39	57.03
	Ours ($m = 2$)	65.14	67.65	69.52	69.19	72.06	59.92	62.84	64.06	65.33	67.10
	Ours ($m = 3$)	65.10	76.51	75.54	68.45	68.97	59.80	81.12	71.03	64.74	70.46
	Ours ($m = 4$)	64.83	78.23	76.48	75.41	76.86	59.72	88.89	79.53	72.64	82.25
	Ours ($m = 5$)	75.56	79.09	77.13	75.61	77.34	78.06	91.04	86.73	72.35	86.68
	Ours ($m = 6$)	75.88	79.01	78.65	78.74	75.97	79.11	91.40	87.56	83.96	86.08
	Ours ($m = 7$)	75.23	77.14	76.71	78.34	78.89	80.37	88.00	85.47	85.62	89.86
	Ours ($m = 8$)	74.71	79.65	82.07	79.45	76.18	80.23	93.47	92.61	91.15	90.11
	Ours ($m = 9$)	69.88	79.65	81.39	79.71	77.19	69.23	93.47	91.37	88.30	89.03
	Ours ($m = 10$)	68.55	79.65	81.43	77.74	78.77	64.26	93.47	93.16	86.26	92.06
	Ours (Ensemble)	**71.86**	**80.46**	**79.33**	**77.18**	**77.69**	70.91	**91.84**	**89.74**	**84.24**	**88.07**

6   Conclusion

In this work, we attempt to bridge the gap between noisy ECG signals detection and deep learning and aimed to automatically detect the ECG signals contaminated by noise artifacts as they can affect the diagnosis. We present a two-stage deep learning-based method to detect noisy ECG samples. We conducted exhaustive experiments on two different ECG datasets composed of slightly noisy and highly noisy ECG samples to demonstrate the effectiveness of the two-stage framework in detecting the diverse noisy ECG samples. We also present a PCA analysis to justify the performance of the framework. To further bolster the effectiveness of the framework, we studied the transfer of the framework trained on one dataset to another dataset and observed that the framework can still identify the noisy samples. We hope that our work will open up a broader discussion around automatic detection of noisy ECG signals.

Acknowledgements. This work was supported by Institute of Information & Communications Technology Planning & Evaluation (IITP) grant (No.2019-0-00075, Artificial Intelligence Graduate School Program(KAIST)) funded by the Korea government (MSIT) and by Medical AI Inc.

References

1. Abd Sukor, J., Mohktar, M.S., Redmond, S.J., Lovell, N.H.: Signal quality measures on pulse oximetry and blood pressure signals acquired from self-measurement in a home environment. IEEE J. Biomed. Health Inform. **19**(1), 102–108 (2014)
2. Ayat, M., Shamsollahi, M.B., Mozaffari, B., Kharabian, S.: Ecg denoising using modulus maxima of wavelet transform. In: International Conference of the IEEE Engineering in Medicine and Biology Society, pp. 416–419. IEEE (2009)
3. Donoho, D.L.: De-noising by soft-thresholding. IEEE Trans. Inf. Theory **41**(3), 613–627 (1995)
4. Dua, R., sil Yang, S., Li, Y., Choi, E.: Task agnostic and post-hoc unseen distribution detection (2022)
5. Kuzilek, J., Kremen, V., Soucek, F., Lhotska, L.: Independent component analysis and decision trees for ecg holter recording de-noising. PLoS ONE **9**(6), e98450 (2014)
6. Lee, J., McManus, D.D., Merchant, S., Chon, K.H.: Automatic motion and noise artifact detection in holter ecg data using empirical mode decomposition and statistical approaches. IEEE Trans. Biomed. Eng. **59**(6), 1499–1506 (2011)
7. Lee, K., Lee, K., Lee, H., Shin, J.: A simple unified framework for detecting out-of-distribution samples and adversarial attacks. In: Proceedings of the Advances in Neural Information Processing Systems (NeurIPS) (2018)
8. Lu, G., et al.: Removing ecg noise from surface emg signals using adaptive filtering. Neurosci. Lett. **462**(1), 14–19 (2009)
9. McSharry, P.E., Clifford, G.D., Tarassenko, L., Smith, L.A.: A dynamical model for generating synthetic electrocardiogram signals. IEEE Trans. Biomed. Eng. **50**(3), 289–294 (2003)
10. Nemcova, A., Smisek, R., Opravilová, K., Vitek, M., Smital, L., Maršánová, L.: Brno university of technology ecg quality database (but qdb). PhysioNet (2020)

11. Orphanidou, C., Bonnici, T., Charlton, P.H., Clifton, D.A., Vallance, D., Tarassenko, L.: Signal-quality indices for the electrocardiogram and photoplethys-mogram: Derivation and applications to wireless monitoring. IEEE J. Biomed. Health Inform. **19**, 832–838 (2015)
12. Panigrahy, D., Sahu, P.: Extended kalman smoother with differential evolution technique for denoising of ecg signal. Australasian Phys. Eng. Sci. Med. **39**(3), 783–795 (2016)
13. Rodrigues, R., Couto, P.: A neural network approach to ecg denoising. ArXiv abs/1212.5217 (2012)
14. Sameni, R., Shamsollahi, M.B., Jutten, C., Clifford, G.D.: A nonlinear bayesian filtering framework for ECG denoising. IEEE Trans. Biomed. Eng. **54**(12), 2172–2185 (2007)
15. Satija, U., Ramkumar, B., Manikandan, M.S.: A simple method for detection and classification of ecg noises for wearable ECG monitoring devices. In: 2015 2nd International Conference on Signal Processing and Integrated Networks (SPIN), pp. 164–169 (2015)
16. Satija, U., Ramkumar, B., Manikandan, M.S.: Real-time signal quality-aware ECG telemetry system for IoT-based health care monitoring. IEEE Internet Things J. **4**(3), 815–823 (2017)
17. Satija, U., Ramkumar, B., Manikandan, M.S.: Automated ECG noise detection and classification system for unsupervised healthcare monitoring. IEEE J. Biomed. Health Inform. **22**, 722–732 (2018)
18. Satija, U., Ramkumar, B., Manikandan, M.S.: A new automated signal quality-aware ECG beat classification method for unsupervised ECG diagnosis environ-ments. IEEE Sens. J. **19**(1), 277–286 (2018)
19. Satija, U., Ramkumar, B., Manikandan, M.S.: A review of signal processing tech-niques for electrocardiogram signal quality assessment. IEEE Rev. Biomed. Eng. **11**, 36–52 (2018)
20. Sayadi, O., Shamsollahi, M.B.: ECG denoising with adaptive bionic wavelet trans-form. In: International Conference of the IEEE Engineering in Medicine and Biol-ogy Society, pp. 6597–6600. IEEE (2006)
21. Sehwag, V., Chiang, M., Mittal, P.: SSD: A unified framework for self-supervised outlier detection. In: Proceedings of the International Conference on Learning Rep-resentations (ICLR) (2021)
22. Thakor, N.V., Zhu, Y.S.: Applications of adaptive filtering to ECG analysis: noise cancellation and arrhythmia detection. IEEE Trans. Biomed. Eng. **38**(8), 785–794 (1991)
23. Xiao, Z., Yan, Q., Amit, Y.: Do we really need to learn representations from in-domain data for outlier detection? ArXiv abs/2105.09270 (2021)
24. Yoon, H., Kim, H., Kwon, S., Park, K.: An automated motion artifact removal algorithm in electrocardiogram based on independent component analysis. In: Pro-ceedings of the 5th International Conference on eHealth, Telemedicine, and Social Medicine (eTELEMED'2013), pp. 15–20 (2013)

International Workshop on Industrial Machine Learning (IML)

Preface

With the advent of Industry 4.0 and Smart Manufacturing paradigms, data has become a valuable resource, and very often an asset, for every manufacturing company. Data from the market, from machines, from warehouses and many other sources are now cheaper than ever to be collected and stored. A study from Juniper Research has identified industrial internet of things (IIoT) as a key growth market over the next five years, accounting for an increase in the global number of IIoT connections from 17.7 billion in 2020 to 36.8 billion in 2025, representing an overall growth rate of 107%.

With such an amount of data produced every second, classical data analysis approaches are not useful and only automated learning methods can be applied to produce value, a market estimated in more than 200B$ worldwide. Using machine learning techniques manufacturers can exploit data to significantly impact their bottom line by greatly improving production efficiency, product quality, and employee safety.

The introduction of ML to industry has many benefits that can result in advantages well beyond efficiency improvements, opening doors to new opportunities for both practitioners and researchers. Some direct applications of ML in manufacturing include predictive maintenance, supply chain management, logistics, quality control, human-robot interaction, process monitoring, anomaly detection and root cause analysis to name a few. This workshop will ground on the successful story of the first edition, with 19 oral presentations and 3 invited talks, to draw attention to the importance of integrating ML technologies and ML-based solutions into the manufacturing domain, while addressing the challenges and barriers to meet the specific needs of this sector. Workshop participants will have the chance to discuss needs and barriers for ML in manufacturing, state-of-the-art in ML applications to manufacturing, and future research opportunities in this domain.

August 2022

Francesco Setti
Paolo Rota
Vittorio Murino
Luigi Stefano
Massimiliano Mancini

On the Use of Learning-Based Forecasting Methods for Ameliorating Fashion Business Processes: A Position Paper

Geri Skenderi[1]([✉]), Christian Joppi[2], Matteo Denitto[2], and Marco Cristani[2,3]

[1] Department of Computer Science, University of Verona, Verona, Italy
`geri.skenderi@univr.it`
[2] Humatics Srl, Verona, Italy
`{christian.joppi,matteo.denitto,marco.cristani}@sys-datgroup.com`
[3] Department of Engineering for Innovation Medicine of the University of Verona, Verona, Italy
`marco.cristani@univr.it`

Abstract. The fashion industry is one of the most active and competitive markets in the world, manufacturing millions of products and reaching large audiences every year. A plethora of business processes are involved in this large-scale industry, but due to the common short lifecycle of clothing items, supply-chain management and retailing strategies are crucial for good market performance. Correctly understanding the wants and needs of clients, managing logistic issues and marketing the correct products are high-level problems with a lot of uncertainty associated to them, most notably due to the unpredictability often associated with the future. It is therefore straightforward that forecasting methods, which generate predictions of the future, are indispensable in order to ameliorate all the various business processes that deal with the true purpose and meaning of fashion: having a lot of people wear a particular product or style, rendering these items, people and consequently brands fashionable. In this paper, we provide an overview of three concrete forecasting tasks that any fashion company can apply in order to improve their industrial and market impact. We underline advances and issues in all three tasks and argue about their importance and the impact they can have at an industrial level. Finally, we highlight issues and directions of future work, reflecting on how learning-based forecasting methods can further aid the fashion industry.

Keywords: Forecasting · Fashion AI · Industrial Machine Learning

1 Introduction

The technological evolution of the fashion industry has been nothing short of remarkable. Electronic retail, also known as e-commerce, is such a normal commodity nowadays that it's hard to believe that the first e-commerce websites

© Springer Nature Switzerland AG 2023
J.-J. Rousseau and B. Kapralos (Eds.): ICPR 2022 Workshops, LNCS 13644, pp. 647–659, 2023.
https://doi.org/10.1007/978-3-031-37742-6_50

were introduced less than thirty years ago. E-commerce is evergrowing and it is predicted to be worth 24.5% of the whole apparel industry by 2025 [2]. Constant innovation has rendered the Fashion & Apparel industry one of the most lucrative industries in the world [1], and it is expected to keep rising in the following years. Nevertheless, this industry has been widely criticized for its large waste generation [3], because of phenomena like overproduction and product returns [19]. The main reason for this can be tied back to customer dissatisfaction [23], whether that relates to size, color, style, or textile quality. As a result, for the sector to successfully regulate environmentally friendly production methods and be as efficient as possible, it must become fully customer-centric and understand its clients at a profound level. Exploiting the extensive advances in machine learning solutions in the past few years is one of the better ways to achieve this goal.

In this paper, we explore the particular utility of forecasting, a discipline that has remained closely related to retail ever since its early days throughout the 20th century [6,34] until recent years, where multiple forecasting systems are present [25,28,33]. Specifically, we will detail how forecasting models that are based on machine learning can massively improve business processes in fashion, from supply chain and inventory management to marketing policies. The main reason why we argue in favor of these models is that they can bypass several limitations of established and well-known time series analysis methods like AR, MA or ARIMA [6]. To discuss these limitations and discuss why solutions to them are crucial, we will consider three different tasks in this paper:

1. New product demand forecasting, where the future sales of a new product have to be estimated without having any historical data;
2. Short-term new product forecasting, where the future sales of a recently published product have to be estimated based on only a few observations;
3. Product recommendation, where the future preferences of a user have to be predicted based on their past purchases or similarity with other users.

In the following chapters, we will first talk about the advances in each respective task and then argue why these tasks are important and why they can accurately and efficiently be solved using deep learning methods. We then talk about open issues in each task and wrap up the paper by discussing future possibilities of forecasting with deep learning for fashion. We hope that this paper can motivate further research in this field by laying out a series of arguments backed up by concrete results, while also acting as a short survey on these particular tasks that can be considered "edge-cases" of forecasting in fashion.

2   New Product Demand Forecasting

Sales forecasting is one of the most typical and important forecasting applications in fashion retail [5,9]. The ability to predict client demands and behavior can make a huge difference in commercial activity, especially when vast volumes of items need to be controlled, for a variety of economic and financial reasons.

While the forecasting of time series with a known historical past is an extensively studied topic [6,16,20], another practical and much harder case has received very little attention: the forecasting of *new items* that the market has yet to witness. Experts create judgmental projections in these circumstances [16], taking into account the characteristics of the freshly designed product as well as information on what is currently trending in the market to make an educated guess. In simpler words, the *demand* for a new product is foretasted based on an expert's experience.

Under this last formulation, it starts to become clear why machine learning can help in this scenario: It is possible to design models in such a way that they learn this judgmental process. The intuition behind models that can help in solving this task is that generally, new products will sell comparably to similar, older products; consequently, these models should be able to understand similarities among new and older products and understand how trends evolve with time. We will now demonstrate how this task has been tackled in the literature, in order to then provide insight on what can be additionally be done.

In [29], a variety of machine learning models are taken into consideration such as boosting algorithms (XGBoost, Gradient Boosted Trees) and Neural Networks (MLP, LSTM). The authors propose to simulate the expert judgment by utilizing the textual attributes related to category and color, and merchandising factors such as discounts or promotions. In this case, it is possible to train a model using a batch of products, where of course the object's release date is also clearly stated, such that the models can process each ground truth time series and learn inter-product correlations based on their common textual attributes. This is something that classical methods like ARIMA *simply cannot achieve*, as they cannot be fit on multiple series in different time frames, but most importantly they *cannot be utilized* when we have no past observations. In this scenario, relying on a machine learning solution is the most efficient and performing solution.

A big problem with the work of [29], is that they do not consider any visual information. Even though textual attributes are important, they can never create a good enough representation for a fashion item like visual attributes. A picture is, after all, worth one thousand words. In [10], the authors make a big step forward and use an autoregressive RNN model that takes past sales, auxiliary signals like the release date and discounts, textual embeddings of product attributes, and the product image as input. The model then uses an additive attention mechanism [4] to understand which of the modalities is the most important to the sales and combines all these attended features into a feature vector which is fed to a GRU [7] decoder. This Recurrent Neural Network based architecture is indeed an accurate model for expert judgments. Each product is represented by its visual, textual, and temporal attributes, which creates fine-grained groups of similar products. The autoregressive component of the RNN allows the model to take past predictions into account, therefore generating a forecast which is reliant on the initial guess. One of the most important aspects of this work is that the attention mechanism also provides an interpretability component, demonstrating which modality is the most important at each fore-casting step. The authors try out different variations of the architecture and their best performing model, Cross-Attention Explainable RNN, reports less than 40% weighted Mean Absolute Percentage Error (wMAPE) in some partitions of an *unshared, proprietary dataset.*

A few issues that were not considered in the aforementioned papers, are the concept of trends and popularity, as well as a benchmark where the new product demand forecasting task could be tested. In [30], the authors tackle all of these problems, proposing a Transformer-based, multimodal architecture that can also process exogenous Google Trends signals. These signals bring the idea of the fashion expert judgment full circle, as now the model can reason based on the past performances of similar products in the dataset, as well as the online popularity of the different attributes that make up the product. Additionally, to avoid the error accumulation problem of autoregressive RNNs, the authors propose a generative approach where the whole demand series is forecasted in one step. Finally, the authors render their dataset, named Visuelle, public. This is an important aspect as it promotes further research on the methodological aspect of this challenging task, by relying on a dataset that is actually based on the real sales of a fast-fashion company. On Visuelle, the GTM-Transformer model of [30] reports a wMAPE of 55,2%, compared to 59% of Cross-Attention Explainable RNN, as shown also in Table 1. Recent work delves even deeper in the idea of online popularity as a forecasting proxy, with [18] introducing a data-centric pipeline able to generate a novel exogenous observation data (POP), comparing directly the new product image with the images uploaded on the web in the past. The POP signal fed into the GTM-Transformer model represents the state-of-the-art on this task, with a wMAPE of 52,39%. In [26] a novel Multimodal Quasi-AutoRegressive deep learning architecture (MuQAR) has been proposed. The model uses attributes and captions automatically extracted from the product image by the use of image classification and captioning methods. Attributes are used both to broaden the set of google trends and as input to the model together with the image captions. MuQAR model reports a wMAPE of 52,63% (Table 1).

These results demonstrate that the problem of new product demand fore-casting benefits greatly from machine learning and computer vision. It is also very important to consider multi-modality and augment the model reasoning power by using exogenous data that can act as a proxy for the notion of popu-larity. Figure 1 shows different demand forecasting systems at work when they perform the forecasting of new product sales. The best-performing architecture is able to produce forecasts that closely resemble the testing ground truth series, showing how multi-modality and exogenous information helps in improving fore-casting performance. Figure 2 shows the results with different exogenous signals used with the GTM-Transformer architecture. POP provides the most accurate curve. To provide a concrete example as to why performing well on this task is important, we report here a result from [30]. A typical supply chain opera-tion related to new product demand forecasting is the first order problem, i.e., ordering a number of products that matches the sum of future sales, without

Table 1. New Product Demand Forecasting results on Visuelle in terms of Weighted Mean Absolute Percentage Error (WAPE) and Mean Absolute Error (MAE). The lower the better for both metrics.

Method	Input	WAPE	MAE
Attribute KNN [10] 2020	[T]	59,8	32,7
Image KNN [10] 2020	[I]	62,2	34,0
Attr+Image KNN [10] 2020	[T+I]	61,3	33,5
GBoosting [13] 2001	[T+I+G]	63,5	34,7
Cat-MM-RNN [10] 2020	[T+I+G]	65,9	35,8
CrossAttnRNN [10] 2020	[T+I+G]	59,0	32,1
MuQAR [26]	[T+I+G+A+C]	52,6	28,8
GTM-Transformer [30]	[T+I+G]	55,2	30,2
GTM-Transformer [18]	[T+I+POP]	**52,4**	**28,6**

exceeding or underestimating in the best case. By using a typical supply chain policy instead of forecasting based first order, the company would lose 683,372\$, while the seemingly small improvement of 5% in wMAPE terms, results in more than 156,942\$ spared. It is clear to see how this forecasting task can massively help in sorting out initial doubts regarding early supply chain operations, which can translate into a lot of money-saving and efficient decisions.

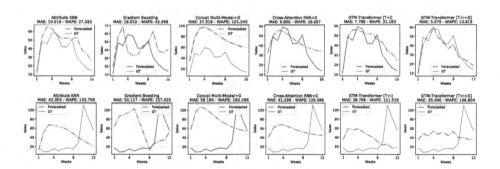

Fig. 1. Qualitative results for the New Product Demand Forecasting of two different products on VISUELLE.

3   Short-Observation New Product Forecasting

Short-observation new product forecasting (SO-fore) aims at predicting future sales in the short term, having a past statistic given by the early sales of a given product. In practice, after a few weeks from the market delivery, one has

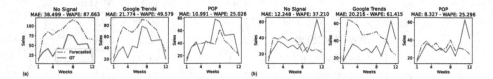

Fig. 2. Qualitative results for the New Product Demand Forecasting of two different products on VISUELLE with different exogenous signals.

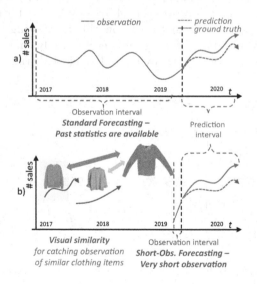

Fig. 3. Illustration of the Short-Observation New Product Forecasting task from [31]. In a), the standard forecasting setup is reported. In b), SO-fore is sketched, focusing on a very short observation window (2 weeks) to predict sales. The authors show that relying on visual similarity to extract information from similar data improves forecasting.

to sense how well a clothing item has performed and forecast its behavior in the coming weeks. This is crucial to improve *restocking policies* [22]: a clothing item with a rapid selling rate should be restocked to avoid stockouts. The same reasoning can be applied to the opposite case, where a product with a slow-selling rate might not necessarily be a focus point for restocking in the near future. Restocking policies are typically processes that are always associated with high uncertainty, because of constantly shifting market dynamics. While it is simpler, in principle, for companies to make an initial guess when having to perform their first restock, i.e., new product demand forecasting, managing restocks while a product is selling can get complicated.

To assess short-term restocking problems, we argue that it is useful to consider two particular cases of the SO-fore problem, based on the estimated lifetime of the product under consideration. Consider a product p that will sell for a pre-defined amount of timesteps t (these can be days, weeks, months, etc.). Given only a few observations, $t' : t' \ll t$, the first set-up would be SO-fore$_{t'-(t-t')}$, in which the observed window is t' weeks long and the forecasting horizon is $t - t'$ weeks long (the remaining, unseen observations), required when a company wants to implement few restocks [12]. This corresponds to forecasting the sales based on the few available observations until the end of the product's lifetime, focusing on the estimation of major restocks.

The second set-up would be SO-fore$_{t'-1}$, where the forecasting horizon changes to a single timestep (at a time), and is instead required when a company wants to take decisions on a frequent basis, as in the *ultra-fast fashion* supply chain [8,32]. This corresponds to forecasting the sales for each timestep based on the t' ones before it, focusing on the estimation of a minor, more frequent, restocks.

In these scenarios, because we have past observations, we can consider *some* classical forecasting approaches, such as Naive method [17] (using the last observed ground truth value as the forecast) or Simple Exponential Smoothing (SES) [15,17]. It is still impossible, in practice, to fit models that make assumptions about the process that generates the time series such as AR, MA, or ARIMA models. Even though in theory having more than one observation is sufficient, a larger sample is required to estimate statistically significant parameters ($t' = 50$ [6]). Therefore, without relying on ML approaches, the forecasting practitioner in this case would have to rely on methods that calculate simple statistics based on the last observed values. On the other hand, similarly to the task of New product demand forecasting, learning-based approaches can exploit inter-product similarity and also the similarity between the initial sales period in order to provide much more accurate forecasts. This problem is of course, simpler than new product demand forecasting, since knowing the initial t' observations can greatly benefit forecasting, without acting purely in a judgmental guessing framework such as the models from [30].

Figure 3 from [31] gives a clear visual explanation of this task. The authors of the same paper introduce Visuelle 2.0, a second version of the homonym dataset, where the time series data are disaggregated at the shop level, and include the sales, inventory stock, max-normalized prices, and discounts. This permits to perform SO-fore considering every single store. The authors then implement on Visuelle 2.0 one ML and one DL approach from [10]: k-Nearest Neighbors and Cross-Attention Explainable RNN. Given that each product in the dataset is known to sell for $t = 12$ weeks, it is assumed that two weeks of sales are observed ($t' = 2$ weeks). In both cases, i.e., SO-fore$_{2-1}$ and SO-fore$_{2-10}$ the authors show that the RNN approach outperforms the others by a significant margin, while the usable classical forecasting approaches give poor performances. It is also worth noticing that exploiting image embeddings proves to be crucial to further improve the performances in the case of longer horizons.

Short-observation new product forecasting is a task of high importance especially in the industry of fast-fashion, for several reasons. Firstly, it is necessary to have estimates about restocking policies when the product lifecycle is so dynamic. Secondly, given that most fast-fashion companies have multiple shops, it is necessary to understand how different products sell in each shop. Finally, utilising forecasting approaches continuously is very important for marketing reasons in specific shops, because if the company knows how much a given product will sell in advance, they can try to make it sell more or less by changing the item's position within the shop. It is therefore very important to have benchmarks that can capture these different elements, in order to advance this particular area of fashion forecasting. We believe that Visuelle 2.0, as mentioned before, contains a lot of data and information and it is the first of its kind, but it is important for industrial practitioners to try and create other datasets that might present different forecasting challenges in the short term.

4   Product Recommendation

So far we have explored problems that deal a lot with the supply chain. Of course, this is not the only aspect that a company would have to manage in the real world, given that the main goal is to sell a particular product. The biggest issue with fashion is that it represents a form of expressiveness and like any other form of expressiveness, it is quite subjective and often defined by different societal biases. It is therefore useful to continuously have an idea as to what particular clients like and tailor new products that are specific to some client base. This is by no means a new idea, yet given the abundance of choices when looking at clothing items, a good recommendation system is required to correctly sort, order, and deliver relevant product content or information to users. Effective fashion recommender systems may improve the purchasing experiences of billions of customers while also increasing supplier sales and income. Deploying such systems in the fashion industry is not trivial, often because the purchase history for a customer is very sparse and because most customers do not define themselves based on a single style. The biggest issue of these mining and retrieval systems is that often they might categorize users as actually belonging to a particular style or group of clients and immerse them in a "bubble of information", where the user keeps getting similar recommendations. On the other hand, the systems must also maintain a relatively conservatory notion of novelty and not recommend random things to a user.

We believe that several of these issues can be bypassed if the temporal aspect were to be considered instead of treating product recommendation as a static problem. Most recommender approaches deployed in practice are instances of collaborative or content filtering, where the systems often relied on user or item similarity to perform recommendations. As an illustrative example, consider a client who typically buys sportswear, but recently bought a suit jacket and a shirt. Considering user-user similarity, the system will probably provide a recommendation that is related to sportswear, since that is what other similar users have provided. The same thing can be said about the items, where most of the population is made up of a particular type of article. What is often missing in these cases, is the notion of the time of purchase of each product. Using temporal continuity in recommender systems is nothing novel, as seen in the field of research of session recommendations [21,27], but actually relying on the temporal properties of purchases to characterize users is something that is not deployed in typical systems. We like to refer to this notion as similarity-over-time.

If the recommendation task was cast as a forecasting task, a model would also have to keep in mind the temporal relationship between the purchases (or ratings) and similarity-over-time. In this scenario, a simple idea could be to give more weight to later observations or, given enough data, understand the seasonal trends of the users. It is, therefore, crucial to have data on which to learn or try these approaches. A real-case scenario of such datasets for fashion is Visuelle 2.0 [31] and the Amazon reviews dataset [24]. A graphical example of customer data from Visuelle 2.0 is reported in Fig. 4, where it is visible that some users have marked preferences: The recent purchases of user 10 are all greyish items.

Product recommendation as suggested here would consist in defining a particular time index t_{rec}, when the historical data of all the past purchases (older than t_{rec}) of all the customers will be taken into account. Therefore, two types of inferences will be possible: 1) to suggest which product (or category, or attribute) z_k a specific customer u_i could be interested in; a positive match will be in the case of an effective purchase of z_k (or some item which is in the category z_k or that expresses the attribute z_k) by u_i after time t_{rec}; 2) same as before, but including a specific time interval T_{buy} within which the customer will buy. In practice, a positive match will be in the case of an effective purchase of z_k (or some item which is in the category z_k or that expresses the attribute z_k) by u_i *in the time interval* $]t_{\text{rec}}, t_{\text{rec}} + T_{\text{buy}}]$. This creates a system that can provide more novelty and also interaction with users, since as the purchase data grow, so does the system's ability to understand the user's preferences over time. Because this is the idea of casting recommendation as forecasting [11,14] is inherently quite multi-modal, the use of machine learning techniques, especially deep learning, can provide optimal solutions, even though in principle the recommendation itself can still be carried out by slightly tuning standard techniques. This interplay could be certainly explored using on the Visuelle datasets proposed in [30,31].

Fig. 4. Consider a random sampling of users purchases. Personal styles do emerge: users 1 and 10 have no trousers in their logs, user 6 has bought almost short sleeves and no trousers, while user 7 seems to prefer long sleeves and several trousers; user 10 has a marked preference for light yellow-grayish colors. (Color figure online)

5   Conclusion

5.1   Future Work

In general, learning forecasting models for fashion products is a very challenging task. The sales dynamics often have high variance and they are quite different from one company to another. A primary focus should be put into creating datasets that contain sales information from multiple platforms, in order to create forecasting models that generalize better. Of course, a model has to be fit to a specific series to get the best performance, but for small start-ups, it is very important to have analytical support as early as possible. This means having models that can be fine-tuned on small datasets and so far this issue is yet to be explored in industrial forecasting scenarios.

New product demand forecasting can be further improved by reasoning on other shared, prior factors of the products. The authors in [30] suggest popularity, but item availability and also price series play an important role. Considering the price, future work should pay attention to multivariate forecasting of the sales and the price. This allows companies to understand the dynamics of the sales and the evolution of the price, which aids discount campaigns and profit understanding. The same can be said about Short observation of new product forecasting.

Temporal fashion recommendation is a relatively new field, but one promising direction of future work is the forecasting of irregular and sparse time-series. Since most users buy items in a sporadic way, it is hard for any model to learn temporal dependencies other than an order for most users. These models should therefore reason also in terms of similarity-over-time, recommending items that similar users with more purchases bought at that time. In this way, the recommendation can improve interactions with users, but also avoid recommending only evergreen products and present new products to their users.

5.2 Ethical Issues

From the point of view of societal impact, we believe that forecasting approaches can be highly beneficial for reducing pollution since fashion is the third most polluting industry in the world. Having a precise estimation of sales or popularity can improve the situation by solving supply chain issues. The economical aspect is also very important since accurate forecasts can lead to millions of spared USD, as reported in [30]. Nevertheless, forecasting models do bring about ethical implications. The first one is the reduced attention toward industry experts because if the models start to perform well, companies might start cutting departments that only deal with judgmental forecasts. In the case of product recommendations, information bubbles can be produced and limit both the user and the company, since a lot of products will not be seen or recommended. Finally, basing all decisions based on forecasts leads to a phenomenon that is well known in finance, which is that they become self-confirmed, i.e., the forecasts become real because every action becomes based on them. It is preferred to use these tools as decision-making helpers rather than oracles and use probabilistic forecasting to understand the uncertainty related to the predictions.

5.3 Final Remarks

In this position paper, we discuss about learning-based forecasting methods for the fashion industry, and we argue why their use is absolutely necessary for different scenarios. Machine learning is increasingly becoming more important in other aspects of FashionAI such as clothing generation, virtual try-on, and product search, yet supply-chain operations and business processes related to restocking and selling are often still tackled with specific company policies. We believe that forecasting solutions should be carefully implemented at different stages of the product lifecycle and guide companies towards more informed decision-making, ultimately leading to a more efficient and productive world of fashion.

Acknowledgements. This work has been partially supported by the Italian Ministry of Education, University and Research (MIUR) with the grant "Dipartimenti di Eccellenza" 2018–2022.

References

1. Apparel market worldwide (2022). https://www.statista.com/topics/5091/apparel-market-worldwide/

2. E-commerce market worldwide (2022). https://www.statista.com/topics/871/online-shopping/
3. Pollution: the dark side of fashion (2022). https://www.vam.ac.uk/articles/pollution-the-dark-side-of-fashion
4. Bahdanau, D., Cho, K., Bengio, Y.: Neural machine translation by jointly learning to align and translate (2016)
5. Beheshti-Kashi, S., Karimi, H.R., Thoben, K.D., Lütjenband, M., Teucke, M.: A survey on retail sales forecasting and prediction in fashion markets. Syst. Sci. Control Eng. **3**, 154–161 (2015). https://doi.org/10.1080/21642583.2014.999389
6. Box, G.E., Jenkins, G.M., Reinsel, G.C., Ljung, G.M.: Time Series Analysis: Forecasting and Control. Wiley (2015)
7. Cho, K., et al.: Learning phrase representations using RNN encoder-decoder for statistical machine translation (2014)
8. Choi, T.M., Hui, C.L., Liu, N., Ng, S.F., Yu, Y.: Fast fashion sales forecasting with limited data and time. Decis. Support Syst. **59**, 84–92 (2014)
9. Choi, T.M., Hui, C.L., Yu, Y.: Intelligent Fashion Forecasting Systems: Models and Applications. Springer, Heidelberg (2013). https://doi.org/10.1007/978-3-642-39869-8
10. Ekambaram, V., Manglik, K., Mukherjee, S., Sajja, S.S.K., Dwivedi, S., Raykar, V.: Attention based multi-modal new product sales time-series forecasting. In: Proceedings of the 26th ACM SIGKDD International Conference on Knowledge Discovery & Data Mining, pp. 3110–3118 (2020)
11. Fayyaz, Z., Ebrahimian, M., Nawara, D., Ibrahim, A., Kashef, R.: Recommendation systems: algorithms, challenges, metrics, and business opportunities. Appl. Sci. **10**(21), 7748 (2020)
12. Fisher, M., Rajaram, K., Raman, A.: Optimizing inventory replenishment of retail fashion products. Manuf. Serv. Oper. Manage. **3**(3), 230–241 (2001)
13. Friedman, J.H.: Greedy function approximation: a gradient boosting machine. Ann. Stat. **29**(5), 1189–1232 (2001). https://doi.org/10.1214/aos/1013203451
14. Hu, Y., Peng, Q., Hu, X., Yang, R.: Web service recommendation based on time series forecasting and collaborative filtering. In: 2015 IEEE International Conference on Web Services, pp. 233–240. IEEE (2015)
15. Hyndman, R., Koehler, A.B., Ord, J.K., Snyder, R.D.: Forecasting with Exponential Smoothing: The State Space Approach. Springer, Heidelberg (2008). https://doi.org/10.1007/978-3-540-71918-2
16. Hyndman, R.J., Athanasopoulos, G.: Forecasting: Principles and Practice. OTexts (2021)
17. Hyndman, R., Athanasopoulos, G.: Forecasting: Principles and Practice, 2nd edn. OTexts, Australia (2018)
18. Joppi, C., Skenderi, G., Cristani, M.: POP: mining POtential Performance of new fashion products via webly cross-modal query expansion. arXiv preprint arXiv:2207.11001 (2022)
19. Lane, H.C., D'Mello, S.K.: Uses of physiological monitoring in intelligent learning environments: a review of research, evidence, and technologies. In: Parsons, T.D., Lin, L., Cockerham, D. (eds.) Mind, Brain and Technology. ECTII, pp. 67–86. Springer, Cham (2019). https://doi.org/10.1007/978-3-030-02631-8_5
20. Lara-Benítez, P., Carranza-García, M., Riquelme, J.C.: An experimental review on deep learning architectures for time series forecasting. CoRR abs/2103.12057 (2021). https://arxiv.org/abs/2103.12057

21. Li, J., Ren, P., Chen, Z., Ren, Z., Lian, T., Ma, J.: Neural attentive session-based recommendation. In: Proceedings of the 2017 ACM on Conference on Information and Knowledge Management, pp. 1419–1428 (2017)

22. Maaß, D., Spruit, M., de Waal, P.: Improving short-term demand forecasting for short-lifecycle consumer products with data mining techniques. Decis. Anal. **1**(1), 1–17 (2014). https://doi.org/10.1186/2193-8636-1-4

23. Masyhuri, M.: Key drivers of customer satisfaction on the e-commerce business. East Asian J. Multidisc. Res. **1**(4), 657–670 (2022)

24. Ni, J., Li, J., McAuley, J.: Justifying recommendations using distantly-labeled reviews and fine-grained aspects. In: Proceedings of the 2019 Conference on Empirical Methods in Natural Language Processing and the 9th International Joint Conference on Natural Language Processing (EMNLP-IJCNLP), pp. 188–197 (2019)

25. Oreshkin, B.N., Carpov, D., Chapados, N., Bengio, Y.: N-BEATS: neural basis expansion analysis for interpretable time series forecasting. In: International Conference on Learning Representations (2020). https://openreview.net/forum?id=r1ecqn4YwB

26. Papadopoulos, S.I., Koutlis, C., Papadopoulos, S., Kompatsiaris, I.: Multimodal quasi-autoregression: forecasting the visual popularity of new fashion products. arXiv preprint arXiv:2204.04014 (2022)

27. Ren, P., Chen, Z., Li, J., Ren, Z., Ma, J., De Rijke, M.: RepeatNet: a repeat aware neural recommendation machine for session-based recommendation. In: Proceedings of the AAAI Conference on Artificial Intelligence, vol. 33, pp. 4806–4813 (2019)

28. Salinas, D., Flunkert, V., Gasthaus, J., Januschowski, T.: DeepAR: probabilistic forecasting with autoregressive recurrent networks. Int. J. Forecast. **36**(3), 1181–1191 (2020)

29. Singh, P.K., Gupta, Y., Jha, N., Rajan, A.: Fashion retail: forecasting demand for new items. arXiv:1907.01960 [cs], June 2019. http://arxiv.org/abs/1907.01960

30. Skenderi, G., Joppi, C., Denitto, M., Cristani, M.: Well googled is half done: multimodal forecasting of new fashion product sales with image-based google trends. arXiv preprint arXiv:2109.09824 (2021)

31. Skenderi, G., Joppi, C., Denitto, M., Scarpa, B., Cristani, M.: The multi-modal universe of fast-fashion: the Visuelle 2.0 benchmark. arXiv preprint arXiv:2204.06972 (2022)

32. Taplin, I.M.: Global commodity chains and fast fashion: how the apparel industry continues to re-invent itself. Compet. Change **18**(3), 246–264 (2014)

33. Taylor, S.J., Letham, B.: Forecasting at scale. Am. Stat. **72**(1), 37–45 (2018)

34. Yule, G.U.: On a method of investigating periodicities in disturbed series, with special reference to Wolfer's sunspot numbers. Philos. Trans. R. Soc. Lond. Ser. A (Containing Papers of a Mathematical or Physical Character) **226**, 267–298 (1927). http://www.jstor.org/stable/91170

Toward Smart Doors: A Position Paper

Luigi Capogrosso[1(✉)], Geri Skenderi[1], Federico Girella[1], Franco Fummi[1],
and Marco Cristani[2]

[1] Department of Computer Science, University of Verona, Verona, Italy
{luigi.capogrosso,geri.skenderi,federico.girella,franco.fummi}@univr.it
[2] Department of Engineering for Innovation Medicine of the University of Verona,
Verona, Italy
marco.cristani@univr.it

Abstract. Conventional automatic doors cannot distinguish between people wishing to pass through the door and people passing by the door, so they often open unnecessarily. This leads to the need to adopt new systems in both commercial and non-commercial environments: *smart doors*. In particular, a smart door system predicts the intention of people near the door based on the social context of the surrounding environment and then makes rational decisions about whether or not to open the door. This work proposes the first position paper related to smart doors, without bells and whistles. We first point out that the problem not only concerns reliability, climate control, safety, and mode of operation. Indeed, a system to predict the intention of people near the door also involves a deeper understanding of the social context of the scene through a complex combined analysis of proxemics and scene reasoning. Furthermore, we conduct an exhaustive literature review about automatic doors, providing a novel system formulation. Also, we present an analysis of the possible future application of smart doors, a description of the ethical shortcomings, and legislative issues.

Keywords: Smart Doors · People Detection · Trajectory Forecasting · Industrial Machine Learning

1 Introduction

An *automatic door*, also known as an auto-door, is a door that opens automatically by sensing the entrance of a person or an object in a small area close to the door. Automatic doors have been in existence for many centuries. We have to go back to the first century AD in Roman Egypt. It was here that a mathematician, Heron of Alexandria, invented the first known automatic door: a mechanism employed to open a temple's doors when a fire was lit at the altar [40].

In the last decade, automatic doors are found in many different places, spanning from airports, residential areas, banks and hospitals, to offices and industrial units. They automatically detect the presence of an agent (a person or a big object) nearby, using sensors (infrared, ultrasonic) and other components. Even though these techniques are effective and successful in detecting people, they fail

© Springer Nature Switzerland AG 2023
J.-J. Rousseau and B. Kapralos (Eds.): ICPR 2022 Workshops, LNCS 13644, pp. 660–673, 2023.
https://doi.org/10.1007/978-3-031-37742-6_51

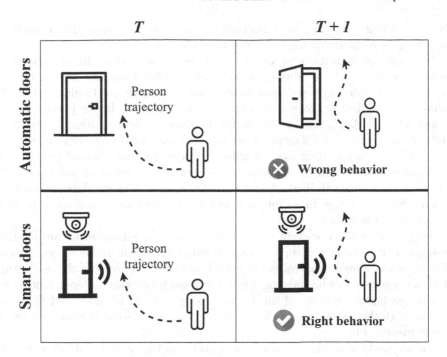

Fig. 1. *Smart door* teaser: the image shows the behavior of a conventional and a smart door in the case of a tangent trajectory by a person. In none of the depicted examples there is an intention to enter the door. As we can see, the behavior of conventional automatic doors at instant $T + 1$ is wrong, *i.e.*, the door opens at the moment the person starts to approach, creating a false positive. On the other hand, the smart door, predicts the intention of the people approaching the door, and by rationally deciding whether or not to open the door, understands that the person does not want to enter (only passing nearby) and does not open.

to understand their intention to enter or exit with respect to the surrounding environment [34].

In these scenarios, we can identify two main challenges. The first one is that an automatic door cannot decide whether it should open or not based on the people's intention, especially when the person is approaching quickly [48] (if a person just passes by a door and has no intention of entering it, the door will open unnecessarily). The second one is that an automatic door cannot distinguish between the different actors that can interact with it [60] (we might not want to open the door for a 2-year-old child) (Fig. 1).

Based on what has been said so far, there is a clear need to incorporate the decision-making process to make automatic doors intelligent: we are moving into the era of *smart doors*. Let's define a smart door as a system that predicts the *intention* of people near the door based on the social context of the surrounding environment and then makes rational decisions about whether or not to open the door. Eventually, it should also hold the door open for several seconds until no person is in the detection area, and then close.

To ease the transition to smart doors, researchers need to provide these systems with a sort of "human intelligence". Therefore, the key is to add machine/deep learning algorithms to automatic doors. In particular, automatically predicting future movements of people is a hot topic in the pattern recognition field [32]. Applying this, in a nutshell, gives the door system the ability to understand humans by following a pedagogical [29] and psychological [54] process. In fact, a smart door system able to predict the intention of people near the door requires a complex combination of *proxemics* and *scene reasoning*: the former considers that individuals behave differently if they are alone, in a group, or a crowd. The latter takes into account the constraints of the scene (people cannot cross the walls).

Furthermore, the use of smart doors with synergies among other automation systems (motorized lock and pressure pad) can allow for the remote management of door access, climate control, and safety. It could be argued that the realization of these concepts will be most significant toward promoting independent living and increasing the quality of life for the rising number of older and impaired people, with the prevalence of chronic conditions such as cardiovascular disease and dementia [14].

Smart doors can also be used as a cost-effective and reliable method of using machine/deep learning algorithms and sensors to build a healthy environment [52] (a smart entry device in a shop center that automatically counts people, monitors human body temperature, and detects a mask at the door opening system).

Finally, we emphasize that smart doors are ideal for commercial and public sector buildings and installations that may involve a large number or variety of users, such as able-bodied, disabled, young, and elderly [35]. There is an absolute need to ensure safe and easy access for all, yet special attention must be paid to the application of these systems [41]. This requirement impacts architects and specifiers who, in addition to meeting the conflicting needs of a range of stakeholders, must also ensure that legal duties are met to minimize the risks of dangerous situations.

2   Related Work

The automation of doors has seen numerous approaches and evolution throughout the years, with smart doors being the latest iteration in the innovation process. This section focuses on the research efforts that precede this work. It includes studies dedicated to several automatic door systems proposed by researchers in previous years and the first attempts that use machine/deep learning in developing smart door systems. These deep learning models are trained using datasets like the ones we will introduce in Sect. 2.5, allowing smart doors to learn automation through proxemics and scene reasoning.

The different automation approaches can be grouped into the following four different categories: *(i)* automation through sensors, *(ii)* automation through detection, *(iii)* automation through intention, and *(iv)* automation through proxemics. For each one, we will indicate their methodologies, strengths, and weaknesses.

2.1   Automation Through Sensors

Automation through sensors is the most common approach. It uses sensors, such as motion or infrared, to trigger the door opening. This category has seen some evolution over the years, particularly in the use of different sensors: starting with classic infrared (IR) sensors [20], the methodology has progressed by using other sensors to improve performance. For example, in [46] and [28] the use of ultrasonic sensors brought an improvement in motion detection, especially in outdoor scenarios where IR light from the sun would interfere with the door's IR sensor.

More recently, there has been a shift to the use of temperature sensors: these open the door if and only if the temperature does not exceed a maximum threshold [25]. This method was invented and used to reduce the spread of COVID-19 virus by avoiding opening the door to feverish people [49].

Unfortunately, this category of approaches produces a high number of false positives (unnecessary door openings) since they do not classify the subjects generating the detected motion. This causes the door to open even when it is not necessary if the sensors detect motion.

2.2   Automation Through Detection

With detection, we refer to the task of recognizing people in a custom scenario (see Sect. 3.1 for more details). With this definition, we can describe the approach in this category as using cameras such as RGB or RGB-D to detect people and open the door.

The most common approach is based on cameras whose output is sent to a machine learning detection model, whose task is to predict whether the scene contains a person. For example, such an approach is presented in [17] and [16], where a Kinect and its API are used to detect people in the scene and open a door accordingly. Another similar implementation is presented in [34], where a camera is used to perform face detection and recognition.

While reducing the number of false positives compared to the sensor-based method, this category still suffers from false positives, for example, when a person walks past the door without intending to walk through it. Therefore, the intention is a crucial factor to consider when the goal of the system is oriented toward reducing the number of false positives.

2.3   Automation Through Intention

As mentioned several times above, a person may walk past a door without intending to go through it. In such cases, an automatic door should not open, and if it does, it should be considered a false positive, meaning that the system incorrectly predicted that the person would need to open the door. The use of intention-based systems has seen a recent rise in popularity, mainly due to the increase in computing power that allows for the training of a model and the use of more complex algorithms in a real-time scenario.

Although studying people's intentions is difficult, it can be made easier by making them explicit to users. In [27] and [58] a speech recognition model is used to recognize user commands and open doors accordingly. Another approach is to make intentions explicit by asking the user to show a token [62], assume a predefined pose [50], or perform a predefined gesture [8], all of which must be recognized by machine learning models.

While these approaches reduce the number of false positives compared to previous ones, they introduce the risk of increasing the number of false negatives when the door does not open due to misidentification of the necessary commands caused by the innate complexity of these tasks. Another problem with these systems is the need for explicit user interactions, which makes them unusable in an everyday life scenario where users may not be able to perform the necessary gestures or people would not be able to know what gesture to make.

2.4 Automation Through Proxemics and Scene Reasoning

To ease the transition to smart doors and predict the intention of people approaching the door, without them having to perform tasks out of the ordinary, a system capable of performing a combination of proxemics and scene reasoning is needed.

One of the first attempts in this direction is the one made by us in [45]. The system aims at assisting elderly and impaired people in co-housing scenarios, in accordance with privacy design principles. This approach estimates user intention through a trajectory forecasting algorithm, predicting the trajectory of people and using this information to infer the intention to use (or not use) the door. These methods result in a seamless experience for the user, who no longer has to worry about interrupting their workflow to issue commands to the system. However, some aspects of this work need to be improved. The first is that the proposed system focuses only on the analysis of elderly and disabled people. The second is that to use these systems we need datasets on which to train our models, and state-of-the-art research has produced only a few benchmarks to date, as we will see in the next section.

2.5 Testing Automatic Doors

All systems that implement the methods presented above must undergo a validation process to confirm that they work properly. For the traditional automatic doors (with sensors), the validation process generally evaluates the performance of the sensors, motors, and safety measures for a given door. These performances need to comply with a set of guidelines to ensure the safety of operations (as discussed in Sect. 4).

However, for smart doors, this validation process involves additional steps given the introduction of a machine or deep learning models. These models, as presented in the previous section, are used to assess the presence and intention of people and operate the doors accordingly. In order to train these models and validate their performance offline, we require datasets.

For smart doors models, datasets are composed of videos and images accompanied by ground truth annotations, meaning that each element of the dataset is annotated with the correct behavior expected from the model. For example, a model trained to detect people through a camera will use a dataset containing images (or videos) of people in a similar situation to the one it will be installed in.

Especially for deep learning models, large datasets are needed to perform meaningful training. As such, deep learning models have seen limited application to trajectory forecasting. In [47], the authors address the lack of training data by introducing a scalable machine annotation scheme that enables our model to be trained using a large dataset without human annotation.

In [15], a framework is developed for smart homes dataset analysis to reflect their diverse dimensions in a predefined format. It analyzes a list of data dimensions that covers the variations in time, activities, sensors, and inhabitants.

As we can see, the state of the art regarding datasets to train intelligent models for smart door systems is also still in a flux. We note a surprising absence of indoor trajectories datasets. The only work that comes close in this regard is [15], whose results are useful for upcoming researchers to develop a better understanding of the characteristics of smart home datasets and classifier performance.

3   Toward Smart Doors

The creation of a smart door requires solving classical computer vision and forecasting tasks, namely people detection/tracking (Sect. 3.1) and trajectory forecasting (Sect. 3.2).

In the following, we will describe these two modules in detail re-targeting, when possible, previous computer vision and forecasting methods that can provide a solution to these problems.

3.1   People Detection and Tracking

Detecting and tracking people is an important and fundamental component of many interactive and intelligent systems [31]. In particular, the problem of detecting a person can be stated as: given a video sequence or an image, localize all the subjects that are humans [6]. So then, for tracking people, we start with all possible detections in a frame and assign them an ID, which we try to carry forward into subsequent frames. If the person has moved out of the frame the ID is dropped, and if a new person appears, we assign them a new identifier [61].

Both detection and tracking are challenging problems, especially in complex real-world scenes that commonly involve multiple people, changes of appearance, complex and dynamic backgrounds, and complicated occlusions [2]. Nonetheless, people detection has reached impressive performance in the last decade given the interest in the automotive industry and other application fields [4]. At the same time, people tracking systems have become increasingly robust even in crowded scenes due to the extensive efforts in video surveillance applications [19].

Different people detection techniques have been designed to work indoor [51], outdoor [26] and in crowded scenes [55]. When the image resolution becomes too low to spot single people, regression-based approaches are used [5,7], also providing, in some cases, density measures [33,59].

In general, the process of detecting people from video (or images) can be performed with the following four sequential steps: *(i)* extracting candidate regions that are potentially covered by human objects [12], *(ii)* describing the extracted region [39], *(iii)* classifying or verifying the regions as human or non-human [63], and *(iv)* post-processing (merging positive regions [13] or adjust the size of those regions [30]).

Once the people within the image have been identified, if the work imposes the assumption that the ground plane is planar, it is necessary to estimate a homography given by some reference features or using information from the vanishing points detected in the image [11,42].

On the other hand, a simple method for tracking multiple objects is using the Euclidean distance between the centers of bounding boxes at successive frames. Thus, an object in a frame is considered the same as an object in a previous frame if the Euclidean distance between their bounding box centers is small [10]. An improvement to this method can be made using a Kalman filter [56], which is able to predict the future position of objects based on their past trajectory. These presented are very simple tracking methods, which therefore do not allow for the accurate implementation of a smart door system. So, it is necessary to use more advanced systems such as DeepSORT [57] that do not rely solely on the objects position and movement but introduce a metric which compares two people regarding their visual features.

3.2   Trajectory Forecasting

Forecasting people's trajectories has been a topic of studies for over two decades. For an in-depth dive into the detailed methodological aspects, the interested readers can refer to various surveys [3,38], and [18]. In its essence, trajectory forecasting is a multivariate time-series forecasting task, considering that in most applications the system has to predict the x and y coordinates of a tracked object of interest over time. This means it is necessary to jointly forecast the x and y signals and understand the intricate relationship between them. These predictions can be made in a probabilistic manner or by simply estimating the expected values (point forecasting). In the first case, we try to forecast the parameters of the assumed distribution of the future trajectory. Because this is often assumed to be a Gaussian, the predictions are therefore the respective means and the diagonal covariance matrix.

In the literature, there are two main aspects that go into modelling trajectories in an optimal manner: the first one is using or producing well-performing sequence models and the other is using multi-modality and modeling the social information available in the scene. The impressive performance of gated recurrent neural networks such as LSTMs [24] and GRUs [9] on sequential tasks quickly made its way into trajectory forecasting, with several pioneering works [1, 43] using these RNN variants. Little after their massive success in NLP, the Transformer [53] made its way into trajectory forecasting as well [22]. To take another step further in modeling social interactions, the seminal work of [23] proposed to use a GAN-based approach and generate plausible trajectories.

Large improvements in trajectory forecasting came with endpoint-conditioned models, which try to estimate the final goal of the moving agent and then its trajectory [36,37]. We argue that in the case of smart doors, this approach is crucial to allow the application of intelligent doors. The reasoning behind this is that the social interactions in a closed world are much more limited than in open scenarios, which are the cases considered in the benchmark dataset of all the works cited above. There is of course less variability in an office than out on the streets, but much less space. To provide an optimal trajectory estimation, the model needs to estimate where the agent is heading first. This is even more important for smart doors since the goal estimation is already half of the job: If the system knows the agent will reach the door, then it is simply a matter of understanding how many time steps it will take *i.e.*, knowing its trajectory. Probabilistic forecasting of trajectories is important for indoor scenarios and smart doors, as it is for its outdoor counterpart. In industrial settings, most decisions will be made based on the confidence interval of the trajectory. We believe that the advantage of being indoors is that, given an optimal forecasting model, there is little variance to particular trajectory types and therefore the corresponding confidence intervals will be relatively narrow. This is turn translates to high-confidence decisions.

The problem can also be tackled in alternative ways, as demonstrated by [45], where we try to cast the trajectory forecasting problem directly as a time-series classification task. This is done by labeling different trajectories that are extracted via a detection and tracking module from a camera inside a room. This approach produces excellent results utilising a very efficient Random Forest model, which also provides interpretability for shorter trajectories. In general, however, the acquisition of trajectories must take place at an adequate distance to allow the system to make the prediction and consequently then open or not open the door. By considering the problem purely as a trajectory forecasting task, the decision then becomes a variable that can be decided based on the industrial set-up, which provides even more flexibility. These learning-based approaches open up a world of new possibilities for smart doors in large commercial settings, creating energy-efficient solutions.

4 Legislative Issues

The implementation and use of automatic doors are subject to legislation, enforcing guidelines on the installation and correct behavior needed to ensure easy and safe interactions with users under different circumstances. We argue that smart doors, seen as an evolution of the conventional automatic door, must also comply with these guidelines and that the presence of this legislation demonstrates the feasibility of the proposal of this position paper. Additionally, we will address the privacy aspect of these smart systems in Sect. 5, introducing ways to avoid privacy concerns over the data being used. Given that laws may vary from country to country, we will only mention general aspects that can be taken into account in the software used to operate the doors, as the production and physical installation of the doors are beyond the scope of our work.

The most important aspect is the *overall safety* of the users during daily operations. It includes safety for the users operating the door as well as people in the vicinity of the door, defining areas of operation in which the system needs to take care to not cause harm. The first area of operation is the one users cross to reach other rooms. A system needs to be able to detect people in this area to avoid closing the door and injuring them. A combination of pressure and IR sensors is usually present in automatic door systems, allowing the system to detect people and revert to the open state. The second one is the area of operation of the door itself. In sliding doors, for example, this includes the area in which the door slides while opening. In a revolving door, this is the area where the door swings while opening. If people find themselves in these areas they risk being hit, crushed, or severed by the door itself. Many laws are in place enforcing physical boundaries for the regions surrounding these areas. In European legislation, laws are in place to limit the maximum speed of automatic doors, limiting the damage to users being hit. Other laws define distances between the doors and other hard surfaces, limiting the risk of crushing.

Finally, another crucial aspect is *behavior during emergencies*. With emergencies, we refer to situations in which either an emergency signal is being sent to the door (manually or by another system), or the system detects that it can no longer operate correctly. An example of this may be a fire alert, where an outside system (or an operator) signals the door that an emergency is taking place. Another instance of an emergency might be a power outage, where no signal is being sent but the door can no longer operate normally. In these cases, according to European legislation, doors must switch to a safe state that allows them to be used even in the absence of power. This safe state can be an open state, in which the door remains open, or a manual state, in which the door can be operated manually.

Another similar issue is related to the *detection of malfunctions* in the system (not opening the door when needed). In this case, the system needs to detect its malfunction and change its behavior accordingly, for example by default to the safe states previously mentioned.

All these problems can be further mitigated through proper implementation of the smart door control system. Interaction with emergency systems is clear, and default safe states can be implemented even without power. Proper detection of people in the areas of operation (using the method presented in Sect. 3.1) can prevent smart doors from opening and closing when they detect people in these areas, aiding traditional sensors and further limiting the risk of injuries. As such, we argue that smart doors, as presented in this work, would not only follow the requested legislation but provide additional safety features, thanks to their control system and use of cameras.

5 Discussion

Major advances in computer vision have set the stage for the widespread deployment of connected devices with *always-on* cameras and powerful visualization capabilities. While these advances have the potential to enable a wide range of novel applications and interfaces, such as smart doors, privacy and security concerns surrounding the use of these technologies threaten to limit the range of places and devices where they are adopted.

Optical cameras can be the most suitable sensors for a smart door system, but the acceptance of this technology can be difficult since it raises privacy concerns. Video footage can reveal the identity of the people being filmed, and in general, nowadays, recording is regulated by strict laws, both nationally and internationally. In addition, potential attacks on video transmission channels and storage servers can be a serious security problem.

We believe that, despite the widespread cloud-centered application, this should not be the only paradigm to refer to and that a new approach to decentralization is needed. In particular, by adopting the *edge-centric computing* paradigm, we will push the frontier of computing applications, data, and services away from centralized nodes to the periphery of the network. This allows the implementation of the *privacy-by-design* principle, as is shown in [45]. So, first, processing the video internally (through an edge device) and then, transmitting only the result of the computation to the remote server, without any sensible information.

While great strides have been made in lowering the power requirements of on-board processing by novel, highly efficient microcontrollers [21], one of the most severe energy efficiency bottlenecks is the need to periodically process data found in traditional polling-based systems [44]. One approach to reducing the amount of data that needs to be processed is *event-driven processing*, where data is only processed if certain activity conditions are met, like motion in a video stream.

At the same time is worth nothing that current computer vision technology is now mature enough to handle privacy issues. In addition, the legislative and legal conditions are also extremely specific in order to minimize any risks to people as much as possible. So, through the intersection of different research fields, combining their respective paradigms and technologies, nowadays it is possible to create a smart camera system that is fully secure from the perspective of privacy and ethics.

6   Conclusion

In this position paper, we introduce smart doors as systems that predict the intention of people near the door, following the social context of the surrounding environment, and making rational decisions relative to whether or not to open. We have seen how social context requires such systems to optimize processes like climate control and security or develop emerging application scenarios to improve our quality of life.

In addition, the implementation of these systems allows for the analysis of social context, and thus advances research in this sociological regard as well. Smart doors cover to date, and will do so even more in the future, an important role in several fields, thus providing a continuous source of interest in this multidisciplinary problem.

Acknowledgements. This work has been partially supported by the Italian Ministry of Education, University and Research (MIUR) with the grant "Dipartimenti di Eccellenza" 2018–2022.

References

1. Alahi, A., Goel, K., Ramanathan, V., Robicquet, A., Fei-Fei, L., Savarese, S.: Social lstm: human trajectory prediction in crowded spaces. In: Proceedings of the IEEE Conference on Computer Vision and Pattern Recognition, pp. 961–971 (2016)
2. Andriluka, M., Roth, S., Schiele, B.: People-tracking-by-detection and people-detection-by-tracking. In: 2008 IEEE Conference on Computer Vision and Pattern Recognition, pp. 1–8. IEEE (2008)
3. Becker, S., Hug, R., Hübner, W., Arens, M.: An evaluation of trajectory prediction approaches and notes on the trajnet benchmark (2018). arXiv preprint arXiv:1805.07663
4. Benenson, R., Omran, M., Hosang, J., Schiele, B.: Ten years of pedestrian detection, what have we learned? In: Agapito, L., Bronstein, M.M., Rother, C. (eds.) ECCV 2014. LNCS, vol. 8926, pp. 613–627. Springer, Cham (2015). https://doi.org/10.1007/978-3-319-16181-5_47
5. Boominathan, L., Kruthiventi, S.S., Babu, R.V.: Crowdnet: a deep convolutional network for dense crowd counting. In: Proceedings of the 24th ACM International Conference on Multimedia, pp. 640–644 (2016)
6. Brunetti, A., Buongiorno, D., Trotta, G.F., Bevilacqua, V.: Computer vision and deep learning techniques for pedestrian detection and tracking: a survey. Neurocomputing **300**, 17–33 (2018)
7. Chan, A.B., Liang, Z.S.J., Vasconcelos, N.: Privacy preserving crowd monitoring: counting people without people models or tracking. In: 2008 IEEE Conference on Computer Vision and Pattern Recognition, pp. 1–7. IEEE (2008)
8. Chiu, S.Y., Chiu, S.Y., Tu, Y.J., Hsu, C.I.: Gesture-based intention prediction for automatic door opening using low-resolution thermal sensors: a u-net-based deep learning approach. In: 2021 IEEE 3rd Eurasia Conference on IOT, Communication and Engineering (ECICE), pp. 271–274. IEEE (2021)
9. Cho, K., et al.: Learning phrase representations using rnn encoder-decoder for statistical machine translation (2014). arXiv preprint arXiv:1406.1078

10. Cojocea, M.E., Rebedea, T.: An efficient solution for people tracking and profiling from video streams using low-power computer. In: Hernes, M., Wojtkiewicz, K., Szczerbicki, E. (eds.) ICCCI 2020. CCIS, vol. 1287, pp. 154–165. Springer, Cham (2020). https://doi.org/10.1007/978-3-030-63119-2_13

11. Criminisi, A., Reid, I., Zisserman, A.: Single view metrology. Int. J. Comput. Vision **40**(2), 123–148 (2000)

12. Dalal, N.: Finding people in images and videos. Ph.D. thesis, Institut National Polytechnique de Grenoble-INPG (2006)

13. Dalal, N., Triggs, B.: Histograms of oriented gradients for human detection. In: 2005 IEEE Computer Society Conference on Computer Vision and Pattern Recognition (CVPR 2005), vol. 1, pp. 886–893. IEEE (2005)

14. Donnelly, M., Paggetti, C., Nugent, C., Mokhtari, M. (eds.): ICOST 2012. LNCS, vol. 7251. Springer, Heidelberg (2012). https://doi.org/10.1007/978-3-642-30779-9

15. Fatima, I., Fahim, M., Lee, Y.-K., Lee, S.: Analysis and effects of smart home dataset characteristics for daily life activity recognition. J. Supercomput. **66**(2), 760–780 (2013). https://doi.org/10.1007/s11227-013-0978-8

16. Feng, X., Yazawa, Y., Kita, E., Zuo, Y.: Control of automatic door by using kinect sensor. Bull. Netw. Comput. Syst. Softw. **6**(1), 17–21 (2017)

17. Fosstveit, H.A.: Intelligent sliding doors. Master's thesis, Institutt for datateknikk og informasjonsvitenskap (2012)

18. Franco, L., Placidi, L., Giuliari, F., Hasan, I., Cristani, M., Galasso, F.: Under the hood of transformer networks for trajectory forecasting. arXiv preprint arXiv:2203.11878 (2022)

19. Fuentes, L.M., Velastin, S.A.: People tracking in surveillance applications. Image Vision Comput. **24**(11), 1165–1171 (2006)

20. García, V.H., Vega, N.: Low power sensor node applied to domotic using IoT. In: Mata-Rivera, M.F., Zagal-Flores, R. (eds.) WITCOM 2018. CCIS, vol. 944, pp. 56–69. Springer, Cham (2018). https://doi.org/10.1007/978-3-030-03763-5_6

21. Gautschi, M., et al.: Near-threshold risc-v core with dsp extensions for scalable iot endpoint devices. IEEE Trans. Very Large Scale Integr. (VLSI) Syst. **25**(10), 2700–2713 (2017)

22. Giuliari, F., Hasan, I., Cristani, M., Galasso, F.: Transformer networks for trajectory forecasting. In: 2020 25th International Conference on Pattern Recognition (ICPR), pp. 10335–10342. IEEE (2021)

23. Gupta, A., Johnson, J., Fei-Fei, L., Savarese, S., Alahi, A.: Social gan: socially acceptable trajectories with generative adversarial networks. In: Proceedings of the IEEE Conference on Computer Vision and Pattern Recognition, pp. 2255–2264 (2018)

24. Hochreiter, S., Schmidhuber, J.: Long short-term memory. Neural Comput. **9**(8), 1735–1780 (1997)

25. Iskandar, D., Nugroho, E.W., Rahmawati, D., Rozikin, I.: Automatic door control system with body temperature sensor. Int. J. Comput. Inf. Syst. (IJCIS) **2**(4), 111–114 (2021)

26. Jafari, O.H., Mitzel, D., Leibe, B.: Real-time rgb-d based people detection and tracking for mobile robots and head-worn cameras. In: 2014 IEEE International Conference on Robotics and Automation (ICRA), pp. 5636–5643. IEEE (2014)

27. Jimoh, I., Joshi, A., Mikail, O.O.: Intelligent voice-based door access control system using adaptive-network-based fuzzy inference systems (anfis). J. Comput. Sci. **3**(5), 274–280 (2007)

28. Kim, G.D., Won, S.Y., Kim, H.S.: An object recognition performance improvement of automatic door using ultrasonic sensor. J. Inst. Electron. Inf. Eng. **54**(3), 97–107 (2017)
29. Kiru, M.U., Belaton, B., Mohamad, S.M.S., Usman, G.M., Kazaure, A.A.: Intelligent automatic door system based on supervised learning. In: 2020 IEEE Conference on Open Systems (ICOS), pp. 43–47. IEEE (2020)
30. Leibe, B., Seemann, E., Schiele, B.: Pedestrian detection in crowded scenes. In: 2005 IEEE Computer Society Conference on Computer Vision and Pattern Recognition (CVPR 2005), vol. 1, pp. 878–885. IEEE (2005)
31. Liciotti, D., Paolanti, M., Frontoni, E., Zingaretti, P.: People detection and tracking from an RGB-D camera in top-view configuration: review of challenges and applications. In: Battiato, S., Farinella, G.M., Leo, M., Gallo, G. (eds.) ICIAP 2017. LNCS, vol. 10590, pp. 207–218. Springer, Cham (2017). https://doi.org/10.1007/978-3-319-70742-6_20
32. Lin, T., Wang, Y., Liu, X., Qiu, X.: A survey of transformers (2021). arXiv preprint arXiv:2106.04554
33. Liu, J., Gao, C., Meng, D., Hauptmann, A.G.: Decidenet: counting varying density crowds through attention guided detection and density estimation. In: Proceedings of the IEEE Conference on Computer Vision and Pattern Recognition, pp. 5197–5206 (2018)
34. Lwin, H.H., Khaing, A.S., Tun, H.M.: Automatic door access system using face recognition. Int. J. Sci. Technol. Res **4**(6), 294–299 (2015)
35. Lymperopoulos, P., Meade, K.: Pathpass: opening doors for people with disabilities. In: 2014 4th International Conference on Wireless Mobile Communication and Healthcare-Transforming Healthcare Through Innovations in Mobile and Wireless Technologies (MOBIHEALTH), pp. 32–35. IEEE (2014)
36. Mangalam, K., An, Y., Girase, H., Malik, J.: From goals, waypoints & paths to long term human trajectory forecasting. In: Proceedings of the IEEE/CVF International Conference on Computer Vision, pp. 15233–15242 (2021)
37. Mangalam, K., et al.: It is not the journey but the destination: endpoint conditioned trajectory prediction. In: Vedaldi, A., Bischof, H., Brox, T., Frahm, J.-M. (eds.) ECCV 2020. LNCS, vol. 12347, pp. 759–776. Springer, Cham (2020). https://doi.org/10.1007/978-3-030-58536-5_45
38. Morris, B.T., Trivedi, M.M.: A survey of vision-based trajectory learning and analysis for surveillance. IEEE Trans. Circ. Syst. Video Technol. **18**(8), 1114–1127 (2008)
39. Nguyen, D.T., Li, W., Ogunbona, P.O.: Human detection from images and videos: a survey. Pattern Recogn. **51**, 148–175 (2016)
40. Papadopoulos, E.: Heron of alexandria (c. 10–85 ad). In: Distinguished Figures in Mechanism and Machine Science, pp. 217–245. Springer, Heidelberg (2007). https://doi.org/10.1007/978-1-4020-6366-4_9
41. Robles, R.J., Kim, T.H., Cook, D., Das, S.: A review on security in smart home development. Int. J. Adv. Sci. Technol. **15** (2010)
42. Rother, C.: A new approach to vanishing point detection in architectural environments. Image Vision Comput. **20**(9–10), 647–655 (2002)
43. Salzmann, T., Ivanovic, B., Chakravarty, P., Pavone, M.: Trajectron++: multi-agent generative trajectory forecasting with heterogeneous data for control (2020)
44. Scherer, M., Mayer, P., Di Mauro, A., Magno, M., Benini, L.: Towards always-on event-based cameras for long-lasting battery-operated smart sensor nodes. In: 2021 IEEE International Instrumentation and Measurement Technology Conference (I2MTC), pp. 1–6. IEEE (2021)

45. Skenderi, G., et al.: Dohmo: embedded computer vision in co-housing scenarios. In: 2021 Forum on specification & Design Languages (FDL), pp. 01–08. IEEE (2021)
46. Song, D.H., Chang, B.K.: Development of on intelligent automatic door system using ultrasonic sensors. J. Kor. Inst. Illuminat. Electr. Install. Eng. **23**(6), 31–39 (2009)
47. Styles, O., Ross, A., Sanchez, V.: Forecasting pedestrian trajectory with machine-annotated training data. In: 2019 IEEE Intelligent Vehicles Symposium (IV), pp. 716–721. IEEE (2019)
48. Sümbül, H., Coşkun, A., Taşdemir, M.: The control of an automatic door using fuzzy logic. In: 2011 International Symposium on Innovations in Intelligent Systems and Applications, pp. 432–435. IEEE (2011)
49. Supriana, A., Prakosa, B.A., Ritzkal, R.: Implementation of body temperature checking system with automatic door lock web and arduino assistance. Jurnal Mantik **5**(3), 1915–1921 (2021)
50. Terashima, T., Kawai, Y.: A proposal for an automatic door opening and closing interface based on speech recognition and pose estimation. In: Proceedings of the 9th International Conference on Human-Agent Interaction, pp. 283–285 (2021)
51. Tseng, T.E., Liu, A.S., Hsiao, P.H., Huang, C.M., Fu, L.C.: Real-time people detection and tracking for indoor surveillance using multiple top-view depth cameras. In: 2014 IEEE/RSJ International Conference on Intelligent Robots and Systems, pp. 4077–4082. IEEE (2014)
52. Varshini, B., Yogesh, H., Pasha, S.D., Suhail, M., Madhumitha, V., Sasi, A.: Iot-enabled smart doors for monitoring body temperature and face mask detection. Global Trans. Proc. **2**(2), 246–254 (2021)
53. Vaswani, A., et al.: Attention is all you need. Adv. Neural Inf. Process. Syst. **30** (2017)
54. Walther, D.: Interactions of visual attention and object recognition: computational modeling, algorithms, and psychophysics. California Institute of Technology (2006)
55. Wang, X., Xiao, T., Jiang, Y., Shao, S., Sun, J., Shen, C.: Repulsion loss: detecting pedestrians in a crowd. In: Proceedings of the IEEE Conference on Computer Vision and Pattern Recognition, pp. 7774–7783 (2018)
56. Welch, G., Bishop, G., et al.: An introduction to the kalman filter (1995)
57. Wojke, N., Bewley, A., Paulus, D.: Simple online and realtime tracking with a deep association metric. In: 2017 IEEE International Conference on Image Processing (ICIP), pp. 3645–3649. IEEE (2017)
58. Wu, S.Y., Wang, Y.Y.: Design of a new intelligent electronic door system. Comput. Modern. **251**(07), 115 (2016)
59. Xu, B., Qiu, G.: Crowd density estimation based on rich features and random projection forest. In: 2016 IEEE Winter Conference on Applications of Computer Vision (WACV), pp. 1–8. IEEE (2016)
60. Yang, J.C., Lai, C.L., Sheu, H.T., Chen, J.J.: An intelligent automated door control system based on a smart camera. Sensors **13**(5), 5923–5936 (2013)
61. Yilmaz, A., Javed, O., Shah, M.: Object tracking: a survey. ACM Comput. Surv. (CSUR) **38**(4), 13-es (2006)
62. Yoon, S.H., et al.: IoT open-source and AI based automatic door lock access control solution. Int. J. Internet Broadcast. Commun. **12**(2), 8–14 (2020)
63. Zhao, L., Thorpe, C.E.: Stereo-and neural network-based pedestrian detection. IEEE Trans. Intell. Transp. Syst. **1**(3), 148–154 (2000)

Intuitive Physics Guided Exploration for Sample Efficient Sim2real Transfer

Buddhika Laknath Semage$^{(\boxtimes)}$, Thommen George Karimpanal ,
Santu Rana , and Svetha Venkatesh

Applied Artificial Intelligence Institute, Deakin University, Geelong, Australia
bsemage@deakin.edu.au

Abstract. Physics-based reinforcement learning tasks can benefit from simplified physics simulators as they potentially allow near-optimal policies to be learned in simulation. However, such simulators require the latent factors (e.g. mass, friction coefficient etc.,) of the associated objects and other environment-specific factors (e.g. wind speed, air density etc.,) to be accurately specified. As such a complete specification can be impractical, in this paper, we instead, focus on learning task-specific estimates of latent factors which allow the approximation of real world trajectories in an ideal simulation environment. Specifically, we propose two new concepts: a) action grouping - the idea that certain types of actions are closely associated with the estimation of certain latent factors, and; b) partial grounding - the idea that simulation of task-specific dynamics may not need precise estimation of all the latent factors. We demonstrate our approach in a range of physics-based tasks, and show that it achieves superior performance relative to other baselines, using only a limited number of real-world interactions.

Keywords: Reinforcement learning · Physics · Sample efficiency · Exploration

1 Introduction

One of the defining characteristics of human learning is the ability to leverage domain knowledge to learn quickly and with very little data. This is a key characteristic many machine learning models, including reinforcement learning (RL), lack [19,21]. For example, to attain similar levels of performance in video-game playing, deep Q-networks (DQN) [22] have been reported to require 50 million frames of experience (38 days of gameplay in real-time), which stands in stark contrast to the less than 15 minutes of gameplay required by human players [29]. This difference has largely been attributed to the fact that humans leverage prior knowledge [11] for tasks, allowing for more efficient exploration during learning. Incidentally, current industrial applications of RL are hampered by the same issue of sample inefficiency when adapting to unknown conditions or tasks, which needs to be improved in order to build robust and multi-tasking RL agents.

© Springer Nature Switzerland AG 2023
J.-J. Rousseau and B. Kapralos (Eds.): ICPR 2022 Workshops, LNCS 13644, pp. 674–686, 2023.
https://doi.org/10.1007/978-3-031-37742-6_52

In physics-based problems, one can leverage the known laws governing the physical world, as described by classical mechanics. This structured prior knowledge can be assumed to be encapsulated in physics simulators, and can be leveraged for training artificial agents on physics based tasks [12,31]. For example, when training a robot to play golf, with good estimates of the latent factors (eg., mass, friction) associated with the ball, club and turf, a physics simulator would be able to compute the approximate ball trajectory. Such approximations allow the possibility of learning approximate policies solely in the simulator, obviating the need for extensive interactions with the real world. Recently proposed methods such as domain randomisation (DR) [25,28] operate precisely on such a basis, where a simulation policy is trained on a variety of simulation environments, each of which is generated using randomly sampled latent factors.

Fig. 1. Action groupings represented by (a) rolling and (b) collision action types. Due to partial grounding, only rolling needs to be explored for a 'putt' shot in golf.

While DR produces robust policies against environmental variations, the resulting policy does not behave optimally in the given real environment. To achieve this, DR agents require further training using real-world interactions, which in some cases can be prohibitively expensive. Instead, using fewer interactions, if we were able to learn latent factors to closely reproduce realistic task-specific trajectories in simulation, the corresponding simulation policy would transfer seamlessly to the real environment. Here, we propose an *Intuitive Physics Learning Workflow (IPLW)* to learn such a simulation policy (a) by using intuitive *action groupings*, according to which, specific latent factors are associated with specific types of actions and (b) by using the fact that depending on the task, certain latent factors may be more useful to estimate than others, an idea we term *partial grounding*. For example, through intuitive action groupings, we may assume that rolling and collision actions are typically associated with estimating friction and coefficient of restitution (CoR) respectively. Partial grounding is based on the observation that depending on the task under consideration, it may not be necessary to treat each latent factor with equal importance. That is, for a rolling-intensive task (e.g. a 'putt' shot in golf, as shown in Fig. 1), one need not spend considerable effort on estimating CoR, as it is likely to be less relevant to the task. Similar ideas proposed in concepts such as observational dropout [15] have previously been shown to be useful for model estimation.

To implement IPLW, actions are first ranked according to simple heuristics such as the number of collisions or the rolling time experienced during a trajectory. The top-ranked subsets of these actions are then classified as either collision or rolling action types, each of which is associated with the estimation of a specific latent factor (i.e., CoR and friction respectively). In this way, we use knowledge of physics relationships to remove less informative actions from consideration, which constrains the action space significantly. Furthermore, such action categorization fits naturally with the idea of partial grounding, as it allows agents to interact with the environment based on the specific latent factors to be estimated. In implementing partial grounding, we use task-specific knowledge from a given environment to accelerate learning in another environment, which may differ in terms of the unmodeled factors (e.g. air resistance, surface roughness etc.). Specifically, we first characterize the known environment through its empirically estimated transfer performances for various latent factor values on an ideal simulator (i.e. without the unmodeled factors). Using this performance surface, we compute the gradients of the transfer performance with respect to latent factors, and use these as exploration cues to choose specific action types when exploring the new environment.

In summary, the main contributions of this work are:

- Proposing a paradigm of intuitively biased action selection for task-specific grounding in physics based RL tasks.
- Developing a novel interaction strategy that estimates relevant latent factors to closely approximate real world trajectories in the simulator.
- Empirical demonstrations of the framework through superior jump start improvements in a range of different physics based environments.

2   Related Work

Studying human understanding of physics dynamics and the learning process has provided useful insights that have been used to improve physics related machine learning models. These models can be classified into two categories as top-down and bottom-up approaches: bottom-up approach attempt to learn physics representations without providing external biases [14,16,18], whereas top-down tries to build improved physics models using the physics knowledge we possess. Our study adopts a top-down approach aiming to construct a better bias similar to *Sample, Simulate, Update* model [3], but instead of using an object specific spatial bias, we define bias in terms of physics latent factors and their relationship to the task.

Galileo [31] was an early attempt at learning simple physics dynamics that comprised a physics simulator and utilised sampling to estimate latent factors of the objects. *Perception-Prediction Networks* [34] is another attempt at estimating latent physics factors by using Graph Neural Networks to build an inductive bias by observing object movement dynamics. DensePhyNet [32] extends this concept by allowing iterative actions on objects to learn a latent representation indicative of latent physics factors of the objects using a deep learning architecture. We use a similar idea as *Galileo*, but we evaluate latent factors in a task oriented manner by combining ideas from transfer learning in RL [13,27,36].

When training robots in simulated environments for transfer, domain randomisation [2,23,25,26,28] and domain adaptation [6] are generally the two main approaches adopted. Domain randomisation trains robots with randomised latent factors, whereas domain adaptation attempts to match the data distribution in the simulator to the real-world. Grounded learning [12] is a domain adaptation technique that trains robots in a simulated environment by attempting to reduce the trajectory difference between simulated and the real worlds. Various extensions of this concept have been used to identify system parameters in robotic applications [4,33]. In this study, while adopting a simulation based approach similar to grounded learning, we utilise the knowledge of physics to select better actions that expedite the latent factor estimation process.

Improving the efficiency of exploration has been the focus of curiosity based [24] and other methods [8,35]. Our method also aims to improve the sample efficiency through improved exploration, albeit through the preferential selection of action types based on physics knowledge.

3 Approach and Framework

In this work, similar to the setup used in PHYRE [5], we consider physics based tasks where a single action is executed to solve the task under consideration. Although this corresponds to a contextual bandit setting [20], we train the agent using RL, as it has been shown to be effective for such problems [5]. Accordingly, we formalize our problem as a Markov Decision Process (MDP) $\mathcal{M}$, represented as a tuple $< \mathcal{S}, \mathcal{A}, \mathcal{R}, \mathcal{P} >$, where $\mathcal{S}$ is the state space, $\mathcal{A}$ is the action space, $\mathcal{P}$ is the transition probability function and $\mathcal{R}$ is the reward function.

In physics based tasks, the transition function $\mathcal{P}$ depends on: (a) modelable latent factors L (mass, coefficient of restitution, friction, etc.) of the various objects involved, (b) unmodelled factors U specific to the scenario (e.g.: wind resistance) and the simplification of simulator, and (c) the underlying rules ρ that govern the dynamics of the physical world (e.g.: Newton's laws of motion). Thus, $\mathcal{P}$ can be represented as:

$$\mathcal{P} = \rho(\phi) \tag{1}$$

where $\phi = [L, U]$. The benefit of the above representation is that ρ is universally consistent, and can thus be incorporated as a prior. For instance, in our approach, we encode this prior by means of a physics simulator, using only factors in L, which inherently accounts for our knowledge of object interactions. The incorporation of such prior knowledge allows us to build a model of the real world in a structured manner, by leveraging the universal nature of ρ.

Similar to the task in the real world, a simulated task can also be framed as an MDP $\mathcal{M}_{sim} = < \mathcal{S}, \mathcal{A}, \mathcal{P}_{sim}, \mathcal{R} >$. Such an MDP shares the same state space $\mathcal{S}$, action space $\mathcal{A}$ and reward function $\mathcal{R}$ as the real world MDP $\mathcal{M}$, and differs solely in the transition function.

The transition function used in simulation is given by $\mathcal{P}_{sim} = \rho(\theta)$, where θ represents latent factor estimates corresponding to an ideal simulation environment devoid of the unmodelled factors U. The intuition is that unmodelled factors, due to its nature, may vary drastically in different scenarios, and the relative gain in accurate simulation is much smaller than the complexity needed to incorporate them. Hence, by learning the equivalent latent factors θ in an ideal simulated environment, one can proceed to approximate $\mathcal{P}$ without any inherent assumptions about the environment in question. Finally, using the latent factor estimate θ, we learn a policy π^* within the simulated environment, and use it to initialize learning in the real world. If π^* corresponds to a good policy, we expect it to result in jump-start improvements in the real world learning performance.

In the following section, we describe in detail our proposed approach to determine θ. The overall algorithm (IPLW), is summarised in Algorithm 2.

3.1   Latent Factor Estimation

In IPLW, first the real world trajectories $\tau \in D$ are generated using action selection strategies, described in Sect. 3.2. In order to obtain reasonable estimates of latent factors that minimize the difference between $\mathcal{P}$ and $\mathcal{P}_{sim}$, we then generate simulated trajectories τ_{sim} corresponding to τ and some sampled latent factors θ. By comparing τ_{sim} to corresponding real-world trajectory τ, we can compute the residual as:

$$\nabla(\theta) = \frac{1}{|D|} \sum_{\tau \in D} d(\tau, \tau_{sim}) \qquad (2)$$

Here, d is measured as the sum of squared difference between the states in the simulated and real-world trajectories.

The computed residual is then minimized using an optimiser to yield updated values for the latent factors:

$$\theta^* \leftarrow \underset{\theta}{argmin} \nabla(\theta) \qquad (3)$$

By updating θ as per the above equation, we obtain improved estimates θ^* that allows τ_{sim} to closely match the sampled real world trajectories τ.

Algorithm 1 Gradient Based Action Selection

Input:
1: $\hat{\theta}$: $\mathbb{R}^N$ vector of estimated latent factors
2: $\mathcal{J}(\theta)$: function that returns jump start performances for latent factors θ
3: **Output:** P : vector of action type probabilities corresponding to N latent factors
4: $X \leftarrow []$
5: **for** $k \leftarrow 1$ to N **do** $X_k \leftarrow \frac{\partial \mathcal{J}(\theta)}{\partial \theta_k}$ evaluated at $\hat{\theta}$
6: **end for**
7: $Z \leftarrow \sum_{n=1}^N X_n$
8: return $P = [\frac{X_1}{Z}, ..., \frac{X_N}{Z}]$

3.2 Action Selection Strategies

In rolling out trajectories to estimate θ^*, the type of actions chosen could be important, depending on the scenario. For example, for a task that is primarily dependent on rolling actions, rolling out collision-heavy trajectories without much rolling is not likely to be useful. This is because collision-heavy trajectories are unlikely to improve friction-related latent estimates. Hence, the choice of action types can significantly influence latent factor estimates. Using this intuition, we design a number of action selection strategies (Algorithm 2, line 3) that could be used for latent factor estimation:

1. *Collisions* - actions that cause the most number of collisions among balls are preferentially selected.
2. *Rolling* - actions that keep the balls in contact with the floor for the longest cumulative duration during simulation are selected.
3. *Random* - actions are selected randomly.
4. *Mixed* - collision and rolling actions are selected in equal proportion.
5. *Gradient based* - Ideally, action types should be selected in accordance to the performance improvements they facilitate. If an estimate of the transfer performance ($\mathcal{J}(\theta)$) as a function of the latent factors θ is available, it can be used to generate selection probabilities (e.g. probability of choosing rolling actions) corresponding to each action type. For example, if $\theta = [\theta_{CoR}, \theta_{friction}]$, the probabilities of selecting collision and rolling action types can be given by $\frac{\partial \mathcal{J}(\theta)}{\partial \theta_{CoR}}/(\frac{\partial \mathcal{J}(\theta)}{\partial \theta_{CoR}} + \frac{\partial \mathcal{J}(\theta)}{\partial \theta_{friction}})$ and $\frac{\partial \mathcal{J}(\theta)}{\partial \theta_{friction}}/(\frac{\partial \mathcal{J}(\theta)}{\partial \theta_{CoR}} + \frac{\partial \mathcal{J}(\theta)}{\partial \theta_{friction}})$ respectively. This strategy samples action types in accordance to the relative importance of different latent factors for achieving a task (Algorithm 1).

4 Experiments

Experiment Setup: To demonstrate the general nature of our approach, we select two distinct physics based tasks: (a) Basketball, a collision intensive task, and; (b) Bowling, a task involving both rolling and collision actions. In the task (a), a free falling ball must be positioned together with a plank fixed at 45°, so

---

Algorithm 2 Intuitive Physics Learning Workflow

Input:
1: E, E_{sim} - Real and simulated environments
2: $min\_residual > 0$, $max\_attempts > 0$ - Interrupt thresholds
3: $action\_selection\_strategy$ - Strategy to select an action type (e.g. collisions, rolling .etc)
4: $optimizer$ - The CEM optimizer used to improve latent factors
5: N - Number of actions to use for $optimizer$
6: **Output:** Simulation policy π^*
7: $\theta \leftarrow Random()$; $num\_rounds \leftarrow 0$
8: **while** True **do**
9:     $exploring\_actions \leftarrow$ Sample actions on E_{sim} initialized with θ
10:     $exploring\_actions \leftarrow$ Rank $exploring\_actions$ according to $action\_selection\_strategy$ and select best N actions
11:     $D \leftarrow$ Rollout $exploring\_actions$ on environment E and collect trajectories
12:     $\theta_{sampled}$, $residuals \leftarrow$ Sample θ in E_{sim} with $exploring\_actions$
13:     θ, $residual_{min} \leftarrow optimizer(\theta_{sampled}, residuals)$
14:     Increment num_rounds
15:     **if** $residual_{min} < min\_residual$ or $num\_rounds > max\_attempts$ **then**
16:         Train DQN on E_{sim} with θ to learn policies π^*
17:         Transfer trained policies π^* to real-world E
18:         Break
19:     **end if**
20: **end while**

---

that the ball bounces off the plank and into a basket set up some distance away (Fig. 2(a)). For the task (b), we consider a 0000 PHYRE template [5] based task consisting of 3 balls, where the goal is to keep two of the balls in contact by controlling the position and size of the red ball (Fig. 2(b)).

For this study, both the simulated and real-world data are generated using Pymunk physics simulator [1]. The simulated world is set up to differ from the real world through a different value of a "damping" factor. The damping factor (u) introduces an additional drag force on objects, i.e. a value 1 represents no drag while 0.9 means each moving body will lose 10% of its velocity per second. In the context of real-world forces, the damping factor represents physics factors that are difficult to model universally, e.g. rolling friction, air-resistance.

The transfer performance of the simulator trained policy is evaluated in terms of an $AUCCESS$ score, which is a weighted average score that emphasizes the speed of learning. Given a range of attempts $k \in \{1, .., 100\}$ at solving a given task, we determine weights w_k as $w_k = log(k+1) - log(k)$, and compute the $AUCCESS$ score as **AUCCESS** $= \sum_k w_k.s_k / \sum_k w_k$, where s_k is the success percentage at k attempts [5, Sec. 3.2].

4.1   Effect of Action Type Selection

In this section, we consider both Basketball and Bowling tasks (Fig. 2), in which, each of the action selection strategies (collisions, rolling, random, mixed and

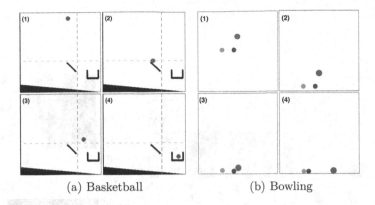

(a) Basketball   (b) Bowling

Fig. 2. Physics tasks for evaluating the sample efficiency of RL agents. 1) The ball and the angled plank (constrained to be below the horizontal green line and to the left of the vertical gray line) need to be positioned so that the ball bounces into the basket. 2) An agent can place the red ball (x, y coordinates and the radius) with the aim of keeping the blue and green balls in contact for 3 s (Color figure online).

gradient based) is allowed to interact with the real environment for 500 interactions, based on which the latent factors are estimated using IPLW. The obtained latent factor estimates are then used to learn policies in simulation, which are then transferred to the real environment to measure the jump start improvement in learning performance. For both tasks, the real world is set to damping (u) 0.8 and the simulated environment has no damping (i.e. ideal).

Figure 3(b) shows the transfer performance surface for the Basketball task. As inferred from the figure, this task requires a significant level of accuracy in the CoR estimate, whereas the friction estimate is inconsequential (real-world latent values: friction 0.2, CoR 0.7). This is further confirmed in the jump start transfer performance plots in Fig. 3(a), where estimates from rolling actions achieve 0 performance, whereas those from collisions appear to significantly improve the performance. Compared to random exploration, Gradient-7 and Gradient-6 plots demonstrate the efficacy of biasing action selection using gradient ratios from relatively similar environments ($u = 0.7$ and 0.6 respectively).

The jump start plot for the Bowling task (real-world latent values, friction 0.707 and CoR 0.447) is depicted in Fig. 3(c), and suggests that the gradient based methods perform the best, followed by the mixed strategy. Action selection strategies that used only one action type (rolling or collisions) for estimation performed relatively worse, probably due to the fact that these strategies led to some of the latent factors to be poorly estimated.

Among the action selection strategies, the gradient based strategy relied on previously obtained characteristics of transfer performances as a function of the different latent factors. Although such a detailed characteristic may be expensive to obtain in terms of the number of real world interactions, it may allow one

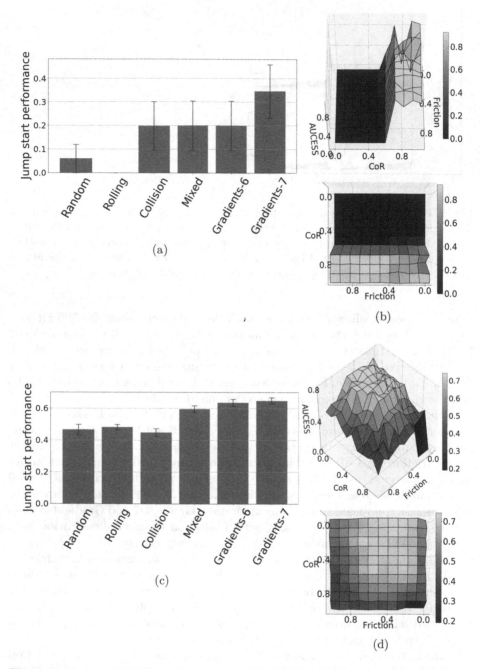

Fig. 3. Evaluating IPLW based learning for (a)–(b) Basketball task and (c)–(d) Bowling validation tasks. (a),(c): Evaluating action selection strategies on jump start, using 10 iterations of 50 actions/iteration. Gradient-7 and Gradient-6 refer to $u = 0.7$ and $u = 0.6$ environments respectively. (b), (d): Jump start performances of friction vs. CoR combinations in $u = 0.7$ environment for respective task. This illustrates the performance in different regions of the latent space, which could inform *intuitive action grouping* and *partial grounding*.

to select appropriate action types in the presence of the unmodeled factors that vary across environments.

Implementation Details: We use cross-entropy (CE) method [7] as the optimizer in IPLW, using 10 rounds of 1000 multivariate normal sampled mass, friction and COR estimates with 200 elite samples selected at each round. We take 5 IPLW based estimates using different random number generator seeds (50, 100, 150, 500, 1000), run 3 RL trials from each estimate and average the jump start performances. In IPLW, 10 rounds of iterations are used.

Basketball Task: Contains 25 total tasks, with varying basket positions, split into 15 training, 5 validation and 5 test tasks, with an action space of 40,000 discretised actions (ball and the plank each can take 200 positions). If an action does not achieve the goal, a trajectory produces 10 observations corresponding to 500 time steps observed at 50 step intervals, whereas completion of the goal will terminate the trajectory immediately. For the purpose of this study, we use a simplified scenario where both the ball and the plank are made of the same material, with friction = 0.2 and CoR = 0.7, and the agent is aware of the latent factor values of rest of the objects in the task (e.g. walls, floor, basket). Here, we use an initial normal distribution with mean and standard deviation set to (0.5, 0.25) for the friction estimate in the CE optimiser. When pretraining the DQN, we use 1000 of 32 size batches, for both IPLW and gradient plots (Fig. 3 (b)).

Bowling Task: Contains 100 total tasks, with varying green and blue ball positions and sizes, split into 60 training, 20 validation and 20 test tasks, with an action space of 50,000 discretised actions. Each trajectory contains 68 observations corresponding to 4000 time steps observed at 60 step intervals, equivalent to approximately 16.6 s of real-world play. When pretraining the DQN, we use 1000 of 16 size batches, for both IPLW and gradient plots (Fig. 3 (d)).

5   Discussion

From a broad perspective, in this study, we try to decompose the complex relationship between the action types, the latent factor information associated with an action type and the latent factor information most relevant to a given task. A standard approach is to iteratively learn a simulated policy, deploy it in the real-world and minimise the difference between the real and simulated trajectories [9,10,17]. Instead, by decomposing this complexity, we believe it is possible to make solutions more generally applicable. For example, latent factor dependencies from a sport such as Golf may be transferable to billiard sports (e.g. snooker, carom), due to the similarity between tasks' friction dependency (rolling motion) and CoR dependency (initial strike on the ball). Such a task-specific latent factor dependency prior can be combined with an action type prior from the billiard sports domain where it uses a billiard cue to hit the ball instead of a golf club. The reuse of such invariant priors could address the issue of sample efficiency, which has been the bottleneck when applying RL to industrial applications. It is particularly true in physics-based systems (e.g., robotic systems) used in manufacturing and prototyping, which a vast number of industrial systems are based on. Hence, we posit our proposed IPLW framework would have particular significance to real world industrial applications.

When learning task-specific latent factor dependencies, our current implementation uses a considerable number of transfer performance samples to generate the performance surfaces shown in Fig. 3(b),(d). However, it may not be possible to recreate similar surfaces when a large number of latent factors are involved. Such scenarios may demand uncertainty-based sampling techniques to focus on specific regions of the performance surface or function approximations. Dedicated attention mechanisms [30] to identify relevant objects to a task may also be useful in this regard. Interestingly, mixing action types in equal proportions can be a reasonably sample efficient and low cost exploration method.

Apart from the latent factors, the dimensionality of the unmodelled factors (damping) may also affect Sim2real transfer. Our evaluation environments consider only a single unmodelled factor. However, in practice, these factors could be multidimensional (e.g. wind speed and direction). Although we believe a sufficient degree of similarity between real and simulated environments would ensure the handling of an arbitrary number of unmodelled factor dimensions, it presents an open issue and a potential topic for future work.

6   Conclusion

In this work, we proposed an approach to efficiently explore physics-based tasks based on task-specific estimates of latent factors. We introduced the ideas of intuitive action groupings and partial grounding, which formed the basis for IPLW, our proposed workflow to achieve improved exploration during learning. We empirically evaluated our proposed approach in two types of physics based learning environments and demonstrated its superior sample efficiency compared to various baselines.

Acknowledgements. This research was partially funded by the Australian Government through the Australian Research Council (ARC). Prof Venkatesh is the recipient of an ARC Australian Laureate Fellowship (FL170100006).

References

1. Pymunk. http://www.pymunk.org/
2. Akkaya, I., et al.: Solving rubik's cube with a robot hand. arXiv preprint arXiv:1910.07113 (2019)
3. Allen, K.R., Smith, K.A., Tenenbaum, J.B.: Rapid trial-and-error learning with simulation supports flexible tool use and physical reasoning. Proc. Natl. Acad. Sci. **117**(47), 29302–29310 (2020)

4. Allevato, A., Short, E.S., Pryor, M., Thomaz, A.: Tunenet: one-shot residual tuning for system identification and sim-to-real robot task transfer. In: Conference on Robot Learning, pp. 445–455. PMLR (2020)
5. Bakhtin, A., van der Maaten, L., Johnson, J., Gustafson, L., Girshick, R.: PHYRE: a new benchmark for physical reasoning. In: NeurIPS, pp. 5082–5093 (2019)
6. Carr, T., Chli, M., Vogiatzis, G.: Domain adaptation for reinforcement learning on the atari. In: AAMAS 2019, Richland, SC, pp. 1859–1861 (2019)
7. De Boer, P.T., Kroese, D.P., Mannor, S., Rubinstein, R.Y.: A tutorial on the cross-entropy method. Ann. Oper. Res. **134**(1), 19–67 (2005)
8. Denil, M., Agrawal, P., Kulkarni, T.D., Erez, T., Battaglia, P.W., de Freitas, N.: Learning to perform physics experiments via deep reinforcement learning. In: ICLR. OpenReview.net (2017)
9. Desai, S., Karnan, H., Hanna, J.P., Warnell, G., a. P. Stone: stochastic grounded action transformation for robot learning in simulation. In: 2020 IEEE/RSJ International Conference on Intelligent Robots and Systems (IROS), pp. 6106–6111 (2020). https://doi.org/10.1109/IROS45743.2020.9340780
10. Du, Y., Watkins, O., Darrell, T., Abbeel, P., Pathak, D.: Auto-tuned sim-to-real transfer. arXiv preprint arXiv:2104.07662 (2021)
11. Dubey, R., Agrawal, P., Pathak, D., Griffiths, T.L., Efros, A.A.: Investigating human priors for playing video games. arXiv preprint arXiv:1802.10217 (2018)
12. Farchy, A., Barrett, S., MacAlpine, P., Stone, P.: Humanoid robots learning to walk faster: from the real world to simulation and back. In: AAMAS, pp. 39–46 (2013)
13. Fernández, F., Veloso, M.: Probabilistic policy reuse in a reinforcement learning agent. In: AAMAS, pp. 720–727 (2006)
14. Fragkiadaki, K., Agrawal, P., Levine, S., Malik, J.: Learning visual predictive models of physics for playing billiards. In: Bengio, Y., LeCun, Y. (eds.) ICLR 2016, San Juan, Puerto Rico, 2–4 May 2016 (2016)
15. Freeman, D., Ha, D., Metz, L.S.: Learning to predict without looking ahead: world models without forward prediction (2019)
16. Grzeszczuk, R., Terzopoulos, D., Hinton, G.: NeuroAnimator: fast neural network emulation and control of physics-based models. In: SIGGRAPH 1998, pp. 9–20. Association for Computing Machinery, New York (1998)
17. Hanna, J.P., Stone, P.: Grounded action transformation for robot learning in simulation. In: AAAI, pp. 4931–4932. AAAI Press (2017)
18. Janner, M., Levine, S., Freeman, W.T., Tenenbaum, J.B., Finn, C., Wu, J.: Reasoning about physical interactions with Object-Oriented prediction and planning (2018)
19. Lake, B.M., Baroni, M.: Generalization without systematicity: on the compositional skills of sequence-to-sequence recurrent networks. In: Dy, J.G., Krause, A. (eds.) ICML, Proceedings of Machine Learning Research, vol. 80, pp. 2879–2888. PMLR (2018)
20. Li, L., Chu, W., Langford, J., Schapire, R.E.: A contextual-bandit approach to personalized news article recommendation. In: Proceedings of the 19th International Conference on World Wide Web, pp. 661–670 (2010)
21. Loula, J., Baroni, M., Lake, B.: Rearranging the familiar: testing compositional generalization in recurrent networks. In: Proceedings of the 2018 EMNLP Workshop BlackboxNLP: Analyzing and Interpreting Neural Networks for NLP, pp. 108–114 (2018)
22. Mnih, V., et al.: Human-level control through deep reinforcement learning. Nature **518**(7540), 529–533 (2015)

23. Muratore, F., Eilers, C., Gienger, M., Peters, J.: Data-efficient domain randomization with bayesian optimization. IEEE Rob. Autom. Lett. **6**(2), 911–918 (2021). https://doi.org/10.1109/LRA.2021.3052391

24. Pathak, D., Agrawal, P., Efros, A.A., Darrell, T.: Curiosity-driven exploration by self-supervised prediction. In: Proceedings of the 34th ICML, ICML 2017, vol. 70, pp. 2778–2787. JMLR.org (2017)

25. Sadeghi, F., Levine, S.: CAD2RL: real single-image flight without a single real image. In: Amato, N.M., Srinivasa, S.S., Ayanian, N., Kuindersma, S. (eds.) Robotics: Science and Systems XIII, MIT, USA, 2017 (2017)

26. Sheckells, M., Garimella, G., Mishra, S., Kobilarov, M.: Using data-driven domain randomization to transfer robust control policies to mobile robots. In: 2019 International Conference on Robotics and Automation (ICRA), pp. 3224–3230 (2019). https://doi.org/10.1109/ICRA.2019.8794343

27. Taylor, M.E., Stone, P.: Transfer learning for reinforcement learning domains: a survey. J. Mach. Learn. Res. **10**, 1633–1685 (2009)

28. Tobin, J., Fong, R., Ray, A., Schneider, J., Zaremba, W., Abbeel, P.: Domain randomization for transferring deep neural networks from simulation to the real world. In: 2017 IEEE/RSJ International Conference on Intelligent Robots and Systems (IROS), pp. 23–30 (2017)

29. Tsividis, P.A., Pouncy, T., Xu, J.L., Tenenbaum, J.B., Gershman, S.J.: Human learning in atari. In: 2017 AAAI Spring Symposium Series (2017)

30. Vaswani, A., et al.: Attention is all you need. In: Proceedings of the 31st International Conference on Neural Information Processing Systems, NIPS 2017, pp. 6000–6010. Curran Associates Inc., Red Hook (2017)

31. Wu, J., Yildirim, I., Lim, J.J., Freeman, B., Tenenbaum, J.: Galileo: perceiving physical object properties by integrating a physics engine with deep learning. In: Cortes, C., Lawrence, N.D., Lee, D.D., Sugiyama, M., Garnett, R. (eds.) Advances in Neural Information Processing Systems, vol. 28, pp. 127–135. Curran Associates, Inc. (2015)

32. Xu, Z., Wu, J., Zeng, A., Tenenbaum, J.B., Song, S.: Densephysnet: learning dense physical object representations via multi-step dynamic interactions. In: Bicchi, A., Kress-Gazit, H., Hutchinson, S. (eds.) Robotics: Science and Systems XV, University of Freiburg, Freiburg im Breisgau, Germany, 22–26 June 2019 (2019). https://doi.org/10.15607/RSS.2019.XV.046

33. Zeng, A., Song, S., Lee, J., Rodriguez, A., Funkhouser, T.: Tossingbot: learning to throw arbitrary objects with residual physics. IEEE Trans. Rob. **36**(4), 1307–1319 (2020). https://doi.org/10.1109/TRO.2020.2988642

34. Zheng, D., Luo, V., Wu, J., Tenenbaum, J.B.: Unsupervised learning of latent physical properties using Perception-Prediction networks. In: Globerson, A., Silva, R. (eds.) Proceedings of the Thirty-Fourth UAI 2018, Monterey, California, USA, 6–10 August 2018, pp. 497–507. AUAI Press (2018)

35. Zhou, W., Pinto, L., Gupta, A.: Environment probing interaction policies. In: International Conference on Learning Representations (2018)

36. Zhu, Z., Lin, K., Zhou, J.: Transfer learning in deep reinforcement learning: a survey. arXiv preprint arXiv:2009.07888 (2020)

Gym-DC: A Distribution Centre Reinforcement Learning Environment

Saeid Rezaei$^{(\boxtimes)}$ [ID], Federico Toffano [ID], and Kenneth N. Brown [ID]

Confirm Centre for Smart Manufacturing, School of Computer Science & IT
University College Cork, CorkT12 XF62, Ireland
{saeid.rezaei,federico.toffano,k.brown}@cs.ucc.ie
https://confirm.ie/

Abstract. Distribution centres in supply chains receive shipments and forward them to transport providers for the next part of their journey to their final destinations. In some Physical Internet proposals, distribution centres will be autonomous. The decision system should choose a transport provider for each packet. Reinforcement learning is a well-established method for learning policies by acting in an environment and observing states. Coupled with Deep Learning, it has shown significant results in competitive environments like board games. To develop and evaluate Reinforcement Learning solutions for managing a distribution center on the Physical Internet, we need a simulated environment that should be as close as possible to real-world conditions. We present Gym-DC - the first framework for Reinforcement Learning research for distribution centres and Physical Internet hubs, based on the OpenAI Gym.

Keywords: Physical Internet · simulator · OpenAI gym · Reinforcement Learning

1 Introduction

It is estimated that the global freight demand will triple between 2015 and 2050 [12]. Significant improvements in transport and logistics services will be required to manage this growth. The Physical Internet (PI) is a proposal for an open global logistics system founded on physical, digital, and operational interconnectivity [11]. It envisages an interconnected network of hubs and logistics providers that transport goods in standardized nested containers, inspired by the transmission of packets in the communications internet. One of the main components of the PI is the transshipment hub, which acts as a router, receiving packages and forwarding them to other hubs to move the packages closer to their final destination. The intention is that these hubs are autonomous, deciding for each package or group of packages what the next hub on their journey should be. The hubs may also have to decide on a specific transport service provider for the next journey for the packages. Fast and efficient decision-making processes in the hubs will be required for the PI to be a success. The economic

© Springer Nature Switzerland AG 2023
J.-J. Rousseau and B. Kapralos (Eds.): ICPR 2022 Workshops, LNCS 13644, pp. 687–699, 2023.
https://doi.org/10.1007/978-3-031-37742-6_53

version of this problem is a two-sided market that is managed by centralized or decentralized agencies [10] [19] [18]. The hubs are unlikely to have full knowledge of the network or of the availability and reliability of service providers on that downstream journey, so classical optimization methods will not be applicable. Reinforcement learning (RL) is a well-established technique for decision-making in complex and unknown environments [17], in which an agent learns policies for behavior through interacting with its environment. RL has been proposed for various functions related to the PI, including synchronized multi-modal replenishment [7], two-sided markets [1,18] and internet congestion control [6,15], and has shown recent success in competitive environments [16]. We propose using Reinforcement Learning for transshipment hub or Distribution Centre decision-making, using a virtual environment so that an agent does not suffer from poor choices in its exploration phase. We propose a simulator for a PI distribution center, Gym-DC, based on the OpenAI Gym framework. The paper is structured as follows: Sect. 2 provides a literature review; Sect. 3 provides an overview of the framework for a simulation of a distribution center. Section 4 describes a first RL agent for that environment, and empirical results are shown in Sect. 5.

2   Background and Related Work

2.1   Physical Internet Hub

The PI is modeled as the logistics equivalent of the Internet [5]. [11] proposed a seven-layer Open Logistics Interconnection (OLI) model similar to the Open Systems Interconnection (OSI) model. OLI model is summarized in table 1 .

Table 1. OLI model

No.	Layer	Functionality provided to the upper layer
7	Application	Purchase order with delivery requirements
6	Presentation	Order monitoring
5	Shipping	Shipment and π–container assignment and monitoring assignment and monitoring
4	Routing	Route assignment and monitoring for each shipment and π–container
3	Network	Network state monitoring, Route segment, assignment and monitoring
2	Link	Validation and monitoring of each flow link state and route segment move orders
1	Physical	π–container and π–means, state monitoring and move order tracking

The main role of an internet router is to receive and transmit digital packets through ports. Forwarding, routing, and (de)encapsulations are considered the main operations in the router. For the Physical Internet hub, different types and features have been proposed in different scenarios. The abstract form of the PI hub is shown in Fig. 1.

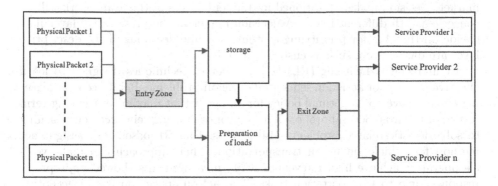

Fig. 1. Conceptual diagram for hub

2.2 Related Work

[11] defined the routing layer as a functional provider for a set of π-containers in an efficient and reliable manner. However, there are some alternative visions for the routing layer. [9] proposed three different candidates for autonomous decision-making in routing: the π-node, π-container, and π-transporter. The π-node is the hub as described above. The π-container encloses the freight items and makes decisions at each interconnection point on its next intermediate destination. The π-transporter is the logistics transport, which monitors traffic conditions, exchanges information with other π-transporters, and determines routes, times, and interchange points. An evaluation study in [9] with a range of stakeholders identified advantages and disadvantages for each entity in different criteria and noted that AI and Game Theory methods could improve decision-making to create a more efficient marketplace and that some criteria could only be judged by physical implementation or simulation.

The traditional 3rd party logistics provider (3PL) are service providers that own or lease and operate storage warehouses or distribution centers. They have a range of customers, including producers, distributors, retailers, etc. Traditionally 3PLs prefer long-term agreements with customers to enable efficiencies through planning. However, volatility, uncertainty, complexity, and ambiguity are characteristic of today's logistics environment. Fluctuations in demand for logistic services and capacity may result in overflowing of unused capacity [2]. This is an important issue in logistic optimization, balancing business needs on the one hand and transport, inventory, and facility costs on the other [4].

[2] introduced a three-layer decision-making model for an advanced hyperconnected logistics service provider on the Physical Internet. The descriptive layer

monitors the current activity of the overall market. The predictive layer predicts forthcoming capacity and throughput demand to help capacity utilization, future service levels, and flows throughout the network. The prescriptive layer is set up for decision facilitation capability, especially support in decisions concerning the market. Decision-makers positioned in different layers of this framework will be concerned with different issues. A decision-maker in the prescriptive layer may decide on the plan for prioritizing customers, while decisions in the descriptive layer are data-driven, such as customer activities.

Reinforcement Learning (RL) [17] is a set of techniques designed to learn effective policies for action in sequential decision problems. Reinforcement learning aims to develop an optimal policy for an agent that maximizes the long-term return of rewards. Several proposals have proposed using reinforcement learning to solve logistic-related problems. [14] proposed an RL-based task assignment method for vehicles in urban transportation. Their approach can make vehicle operators achieve higher revenues while measurements showed appropriate response time to transportation tasks. The action space consists of accepting or rejecting assigned tasks by nodes. The reward signal is determined by the node state and actions simultaneously. [7] developed a synchronized multi-modal replenishment model using deep reinforcement learning. They compared the performance of the proposed model with state-of-the-art heuristic policies. OpenAI Gym [3] is a standard framework helping the implementation and reproducibility of a reinforcement learning environment. There are various methods to define environments and action and state spaces. [8] implemented a library of open AI Gym simulators for reinforcement learning environments consisting of classic operations research and optimization problems, including Knapsack, Online Knapsack, and Virtual Machine Packing. They provided benchmarks for their proposed problems to compare RL, heuristics, and optimization models. [13] presented a simulator for the beer game, a decentralized, multi-agent, cooperative supply chain problem. They used a deep reinforcement learning algorithm to get near-optimal order quantities and compared their results with a real-world dataset and observed some similarities.

3   System Design

We next provide a high-level overview of motivations for an open-source distribution center and briefly introduce the distribution center simulator.

3.1   Motivation for Distribution Center Simulator

In the vision for the Physical Internet, autonomy will be widely distributed over different locations and different entity types, each competing for profit and rewards. Individual decisions in a distribution centre must be made in the context of those competing agents, and so there will significant uncertainty about the consequences of any action. In order to develop effective policies, we need a simulated environment in which to evaluate their performance. The simulation should allow different models for incoming service requests and packet arrivals, and different models for service provider behaviour and the downstream behaviour of other centres and providers. In any realisation of the Physical Internet, simulated environments will also be required for evaluating machine learning systems that infer new policies, since there will be financial penalties for poor decision making during any exploration phase. Rather than jump to a full simulation which includes all possible autonomous agent types across the PI, we start by focusing on Distribution Centre. The first version described here provides statistical distributions for upstream and downstream behaviour of other agents; later versions will be developed to act as a single agent in a wider multi-agent Physical Internet simulation.

3.2   Distribution Center Modeling

The aim of the Distribution Centre is to find the best transportation services for the set of packets it receives. It is an online decision problem, with some decisions being required before all packets are known, and before the results of some previous decisions are known. We assume discrete time steps. At each step, the hub will receive some packets, and must make a decision on some of those packets and those in storage as to which service provider they will be allocated. Packets which have arrived but not yet dispatched will be stored for future time steps. The hub knows the schedule of service providers for the next few days. Each packet is characterized by an id, an ultimate destination, a budget for transportation, its weight, its arrival time at the hub, a deadline for delivery, and penalties to be incurred when a packet exceeds its due date or is not delivered. Each service provider is characterized the destinations it offers, a price it charges per kg for each destination, an expected delivery time per destination, a departure time, and the number of packets it can accept.

The capacity of service providers and storage services will be updated after each round of matching. The decision system gains profit based on the difference between the budget of the packet and the service provider charge, and is penalized for dropped or late packets. These penalties are reported at a later time step, when the final status of the relevant packets are known. The main parameters are shown in Table 2.

Table 2. Important simulator parameters

Parameter	Description
num packets	Number of packets in the which are arrived in the simulation period.
num sp	Number of service providers.
num days	Number of days of the period.
num departures sp	Number of departures for every service provider in the simulation period.
num destination	Total number of destinations.
mean packet weight	Mean parameter of weight for packets.
stddev packet weight	Standard deviation of weight for packets.
mean packet budget	Mean parameter of budget for packets.
stddev packet budget	Standard deviation of budget for packets.
mean packet penalty	Mean parameter of penalty.
stddev packet penalty	Standard deviation of penalty.
mean packet time to deadline	Mean parameter of time to deadline from arrival time.
stddev packet time to deadline	Standard deviation of time to deadline from arrival time.
mean service provider price per kg	Mean parameter of price per KG of service provider.
stddev service provider price per kg	Standard deviation of price per KG of service provider.
mean service provider time	Mean parameter of delivery service provider delivery time.
stddev service provider delivery time	Standard deviation of service provider delivery time.
mean service provider capacity	Mean parameter of service provider capacity.
stddev service provider capacity	Standard deviation of service provider capacity.
storage capacity	The value for the storage capacity.
window time	Number of following days which the providers schedule of service are known for the system

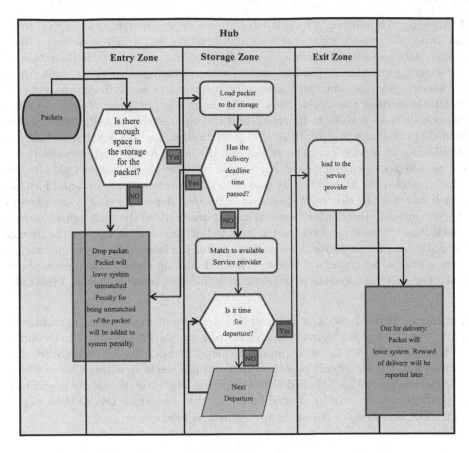

Fig. 2. Flow diagram from the point of view of the packet

Algorithm 1 Matching Algorithm

1: Given: list of available service providers, hyperparameters for matching, capacity of storage, list of packets
2: sort the list of packets based on the hyperparameters for matching
3: sort the list of available service providers based on the hyperparameters for matching
4: **for** packet with highest priority do **do**
5:     **for** service provider with highest preference do **do**
6:         check destination and deadline of packet
7:         **if** *matched* **then**
8:             Pair packet to service provider
9:             Update service provider capacity
10:            break
11:        **end if**
12:    **end for**
13: **end for**

Matching Algorithm. The simulator allows for any matching algorithm to be deployed. We provide a parametrised matching system, which separately priorities packets and service providers based on specified parameters. It then iterates by selecting the highest priority packet, and allocating it to the highest priority service provider, until all known service providers are full. Any packets for which the earliest possible delivery would incur a lateness penalty greater than the non-delivery penalty is discarded, and the non-delivery penalty incurred. We provide packet ordering priorities of highest budget, highest penalty, and closest deadline, and service priorities of earliest dispatch, lowest cost, earliest delivery and highest remaining capacity. Simple baseline algorithms include Greedy, which matches the highest budget packet to the lowest cost provider, and Fastest, which matches the closest deadline to the earliest departure that is expected to deliver on time. In addition, we provide a parametrised dynamic match, which checks the hub storage level, and if it is below threshold it applies the greedy heuristic, and if it is above threshold, it applies the fastest dispatch heuristic. In later sections, we describe a Reinforcement Learning agent, which attempts to learn the best combination of heuristics for different possible states of the hub.

Problem Objectives. It is assumed that the aim of the hub is to maximise its profit minus its penalties over the lifetime of a simulation episode. At the end of each episode, the simulator computes the profit and penalty for each packet that arrived into the hub. Some packets will remain in the hub, without having been dispatched, but without their deadline expiring. For those packets, a percentage of profit or penalty will be applied based on the number of days to their expiry time. The performance measures are defined as follows:

$$Performance = Profit(sent) - Penalty(dropped) - value(remaining) \quad (1)$$

$$Profit = \sum_{i=1}^{m}[budget(p(i)) - (weight(p(i)) \times Cost(sp))] \quad (2)$$

$$Penalty = \sum_{i=1}^{m}[penalty(p(i))] \quad (3)$$

4   Rinforcement Learning Agent

We now present a first RL agent intended to learn effective policies for managing the distribution centre.

Table 3. Parameters of simulation settings

Parameter	Simulation setting 1	Simulation setting 2	Simulation setting 3	Simulation setting 4
num packets	500	500	500	500
num sp	5	5	5	5
num days	10	10	10	10
num departures sp	10	10	10	10
num destination	5	5	5	5
mean packet weight	10	10	10	10
stddev packet weight	2	2	2	2
mean packet budget	35	35	35	35
stddev packet budget	3	3	3	3
mean packet penalty	5	5	5	5
stddev packet penalty	1	1	1	1
mean packet time to deadline	5	5	5	5
stddev packet time to deadline	3	3	3	3
mean service provider price per kg	15	15	15	20
stddev service provider price per kg	2	2	2	2
mean service provider delivery time	5	5	5	1100
stddev service provider delivery time	2	2	2	15
mean service provider capacity	100	100	100	1100
stddev service provider capacity	15	15	15	15
storage capacity	5500	5500	500	10500
window time	11	13	7	11

Defining the Environment State Reinforcement Learning assumes that an agent in a dynamic system traverses through a sequence of states, and at each stage applies an action which influences the next state in the sequence. Defining the appropriate state set for a wider environment is a challenging issue. The planning in this problem may be adjusted based on storage capacity, estimation of arriving packets, and profit and penalty in the future. One simple set for Gym-DC is introduced here, based on three features extracted from the simulator: the trend of the arrival of packets, the capacity of distribution center storage, and the ratio of profit/penalty in a greedy policy. The state is characterise by three integers:

Table 4. Comparison of system performance between heuristics in each setting

Heuristic	Simulation setting 1	Simulation setting 2	Simulation setting 3	Simulation setting 4
Greedy policy	206.8438	200.8105	179.4298	259.5055
Fastest_departure policy	209.8950	197.6339	202.7647	241.2827
Random policy	203.6878	194.4256	192.7215	246.6060
Conditional-20	206.8438	200.8105	189.9368	259.5055
Conditional-40	206.8438	200.8105	196.2332	259.5055
Conditional-60	206.8438	200.8105	201.4573	259.5055
Conditional-80	206.0814	198.6412	202.5235	259.5055
RL agent	218.8146	205.8024	208.9052	257.7658

- $d_1 \in \{0,1\}$: the variable equals 1, if trend of arriving packets is increasing and 0 if it is decreasing.
- $d_2 \in \{0,1,\ldots,99\}$: the percentage capacity occupied
- $d_3 \in 0,1,\ldots,9$:
  Profit=(estimated profit for greedy action)
  Penalty=(penalty for packets in storage)
  d_3 is 9 if profit/penalty is greater than 10
  d_3 will be mapped to range (5,9) if the ratio is between (1,10)
  d_3 will be mapped to range (0,4) if the ratio is less than 1

The Agent Actions. The agent specifies the matching policy by choosing appropriate matching hyperparameters. The action space can be modeled in a discrete or continuous way. In the discrete case, the actions are the direct switching from a greedy approach to fast_departure or reverse. In the continuous case, the action is the selection of values for the weights in of the different parameters in the ranking. In the case of packets, we rank them by their budget and by their penalty. In the case of service providers, we rank them by their departure time and by the cost of service.

Reward Function. Choosing an appropriate reward function is crucial for the agent to learn an optimal policy. One idea is to consider the performance of each simulation period as a reward. The agent will receive zero in each timestep until the simulation time for one period is over. The agent will receive the performance of the system in that period at the end of the episode. The value of performance will be mapped to a float value between 0 and 1000 and will return to the agent at the end of each episode. In this simple agent we apply the reward to the final action only. We rely on the distribution of states in the episode initialisation to ensure a wide coverage of state-action pairs receive feedback, and so we expect to require many episodes before convergence occurs.

5   Results

5.1   Discussions and Results

To demonstrate the framework and evaluate the performance of the RL agent, several heuristics are defined and their average performance in four different simulation settings is calculated. Table 3 summarizes the parameters for these settings. The heuristic used in Conditional-20, Conditional-40, Conditional-60, and Conditional-80 is defined as follows: First, the ratio value will refer to the relative percentage of available capacity storage; second, if the ratio is higher than the indicated value, the agent will behave as if using greedy policy, otherwise, it will switch to fastest-departure.

Each episode lasts for 100 timesteps. The RL agent is trained using the A2C algorithm. For each setting, the RL agent explored six million timesteps in training. The test process includes 100 episodes with different random seeds in each simulation timestep for each setting. Table 4 summarizes the average performance of each policy for each setting. It can be observed that the RL agent converges to approximately the optimal policy in each setting.

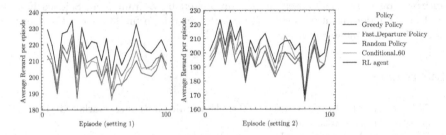

Fig. 3. Plotting performance of different policies for settings 1 and 2.

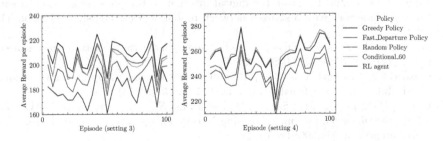

Fig. 4. Plotting performance of different policies for settings 3 and 4.

6 Conclusion

This work is motivated by the increasing interest in RL solutions for sequential decision problems in which the decision maker's available choices and rewards in the future are affected by current decisions. The decision-making system should balance customer expectations with the costs of different options to meet the required performance objectives and may be penalized for any downstream delay or loss of packets. In its ultimate form, the decision-maker does not have full knowledge about the behavior of third-party agents such as service providers or other distribution centers, and so must learn the consequences of each choice. Gym-DC will help researchers to evaluate decision-maker in different situations and options. Current gap associated with RL research, We took steps towards covering this gap by first RL benchmarking simulation framework. Experiment reproducibility in the case of simulator and RL frameworks will help to compare different RL algorithms or other heuristics and methods with the same benchmark. We describe our modeling for the Distribution center simulator and present an illustrative example. The code is open-sourced under a GPL license as an OpenAI Gym environment and accompanying testing module.

Acknowledgment. This research was supported by a grant from Science Foundation Ireland under Grant number 16/RC/3918 which is co-funded under the European Regional Development Fund.

References

1. Akbarpour, M., Li, S., Gharan, S.O.: Dynamic matching market design. arXiv preprint arXiv:1402.3643 (2014)
2. Boerger, J., Montreuil, B.: Data-driven analytics-based capacity management for hyperconnected third-party logistics providers. In: International Physical Internet Conference, pp. 222–232 (2020)
3. Brockman, G., et al.: Openai gym. arXiv preprint arXiv:1606.01540 (2016)
4. Davydenko, I.Y.: Logistics chains in freight transport modelling (2015)
5. Dong, C., Franklin, R.: From the digital internet to the physical internet: a conceptual framework with a stylized network model. J. Bus. Logist. **42**(1), 108–119 (2021)
6. Gawłowicz, P., Zubow, A.: ns3-gym: extending openai gym for networking research. arXiv preprint arXiv:1810.03943 (2018)
7. Gijsbrechts, J., Boute, R.: A Deep Reinforcement Learning Approach for Synchronized Multi-modal Replenishment, vols. 1–4, p. 151 (2018)
8. Hubbs, C.D., Perez, H.D., Sarwar, O., Sahinidis, N.V., Grossmann, I.E., Wassick, J.M.: Or-gym: a reinforcement learning library for operations research problems. arXiv preprint arXiv:2008.06319 (2020)
9. Kaup, S., Ludwig, A., Franczyk, B.: Design and evaluation of routing artifacts as a part of the physical internet framework. arXiv preprint arXiv:2011.09972 (2020)
10. Khezerian, P.: Exploring theoretical models with an agent-based approach in two sided markets (2017)

11. Montreuil, B., Meller, R.D., Ballot, E.: Physical internet foundations. In: Service Orientation in Holonic and Multi Agent Manufacturing and Robotics, pp. 151–166. Springer, Heidelberg (2013). https://doi.org/10.1007/978-3-642-35852-4_10
12. OECD. ITF transport outlook (2017)
13. Oroojlooyjadid, A., Nazari, M., Snyder, L.V., Takáč, M.: A deep q-network for the beer game: deep reinforcement learning for inventory optimization. Manufact. Serv. Operat. Manag. **24**(1), 285–304 (2022)
14. Qin, W., Sun, Y.N., Zhuang, Z.L., Lu, Z.Y., Zhou, Y.M.: Multi-agent reinforcement learning-based dynamic task assignment for vehicles in urban transportation system. Int. J. Prod. Econ. **240**, 108251 (2021)
15. Ruffy, F., Przystupa, M., Beschastnikh, I.: Iroko: a framework to prototype reinforcement learning for data center traffic control. arXiv preprint arXiv:1812.09975 (2018)
16. Schrittwieser, J., et al.: Mastering atari, go, chess and shogi by planning with a learned model. Nature **588**(7839), 604–609 (2020)
17. Sutton, R.S., Barto, A.G.: Reinforcement Learning: An Introduction. MIT Press (2018)
18. Taywade, K., Goldsmith, J., Harrison, B.: Multi-agent reinforcement learning for decentralized stable matching. In: Fotakis, D., Ríos Insua, D. (eds.) ADT 2021. LNCS (LNAI), vol. 13023, pp. 375–389. Springer, Cham (2021). https://doi.org/10.1007/978-3-030-87756-9_24
19. Wang, X., Agatz, N., Erera, A.: Stable matching for dynamic ride-sharing systems. Transport. Sci. **52**(4), 850–867 (2018)

IndRAD: A Benchmark for Anomaly Detection on Industrial Robots

Edoardo Fiorini, Davide Tonin, and Francesco Setti[✉]

Department of Computer Science, University of Verona, Verona, Italy
`francesco.setti@univr.it`

Abstract. Many approaches for fault detection in industrial processes has been presented in the literature, with approaches spanning from traditional univariate statistics to complex models able to encode the multivariate nature of time-series data. Although the vast corpus of works on this topic, there is no public benchmark shared among the community that can serve as a testbench for these methods, allowing researchers to evaluate their proposed approach with other state of the art approaches. In this paper we present the Industrial Robot Anomaly Detection (IndRAD) dataset as a benchmark for evaluating fault detection algorithms on industrial robots. The dataset is composed by 13 nominal trajectories and 3 trajectories with structural anomalies. We also propose a protocol to inject sensory anomalies in clean data. The dataset, code to reproduce these experiments and a leaderboard table to be used for future research are available at https://github.com/franzsetti/IndRAD.

Keywords: Fault detection · anomaly detection · time series analysis · industrial robots

1 Introduction

Industrial robots play an increasingly important role in manufacturing as they allow to increase productivity preserving high quality standards. Industrial robots are widely used in repetitive tasks, such as pick-and-place, welding, painting, *etc.* However, hardware and software issues can produce failures of the system, that easily translate in significant interruption of the entire production line with an associated loss of money for the company. Robotic failures can have even more dramatic consequences when dealing with collaborative robots, *i.e.* robots that can cooperate with human operators sharing the workspace. In this case, robot's failures can easily lead to serious injuries for the human operator.

For this reason it is of primary importance to identify on time faults that can potentially lead to a failure. Unfortunately, this is not a trivial task since in most of the cases these faults do not produce a failure immediately, but they will lead to a failure postponed in time [7]. To limit the probability of failures, many industries implement a scheduled preventative maintenance program, that

© Springer Nature Switzerland AG 2023
J.-J. Rousseau and B. Kapralos (Eds.): ICPR 2022 Workshops, LNCS 13644, pp. 700–710, 2023.
https://doi.org/10.1007/978-3-031-37742-6_54

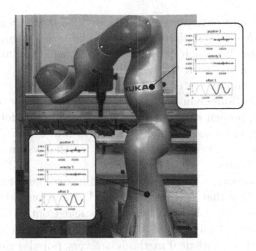

Fig. 1. Graphical representation of our data acquisition setup. We collect information on position, velocity and torque of each joint of a Kuka LBR iiwa 14 robot.

is often inefficient as it generates unnecessary operations and downtimes. It is instead widely desired to perform maintenance operations based on the current status of the robot, minimizing both unscheduled breakdowns and production donwtimes. This approach is called Condition-Based Maintenance (CBM) [9] and it requires a monitoring system that automatically detects incipient failures by processing time series data collected from the robot.

The main task of such a monitoring system is to perform real-time anomaly detection from the collected time series data, identifying any fault data that do not conform to historical patterns, and raise an alert to the human operator. Such a system should be computationally light, to provide fault detection in real time; it should detect faults with high precision and recall; and, most important, it should be able to detect contextual failures, *i.e.* when a faulty sensor reports valid readings, that become invalid when analyzed as correlated with the other sensors.

There are three main challenges in fault detection on industrial robots: *(1) Unbalanced data*: the number of anomalous samples is very limited because for most of the time the robot is running under nominal conditions. Besides, recording instances of faults on industrial robots can be costly and dangerous. *(2) Non-stationary signals*: each joint rotates at different angles, with different speed and requires different currents in different robot motions. *(3) Real-time response*: a fault must be identified as quick as possible, avoiding the fault to evolve in a failure with potentially catastrophic consequences. As a result of these challenges, traditional supervised learning methods are generally unfeasible as they require balanced datasets to train properly. Moreover, the anomaly detection method should learn a feature representation that can separate signals related to faults from robot motions. Finally, the algorithm should be suitable for online anomaly detection rather than processing accumulated data.

Fault detection approaches are typically divided into three categories: *model based, knowledge based* and *data driven*. Model-based algorithms are potentially very accurate, but their performance is strongly related to the fidelity of the underlying model with the monitored system. This model can be difficult to build for complex systems, and the computation can also be too hard for real-time applications. Knowledge-based algorithms rely on rules generated by experts. This approach is usually good in detecting predefined faults, but it fails in detecting unexpected anomalies. Finally, data-driven algorithms rely on statistical information taken from the history of the system to detect outliers and label them as faults.

Data-driven approaches are usually divided in two families. Statistical methods detect data points that deviate from the distribution of the historical data. These methods used for robots include Statistical Control Charts (SCCs) [8], Principal Component Analysis (PCA) [13], and Partial Least Squares (PLS) based approaches [11]. Statistical methods are very popular due to their computational efficiency. However, most of them assume that all the data are accumulated before faults can be detected, which make them unsuitable for real-time anomaly detection. Furthermore, they assume that normal data are generated from a known distribution. In contrast, machine leaning based methods classify faults either in a supervised or unsupervised setup. Supervised methods, like [16], are only feasible when there is a high volume of labeled data including sufficient normal and abnormal data, because they only learn from examples where the desired outcomes are already known. Therefore, unsupervised methods are preferable. Among them, distance-based methods [10] may work well yet are not suitable for high dimensional data streams. Other popular methods feasible for highly unbalanced dataset are One-Class Support Vector Machines (OCSVM) [14] and reconstruction-based approaches like Autoencoder [5] and Variational autoencoder [2]. Some recent models based on these methods can capture temporal dependencies by handling time series data using variational inference [15] or variational autoencoders [12].

2   IndRAD Dataset

We acquired the Industrial Robot Anomaly Detection (IndRAD) dataset at the ICELab of the University of Verona. We used the very popular LBR iiwa 14 R820 collaborative robot produced by KUKA AG. This is a 7 axis collaborative industrial robot specifically designed for assisting human operators in high precision assembly tasks. With a workspace radius of 820mm and a maximum payload of 14kg, this robot represents a perfect case study since faults in its hardware and software components can easily lead to severe injuries for the operator.

The dataset is composed of 16 trajectories lasting for approximately 30 s each. In all trajectories, each joint of the robot performs an independent sinusoidal function with random amplitude and frequency (we only verified in advance that these trajectories were compliant with spatial constraints, *i.e.* did not cause collisions with the environment or with the robot itself). The main idea behind this strategy is to span the most part of the robot's workspace. We decided not to use standard tasks, such as pick & place, or predefined trajectories in the cartesian space to avoid overfitting on standard motion of the end effector. We collected measurements about the angle, velocity and torque applied to each joint of the robot for a total of 21 signals available at each time frame. These data are logged at a frequency 500 Hz. We collected 13 trajectories with the robot working under nominal conditions. We also simulated two different kind of anomalies: structural and sensory anomalies. As for *structural anomalies*, we collected 3 trajectories where we added unexpected loads on the last links of the robot. This simulates an effect where the robot picks a load, either on purpose or accidentally, that is not expected from the process. We also added *sensory anomalies* in post processing by manipulating the collected time-series to impose anomalies on the readings of some sensors. While this part can be added arbitrarily, we propose here a strategy to unify the generation of such anomalies in order to guarantee comparability of different methods.

2.1   Sensory Anomaly Generation

Inspired by [4], we identified 5 kinds of sensory faults:

bias from a certain time instant, the sensor outputs a value which is the true value with an additive offset;

drift the output of the sensor is again affected by an additive bias, while in this case the offset is increasing over time;

degradation the noise on the sensor output, associated to the sensor calibration, increases for external reasons;

freeze the sensor outputs the exact same reading for a certain time interval;

spike the sensor provides an instantaneous reading which is outside a reasonable range for the specific actuator.

We assume here that the anomaly will always appear within the observation period, *i.e.* at the beginning of the observation the system is running under nominal conditions. Thus, we let the fault to appear at a random time between 10% and 90% of the observation period. We also assume that a single reading is affected by the fault, which means we introduce the anomaly on a single signal, randomly chosen within the 21 channels. When applicable, we also randomize the entity of the fault. We first compute the average amplitude and the standard deviation of the nominal signal. For bias we apply a constant offset of a random value from 25% to 50% of the average amplitude of the signal. For drift we apply a linearly increasing offset from 0 to 100% of the average amplitude of the signal. For degradation we apply an additive white noise with a random amplitude of 40% to 80% of the standard deviation of the signal. For freeze, we just repeat the value of the signal at the time the fault appears. For spike, we apply an instantaneous reading with a multiplicative offset of 5 to 10 times the average amplitude of the signal. An example of each kind of sensory fault is shown in Fig. 2.

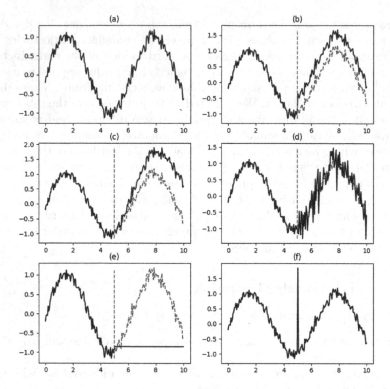

Fig. 2. Examples of sensory faults. (a) nominal signal, (b) bias, (c) drift, (d) degradation, (e) freeze, (f) spike.

3   Benchmarking Anomaly Detection

Let $S = \{p_1, \ldots, p_7, v_1, \ldots, v_7, t_1, \ldots, t_7\} \in \mathbb{R}^{21}$ be the set of 21 signals that we are monitoring, where p, v and t refer to position, velocity and torque respectively, and the numerical index refers to the specific joint. An input vector $i_t = \{i_{t,1}, \ldots, i_{t,21}\} \in \mathbb{R}^{21}$ is given at each time step, where $i_{t,j} \in \mathbb{R}$ denotes the value of signal j at the current time t. The anomaly detection problem is to decide for each given i_t, whether or not it is anomalous with respect to the nominal behavior of the system.

In this paper we provide anomaly detection experiments with a set of baselines that are considered as standard in the literature, together with some state of the art approaches for multivariate anomaly detection. For all the following methods we adopt a sliding window strategy. Thus, we feed each approach with a matrix $I_t = \{i_{t-T}, \ldots, i_t\} \in \mathbb{R}^{21 \times T}$ representing the recent history (the last T time frames) of the input vector.

Given the inherent high dimensionality of the data and the strict time constraint for real time detection, most of the methods in the literature apply some dimensionality reduction techniques to extract informative features and reduce noise at the same time. The most common techniques are Principal component analysis (PCA) or deep autoencoders (AE). In both cases, the input I_t is transformed in a compact representation of it $H_t = \{h_1, \ldots, h_K\} \in \mathbb{R}^K$ with $K << 21T$.

3.1 Baselines

We explore three main families of anomaly detection methods reported in the literature, namely PCA based, deep autoencoders, and one-class classification.

Principal Component Analysis (PCA). By projecting process variables into a lower-dimensional subspace, PCA reveals the inherent cross-correlation among process variables [1]. In this regard, principal components can efficiently describe a process in a reduced subspace. The aim of PCA is to find the subspace of maximum variance in the input matrix. The measurement matrix I_t is first normalized to unit variability, and then decomposed to the product of two factors, $I_t = PW_t'$, where $P \in \mathbb{R}^{21 \times T}$ represents a matrix of the principal components (PCs) and $W_t \in \mathbb{R}^{T \times T}$ is the loading matrix. In presence of cross-correlated multivariate data, the first k PCs (with $k << T$) are sufficient for preserving relevant information in the original data. Thus, after selecting the appropriate number k of PCs to include in the model, the data matrix I_t can be expressed as a sum of an approximated matrix $\hat{I}_t$, and residual data E_t.

$$I_t = PW_t' = \hat{I}_t + E_t \tag{1}$$

In PCA-based systems one can monitor either the residuals or the scores. Although it is widely recognized that the residuals provide superior detection capability [17], both statistics are complementary are worth to be monitored.

At training time, analyzing only nominal data, we compute a statistical model of the signals. At testing time, an anomaly is detected when the new signals do not conform with the model. To this aim, we need to define some acceptability criteria to be used. In this work we use three different approaches for detecting the anomaly, namely *median*, *quantile* and *gaussian*.

With *median* we raise an alert whenever the L^2 norm of the residuals at testing time exceeds the median of the same values computed at training time multiplied by a constant safety factor. In this case all features are considered together at each time frame, since all the signals collapse to a single value when computing the norm of the residuals.

For *quantile* we again analyse the L^2 norm of the residuals at testing time. At training time we compute the control limits as the 5% and 95% quantiles of the distribution on the nominal data. In this case each PC is processed separately, thus this is a univariate monitoring approach.

Finally, in *gaussian* we fit the approximated matrix $\hat{I}_t$ with a mixture of multimodal gaussian distributions at training time. At testing time, we compute the Mahalanobis distance from the current approximation of the measurement matrix and each component of the gaussian mixture model; finally, we keep the minimum distance as the anomaly score and we compare it with a fixed threshold set in advance. In this way we analyse whether the measurement matrix can fit at least one of the gaussian models within the mixture, assuming that anomalies lie far apart from them.

Deep Autoencoders. An alternative approach to reduce the dimensionality of a signal is using deep autoencoders (AE) [3]. AEs are a family of neural network architectures characterized by two parts: an encoder and a decoder. The general idea is that the encoder is able to compress the information provided by the input signal into a lower dimensional feature space, while the decoder is then able to reconstruct the high dimensional input. The weights of these networks are learnt by feeding the model with nominal data and using a loss function based on some "reconstruction quality" measure, *i.e.* a measure of the difference between the input and the reconstructed output. The reconstruction quality measure is then used also to compute the residual matrix. In our baselines we consider the L^2 norm of the difference between the input and reconstructed signals.

$$\mathcal{L} = \|I_t - \hat{I}_t\|_2 \tag{2}$$

At testing time, anomalies are detected using the same criteria (median, quantile and gaussian) exposed above for PCA based methods. The idea behind this detection is that an AE trained purely on nominal data cannot reconstruct unforeseen patterns of anomalous data well.

When dealing with time-series, one may use Long Short-Term Memory (LSTM) layers [6], a specific model of Recurrent Neural Network (RNN). For encoding, an LSTM-AE projects multimodal observations and their temporal dependencies at each time step into a latent space using serially connected LSTM layers. For decoding, it estimates an approximation of the multimodal input from the latent space representation.

One-class Support Vector Machines. One-Class Support Vector Machines (OCSVMs) [14] are an unsupervised variation of the supervised Support Vector Machines. OCSVMs build a model that describes only normal operating conditions and uses it to flag out data points that do not conform to the reference model. The OCSVM procedure, inherited from standard SVMs, uses a kernel function for projecting input data points to a higher-dimensional feature space, where the discrimination of normal from anomalous data becomes clearer and easier, leveraging the capacity of the kernel functions to model the process non-linearity of normal behavior. OCSVM identifies anomalies in the feature space based on the construction of a hyperplane (or a hypersphere, depending on the implementation) that appropriately separates the data from the origin. In fact, the OCSVM procedure learns a decision function $\mathcal{D}(x)$ that returns 1 or -1 to respectively show whether the data is nominal or anomalous.

The input data x is first projected into the higher dimensional feature space $\mathcal{F}$ based on the kernel function $\mathcal{K}(\cdot, \cdot)$. The decision function $\mathcal{D}(x)$ intends to maximize the Euclidean distance between the origin and the separating hyperplane H, subject to the constraints that all nominal points must lie in the outer region. Operatively speaking, one wants to allow a small portion of nominal data to be classified as anomalies, thus to achieve better global performances. Thus, the objective function to be optimized is:

$$\min_{w,\xi,\rho} \frac{1}{2}\|w\|^2 + \frac{1}{\nu l}\sum_{i=1}^{l}\xi_i - \rho, \quad \text{subject to } \langle w, \mathcal{K}(x) \rangle \geq \rho - \xi_i, \; \xi_i \geq 0 \qquad (3)$$

where w denotes a support vector, ρ refers to an offset from the origin, l is the number of samples taken into account, ξ_i is the distance of the i-th sample from the decision buondary, and $\nu \in [0,1]$ refers to a parameter characterizing the solution.

4 Experiments

In all our experiments we used a sliding window approach with window size of 2000 samples (4 s) and stride 50 samples (0.1 s). For PCA, we used 21 PCs, while for AEs we used an architecture with three LSTM layers in both encoder and decoder with 64, 32 and 16 nodes respectively. As performance metrics we used standard classification measures precision, recall and F_1-score, which is the harmonic mean of precision and recall.

Quantitative results are reported in Table 1. One key outcome of this results is that PCA consistently outperforms AEs approaches. We hypothesize that this is mostly related to two facts: on the one hand PCA is less sensitive to the training procedure, including the amount of data used in fitting the model, while AE models require possibly more data at training time and more accurate tuning of the hyperparameters. On the other hand, we are using a simple architecture, yet very common in time series analysis; more sofisticated architectures like Variational or Contrastive AutoEncoders will probably outperform both AE and PCA. A second finding from these results is that OCSVM has a clear tendency towards high recall performance, generating a high number of false positives as well. This is mostly related to the choice of parameter ν in Eq. (3); nevertheless, it is always preferable for a real monitoring system to generate false positives than misdetections.

We also report qualitative results on a sample trajectory of our dataset. The trajectory in Fig. 3 is corrupted with a bias anomaly on the torque reading of the second joint (label 'effort1', second row right column). PCA is then used for reconstructing the approximated signal after computing the principal components from nominal data only, in yellow in Fig. 4. As we can clearly see, the anomaly on one sensor generates erroneous reconstruction on many other signals. The type of error on these signals is non necessarily the same as the imposed anomaly, e.g. many plots show a degradation of the signal rather than a bias. Finally, the anomaly score and the thresholds computed with median, quantile and gaussian criteria are reported in Fig. 5.

Table 1. Average precision, recall and F_1-score of all the baseline approaches.

Approach	Criterium	Precision	Recall	F_1-score
PCA	Median	0.67	0.65	0.66
	Quantile	0.47	0.93	0.57
	Gaussian	0.33	0.50	0.33
Autoencoder	Median	0.57	0.49	0.52
	Quantile	0.56	0.41	0.45
	Gaussian	0.24	0.27	0.25
One-class SVM		0.11	0.85	0.17

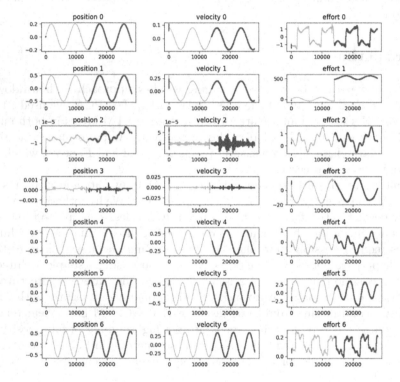

Fig. 3. Signals acquired from a sample trajectory with sensor anomaly on the torque of the second joint ('effort 1')

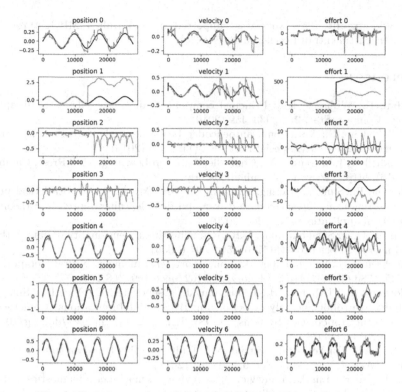

Fig. 4. Signal reconstruction with PCA using 21 components.

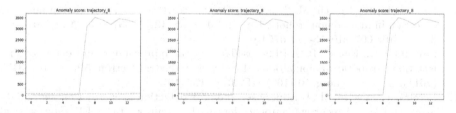

Fig. 5. Anomaly score and thresholds for median, quantile and gaussian criteria.

5 Conclusion

In this paper we presented the Industrial Robot Anomaly Detection (IndRAD) dataset, a novel benchmark for evaluating fault (*i.e.* anomaly) detection on industrial robots. To the best of our knowledge, this is the first public dataset specifically released for this purpose. The dataset comes with 13 nominal trajectories and 3 trajectories with structural anomalies. We also propose a protocol for injecting sensory anomalies. A public repository, continuously updated, reports results with both baselines and state of the art approaches.

Acknowledgment. This work was supported by the Italian MIUR through the project "Dipartimenti di Eccellenza 2018-2022".

References

1. Abdi, H., Williams, L.J.: Principal component analysis. Wiley Interdisciplinary Rev, Comput. Stat. **2**(4), 433–459 (2010)
2. An, J., Cho, S.: Variational autoencoder based anomaly detection using reconstruction probability. Special Lect. IE **2**(1), 1–18 (2015)
3. Goodfellow, I.J., Bengio, Y., Courville, A.: Deep Learning. MIT Press, Cambridge (2016). http://www.deeplearningbook.org
4. Harrou, F., Sun, Y., Hering, A.S., Madakyaru, M., Dairi, A.: Statistical process monitoring using advanced data-driven and deep learning approaches: theory and practical applications. Elsevier (2020)
5. Hinton, G.E., Salakhutdinov, R.R.: Reducing the dimensionality of data with neural networks. Science **313**(5786), 504–507 (2006)
6. Hochreiter, S., Schmidhuber, J.: Long short-term memory. Neural Comput. **9**(8), 1735–1780 (1997). https://doi.org/10.1162/neco.1997.9.8.1735
7. Hornung, R., Urbanek, H., Klodmann, J., Osendorfer, C., Van Der Smagt, P.: Model-free robot anomaly detection. In: IEEE/RSJ International Conference on Intelligent Robots and Systems (IROS), IEEE (2014). https://doi.org/10.1109/IROS.2014.6943078
8. Jaber, A.A., Bicker, R.: Industrial robot fault detection based on statistical control chart. Am. J. Eng. Appl. Sci. **9**, 251–263 (2016)
9. Jardine, A.K., Lin, D., Banjevic, D.: A review on machinery diagnostics and prognostics implementing condition-based maintenance. Mech. Syst. Signal Process. **20**(7), 1483–1510 (2006)
10. Khalastchi, E., Kalech, M., Kaminka, G.A., Lin, R.: Online data-driven anomaly detection in autonomous robots. Knowl. Inf. Syst. **43**(3), 657–688 (2014). https://doi.org/10.1007/s10115-014-0754-y
11. Muradore, R., Fiorini, P.: A PLS-based statistical approach for fault detection and isolation of robotic manipulators. IEEE Trans. Industr. Electron. **59**(8), 3167–3175 (2011). https://doi.org/10.1109/TIE.2011.2167110
12. Pereira, J., Silveira, M.: Unsupervised anomaly detection in energy time series data using variational recurrent autoencoders with attention. In: IEEE International Conference on Machine Learning and Applications (ICMLA). IEEE (2018)
13. Sathish, V., Ramaswamy, S., Butail, S.: Training data selection criteria for detecting failures in industrial robots. IFAC-PapersOnLine **49**(1), 385–390 (2016). https://doi.org/10.1016/j.ifacol.2016.03.084
14. Schölkopf, B., Platt, J.C., Shawe-Taylor, J., Smola, A.J., Williamson, R.C.: Estimating the support of a high-dimensional distribution. Neural Comput. **13**(7), 1443–1471 (2001)
15. Sölch, M., Bayer, J., Ludersdorfer, M., van der Smagt, P.: Variational inference for on-line anomaly detection in high-dimensional time series. arXiv preprint arXiv:1602.07109 (2016)
16. Vallachira, S., Orkisz, M., Norrlöf, M., Butail, S.: Data-driven gearbox failure detection in industrial robots. IEEE Trans. Industr. Inf. **16**(1), 193–201 (2019)
17. Wise, B.M., Ricker, N., Veltkamp, D., Kowalski, B.R.: A theoretical basis for the use of principal component models for monitoring multivariate processes. Process Control Qual. **1**(1), 41–51 (1990)

Author Index

© Springer Nature Switzerland AG 2023
J.-J. Rousseau and B. Kapralos (Eds.): ICPR 2022 Workshops, LNCS 13644, pp. 711–713, 2023.
https://doi.org/10.1007/978-3-031-37742-6

Printed in the United States
by Baker & Taylor Publisher Services

Printed in the United States
by Baker & Taylor Publisher Services